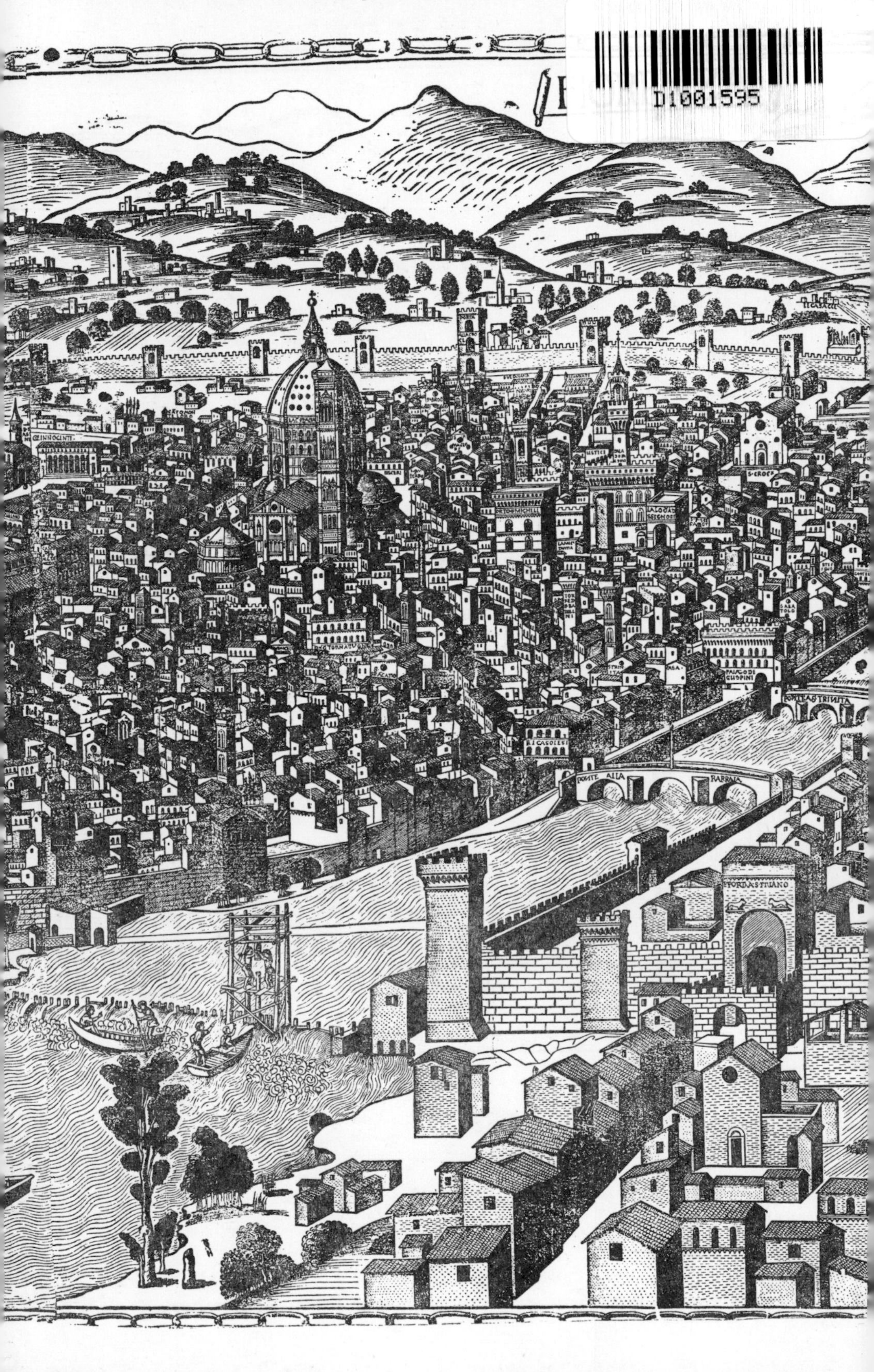
PONTE ALLA
PORTA·S·FRIANO

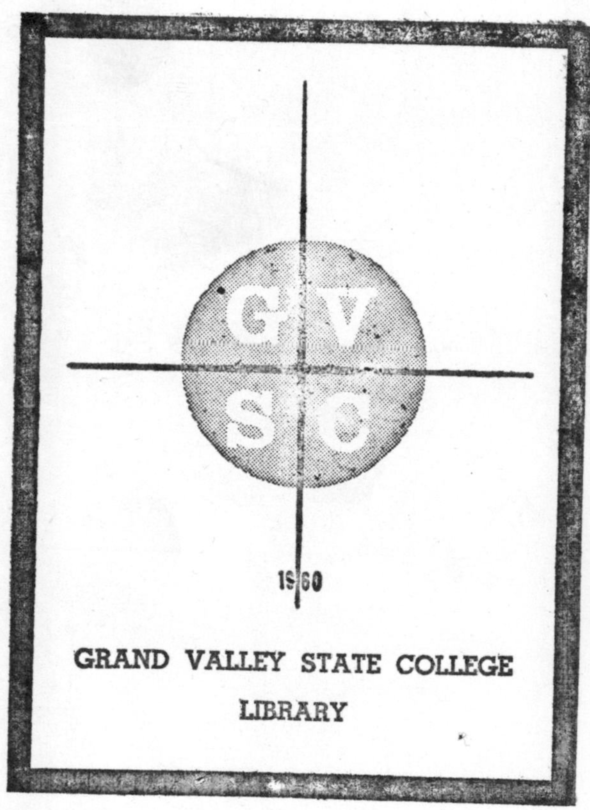

The Taste of Angels

STUDY FOR THE LIBYAN SIBYL

Drawing by Michelangelo for the fresco in the Sistine Chapel. Formerly in the Beruete Collection, Madrid
Metropolitan Museum of Art

The Taste of Angels

A HISTORY OF ART COLLECTING FROM RAMESES TO NAPOLEON

Francis Henry Taylor

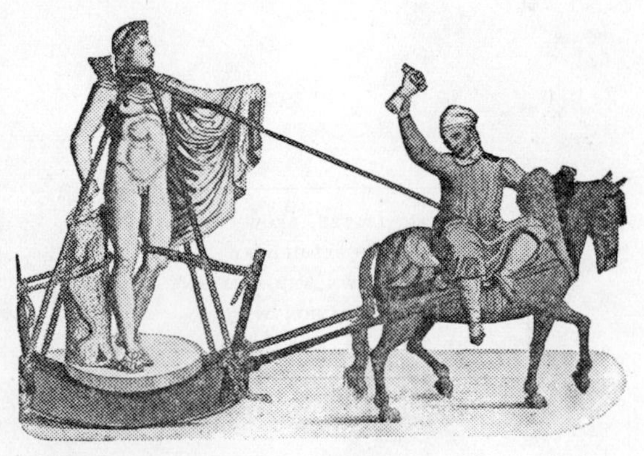

An Atlantic Monthly Press Book

Little, Brown and Company · *Boston* · 1948

FIRST EDITION

Published September 1948

ATLANTIC–LITTLE, BROWN BOOKS
ARE PUBLISHED BY
LITTLE, BROWN AND COMPANY
IN ASSOCIATION WITH
THE ATLANTIC MONTHLY PRESS

Published simultaneously
in Canada by McClelland and Stewart Limited

PRINTED IN THE UNITED STATES OF AMERICA

TO

THE COLLECTORS OF THE PAST
WHO IN THEIR INNOCENCE HAVE
RISKED THEIR LIVES AND FORTUNES
TO ENCOURAGE ART,

AND TO THE

PATRONS AND CRITICS OF THE PRESENT,
THIS BOOK IS DEDICATED

. . . in all these things we are more than conquerors . . . neither death, nor life, nor angels, nor principalities, nor powers . . . shall be able to separate us . . .

—ROMANS VIII. 37–39

Notice to the Reader

In the turbulent days of Fascist Italy, immediately preceding World War II, a legend persisted in artistic circles concerning an American tourist in Florence who had purchased a painting by Titian. In order to confound the authorities and take the picture out of the country he had a restorer cover it with a thick varnish and, after it had dried out thoroughly, paint a modern landscape on the surface. The picture sailed through the customs at Modane and soon arrived in Paris. Thereupon the collector sought out another restorer who was even more skillful and ordered him to remove the covering and bring the picture to its original condition. The artist worked for several weeks: first disappeared the modern landscape and then appeared the Titian. He kept on cleaning, not satisfied with what he found, until, finally, beneath it, hard up against the very canvas itself, was a portrait of Mussolini. Now while the legend may very well be apocryphal, the moral to be drawn from it is far from doubtful, for it bears a stamp of authenticity which goes far beyond the certificates of scholars which are peddled so promiscuously in the auction room.

The moral, in effect, is the motive which inspired this book. Twenty years' experience as curator and director in American museums has convinced me that the phenomenon of art collecting is too instinctive and too common to be dismissed as mere fashion or the desire for fame. It is a complex and irrepressible expression of the inner individual, a sort of devil of which great personalities are frequently possessed. It is a curious coincidence that all of the men and women dealt with in these pages were highly interesting in their own right and would, indeed, have been so even had they never collected anything in their entire lives.

How different are these individuals and yet how representative of their times and countries – the Pharaohs of ancient Egypt, the early Hellenic priests and treasurers of the sanctuaries, the Tyrants of early Athens, Pericles, Alexander the Great and his generals. With the Roman conquest of the ancient East, new plunder and new cultures pour into Rome – the soldiers and senators of the Republic, Julius Caesar, Augustan Emperors and private citizens like Vergil and Cicero enter the list of the foremost art collectors of antiquity. The climax is reached in the fastidiousness and greed of the Proconsul Verres, whose indictment by Cicero recalls the trial of Hermann Goering for similar crimes against society and the arts at Nuremberg.

The saints and sinners of the Middle Ages add their own flavor to the art of collecting; Abbot Suger of Saint Denis, Jean, Duc de Berry, the Dukes of Burgundy and the German princelings bring into their cabinets a combination of superstition and reality which ultimately lay the foundations for the museums of natural history and science. They, in turn, are counterbalanced by the art galleries of the Renaissance to which the Medici in Florence and the Popes of Rome contribute their humanism and their lavish patronage.

These are the stories familiar to the student of art history. What is less known is the pattern of the men who follow in their footsteps: of the accumulations of treasures by the Hapsburgs who ruled in various parts of Europe from 1273 to 1918, leaving behind them the Prado and the galleries of Vienna and the Low Countries; of the great triumvirate in England – Charles I, Buckingham and Arundel. Again, France over half a dozen centuries under the Valois and Bourbon kings gathers into her churches, palaces and museums the masterpieces of Gallic culture. Richelieu, Mazarin, Colbert, set the pace and Napoleon marks the zenith of her aspirations, making possible the development of the nineteenth century and preparing the soil for modern art.

But more particularly it is our own English heritage which is to play so marked a role in the politics, life and letters of our own day. For the British understand the imperialism of the arts and their function in society, a society that reached its ultimate fulfillment in the gentleman – a citizen of the world in whom are combined both the intellectual ideals of the Greek and the chivalry of the medieval knight. If Horace Walpole has been chosen in this study as the instrument to interpret the hereditary attitude towards possessions of the English, it is because he emerges not only as the epitome of these conventions but also as the greatest art critic in the mother tongue.

These are the elements of which the history of collecting is composed. Naturally, however, the two most essential ingredients are the artists themselves and the patrons and men of wealth and learning who brought their genius to flower.

Since it is a commonplace that every work of art requires both a creator and a spectator, it became evident that some exploratory inquiry was in order to determine the role of the patron or collector. Through the centuries he has held the balance between the artist and the layman and has handed down with courage and a spirit of adventure the tangible remnants of the history of civilization. Thus, over the past ten years, precious moments stolen from administrative cares have been devoted to the single purpose of penetrating the varnish which has obscured the canvas, and of going still further in the hope of finding the man behind the picture.

No general history of collecting has been written in the English language. And while there is a vast bibliography (of which a selection is given in the Appendices) on special phases of collecting in various European countries and epochs, no general work in any language has appeared. During the nineteenth century our thinking was revolutionized by the emergence of the modern science of economics. In its wake has followed a revaluation of historical and political motives and events; Spengler and Toynbee, to name but two, have recognized the interplay between social history and the rise and fall of capital. Money has suddenly seemed to come into its own in the academic world. But the history and criticism of art have been curiously exempted from the impact of economics and the social sciences. Writers and teachers of the humanities have been content to abide by time-worn conclusions and formulae; and, in order to while away the tedium of the dead-end street in which they have arrived, have invented the game of iconology, a form of intellectual hopscotch played upon the sidewalks of eternity.

For more than a hundred years it has been fashionable to consider the periods of creation as the very antithesis of periods of collecting and eclecticism. This is a doctrine which has had general currency and acceptance by the scholars of all nations; it seemed, moreover, like a good theory in view of the fact that the periods of the greatest production of creative art appear to have come at times when civilization was upon its decline. Historians of the mid-nineteenth century had failed, for example, to recognize in the Hellenistic period that the great era of spending coincided with the seizure of Persian gold in the conquests of Alexander the Great, and that the ancient world had been thus precipitated into a profit inflation, and an attendant era of luxury among the very rich (contrasted with pitiable conditions among the very poor), seldom seen in other periods of history. Yet today we have learned to recognize the cyclical character of these periods of inflation and deflation. In Egypt the XVIIIth Dynasty produced a revival of the arts which was based upon the plunder of the Theban kings. Roman collecting was the booty, primarily in gold and silver, of the conquest of Greece and the expansion of the Empire. Lord Keynes has advanced a very cogent argument for believing the Dark Ages to be not so much a period of religious and cultural decline as it was the most catastrophic deflation (following the prosperity of Rome) that the world had ever seen. Then, as a consequence of the revival of trade through improved communications, shortly after the year 1000, the economy of the Holy Roman Empire, depending upon a finely balanced ratio of gold and silver to agriculture and manufacturing – a balance not to be upset until the discovery of America – laid the foundations for the rise of modern capitalism.

Within ten years of Christopher Columbus's historic voyage, the first convoys of gold and silver from the New World were already on their way to Spain. Then followed the treasure of Montezuma in 1519 and that of the Incas of Peru in 1534; during the sixteenth century more bullion arrived annually on the treasure ships of Charles V and Philip II than was produced in any one year in all of the mines of Europe put together. The importations from 1503 to 1660, according to Hamilton, amounted to somewhere between a half a billion and a billion gold pesos. The glut of gold became still more critical because of the stupid fiscal policies of the Spanish crown, which forbade its being shipped out again from the country to ease the general credit situation of the continent. After an unprecedented boom at the Spanish dominated Antwerp Bourse, the first great stock market boom in history, there was a crash in 1557, which precipitated the three successive bankruptcies of Philip II and destroyed at the same time the power of Florence, then the collecting center of the revenues of the Church, and of the Augsburg bankers. A loaf of bread in Madrid was worth eleven dollars in today's money. The price revolution and the general disaster added fuel to the flames of Reformation. The theories of Sombart, Tawney and Max Weber, attributing the rise of capitalism so directly to the rise of Calvinism, have obscured the more realistic reasons caused by the surplus of precious metal from America.

* * * * *

To determine the value of money in former times a great many variable factors must be taken into account; for while the volume of money has changed greatly and quickly since the Middle Ages, the effect on prices has been equally manifest. The trend has been upward. Irving Fisher (writing in 1912) maintained "that prices are now about ten times as high as they were in the period between 1200 and 1500 A.D." If one allows for the inflation following the two World Wars and the depreciation of the gold content of the United States dollar by approximately 50 per cent, it is fair to argue that the ratio Fisher quoted has been doubled in the past thirty years. Preserved Smith has stated that "there was hardly wealth at all in the Middle Ages, only degrees of poverty, and the sixteenth century first began to see the accumulation of fortunes worthy of the name." In 1909 there were 1100 persons in France with an income of more than $40-000 per annum. Among them 150 with an income of more than $200-000. In England in 1916, 79 persons paid income taxes on estates of more than $125,000,000. The richest man in France in the fifteenth century, Jacques Coeur, had amassed a capital of only $5,400,000. The total wealth of the House of Fugger about 1550 has been estimated at $32,000,000, though the capital of their bank was never anything like that.* Agostino Chigi, the treasurer of Pope Julius II, was said to have an income of $2,000,000 a year. On the other hand there was no prosperous middle class. The rich were very very rich; and the poor were destitute. How little actual money was in circulation may be judged from the fact that the total revenue from taxes of Francis I and Henry II was approximately $256,000.

The problem of the historian is to reconcile the value of money at different periods to the value of human labor and the prices of the necessities of life. For the purposes of this book, which seeks only to establish, however vaguely, the relative value of the work of art to the society in which it was created or acquired, it will be necessary to make certain arbitrary assumptions in regard to the value of money. The standard coinage to be considered is that of Italy, which was dominated by the gold gulden or florin of Florence and the Venetian ducat which from medieval times had a gold content of $2.25.† Roughly speaking, the ducat, the florin, the gulden, the French livre, the English pound and the Spanish-Austrian taler, while their actual gold and silver content varied greatly (according to the policies of the several countries in regard to the debasing of coins), were used more or less interchangeably for nearly three hundred years. None of the modern refinements of foreign exchange had been worked out. The economy between countries was limited and it became convenient to approximate the values of all these countries into a whole lump unit of currency. Obviously the work of art (and the jewel or goldsmith's weight of metal in a gold chain or reliquary) was a firmer medium for international exchange and was also more freely transported from one country to another with less fear of piracy. I believe we may fairly consider the purchasing power of the ducat or the florin at $20 from the period of the Renaissance to the French Revolution.‡ Such a rule of thumb is no more than a relative convenience

* Preserved Smith, *The Age of the Reformation.* Henry Holt and Co., 1920, pp. 460–461.

† The livre tournois in France was valued in 1500 at about $1.00. The cost of living in France during the Renaissance was much lower. So it was in Spain, England and the Low Countries until the importation of American gold. In Germany, the gulden, because of the close association between the Empire and the Papacy, favored the currencies of Italy.

‡ Burckhardt put the gold florin or *fino d'oro*, the ducato and the scudo at between 55 and 60 French gold francs at the par value of 1870. That would have been approxi-

which will enable the reader's imagination to make some vague comparison of the wealth of former times with the fortunes of the art patrons of the present day. For brevity this generality (unless otherwise stated) will be followed throughout this study.

* * * * *

Since the fall of Rome, works of art had never had any real market value. The artist of Gothic and Renaissance times was attached to the household of the prince as a personal servant, and he produced his wares purely and simply on the basis of production costs. He received his board and lodging, a living wage, and certain perquisites depending upon the liberality and enlightenment of his patron. For the rest he received fixed amounts to cover the costs of his materials and usually established schedules for special commissions according to size and subject matter, and so on. The works of art thus made became part of the general ambience of the court and were more or less taken for granted.

But the Renaissance princes, particularly those of Italy, were ruined by the depression of the fifteenth century and the bankruptcies of the sixteenth. World finance had slipped from their control; England, the Low Countries, France and Germany emerged as modern capitalistic powers. The disastrous consequences of the Hundred Years' War and the Wars of the Roses were long over. There was an era of profligate spending in these countries and a frantic effort on the part of Italy to sell them whatever assets could be salvaged from the wreck. The chief of these were the works of art which the later generations of Renaissance patrons had inherited and were able to convert into immediate cash.

Our information regarding the artist and the value of works of art during the Renaissance is all too fragmentary. By the middle of the fifteenth century the artist had reached the economic level of the small shopkeeper. According to the Vicomte d'Avenel* the dowries which the artists gave their daughters varied from 5400 French gold

mately $10 in gold at that same date. A general increase in prices has occurred since 1870 and the dollar was devalued in 1933 by nearly one half. Cf. Appendix A.

* G. d'Avenel, *Les riches depuis sept cents ans*. Paris, 1909.

francs (computed as of 1909) to 10,800. Mantegna gave his daughter a dowry of 13,400 French francs in 1499.

Raphael, Michelangelo and Titian were the first artists to have a lucrative situation. Raphael, who left an estate of $140,000, demanded 100 ducats ($2000) from Agostino Chigi for each head in the frescoes of Santa Croce in Rome. "Be sure," Chigi said to his agent, "that Raphael is satisfied for if he charges me as much for the drapery I am ruined." Leonardo and Michelangelo each received a salary of $129 a month for work executed for a prince. And Michelangelo was paid 280,000 francs ($56,000) for the ceiling of the Sistine Chapel. It took him four years and he was obliged to pay his assistants out of that sum. While he was painting the *Last Judgment*, on the other hand, he got nothing beyond his salary as Chief Architect, Sculptor and Painter of the Apostolic Household. He left an estate of 180,000–200,000 francs, the house which Bramante had built for him and some other parcels of real estate. Pope Paul III had given him the enormous pension of $5200. Titian's more lavish patronage by the Emperor Charles V is described in Chapter IV, Book III.

Dürer left an estate of $32,000 – mostly from the sale of his prints. He had received a pension of $600 from the Emperor and had sold pictures for as much as $375 each. Rubens's average price for a picture was from $300 to $800. Van Dyck was paid $250 for the portrait of *Charles I* now in the Louvre and Rembrandt approximately the same for his portraits. The *Night Watch* brought him only slightly more than $1200. Velasquez received a salary of about $2000 as Aposentador of the Palace in addition to full perquisites of living. The court painters of Louis XIV received annual salaries of $3000, quarters, servants and similar perquisites.

But after 1550 as new fortunes arose to replace the hereditary ones, little by little works of art were sold to meet debts, to finance military campaigns and to provide dowries for ugly ducklings. The most spectacular sale was that in 1627 of the hereditary collections of the Dukes of Mantua, comprising the incredible treasures of the Gonzaga and the d'Este houses accumulated over a period of nearly three hundred years, to Charles I of England. From then on the history of collecting of the seventeenth and eighteenth centuries becomes the history of the liquidation of the family holdings of southern Europe to the prosperous parvenus of the capitalistic north.

Collecting, like history, is the result of neither cause nor effect; and it is not concerned with which came first, the chicken or the egg. The doctrine of periods of creation *versus* periods of eclecticism, even if it bears any germ of truth, is quite irrelevant. The collections are merely the tangible illustrations to the ordinary processess of economic history and show the trends of historic taste. They form the records of the life story of successful men in successful times. That the pattern varies in different countries is entirely consonant with the other variable factors of history. If Queen Elizabeth was able to weather the price revolution of her day, it is because of her financial wisdom and that of Sir Thomas Gresham. Keynes has shown how Elizabeth used the booty captured from the Spanish by Drake on the *Golden Hind* to pay off her foreign debt and invested the balance of about £42,000 in the Levant Company. Largely out of the profits of the Levant Company there was formed the East India Company, the profits of which during the seventeenth and eighteenth centuries were the main foundations of England's foreign connections. Since 1580, the £42,000 invested by Elizabeth out of Drake's booty had accumulated by 1930 to approximately the actual aggregate of Britain's foreign investments before the First World War – namely £4,200,000,000 or, say, a hundred thousand times greater than the original investment.* What I am suggesting is that the economy of each nation will shed a revealing light upon the direction of its national taste and artistic styles.

This book will inevitably lay itself open to the charge of wandering over the face of the earth and inquiring into many divergent fields in which no single person can have universal competence. But in doing so, it is hoped that it will show that men of affairs in any country and at any time are very much alike; their tastes and their ambitions are the same. It is addressed neither to the art historian nor to the businessman, but to those who care for art and have a curiosity about those who likewise cared before them. In turning through its pages may the reader share some of the author's pleasurable surprise in the

* J. M. Keynes, *A Treatise on Money*. Harcourt, Brace and Co., 1930. II, p. 30.

acquaintances he has made. The present work deals with those collectors and personalities of history from Ancient Egypt to the Napoleonic Wars. A subsequent volume will deal with European collectors of the Industrial Revolution and the rise of collecting in America.

Contents

List of Illustrations

Unless otherwise stated, the illustrations are taken from the Print and Photographic Collections of the Metropolitan Museum of Art and the personal collection of the author. The color illustrations have been made from objects in the possession of the Museum.

BOOK ONE

Origins of the Classical Tradition

CHAPTER I

The Earliest Collections

THE earliest collections of mankind were inevitably associated with religion and the public treasury. The plunder of war and the tangible fruits of industry have always passed from one generation to the next, and works of art, being constantly associated with power, served as a medium of exchange; at the same time, by virtue of their intrinsic worth, based primarily upon the precious metals and rare stones of which they were composed, they served as a reserve of public wealth and a symbol of the nation's credit. Inescapably the treasury proper outgrew the vault or strong room and invaded the sanctuary and the temple. They were neither actually museums nor theoretical creations for cultural delectation; they were part of ordinary everyday life, lying halfway between the savings bank and the sacristy.

The royal tombs of the Valley of the Kings stand as mute testimony to the transitoriness of human beings, yet at the same time offer proof of their belief in the permanency of material things. Let no one think that the Pharaoh's concern for his physical well-being in the life to come prevented his laying up for himself treasures on this earth. The Egyptian kings have left records of collections of votive offerings which they had assembled to placate the gods. They differ, however, from the votive offerings of the Buddhist or Christian dispensations in that the objects themselves seem scarcely capable of working miracles, but rather they were part of the practical and comfortable furniture of the spirit of the departed. They were associated with everyday life; they were the objects which the deceased had known and used during his mortal existence and as such were embellished and decorated with a dignity and profusion that were fitting to his rank. If the fastidiousness of the Egyptian mummy is surprising, it is more especially because of the sense of continuity of property which he chose to carry with him to the tomb. "The God lives in his temple like a king in his palace," says Jean Capart, "and the temple itself is nothing but a replica constructed for eternity of the ephemeral in which the Pharaoh resides." "You can't take it with you" is a concept which was wholly foreign to the Egyptian and one which he could never have understood.

It was therefore possible for the Egyptian and his "Ka," or soul, the spiritual double of his mortal self, to live happily together through a limited partnership of intense accretion with a comfortable certainty that the capital which the firm had compounded would not diminish in the passing centuries. In his triple role of god, priest and temporal King of Egypt, the Pharaoh operated upon principles of sovereignty and of economy that were entirely sound; what he did not attribute to his temporal needs, he found imperative as part of the equipment for his life hereafter. While he sought to surround himself with the very finest and most luxurious products of the artist and the artisan, he was not a collector in the modern sense. The work of art was either an object of domestic utility or an object of the cult.

Egypt had reached the zenith of her power and luxury in the New Kingdom. The Pharaohs of the XVIIIth Dynasty built huge palaces at Thebes, which they filled with booty, and erected temples to the gods of victory. Across the river their generals installed themselves in sumptuous villas whose gardens touched upon the waters of the Nile. A fashion for naturalism in all its manifestations soon tended to break down the hieratic splendor and formality of the earlier dynasties. Plant forms and animals appeared in profusion upon the walls and columns of the palaces. Yet, at the same time, the traditional severity remained in their temples, and throughout the later periods of Egyptian art a certain atavism prevented their departing too radically from long established models. This antiquarianism is often found in the Stygian accumulations of the Valley of the Kings, for the Pharaoh did not limit himself to the latest streamlined gadgets of his particular dynasty. He took with him to the tomb statuettes of ancestors, unguent pots of an earlier queen, the charms and amulets which had given occult powers to his predecessors. The most spectacular collection, because it is the largest ever found intact, that of Tutankhamun, has been described as a "dynastic museum established possibly for political reasons." It was a collection, said Howard Carter, "of the art of various periods and even of various nations – in short a collection of the palace heirlooms gathered by Pharaoh after Pharaoh over a considerable period." While it is fashionable today for us to see in this loosening up of traditional forms in the art of the XVIIIth Dynasty the elements of decay and a surrender to the siren call of naturalism, it is nevertheless difficult to escape the breathless beauty of the birds and animals and of the portraits that gave such color and gaiety to the palaces of Thebes and Amarneh.

Despite their awesome majesty, the Pharaohs were prone to human weaknesses and, like the more mortal monarchs of a later day, indulged in fantasy. The young Tutankhamun, it appears, was an amateur collector of walking sticks and staves, for in the annex to his tomb and in its antechamber were found a great number. His predecessor, Amenhotep III, was something of a collector and had a passion for blue enamel. Thutmose III was interested in nature and brought back from his campaigns a series of rare and exotic plants, ordering a catalogue of his botanical and biological specimens to be carved upon the walls of the temple at Karnak. With this interest in natural philosophy it followed that there should be awakened an intellectual curiosity in regard to books and the accumulated knowledge of mankind. Thus at Thebes, and up and down the Valley of the Nile, the great new buildings of the Pharaohs contained as part of the palace enclosures vast libraries and treasure rooms where historical works began to find a logical and quite natural setting. At the Metropolitan Museum the celebrated collection of Lord Carnarvon, as well as the fruit of fifty years of systematic excavating by its staff, imposes upon the most casual visitor the stupendous capacity of these early monarchs for personal adornment and fastidious abode. At no other time, indeed, in history has the general ambience of the collector been more marked in daily life, more deeply acquisitive, more conscious of the continuity of property to meet the perpetual care and needs of the collector in the life beyond the tomb.

Five hundred years before Christ, Hecataeus of Miletus described a noble temple in Egypt containing a library; over its entrance was carved the motto, "The Place of Healing of the Soul." Strabo towards the close of the first century described a similar temple but called it the Memnonium of Thebes. Shortly afterwards, Diodorus of Sicily left a very minute description of what he called "the tomb of Osymandyas." This tomb was nothing else than the great palace and library of Rameses II. Connected with it was the most famous library in the world and the earliest of which we have any record that has come down to us from antiquity.*

It was this same Osymandyas of whom Shelley wrote:

> I met a traveller from an antique land
> Who said: Two vast and trunkless legs of stone
> Stand in the desert. . . . Near them, on the sand,
> Half sunk, a shattered visage lies, whose frown,
> And wrinkled lip, and sneer of cold command,
> Tell that its sculptor well those passions read
> Which yet survive, stamped on those lifeless things,
> The hand that mocked them, and the heart that fed:
> And on the pedestal these words appear:
> "My name is Ozmandias, King of Kings:
> Look on my works, ye Mighty, and despair!"
> Nothing beside remains. Round the decay
> Of that colossal wreck, boundless and bare
> The lone and level sands stretch far away.

The accounts of the Ramesseum, with its great peristyles and palace rooms and its library and galleries of sacred objects, have something of fact but are nevertheless subject to poetic imagination and the dragoman's touch. The only inscription remaining which suggests the quotations of Hecataeus and Diodorus is:

> The writings of Thot [the god of wisdom]
> May they give everlastingness and an eternity of jubilees.

More telling, however, because they are contemporary documents, are the scenes still preserved in the tombs of the viziers of some of the XVIIIth Dynasty kings. It was one of the functions of the vizier to present to the king ambassadors from foreign lands and they are

* Cf. Appendix A.

shown in several instances bearing gifts from Nubia, Asia and the Islands of the Mediterranean. These are in part "goods" such as ebony and ivory from the south and ingots of copper and gold from the north. Far more interesting are the gold and silver vessels of beautiful design and intricate workmanship which were brought to propitiate the Pharaoh and delight his eye. Were it not for these representations our knowledge of the Minoan civilization, for example, would be far less than it is now, in regard to both what it produced and the time at which it flourished.

Coupled with these is another scene in which are pictured hundreds of objects: jewelry, toilet articles, statues, arms, and such, which were made in the royal ateliers and presented to the king at the New Year feast. The palace must have contained a veritable "museum of modern art," both domestic and foreign, and, as one king succeeded another, through dynasties like the XVIIIth and XIXth, the collections came to include ancient as well as contemporary art.

Sir Leonard Woolley has found evidences that the collecting tradition of the Egyptians was repeated in Mesopotamia in very early times. At Uruk, the Erech of the Bible, at Ur of the Chaldees and at various other sites he has found the hereditary collections of the kings of Sumeria, of Babylon and of Syria. Among them was a stone cup that had belonged to the King of Akkad which had been carefully prized and handed down from generation to generation for over a thousand years. At Ur was a clay drum which proved to be the earliest museum label known. But above all, it is in the public libraries of Babylonia and Assyria that we find the most extravagant collections of early antiquity. The library of Ashurbanipal, for instance, contained something over 30,000 clay tablets devoted to the entire range of Mesopotamian literature, history, science and religion. There were copies of ancient Sumerian texts, temple archives, collections of birds, omens, moral precepts, incantations, medical texts, legal documents and legendary literature. In short, as the Rigbys have pointed out, the Sumerians incorporated in their libraries everything and anything. They were the forerunners and the prototypes of the great public libraries of the present day.*

* D. and E. Rigby, *Lock, Stock and Barrel*, J. B. Lippincott Co., 1945, Chapters I–X.

It is not until we reach the Hellenistic world of Alexandria that we find the heritages of ancient Egypt and Mesopotamia blended together in the great library and museum of that city. It was one of the Seven Wonders of the ancient world. Strabo, the ubiquitous geographer, described "the most beautiful public precincts and also royal palaces," showing that each king at his expense had added some adornment to the public monuments for the purpose of immortalizing his reign:

> The museum is also a part of the royal palaces, it has a public walk, an exedra with seats and a large house in which is the common mess hall of the men of learning who share the museum. This group of men not only hold property in common but also have a priest in charge of the museum who formerly was appointed by the king but is now appointed by the Caesar.*

Philo, writing in the first century A.D., speaks with rapture of the city:

> There is not in the world such a precinct as the so-called Serapaeum, temple of Caesar, patron of mariners, which rises conspicuously opposite the excellent harbors, very large and noticeable, and unmatched for the wealth of its votive offerings, being surrounded with pictures, statues, silver and gold. In the extensive precinct are porticos, libraries, men's apartments, baths, sacred groves and propylaea, open spaces and halls open to the sky. In fact it is embellished in the most sumptuous way and gives hope of safety alike to those who set out and to those who disembark.†

Few centers have aroused such astonishment among the travelers and writers of antiquity, and a visit to Alexandria was generally considered one of the requirements of the educated citizen. The inspiration for the museum, it is believed, was the Athenian Mouseion, founded by Aristotle, and Ptolemy Soter called to his court a follower of Aristotle, Demetrius Phalereus, for the purpose of re-creating it in the Egyptian capital. The library, which by Roman times counted hundreds of thousands of rolls, was likewise one of the great wonders of the world. But the Alexandrian Museum differed from its Aristo-

* Strabo, *Geography*, XVII (Alexandria).
† Philo, *On the Seven Wonders of the World* (Alexandria).

telian model in many ways. It was far richer and far larger. The funds were administered by a priest who was appointed by the king, and it was essentially a court institution under palace control and knew both the advantages and the disadvantages of royal patronage. In some ways it resembled a modern university but the scholars and scientists and literary men whom it supported were under no obligation to teach. They had only to pursue their studies to the greater glory of the Ptolemy. Whatever the palace required, Forster declares,

it had only to inform the Mouseion, and the subsidized staff set to work at once. The poets and scientists there did nothing that would annoy the royal family and not much that would puzzle it, for they knew that if they failed to give satisfaction, they would be expelled from the enchanted area and have to find another patron or starve. It was not an ideal arrangement, which outsiders were prompt to point out, and snobbery and servility taint the culture of Alexandria from the first. It sprang up behind walls, it never knew loneliness nor the glories and the dangers of independence, and the marvel is that it flourished as well as it did. At all events, it is idle to criticize it for not being different, for if it had been different, it would not have been Alexandrian. In spirit and in fact the palace and the Mouseion touched, and the palace was the stronger and the older. The contact strangled philosophy and deprived literature of such sustenance as philosophy can bring to her. But it encouraged science and gave even to literature certain graces that she had hitherto ignored.*

If there was a museum of objects at all in the modern sense, it was confined to the votive offerings, the statues and the works of art that enriched the Serapeum and the various temples of the palace enclosure. Nowhere among the records which have survived does there appear to be a detailed list of any collection of objects, interesting for their own sake, to which students or scholars addressed themselves as works of reference. It is curious, indeed, that whereas in Athens and Pergamon, and even in Antioch, there seems to have been a lively interest in art theory and in aesthetics, Alexandria should have been so completely devoid of it.

* E. M. Forster, *Alexandria: A History and Guide*. Whitehead Morris, Ltd. (Revised ed. 1938), p. 26.

CHAPTER II

The Hellenic Contribution

IF the cult of death seems to have dominated every phase of Egyptian life, it was almost totally absent from Greek thought. There was a friendliness to Greek religion, a camaraderie with the gods and goddesses of Mount Olympus who, being both mortal and immortal at the same time, shared with the Arcadian shepherds and shepherdesses the same passions and appetites, the same fears and weaknesses; they had a mutual sympathy for beauty and freedom of the spirit. The ancient Greeks were "extroverts" in the most complete sense of the word, living their lives in the open, concealing nothing from each other, and were entirely free from those inhibitions which Semitic insecurity and Christian penitence have, over the centuries, added to the complexities and frustrations of modern life.

This ultimate expression of anthropomorphism may be found in Greek art, which, too, was shared in common between divinities and common men. It was an art which differed from that of Egypt as greatly as did the religious beliefs of Hellas differ from those of the Nile Valley. Just as he wished to share his carnal pleasures with his god, the Greek offered his works of art to the temples for their common use. The Homeric poems leave no doubt about the sensuous pleasure which he took in luxurious and fine craftsmanship, and if the Greek expected quality for himself, he was shrewd enough to know that the god, whose all too human vengeance he was seeking to placate, would be satisfied with nothing of a lower standard of perfection. Whether or not these objects served a useful purpose in the life to come was unimportant if only they obtained favors for the donor in this world.

Since the Muses were usually associated with springs and rivers, it became the custom to establish shrines in their honor in shady groves, often high on mountaintops, where the spirits of the nine learned maidens of mythology might inspire the artists to their highest endeavors. Special cults and altars adorned with images were dedicated to them. Soon schools were established, such as the Orphic School on Mount Olympus and that of Hesiod on Helicon; these became gathering places for the devotees of art. Later they grew into the treasuries of the great sanctuaries at Delphi and Olympia which were filled, particularly at the latter place, with votive statues of the athletes who had won distinction in the Pan-Athenaic games. These shrines were scattered over the Greek landscape, the most famous ones being dedicated to Athena or Hera, and their sculptural decoration, particularly the friezes which adorned the temples, have today become the pride of the museums of Paris, London and Munich.

As in Egypt, religious conservatism and the custodianship of the various priesthoods were largely responsible for the character and nature of these treasury collections. Anything that had to do with ancestral gods and their cults was carefully and reverently preserved. Some of the most exquisite and precious painted vases, as well as vessels of gold and silver, have been recovered from pits close by the sanctuaries where they had been buried to keep them from profane hands, once their usefulness was ended. By and large, as Dinsmoor has shown,* the sanctuaries were haphazard accumulations of treasure, plate, weapons and furniture. In the larger religious centers the treasuries were connected with each other by long galleries, usually open to the sky, in which were shown the votive statues. Since the priests valued anything that was rare or seemed at the time to have intrinsic value, specimens of natural history, particularly rare and precious stones and substances to which some medicinal lore was attached, crept into the collections. The early treasuries soon came to have something of the character of the *Wunderkammer* of the north German princes of the sixteenth century.

The annual financial records of the treasurers, not unlike the dry reports of their descendants, served as catalogues of these earliest

* Professor William B. Dinsmoor has very generously given the writer access to notes of an unpublished lecture delivered by him at the Frick Collection, New York, in 1941.

Greek museums. Pausanias, in his accounts of the Acropolis in Athens and of the sanctuaries of Apollo at Delphi, of Hera at Samos and of Zeus at Olympia, enumerates not only the votive statues he has seen, and the pictures and precious objects in gold and ivory, in bronze and inlaid woods, but he gives detailed accounts of the history and provenance of each piece so far as legend or hearsay can support it. Before proceeding, for example, with his description of the contents of the Temple of Athens, he pauses in the Propylaea:

> On the left of the gateway is a building with pictures. Among those not effaced by time I found Diomedes taking the Athena from Troy and Odysseus in Lemnos taking away the ball of Philoctetes. There in the picture is Orestes killing Aegisthus, and Pylades killing the sons of Nauplius who had come to bring Aegisthus succor. . . . There are other pictures, including a portrait of Alcibiades, and in the pictures are emblems of the victories his horses won at Nemea. . . .*

The treasuries served also another purpose beside that of religion; the city-states used them as branch banks or deposits in the Panhellenic sanctuaries dedicated to their particular local gods. Thus, under the direction of the priesthood, was established a system of primitive banks for international settlement upon which much of the early Greek economy was based. These banks also became a place for the reception of hostages of battle and the spoils of war, for Pausanias records methodically the items taken in various campaigns, such as the statues of Phidias which had been carried off to Delphi.

It is important to remember that the art collections of Greece, which at first so resembled the early temple collections of Egypt and Mesopotamia, were essentially public property and were displayed, if not in the religious shrines themselves, in the agorae or pinacothecae and in the gymnasia. The early Greek citizen, living his life for the most part in the open, did not require the type of house suitable to decoration and embellishment which became fashionable in Hellenistic times. His wants were simple, sculpture and painting were communal considerations, not private, and the idea of family portraits or such sentimental memorabilia, except in funerary monuments, did not exist.

These accumulations of treasure were, if anything, informal and

* Pausanias, *Description of Greece*. I, 41.

free from the self-consciousness of the modern collector. Consideration of the work of art was purely objective and the Greeks until well beyond the time of Alexander were little concerned with theories of beauty or with the emotional and intellectual processes of the artist. The work of art was admired for its own sake and not, as is so often the case today, because of the prestige or importance of the person who created it. Socrates, originally a sculptor, "gave up the calling as low and ignoble," and in Plato's *Republic* the artist was looked upon as the lowest order of citizen. Plutarch put the artists on a level with the greatest poets but he was an exception among the ancient authors. Seneca on the other hand said, "While we adore idols, we despise those who fashion them." Philostratus and Galen give them a cautious and provisional status in intellectual society. While in recent years evidence has turned up to show that citizenship was conferred on exceptional artists like Phidias and Polygnotus, generally speaking the artists were thought of as common laborers and artisans. Miss Gisela M. A. Richter has suggested that the social position of the artist in Athens at the time of Pericles was not unlike that of the physician (or in fact any professional man) in prewar, Edwardian London – that is to say that only the most notable talents were received in the world of fashion and then only grudgingly and with an air of patronizing enthusiasm. Lions have roared from time immemorial, only to be patted on the head by the brave and the very, very rich.

The economic situation of the artist in antiquity is one that is particularly difficult for us to understand today. Ludwig Friedländer in his *Roman Life and Manners** has gone far towards lifting the veil of obscurity under which the artist labored:

> The fact that works of art were in the main produced by slave labor, and were generally in use, made such labor cheap. But even free artists were not too well paid. In the Edict of Diocletian the daily wage of the workmen who attended to the artistic decoration of houses is based upon the supposition that they like the rest received their board from the land-

* Ludwig Friedländer, *Roman Life and Manners*. E. P. Dutton and Co., Inc., [1908]–1913 (4 vols.). II, 3; I, 1; d., pp. 319–321. The reader's attention is also called to the chapter on artistic patronage in the age of Pericles in Martin S. Briggs, *Men of Taste*, Charles Scribner's Sons, 1947.

lord. The pay of the stucco worker is the same as that of the bricklayer, carpenter, lime-burner, carriage maker, baker and smith; that of the mosaic worker is a fixed hire, that of the clay and stucco modeler half as much again, that of the portrait painter, three times as high. The casting of statues in bronze was paid by the pound. In the case of statues, the result of their production on a large scale was a great lowering of price. In the time of Alexander the Great, 3000 drachmae($600) seems to have been the usual price for a statue; whereas Dial of Prusa in his Rhodian speech says that a bronze statue could be erected for 1000 drachmae, that is $200, or even 500 drachmae($100). The extent to which art as a mechanical profession occupied the field of art proper and the humble position of the majority of those who practiced both, could not fail to influence the estimation in which art was regarded by persons of education.

Upon her noblest monuments the artisans of Athens worked for little recompense. In the accounts of the cost of the frieze of the Erechtheum during the last quarter of the fifth century when artists were working side by side upon the frieze of the Parthenon, "the sum for a single figure without accessories is 60 drachmae ($12), for a man on horseback, 120 drachmae; for a chariot with two horses and a youth, 24 drachmae; for a woman with a child, 80 drachmae; the figures are two feet high, very finely worked in front but left flat behind." Friedlander insists that since the price was so low it is fair to suppose that these prices were only for the workmanship and did not include the cost of the material. During the Roman occupation of Greece the average price for a life-size marble figure was 4000 sesterces, or about $200, and the same prices prevailed in Rome.

Since the early Greeks had no high opinion of the artisan as an individual, and few theories about taste, they obviously did not become collectors; for the collector is, first and last, a theorist of taste upon whose acceptance or rejection the fashionable judgment of the art market fluctuates, up or down. The work of art then remained until the time of Alexander either an oblation to the god or part of the public wealth to be guarded in the treasury of the temple and reckoned only in terms of its monetary value. So little in fact were the productions of the artists estimated for their own worth that when the citadel of Athens was destroyed by the Persians in 480 B.C.

the Greeks used the fallen statues to fill in the soil for rebuilding the temple.

Centuries later when the new cities founded by Alexander the Great and his generals were being built, they were eager to acquire the reputation for a culture which hitherto they had not possessed. Already art was destined to be the handmaiden of political and military conquest. Alexander at Pella, moved by a nostalgia for the purity of ancient Athenian civilization, became a collector of antiquities. The Hellenistic monarchs began systematically and reverently to collect the ruins and the fragments of the classic age and Sicyon became the gathering place for the art dealers of the empire. Mahaffy has described this city as "a Renaissance Florence of the Hellenistic age." No king or satrap of Alexander's empire, he pointed out, would overlook the fashionable necessity of having works of art, particularly bronzes from Sicyon, brought to his collection. It was indeed here that the vogue of art collecting, as it was to be carried on in Roman times, had its origin. According to Plutarch, Aratus procured from the Ptolemies of Alexandria a fine collection of pictures and thereby sealed a long sought for political alliance. The temples and palaces of Daphne at Antioch in Syria opened on long galleries of paintings and sculpture of an unprecedented scale, as did the residence of King Pyrrhus in Ambracia. An interest in art and in collecting became widespread throughout Alexander's empire. But as yet there appeared to be no centralization as there had once been in Athens or was to come in Rome.

Ideas of luxury generally seem to come from the Orient. It was the contact of Alexander's generals with the absolute monarchies of the East, particularly of Persia, which gave them new and sumptuous appetites. Furthermore, the amount of gold and silver that poured into Greece was phenomenal. No comparable influx of precious metals has ever been seen except in the sixteenth century when American and Indian gold poured into Spain. The adventurers brought home with them large fortunes and the traders and purveyors of the army increased their own already considerable wealth. "With these eastern fortunes," says Mahaffy, "must have come in the taste of all superior comforts and luxuries which they found among the Persian grandees. Not only the appointments of the table in the way of plate and pottery but the very tastes and flavors of Greek cookery must have profited by comparison with the knowledge of the East. So also the furniture, especially in carpets and hangings, must have copied Persian fashion just as we still affect oriental stuffs and designs." * Pictures and statues began for the first time to adorn private houses. The sumptuousness of the furniture and of the equipment of everyday life passed beyond all limits and a revolution in architecture and domestic taste accompanied it.

Nowhere was the luxury and cultivation of the Hellenistic world more marked than in Pergamon, where, according to Vitruvius, the Attalid kings, "attracted by the great sweetness of the science of philology, founded an excellent library for the enjoyment of the public." In this library, adjoining which, as in Alexandria, was the great sculpture collection, were monuments, copies of the greatest works by Phidias. The latter were esteemed among the ancients as highly as we in the present day consider the Elgin marbles. They were the first monarchs of whom we have any record to conduct excavations to recover works of art of an earlier age, and it was in their library that were formulated the aesthetic judgments which later were passed on to Cicero and Quintilian, setting up standards of perfection in sculpture and in painting. Strabo tells us how the libraries of Aristotle and Theophrastus were buried to hide them from the rapacity of the Attalids, and Pausanias, Tacitus, and Pliny the Elder describe historic paintings which recorded their political and military campaigns. The great altar of Zeus, for so long the chief ornament of the classical museum in Berlin and which the Russians have sent on flatcars to the east, is perhaps the most notable example of the Pergamene school.†

* J. P. Mahaffy, *Greek Life and Thought.* The Macmillan Co., 1896, p. 113.

† The most recent authority on Pergamon, Miss Hansen, has given the following account of collecting by the Attalid kings (E. V. Hansen, *The Attalids of Pergamon,* Ithaca, Cornell University Press, 1947, pp. 289–290, 332–333):

"To Attalus I belongs the credit of having begun the collection of famous works of earlier art from other places, the first of its kind in antiquity. From Aegina, which he obtained in 210 B.C. by purchase from the Aetolians, the king transported to Pergamon several works, among them the colossal bronze statue of Apollo by the early fifth century sculptor Onatas, son of Micon. In the Aeginetan plunder was also a statue by Theron, a Boeotian who lived in the second half of the third century and made por-

TRIBUTE GIFTS OF THE NEW YEAR

THE LIBRARY IN THE PALACE OF RAMESES II

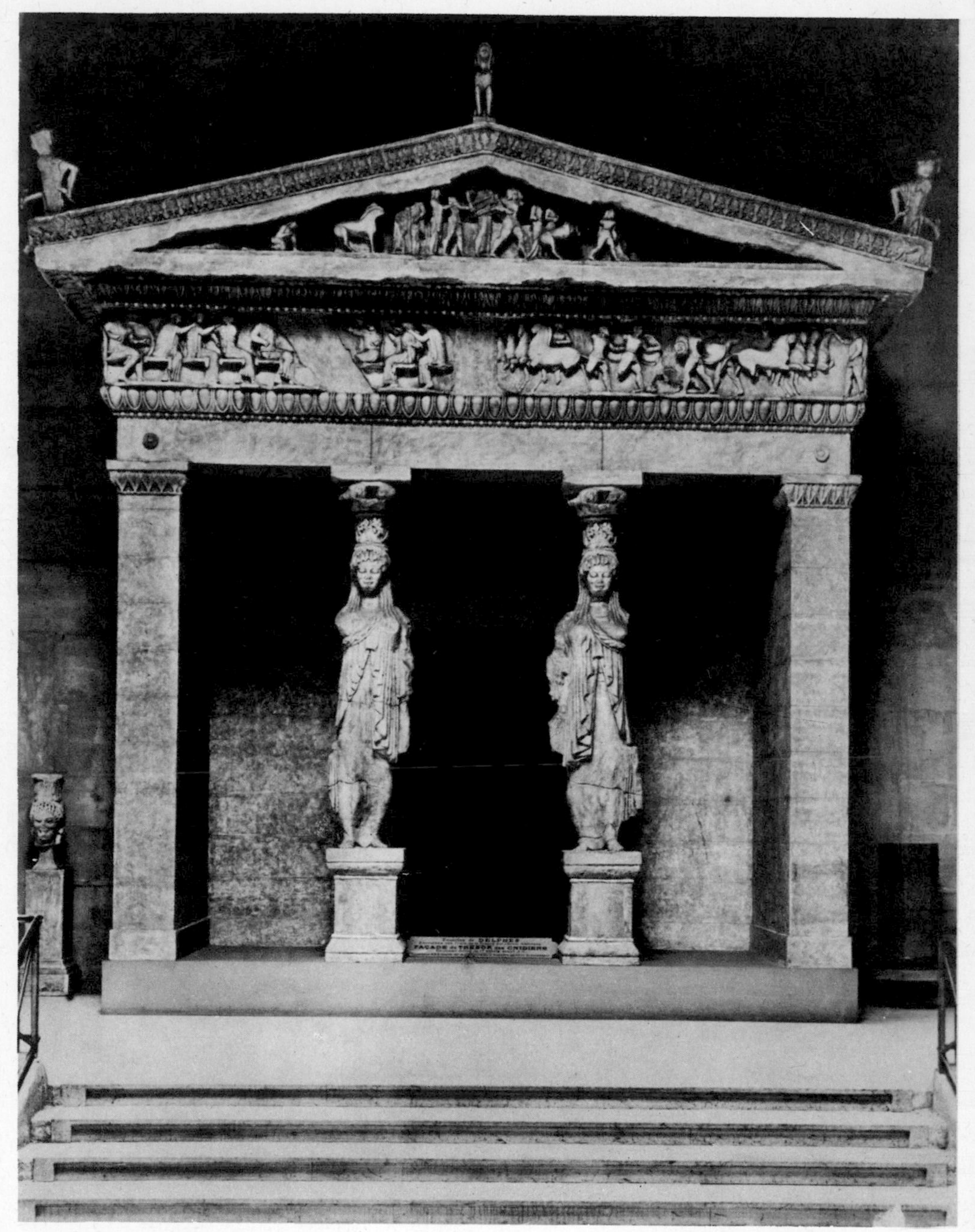

THE TREASURY OF THE CNIDIANS AT DELPHI

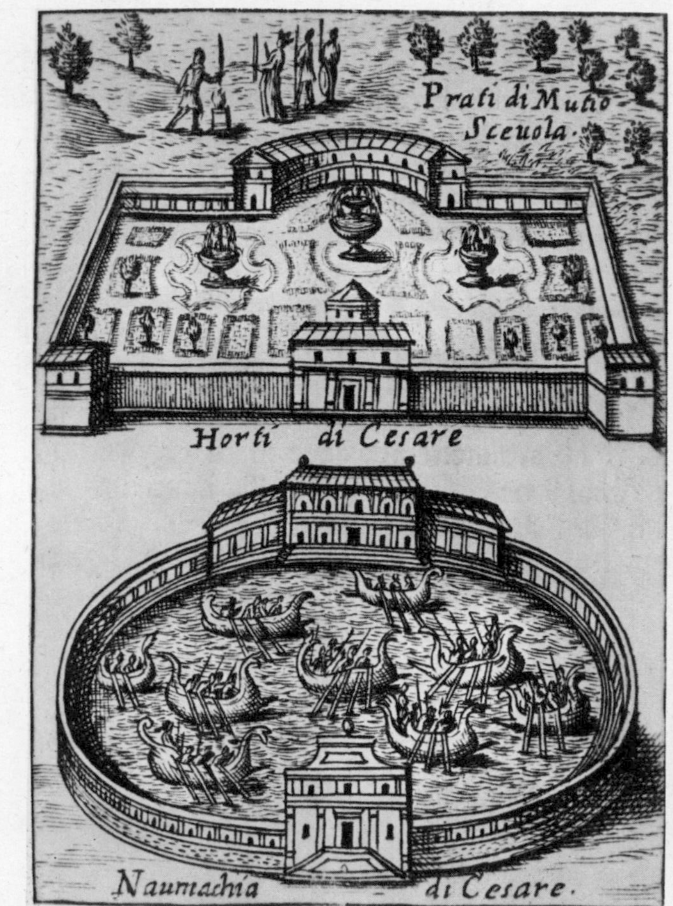

THE GARDENS OF SALLUST AND OF JULIUS CAESAR

From the *Ritratto di Roma Antica*, 1689

THE HORSE TAMERS (CASTOR AND POLLUX) OF THE MONTE CAVALLO

Attributed to Praxiteles after an engraving by Lafreri, sixteenth century

As Rome was to conquer the Hellenic world, so did she feel called upon to appropriate to her own needs the cultures which she had despoiled. Many indeed of the objects here discussed turn up again in Roman times only to be buried and resurrected by the humanists of the Renaissance.

---

traits of Olympic victors. . . . Ten years later, when Attalus obtained the Eubeoan town of Orens, he carried off the works of the Athenian sculptor Silanon, and these were included in the art collection which Eumenes II set up in the precinct of Athena. . . .

"As Attalus I and Eumenes II collected specimens and had copies made of earlier sculpture, so Attalus II was a connoisseur of paintings. Besides the well known story of his offer of a hundred talents for the painting of Dionysus by Apelles' contemporary Aristides when Corinth was sacked in 146 B.C., we have an inscription of the year 141/0 B.C. enumerating the honors paid by the Delphians to three Pergamene artists sent by Attalus II to copy paintings in Delphi, probably the famous frescoes in the Lesche of the Cnidians, painted by Polygnotus about 460 B.C."

A more vivid picture of the wealth and eclectic taste of Hellenistic Antioch has been provided in recent years by the splendid series of mosaics now at the Louvre, the Worcester Art Museum and the Baltimore Museum of Art which were unearthed in the 1930's. Cf. C. R. Morey, *The Mosaics of Antioch*, Longmans, Green, 1938, and the several volumes which have already appeared of *Antioch-on-the-Orontes* published by the Committee for the Excavation of Antioch and Its Vicinity. Princeton University Press, 1934 to date.

CHAPTER III

Roman Holiday

WORSHIPING the same gods as the Greeks, the Romans were at first conscience-stricken at the thought of plundering the shrines of divinities whose protection they too implored. Upon the advice of their priests they had adopted a fine method of distinguishing between sacred and profane and, when a foreign sanctuary proved too tempting to pass by, they gave to the gods at home a substantial portion of the booty. Quite often a Roman general would guarantee in advance the protection of a god; he would agree with the priests at Rome upon the particular shrines that offered the greatest benefits and then prorate the anticipated gold and silver booty before the campaign started. Thus Marcellus, the first Roman to conquer a Greek city, gave all the treasures he carried off from the temples of Syracuse to the Temples of Honor and Virtue on the Appian Way, keeping only an astronomical globe for himself.

As the taste for conquest spread so did the Roman taste for art increase and become more catholic; the city gradually overflowed with trophies taken from the subject peoples. They served as monuments in honor of the State and of the gods. But in the later years of the Republic, when the importance of the individual demanded greater recognition, these collections likewise served as monuments to personal ambition. They were frequently named after the general who had brought them home, and people referred casually to a particular statue in a temple as "the *Apollo* of Socius" or to "the monuments of Parius." Prominent Romans vied with each other in the erection and lavish decoration of their temples. Lucullus, for example, borrowed a series of Corinthian statues from his friend Mummius for the opening of his newly built Temple of Fortuna. He never returned them and Mummius was both wise and generous enough not to remind him of his promise. Other temples which in this way became religious or cult museums were those of Castor and Pollux, of Concord, of Venus Genetrix in the Forum of Caesar, and that of Mars in the Forum of Augustus. Among the nearly score of others were those of Isis and Serapis which were devoted almost entirely to Egyptian art.

This enthusiasm for antiquities which had begun originally as a hobby of the nobility took a wholly unexpected turn. It became the symbol of political and military authority, just as it did in Nazi Germany. The demand for works of art spread with epidemic swiftness. Rome had become a Hellenistic city in the image of Pergamon, and Antioch and Alexandria. Fortunately for the Roman conscience, still a little superstitious about looting Greece, Cleopatra had taken her share of the Hellenic monuments and it was considered only fair that Egypt should yield to Octavian the treasures which she had acquired. Following the example of the generals of the Republic, the age of the Caesars expanded and crystallized this fever for collecting and for the establishment of new institutions. On the very day of the battle of Pharsalus, Julius Caesar vowed to erect a temple to Venus while Octavian at Philippi promised one to Mars.

In connection with the temples themselves there were areas and halls specially prepared for the safekeeping and display of works of art. In one of these halls of Venus, Caesar deposited his own superlative collections of carved gems. The Temple of Apollo on the Palatine was the most famous of these religious monuments, later containing the Greek and Latin library of Augustus. Among other famous works it boasted a sculpture by Scopas; its great doors paneled in carved ivory represented the story of the *Niobids;* the pediment sculptures were Greek works from Chios and bronze bulls by Myron stood at the entrance.

But if these Roman temples were in a sense museums, as were the treasuries of the Hellenic sanctuaries, they were established from rather different motives in that the Greek foundations were local and spontaneous, whereas the Roman temple was a unit in a carefully planned program of a state religion. Yet, in the steady march of events from the days of the Republic on, there is visible a change in sentiment towards the possession of collections. The religious aspect falls into the background and the objects are looked upon as public wealth or treasure. The great baths, which were secular and semipublic, had many of the most magnificent collections of painting and sculpture in the city, and their "club rooms" were lavishly appointed with plate and tapestry taken from the entire Mediterranean world. The *Laocoon* was found in 1503 in the Baths of Titus; Lysippus's masterpiece adorned the Baths of Agrippa. Julius Caesar urged Asinius Pollio, the distinguished patron of art and letters who had founded the first public library in Rome, to open both his art collections and his books to the public. Agrippa later advocated making all collections of painting and sculpture state property and exhibiting them in Rome, instead of having the most precious relics of antiquity hidden in the country villas of the rich. This threat was not carried out, the later emperors continuing to loot the distant provinces for the embellishment of their palaces. Local governors sought to keep in favor by aiding them in their plunder. Five hundred bronze statues were carried off from Delphi alone and the culmination of these imperial appetites may still be seen in the vestiges of the palace of Diocletian at Spalato and in the ruins at Tivoli of the Villa of Hadrian.*

It was in this villa, spreading over an area of seven square miles on the banks of the Tiber, that this Emperor who had pushed the Roman frontiers to their farthest limits spent the late afternoon of his life. Having spent eighteen years of travel in every part of the Empire, where he had contributed to the architecture and beauty of the cities, he sought to recapture them by rebuilding facsimiles of the loveliest monuments he had seen. He reproduced the most celebrated halls of Athens and of Delphi, and even went so far as to reproduce the Vale of Tempe in Thessaly. He was a patron not only of architecture but of learning, forming libraries which he endowed and writing, like so many patrons of the arts, indifferent verse; soldier, traveler, philosopher and man of letters, he was a Hellenist who spoke Greek better

* Pliny, writing about A.D. 72, stated that "Mummius filled all Rome with sculptures after the conquest of Achaea. . . . The Luculli, too, brought over a number of statues; 73,000 are still to be seen at Rhodes, according to Mucianus, who was three times consul, and it is supposed that at least as many still remain at Athens, Olympia and Delphi." (K. Jex-Blake, *The Elder Pliny's Chapters on Art*, London, 1896, p. 29.)

than Latin. If for nothing else, the museums of the present day are indebted to him for the idea of the "period room."

It was inevitable that official patronage of art should affect the taste and character of the private citizen. No Roman of quality could permit himself to be left out of the fashionable world of art and letters, and we find, over a period of nearly three hundred years, throughout Latin literature an obsession with rare books and works of art.

The Roman world of fashion was very much like that of New York at the present time – money, comfort and the highest standards of luxury that money can buy being the primary consideration. The plumbing was elaborate and functioned perfectly; only the finest marbles were admitted. It was an age in which bronze and alabaster were flourished with the same abandon with which we use plate glass and chromium steel. Society, though addicted to the market place, a tradition which has persisted to this day in the arcades of Milan and Rome, confined itself to a lavish hospitality in private houses with *triclinia* or dining rooms arranged for every season of the year, and to the gardens and swimming pools of country villas. Public bars and restaurants, while they may have existed to some degree, did not occupy an important role in daily life. When the Roman was not at home he passed his time in the temples or the forums and then spent his leisure in the great public baths which resembled closely the athletic clubs and casinos of the present day.

Nothing was too good or too expensive for the citizens of Rome and they had the whole world which they had conquered to draw upon. It is curious, however, with all their fastidiousness and wealth, how relatively few types of luxury articles they had available. Of course horses, fine women, food and drink occupied a goodly portion of their fortunes and attention. Jewelry, works of art and bacchanalian feasts helped them to get rid of another portion of their wealth. There were no income taxes and no automobiles; the idea of the mink coat had not yet become the fixation that it is today and the deadly fear of alimony was virtually unheard of. There was nothing to do with money except to lavish it upon the most minute and incidental articles of daily use: Aeginetan candelabra at 25,000 sesterces, murrhine cups of agate for which collectors paid from 300,000 to 1,000,000 sesterces a piece, Babylonian embroidered coverlets, woven in gold, ranging from 800,000 to 1,000,000 sesterces, and tables of citrus wood inlaid with ivory, gold, silver, for twice that amount. Seneca was said to have had 500 such tables in his collection.

Luxury abounded everywhere; it was not confined to emperors or senators, or to the generals of the victorious armies. Martial's shorter poems and epigrams expose unmercifully the snob who exaggerates the quality and cost of all he owns: he buys slaves for 200,000 sesterces, drinks old vintages, has plate worth 5000 sesterces a pound, a gilded coach worth as much as an estate, a mule bought for the price of a house, and all his not very large possessions cost a million in our cash. This sum, says Friedländer, "must have been sufficient to furnish a fine house, if not a palace."

Of all the various types of art objects upon which the Romans set their hearts, the famous Corinthian bronzes were the most coveted, the most highly valued. Mummius, who was Consul in 146 B.C., had conquered Greece. After defeating the army of the Achaean League at the Isthmus of Corinth, he entered the city without opposition. The city was burned, abandoned to pillage; the native Corinthians were sold for slaves, and the rarest specimens of Grecian art were given up to the rapacity of an ignorant conqueror. Polybius the historian saw Roman soldiers playing at draughts upon the far-famed picture of *Dionysus* by Aristeides; and Mummius himself was so unconscious of the real value of his prize that he sold the rarer works of painting, sculpture and carving to the King of Pergamon, and "exacted securities from the masters of vessels, who conveyed the remainder to Italy, to replace by equivalents any picture or statue lost or injured in the passage."

According to legend the composition of Corinthian bronze, which was fused with gold and silver, and had by Imperial times become a lost secret of antiquity, was the accidental result of the burning of Corinth by Mummius. For the next two centuries the patina and color of Corinthian vessels gave a distinction to a collection which was not readily accorded to any other form of art. Seneca records the fabulous prices fetched by these items "through the insanity of a few" and Pliny the Younger wrote a letter to his friend Annius Severus about a bronze which he had just acquired:

I have lately purchased with a legacy that was left me, a statue of Corinthian bronze. It is small, but pleasing, and finely executed, at least, if I have any taste; which most certainly in matters of this sort, as perhaps in all others, is extremely defective. However, I think even I have enough to discover the beauties of this figure; as it is naked, the faults, if there be any, as well as the perfections, are more observable. It represents an old man in a standing posture. The bones, the muscles, the veins, and wrinkles are so strongly expressed, that you would imagine the figure to be animated. The hair is thin and failing, the forehead broad, the face shrivelled, the throat lank, the arms languid, the breast fallen, and the belly sunk; and the back view gives the same impression of old age. It appears to be a genuine antique, alike from its tarnish and from what remains of the original colour of the bronze. In short, it is a performance so highly finished as to fix the attention of artists, and delight the least knowing observer; and this induced me, who am a mere novice in this art, to buy it. But I did so, not with any intent of placing it in my own house (for I have as yet no Corinthian bronzes there) but with a design of fixing it in some conspicuous place in my native province, preferably in the temple of Jupiter; for it is a present well worthy of a temple and a god.

Pray, then, undertake this, as readily as you do all my commissions, and give immediate orders for a pedestal to be made. I leave the choice of the marble to you, but let my name be engraven upon it, and, if you think proper, my titles. I will send the statue by the first opportunity; or possibly (which I am sure you will like better) I may bring it myself; for I intend, business permitting, to make an excursion to you. This is a promise which I know you will rejoice to hear; but you will change your countenance when I add that my visit will be only for a few days, for the same affairs that now detain me here will prevent my making a longer stay. Farewell.*

A whole quarter of Rome in the vicinity of the Villa Publica was devoted to art dealers, booksellers and antiquarians – a quarter which was rife with the time-honored practices of falsification and forgery, of "phony" restorations and rigged auction sales. All of the practices of Fifty-seventh Street, for better or worse, appear in the writings of

* Pliny the Younger, *Letters*. Ed. William Melmoth. Heinemann, 1915. II, 205.

the satirists. Suetonius describes a scene in a Roman auction room which in the days of Mr. Hearst might have had its counterpart in New York. The Emperor Caligula, who was constantly in need of money, announced a sale of the spurious objects of his collection in which he himself would act as auctioneer. All of the members of his court were invited to be present and were obliged to buy well beyond the reserve price. One poor courtier fell asleep and Caligula thereupon called the attention of the barker to the fact that every time the man nodded in his sleep he raised his bid. When he awoke he had acquired some $5,000,000 worth of trash from the Emperor's collection.

But the buying was not always on this scale; hundreds of little shops abounded with works of art to fit every purse and every taste. The commentaries and the plays frequently poke fun at the ignorance and pretension of collectors, at their vanity and unwillingness to take advice, and at their pompous parade of misinformation. Petronius has immortalized this class of connoisseur in the *Satyricon* where Trimalchio, the ludicrous parvenu and buffoon, is the archetype of all such collectors of ancient and modern times.

The guests had assembled for the banquet, observed Petronius:

At last then we sat down, and boys from Alexandria poured water cooled with snow over our hands. Others followed and knelt down at our feet, and proceeded with great skill to pare our hangnails. Even this unpleasant duty did not silence them, but they kept singing at their work. I wanted to find out whether the whole household could sing, so I asked for a drink. A ready slave repeated my order in a chant not less shrill. They all did the same if they were asked to hand anything. It was more like an actor's dance than a gentleman's dining room. But some rich and tasty whets for the appetite were brought on; for everyone now had sat down except Trimalchio, who had the first place kept for him in the new style. A donkey in Corinthian bronze stood on the side-board, with panniers holding olives, white in one side, black in the other. Two dishes hid the donkey; Trimalchio's name and their weight in silver was engraved on their edges. There were also doormice rolled in honey and poppy-seed, and supported on little bridges soldered to the plate. Then there were hot sausages laid on a silver grill, and under the grill damsons and seeds of pomegranate.

While we were engaged in these delicacies, Trimalchio was conducted in to the sound of music, propped on the tiniest of pillows. A laugh escaped the unwary. His head was shaven and peered out of a scarlet cloak, and over the heavy clothes on his neck he had put on a napkin with a broad stripe and fringes hanging from it all round. On the little finger of his left hand he had an enormous gilt ring, and on the top joint of his next finger a smaller ring which appeared to me to be entirely of gold, but was really set all round with iron cut out in little stars. Not content with this display of wealth, he bared his right arm, where a golden bracelet shone, and an ivory bangle clasped with a plate of bright metal.

As the gaiety of the evening wore on, Trimalchio boasted of his possessions. "I am the sole owner of Corinthian plate . . . You may perhaps inquire," he declared, how I come to be alone in having genuine Corinthian stuff: the obvious reason is that the name of the dealer I buy it from is Corinthus. But what is real Corinthian, unless a man has Corinthus at his back? Do not imagine I am an ignoramus. I know perfectly well how Corinthian plate was first brought into the world." Then after he had lectured his friends upon this subject he turned to silver, for which "I have a great passion. I own about four hundred four gallon cups engraved with Cassandra killing her children, and they lying there dead in the most life-like way. I have a thousand jugs which Mummius left to my patron, and on them you see Daedalus shutting Niobe into the Trojan horse. And I have got the fights between Hermeros and Portraites on my cups, and every cup is a heavy one; for I do not sell my connoisseurship for any money." Trimalchio's treasures are no more but the species is not extinct. It lives on in the dinner parties of Palm Beach and Park Avenue.*

We must not, however, suppose that all the Romans were necessarily vulgar and that there were not among them collectors of knowledge and sensibility comparable to those of the Renaissance. The tradition was long in developing and had been firmly planted on Latin soil as early as the second century B.C. when Eumenes II sent his grammarian and librarian, Crates of Mallos, from Pergamon as ambassador to Rome. The impetus given by this early humanist set in flame a desire for learning and cultivation which, though largely im-

* Petronius, *The Satyricon*, trans. by Michael Heseltine. Loeb Classical Library, 1913.

ported from the other centers of antiquity, was surely no less genuine. History has often seen these phenomena of nations turning to the arts in their prosperity – Florence under the Medici, England under the Stuart and Georgian kings, and France in the reign of Louis XIV. We in the United States, too, are now seeing this same development take place. It is a form of intellectual compensation or atonement for dominating the world at a given period – tempered perhaps with an all too human instinct for the display of wealth.

From the days of the Republic, Greek libraries were being constantly transported as organized units to Rome. Lucius Aemilius Paulus had seized for himself the library of Perseus, King of Macedon. He bequeathed it to his sons, one of whom was the younger Scipio, conqueror of Carthage. Lucullus had obtained a rich library in Asia Minor which he brought home and opened up to scholars. Sulla, capturing Athens in 86 B.C., took with him Aristotle's library which he established in his spacious palace in Rome under the care of two learned scholars, Andronicus of Rhodes, the Aristotelian commentator, and Tyrannion, later Cicero's literary adviser. It is hardly necessary to point out that to possess a library at this time was a badge of cultivation and of personal achievement. Thompson contends that "in the case of men of genuine culture the nucleus of these books was, no doubt, a working library; but even such men, in the spirit of their age, often collected extravagantly for the mere luxury of possession. The correspondence of Cicero, for example, teems with references to this enthusiasm. In each of his villas (he had eighteen in different parts of Italy), there was a permanent library. Yet in his bookish extravagance, Cicero seems to have been merely typical of his social class, whose practices, as always, were grotesquely imitated by the crude and newly wealthy." *

The world has seldom seen, before or since, such extravagance and luxury or such a blatant disregard for the property of others. These villas and palaces were not confined to Rome but may still be seen throughout the length and breadth of the Empire wherever money was made. It was the pride of the local governor or banker to outdo

* James Westfall Thompson, *The Medieval Library*. University of Chicago Press, 1939, p. 5.

the capital itself. And in the baths of Pompeii and Herculaneum (and the even more exclusive Baiae) the makers of the Roman Empire spent their declining years on a diet of soft foods, soft women and still softer intellectuality.

Thanks to Pliny and Vitruvius we have a pretty good picture of what these villas and collections looked like and how the owners and their households lived in the midst of so much borrowed finery from Greece and Asia. By the time of Augustus picture galleries were so common that in Vitruvius's plan of a great house "a large hall towards the north for this purpose was considered indispensable; in later times, collections of sculpture also became general." The taste invariably was for the antique. Young Roman citizens went to Greece, to Africa and to Asia Minor in much the same spirit in which the Whig aristocrats of the eighteenth century took the grand tour to Italy. Their quest was primarily literary, to tie up the fragments of their schooling with the vestigial beauties of the classic past; and the accumulation of works of art was no proof of their artistic feeling but rather a means of satisfying newly aroused curiosities and of acquiring the necessary superficial background for their social and political position. Like their Georgian successors they also gave scanty consideration to the masterpieces of their contemporaries. If they suffered modern art at all, it was in the fields of decoration and architectural embellishment and not because they believed in the immortality of an undiscovered talent. Antiquity then as always offered a special and appealing opportunity for veneration. Pliny maintained that the picture galleries were stuffed with old pictures; Quintilian ridicules the enthusiasts for "primitives" and during the reign of Hadrian there was a raging fashion for Hellenistic art, particularly the pictures and statues of the period of the Diadochi.

The snobbery of possession shining through the pages of the Latin commentators far surpassed anything which we know today. Martial said of a man who boasted too loudly of his treasures that his friends were just as genuine as his collection. During the reign of Hadrian it even became common practice to inscribe statues with signatures of the great artists of the past. Possibly this was done not so much with intent to deceive but rather in the way that the Chinese emperors for a thousand years stamped their scrolls with attributions and official seals as proof of their own admiration and superior connoisseurship. And in this connection, too, "provenance" and pedigree became indispensable attributes of antiquity and importance. Friedländer tells how objects with personal and historic association were highly prized — an earthen lamp of Epictetus, the jewels of Germanicus, silver vessels belonging to Philip of Macedon which were recovered from a shipwreck. Caracalla had some weapons said to have belonged to Alexander the Great; a little *Hercules* by Lysippus in the collection of Novius Vindex was claimed to have come from the same source. These vaunted claims aroused the scorn of the irreverent, for when Martial was asked to look with respect upon "a plank from the ship *Argo*," he said he was unwilling to listen further to the "smoke-begrimed genealogies" of silver cups supposed to have belonged to Nestor, Achilles and to Dido.

The pattern of Roman collecting had early been laid out by Sulla, the first of the private connoisseurs on the grand scale. A great noble and warrior, he had spared nothing either public or private in Greece if he could take some profit for himself. Among his treasures were the *Hercules* by Lysippus which had belonged first to Alexander the Great and later to Hannibal, and a small golden statue of *Apollo*, stolen from Delphi, which went with him on all of his campaigns. Before each battle he would pray to it and kiss it reverently. His lieutenants Verres and Murena were obviously well trained in the art of plunder. Sulla's heir and son-in-law, Scaurus, staggered even his contemporaries by building a theater for a single performance to seat 80,000 persons which he decorated with 3000 statues and 360 columns. His collection of engraved gems at Tusculum, the first to be made in Rome, and rivaled only by the six collections of cameos and intaglios given by Julius Caesar to the Temple of Venus, were valued together with his furniture, paintings (which included those brought from Sicyon by Pausias) and gold thread tapestries from Messina at something around $10,000,000 in today's money. The gardens of Lucullus, described by Plutarch, which extended down the slopes of the Pincio, later occupied by the Villa Medici, were filled not only with statues and works of art but with exotic plants and wild beasts from distant parts of the Empire. Pompey's gardens on the Janiculum boasted many splendid pieces. The colossal *Melpomene* in the Louvre and the bronze *Hercules* acquired by Pope Pius IX for the Vatican decorated his private theater, which was said to have a portico of 300 columns of rose marble.

Among the possessions of Julius Caesar, according to Bonnaffé, were the head of *Jupiter* in the Louvre, the statue of *Meleager* in the Vatican and the lovely *Venus* of the Hermitage in Saint Petersburg.* The gardens of Sallust on the Quirinal contained likewise examples which have survived the centuries, including such famous groups as the *Dying Gaul* and the *Venus and Cupid* in the Belvedere of the Vatican, besides a number of other antiquities found in the Villa Ludovisi which later occupied this site.

These are but a few of the masterpieces which peopled the residences of the wealthier Romans and which have provided such a field day ever since for scholars and collectors. But even these pale beside the collections amassed by the Proconsul Verres. Son of a patrician, he was destined to public life and rose to be Governor of Sicily. There was nothing which escaped his grasp. He was ruthless, fastidious, and possessed probably the finest eye for works of art of anyone in the ancient world. His collection epitomized not only the gigantic cultural appetites of his countrymen but the abysmal depths to which they would stoop in order to satisfy them. Cicero, whose merciless prosecution of him is contained in the celebrated orations *In Verrem* sought an indemnity of 100,000,000 sesterces (about $25,000,000) for his Sicilian thefts alone. These orations, with their invective and devastating criticism, give a vivid description of Verres's palace and

* The Louvre head of *Jupiter* has had a long romantic history. Marc Antony brought both the head and the figure to which it belongs to Italy from Samos. Augustus, the first of the emperors to covet it, placed it in the Capitol at Rome where it remained until the sixteenth century, when it found its way to the cabinet of Margaret of Antioch, Duchesse de Camarion. She in turn gave it to Cardinal Granvella, the Minister of the Emperor Charles V, who placed it in his gardens at Besançon. When Louis XIV took this city in the seventeenth century the magistrates presented the statue to the King for the gardens at Versailles. The head is today intact, but the torso, damaged in the course of time, was restored by the sculptors Girardon and Drouilly. Cf. E. Bonnaffé, *Les Collectionneurs de l'ancienne Rome*, Paris, 1867. It must be remembered that the writer, working at a time when archaeology was still an art and not a laboratory science, was more concerned with fiction than with fact.

its contents. The entrance to it was through the ivory and gold doors of the Syracusan Temple of Minerva, above which was a superb Gorgon's head carved in ivory. The tapestries of the entrance hall, stolen from Messina, from the palaces of Malta and Syracuse, were woven with gold thread and reputed to be worth 200,000 sesterces. His finest furniture was bequeathed to him by the beautiful courtesan Chelidon, and the curtains and upholstery had been the product of three years' work by the noblest ladies of Sicily.

The palace, fantastic in scale, followed the usual Roman plan of wings and buildings giving upon an atrium or court. Disposed about its peristyle of columns was the finest collection of statues in Italy. What Verres had not acquired by confiscation in the lands which he had governed he later acquired by purchase and by blackmail. One wing of the villa was devoted to the *pinacotheca* or picture gallery for which he had ransacked the East; the paintings included, among others, the twenty-seven portraits of the Kings of Sicily from the Temple of Minerva in Syracuse. The cabinet of bronzes and candelabra was no less fine than the sculptures in marble, being particularly rich in Corinthian bronzes. Terra cottas, vases and engraved stones occupied special halls, and the living apartments, with a series of dining rooms for every season, were sumptuously appointed with gold and silver plate in which Verres's connoisseurship was unsurpassed.

But all these riches were to bring him nothing but sorrow and disgrace. Banished from Rome in 70 B.C. as the result of Cicero's prosecution, Verres lived in exile for twenty-seven years. When he returned after the assassination of Cicero, Marc Antony, who was then in power, asked Verres to give him some of his Corinthian bronzes. Although he knew what the consequences would be if he refused, Verres nevertheless decided not to part with them, and he was placed upon the proscription lists and condemned to death. The story is told that when Marc Antony sent him the poison to drink in a murrhine cup, the most valuable article in his collection, Verres drank the poison quickly and dashed the cup upon the marble floor, smashing it into a thousand pieces.

The greed of provincial governors and their insatiable appetite for art may well have contributed to the suddenness with which the Roman Empire fell into a decline. Cicero in his prosecution of Verres did not confine his indictment to the Proconsul of Sicily, but inveighed against the spoils system as a whole. "Year after year," he said, "we have seen all the wealth of all the world become the property of a mere handful of men; and our readiness to tolerate and permit this is the more apparent because none of those persons conceals his cupidity, none is concerned to throw any doubt on the fact of it. Among all the treasures that so richly adorn this beautiful city of ours, is there one statue, one picture, that has not been captured and brought hither from the enemies we have defeated in war? Whereas the country houses of the men of whom I refer are furnished to overflowing with the countless beautiful things of which they have robbed our most loyal allies. What do you suppose has become of the wealth of the foreign nations who are now so poor, when you see Athens, Pergamum, Cyzicus, Miletus, Chios, Samos – nay, all Asia and Achaea, all Greece and Sicily, concentrated in these few country-houses? Yet I repeat, gentlemen, that today your allies are not attempting, and not caring, to recover any of these treasures. By their loyalty and good service they guarded themselves against being deprived from them by public decree of the Roman nation. The time came when they could not resist the greed of this man or that, but in one way or another they were able to gratify it. Today they have lost the power not only of resisting but even of supplying the demands made of them." *

The taste for collecting continued through the days of the Empire. But as the imperial structure placed more and more emphasis upon the person and court of the emperor, private collecting became relatively less and less important. By the time of Constantine the Great in the fourth century A.D. new interests had arisen and already the decline of Roman culture was apparent. With the transfer of the capital to Byzantium in 476 A.D., Rome had entered into its thousand years of medieval slumber. The City of Ruins had already become a fact and not even the splendor of the Byzantine court could retard the steady progress of disintegration. Rome was the quarry from which the new world of Christendom was to be built. The Hippo-

* *Cicero: The Verrine Orations* (English trans. by L. H. G. Greenwood). The Loeb Classical Library. II, pp. 606, 607.

drome in Constantinople, containing some 60 statues that had once graced the Forums of the Caesars, and Hagia Sophia (with its 420 antique sculptures) which later on was to yield its multicolored veneer of marble to Saint Mark's in Venice, were foundations in the Roman pattern. But they were none the less museums dedicated to a different God. Constantine's determination to make Byzantium the capital of the world was the very thing which killed Rome. It took many centuries for the tastes and curiosities of her period of supremacy to be reawakened and to recover from the fanaticism of early Christianity. The social and economic conditions upon which the collector thrives were gone and not to be recaptured until the Renaissance.

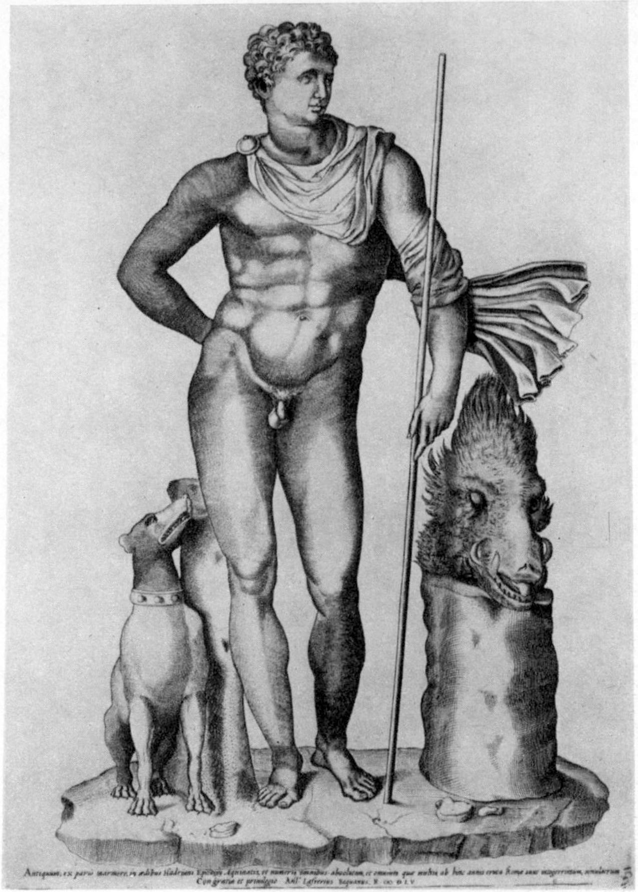

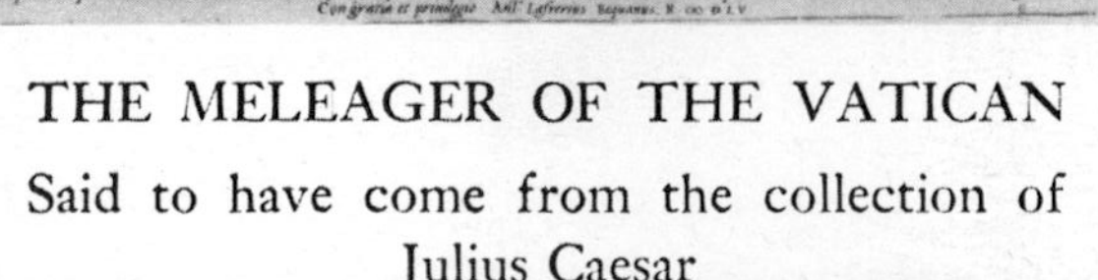

THE MELEAGER OF THE VATICAN

Said to have come from the collection of Julius Caesar

THE MELPOMENE OF THE LOUVRE

Said to have been found in the Gardens of Pompey on the Janiculum

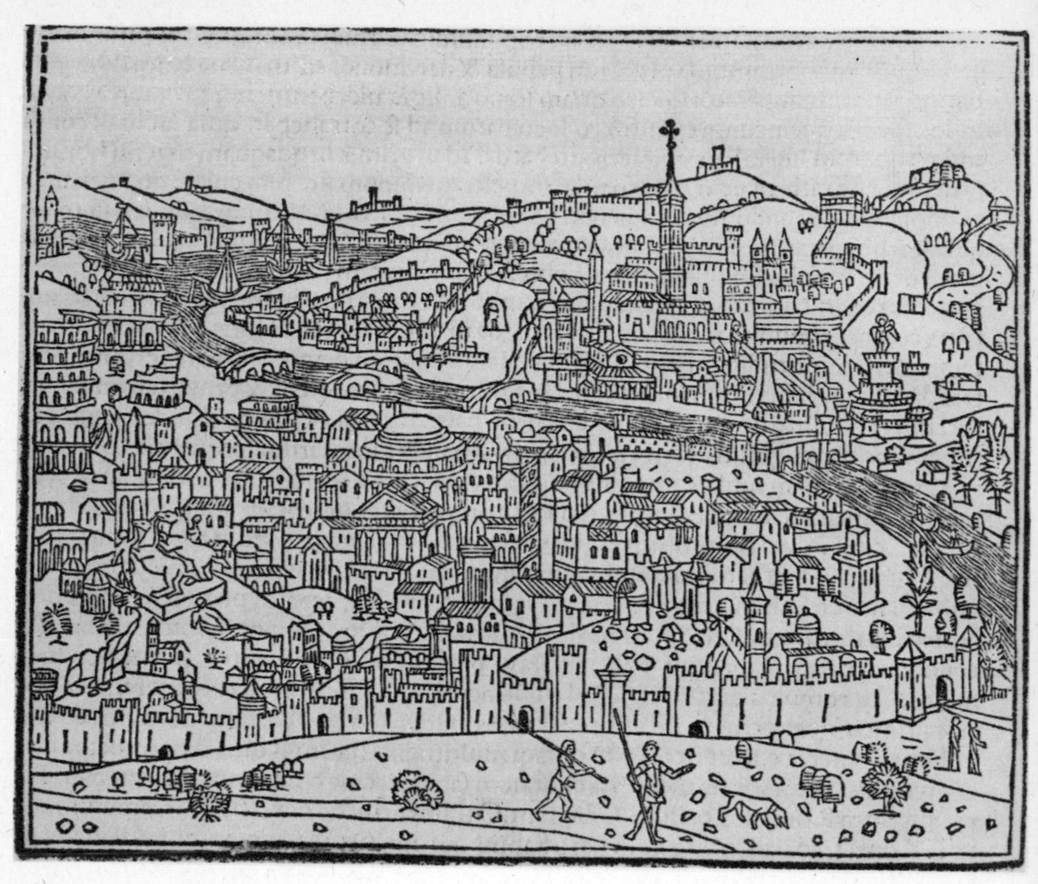

ROME AT THE CLOSE OF THE MIDDLE AGES

The earliest printed view of Rome taken from the *Bergamensis Chronicle*, A.D. 1493. In the foreground may be seen the Pantheon and Trajan's Column; across the Tiber the ancient basilica of Saint Peter's, the medieval buildings of the Vatican and the Castel Sant' Angelo

CHAPTER IV

The Middle Ages

THE Middle Ages open another vista in the history of collecting, that "squirrel instinct" of the human mind. Collecting continued in a thin trickle for another thousand years. The decline of Rome was after all a lengthy process of decay and we must not assume that the curtain was rung down on a certain evening of the fifth century and that the comedy was ended. Even if the actors lacked the talent of their predecessors and the chorus sang off key, the audience still demanded some kind of performance. It was, moreover, the responsibility of the Church to see that during the dark night of barbarism the lamp of classic learning was not totally extinguished.

The Christian communism of the Middle Ages had put an end to private wealth, and Europe was not to see a bourgeoisie again until the formation of the Italian republics. Only the hereditary rulers and the prelates of the Church were in a position to patronize the arts. Then too, the struggle for survival of primitive Christianity, first against the persecutions of the emperors and later against the persistence of paganism and idolatry, compelled a strict censorship in subject matter. It necessitated, in a community in which the ability to read was confined to the clergy, a mobilization of all of the means of visual expression for the propaganda of the new religion. There was little place in the medieval system for the gods and goddesses of classical antiquity. In the Byzantine palaces at Ravenna and in the East, particularly in the great cosmopolitan centers on the Bosporus and in Antioch and Alexandria, there lingered on a persistent nostalgia for classical antiquity. The saints of Christendom appear with a new hieratic splendor. Their glory is the glory of the new faith but their forms follow implicitly the patterns of the past. Since ecclesiastical authority was never able to dispense entirely with hoary tradition, we see for example the classical pictures of the philosophers of Greece transformed into the seated Evangelist portraits which preface the Gospels in the early manuscripts of the New Testament.

But there were profounder and more philosophic reasons for the change in taste during the early centuries of the Christian era. The sense of sin which had taken possession of men's minds, and the urgency for salvation through expiation, had brought the citizens of the dismembered and decaying Empire to look with disfavor upon personal luxury and its attendant evils. The Fathers of the Church lamented the wickedness about them and Saint Augustine, who in his youth had admired Plato and Cicero, condemned the ancient culture. "The Greek philosophers," he said, "would tremble among the dead to hear the name of Christ. The poets were inventors of lies and immorality. The pagan gods were demons, and pagan statues demons in stone." In his *Confessions* he wrote: "What innumerable toys made by divers arts and manufactures in our apparel, shoes, utensils, in pictures and divers images, and these far exceeding all necessary and moderate use and all pious meaning have men made to tempt their own eyes withal. The beauty of God's temple is the beauty of righteousness. . . . God's holy temple is marvelous, not in pillars, marbles and in gilded ceilings, but in righteousness." *

Yet if the aesthetic consciousness endured longer in the Byzantine Church because of the proximity of Oriental cultures, it was quickly forgotten in the outposts of Latin Christianity. Waves of barbarians from the plains of northern and central Europe swept down upon the Italian peninsula, taking possession of Lombardy and of the Roman colonies in Spain and Provence. Gaul and the colonies beyond the Rhine had preserved little of the civilizing influences of the Roman occupation, and the craftsmen of these countries were primarily concerned with tribal decorations and designs of jewelry and personal articles which the horsemen carried with them on their migrations. Rome fell repeatedly before the storming of the Hun; in the wake of the economic devastation of the once prosperous Empire there

* Saint Augustine, *De Pulchro et Apto*. Cf. André Fontaine, *Doctrines d'art en France* (Renouard), 1909, and Frank P. Chambers, *The History of Taste*, Columbia University Press, 1932.

followed pestilence and famine. The soil of Europe so beautifully husbanded by Roman colonizers turned sour from neglect; in order to nourish it, the peasants, who had taken possession of these once gracious villas, burned for lime the statues which had originally peopled their formal *allées* and colonnades. How much of the collections of classic times was thus turned into fertilizer we can never say, but if the practices which still continue in Greece and in the Middle East are any indication, it is safe to assume that the greater part was thus destroyed.

It was not until the time of Charlemagne that there was at last some semblance of a European state. Ephemeral kingdoms and duchies had risen to power only to fall to the depredations of their neighbors. The Church was the only link with the past, and acknowledging at least a titular submission to the Bishop of Rome, the prelates of the secular dioceses provided the only organized authority on the Continent. Even the self-contained agricultural communities founded upon the remains of the Roman estates failed to provide anything more than a local paternalism. Statecraft had died out and feudalism, so highly perfected by the time of the Norman Conquest, had far to go before being accepted as a political ideal.

Side by side with the secular bishops arose the abbots who, answerable directly to Rome, gradually gathered into their monastic establishments all that was left of the vast culture of antiquity. The Benedictines, first setting out as missionaries from the mother house of Monte Cassino near Naples, spread their authority over western Europe and the British Isles. To these monks must be given full credit not merely for having preserved the remnants of the classics, but also for having kept alive the incentive for learning. Without them the art of reading and writing would have perished in the West with the fall of Rome. They established libraries and copying rooms. The illustrations to their books of devotion, their theological commentaries and their bestiaries, together with whatever copies of the classics fell into their hands from pilgrims and travelers from the East, served as the texts for the education of the nobility and clergy and were the models for the works of art developed under their direction. The great murals and sculptured portals, the stained glass and tapestries of the medieval churches which were the poor man's Bible, all derived their inspiration from the manuscripts illuminated in the monasteries. It has been said, and with justice, that the miniatures of European manuscripts were the backbone of medieval art from which all the variations of style and iconography depended.

Towards the period of the "Carolingian Renaissance" (Charlemagne was crowned Emperor by the Pope in Saint Peter's in the year 800 A.D.), society had already begun to re-establish itself on the wreckage of the Roman Empire. The Benedictine Order was in its full prosperity. The feudal nobles through the fortunes of guerilla warfare had managed to acquire a new and often ill-gotten wealth which they lavished upon the religious foundations in the hope of gaining the security of heaven after a reasonably short delay in purgatory. Their gifts and bequests took various forms; the most important were, of course, the architectural additions to church property, dependencies of abbeys, the rebuilding of cloisters, memorial chapels and stained-glass windows. But equally important in the eyes of the clergy were precious books and relics from the East; textiles, fragments cut from the shroud of a martyr, a drop of the Blessed Virgin's milk, a fragment of the True Cross or the decayed tooth of a local worthy, who, like Saint Patrick, might have driven the snakes from his native country. Encased in delicately wrought shrines of gold and silver and encrusted with rubies, pearls and antique cameos, they became the nucleus of church treasuries and paralleled the religious collections of the Greek and Roman temples.

Among the greatest of these medieval treasuries was that of the Royal Abbey of Saint Denis, whose twelfth-century Abbot Suger rebuilt the church and provided it with a collection of liturgical vessels of the utmost preciousness. Some of them have come down to us: the ewers and vessels in the Galerie d'Apollon of the Louvre, and the agate and gold chalice set with antique gems in the Widener Collection at Washington.

We have thought it proper to place on record the description of the ornaments of the Church by which the Hand of God, during our administration, has adorned His Church, His Chosen Bride; lest Oblivion, the jealous rival of Truth, sneak in and take away the example for further action. Our Patron, the thrice blessed Denis, is we confess and proclaim, so generous and benevolent that we believe him to have prevailed upon God to such an extent, and to have obtained from Him so many and so great things, that we might have been able to do for his church a hundred times more than we have done, had not human frailty, the mutability of the times, and the instability of manners prevented it. What we, nevertheless, have saved for him by the grace of God is the following.*

There follows a list of the objects which embellished the church — the golden altar frontal in the upper choir and the golden crucifix. Suger describes the gems applied to the crucifix, and the quality of workmanship in gold and enamel of the various objects made under his direction. Then he says:

Also with the devotion due to the Blessed Denis, we acquired vessels of gold as well as precious stones for the service of the Table of God, in addition to those which the kings of the Franks and those devoted to the church had donated for this service. Specifically we caused to be made a big golden chalice of 140 ounces of gold adorned with precious gems, viz., hyacinths and topazes, as a substitute for another one which had been lost in the time of our predecessor.

The enumeration continues of the other treasures: a "vessel of prase, carved in the form of a boat, which King Louis, son of Philip, had left in pawn for nearly ten years"; a "pint bottle of beryl or crystal, which the Queen of Aquitania had presented to our Lord King Louis as a newly wed bride on their first voyage" (the *Juste* of the Louvre); "a precious chalice out of one solid sardonyx" (the Widener chalice); and "a porphyry vase, made admirable by the hand of the sculptor and polisher, after it had lain idly in a chest for many years, converting it from a flagon into the shape of an eagle" (Louvre).

Abbot Suger concludes this inventory of the treasures of Saint Denis in the middle years of the twelfth century with the following pious exhortations:

. . . For all this we thank Almighty God and the Holy Martyrs, since He has not refused abundantly to bestow upon the most sacred altar, at which He wanted us to be offered as a child under the precepts

* Suger, *De Administratione*.

of our holy rule, that which we may serve Him in worthy manner.

And since we are convinced that it is useful and becoming not to hide but to proclaim Divine benefactions, we have destined (for this purpose) that increase in textiles which the hand Divine has granted to this sacred church in the time of our administration; we urge that they be laid out on our anniversary in order to propitiate the supreme power of Divine Majesty and to enhance the devotion of the brethren, and as an example for the succeeding abbots. For late and scanty penance cannot atone for so many and so great sins as I have committed, nor for the enormity of my crimes, unless we rely upon the intercession of the Universal Church.*

* * * * *

Mediterranean commerce, through new inventions in the rigging of sailing vessels which had replaced the painful galleys of Roman days, and through advances in the science of navigation, had taken a new impetus. Contacts with the Eastern world which had been almost broken off were once again resumed. Overland trade routes were opened up connecting seaports with inland waterways, and the Church once more took the leadership by cornering the travel business of the Middle Ages. The abbeys and convents which dotted the trade routes at convenient intervals served not only as inns and hostels for commercial travelers, but as hospitals and asylums for pilgrims who were beginning to look for salvation amid the hallowed ruins of Palestine and Rome.

Around the year 1000, when all good men had believed the world would end, another discovery was made which brought about an industrial revolution almost as fundamental and far-reaching in its implications as the invention of the steam engine eight hundred years later. This was the discovery that the traditional harness, handed down from antiquity and fitting tightly around the animal's throat, did not give adequate play to the traction powers of the horse. Any heavy pull would immediately strangle him. The economy of Europe was thus dependent upon the slow-moving oxcart to draw the heavy loads, the horse being reserved for the lighter and more mobile uses of cavalry warfare. To meet this difficulty the modern horse collar was

* E. Panofsky, ed. and trans. *Abbot Suger on the Abbey Church of Saint Denis and its Art Treasures*. Princeton University Press, 1946, pp. 53, 77, 81.

invented; lying flat against the chest and shoulders of the horse, it left his windpipe free and permitted him to pull a load upwards of a thousand pounds. From the discovery of this simple device, which quickened many times the movement of goods, as Lynn White points out, the prosperity of the Middle Ages grew, for from it dated the era of horse-drawn transportation, the basis of the new and revitalized economy which dominated Europe until well into the nineteenth century.*

There were other advances and discoveries in science which added to the commercial and intellectual ferment of Europe. The grinding of lenses for eyeglasses alone was a discovery which gave twenty years of additional reading to the average student, a factor of incalculable importance in hastening the Renaissance. Much of this science was filtered through the highly civilized Norman court at Palermo where the Hohenstaufen emperor and the Kings of Sicily had given refuge to Arabian and Jewish scientists, physicians and philosophers. The Moslems in Spain, taking their direction from the Caliphate of Cordova, likewise patterned their culture on Eastern models. The wisdom and culture of the world of Islam were blended with the learning of the Christian monks and penetrated through the hangover of the classic past. Palermo, indeed, was to the later phases of Byzantine art what Ravenna was to the sixth and seventh centuries. It was the crucible in which were melted down the elements of the fast approaching Italian Renaissance. Yet Sicily and Malta were merely way stations to the Holy Land. The restlessness which had seized Europe upon the ultimate maturing of the feudal system carried the Mediterranean spirit of inquiry into France and Spain as well as to the northern countries. The Crusades which occupied the knights of the Continent for nearly two hundred and fifty years, and which brought some hundreds of thousands of pilgrim warriors into contact with the civilizations of the East, finished the task of preparing the soil for the revival of learning.

Stripped of their romantic glamour of the nineteenth century and freed from the trappings of Sir Walter Scott and Howard Pyle, the

* Lynn White, "Technology and Invention in the Middle Ages," in *Speculum*, April 1940. Vol. XV, pp. 141–159.

Crusades must be looked upon not so much as a spiritual movement but rather a reaction against the artificial self-sufficiency of feudal economy. The château, which had dominated the village and the fief, was a unit which left little to the imagination or enterprise of the individual. Every county or dukedom was separated from its neighbor not merely in matters of allegiance but by high tariff walls; what opportunity there was for free taxation was limited to arbitrary levies on the movement of goods as they traveled through private estates from the free incorporated cities, then in the process of formation, or from the East. Already we hear the cry of "free enterprise" raised against the barons, for there was no interchange of capital or goods as in Roman or modern times. Each community lived almost exclusively on what it produced and widespread distribution of food and goods was virtually unknown. Society had reached one of those periodic stalemates between production and consumption which inevitably result in the great upheavals of history. The Crusades were an easy way out since they offered the nobles an outlet for their courtly militarism and new lands to plunder in the name of Christ.

The Crusades, like all military campaigns, required extraordinary financing; the underwriters for this lucrative venture were the merchants and bankers of the Venetian Republic. Venice had maintained her maritime supremacy unbroken from the last days of the Byzantine capital at Ravenna. Mistress of the Adriatic, she gradually dominated the whole of the Mediterranean basin. Her barques and naval vessels entered every sea; her traders were the chief men of affairs in every port. Her trade with Alexandria, still the most prosperous manufacturing and exporting center of the Levant, was virtually a monopoly. Venice played her cards both ways and took a profit wherever it was to be found. She transported at exorbitant rates the knights of western Europe to the Holy Land to fight the Saracen and Turk. She had carried Saint Louis's crusading army of 10,000 men and 4000 horses with only 15 vessels. Villehardouin tells us that the Venetians had charged 85,000 silver marks for embarking in their fleets the soldiers of the Cross during the Fourth Crusade. In addition, they had bargained for a share of the booty.*

* Albert Malet, *Moyen Âge*. Hachette, 1926.

Yet Venice remained strictly neutral by selling Christian women and blond Nordic eunuchs to the Oriental harems. In the matter of arms she sold and manufactured them, of course, for both sides with complete impunity. Not until the last and Fourth Crusade in the thirteenth century did she hearken to the call of the True Faith and pounce upon the city of Constantine itself; here her merchants and sea captains had been received like brothers by the Greeks for seven hundred years. The fruits of this despicable act may still be seen in the Cathedral of Saint Mark, which gained not only the bronze horses of Nero from the Hippodrome but also the marble facing and incrustation that had been carefully pried off the exterior of Hagia Sophia and brought to Venice in the bottoms of her warships.

From the prosperity of selling Christian slaves to Moslems along with grain from the plains of France and Spain, woolen cloth from Florence and the Low Countries, glass from the factories of Torcello and Murano, and of the importation in her returning galleys of spices, gold and silver, silks and precious jewels, the Queen of the Adriatic luxuriated in truly Oriental splendor. Each year the "Caravan of the Levant" set out with naval convoy for the Eastern ports. Unending was the speculation regarding their safe return and side bets and other forms of primitive insurance against the pirates of the Barbary Coast gave rise to a host of business enterprises. When the galleons finally arrived in Venice and were unloaded at the private quays of the patrician palaces, the city was in a mood for revelry.

Gold filled the strong boxes of the merchants. Their families donned garments so gorgeous that city-fathers, fearing the new-won wealth might demoralize the rest of the population, passed sumptuary laws forbidding boys under twelve to wear pearl-covered belts and limiting the quantities of gold tissue which patrician ladies might wear in public.

Worthy of their riches were the palaces built by these parvenus, one of which the Golden House, the *Ca' d'Oro*, still stands. Each of the palaces, with its balconies upheld by delicately cut Moorish pillars and walls brilliant with gold-leaf and bright frescoes, was rendered doubly magnificent by having a twin, mirrored in the waters of the canal below.*

* Miriam Beard, *A History of the Business Man.* The Macmillan Co., 1938, pp. 110, 111.

This parade of wealth received the confirmation of the State. Only a merchant who could build a golden house could have his name inscribed in the Golden Book of the patricians and by means of decrees the richer families of Venice closed their ranks to outsiders and proclaimed a monopoly of public offices. Thus the Republic was governed by "an elite of about a thousand men and their families, having incomes ranging from 200,000 to 500,000 lire a year, who formed the *nobile* in a population of perhaps 190,000."

Such a society was ripe for the pleasures of collecting. Following the medieval custom the church treasuries in the Veneto housed the first assemblages of works of art. Cesare Augusto Levi has shown that in this early period of the Crusades the treasury of San Marco was more than a collection; it was a *Monte di Pietà*, a pawnbroker's bank in which were deposited relics and objects of precious value from the churches of western Europe. This the Crusaders put up as collateral for passage on Venetian ships for themselves and their armies to the Holy Land. These relics often remained unclaimed in the centuries that followed. The first public collections, however, were those formed by the Doges, consisting usually of gifts from Oriental sovereigns or works of art acquired by conquest, which were housed in the Ducal Palace. This latter was several times destroyed by fire, most seriously under the Doge Sebastiano Venier, so that little has come down to us. Then followed the corporate collections of the guilds of merchants and craftsmen, the *Scuole* who commissioned important works of art for the churches. Certain of these guilds, such as the *Corpo degli Orefici*, which included the goldsmiths, bankers and jewelers, were exceedingly powerful and commanded enormous resources.*

But it was among private individuals that we find the greatest interest and activity, particularly with families like the Falieri, Mocenigo, Contarini, Tiepolo and Michiel who, for a period of two centuries, had provided Doges to the Republic. It was, in fact, under the Michiel and Dandolo Doges that Constantinople was looted. What did not go into the custody of the State found its way into the hands of their

* C. A. Levi, *Collezioni Veneziane*. F. Ongania, 1900. (2 vols.)

descendants. Marco Polo, the fabulous merchant and explorer who visited the court of the Chinese emperor at Peking, brought back the treasures of the Orient and became the prototype of the typical Venetian man of wealth. His most valuable manuscripts passed into the collections of the Falieri, and another portion, later the property of Petrarch, was given by the poet to the Library of the Ducal Palace. Once the fashion was established, it is safe to assume that no patrician sent a ship out from Venice to the Levant without its returning laden with antique marbles, fragments of inscriptions and works of art of every kind, which also served as ballast to the comparatively light but precious cargo of silks and spices which she carried.

Whereas in Venice collecting was both widespread and unselfconscious, it was nothing more than a reflection of prosperity and the type of internationalism which such maritime prosperity always breeds. In Florence, on the other hand, there was a deliberate humanistic program among the collectors even of the fourteenth century. Venice showed little interest in the Renaissance until the visit of Donatello to Padua in 1434 to make the bronze equestrian statue of Gattamelata. To be sure in this city of commerce there had been for a century or more a small group of *cognoscenti* who held a more enlightened point of view than that of the majority of businessmen. The influence of the University of Padua was very great; Giotto had been painting about the turn of the fourteenth century the wonderful frescoes of the Arena Chapel when Dante visited him there. All through the Veneto there were individuals like Oliviero Forzetta, the notary and physician of Treviso, who formed an important collection of antiquities and drawings. The catalogue of his possessions, published in 1369, is the earliest such catalogue to have existed to this day. Petrarch is known to have been collecting books and works of art in Venice in 1345 and Marco Polo had already set a standard for the Venetian collector – a type which was frequently repeated and exemplified by personalities like the Doge Benedetto Dandolo, who traveled through Asia, Syria and the Germanies constantly looking for works of art. This interest increased with each generation and, following Donatello's visit, we see a change in Venetian painting.

Byzantine conventions gave way to that freedom of individual expression which was emerging in lower Italy.* The authority of the artist in the community, however, finally became established in 1474 when Gentile Bellini was put in charge of improvements and embellishments of the Ducal Palace and given charge of the collections belonging to the State.

During the fifteenth and sixteenth centuries the wealth and culture of the Venetians had reached their full maturity. It was the moment of the great colorists and all of the golden houses of the *nobili* were filled with the canvases of their contemporaries: Cima, Giorgione, the Bellinis, Titian, and later, Tintoretto and Veronese. These paintings which they commissioned from the artists they interspersed with antiquities inherited from their ancestors and Byzantine icons encrusted with gold and silver. It was, in fact, the Venetian trade which had introduced the taste of portable panel pictures to the Italian peninsula.

Venice was never strong in sculpture and the tombs of the Frari are, for the greater part, by artists trained in Lombardy where this stonemason's tradition was firmer than in the lagoons. Other aspects of the Oriental heritage were, of course, the famous skills in the blowing of glass and in mosaic work which conspired to give Venice that sparkle and glitter which attracted to her the whole of western Europe like moths before a candle flame. The palaces of the ducal families vied with each other in the sumptuousness which we see even today in houses and gardens such as those of the Dandolos in the Giudecca, the Contarini at Santa Maria del Orto and of the Foscarini. Palaces like those of the Malipiero, Vendramin, Ruzzini and Grimani were to become the happy hunting ground of the English and Austrian collectors of the eighteenth century.†

But it is significant that, despite their love of the sensuous, there

* Francesco Squarcione at Padua was the founder of an atelier which produced Marco Zoppo, Mantegna, Carlo Crivelli, Ansovino da Forlì, Cosimo Tura and Jacopo da Montagna. Part of their training was copying the antiquities which Squarcione had lovingly collected over many years.

† No account of the history of taste in Europe can be given without reference to the *Description of Venice* by Francesco Sansovino, son of the architect and sculptor. So complete and perfect is the account of the life and wealth of the city at the end of the sixteenth century that Book IX has been added as Appendix C, p. 607. *Venetia Citta Nobilissima e Singolore, descritta de XIII libri da Mr. Francesco Sansovino*, Venice 1581 (Book IX), is here translated into English for the first time.

was a lack of program and purpose to Venetian collecting which sets it apart from the activity of the Medici in Florence, or from the humanistic courts of Mantua and Ferrara. In the first place there was an absence of dynastic interest since the doge was elected, and although we see the same names returned to office over and over again, there was not the incentive to build a collection around a single succession, particularly since the law of primogeniture did not exist and family property was divided equally among the heirs. Thus we see the paradox that while Venice during the centuries of the Renaissance probably contained *en gros* the most fantastic collections in Europe, she had fewer "collectors" in our modern use of the word than any great city in Europe. Their artistic possessions meant little more to them than luxurious household furnishings. The proof of this contention lies in the curious fact that the two most celebrated Venetian collections were formed not in Venice but in Rome by the Cardinals Barbo and Grimani, who had learned their role from their humanistic competitors in the Sacred College. For many years the Palazzo di Venezia in Rome contained a greater museum than could be found under any one roof in Venice. The Grimani collection later was transported home and left to the Ducal Palace; but that of Pietro Barbo, later Pope Paul II, was dispersed after his death and was in large part acquired by the Medici Pope Clement VII for the Palazzo Madama. Likewise the two great libraries of the Ducal Palace were formed and given to Venice by humanists from out of town, Petrarch, and the Greek Cardinal, Bessarion.

CHAPTER V

The Feudal North – A Contrast to the Venetian Sea Power

IT must not be assumed that the sophistication of Venetian life extended into western Europe. There, other factors had conspired to give a different flavor to society. Feudalism was essentially the contradiction to it, for instead of allowing the untrammeled play of free enterprise, characteristic of the maritime capitalists of the Adriatic, the French or Flemish noble exercised a dictatorial paternalism beneath which everything depended from him and the officers of his court. The self-sufficiency of the medieval community which had had to find an outlet of reaction in the Crusades was, in the fourteenth and fifteenth centuries, applied to the court itself. Each noble not only surrounded himself with a household of courtiers and politicians, military men and clergy, but it became necessary for him to emphasize the traditional authority of his dynasty by becoming the fountainhead of learning and the arts. Two institutions which had grown and prospered during the earlier Middle Ages served him in establishing his position: one the pattern of the monastic library and artist's atelier, the other the Code of Chivalry which had come to northern Europe from the Arabic courts of Sicily and Spain.

Already a change had taken place in architecture; the principles of Gothic construction had enabled a greater economy in masonry and opened up, through the use of the groined vault, larger spaces for mural, glass and tapestry decoration. Moreover, the growing power of the guilds and corporations, through the example of the free cities of Germany and Italy, had produced a demand for new building into which much of the newly made wealth of the Continent was poured. Another change took place in domestic architecture, for during the early years of the Hundred Years' War great advances had been made in engines of destruction. The fortified castle no longer afforded the protection from siege which it had enjoyed in the past and, particularly in France where Louis XI had sought to solidify the position of the French monarchy by reducing the power of the nobles, the *châteaux forts* of medieval times were gradually being replaced by *châteaux de plaisance*, or villas in the style of the country palaces of Italy.

But the tradition of feudalism was opposed both in principle and in practice to the rise of the middle class; for chivalry, despite the picturesqueness of its code and the charming manners of the Court of Love, was the prinicipal weapon to keep the bourgeois under heel. In its very essence chivalry was a form of "exclusion act" which imposed through a system of freemasonry and segregation the authority of the knight or courtier. It lifted him by successive titles, mystical degrees and incantations to privileges and rights above his fellow men. The struggle for the preservation of those hereditary perquisites was the history of the fifteenth-century fight for personal liberty. That this liberty was first won in the city republics of Italy, freed from the tyranny of the *condottieri*, was one of the chief reasons why the Renaissance first found itself on Italian soil.

Nowhere does this social change reveal itself more clearly than in the status of the artist. No longer the manly and intelligent artisan of the age of the cathedral builders, he becomes a skillful valet, fit for all kinds of services, "adding saddlery to painting and secret commissions to works of real art; a man who ranks in the prince's household with the fool, the minstrel and the tailor." The distinction between the artist and the laborer was not apparent until well on in the fourteenth century in the courts of Jean le Bon and his son Charles. At the rival court of Burgundy the ultimate expression of feudal chivalry was reached in the Order of the Golden Fleece. There in the span of three generations was developed the highest state of later medieval culture. The intellectual curiosity that was to carry the Valois kings to Italy was kindled and we see the first stirrings of the northern Renaissance. However, under the protection of Philip the Good and Charles the Bold the artist regained something of his former stature and added new laurels to his crown.

Renan observes in his *Discours* that "the artist becomes the favorite, the guest, and often the secret agent and confidant of the princes; the architect has the title of sergeant-at-arms; the painter is a *valet-de-chambre*. They enter the royal households side by side with the lower attendants – spicers, tailors, etc." * These, however, were not empty offices; they carried great weight at court as may be seen in the contrast of the status of those artisans in the community who did not enjoy these princely favors. Yet the social position of the artist, however intimate his influence and authority, was slow in gaining the exaltation of the Renaissance, for, as Coulton has pointed out, as late as the reign of Pope Pius II, the enlightened Aeneas Sylvius Piccolommi, only such a painter as Paolo Romano could be admitted to the great hall. "Master Giovanni, who bore the title of 'Sculptor of the Apostolic Palace,' was relegated to the second hall with tailors, cooks, porters, couriers, grooms, sweepers, muleteers, water-carriers and so forth." †

* * * * *

Together with this cavalier treatment of the artist, collecting in feudal society had another meaning and purpose than it had in Italy. What collections there were, and they were few indeed, consisted chiefly of gifts of ambassadors and visiting sovereigns or occasional works of art, usually in gold and silver, taken as plunder in military excursions. Reliquaries and liturgical vessels were deposited in the chapel of the castle but other objects were distributed through the living apartments or stored with weapons and other curios in the armory. Rare coins and medals formed the nucleus of the earliest cabinets, and oddities of natural history were especially popular. These collections, particularly in Germany, portray the literalness of the Teutonic mind and prepare the way for the *Wunderkammer* of the sixteenth century. From these emerge the science museums of modern times.

Like the humanists of the north, the collectors in those lands were more concerned with the dawn of science than with beauty. The in-

* Ernest Renan. *Discours sur l'État des Beaux Arts*. Lévy, 1865. II, 208.

† G. G. Coulton, *Art and the Reformation*. Alfred A. Knopf, Inc., 1928. Appendix 7, p. 254.

IC XC

BYZANTINE ENAMELS ON GOLD

Ornaments from a book cover, eleventh century. Formerly in the Pierpont Morgan Collection. Metropolitan Museum of Art

tellectual movements were essentially religious and developed a rational spirit of inquiry which helped in many ways to bring about the Reformation. The collections were curiously catholic in their accumulation; they comprised gifts of all sorts, sea shells, fossils, stuffed alligators, minerals, works of gold, silver and glass, as well as a hodgepodge of painting and statuary. The Archduke Albrecht of Bavaria possessed, for example, 3407 objects which included, in addition to 780 paintings, "an egg which an abbot had found within another egg; manna which fell from Heaven in a famine; a stuffed elephant, a hydra and a basilisk." Like the old apothecary's shop in Garth's *Dispensary:*

> Here Mummies lay most reverently stale,
> And there the Tortoise hung her Coat o'Mail;
> Not far from some huge Shark's devouring Head
> The Flying-Fish their finny Pinions spread.
> Aloft in rows large Poppy Heads were strung,
> And near a scaly Alligator hung.*

Nor were church treasuries entirely free from the cult of the curious, for in the early eighteenth century a learned Scottish judge implores a friend while visiting the Royal Abbey of Saint Denis "to take notice of Charles the Great's Crown in which there is a Rubie of the Bigness of a Pidgin's Egg; A large Cup of oriental Aggat,† which they count much of; One of the Nails that fixed our Saviour's Bodie to the Cross, sent to Charles the Great by Constantine V, Emperour of Constantinople; One of the Potts wherein our Saviour changed the water into wine at the marriage of Cana in Galilee; the Pucel of Orléans Sword, wherewith she overcame the English; the Lantern that was carried before Judas, when He betrayed our Saviour; and a thousand other things of great value." ‡ More recently Mark Twain records that it was possible to see in the sacristy of Cologne Cathedral the skull of a child in an elaborate reliquary, labeled "Head of Saint John the Baptist at the age of twelve years."

* Garth, *The Dispensary*. London, 1720. Canto II, p. 17.

† This refers possibly to the agate chalice from Saint Denis in the Widener Collection, now in the National Gallery of Art, Washington. Cf. p. 37.

‡ David Murray. *Museums: Their History and Their Uses*. Maclehose, 1904. I, 198.

One name stands out in this welter of anonymity of the later Middle Ages as the archetype of the collector, that of Jean de France, Duc de Berry. In him may be seen combined the connoisseurship of the Valois, of the English kings and of the House of Burgundy. He embodies both the breadth and the fineness of their interests and, fortunately, through the careful inventory of his collections made by Robinet d'Estampes in 1416, we are able to form some picture of his personality. His principal passion was for books and beautifully illustrated manuscripts which he collected assiduously – it was for him that the great *Book of Hours* at Chantilly was made. He had also the light finger of the true collector, for it was only on his deathbed that his confessor forced him to return to the Abbey of Saint Denis the *Chroniques de France* which he had "borrowed." During the wars with the English under a flag of truce, Berry and the Duke of Bedford would meet in one another's tents to compare the miniatures of a newly acquired *Book of Hours*, only to return to battle on the following morning. His collection of antique gold and silver coins (a part of which had been melted down after his defeat at Agincourt) later elicited the admiration of Filarete, who also admired his cabinet of some fifteen hundred cameos and intaglios. The incomparable *Gemma Augustea* in the Vienna Museum is first recorded in this inventory. Berry was the first Frenchman to send agents to Italy to purchase works of art, chiefly antiquities in sculpture, inscriptions and vases. The altar which he gave to the Abbey of Poissy, now preserved in the Cluny Museum, was bought for him from the Venetian workshop of Baldassare degli Embriachi. Like all medieval princes, he was inordinately fond of jewels and precious stones, many of which were incorporated in the bindings of his beloved manuscripts. The inventory included references to paintings on panels as well as in the form of miniatures. The Van Eyck wings, formerly in the collection of the Hermitage, now at the Metropolitan Museum, may possibly be one of the items listed. Berry also employed one of the earliest art dealers recorded – Jean Auchier (Giovanni Alcherio) – who was prominent as a *curieux* in Paris around the year 1400 and who voyaged back and forth constantly between Lombardy, France and Burgundy. His primary interest was the study of the differences in technique between the Flemings and Italians.

But despite the enlightened taste which he showed in art, Berry was not immune from the fascination of the *Wunderkammer* and the essential medievalism of his collecting shines through the pages of the inventory.* All of the gadgets so close to the hearts of the German princelings are there: jeweled chessboards, gaming tables, fantastic clocks and timepieces, elaborate hot-water bottles in gold and silver (*scaldamania*), perfumes in exotic containers, bags filled with lapis lazuli for making pigments, bowls of porcelain and agate. The relics included the engagement ring of Saint Joseph, a fact which the faithful Robinet qualifies with the phrase "*si comme disait la Dame de St. Just, qui donna ledit à Mgr. aux étrennes 1406*," and the Gospel according to Saint John written on a piece of parchment "not bigger than a silver coin." Coconuts, the teeth of walfish, crystals, ostrich eggs, shells from the Seven Seas, the hides of polar bears and the horn of a unicorn held equal authority with the most precious panels and illustrated books. It was first and last the collection of a feudal lord into which as yet had blown no faint breath of the humanism of Renaissance Italy.

* Jules Guiffrey, *Inventaires de Jean, duc de Berry*, 2 vols. Paris, 1894–1896.

BOOK TWO

Italy and the Rise of Capitalism

CHAPTER I

The Medici

In western and northern Europe the Dark Ages had overwhelmed the earlier Greco-Roman civilization with a pall of ignorance, but in Italy the constant survival of antiquity in ruins, language and daily traditions had reflected itself in an almost unbroken stream of memories of which that of the City of Rome was the most vivid and appealing. To the men of the Middle Ages, Haskins has pointed out, Rome was the great fact in their immediate past, "for the Roman Empire had for several centuries been conterminous with the civilized world and had handed on conceptions of unity, universality, order and authority from which Latin Europe could not escape. Rome was their common memory, Rome not fallen, Rome eternal. Whenever they looked back they saw Rome and heard her voice, 'the voice of murmuring Rome.' " *

Roma stat, orbis apex, gloria, gemma, decus . . .

But the imperial city had indeed fallen into decay. Her splendid buildings had been pillaged by lime burners and marble cutters to provide the façades of cathedrals at Pisa, Lucca and Salerno. Desiderius had purchased "columns, bases, capitals, and marbles of various colors" for the abbey church of Monte Cassino. Suger, the great twelfth-century abbot and connoisseur of Saint Denis, had entered into negotiations for the columns from the Baths of Diocletian. Even in far-away England fragments of Rome had found their way to Westminster and Canterbury, and the brother of King Stephen, Bishop Henry of Winchester, had brought the first collection of antiquities from Italy, gathered from among the statues scattered on the Aventine and Caelian hills by the Normans under Robert Guiscard.

* Charles Homer Haskins, *The Renaissance of the Twelfth Century*. Harvard University Press, 1927, pp. 117–118.

Yet there was an irresistible fascination to these ruins which continued to attract the pilgrims and tourists of the Latin-speaking countries. For their edification there were compiled guidebooks and descriptions which, like the *Mirabilia Urbis Romae* of William of Malmesbury, underscored the contrasts with her ancient greatness as mistress of the world and her present plight. "This extraordinary combination of fact and fable, pagan and Christian," says Haskins, "falls into three parts. The first, after describing the foundation of Rome on the Janiculum by Janus, son of Noah, lists its gates and arches, the baths, palaces, theatres, and bridges, its Christian cemeteries, and the places where the saints suffered martyrdom. The second comprises various legends of emperors and saints, especially legends of statues, including the popular *Salvatio Romae*, a set of bells attached to the statues of the several provinces on the Capitol so as to give alarm whenever a province revolted; the philosophers Phidias and Praxiteles in the time of Tiberius; the passion of the martyrs under Decius; and the foundation of the three great churches by Constantine. The third part takes the reader through the various quarters of the City and points out the striking monuments and ancient traditions connected with them, concluding:

> These and many more temples and palaces of emperors, consuls, senators, and prefects were in the time of the heathen within this Roman city, even as we have read in old chronicles, and have seen with our eyes, and have heard tell of ancient men. And moreover, how great was their beauty in gold, and silver, and brass, and ivory, and in precious stones, we have endeavored us in writing as well as we could to bring back to the remembrance of mankind.*

Another guidebook by "Master Gregory on the Marvels of Rome whether made by magic art or by human labor" groups the ruins by classes, listing the bronze beasts, the marble statues which by reason of their idolatry had been destroyed by Gregory the Great, the palaces, triumphal arches and pyramids. "The fate of ancient buildings," continues Haskins, "is illustrated by the temple of Pallas, torn down with much labor by the Christians and much injured by time, leaving only the portion which serves as a granary for the cardinals, and sur-

* Haskins, *op. cit.*, 122.

rounded by heaps of broken statues, among them the headless image of the Goddess before which Christians had once been brought to test their faith. Already we see that neglect of ancient ruins which Poggio was to lament in the fifteenth century; the Rome, once golden, now mellow with the decay etched by Piranesi – which led Gibbon to plan his *Decline and Fall* as he sat 'musing in the Church of the Zoccolanti or Franciscan fryars, while they were singing Vespers in the Temple of Jupiter on the ruins of the Capitol.' "

The idea of glory never dies and the pontiffs had become accepted as the true successors of the Caesars. The *Ordo Romanus* shows that when they went about on their state processions within the city their way led through the triumphal arches of ancient paganism; "a new Via Sacra had arisen for Christian pomps." The humanism of the fifteenth century had not yet arrived but the trail was already well blazed, and throughout the Italian peninsula we see a revival of the glory of antiquity. The decree of the Roman Senate in 1162 that "Trajan's column should never be destroyed or mutilated but should remain as it stands to the honor of the Roman people as long as the world endures" was but the forerunner of similar measures. There were monuments to Latin poets erected in Italian cities: to Vergil in Mantua, to Pliny in Como and to Ovid in Sulmona. According to tradition, the classical figure incorporated in the *Fonte Gaia* in Siena was a statue by Lysippus, and without a rigid schooling among the antique marbles in the Campo Santo at Pisa, Nicolò Pisano would never have produced his famous pulpits.

If we are surprised at the sophistication and classical consciousness which burst upon Italy in the fifteenth century, we must remember that it was preceded, to borrow a term from modern psychology, by a steady stream for a thousand years of the "classical *unconscious*." We can no longer accept the simple and convenient definition of the Renaissance as a revival of classical antiquity which took place in the year 1453. It must be considered as a steady movement towards the growth of the individual and of individual freedom which had started fermenting in men's minds shortly after the year 1000. It was made possible by the economic prosperity of the later Middle Ages, a prosperity which brought with it the inevitable baggage of world problems – religious ideologies, labor disputes and organized opposition to the nobles, particularly in the larger cities, and the rise of modern capitalism. "Rugged individualism," so dear to the hearts of our American industrialists, has never known a period of such unbridled opportunity. To be sure it generated its own philosophy and code of ethics. Joachim of Flora in the thirteenth century summed it up by saying, "The Gospel of the Father is past, the Gospel of the Son is passing, the Gospel of the Spirit is to be." John Addington Symonds in recalling the classic phrase of Michelet stated that "the great achievements of the Renaissance were the discovery of the world and the discovery of man. . . . By discovery of the world is meant, on the one hand, the appropriation by civilized humanity of all corners of the habitable globe, and on the other, the conquest by Science of all that we know about the nature of the universe. In the discovery of man, again, it is possible to trace a twofold process. Man in his temporal relations, illustrated by Pagan antiquity, and man in his spiritual relations, illustrated by Biblical antiquity; these are the two regions, at first apparently distinct, afterwards found to be interpenetrative, which the critical and inquisitive genius of the Renaissance opened for investigation." *

Such a program could not fail to produce a new beauty or new conceptions of beauty. Man was immediately liberated from the factual considerations of the medieval craftsman. His product contained a new content, something other than what the priest had directed him to use as subject matter; and he imparted to his work his own essence as an individual and as a member of society. Anonymity of authorship, required by the conventions of the Church, and which for many centuries had stamped so authentically the work of religious art, gave way to the type of reflective interpretation which was possible only when the artist enjoyed a liberty of conscience that was previously unknown. Saint Thomas Aquinas, who had so dominated the medieval mind, said in the *Summa Theologica*, "The name of art should be applied to those arts only which contribute towards and produce the necessaries of life." Elsewhere he insisted that "art is nothing else but

* John Addington Symonds, *Renaissance in Italy: The Age of the Despots.* Henry Holt and Co., 1888, pp. 15, 17.

the right reason about things to be made," and in his confusion between the beautiful and good he allowed little play for aesthetic emotion. Grudgingly enough he speaks of the "lustre of beautiful objects" and of "the integrity, perfection, proportion and harmony of beautiful things," but it was not until the humanism of the Renaissance, which through "the study of classical records and the development of the spirit of scientific observation and experiment had brought about a more accurate knowledge of the world of nature and of men," that the creation of beauty as a worth-while end in itself was tolerated.

Chambers has shown in his *History of Taste* that the Renaissance in reawakening aesthetic consciousness, which had lain dormant since Greco-Roman times, urgently sought to re-create in art and literature the concept of "fine art." Naturally it clothed the new forms in the traditions of Italy's great past. "The Renaissance," he says, "was not the discovery of the ancient classics, long since buried in darkest ignorance, but the discovery that the ancient classics were beautiful. The Middle Ages had read the classics for 'what they spake,' the Renaissance read the classics for 'how they spake.' " It was its business, he adds, "to create an idea of art as a thing of beauty, justified by beauty, to be seen and praised as such, the idea of art satisfying in the mere contemplation, the idea of pictures for the picture gallery, architecture for the street front, plays for the theater, music for the concert-chamber." *

This spirit affected not only the producer but the consumer. For the first time since the fall of Rome we see again the conditions upon which art collecting, as it has been practiced in antiquity and in modern times, was possible. While we have shown that during the period of a thousand years from the death of Constantine the Great the taste for treasures never died, and that collecting is indeed a subconscious instinct of the man of property, the differences between collecting in the grand manner and the haphazard accumulation of works of art characteristic of feudal princes are very great. The collections of the Renaissance were not the result of the seizure of political and financial power by new hands alone, but are the truest concrete expressions of

* Frank P. Chambers, *The History of Taste*. Columbia University Press, 1932, pp. 29, 37.

the humanism which had captured the imagination of Italy. The embodiment of these principles is seen in the results of eleven generations of collecting by a single Florentine family who were to set the pattern for the art collections and princely galleries of the Western world.

THE CLIMATE OF FLORENTINE ECONOMY

Contrary to most popular belief, the Medici alone did not create the wealth of Florence. Arriving comparatively late on the scene as wool merchants and textile manufacturers, by cleverness and trickery they slowly acquired control over their competitors and became the bankers of Europe. But the economy of Tuscany and likewise the business tastes and habits of the Tuscans were very ancient, finding their origins in the business rivalry between the early Roman and Etruscan merchants, who, according to Miss Beard, worshiping the Goddess Fortuna,* were never willing to submit to the agrarian policies of Rome. During the early Middle Ages when the capital was constantly being invaded and the seat of political and financial policies directed from Byzantium, Florence established the foundations of her fortunes as the money market of western Europe. Gradually, as money economy succeeded barter and exchange, she entered into the more lucrative fields of manufacturing and of the export and import trade. Where the Venetians dominated the markets east of Italy and the commerce of the Levant, Florence extended her authority from Spain to Scandinavia and the Germanies, bringing the monarchies and nobles one by one into her power. As bankers for the Church and collectors of the papal revenues, particularly of tithes and "Peter's pence," she was never at a loss for ready cash with which to play one power against another or to control the election of pope or emperor. Her customary procedure was to lend money to the land-poor feudal nobles at excessive rates of interest (which to be sure was strictly forbidden by the Church) and to threaten foreclosure if the nobles did not bring their armies to support her political ambitions. In this way, like Venice, Florence cashed in on the Crusades for, while Venice charged exorbitantly for passage in her ships to the Holy Land, Flor-

* Beard, *op. cit.,* 124 ff.

ence advanced the cash against which her merchants and manufacturers billed the knights for equipment, food and munitions of war. Her policies were constantly being thwarted by the Emperor, who, as theoretical suzerain of Tuscany and champion of the chivalric debtors of an older Europe, lent his support to the Ghibellines against the Guelfs, the party of the merchants, bankers and the Papacy. Dante, espousing the emperor's cause, has become the classic mouthpiece for this economic warfare which, lasting for more than three hundred years, shook not merely Florence but the entire continent of Europe.

Miss Beard, in her fascinating *History of the Business Man*, has summarized the recent investigations and literature on Florentine commercial activity in the thirteenth and fourteenth centuries and has shown how the chief families, by a judicious diversification of their interests as merchants, inevitably ended up as bankers.* The Scali family, for example, beginning as importers of raw materials established in the Arte de Calimalà, the Florentine Rialto, immediately allied themselves with the wool guild and engaged in that trade with England. Soon they lent money to the British crown and received in return large interests in Aquitaine, Poitou and Normandy, as well as the right to farm taxes in Paris, Toulouse, Narbonne and Bordeaux. This was in addition to their being allowed to form a consortium for collecting taxes in Florence and to coin money at Naples. The Medici in their early days were typical of the other commercial families and diversified their risks in many directions. "As manufacturers, they ran silk and wool plants. As traders, they had extensive connections; the Bruges office, for example, shipped oriental spices, almonds, sugar and cloth to London in exchange for wool and hides. The head of the Medici had the books of all branches sent to him for yearly inspection and in the late 1400's these included 24 from France, 37 from Naples and 50 from Turkey. As bankers, they were involved in foreign diplomacy; thus the Medici forced a branch office upon Milan by sup-

* The literature on the Florentine economic climate produced during the last half century is very considerable, and nowhere, perhaps, has it been more thoroughly explored, particularly in its relation to the Renaissance of art and letters, than at the Warburg Library, formerly in Hamburg, now connected with the Courtauld Institute in London University. Another fruitful source, and one containing a wealth of material included here, is the recent work by Martin Wackernagel, *Der Lebensraum des Künstlers in der Florentinischen Renaissance*. Leipzig, E. A. Seeman, 1938.

porting a tyrant, Sforza, who protected them while they induced courtiers and clerics to buy shares in their bank." *

Earlier, the Bardi family, upon whose ruins the Medici were to climb to fortune in another generation, illustrate even more clearly the extent of Florentine interests abroad; for they were the financiers of the Hundred Years' War, providing cash and provisions to both sides in the battles of Crécy and Agincourt. The Bardi were utterly without scruple and when Pope Urban IV, because of Neapolitan intrigues with the Turk, offered the throne of Naples to Henry III of England for his son, they saw the opportunity of cashing in on a Holy War. Together with the Peruzzi, the Frescobaldi and a group of other Florentine merchants, they lent money at a mere 180 per cent interest, taking as security not only the wool from English sheep but the animals and grazing lands as well. They demanded the wine monopoly and the right to collect the customs at the ports of the British Isles in addition to placing a lien on the state income. But this fall of manna was, unfortunately for them, just a flurry and not a real blizzard, since Edward III, when he succeeded to the throne, soon repudiated every penny of the English debt and threw the Italian agent into the Tower. The Bardi and Peruzzi failed but in their bankruptcy the Bardi were still able to pay 46 per cent to their shareholders.

Such percentages were, in fact, the order of the day. A proverb quoted by Miss Beard maintained that "25 percent is nothing at all; 50 percent will pass the time away; 100 percent is interesting," and she has also shown that in the case of particularly bad risks the Peruzzi and Frescobaldi banks had charged as high a rate as 266 per cent. This was, of course, in direct contradiction to the laws of the Church against usury. However, business is business and what could not be concealed from their confessors in tricks of the trade such as the *barrato* (a form of discounting against futures in the commodity markets) they brazenly admitted by contributing to charitable endowments. While it is, of course, unkind to shatter the world of make-believe of Ruskin and the Pre-Raphaelites, the epidemic contri-

* Beard, *op. cit.*, 131. Also cf. J. Burckhardt, *The Civilization of the Renaissance in Italy*. Much of Miss Beard's material is taken from the latter work.

butions to the churches, convents and hospitals of Florence at this period were in reality a form of hallowed hush-money and not the expression of any sudden wave of religious fanaticism. The Bardi and Peruzzi chapels in Santa Croce, to name but a single church, were paid for with interest charges on these loans to England. The contributions of the guilds and corporations were no less lavish and largely for the same reason, for the clergy, with God's high purpose ever before them, were willing to encourage business if business would encourage them.

It was this practice of decorating churches which gave such monumentality to the early art of Florence. The painters and sculptors thought in staggering dimensions and were easily able to master large wall surfaces. The taste for public buildings also accounts for the paucity of private collections which were not to become important until the time of Lorenzo the Magnificent when, having put the clergy completely in their pockets, the Italian merchants and *condottieri* turned away from decorating the churches; for they now could spend their money with impunity on their villas in the country and on the personal pleasures of their palaces in town.*

This new and tremendous wealth was not produced, however, without a great deal of hard labor, for one must not suppose that even in the enlightened days of the Renaissance ducats, any more than dollars, grew on trees. As prosperity increased for the merchants, the conditions of the poor became intolerable. Machiavelli divided the citizenry between the *popolo grosso*, the fat people, and the *popolo minuto*, or the thin. The rapid expansion of the weaving industry had resulted in the inauguration of the "putting out" or "cottage system" which instantly lent itself to the same abuses which in the Industrial Revolution of the nineteenth century made Manchester and the spinning towns of Old and New England so infamous. The fourteenth century was indeed one of constant turmoil and labor trouble. Jurisdictional fights between the guilds were not unlike the rowing today between the A.F. of L. and the C.I.O. in the United States and the

* Wackernagel, *op. cit.*, gives the roster of most of the large commissions and shows the gradual change in the point of view of patronage and ownership between the times of Cosimo and Lorenzo.

trade-unions councils in Britain, and in the relations between employer and employee only the Church from time to time stepped in, quite gingerly to be sure, to give a word of warning against abuses that seemed too flagrant. Notwithstanding, the usual working day was from twelve to fourteen hours and there were, of course, no provisions against child labor or for the protection of women. Florentine industry in the end revolted and the bankers could think of nothing better than to bring in the Duke of Athens, a genteel thug, half French, half Levantine, as "Conservator of the City of Florence." But, like all fascist dictators, he had delusions of grandeur and quickly bit the hand that fed him. The story of Hitler and the German bankers was already told in 1343; for the families who had employed the Leader were obliged to get rid of him. A conspiracy composed of members of the most prominent business families (Bardi, Frescobaldi, Scali, Strozzi, Altoviti, Rucellai, Pazzi, Acciaiuoli) and the Medici, under the leadership of the Bishop of Florence, beseiged him in the Palazzo Pubblico and regained the power he had taken from them. This did not, however, put an end to the labor troubles and for the next thirty-five years we see the Medici, by treachery and bribery, fomenting the distress which brought about the revolution of 1378 through which they finally took possession of the government of Florence. They did not relinquish it, except for a short interval of twenty years, until the middle of the eighteenth century.

THE MEDICI IN FLOWER

Though the origins of the Medici are still obscure they had enjoyed a substantial position in the community for two hundred years before the Renaissance. Chiarissimo, the eldest son of Giambuono de Medici, was a member of the Town Council in 1201 and doing a thriving business in the Mercato Vecchio. From then on whenever there was a smell of profit or dissension to be manipulated in their favor, the Medici name can always be found in the record. The fortunes of the family increased as the magic of the name spread over the commercial map of Europe. In 1378 when Silvestro de Medici led the riots of the Ciompi, or workers of the woolen industry, thus breaking the power

ABBOT SUGER'S CHALICE FROM SAINT DENIS

Washington, National Gallery of Art

CHINESE VASE FROM THE COLLECTION OF MARCO POLO

Venice, Treasury of San Marco

JEAN, DUC DE BERRY, AND HIS COURT PAINTER

Detail from the *Très Riches Heures,* Chantilly

THE *WUNDERKAMMER* OF DR. HANS WORMS

A typical cabinet of the German physician and collector

RAPHAEL: SAINT GEORGE AND THE DRAGON

No other picture epitomizes more thoroughly the development of taste produced by the political and economic rivalries between different countries and collectors in successive ages. Commissioned from the artist by the Duke of Urbino, Federigo da Montefeltro, it was taken to England as a gift from the Duke to Henry VII by the Perfect Courtier, Count Baldassare Castiglione. The King had conferred the Order of the Garter on Federigo, and in the painting Saint George is seen wearing the Garter below his left knee. The young Raphael at this time was in the Duke's regular employ and received for it probably less than the 100 ducats ($2000) he later asked in Rome of Agostino Chigi for each figure in the Farnesina murals. A pen and ink drawing for the picture is in the Uffizi; a reduction of the painting by the miniaturist Peter Oliver is preserved in the Royal Library at Windsor, and it was also reproduced in tapestry at the Mortlake factory. Passing temporarily from the royal collections, the picture was retrieved by Charles I from the Earl of Pembroke by exchanging for it a group of Holbein drawings. After the King's execution it was sold by Parliament in 1653 for £150, to the Cologne banker Evrard Jabach, for the account of Cardinal Mazarin. With the dispersal of the latter's collection it changed hands frequently. Madame de Noüe acquired the painting for 500 pistoles and had a copy of it made by Philippe de Champaigne for the Jansenist Church at Port-Royal. Then it passed into the celebrated Crozat collection, to be sold by the Crozat heirs in 1772 to Catherine the Great for the Hermitage. It was one of a lot of 400 pictures for which the Russian Empress paid 400,000 livres. Finally in 1930 a New York dealer purchased it from the Soviet Government and sold it to the late Andrew W. Mellon for a price, as reported in the *Congressional Record*, of $747,500. Washington, National Gallery of Art (Mellon Collection)

A CONSISTORY IN THE SISTINE CHAPEL, 1582

After an engraving by Lafreri. Metropolitan Museum of Art

of the nobles and destroying the *Parte Guelfa*, the Medici emerged as the champions of the people.

Florence was at this time without question the most prosperous state in Europe. According to Macaulay, "The revenue of the Republic amounted to three hundred thousand florins . . . a sum which was at least equivalent to six hundred thousand pounds sterling: a larger sum than England and Ireland, two centuries later, yielded to Elizabeth." The annual income of Florence was very much greater than the estimate of Macaulay a century ago and it was upon the extraordinary wealth of this community that the future history of artistic patronage was to a large extent predicated.*

The history of the Medici collections begins with Cosimo Pater Patriae, who inherited from his father, Giovanni di Bicci, not only the family banking house but the power won by the Medici from the revolution. In him we see for the first time the full play of political and diplomatic talents which characterized the later members of the family. Not satisfied by the ruin caused the nobles during the revolt, he pleased the working people by instituting in the Signoria a bill for a graduated income tax and thus wiped out any chance of the return of his rivals to power. He accomplished other much needed reforms but kept his eyes carefully glued upon the family business, his most important excursion in the arts being the direction in 1407 of the competition for the bronze doors of the Baptistry, which, won by Ghiberti, triumphantly announced that the Renaissance had at last begun.

According to Salviati's *Zibaldone*, Cosimo's attitude towards the good works to which he had given so much time and money set a pattern of complacency for all future tycoons. "All those things have given me the greatest satisfaction and contentment (*grandissima contentamento e grandissima dolcezza*)," he said, "because they are not only for the honor of God but are likewise for my own remembrance." And to this he added the pious thought: "For fifty years I have done nothing else but earn money and spend money; and it became clear that spending money gives me greater pleasure than earn-

* Burckhardt, *op. cit.*, 98–104. The footnotes provide very valuable data for the estimate of Florentine wealth and industry.

ing it (*ed accorgomi che ancora sia maggior dolcezza lo spendere che il guadagnare*)." *

To the complaints of the nobles about his business methods, he replied, "If you have gained less, you will have less to pay under a graduated income tax, so you have no cause to grumble." He died in 1429, leaving to his sons, Cosimo and Lorenzo, 179,221 gold florins ($3,600,000) and a few precious platitudes. "I leave you in possession of the great wealth which my good fortune has bestowed upon me, and which your good mother and my own hard work have enabled me to preserve. I leave you with a larger business than any other in the Tuscan land. . . . Be charitable to the poor, speak not as though giving advice, not puffed with pride at receiving many votes. Avoid . . . litigation. Be careful not to attract attention." †

The fortunes grew and Cosimo practiced the preachment of his father. In 1440 his brother Lorenzo left nearly double his inheritance, some 235,000 ducats, and Piero, Cosimo's son, in 1469 bequeathed a similar amount. These were, of course, their private fortunes separate from their capital interest in the family business. Cosimo left a very large sum in addition to 37,238 ducats' worth ($750,000) of jewels, rings, pearls, cameos, books and silver plate. Part of the goldsmith's work, according to the inventory, came from Paris and from Avignon. Items listed as "*Cose di damasche*" show that Asia Minor was represented. The collections of armor were divided into three catagories, *arme de piazza*, *arme de giostra* and *arme di battaglia*. The lists included clocks and astronomical instruments, the exquisitely wrought cup now in the Naples Museum called the *tazza Farnese* and valued at 10,000 gulden. To all of this Lorenzo later added, beside other antiquities which upon the advice of Donatello he had placed in houses of his friends and relatives throughout Florence, a collection of 176 gems, cameos and intaglios formed by the Cardinal of Mantua. They were placed in a special shrine and when in 1494 Pietro had to flee his native city he took these gems with him and sold them with great advantage to the Roman banker, Agostino Chigi. These were the

* Wackernagel, *op. cit.*, 234.

† Beard, *op. cit.*, 152. Also cf. Eugene Müntz, *Les collections des Medicis*, Paris, 1888.

modest beginnings of the Medici collections which we are able to reconstruct, with the help of Müntz's study of the inventories, and to learn something of their character.*

The works of art, like those of their princely contemporaries in northern Europe, were valued only for their intrinsic worth in precious metal. Another generation would see the collection emerge as a gallery of objects precious for their own sakes and not merely counted as tangible and negotiable assets of the family treasury.

If in his business dealings with his fellow countrymen Cosimo followed too closely the classic pattern of the modern banker or corporation chairman to be either attractive or lovable, one cannot take away from him his claim to be the first of the great humanistic patrons of the Renaissance. The intimate of Fra Angelico and Lippo Lippi, Cosimo encouraged likewise the sculptors Ghiberti and Donatello, and the architects Michelozzo and Brunelleschi, with the same zeal with which he worshiped at the fount of classic learning. He wrote in his old age to his tutor, Marsilio Ficino:

> Yesterday I came to the villa of Carreggi, not to cultivate my fields but my soul. Come to us, Marsilio, as soon as possible. Bring with thee our Plato's book *De Summo Bono*. This, I suppose, you have already translated from the Greek language into Latin as you promised. I desire nothing so much as to know the best road to happiness. Farewell and do not come without the Orphean lyre.†

Cosimo gave great fortunes to charity and public welfare. He saw to the rebuilding of the Dominican Monastery of San Marco where he maintained a cell for retreat and meditation. The foundation of the Library of San Marco was the library of the humanist Niccolò Niccoli which he had purchased from the latter's heirs and which Cosimo bequeathed to the monastery. He remodeled the Badia of Fiesole and the Church of San Lorenzo. He stated in his *Ricordi* that the Medici from 1434 to 1471 spent no less than 636,755 gold florins (approximately $13,000,000) on buildings and charities alone.

In 1444 Cosimo crowned his career by founding the celebrated Medici Library, the first public library to exist in Europe since Roman

* Cf. Appendix C, Bibliography.
† Trans. by M. Beard, *op. cit.*, 154.

times and upon the pattern of which Pope Sixtus IV, thirty years later, was to establish the reorganized Library of the Vatican. This library, at first housed in the Medici Palace, was steadily added to by the family in each succeeding generation. In collecting manuscripts and commissioning specially illustrated and illuminated editions of the classic texts which were pouring into Florence from Europe and the Byzantine Empire, it is estimated that the Medici spent, from the recall of Cosimo in 1434 to the death of Piero in 1469, some $15,000,000. Cosimo's grandson, Lorenzo the Magnificent, later added during his rule an annual expenditure for books alone of from $3,250,000 to $3,750,000. He twice sent the humanist Lascaris to the Orient to discover and purchase ancient manuscripts. On his second voyage, Lascaris brought back two hundred Greek works, as many as eighty of which up to that time were unknown. The role which this library was to play in the spread of Italian humanism would indeed be hard to estimate, for, both in fact and in spirit, it shares with the Vatican the parentage of all the great libraries of Europe. It contains some ten thousand Greek and Latin manuscripts, many of which are unique; among these is the original copy of the *Pandects* of Justinian (A.D. 533), a discovery which caused a revolution in the course of jurisprudence. "It contains also the best manuscript of Cicero's letters, two manuscripts of Tacitus, one of them being the sole existing copy of the first five books of the *Annals;* a very ancient copy of the tragedies of Sophocles; a most important manuscript of Aeschylus; a Greek treatise on surgery; the *Commentaries* of Julius Caesar; a Virgil of the fourth century and a Syriac Gospel of the sixth; the Bible copied by Ceolfrid, Abbot of Wearmouth, and called the *Codex Amiatinus* (c. 700 A.D.), a Pliny of the tenth century and numerous literary treasures associated with the Florence of Petrarch and Dante." * Confiscated by the Signoria when the Medici were banished from Florence in 1494, the library was purchased twenty years later by Pope Leo X, transported to Rome and returned to Florence again by another Medici Pope, Clement VII, where finally, in 1524, the Cloisters of San Lorenzo were built by Michelangelo to receive it, whence it derives its name as the Laurentian Library.

* Col. G. F. Young, *The Medici.* Random House, The Modern Library, 1933, p. 68.

The progress of the Renaissance was linked with the palace of the Medici no less than it was with their library. Their house in the Via Larga, better known by the name of its later owners as the Riccardi Palace, was built by Cosimo about 1430 as a model of the architecture of the period. Donatello's *David* stood in the center of the *cortile*. It bears above the entrance the inscription, "The Nurse of All Learning." This was to be the home of the family for a hundred years until, in 1539, the first Grand Duke, Cosimo I, moved to the Palazzo Vecchio preparatory to occupying the new and larger Pitti Palace on the other side of the Arno. Here in the Medici (Riccardi) Palace, Cosimo Pater Patriae passed his strenuous years, and Lorenzo the Magnificent gathered round him the most brilliant intellects of his day. Popes, emperors, kings and princes came to this palace together with merchants, scholars and scientists to pay tribute to the new learning and to see with their own eyes the works of art which the almost legendary wealth and acumen of the Medici had assembled. The house was in reality the first museum of Europe and, so far as the art of Italy and Flanders of the fifteenth century is concerned, has never been equaled since, nor can it be again. The bronzes and antique gems collected by Cosimo and Lorenzo, now in the Archaeological Museum of Florence, formed part of the family cabinet. Sculptures, tapestries, paintings, furniture and the most precious workmanship of goldsmith, enameler and jeweler were crowded into the rooms and galleries of this spacious yet relatively modest house, which, Miglione said, came to be known as "the Hotel of the Princes of the whole world."

The individual artists who labored for and were befriended by the Medici were legion. Donatello, Botticelli and Bertoldo, to be sure, were marked for special intimacies but to recall them all would virtually require the repetition of Vasari's *Lives*. Suffice it to say that over a period of one hundred and fifty years few artists in Europe of major reputation were left untouched by the finger of the Medici and, while the roster of the men whose work adorned the palace is lacking, it is safe to assume that they were all for the greater part represented in this gallery.

In 1489, the year following his wife's death, Lorenzo conceived the idea of converting the suburban villa which he had built for her near San Marco into an academy for the training of young artists. It was in this *cortile* that Lorenzo had placed his antique marbles; and the larger paintings and drawings, cartoons for murals, and other works of art for which he had no room in the Medici Palace were disposed about the apartments and *loggie* of this villa. Bertoldo (the sculptor who had worked at Padua with Donatello) was made the master of this first art academy of modern times and in it he received as pupils, according to Vasari, the great men of the *cinquecento:* Lorenzo di Credi, Granacci, Bugiardini, the sculptors Rusticci, Torrigiano, Baccio di Montelupo, and above all the young Michelangelo whose mask of a Faun is said to be the one preserved today in the Bargello. As a *pensionnaire* of the academy, Michelangelo, then a youth of eighteen, met the leading scholars and humanists of the day, and here it was that Poliziano urged him to try his first classic subject, the *Battle of the Centaurs*, now in the Casa Buonarotti.* That there was a lighter side to the art student's life at this period may be attested by the fact that in these gardens Torrigiano had his famous fight with Michelangelo, breaking the latter's nose; he fled from Florence, first to Spain, and thence to England where he worked upon Henry VII's tomb. And in the winter of 1492–1493, during one of the rare heavy snowfalls recorded in Florence, Michelangelo received one of his earliest commissions, that of making a statue out of snow for the *cortile* of the academy. In fact, Landucci states in his diary that snowmen were the rage that winter in Florence.†

With Lorenzo the Magnificent the Medici had reached their zenith. A handsome, charming and often jovial young man, he lacked none of the shrewdness and wisdom of his grandfather, Cosimo. Piero il Gottoso, his sickly father, had carried on the family tradition both as businessman and as Renaissance patron, but of himself he had little to contribute. This generation was bent on spending money rather than making it, for by this period the Medici had become so rich that they were growing careless. Lorenzo dipped too freely in the city

* A work which bears a close affinity to it is the bronze of the Foulc Collection in the Philadelphia Museum of Art, by his master Bertoldo.

† Wackernagel, *op. cit.*, 270.

treasury and "the crisis which produced Savonarola, the fanatical foe of big business, occurred when the city bonds of Florence depreciated and Lorenzo was forced to lower the interest rate from 5 to 1½ per-cent." * Foreign wars, the transfer of the English wool trade to Flanders, and the opposition of Pope Sixtus IV, through the diabolical conspiracies of his nephews, brought about a series of economic storms which required the manipulation of a skillful pilot. "Under Lorenzo," Miss Beard has shown, "superb pageantry was offered to the public as glorious propaganda and beguilement, since it was on the favor of the public that the Medici had based their splendor. And while the unparalleled processions and the speed of Medicean building were making Florence the most sumptuous of cities, Lorenzo led her energies outward toward imperialism. Expansion was increasingly necessary, for Lorenzo and his family had ruined so many citizens and engrossed so much of the Government's income for their private use that only foreign adventure promised new resources." †

Already considerable in the time of Cosimo, the family art collections had been doubled before the death of Lorenzo the Magnificent in 1492. Two years later the Medici were banished from Florence, the palace looted, the works of art dispersed and the family properties confiscated by the Signoria. Only the palace itself remained, the medallions by Donatello in the arches of the *cortile* telling of the extravagances of Lorenzo. But the frescoes in the Chapel by Benozzo Gozzoli are perhaps the greatest link now left us with the early Medici. Across the years one stands arrested by the bursting humanism of the Council of Florence they depict, and the marriage of the fresh Italian spirit with the fading and sickly tradition of the Byzantine emperors.

For eighteen years the Medici were exiled from Florence but the power and influence of their house was not relaxed. They merely transferred their activity to the Vatican where as princes of the Church and Popes of Rome they continued to dominate the Renaissance scene. The service of Leo X and Clement VII as patrons of the arts is discussed in another chapter on Roman collecting. This latter is in itself quite another variation of the Italian pattern wherein the

* Beard, *op. cit.*, 157.
† Beard, *op. cit.*, 155.

intellectual curiosity of Florentine humanism gives way to a growing sense of classical authority. The lighthearted paganism of the Arno becomes steeped in the conscious lust for power and self-intoxication for which only God's Vicar may claim indulgence. If the Medici of Florence can be credited with bringing the Renaissance of the arts to flower, their Roman representatives may in turn be held responsible for its decay. But in those twenty years of Roman holiday the greatest masterpieces of European art were executed. In the meantime, as the Papacy was preparing for its Golden Age, the drama of collecting was being played on the stages of the lesser courts of Italy.

ANDREA MANTEGNA: THE NATIVITY (DETAIL)

Formerly in the hereditary collections of the d'Este family in Ferrara. Metropolitan Museum of Art

CHAPTER II

Rival Contenders for the Medicean Spotlight

No account of the history of Renaissance collecting would be complete without acknowledging the supremacy of woman and her ability to fertilize the genius of the statesmen, soldiers, artists and philosophers who made this age so great. The women who dominated the courts of Mantua, Urbino and Ferrara, to say nothing of the ladies who inspired the men of Florence, Rome, Milan and Byzantine Venice, appear to be, in contrast to the medieval chatelaines who commanded the courts of love of the Gothic west, less feminine. There is a masculinity characteristic of Isabella d'Este, of Caterina Cornaro, of the Duchesses of Milan and Urbino, which harks back to an earlier age before the Christian virtues had robbed their sex of its equality. "The woman worship of romantic love is over," says Mrs. Taylor, "but the Renaissance passion for beauty will not let its women be thrust away to breed and be silent. The women do as the men, without such controversy. Policy may make marriages, but the great princes must have beautiful and accomplished ladies to rule their courts of artists, to shine like rose-diamonds in their splendid settings. Women come as equals, wise and learned, and diademed, as the Queen of Sheba came to King Solomon. They come as comrades, too, rather than lovers. In their youth they resemble no more the medieval lady, with her slim bending body, her cleaving soft garments, her sweet smile, but rather are like gallant boys, hunting, hawking, learning classics, as well as dancing and singing. Later they ponder Greek philosophy, they are amateurs of all the arts, they govern states, they go clad in armor to keep fortresses." * In the words of Michelet, "*Elles troublent, elles corrompent, et civilisent.*"

* Rachel Annand Taylor, *Invitation to Renaissance Italy*. Harper and Bros., 1930, pp. 154–155.

It was the death of Il Magnifico in 1492 and the banishment of the Medici from Florence that turned the spotlight away from the Arno to the north and to the east. Italy, it must be remembered, was at this time not unlike the Northern States after the American Civil War. The South was prostrate; the families of the Confederacy were too busy healing their wounds to be concerned with culture. Only in the prosperous and booming cities of the Damyankees was there a rivalry for social and intellectual prestige like that of the independent city-states of the *quattrocento*. No single dynasty dominated the land and no one admitted the sovereignty of any individual ruler. The age of the despots was coming to a close, yet there still lingered the blood lust for self-determination which revealed itself in the rivalries of the ladies who presided at these courts. Through them moved triumphantly the perfect courtiers, Castiglione and Pietro Bembo, flattering, cajoling, pointing out works of art as well as writers with new thoughts and intrigues which for the moment would draw attention to a given city. In this world of *arrivistes* and merchant princes we see once more the eternal conflict between blue blood and yellow gold. In the more ancient dynastic principalities of the d'Este and Gonzaga we find not merely a hidden contempt for the riches of the manufacturing capital of Tuscany, but an overwhelming desire to make Florentine humanism into something nobler, more Ferrarese or Mantuan if necessary, but certainly reflecting the superiority of a culture derived from lineage rather than material resources.

Florence was the New York of its day, the noisy money market, vulgar, blatant and yet the envy of all others. Rome, to carry the analogy another step, was the Washington, the seat of government and of the federalizing influences of the Church. Milan, on the border of France and Germany, was the vigorous crude Chicago of the Renaissance, while Venice stood at the Golden Gate to the Orient. Only in those politically weakened states which later reverted to pope or emperor do we find the smugness and civilized refinements of a Boston or a Philadelphia.

Urbino, Naples, Milan, Modena, were all allied with Mantua by blood, by marriage or by bastardy. The parent strain was that of the d'Este of Ferrara. Beatrice d'Este, the girl bride of the Duke of Milan, was the daughter of Ercole of Ferrara and Leonora of Naples. Her sister, the famous Isabella, was the exquisite Marchioness of Mantua whose bosom friend and sister-in-law, Elisabetta Gonzaga, married Guidobaldo, the son of the great Duke of Urbino, Federigo da Montefeltro. Lucrezia Borgia, the golden-haired daughter of Pope Alexander VI, who beneath the sweetness of her face and body "distilled the purest poison of a venomous age," was married to Alfonso d'Este, whose son Ercole II became the husband of Renata, daughter of Louis XII of France. To these courts, too, came "the armèd woman of Forlì," the battling Caterina Sforza, and the Roman wife of the Marquis of Pescara, the pious Vittoria Colonna, who brightened the last years of Michelangelo. Finally the circle of these women seems to close at Asolo where the ex-Queen of Cyprus, Caterina Cornaro, "daughter of the Republic of Venice," held a court which attracted to it Cardinal Pietro Bembo, the Latinist secretary of Leo X, catalyst of the *Cortegiano* and lover of Lucrezia Borgia.

One thing is common to all these women: they loved art passionately and to the collections which filled their palaces and country villas they brought that informality and intimacy which is the basis of true humanism. The merchant prince of the Renaissance, or the politician, not unlike his successor in New York, was pretty apt, except on state occasions, to put his culture in his wife's name. He left it to the woman of the family to mingle with the artists and establish the reputation of the house.

But the secret of the Renaissance woman was, perhaps, her willingness to listen to the artists. Those of us who buy our wares from dealers on Fifty-seventh Street or Bond Street or the Place Vendôme too often forget the role of the artist in the history of taste. For not only did the artist produce the works of art we covet but he also developed, during the course of his creative effort, a fine sense of discrimination, an instinct for distinguishing the good from the bad. It is not surprising, therefore, to learn that the small collections of works of art assembled by the painters and sculptors attached to princely households very often became the core of the dynastic museums over which their patrons and patronesses ultimately presided. The character and scope of these cabinets varied according to the artist's means, and usually, since they could not afford complete or well-preserved antiquities, consisted of fragments: heads, hands and feet of statues and specimens of drapery and decoration which were of great value for their own studies as well as for their pupils. Ghiberti left many marble and bronze figures, according to Vasari, including a reclining figure by Polyclitus and some Greek vases. Francesco Squarcione, the dean of Paduan artists in the middle of the fifteenth century, was wealthy enough to collect on a larger scale and had traveled through Greece and Italy bringing back antiquities and paintings which he required his pupils to copy. His pupil, Mantegna, developed in the latter's studio his great taste for things of the past. Gentile Bellini was said to possess a torso of Venus by Praxiteles and a marble bust of Plato. The marble reliefs, executed near the Scuola di San Marco in Venice, are proof of the *Anonimo Morelliano's* theory that Tullio Lombardo used a draped antique torso as his model. In Siena, Sodoma's collection included some thirty antique monuments, among them a satyr, two sculptured columns, an assortment of bronzes, reliefs, vases, coins and some medieval works. He also assembled a number of casts in stucco, wax and lead. Giulio Romano's house in Mantua was filled with Roman fragments which he would sell or exchange with members of the court.

All of these collections, large or small, were in one way or another but pale reflections of the Medici whose houses and gardens had become proverbial as a paradise for artist and connoisseur. In them no line was drawn between patronage of the contemporary artist and the taste for antiquity. Works of all periods were shown side by side in the same rooms. There was, likewise, a complete catholicity in regard to artistic media. Fresco painting was at its height but usually reserved for churches and semipublic buildings, such as convents and hospitals, and for the larger palaces. At Florence, according to Burckhardt, there had developed a fashion of sinking rows of pictures into the wall paneling. These generally were of mythological subjects resplendent with nudes as a contrast to the smaller religious pictures of the private chapels and oratories. As the Flemish secret of oil painting on wood became more widely known it caught like wildfire, especially in Venice where the sea air discouraged the fresco painter. Landscape, too, and genre gradually insinuated themselves from the north by way of Venice, although they were instinctively foreign to Italian taste. Indeed the Latin mind never quite grasped the fact that genre requires, as Burckhardt so ably stipulated, "the representation of the whole environment, of a certain aspect of life in its entirety, and not of one scene only," as is the case with most Italian pictures.*

The *guardaroba* was the general name for the portion of the palace in which the princely collections were preserved. It included beautiful and spacious galleries (*gallerie*) for the display of works of art as well as the storage rooms and magazines where vases and other materials were put away. The more intimate objects with which the collector chose to live were reserved for the *studio* or study. If the collections proved too numerous, they overflowed into the *antecamera* where they impressed the courtiers and officials as they cooled their heels outside the inner sanctum.

* * * * *

Of all the nonprincely collections two, more than any others, influenced the course of taste in Italy. One was the collection at Como of the historian Paolo Giovio; the other was in Mantegna's house at Mantua. Giovio, a bishop, a courtier and a scholar, possessed a keen psychological insight and an ability of describing vividly the historical personages with whom he dealt in his studies. It was, therefore, quite natural for him to be interested in portraits and to become an eager collector of them. Italy had always gone in for the cult of "glory" and innumerable portraits of the "*viri illustres*" existed. Murals illustrating ecclesiastical and political events often added the portraits of local celebrities and substantial citizens. Prominent men of letters were portrayed for ducal and monastic libraries, and the artists resorted to their imagination if the patron insisted on having the portraits of great men of the past of whom no authentic likeness remained. The twenty-eight famous half-length portraits by Justus of Ghent (in the Louvre and in the Barberini collection in Rome) were prob-

* Cf. J. Burckhardt, *Beiträge zur Kunstgeschichte* (Das Porträt, Das Altarbild, Die Sammler), Basel, 1898, and J. von Schlosser, *Die Kunst und Wunderkammern der Spätrenaissance*, Leipzig, 1908.

ably executed for the library of the palace at Urbino. Monastic orders made a standard practice of having rows of saints and authors painted as murals for their libraries.

Giovio's description of his collections, in his *Musae descriptio in Pauli Jovii Elogia literaria*, shows that he started collecting in 1521 and continued until a year before his death in 1552. His house was a haven for the humanists of all countries and was considered one of the marvels of the age. He had his contemporaries painted by excellent artists. When portraits were not available, he ordered copies, usually busts one and a half feet high, painted on canvas. Numerous woodcuts were included in the collection and while he had intended originally to bring together only the portraits of poets and scholars, he gradually included celebrities of every country and every field of activity. The Museo is mentioned for the last time in 1589 and there is no report of what happened to it. All traces seem to have disappeared as have the copies of the portrait collection which Cosimo de Medici sent Cristofano dell'Altissimo to Como to make at the time of Giovio's death.

* * * * *

While Giovio represents the scholastic side of humanism, Mantegna is the symbol of the thirst for artistic knowledge and for beauty which gave Mantua such prominence and for which Isabella d'Este has taken all the credit.

The cultural tradition of the Gonzaga house was, after all, of long standing for, from the time of Luigi Gonzaga, who had made himself master of the city of Mantua in 1328, the family was keenly aware of the importance of art in exalting the splendor of their rule; Guido and Ludovico had befriended Petrarch, Gianfrancesco I had collected a library which at his death in 1407 numbered close to four hundred volumes. His son, Gianfrancesco II, founded the *Studio* which was recognized as a university in 1423. A decade earlier he had brought to Mantua the learned professor Vittorino Ramboldoni da Feltre, *uomo di Socratico ingegno*, to educate his children. Vittorino established his school in the Casa Zoisa, "The House of Joy," where he taught Greek, Latin grammar, philosophy, mathematics, logic, music and dancing. Intended at first only for the education of Gianfrancesco's children, the school established a pattern for the teaching of the aristocracy and the roster of pupils soon included the noblest names in all Italy. Such scholars as could afford to paid for their tuition, others Vittorino taught "for the love of God." To this school which emphasized so keenly an interest in athletics, in fencing, and in games of chivalry came the budding courtiers and ladies of the whole peninsula. Vittorino da Feltre was as important to Italy as William of Wykeham, Bishop of Winchester, was to England, for he too believed that "manners maketh man." It was here that Federigo da Montefeltro, Duke of Urbino, the "*condottiere virtuoso*," gained his love of the classics and of books, and developed from his teacher the philosophy which ordered the courts of Urbino and Gubbio. Federigo was, in fact, so deeply attached to him that he placed Vittorino's portrait among those of the world's most celebrated philosophers and poets in his library.

When Mantegna was called to the court of Mantua to decorate the palace, the city took on at last the aspect of a capital. He was among the first in a glorious procession: Costa, Giovanni Bellini, Michelangelo, Leonardo, Perugino, Correggio and Francia adorned the apartments of the palace with triumphs and allegories. Giulio Romano later decorated and enlarged the Palazzo del Tè for Isabella's son. The stipend of fifty ducats a month ($1000) which Mantegna received, plus lodging, grain and wood, was a very good one and indicates the estimation in which he was held by his prince. The latter granted him a coat of arms, gave him special gifts and grants for extra commissions, and allowed him to work at will for other patrons.

Mantegna's house (which is still preserved) was built to serve as a background for his collection of antique sculpture; the plan in fact seems to have been taken from the Belvedere in the Vatican, which the painter had seen in 1490 just after its completion when he was decorating the chapel of the Pope. The collections which the house contained were apparently never inventoried, but they must have been of the first quality, for Lorenzo il Magnifico made a special journey to Mantua to see them and the Duke of Milan sent agents with tempting offers for their purchase. In the miasma of history these items have become merged with the collections of the reigning house which were dispersed, in 1627, by the sale (among hundreds of other priceless works) of the Mantegna *Triumphs* to Daniel Nys for the account of Charles I of England. The latter placed them at Hampton Court. The remainder of the Gonzaga collections were looted by the French, who sacked the city three years later and thus enriched the palaces of Cardinal Richelieu.

Isabella d'Este, with the blood of Naples and Ferrara in her veins, took Mantua, its humanism and its works of art in her stride. "*La prima donna del mondo*," Niccolò da Correggio called her. "She made herself into a kind of burning glass for the art, literature and philosophy of Italy." An exquisite materialist, like so many women who take art passionately, she lost all sense of proportion or morality in satisfying her desires. Her ruthlessness and her diplomacy in regard to acquisition were whetted by the limitations of her purse; for her appetite was Medicean and her means to satisfy it merely those of a first-class adventuress. Manuscripts, bibelots, painting and sculpture, jewels and carefully inlaid musical instruments found their way to her like needles to a magnet. An inventory taken three years after her death gives a full list of her collections.*

It was Isabella's dream to make her *grotta* a place of retreat from the world and she strove with all the perseverance and tenacity of her character to adorn it. Again and again in her letters she importuned her friends and agents in Venice, in Florence, in Ferrara or in Rome to send her "some beautiful thing for the studio." Fra Sabba Castiglione, the Knight of Malta and nephew of Baldassare, was implored to send her antiques from Halicarnassus and the Ionian isles. No entreaty was too much for this indefatigable woman. In 1501 she wrote to an agent in Florence:

> If Leonardo, the Florentine painter, is now in Florence, we beg you will inform us what kind of life he is leading, that is to say, if he has begun any work, as we have been told, and what this work is, and if you think that he will remain for the present in Florence. Your Reverence might find out if he would undertake to paint a picture for our studio. If he consents, we would leave the subject and the time to him; but if he

* Cf. Julia Cartwright, *Isabella d'Este*. New York, 1903.

A VENETIAN PALACE OF THE FIFTEENTH CENTURY

From the painting by Mansueti, Venice, Accademia

COSIMO PATER PATRIAE

By Pontormo

LORENZO THE MAGNIFICENT

By an unknown Florentine

FOUNDERS OF THE MEDICI COLLECTIONS

THE MEDICI LIBRARY

After an eighteenth-century vignette by Zocchi

THE EXPULSION OF THE MEDICI 1494

Detail from the border of Raphael's tapestry at the Vatican

ISABELLA D'ESTE, MARCHIONESS OF MANTUA

By Leonardo da Vinci, Uffizi

FEDERIGO DA MONTEFELTRO, DUKE OF URBINO

By Piero della Francesca, Louvre

declines, you might at least induce him to paint us a little picture of the Madonna, as sweet and as holy as his own nature. Will you also beg him to send us another drawing of our portrait, since our illustrious Lord has given away the one which he left here? For all of which we shall be no less grateful to you than to Leonardo.

Leonardo apparently made no reply and hearing that certain antique vases which had belonged to Lorenzo de Medici, and which had been looted from his palace by the mob, were for sale, Isabella wrote to her agent, Francesco Malatesta, asking him to show these vases to some competent person, "such for instance as Leonardo, the painter, who used to live at Milan, and is a friend of ours, if he is in Florence and consult him as to their beauty and quality."

This lady with a whim of iron would not give up. Three years later she wrote the artist directly:

To Master Leonardo da Vinci, the painter.
M. Leonardo,

Hearing that you are settled in Florence, we have begun to hope that our cherished desire to obtain a work by your hand may be at length realized. When you were in this city, and drew our portrait in carbon, you promised us that you would paint it some day on colors. But because this would be impossible, since you are unable to come here, we beg you to keep your promise by converting our portrait into another figure, which would be still more acceptable to us; that is to say, a youthful Christ about twelve years, which would be the age He had when He disputed with the doctors in the temple, executed with all that sweetness and charm of atmosphere which is the peculiar excellence of your art. If you will consent to gratify this our great desire, remember that apart from the payment, which you will fix yourself, we shall remain so deeply obliged to you that our sole desire will be to do what you wish, and from this time forth we are ready to do your service and pleasure, hoping to receive your answer in the affirmative.

Obviously Leonardo couldn't stand the woman for he never answered her letter. The "portrait in carbon" which has been preserved in the drawing collection of the Louvre reveals a pert, persistent and unsympathetic little face. But if butter would not melt in Isabella's mouth in dealing with Leonardo, her treatment of the aging Mantegna, to whom she owed so much, showed her in her true colors. For years she had coveted an antique marble of *Faustina*, the greatest gem of his collection. He had sworn never to part with it, but at last her chance came when he was in need of money to pay a doctor for his daughter's illness. He wrote to her saying:

> I am pressed on all sides by creditors. . . . So it has come into my mind to help myself as best I can by parting from my dearest possessions, and since I have often been asked at different times, and by many persons of note, to sell my dear Faustina of antique marble, necessity, which compels us to do many things, prompts me to write to your Excellency on the subject, since, if I must part from it, I would rather you should have it than any other lord or lady in the world. The price is 100 ducats, which I might have had many times over from great masters; and I beg of you to let me know your intentions, and commend myself infinite times to your Excellency. Your servant, ANDREAS MANTINA.

After long negotiations, Isabella purchased the *Faustina* and Mantegna died six weeks later.

The humanism of Urbino, though it derived much from the schooling which Federigo da Montefeltro had had under Vittorino in Mantua, differed both in form and in flavor from that of Isabella's court. Elisabetta Gonzaga, Isabella's sister-in-law, had married the young Duke, Guidobaldo II, Federigo's son, and consequently brought to this environment something of the other city. But Federigo, who had commenced to build the palace as early as 1454, stamped upon Urbino the imprint of his own character. Castiglione in his *Cortegiano* spoke of the palace as "the most beautiful in all Italy; and so amply did he provide it with every convenience that it appeared rather a palatial city than a palace. He furnished it not only with the usual plenishings of rich brocades in silk and gold, silver plate and such like, but ornamented it with a vast quantity of ancient marbles and bronze sculptures, of rare pictures and musical instruments in every variety, excluding all but the choicest objects."

Federigo's library, which he had commenced as a boy and which today is incorporated in the Library of the Vatican, was second only to that of the Medici in Florence. Although a man of much smaller means, he nevertheless employed some 30 to 40 *scrittori* and spent yearly more than 30,000 ducats on his hobby. It contained, in addition to a great number of theological and medieval works, every book on medicine which was then available, many Greek manuscripts (including a complete Sophocles, a complete Pindar and complete Menander), the works of twenty-five humanists both in Italian and in Latin with all their translations, and an important modern section in which the works of Dante and Boccaccio were given a prominent place. Here was an ideal type of collector, a cultured man, always eager to increase his own learning, one who loved his books and used them intelligently and preserved them with care. "When he said that he would be ashamed to tolerate a printed volume in his library, it was because he valued and honored the beauty of the manuscript, and not because he was either mercenary or a snob." *

Elisabetta lacked the drive of Isabella, nor did she care so violently for material things. She was a creature of reverie and contemplation but also of deep passion which expressed itself in letters rather than in works of art. Her court and that of her husband have been immortalized by Baldassare Castiglione in his *Cortegiano*, which in effect relates the thoughts and philosophies of those who frequented the palace. It was here that Raphael Sanzio entertained Piero della Francesco and Melozzo da Forlì. Signorelli painted in the Santo Spirito, and Giuliano di Medici, Duke of Nemours, walked in the gardens with Bembo discussing poetry and music.

Into this peaceful reign like a thunderclap came the attack of Cesare Borgia. The city was sacked, the palace looted; Elisabetta fled to Mantua to Isabella for protection, but the eager Marchioness lost no time. Three days after the treacherous conquest of Urbino by Cesare Borgia, Isabella wrote to her brother, Ippolito d'Este:

Most Reverend Father in God, my dear and honored brother, – the Lord Duke of Urbino, my brother-in-law, had in his house a small Venus of antique marble, and also a Cupid,† which were given him some time ago by His Excellency the Duke of Romagna. I feel certain that these things must have fallen into the said Duke's hands, together with all the

* Douglas and Elizabeth Rigby, *op. cit.*, p. 166.

† This Cupid was an early work by Michelangelo. Isabella obtained it and it later passed to Charles I of England with the Gonzaga Collections. It perished presumably in the fire at Whitehall.

contents of the palace of Urbino, in the present revolution. And since I am very anxious to collect antiques for the decoration of my studio, I desire exceedingly to possess these statues, which does not seem to me impossible, since I hear that His Excellency has little taste for antiquities, and would accordingly be the more ready to oblige others. But as I am not sufficiently intimate with him to venture to ask this favor at his hands, I think it best to avail myself of your most revered Signoria's good offices, and pray you of your kindness to ask him for the said Venus and Cupid, both by messenger and letter, in so effectual a manner that both you and I may obtain satisfaction. I am quite willing, if it so please Your Reverence, that you should mention my name and say that I have asked for them very urgently, and sent an express courier, as I do now, for, believe me, I could receive no greater pleasure or favor either from His Excellency or from your most dear and reverend Signoria, to whom I commend myself affectionately.—Your sister, ISABELLA, MARCHIONESS OF MANTUA. Mantua, June 30, 1502.

As suddenly the storm was over with the death of Pope Alexander VI, and Cesare Borgia's magical empire departed from him. Giudobaldo returned from Mantua and, though much of the booty was never returned to him by the Church, he passed the rest of his life among his treasures in the retirement of his court.

Thus comes to an end the short but brilliant story of the collections of the d'Este and Gonzaga families which, in point of quality, yielded to no one, the Medici included.*

* In 1627 the bulk of the Gonzaga collections were sold to England, the balance carried off three years later by the French. The Montefeltros died out with Giudobaldo and the Duchy of Urbino was carried on through the della Rovere until 1624 when it reverted to the Papacy. The collections of the latter, then, for the most part were removed to Rome. Ferrara was claimed by the Pope Clement VIII as a vacant fief in 1597 but the House of d'Este persisted through the descendants of the bastard son of Alfonso I as Dukes of Modena and Reggio. They ruled until the nineteenth century, when by alliance with the younger House of Austria the line became extinct. The last Duke, Ferdinand V, presented to the city of Modena his family's picture gallery in 1869, which, united with collections of the Marchese Campori, became the Galleria Estense.

CHAPTER III

The Popes as Patrons and Collectors

THE progress of the Renaissance in Rome is a story quite different from that of Florence or of the lesser courts of Italy.* It is more stately and less inventive. There is none of the gay independence of the humanism of Lorenzo's court, none of the lightness and grace of Tuscan poetry. Because of the elective character of the Papacy, the sense of dynasty so apparent in the Houses of the d'Este and Gonzaga took another form. Rome produced few artists or scholars of her own; she had instead the "receptivity and sterility of all great capitals, spoiled women of pleasure among cities." But Rome had a unique possession of her own: to her was given the prophetic compensation of a long imperial memory. The eternal spiritual and temporal power of antiquity was hers, and to her were drawn irresistibly all of the arts and talents of an alien world. Her decline, which took so many centuries to accomplish and which was never acknowledged by the Holy See, was sealed by the great schism of the West and the Babylonian Captivity of the Popes at Avignon. During those seventy years when the city was abandoned to the jealousies and conflicts of the Roman nobles, the Renaissance had already established its foothold on the banks of the Arno.†

Odo Colonna was elected Pope in 1417. Taking the name of Martin V, he determined, now that the schism had ended and he could return to Rome, to restore once more the imperial power of the Papacy, to make his authority felt and heeded throughout Chris-

* It has seemed wise for the sake of brevity to omit in this book any discussion of the collections of the Visconti and Sforza in Milan or of the Kings of Naples. The pattern was set by the Medici in Florence and the performance was quite similar to that of Mantua, Urbino or Ferrara. The chapters on Naples and Milan in Burckhardt's *Civilization of the Renaissance in Italy* give an adequate picture of these courts.

† The most important investigations regarding the collections of the Popes may be found in Eugène Müntz, *Les arts à la Cour des Papes*. Paris, 1878.

tendom. He had before him the lesson of fourteenth-century Florence and he saw how Cosimo Pater Patriae, the champion of the people, was winning the hearts and confidence of both the Signoria and the working classes by building the city anew and lavishing his wealth upon her churches and public institutions. Looking about the Seven Hills of Rome the Pope saw nothing but desolation, waste and vandalism on every side. In the city, which Cassiodorus boasted had once contained as many statues as it had citizens, were standing not more than a few dozen ancient monuments and most of these were mutilated. What the bankers of Tuscany could do, the wealth and power of Holy Church could probably do better.

The Sacred College in its exile had not been entirely removed from the intellectual currents and ferments of the age, and the court of Clement VI had welcomed a spirit of scientific inquiry. Curiously enough, Avignon's proximity to the Mediterranean ports of France had brought to the papal court travelers and merchants from the East who carried with them works of art and new ideas which normally would not have passed through Rome. Simone Martini, the Sienese, had painted at this court and so had Lippo Memmi, and many other artists. Petrarch, too, had sung the praises of Provence. Thus, when Martin V decided to make Rome great by importing to it the Florentine Renaissance, the soil was thoroughly prepared for it to take root. His first and immediate care was "for the saddened churches" and in his zeal to restore abandoned sanctuaries he started on the systematic spoliation of pagan monuments which his humanistic successors were to carry to such extremes and then repudiate with laws protecting the very buildings they had stripped. The Pope established ateliers for jewelers, embroiderers, and for goldsmith's work, for which he had a weakness; he also employed the best painters Florence could provide – Masaccio, Pisanello and Gentile da Fabriano.

Martin's successor was Eugenius IV, a Venetian schooled in the sensuous beauty of the lagoons. He continued in the footsteps of his predecessor but concentrated on the rebuilding and enlargement of the Lateran, for which his architects and contractors quarried the travertine facing of the Colosseum. Jean Fouquet took his portrait and Filarete did his tomb. Gentile da Fabriano completed the frescoes in the Lateran and Fra Angelico was called to Rome. The tiara of the Pope, encrusted with jewels and stones to the value of 38,000 golden ducats, weighing over twenty pounds, was made by the Florentine sculptor Ghiberti. It was considered one of the marvels of the age.

But it is not until the reign of Nicolas V of Sarzana that the Renaissance can really be said to have arrived in Rome. In the eight years of his pontificate (1447–1455) the medieval city was transformed. The ancient walls, which during the successive invasions of the barbarians had been breached in many places and were crumbling in decay, were rebuilt; the fountains were restored or adorned with new statues and decorations. Fallen arches and obelisks were re-erected, the ancient cemeteries put in order. This rebuilding program was so extensive that it was necessary to open quarries for tufa and travertine in the Forum, the Circus Maximus and the Colosseum. As many as 2500 wagonloads of stone were drawn from them in a single year. Chief object of Nicolas's attention was the palace of the Vatican, for he wished in establishing the Popes as kings to make their surroundings worthy of the temporal power they were gradually acquiring. For the embellishment of the new papal apartments, Fra Angelico, Piero della Francesco and Andrea del Castagno were employed together with an army of skillful artisans, painters and glaziers; calligraphists and illuminators, goldsmiths and embroiderers were given commissions on a fantastic scale; tapestry looms were set up and the papal agents all over Europe were instructed to acquire for the Vatican everything precious that was obtainable.

A spirit of archaeology was abroad. Donatello and Brunelleschi had already visited Rome for the purpose of studying close at hand the antiquities which were constantly being unearthed in the mad scramble to provide marble for the new palaces and churches. Jean Fouquet, who had painted Pope Eugenius IV, and Rogier van der Weyden came to Rome filled with curiosity for the past. Humanists and scholars pondered over the broken fragments of classical inscriptions and bandied them across the dinner tables, giving the subtlest ending to an unfinished couplet. Refugee scholars from Byzantium, poets and historians from northern Italy, Latinists from France and the Germanies flocked to Rome. Clearly some order had to be made of this welter of undigested learning. Nicolas ordered the creation of the Vatican Library, putting a group of humanists to work – such men as Aurisipa, Manetti, Tiphernias and George of Trebizond – to sort out the accumulation of books and manuscripts which had become the casual property of the Popes during the previous thousand years.*

The three-year pontificate of the Spaniard, Calixtus III, was but a momentary interruption in the revival of the city. Engrossed with a crusade against the Turks, he melted down Nicolas's plate and collections of goldsmith's work to pay for galleys, and he dismissed the artists and craftsmen attached to the Apostolic Household. Fortunately this crude Borgia was succeeded by a Sienese humanist, the great Aeneas Sylvius Piccolomini, whom Symonds described as "the last of the Renaissance Popes whom we can regard with real respect." While still a youthful cardinal, representing Pope Eugenius IV at the Council of Basle, he had given himself up to "diplomacy, gourmandism and the perfection of his exquisite Latinity." No other occupant of the Chair of Peter had so well mastered the language of the Church. Becoming Pius at the age of fifty-three, he was already physically old and tortured with gout and asthma, which probably accounts for the simplicity of his personal habits and those of his court. Gregorovius, in examining the archives of the papal exchequer, found that notwithstanding a household of some 270 servants the daily expenditures of the Pope's table did not exceed an average of 8 ducats. In the matter of intellectual diversions, the Pope was more lavish, befriending scholars and indulging his own antiquarian tastes. On a journey to the Congress of Mantua in 1459, he stopped at Clusium to search for the labyrinth mentioned by Pliny and visited the so-called villa of Vergil on the Mincio. Burckhardt relates how the sickly Pontiff was carried on his litter throughout the Campagna as he familiarized himself with the ancient sites of Tusculum and Alba Longa, of Ostia and Falerii. In his *Commentaries* he described with equal interest the monuments of early Christianity and those of paganism.

A man of small economies, Pius II's early years in Rome were

* Cf. C. B. Stark, *Systematik und Geschichte der Archäologie der Kunst*. Leipzig, 1880.

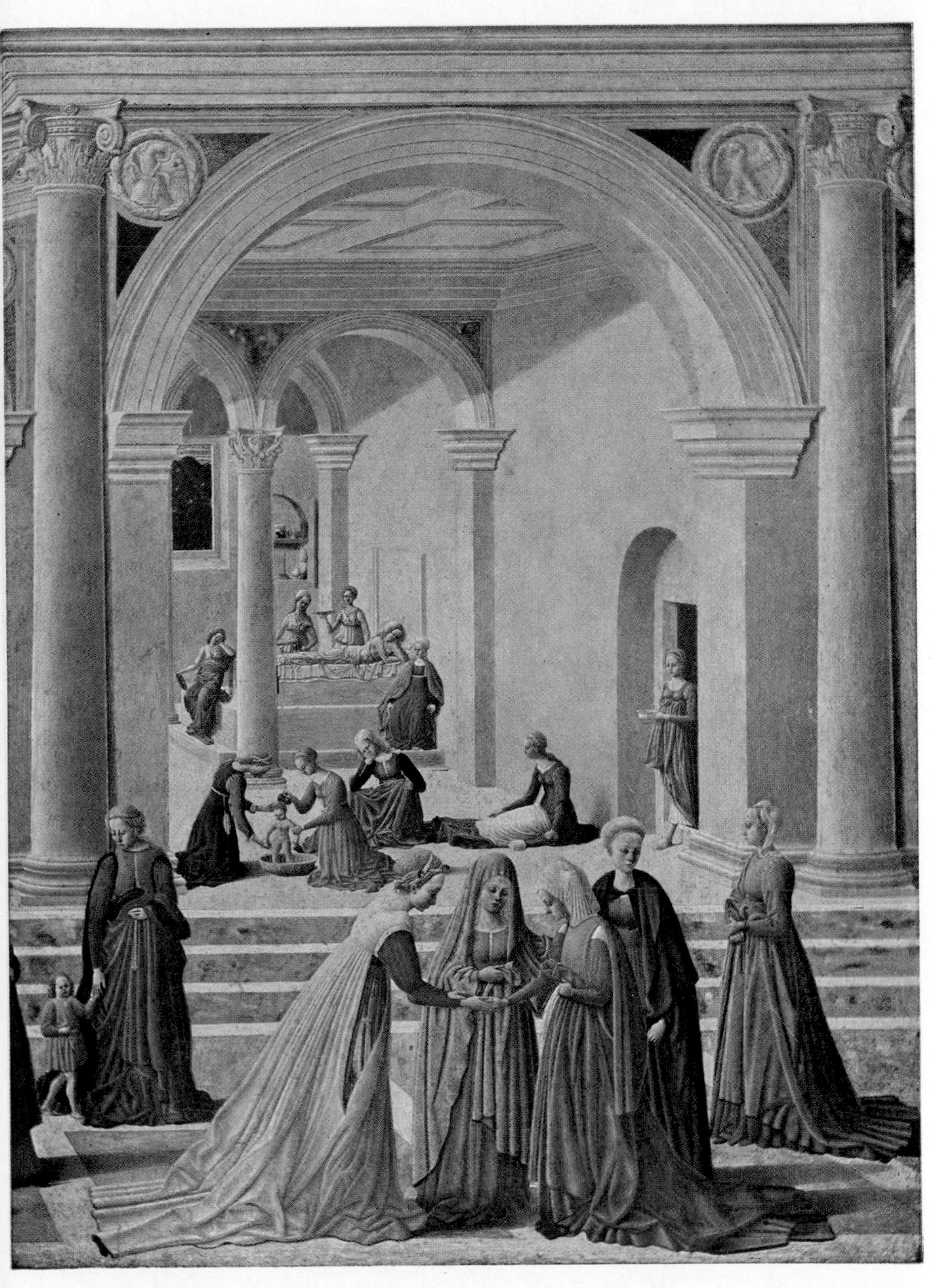

FRA CARNEVALE: THE BIRTH OF THE VIRGIN (DETAIL)

Formerly in the collections of the Dukes of Urbino and the Princes Barberini, Rome. Metropolitan Museum of Art

scholarly and passive. Not until the discovery of gold mines on the papal estate at Tolfa did he begin to carry forward the work of Nicolas V in enlarging and remodeling the Vatican. This windfall, which brought him in 100,000 gold ducats a year, permitted a resumption of the pontifical program on a grand scale. Conscious of the irreparable damage being done to classical Rome by the constant building, Pius II promulgated in 1462 the first of the papal bulls forbidding the quarrying of ancient stone or using any fragment of antiquity in new construction. Ironically enough, the Pope himself, ignoring his own edicts, was the first to plunder the Villa of Hadrian at Tivoli for his own building needs in Rome, Siena, and in his birthplace, Corsignano. To Siena he gave his famous library together with his personal works of art, which included the lovely marble group of the *Three Graces* which must have inspired Raphael's painting now at Chantilly. While part of him may have belonged to Tuscany, "Rome," he said, "is as much my home as Siena, for my house, the Piccolomini, came in early times from the capital to Siena, as is proved by the constant use of the names Aeneas and Sylvius in my family."

If Pius II was the scholar archaeologist of the Papacy, Paul II, who followed him in 1464, was the collector in the truest sense. He had the most voracious appetite for works of art of any of the early Renaissance Popes and was the chief competitor in the salesroom of his contemporary, Lorenzo the Magnificent. As a Venetian cardinal, Pietro Barbo, nephew of Pope Eugenius IV, he created the Palazzo Venezia, recently so publicized as the office of Benito Mussolini, and filled it with what was at that time considered the foremost museum of classical and Byzantine antiquities in Italy. While he did lip service to the cause of humanism by introducing printing from Venice into Rome and reorganizing the University, also by restoring certain antiquities like the statue of Marcus Aurelius and the arch of Titus, he was in reality a vulgar show-off with more instinct for a fine work of art than knowledge. His love for display knew no bounds; one of his tiaras alone was worth 120,000 ducats and in his desire to focus attention on himself he imposed the strictest sumptuary laws upon the papal court to prevent anyone from outshining him in a state procession. Pietro Barbo was a link between the Proconsul Verres and Fifty-seventh Street. While he lacked the sinister grandeur of his immediate successors in the Holy See, he would have been equally at home in a villa in Pompeii or in the showroom of Lord Duveen.

Paul II's collection, which was later sold by Pope Sixtus IV, only to be purchased in large part by the Medici Cardinal, Giuliano (Pope Clement VII), and thus passed on with his property to Florence, was richest in Byzantine objects in gold and ivory, particularly in the rare diptychs of the Eastern consuls. Other items listed in the inventory include 47 bronzes, 25 mosaics or portable altars, a large number of painted icons and panel paintings of religious subjects commissioned by the Cardinal, some 400 cameos and intaglios of both pagan and Christian origin. The collection of medals boasted many items by Pisanello which Barbo had taken away under the nose of Lorenzo the Magnificent while the artist was still lying unburied in his house. But above all else, the collection abounded in objects of gold, silver and precious gems; popular superstition claimed that the Pope was strangled by demons who held the jewels in his rings, and even Platina insists that his death was caused by apoplexy from the great weight of stones in his tiara.

THE GOLDEN AGE OF THE ROMAN RENAISSANCE

When Pius II conferred the red hat on Francesco della Rovere, he little thought that this fifty-seven-year-old Franciscan friar, the son of a fisherman, would succeed him and become the archenemy of the House of Medici. But four years later, in 1471, he ascended the throne of Saint Peter and took the name of Sixtus IV. His contemporaries called him, and quite rightly, "*il Gran Fabbricatore*," for with Sixtus we see the Papacy throwing in its chips upon the gaming table of world politics and playing for higher stakes than ever before. The Popes had tasted the blood of temporal sovereignty and meant to have their share of meat. It is ironical that this Pope, terrible in peace as he was in war, and who, Müntz says, knew only two arguments, "anathema in matters of religion and battle in political affairs," should best be remembered by the most solemn chapel in Christendom, later to become the crowning achievement of Michelangelo's career.

From Sixtus, who died in 1484, to the death of the Farnese Pope Paul III seventy-five years later, Rome was to be abandoned to the license and debauchery of her bishops. But in considering the morality of the time – and its effect upon the history of taste – we must remember that the Popes were morally no better or no worse than the other princes of the Renaissance. They shared the same passion for experiment, the same loving appetite for antiquity. Their enthusiasm for art and humanism was as much a part of their eager vitality as their excesses. What shocked Europe into the Protestant Reformation was not so much what they did, but that they did it "beneath the cloak of sanctity which a sacred tradition had cast upon their shoulders." That their greed should take the form of a demand for the wealth of Germany in order to support and expand their temporal ambitions was, in the eyes of moralists, statesmen and theologians, more serious than carnal sin, which, after all, was a personal affair.

For the history of taste the Popes were important as temporal princes, not as great pontiffs. "Since they had to be either secular lords, or become landless as Christ Himself, and since the heavenly alternative seemed impossible, they preserved that passionate sense of dynasty characteristic of the Italian princes, in itself merely an extension of the fierce Renaissance individualism; and they tore at neighboring states the more feverishly because of the brevity of their tenure, acting at best for the material interests of the Papacy, at worst for the glorification of *nipoti*. So each had an ear for every new invader who would promise part of his plunder, and the Vatican was a centre of foreign intrigue, destined ultimately to rend the great universal medieval Church between the dark fanaticism of Spain and the stolid bigotry of Lutheran Germany. . . . They form, these pontiffs, a strange human procession, crowned with the triple tiara, stiff like dolls in their precious copes closed with marvelous morses, stricken with terrible diseases, racked with rapacities and unseemly desires, yet hungry for the beauty of the past, troubled with grandiose visions, fiercely energetic to create new splendors, unreasonably conscious of bearing some heavenly flame from the very breath of Christ. Look at their heavy heads, arrogantly stamped on their medals – heavy heads charged with animal Caesarian will." *

Sixtus IV was less collector than patron. Claiming to find only 5000 florins in the papal treasury – a claim to which Symonds gives the lie – he immediately sold the collections of his predecessor but on the other hand showed the keenest interest in the monuments of Rome. He opened up the Museum of the Capitol, in which he had gathered such statues as had survived the Middle Ages, and forbade the exportation of antiquities from the city. He reorganized and built the Vatican Library, enlarged the apartments of the palace and completed before his death the construction, though not the painting, of the Sistine Chapel. With Sixtus starts that endless pilgrimage to Rome of artists, architects and craftsmen whom the Popes of the Golden Age were to employ: Botticelli, Signorelli, Perugino, Cosimo Rosselli and Ghirlandajo. Melozzo da Forlì worked for him, painting the celebrated portrait of the Pope surrounded by his nephews and secretaries receiving the humanist Platina. Architects as well as sculptors arrived upon the scene, including Verrocchio and Pollaiuolo. Not satisfied with bringing the artists to the Vatican, Sixtus wished to exercise some measure of control over them; in 1478 he founded the Academy of Saint Luke for the thirty leading artists under his protection. During this pontificate at long last the Roman Renaissance had reached maturity.

The eight years that followed under Innocent VIII merely marked time for the enormity of the "golden monstrous group" with whom Roderigo Borgia surrounded himself. The latter, as Alexander VI, was the Nero among the Popes, one whom Ranke described as a "virtuoso in crime" and the Venetian ambassador as "*molto carnale*." Fascinating as the years of Borgian debauchery may be, and however irresistible the gilded paganism of the Pope and of his children, Caesar and Lucrezia, they contributed comparatively little to the collecting or art patronage of the Holy See. To be sure, the Borgia were munificent patrons for everything that pleased the eye, and artists were employed for their carnivals and balls and for the decoration of their palaces and stately progresses; but in comparison with what went on

* Rachel Annand Taylor, *op. cit.*, 206, 213–214.

before, or with Alexander's immediate successors, the music was played in minor key. This pontiff's monument, aside from the splendid decoration of the Borgia apartments in the Vatican, was not in stone or canvas but in the wider world of politics. "By virtue of his crimes, his ruthlessness, and his ability and perjuries," says Symonds, "Alexander laid the real basis for the temporal power of the Papacy. He achieved for the Papal See what Louis XI had done for the throne of France, and made Rome on its small scale follow the type of the large European monarchies." *

THE CRIMSON DAWN OF THE SIXTEENTH CENTURY

The year 1492, in which Lorenzo the Magnificent died, was one of those prophetic dates which occur from time to time in European history. Just as nearly a half century earlier the year 1453 had marked simultaneously the close of the Hundred Years' War between France and England and the fall of the Byzantine capital to the Turks, so in 1492 we see again the future course of history suddenly explode and capture man's imagination. Granada fell to Ferdinand and Isabella, the Moors were driven out of Spain. In Germany, the Electors and their political associates were occupied with the stirrings and intrigues of an election year which resulted not only in the assumption of Maximilian I to the imperial throne but in the cementing of the fortunes of central Europe with those of Spain and the Low Countries through the Hapsburg dynasty. This year also marked a further revolution in traditional medieval thinking. The world was found to be no longer flat, for Christopher Columbus had sailed beyond the accepted peripheries of polite navigation and had injected a new hemisphere into world politics. The stage was set for the struggles of the sixteenth century, in which the issues of the modern world were to be defined and which, though centering on the timeless battlefields of the Latin peninsula, were destined to leave Italian liberties trailing far behind.

During the period of the Interregnum in Florence the Medici were not exiled in the sense that we are accustomed to today. When they

* Symonds, *op. cit.*, 413.

left Florence the yeast which they had planted continued to work, for the artistic ferment of the Renaissance was a force which no political catastrophe could suddenly annihilate. The artists who owed their instruction and well-being to the ousted rulers continued in their functions, though some, of course, labored in Rome or Milan or elsewhere. But nevertheless this period from 1492 to the Sack of Rome in 1527 was probably the most brilliant golden age since the time of Pericles.

Colonel Young has conveniently listed the artists who were at work in or near Florence in the year 1505 when Leonardo da Vinci and Michelangelo were making the cartoons for the Palazzo della Signoria: Perugino was working at the Annunziata, Raphael, emerging from obscurity, was painting the *Madonna del Gran Duca,* and the *Cardellino.* Botticelli at this time was sixty-one years old, Perugino fifty-nine, Leonardo fifty-three, Michelangelo thirty, and Raphael twenty-two. Among the others present in the city were Lorenzo di Credi, Fra Bartolommeo, Filippino Lippi and Andrea del Sarto. Francia was at work in Bologna, Pinturicchio in Siena and Luini at Milan. Carpaccio, Giorgione, Palma Vecchio and Titian were engaged in setting the final jewels in the crown of Venice. Italy had become the envy of the civilized world and as such laid herself open to the plundering fingers of the rising monarchies of western Europe. The overripe fruit of the Renaissance already bore "the heaviness of rich decay."

During the fabulous decade which turned the century, the Renaissance was nearly over and the Baroque had already started on its way. Italy was torn asunder; the French and Spanish had entered into their death struggle for the domination of the peninsula. As Michelet pointed out, the invasion of Charles VIII was not merely a turning point in the history of Europe, "it was no less than the revelation of Italy to the nations of the world." The Medici had been banished for abandoning Tuscany to the King of France and their palace had been ransacked. Henry VII by his miserliness was laying the foundations for the wealth and greatness of Elizabethan England. Venice, whose power had gradually been declining, was to be crushingly defeated in 1509 at the Battle of Agnadello by the Cambrai

League of Louis XII, Maximilian and Ferdinand. Already shorn of Constantinople, the Adriatic Republic could not well sustain the further loss of Verona, Padua, Bergamo, Cremona and Piacenza. Venice from that moment ceased to be a world power.

It was at this stage that another della Rovere stepped across the threshold of the "Golden Age" and occupied the throne of Peter as Pope Julius II. Symonds has called him "both the saviour of the Papacy and the curse of Italy." From the point of view of art, his reign saw the culmination and fruition of nearly two centuries of humanistic preparation. To him we owe the most splendid works by Michelangelo and Raphael and the very basilica itself of Saint Peter's, "that materialized idea, which remains to symbolize the transition from the Church of the Middle Ages to the modern semi-secular supremacy of Papal Rome."

In 1503, the year of Julius's accession, the *Laocoon* was found buried in the vineyards of a Roman villa. This group of writhing men and serpents, so dear to the hearts of professional archaeologists, has probably elicited more pompous nonsense and more scorn from the irreverent than any other sculpture in the history of art. But whatever one's individual taste may be, or whether one follows the school of Lessing or one's own sense of personal infallibility, it nevertheless is a milestone in the development of criticism, and it projected the pathway of collectors and connoisseurs for the next four hundred years. The Pope, who previous to his election had shown his interest in antiquities by purchasing the *Apollo Belvedere* and other statues, immediately appropriated it, taking it from under the nose of a cardinal who had offered the owner of the villa 600 scudi (c. $3000). The Pope, instead, rewarded the farmer with a lucrative position in the city government, just as a few years later the finder of the *Ariadne* was freed from taxes on his sheep and goats for a period of four years. Transactions of this kind became the classic formulae for the growth of the Vatican collections.

When Poggio, the Florentine humanist and collector, visited Rome in the 1440's, the spirit of archaeological discovery was already stirring. Ciriacus of Ancona had explained the Roman monuments to the Emperor Sigismund, traveling through Italy, Greece and Asia

Minor taking notes of inscriptions and making drawings in order, as he said, "to wake the dead." From these descriptions, and from the rather obscure verses of another traveler, Prospettino Milanese, it is possible to reconstruct a picture of the antique monuments that were visible in the fifteenth century.

The house wrecker was daily taking an enormous toll; the Baths of Diocletian and Caracalla, which still retained their marble facing in Poggio's day, were to be stripped down to the brickwork eighty years later when Raphael came to Rome, and the building program of the Popes was to clear entire areas of the medieval city to make way for large *piazze* with spacious Baroque palaces and churches. Unfortunately Poggio's famous work, *Ruinarum Urbis Romae Descriptio*, was not illustrated, but in 1532 a Flemish artist, Martin van Heemskerck, visited the city and kept a student's notebook filled with drawings of some of the antiquities that were visible in the ruins of public buildings and churches and in the villas and private palaces.* These drawings are of the utmost importance for reconstructing the appearances of the Christian capital just five years after its sack by the armies of the Emperor in 1527.†

Among the earliest collections one that must be mentioned was that of Prospero Colonna, the friend of Poggio, in whose palace at the Santi Apostoli were to be seen the *Apollo Belvedere*, the *Three Graces*, a giant *Hercules* and two statues of barbarian warriors. Later

* Based upon Heemskerck's drawings, a German writer, Hübner, has studied exhaustively the collections themselves, separating out the holdings as far as the documents permitted of each of the great Roman families as well as the personal collections of the princes of the Church. The latter reveled particularly in the more obscure, and therefore obviously more scholarly, representations of deities in their moments of Olympian relaxation and thus gave another twist to the humanism of the day, laying the ground for the sporting iconologists of our own time. Cf. C. B. Stark, *Handbuch der Archäologie der Kunst*, Leipzig, W. Engelmann, 1880, and P. G. Hübner, *Le Statue di Roma*, Klinkhardt and Biermann, 1912.

† Leopold von Ranke, *The History of the Popes*. George Bell, 1908. Appendix, Section 1, No. 13, p. 26. Ranke relates that Venetian ambassadors, sent to Rome to present their allegiance to Pope Adrian VI, describe the newly discovered antiquities in a report to their government. After having given an enthusiastic description of the *Laocoon*, they add the remark "that King Francis I had requested the gift of this noble work from the Pope when they met at Bologna; but His Holiness would not consent to rob his Belvedere of the original, and was having a copy made for the king. They tell us that the boys were already finished, but that if the maestro lived five hundred years and labored a hundred at his copy, it would never attain the perfection of the original."

A TOURNAMENT AT THE VATICAN, c. 1560

The New Saint Peter's is rising in the background. After Lafreri

THE PAPAL COLLECTIONS IN THE GARDENS OF THE BELVEDERE

Painted c. 1550 by Martin van Heemskerck. Vienna

CLEMENT VII

By Sebastiano del Piombo. Naples

LEO X AND NEPHEWS

By Raphael. Pitti

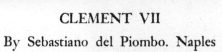

THE MEDICI POPES

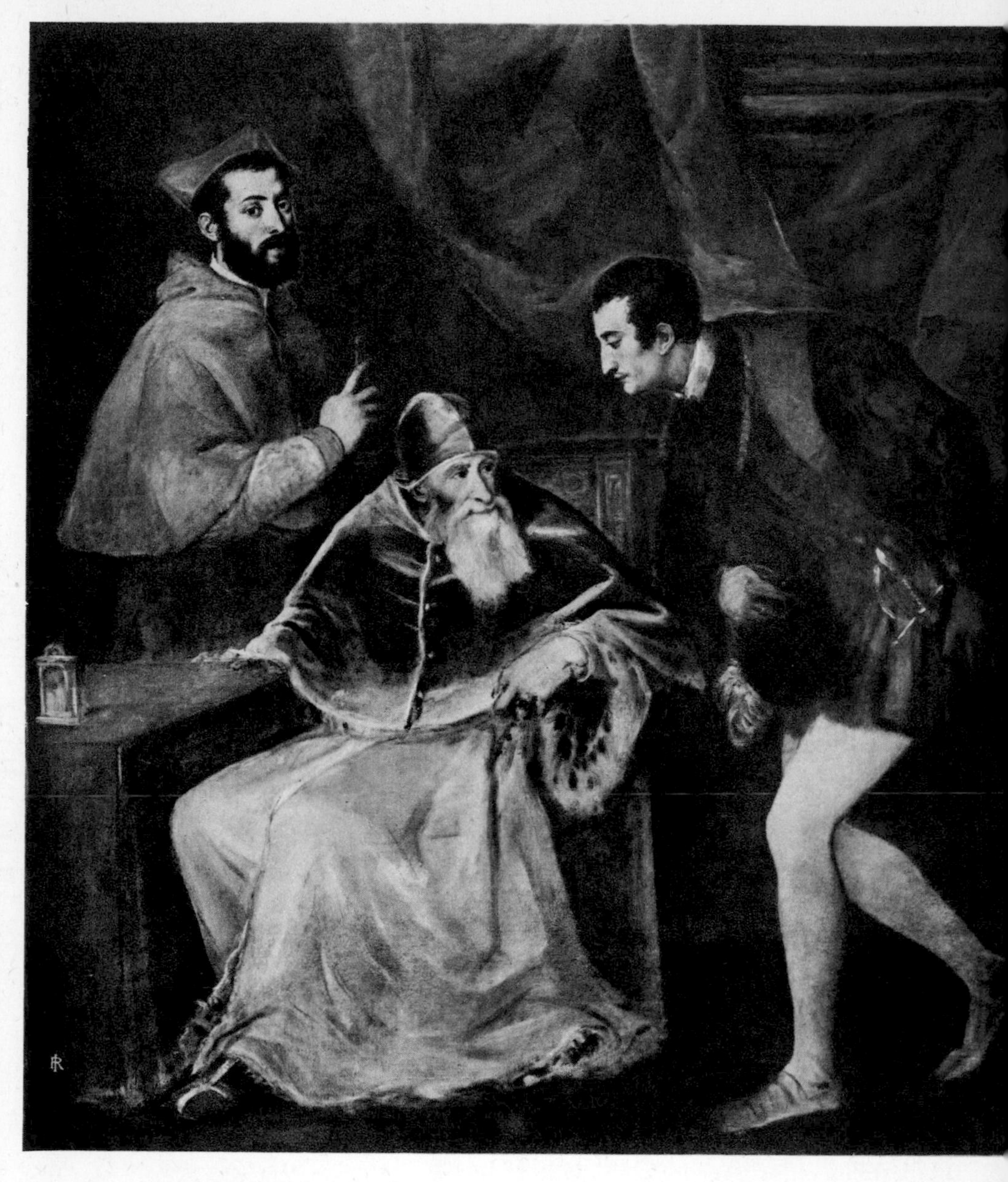

THE FARNESE POPE PAUL III AND NEPHEWS

By Titian. Naples

in the century these were divided between Aeneas Sylvius Piccolomini (Pope Pius II) and Giuliano della Rovere. Another palace famous for its antiquities was that of Rafael Riario, one of the debauched nephews of Sixtus IV. Other houses yielded well-known statues: the Valle, Maffei, Massimo, Caffardiolo, Porcari and Savelli, to pick at random a handful of the several score of names of the more prominent Roman families.

* * * * *

By the turn of the sixteenth century, the extravagance of the Popes and the iniquitous taxation imposed upon the residents of the city gave rise to a phenomenon which had not been seen since the days of the Augustan emperors, namely, the art trade. Appreciation of antiquities, stimulated by a century and a half of self-conscious humanism, had created a group of yearners not merely for the rediscovery of the classical past but for the showy luxury of its most costly emblems. The same Renaissance merchants who had patronized with such reckless extravagance the painters and sculptors of their day had found a new way of immortalizing themselves and, of course, of passing on to their descendants tangible assets which would increase in value. Thus were born in the Golden Age of the Medici Popes the collector and art dealer of modern times. Of the latter we have only fragmentary knowledge but in the beginning the dealers were personages who, as artists like Raphael himself or as ambassadors like the "perfect courtier," Baldassare Castiglione, already enjoyed exalted positions in the world of the great. Such men would indulge in diplomatic negotiations between acquisitive and ruthless bankers like the Medici and impoverished noblemen; their activities at this period being restricted to the most gentlemanly forms of double-dealing. Most active in this field was Giulio Romano, the painter of the exquisite frescoes in the Farnesina Palace, who, among other important transactions, bought in 1520 the large collection of Giovanni Ciampolleri and sold it to Cardinal Giulio de' Medici (Pope Clement VII) for the Villa Madama.

If the earlier Bishops of Rome had blazed the trail of acquisition at the Vatican, Julius II can be regarded as the real architect of the papal collections. He placed the *Apollo Belvedere*, which he had acquired as cardinal, in the court of the Vatican and added gradually the monuments which have given it such lasting fame: in 1503 the *Laocoon*, and the following year the *Hercules* and *Commodus*. In 1512 the large allegorical groups of the *Tiber* and the *Nile* were added. At about the same time two of the finest collections were founded, those of Cardinal Grimani which the latter bequeathed to the Republic of Venice, and is now in the Doges Palace, and that of the Villa Madama, previously mentioned, formed by the Medici Cardinals.

When Raphael was appointed in 1515 Superintendent of Antiquities by Leo X, the Belvedere was, together with the collections of the Capitol (already established as a museum in 1471 by Sixtus IV), the principal official collection of the Papacy. All of that vast body of antiquities which are today scattered through the museums and apartments of the Vatican were to be laboriously gathered in from various sources by the archaeologists of the Apostolic Household in the succeeding centuries. To these collections Leo himself did not contribute greatly, for, like most of the members of the Medici family, the Pope was more interested in personal glory than in the public good. But to archaeology he lent his support wherever discoveries of ancient monuments turned the spotlight directly upon the splendor of his person. "He moved with unprecedented expenditure of processional welcome – frankly enchanted to take his Papal throne, through antique statues, arches, epigrams on Venus and Pallas, trophies and obelisks, effigies of saints and gods."

"Since God has given us the Papacy, let us enjoy it," was Leo's frank apology for a reign which Gregorovius has called a "revelry of culture." Michelangelo was completing the painting of the Sistine Chapel which he had begun in 1508 and Raphael was working on the no less celebrated apartments of the Vatican. The greater part of the talent of Europe, whether in architecture, sculpture or painting, had been recruited to lavish its attentions on the churches and palaces of Rome. The new Saint Peter's was emerging from the scaffolding and the Holy City no longer retained its medieval sweetness; Rome had become once more the capital of the world.*

* *The Catholic Encyclopedia* contends that "Leo X, in keeping with the habits of his family, led the life of a literary and artistic amateur. But though his manner of

To such a capital belonged all the pleasures and excesses which a newly developed lust for power would demand. Leo divided his time between political affairs and carnivals. The accounts of balls, masques and processions defy anything which even the fertile imagination of a Colbert could later devise for the amusement of Louis XIV at Versailles. Hunting and hawking parties in the Campagna, supper parties of Lucullan dimensions at La Magliana, triumphs which gave living pantomimes to the mythologies of Greece and Rome were the order of the day. Even the lovely courtesans of the papal entourage, whose features were as finely chiseled as the hexameters set to music in their honor, appeared as cameos in a setting of pure pagan gold. Restraint was unknown except in the line of the architect or artist or in the subtlety of the musician or man of letters.

Martin Luther, learning of conditions in the Christian capital, wrote to the Pope from Wittemberg:

> I must acknowledge my total abhorrence of your see, the Roman Court, which neither you nor any man can deny is more corrupt than Sodom or Babylon; and which according to the best information I can get, is sunk in the most deplorable and notorious of impiety. Indeed, it is clear as daylight that the Roman Church, formerly the most holy of all, has become a licentious den of thieves. It has become a shameless brothel. It has become a kingdom of sin, of death and of hell, the wickedness of which not even Antichrist himself could conceive.

Another Protestant leader, the late Lord Bishop of London, Dr. Creighton, looking across four centuries, and without condoning Leo's excesses, has expressed a calmer view of the pontiff. Speaking of the personal charm of the man, a combination of the great qualities of his father, Lorenzo the Magnificent, and of the weaker vacillating tendencies of his Orsini mother, he shows that Leo always had a ready smile and a genial remark, and behaved with the dignity and assurance of one who was born to rule:

---

life was quite worldly, he excelled in dignity, propriety and irreproachable conduct most of the Cardinals." The article quotes von Reumont (*Geschichte der Stadt Rom*, II part, 1870): "Leo X is in a great measure to blame for the fact that faith in the integrity and merit of the Papacy, in its moral and regenerating powers, and in its good intentions, should have sunk so low that men could declare extinct the old true spirit of the Church."

In one point Leo was pre-eminently successful; he converted Rome for a brief space into the capital of Italy, and his reputation is chiefly founded on this achievement. Before his pontificate art and letters had been exotics in Rome; under him they were acclimatized. Julius II had been a grim employer of literary and artistic labor; Leo X was a sympathetic friend who provided congenial surroundings. For Leo as a man wished to enjoy life, and as a statesman saw, like Charles II of England, the advantage to be gained from masking political activity under an appearance of geniality, indolence, and easy good nature.*

Leo was a collector in the grand manner – a man of taste and instantaneous decision, he was always ready to pay the asking price for an object even if he had to lie awake at night contriving ways and means of getting even with the man who had sold it to him. The Pope's good humor was contagious; the populace shared his fun and his practical jokes, such as the crowning of the hack poet Baraballa on the Capitol, whither he was to be transported in triumph on the Pope's elephant Hanno. This animal, the gift of King Manuel of Portugal, was the first elephant to be seen in Rome in Christian times and it became not only a delight to the Pope himself but a mascot of the people, featured in public processions, and was popularly supposed to have cost 70,000 ducats. Ulric von Hutten, the phlegmatic Lutheran, grimly reported the pontiff's grief over Hanno's untimely death:

> You have all heard how the Pope had a great animal which was called an elephant, and how he held him in great honor, and how he loved him greatly. Now therefore, you should know that this animal is dead. When he was sick, the Pope was filled with woe. He summoned many doctors, and he said: "If it is possible, cure my elephant!" Then they all did the best they could. They examined the elephant's urine, and they gave him a great purgative which weighted five hundred ounces. But it did not take effect, and so he is dead, and the Pope greatly grieves. They say he would have given five thousand ducats to anyone who cured the elephant for he was a remarkable animal and had an enormous nose. And he always knelt down when he came into the Pope's presence, and trumpeted resoundingly: "Bar, bar, bar!"

* M. Creighton, *A History of the Papacy*. Longmans, Green, 1903. VI, 193.

The Pope ordered Raphael to paint a portrait of Hanno above the elephant's tomb upon which was inscribed the following epitaph:

Beneath this enormous mound, I lie buried, the huge elephant. King Manuel, conqueror of the East, sent me a prisoner to the tenth Leo. I was an animal not seen here for a long time, and the young men of the city admired me because in the body of a beast I had a man's intelligence. Fate envied me my home in fair Latium, and would not permit me to serve my master for as long as three years. Therefore, O Gods, add that time which destiny snatched away from me to the life of the great Leo. – He lived to be seven years old, died of angina, and was twelve palms in height. This monument was placed here on June 18, 1516, by Giovanni Battista of Aquila, papal chamberlain and the elephant's head keeper. What nature took away, Raphael has with his art restored.*

And, as if this elephantine joke were not quite enough, Pietro Aretino, then a humble valet in the Chigi household and later to become the "Scourge of Princes," used this occasion to attract papal recognition by publishing the *Last Will and Testament of the Elephant*, a scurrilous document in which the animal bequeathed the several portions of his anatomy, each with an appropriately insulting word of recollection, to the various members of the Sacred College.

The wealth of Rome was already fabulous. No prince of western Europe could boast the extravagances of the papal court and of the bankers and merchants who manipulated it. "The Pope's income amounted to between 500,000 and 600,000 ducats. The papal household alone, which Julius II had maintained on 48,000 ducats, now cost double that sum. In all, Leo spent about 4,500,000 ducats. On his unexpected death his creditors faced financial ruin. A lampoon proclaimed that Leo had consumed three pontificates; the treasure of Julius II, the revenues of his own reign, and those of his successor." † Agostino Chigi, the Sienese banker who had come to Rome in 1485 and had amassed a colossal fortune, was the archetype of the new capitalistic society that was gradually replacing the old Roman families which had been ruined or driven into exile by the Borgia Pope Alex-

* Thomas Caldecot Chubb, *Aretino – The Scourge of Princes*. Reynal and Hitchcock, 1940, pp. 48–53.

† Klemens Löffler, "Leo X," in *Catholic Encyclopedia*.

ander VI. Originally setting himself up as a moneylender in the Contrada dei Banchi – the Wall Street of the High Renaissance – he twenty years later became papal treasurer under Julius II and an informal secretary of state. In his private business he employed 20,000 men, owned a fleet of 100 vessels, had branch banks throughout Italy. His warehouses scattered from Constantinople to Lyons and from Alexandria to London had taken some of the luster from the Medici houses established in foreign cities a half century earlier. He ran the finances of the Catholic Church, operated the papal mint and the monopoly of the alum mines at Tolfa. Alexander VI had given him the exclusive right to supply grain to the Papal States. His income from rents alone was over 70,000 ducats, how much more from other sources it is difficult to estimate, but a safe guess might be not less than $2,000,000 a year.

Baldassare Peruzzi designed the Farnesina Palace as a setting for this Renaissance jewel – the prince of merchants. Chigi's collections were the envy of Europe; he was the patron of the living at a time when the patron could with difficulty make a mistake. He was also the underwriter of exhaustive excavations for classical antiquities, some of which were found buried in the gardens of his villa. His jewelry, his furniture and his works of art were of the same high quality as the mural decoration painted so lovingly by Raphael. Tempted with the stories of Galatea and of Cupid and Psyche, made flesh by Chigi's installing "for the duration" the painter's mistress, *La Fornarina*, with him, Raphael produced some of his finest and most spirited masterpieces. The house was so closely hung with works of art and tapestries that the Spanish ambassador, calling upon Chigi's ethereal Imperia – the toast of Rome – spat in the majordomo's face because, as he apologized, he "could find no other vacant space." At a banquet given in honor of the Pope, as each course was finished, the servants carried the gold service to the window and threw the dishes into the Tiber. Unfortunately, the next morning Leo passed by and saw fishermen recovering them in a net which had been set in the water to receive them.

* * * * *

But the dark clouds of Protestant reform had long been rumbling in the north. Leo's sudden death in 1523 gave the Emperor (Charles V) the opportunity for which he was looking and he manipulated the election to place Adrian of Utrecht, his tutor, on the papal throne. What might have happened if this violent ascetic had lived more than a few months is difficult to surmise. Perhaps the Church would have hastened its own reform and the Protestant revolt have been averted. But with the Papacy again vacant within the year, the Medici interests were able to marshal their forces and put a member of the family once again in power. While Cardinal Giulio, who took the name of Clement VII, had been an able minister of state for Leo X, he had made his principal occupation that of collecting works of art. He had set the pattern which the Grand Dukes of Tuscany were to follow.

Excellent as he was as a collector, Clement VII proved fatal, however, as a pontiff. As the political horizon grew darker, his earlier political dexterity proved to be his undoing. In 1527 the crash came, and, says Symonds, "by a series of treaties, treacheries, and tergiversations, Clement had deprived himself of every friend and exasperated every foe. Italy was so worn out with warfare, so accustomed to the anarchy of aimless revolutions and to the trampling of stranger squadrons on her shores that the news of a Lutheran troop, levied with the express purpose of pillaging Rome and reinforced with Spanish ruffians and the scum of every nation, scarcely roused her apathy. The so-called army of Freundsberg – a horde of robbers kept together by the hope of plunder – marched without difficulty to the gates of Rome."* For nine months the city was abandoned to this band of 30,000 brigands while the Pope was held prisoner in the Castel Sant'Angelo.

Benvenuto Cellini has given us a vivid picture of the siege in his *Autobiography*. If we are to believe his boasting, he not only slew the Constable of Bourbon with his own musket but was solely responsible for the defense. "I shall skip over some intervening circumstances," he blithely writes, "and tell how

Pope Clement, wishing to save the tiaras and the whole collection of great jewels of the Apostolic Camera, had me called, and shut himself up together with me and the Cavalierino in a room alone. The Cavalierino had

* Symonds, *op. cit.*, 443–444.

been a groom in the stable of Filippo Strozzi; he was French and a person of the lowest birth; but being a most faithful servant, the Pope had made him very rich and confided in him like himself. So the Pope, the Cavaliere, and I, being shut up together, they laid before me the tiaras and the jewels of the regalia; and his Holiness ordered me to take all the gems out of their gold settings. This I accordingly did; afterwards I wrapt them separately up in bits of paper, and we sewed them into the lining of the Pope's and the Cavaliere's clothes. Then they gave me all the gold, which weighed about two hundred pounds, and bade me melt it down as secretly as I was able. I went up to the Angel, where I had my lodging, and could lock the door so as to be free from interruption. There I built a little draught furnace of bricks, with a largish pot, shaped like an open dish, at the bottom of it; and throwing the gold upon the coals, it gradually sank through and dropped into the pan. While the furnace was working, I never left off watching how to annoy our enemies; and as their trenches were less than a stone's throw right below us, I was able to inflict considerable damage on them with some useless missiles, of which there were several piles, forming the old munitions of the castle. I chose a swivel and a falconet, which were both a little damaged in the muzzle, and filled them with the projectiles I have mentioned. When I fired my guns, they hurtled down like mad, occasioning all sorts of unexpected mischief in the trenches. Accordingly I kept those pieces always going at the same time that the gold was being melted down; and a little before vespers I noticed someone coming along the margin of the trench on muleback. The mule was trotting very quickly, and the man was talking to the soldiers in the trenches. I took the precaution of discharging my artillery just before he came immediately opposite; and so making a good calculation, I hit my mark. One of the fragments struck him in the face; the rest were scattered on the mule, which fell dead. A tremendous uproar rose up from the trench; I opened fire with my other piece, doing them great hurt. The man turned out to be the Prince of Orange, who was carried through the trenches to a certain tavern in the neighborhood, whither in a short while all of the chief folk of the army came together.

When Pope Clement heard what I had done, he sent at once to call for me, and inquired into the circumstance. I related the whole, and added that the man must have been of the very greatest consequence, because the inn to which they carried him had been immediately filled by all the chiefs of the army, so far at least as I could judge. The Pope, with a shrewd instinct, sent for Messer Antonio Santacroce, the nobleman who, as I have said, was chief and commander of the gunners. He bade him order all us bombardiers to point our pieces, which were very numerous, in one mass upon the house, and to discharge them all together upon the signal of an arquebuse being fired. He judged that if we killed the generals, the army, which was already on the point of breaking up, would take to flight. God perhaps had heard the prayers they kept continually making, and meant to rid them in this manner of these impious scoundrels.

We put our cannon in order at the command of Santacroce, and waited for the signal. But when Cardinal Orsini became aware of what was going forward, he began to expostulate with the Pope, protesting that the thing by no means ought to happen, seeing they were on the point of concluding an accommodation, and that if the generals were killed, the rabble of the troops without a leader would storm the castle and complete their utter ruin. Consequently they could by no means allow the Pope's plan to be carried out. The poor Pope, in despair, seeing himself assassinated both inside the castle and without, said that he left them to arrange it. On this the orders were countermanded; but I, who chafed against the leash, when I knew that they were coming round to bid me stop firing, let blaze one of my demicannons, and struck a pillar in the courtyard of the house, around which I saw a crowd of people clustering. This shot did such damage to the enemy that it was like to have made them evacuate the house. Cardinal Orsini was absolutely for having me hanged or put to death; but the Pope took up my cause with spirit. The high words that passed between them, though I know what they were, I will not here relate, because I make no profession of writing history. It is enough for me to occupy myself with my own affairs.*

But the heroic bombast of Florence's most noted goldsmith did not deter the Flemish, German and Spanish troops, who having received only promises and no pay for many months were in a state of open mutiny.

When the night came, the pot-bellies who guarded the Sistine Bridge took fright and the army overflowed from the Trastevere into Rome itself. Then you heard the outcries. The gates crashed to the ground. Everyone fled. Everyone hid himself. Everyone wept. Soon blood drenched the ground, people were butchered right and left, the tortured

* Benvenuto Cellini, *Autobiography*, trans. by John Addington Symonds. Brentano, n. d., I, 179 ff.

were screaming out, prisoners were begging for mercy, women were tearing their hair, old men were quaking, the city was turned upside down. Happy was he who was killed by the first blow, or in his agony found someone to dispatch him. But who can tell of the woes of such a night? Friars, monks, chaplains, and the rest of the tribe, armed or unarmed, hid themselves in the sepulchres, more dead than alive, and there was not a cave nor a hole in the ground nor a bell-tower nor a wine cellar nor any secret place which was not filled with all sorts of persons. Respectable men were mocked and with the clothes torn off their backs, were thrown down and searched and spat upon. Neither churches nor hospitals nor private houses were regarded. They even entered those sanctuaries where men are not allowed to enter, and chased women, out of maliciousness, into places where women are excommunicated for going. It was pitiful to see fire consuming the gilded loggias and the painted palaces, and it wrung your heart to hear husbands, red from the blood of their own wounds, crying for their lost wives in a voice that would have made the Colosseum weep, and that is a block of solid marble.*

Clement was forced to an ignominious capitulation. In a few short weeks the Medicean city had been destroyed. The Christian world, both Catholic and Protestant, was visibly shaken by this visitation of Jehovah upon the Sodom and Gomorrah of the Renaissance. Rome's works of art were scattered or destroyed, her artists driven to the protection of Venice and Mantua.

Gregorovius puts the loss from the Sack at £1,500,000 sterling. Thirteen thousand houses were burned or destroyed and 30,000 inhabitants were dead by sword, fire, exposure, hunger or plague. "When at last the barbarians withdrew sated with blood, surfeited with lechery, glutted with gold, and decimated with pestilence, Rome raised her head a widow. From the shame and torment of that sack she never recovered, never became again the gay, licentious lovely capital of letters, the gay gilded Rome of Leo." Clement, who had thus brought to an end the Golden Age of the Papacy, also rang down the curtain on the elder branch of the Medici. His own fabulous col-

* This account, based upon a letter from Sebastiano del Piombo to Aretino, was put in the mouth of Nanna, the lighthearted nun of Aretino's *Raggionamenti*, and may be considered one of the earliest war correspondent's dispatches. The English translation is from Chubb, *op. cit.*, 190.

lections at the Villa Madama were either destroyed in the Sack or sold to be repurchased by another junior line of Medici cardinals.

* * * * *

The election of Alessandro Farnese in 1534, the first Roman to sit upon the chair of Peter in 104 years, was a matter of great rejoicing. The black days of the Sack were over and the spell of misery was broken. Lanciani pointed out that the fifteen years of Paul III's rule mark one of the happiest periods in the history of the city. But it was largely due to the vigorous character of the Pope himself that the reign was so important for the history of art and particularly for the history of collecting. Created a cardinal at twenty-five, he had embarked upon a career of archaeology that quickly removed him from the amateur class and made him the envy of all professionals.

Alexander VI, in return for certain favors, had given him the rights to all the ruins, buildings and fortifications in the vicinity of the Church of San Lorenzo fuori le mura to use as building materials for the Palazzo Farnese. These ruins, the debris of buildings dating from the eighth to the twelfth century, had been thrown together into hastily improvised bulwarks against the Saracens and Teutonic invaders. To strengthen these walls all manner of marble had been thrown into them, and in one wall alone the young Cardinal found twenty portrait heads of Roman emperors. This was the nucleus of the famous Museo Farnesiano; from this point on Alessandro Farnese displayed a mania for excavation. He obtained from the Pope the further right to all antique material which he could cart away in a single night. Carefully laying his plans and surveying the various sites in the city, the Cardinal commandeered a fleet of seven hundred oxcarts and thus in one coup acquired what he needed for his palace. Excavations were conducted in every part of Rome and in the Campagna; the Temple of the Sun in the Colonna gardens on the Quirinal was completely destroyed, as were the Forum of Trajan, the Temple of Neptune and the Portico of the Argonauts in the Piazza di Pietra.

As Pope Paul III, he continued his fanatical interest in unearthing the antiquities of Rome. From the Gardens of Caesar and from the Baths of Diocletian and Caracalla were brought the principal pieces of the present-day Naples Museum. "The number of masterpieces," says Ligorio, "goes beyond the dreams of imagination." All of these collections the Pope left to his own grandson, another Cardinal Alessandro Farnese. In pillaging the ancient ruins, Paul III was careful to improve the sites which he had excavated, and the full measure of his activity is best seen in the preparations which his Commissioner of Public Works made for the triumphal entry of the Emperor Charles V into Rome on April 1, 1536. In less than fifteen weeks, and at the cost of 50,000 ducats, a special highway was constructed three miles long, opened, leveled, paved and decorated with triumphal arches; two hundred houses and four churches were demolished. The Baths of Caracalla, the Septizonium, the Colosseum, the Palace of the Caesars were cleared of their surrounding modern buildings; the Templum Sacrae Urbis (the Church of Saints Cosmas and Damian), the Heroon of Romulus, son of Maxentius, the Temple of Faustina, the Arch of Septimius Severus, the Forum and Column of Trajan were brought into full view. In short, all of the Roman ruins lying between the Piazza San Marco and the Colosseum were opened up by Paul III and left by him in much the condition that those of us who knew Rome before Mussolini remember it. Through this highway the Emperor was escorted from the Appian Way, then on to the Via del Popolo and finally to Saint Peter's. This pageant, the crowning triumph of Charles V's career, marked also the end of the Renaissance in Rome.*

The Farnese collections, passing to the Pope's grandson, were left by him to the city in a will dated 1587:

> It is my solemn will that all my statues of bronze or marble, my Library and the Office of the Blessed Virgin illuminated by Giovio Clovis, shall be preserved and kept forever in the City of Rome, and in the Farnese Palace, and that none of my heirs and successors shall dare to sell or give away, or transfer to other places or pawn any of the objects of art and curiosity which exist at the present moment in my collection.

But despite this will the collections were soon to leave the city. The marriage of the Pope's nephew, Ottaviano Farnese, to the Emper-

* A full account is given in R. Lanciani, *The Golden Days of the Renaissance in Rome*. Houghton Mifflin Co., 1906.

or's daughter, Margaret of Austria, later Margaret of Parma, had opened the collections to litigation and temptation. A Bourbon claim through the House of Parma was made in the eighteenth century and Pope Pius VI, in order not to offend the newly established Bourbon dynasty, ordered their transfer to Naples in 1787.

The latter half of the sixteenth century saw the beginning of the great dispersal to follow in the Augustan Age. Aldrovandi in 1550 listed about a hundred private collections all smaller in size and inferior in quality to the Farnese and Medici or to that of Cardinal Ippolito d'Este at Tivoli. Next in rank to these were possibly the Carpi and the Cesi collections, but these, like so many others, were to be swallowed up a century later by the Borghese, Ludovisi, Barberini and Giustiniani families. Pope Julius III, the successor of Paul III, was interested only in his Villa Giulia at the Porta del Popolo, now filled with such marvelous Etruscan statues. The *Boschetto* in the Belvedere in turn was decorated with objects stolen from this villa by Pius IV, who also made some dramatic purchases between 1550 and 1565. But the great period was over. The Renaissance had spent itself. For the next two hundred years, except for the harvest of the later Medici collectors in Florence, the story moves to the rising monarchies of western Europe.

CHAPTER IV

The Golden Sunset of the Medici

If the elder branch of the Medici family produced the Renaissance of art in Florence, it was the younger branch that reaped the harvest. For in the two centuries following the Interregnum of 1494 the galleries and palaces of the Arno were to receive the collections of the various branches of the family from Rome as well as Florence. The dour, phlegmatic Dukes of Tuscany upon whom the sun was setting were to become the models for the collectors of western Europe, in fact of the whole world.

The sunset of this family was not, however, lacking in brilliance. What the elder branch had succeeded in accomplishing as bankers, humanists and merchants, the Grand Dukes perpetuated as diplomats and marriage brokers. By 1610, within eleven generations of Giovanni di Bicci, a Medici was seated on each of the four principal thrones of Europe: France, Spain, England and Germany.

Upon the death of the bastard Alessandro in 1537, there were no male descendants of the elder branch of the family. Catherine de Medici, the last of the direct line, had become the wife of the French Dauphin. Cosimo, the son of Giovanni delle Bande Nere, claimed descent from both branches since his mother was a granddaughter of Lorenzo the Magnificent. He was therefore elected by the Council of Forty-eight to become the chief of state. First becoming Duke and then Grand Duke of Tuscany, he set out upon his program of expanding the power and influence of the Medici name. By marrying Eleanora of Toledo, the daughter of the Spanish Viceroy of Naples and one of the richest women in Europe, Cosimo found himself in a position to indulge his interests and to carry on the artistic pursuits of the first Cosimo whose name he bore.

The Medici Palace on the Via Larga, although restored to the family by Leo X, had shown itself to be indefensible, and, while he was awaiting the enlargement and alteration of the Pitti Palace, Cosimo I moved to the better fortified and more authoritative Palazzo Vecchio. With the assistance of Vasari and Bronzino, he determined to bring together a collection which would be superior to that of his ancestors. The plunder of the Medici collections which had taken place in 1494, and again in 1527, had dissipated the treasures of the elder branch, scattering far and wide most of what had not been destroyed. Valuable pictures which had once been the property of the Medici even found their way to France and Germany. "But," asserts Colonel Young, "some portion of these art treasures were still in Florence, dispersed among different families, or hidden away elsewhere; and Cosimo had search made for these and bought back as many of them as he could find for the embellishment of his new palace, including portraits of the family, a few statues and busts and objects of art such as the vases which had belonged to Lorenzo the Magnificent." Bronzino was commissioned to paint (from medallions, frescoes or other documentary sources) the portraits of the Medici from Giovanni di Bicci down.

No less intense was Cosimo's zeal for antiquities; he conducted extensive excavations at Arezzo and Chiusi for traces of Etruscan art, while, at the same time, he purchased everything of classical or Egyptian archaeology that came his way. The present Etruscan Museum in Florence, one of the finest in existence, and the Egyptian Museum are largely due to Cosimo I. Among the splendid pieces he discovered are the statue of *Minerva* found near Arezzo in 1541, the fire-breathing *Chimaera* found in the same place three years later, and the *Orator* from Lake Trasimene.

The *Arazzeria* or tapestry works founded by Cosimo was also one of his major contributions to the arts. By paying preposterous salaries, he was able to import two Flemings, Nicholas Karcher and Jean van der Roost. They were given annual salaries of 600 scudi ($12,000), free quarters and permission to undertake private commissions in addition to their work of direction of the factory. In return they bound themselves to teach the secrets of their art to a fixed number of Florentines and to keep twenty-four tapestries always on hand as examples. This factory grew in stature and reputation and continued until the death in 1743 of the Princess Palatine, the Grand Duchess Anna Maria Ludovica.*

What Cosimo I had started his descendants carried on. The palaces were frequently enlarged, additional wings put on the Pitti and the famous covered passage completed across the Arno, linking the two palaces together. This passage was alleged to be in imitation of a similar corridor described by Homer uniting the palace of Hector with that of Priam. The Boboli Gardens were also the object of lavish attention. But it was in the formation and systematization of their collections that their greatest interest lay. Francis I actually began the building and arrangement of the Uffizi as a picture gallery. Prior to this time it had housed the public offices of the State while Cosimo I had used the upper stories as workshops for craftsmen who were furnishing his palaces.

Ferdinand, the fourth son of Cosimo I and Eleanora of Toledo, succeeded his brother in 1587. Fierce, haughty and independent, he had spent thirteen years in the College of Cardinals although he never had taken Holy Orders. But during this period in Rome when he saw the greater part of the collections gathered together by Julius II, Leo X, Clement VII and Paul III, scattered and neglected by their successors, Ferdinand purchased back again everything upon which he could lay his hands. He built the lovely Villa Medici on the Pincio, later the French Academy, and there he collected an immense number of the most priceless works of Greek and Roman sculpture. These included among others the ravishing *Medicean Venus*, found in the Villa of Hadrian at Tivoli, the group of *Niobe and Her Children* discovered in 1583 at the Porta San Paolo, the *Dancing Faun*, the *Knife-Whetter*, and the *Apollino* as well as many other antiquities, statues and busts of Roman emperors, which now adorn the staircases of the Florentine museums. Thus Ferdinand, Colonel Young points out, "before he was

* Two magnificent examples from these looms, so different in texture from the tapestries of Flanders, are now in the Philadelphia Museum of Art, having been formerly in the Edmond Foulc Collection in Paris. These tapestries were woven as decorations for a banquet to commemorate the defeat of Francis I at the Battle of Pavia and are interesting to Americans because the borders of fruits, flowers and birds include wild turkeys, a fowl unknown to Europe, imported from the New World and served at this repast.

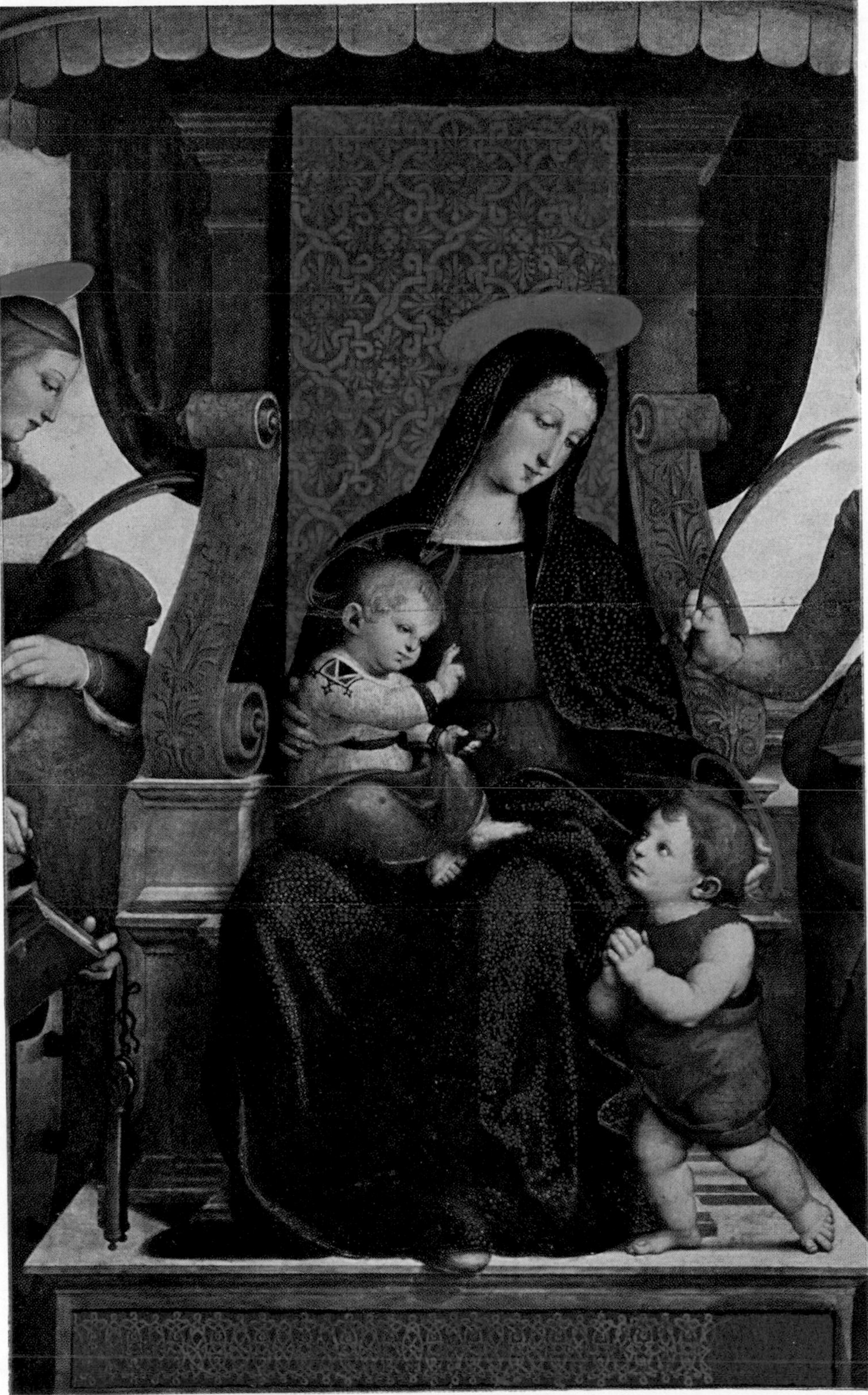

RAPHAEL: THE COLONNA MADONNA (DETAIL)

Painted originally for the nuns of the Convent of Sant' Antonio da Padova at Perugia, who sold it in 1678. It remained in Rome in the Colonna Palace until 1802 when it passed to the King of Naples and the Two Sicilies. His descendant, Francis II (the "Duke of Castro"), sold it to a dealer in Paris for $200,000. Pierpont Morgan shortly afterwards bought it for $500,000 and presented it to the Metropolitan Museum of Art. One of the *predelle* of the same altarpiece, acquired by Queen Christina of Sweden, and which passed into the Orléans collection, is also at the Metropolitan Museum.

Grand Duke, purchased out of his own private funds the six best examples of Greek art Florence now possesses; and except the *Apollo Belvedere*, the *Laocoon*, and the *Torso of Hercules*, the best which were at that time known."

As the ruler of Tuscany, Ferdinand was no less active in the world of art than he had been in Rome. He conveyed a large portion of his Roman possessions to rooms prepared for them in the Uffizi and commissioned Buontalenti to construct additional rooms, including the celebrated Tribuna. He continued to bring together the scattered treasures of his ancestors which were slowly cropping up in the attics and cellars of Florentine houses, whither they had gone after the looting of Lorenzo's palace in 1494.

Cosimo II, who ruled from 1609 to 1620, is better remembered for his interest in science and his protection of Galileo than for his patronage of the arts. Nevertheless, the dignity of his position demanded a polite acquiescence and the palace grew in size if not in stature under his reign. He was the last of the family to be a banker and he withdrew from the private trading which had brought the family fortunes to such fantastic heights. At a time when the Medici were occupying the leading thrones of Europe, Cosimo II felt obliged to close the branches of his family's bank in the foreign capitals to overcome, perhaps, the stigma of eleven generations of trade by members of this bourgeois dynasty.

It was in the fifty-year reign of his eldest son, Ferdinand II, who succeeded him in 1620, that the story of the Medici as collectors comes to its fulfillment. We have seen that the Grand Dukes Francis I and Ferdinand I had begun by placing some of the family pictures in the rooms above the offices of the Uffizi; "but as yet," Colonel Young observes, "there was nothing there which could be called a regular picture gallery. However, in the latter part of Ferdinand II's reign, at the suggestion of Cardinal Leopoldo, he and his brother, Giovanni Carlo, both of whom possessed very large collections of pictures of their own (irrespective of those which were the general property of the family) besides numerous other objects of art, gave the whole of their collections to form the gallery in the Grand Ducal palace itself (the Pitti gallery) and those belonging to Leopoldo to form the Uffizi

Gallery." * At the same time Ferdinand, who had enlarged the palaces in 1640 to receive them, added not only the general collection of pictures which he had inherited as head of the family, but as well the extraordinary treasures of the Dukes of Urbino which came to him with his wife, Vittoria della Rovere.

Although this generation of Medici brothers were not humanists in the sense that their ancestors were in the fifteenth and sixteenth centuries, we cannot overlook their contribution to the history of culture. These galleries which their great-niece, Anna Maria Ludovica, was to make public formed the pattern upon which all the princely galleries of Europe were to be modeled. Already in France, in Spain and England, art had been called to the service of the political ideology of monarchy. Almost everything which we know of the discipline of art history was nurtured in these palaces of the Medici.

Ferdinand had the reputation of being "the most cultured ruler of his time." He may very well have been. But his brothers if anything exceeded him in talents and intellectual curiosity. Cardinal Giovanni Carlo was his minister of finance. Created a Cardinal by Innocent X, he had resided for some years in Rome where he was the instructor of Queen Christina of Sweden, that *curieuse enragée* whom we shall meet again in another chapter, on the occasion of her conversion to the Roman Communion. Cardinal Leopoldo, the political genius of the triumvirate, served as an informal Minister of State. But it was in the furtherance of science, literature and art that they found their real preoccupation. A decade before the Royal Society in London or the French Academy of Sciences was founded, they had established the *Conversazione Filosofica* or Philosophical Society of the Palace, which included the ablest scientific and literary men of the day. This gave place in 1657 to the *Accademia del Cimiento* or Academy of Experiment, the first society for experiments in natural science ever formed in Europe, which adopted the fundamental law that "no special school of philosophy or system of science should be adopted by it and that it bound itself to investigate nature by the pure light of experimental fact." The society was open to all talent and the privilege of selecting experiments lay with the president.

* Young, *op. cit.*, 669.

There is a certain satisfaction in knowing that the Uffizi was host to this learned society whose motto *Provando e Riprovando* has remained a watchword to this day for men of science. Their standards for literary exercise were no less exacting. These academies barely survived the Medici rulers but the mute testimony of their accomplishment may still be seen in the museums of the Arno. The present National Library of Florence has become the repository of the Palatine Library and now houses, together with the collections of these princes, one of the richest bodies of early scientific papers in the world.

The brilliance of the reign of Ferdinand II quickly subsided. It was like the unexpected and late summer flowering of a vine which in the past had borne more than its share of luscious fruit. Weakness, which was Ferdinand's most glaring fault, became in his son, Cosimo III, an active vice. The latter abandoned himself to enormities and imbecilities of every kind, and submitted to religious intolerance and bigotry. The intellectual freedom of his father's reign vanished completely and Cosimo's only interest in art was in removing what statues were left in the Villa Medici in Rome to place them in the Boboli Gardens, where his physicians had ordered him to take his exercise, and in supervising the construction of the family mausoleum.

The days of the political life of the Grand Duchy were numbered while "the European monarchs watched like wreckers the last moments of the foundering Medici." The paramount issue for the next thirty years was to be the question of who would occupy the throne of Florence the moment it fell vacant. The death of Cosimo's eldest son in 1713 and that of Louis XIV two years later jeopardized the future of Tuscany. The Florentine Senate wished the throne to pass upon the death of Cosimo's second son, Giovanni Gastone, to his sister, the Princess Palatine. The principal claimant among the powers was Philip V of Spain, who married the Princess Elizabeth of Parma (she, through Margharita dei Medici, was a granddaughter of Cosimo II) in order to establish the Spanish claim. England and Holland were opposed but failed to act. The wrangling continued, Cosimo opposing the Austrians until his death in 1723. With the accession of Gian Gastone matters went from bad to worse. Each slight illness on the part of the Grand Duke offered a fresh pretext for the invasion of threatening armies of both Austria and Spain. At length, in October 1735, Austria, France, England and Holland agreed that as the basis of a general peace, the Grand Duchy of Tuscany should be given to the Emperor's daughter, Maria Theresa, who was married to Francis, Duke of Lorraine. The latter, in exchange for Tuscany, ceded Lorraine to France, and Tuscany thus became an appanage of the house of Austria. This agreement in which Spain reluctantly joined, was ratified the following year at the Peace of Vienna.

Thus did the independence of Florence, whose liberties and prestige are synonymous with the name of Medici, finally expire. But in this glorious sunset there was a furious afterglow in the munificent, if quixotic, gesture of the last of her race. The rightful heir to the Tuscan throne was Anna Maria Ludovica, the daughter of Cosimo III. Married to the Elector Palatine of the Rhine, she filled an important position in Germany for twenty-six years before returning as a widow to her father's court. She was a woman of firm mind and cultivated tastes upon whom converged the great wealth and properties accumulated by her relatives. A discerning collector, trained as a child by her great-uncle, Cardinal Leopoldo, she proceeded to fill in gaps in the collections, particularly in the field of Flemish and German painting, of which she was most fond. Lavish in her gifts to charity and confident that her fortune would end with her, the Electress spent fantastic sums on *bibelots*, jewels, precious metals, and upon her wardrobe which was one of the wonders of the age. Humiliated beyond endurance by the new Austrian Grand Duke and his vulgar agent, the Prince de Craon, she withdrew entirely from the life of the court and maintained her own separate establishment in a portion of the Grand Ducal Palace. It was here in the midst of the accumulated art of her ancestors that she developed her great design. She gave outright "to the State of Tuscany forever, in the person of the new Grand Duke and his successors" all of the collections of the Medici not only in Florence but in Rome and in the other palaces and villas of the family. She imposed but two conditions, "*None of these collections should ever be removed from Florence, and that they should be for the benefit of the public of all nations.*" Only two men

ex

DU

Henri II
ing of Fran

The Princi
akes no at
ho interma

since have dared to tamper with her will – Napoleon Bonaparte and Adolf Hitler.

By this act Anna Maria Ludovica, "The Last of the Royal Race of the Medici" as her tomb proclaims, earned the undying gratitude of the civilized world and achieved a sweet revenge upon the predatory ambitions of the Hapsburgs.*

* Colonel Young has summarized the terms and items of this testament, written shortly before her death in 1743, probably the greatest single public donation in all history. What its monetary value was either at that time or today it would be impossible to compute. It included, with much besides:

"(a) The whole of the pictures and statues which were in the Uffizi Gallery, the Royal Palace, the Villa Medici at Rome, and the other villas of the family, now forming the Uffizi and Pitti Galleries.

(b) The rare collection of gems and other objects of art, now in the gem rooms of the Uffizi Gallery.

(c) A great collection of cameos, engraved gems and similar articles, now in the Museum of the Bargello, and including the celebrated collection of coins and medallions of Lorenzo the Magnificent, the oldest in Europe.

(d) Statues and busts by Donatello, Verrocchio, Mino da Fiesole and other notable sculptors, now in the Museum of the Bargello.

(e) A great collection of bronzes, now in the Museum of the Bargello.

(f) The New Sacristy, with the masterpieces of Michelangelo.

(g) The whole of the contents of the Library of the Palace and the Medici Library at San Lorenzo.

(h) A large and important collection of Egyptian and Etruscan antiquities now forming the chief part of the Archaeological Museum.

(i) A valuable collection of majolica, Urbino-ware and Faenza-ware, rare suits of armor, and curious and valuable arms, now in the Museum of the Bargello.

(j) A large collection of tapestries now forming the *Galleria degli Arazzi*.

(k) Valuable tables of *pietra dura* work, cabinets and precious furniture now in the Uffizi and Pitti Galleries.

(l) The inlaid tables, valuable cabinets, tapestry and other similar articles, now in the Royal apartments of the Pitti Palace.

(m) The gold dessert service, gold and silver ornaments, rare china, valuable plate, croziers and crucifixes in ivory and amber, the mitre with miniatures made of humming bird's feathers which had belonged to Clement VII, priceless works in *niello*, handsome goblets and vases by Benvenuto Cellini, and many other heirlooms of the family, all now in the Treasure Room of the Pitti Palace.

(n) The reliquaries and other ornaments of the Grand Ducal Chapel in the Pitti Palace.

(o) The immense Medicean wardrobe of costly robes and dresses for state occasions."

In the summer of 1939 a great exhibition was held at Florence – *la Mostra Medicea*. The Medici-Riccardi Palace was made the scene for bringing together as faithfully as possible the personal possessions of the Medici – particularly those items of Lorenzo il Magnifico and of his grandfather which had adorned this palace prior to the Sack in 1494. A similar exhibition of manuscripts, documents, books, family papers and memorabilia was held simultaneously at the Laurentian Library. The student of the history of the Medici will find it rewarding to compare the items given in the illustrated catalogue (*Mostra Medicea – Palazzo Medici 1939*, 2nd ed. Florence, Casa Editrice Marzocco) with the inventories published by Eugène Müntz, *Les collections des Medicis*, Paris and London, 1888.

BOOK THREE

The Long Arm of the Hapsburgs

CHAPTER I

The Strange, the Wonderful, the Curious, the Rare

COLLECTING is not confined to any country or to any region; it seems to be a universal and instinctive avocation; but in every society and time there are certain persons of taste who stand out with such dazzling clarity that they seem to obscure the others. This was particularly true of the dozen or more generations of the Medici, of whom each one, to a greater or lesser degree, contributed to the artistic accumulations of Florence. The same may be said of the Papacy, which in the course of centuries drew to the palaces of the Vatican a never-ending stream of treasure. To be sure the torrent was swollen from time to time by the passionate desire of certain pontiffs to outshine their predecessors, but by and large Rome is artistically the result of the corporate efforts of an undying spiritual and temporal authority.

From 1273 to 1806 another dynasty, the House of Hapsburg (ruling as emperors and princes in every part of Europe and allied to the houses of Saxony and the Wittelsbachs of Bavaria), whose dominions at their apogee stretched from the Baltic to the Mediterranean, and from Gibraltar to the Indies and America, became, after the Medici and the Popes of Rome, the most consistent art patrons and collectors in history. These fortunes were concentrated in the Emperor Charles V (1519–1558), whose grandparents on his father's side were the Emperor Maximilian I and Mary of Burgundy. He was the most universal emperor that Europe had seen since the time of Charlemagne. There descended to him and to his succession not only five hundred years of political experience in every corner of the continent, but the artistic accretions of the monarchs and princes who had preceded him. The museums and picture galleries of Madrid, of Brussels and Vienna, are not alone monuments to the industry and taste of Philip II, of the Archduke Leopold Wilhelm or of the Emperor Rudolph II, but they are the enduring record of a Hapsburg culture which has persisted to our own day.

The German Renaissance had developed a pattern and a formula of living just as authentic and recognizable as that of the Renaissance of Italy. Unlike the similar revival of learning in France, it was not a blend of Gothic and classical survivals but was a contrast of violently conflicting elements – the very elements which produced the Reformation and prevented any rational approach in the Germanies to democratic thought. It was the mirror of a society held firmly in the grasp of the practical, hard-minded merchants and manufacturers who used the courts of the nobility as a fine antiquarian smoke screen for their ambitions and activities. The history of Hindenburg and the industrial backers of the Nazi party, if written once in the sixteenth century, was written a hundred times over.

Nothing shows more clearly the disorder and confusion of the German prince, and his inability to cope with the social revolution of his day, than does the "magpiety" of his *Wunderkammer*. For here we see him face to face with contemporary science, with natural history and philosophy, with art and architectural *tours de force*. But, above all, these manifestations of his ruling wisdom, the artifacts of his collection, are merely embellishments for the glory and authority of his ancestral house. Tied hand and foot to the bankers and iron-masters of his heavily mortgaged lands, his castles provided avenues of escape into a world of make-believe which Wagner and Adolf Hitler were later to turn to such profitable account.

The *Wunderkammer* was the outgrowth of the strong room, the treasury of the castle into which anything of intrinsic value was placed. As the family possessions accumulated through the centuries and expanded beyond the limits of the strong room, the latter was reserved for the more precious objects in silver and gold, while larger items overflowed into the armory and other semipublic rooms. Soon the collections began to assume such proportions that they required some one member of the household to be responsible for them. The treatment varied according to the character and interests of the reigning prince. Occasionally it was the major-domo who administered the collection; at other times it was a trusted servant or soldier whose knowledge of arms was indispensable. More often than not, it was a cleric, usually of a scholarly and scientific turn of mind, attached to the castle as librarian or chaplain, or as tutor for the children. Generally speaking, he was more interested in natural phenomena than in art, and he had a passion for order and classification. Like so many curators, he was less concerned with humanity than with the humanities, and was apt to consider the object more important for what it taught than for its own interest or beauty.

The medieval and superstitious character of the *Wunderkammer* was universally acknowledged in the collections of central Europe. The Elector of Saxony, Augustus I, filled seven rooms of his palace in Dresden with works of art, to which his successors added liberally; his collections became the nucleus about which those later housed in the rococo palace of the Zwinger and in the Grüne Gewölbe (the green treasure room of Saxony) were ultimately established. He was typical of his time and shared something of the blind faith of his Bavarian cousins; in 1611, he accepted from the Bishop of Bamberg a stuffed phoenix and he refused an offer of 100,000 golden florins from the Venetian Council of Ten for a unicorn in his possession. His particular pride, and one that must have made the poor Bishop of Como writhe with envy in his grave, was his "series of portraits of the Roman Emperors from Caesar to Domitian done by Titian from the life."

The epitome of this Teutonic point of view is found in the collections and catalogue of the Archduke Albrecht V of Bavaria, who died in 1579. He had married Anne, the daughter of the Emperor Ferdinand I, brother of Charles V; she was, therefore, the great-niece of the Emperor Maximilian. This collection reflects the atmosphere and purpose of all of the collections in the Germanies, not only in the general authoritarian program common to such cabinets but also in their lavishness and prodigality.

Albrecht, who was well educated as German princes go, having studied at the University of Ingolstadt, made a grand tour in Italy, where he became familiar with the classics. Politically loyal to the

Emperor, profiting where he could from the quarrels of the mighty, he was none the less from head to toe an absolutist, demanding all the perquisites and privileges of the petty sovereign. As a ruler he was benign, looking with favor upon the rise of the middle class and exerting his influence in curbing the nobility. He was a patron of the arts and crafts and introduced into Bavaria the manufacture of glass and tapestry weaving. In his private life Albrecht seems to have been lonely, finding in art what family and friends were unable to give him. He called Orlando di Lasso to his court, and employed Glovio, a friend of Titian's and one of the greatest miniature painters of his day, to illuminate his prayer book. His jewels, of which he had a fabulous group, were chiefly those ornate combinations of ships, mermaids and wild animals, set in pearls, enamels and gold filigree, in which the German taste delighted. Something of an amateur bibliophile, he had tried in vain to buy *en bloc* the libraries assembled by Hartmann Schedel of Nuremberg and by Hans Jakob Fugger.

It was in the frank and unrestrained passion for the strange that Albrecht's cabinet was particularly notable. Formed fully a hundred years later than the collections of Jean, Duc de Berry, its naïveté and superstition are the result of a stubborn medievalism which the Latin countries had long since yielded to the Renaissance. The Thomist search for synthesis, that constant preoccupation of the theologians of the Middle Ages, was applied through some instinctive and subconscious thought transference to the world of science and of art. The German princes and the learned doctors were eager to sift and collect in their outward forms the new discoveries regarding the nature of the universe. Their observations made new instruments necessary for the purpose of describing and defining the motions and positions of the earth and heavenly bodies. The inadequate knowledge that man had of many things, however, and the traditional Teutonic belief in the supernatural, gave rise to the validity of special attributes to human beings and inanimate objects, capable either of malevolent witchcraft and sorcery or of the capacity to heal the sick and enrich the poor. The German taste for alchemy so celebrated by the legend of Dr. Faustus was but another expression of this tentative curiosity.

The plan of a princeling's cabinet was based upon a few funda-

Fred
nant of i
died

Elizabet
aughter o
peror Sigi

JOANNA
(daughte
and

PHI
ing of Spa

PHI
ing of Spa

PHI
ing of Spa

Collect
Hapsburg
Kings
(166

mental and generally accepted precepts. The chief objective was the study of the macrocosm, the all-embracing universe. Next in importance stood the three large kingdoms of nature: animal, vegetable and mineral. New forms or freaks of any of their subdivisions were matters of collector's envy and speculation. Dwarfs, persons exhibiting deformities and abnormalities of any kind, strange animals, stones of unconventional shape, petrifications, ores and coral reefs – all these developed fascinations which soon imbued them with hidden meanings and significance. So the strange, the wonderful, the curious, the rare, were more and more welcomed by the credulous with each passing day. The discovery of whole new sections of the world, the acquaintance with new peoples and their customs, only served to strengthen their predilection for collecting tribal fetishes trimmed and decorated with shells and feathers. Many of the artists, too, succumbed to these enchantments; Dürer not only made an etching of a monster pig but undertook a journey of several days into the Netherlands to draw an Indian prisoner from America who was shown in a triumphal procession of the Emperor Charles V. The marginal decorations which he made for Maximilian's prayer book are also filled with similar excursions in the surrealist world of his day.

To the Teutonic mind it seemed that the work of art was important only for the value of the materials of which it was made or because it represented some phase of cosmic curiosity. The great period of Gothic art was over and the collector-patron, although he still retained his craftsman's sense of the fitness of things, was turning to cultural history and scientific explanation. Statues, busts and portraits were systematically commissioned and acquired to show, after the manner of Paolo Giovio in Como, the authoritarian continuity of great statesmen and philosophers. Coins were valued for the faces stamped upon them, and representations of battles and historical events were popular, particularly if they assisted in any way the dynastic pretensions of the ruler. Intricately wrought and inlaid cabinets and cases filled with secret drawers were crammed to overflowing with oddments of all kinds: mathematical and astronomical instruments, toilet articles, perfume bottles, boxes, games and clocks, all elaborately decorated with agate, jasper and onyx, or inlaid with mother-of-pearl and tortoise shell. As techniques developed, these "gadgets" were fitted with springs and devices to make them work mechanically, striking out the hour or playing melodies in miniature music boxes.

Obviously nothing but a systematic catalogue could bring order out of such a hodgepodge. This task was given by the Archduke to Dr. Samuel Quickeberg, a seasoned collector of no small consequence, who published in Munich in 1567, under the title *Musaeum Theatrum*, the first printed museum catalogue that we know. This plan of arrangement and exhibition became the standard for the next century and reappears with little change in John Tradescant's first catalogue of an English cabinet published in London in 1656. The *first class* of objects consisted of the artifacts of religion, and these stood first in order of arrangement of the exhibition. Next came anything pertaining to the owner or his family. Still another subdivision included all views and descriptions of the landscape, and the flora and fauna of the region; particular emphasis was laid upon local topography and maps. The *second class* concerned itself with sculpture and minor plastic works such as coins, medals and goldsmith's work. The *third class* was devoted to specimens of natural history with its many subdivisions of species and subspecies. In the *fourth class* were found scientific and musical instruments of every variety and description, and finally, in the *fifth class*, are the works of art: paintings, coats of arms and genealogies, landscapes and portraits. These were all held together by appropriate scrolls and legends which, with the help of quotations from the best classical authors, and fulminations from the Prophets and Book of Revelations, proved the inevitable folly of worldly vanity and deplored the practice of laying up for one's self treasures upon this earth.

It would be tedious to enumerate the nearly four thousand items in this cabinet. Albrecht could afford anything he wanted and what he could not he apparently bought anyhow, for he left a debt of 2,360,000 florins to the Fugger Bank. His Italian agents, the Venetian dealers Jacopo Strada and Niccolò Stoppi, had entrée everywhere and bought on sight everything that might please their patron, shipping it all to Germany.

CHAPTER II

Millions and Millionaires

THE consolidation of the Hapsburg dominions about the year 1500 had placed at the disposal of the princes of this house the entire artistic production of Europe. What they did not acquire by patronage and purchase in the free markets of Antwerp, Florence and Augsburg, they took by marriage and by conquest. Maximilian, who married Mary of Burgundy, daughter of Charles the Bold, was a man of inordinate ambition but little business ability. His gifts to the church at Innsbruck testify to his abilities as a patron of sculpture, but he was constantly in debt, pawning much of the Burgundian treasure in his wife's dowry. Maximilian's greatest contributions were in the field of literature as the reputed author of *Der Weisskönig* and of *Theurdank*, and he especially favored the universities of Vienna and Ingolstadt. As patrons of Van Orley, he and his wife lavished their patronage upon the designers of tapestry in Brussels, and his encouragement of Dürer resulted in the incomparable print series of the *Triumph of Maximilian.* But pitted against his rivals in southern Europe, or compared with his daughter Margaret of Austria and his grandchildren and great-grandchildren in Spain and the Low Countries, Maximilian showed himself to be merely a normally acquisitive man of his time and environment. A typical petty German princeling, brought up in Augsburg under the thumb of the Fuggers and the Welsers, to whom he was constantly in debt, he atavistically belonged to the robber barons of the Middle Ages. But the power was passing into the hands of a new type of captain of industry — the millionaire capitalist of modern times. Beside them he seems a weak statesman, an insignificant collector, arrogant, superstitious and insecure.

The basis of Renaissance prosperity was, of course, the carrying trade between East and West. Venice, and to a lesser degree Genoa, had for centuries successfully exploited these markets first opened up by the Crusades. By the fifteenth century the two main import routes to Europe were already clearly established; the water route was by way of the Indian Ocean and the Red Sea to Egypt, where at Alexandria the depots and commercial outposts of Venice collected the traffic for her vessels, the route by land was by caravan across Turkestan to the Caspian, thence, again by camel, to the Black Sea, where it was met by ships of the traders of Genoa, whose colonies at Pera, a suburb of Constantinople, and Caffa in the Crimea enabled her to dominate the waters of the Euxine. In addition to these waterways there were several minor ones; an intermediate path led from the Persian Gulf along the Euphrates, through Damascus to Beirut and other Syrian harbors.*

Aleppo remains even today the western terminus for the caravan route from Tibet, and not far from the railway station where one boards the Taurus Express for Berlin or Bagdad is situated one of the great art collections of the Middle East. Appropriately enough, it belongs to the Marcopoli family, descendants of Marco Polo, who live luxuriously in a Baroque villa built above the Gothic vaulted *souks*, or bazaars, of the city. Next door, occupying another site in these lovely hanging gardens, the English Trading Company of the Gentlemen Adventurers, chartered by Queen Elizabeth, still functions, sending home coffee, tea and spices from the Orient.

Such an expansion of economic life, bringing with it ideas and practices so revolutionary to the feudal system and so threatening to the absolute authority of the medieval guilds, could not be accomplished without an elaborate banking and credit system which took many generations to develop. The bankers had already established themselves in the eleventh and twelfth centuries as money-changers in the north Italian towns of Asti and Chieri. They became known by the collective names of Lombards or Cahorsines (from Cahors in southern France), and carried on a general pawnbroker's business. It is no accident that the Bank of England and the Royal

* Albert Boardman Kerr, *Jacques Coeur*. Charles Scribner's Sons, 1927, pp. 64 ff.

THE GALLERY OF THE UFFIZI

From the eighteenth-century catalogue

GIOVANNI CARLO

LEOPOLDO

THE MEDICI CARDINALS – FOUNDERS OF THE UFFIZI

Painted by Sustermans. Lucca

THE LAST OF THE MEDICI
Anna Maria Ludovica with her husband, the Elector Palatine
By Frans Douven, 1690. Pitti

JACOB FUGGER THE RICH

Painted by an unknown artist, c. 1520

LUCA PACCIOLO – INVENTOR OF DOUBLE ENTRY BOOKKEEPING

By Jacopo dei Barbari. Naples

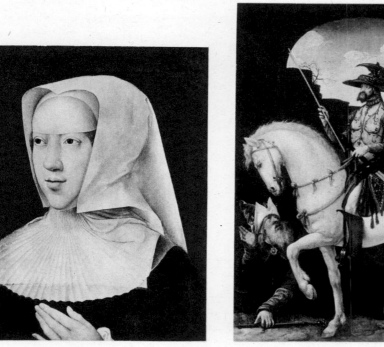

MARGARET OF AUSTRIA

By Bernard Van Orley

CHARLES V

By Jan Vermeyen (?)

MAXIMILIAN I

By Albrecht Dürer

Exchange are situated upon the ancient Lombard Street of medieval London, for it is from this nerve center of empire that international business in countless tongues and currencies has since that day been carried on.

To these brokers the prelates of the Church naturally turned. Not only were the Lombards practiced in the skill of long-term and short-term notes but they had, through their correspondents in every European port and trading center, connections which were both profitable and convenient.

By the end of the Middle Ages the Church had become a gigantic administrative system establishing its own policies of international relations, waging war at will, and controlling education, medicine and every charitable enterprise. To support these vast and widespread institutions a carefully-built-up system of papal taxation was necessary. Innocent III, about the beginning of the thirteenth century, had established regular sources of revenue based upon tithes, Crusaders' contributions, taxes and indulgences which were levied on all Christendom. The clergy thus faced with this complex economic system welcomed any class of operator who could do their financial dirty work for them and yet, at the same time, absolve them of the sin of usury. If, happily, the banker happened to be both a Lombard and a Jew, then God and Mammon could be served with true Christian impartiality.

Into this complicated fabric of pope and emperor, bishop and robber baron, the city merchants of western Europe wove the thread of capitalism and free enterprise. The pattern of activity everywhere was essentially Italian but the coloring in each country was conditioned by climate and the tenacity of local feudal customs. Jacques Coeur of Bourges, *Argentier du Roy* and *Contrôleur des Finances* under Charles VII, and Jakob Fugger of Augsburg (born three years after Jacques Coeur's death in 1456), Imperial Counselor to the Emperors Maximilian and Charles V, built their fortunes as well as their collections of art upon Italian models. Jacques Coeur, by imitating the maritime policies of the Venetians, reorganized the economy of France and, through its power, ultimately drove the English from the Continent. Fugger, carrying on the great financial transactions of the

Hapsburgs, used the same pledges and securities which the Florentines had demanded of the House of Anjou. In each country, it is interesting to note, the financial brains were native-born sons who had grown up with the rapidly developing and changing business conditions of their respective countries.

Two discoveries were largely responsible for the rapidity with which this new capitalism spread throughout Europe – the discovery of time as a potential factor in industrial production, and the invention of double-entry bookkeeping by a Neapolitan monk, Luca Pacciolo. In medieval times, without proper mechanical means for measuring time, the idea of the hourly wage or of piecework had scarcely existed, consequently production and cost could never be reckoned in their accurate relationship to one another. The relation of employer to employee was to a large extent the relation of the bondsman to the master, and the working day and the working week were regulated more or less by the local Christian calendar. It has been pointed out frequently that the number of saint's days in a community were in a sense determined by the good and bad times of a given period. If, because of unemployment and high prices, it were found necessary to shorten the working week, then, happily, a new saint's day to celebrate a local worthy was established, and thus another workless holiday created. "Suddenly the businessman was plunged into a modern world which no longer revolved about the rising and setting of the sun; the angelus gave way to the astrolabe and mechanical clocks, and at one glance he was able to tell from his books the daily position of his business. Jakob Fugger thus increased his fortune from 200,000 gulden in 1511 to 2,000,000 ($40,000,000) in 1527. Had he relied upon the accounting methods of his forefathers, he could never have kept his finger on a world-wide business which earned him an annual profit of 55 per cent." *

Important as were these discoveries to the general spread of capitalism, it was the perfection of the blast furnace which was to set the tone of German economy and, by indirection, the character of the Northern Renaissance. For from that moment German industry was committed to the manufacture of munitions of war, and through their sale achieved a standard of living which, far more than the printing of

* Cf., Beard, *op. cit.*

books from movable type, created the atmosphere for leisure, and the cultivation and patronage of the arts.

Gradually the financial power of Italy moved to the north – Venice was defeated by the League of Cambrai in 1509 and in the same year the Portuguese, defeating the Arabs at Diu, established their supremacy over the Indian Ocean. The trade routes shifted into the North Sea and revolved around the wool trade between Flanders and Britain. Florence still continued to collect the revenues of the Church and maintained her standing as a money market, but the new commercial capitals of Europe were Antwerp, Nuremberg and Augsburg.

Antwerp, the center of the wool industry and the chief point of contact with Britain, had become the brokerage house for weaving and textiles and all phases of commerce. Her port was the principal gateway for copper and spices and for the exchange of manufactured goods between England and Germany. Gradually the power of the Hanseatic cities which had controlled the economy of medieval Germany was broken; and Antwerp reigned supreme until disaster finally overtook the Spanish rule. The bankruptcies of Philip II, precipitated by the same causes, brought about in 1557, after a ten-year boom, the collapse of the Antwerp Bourse, the first great stock market crash in modern history; the city of the Scheldt was forced to yield to the inventive and stubborn wit of the Dutch Republic.

Nuremberg in the sixteenth century was as deceptive as she has been in the days of the Nazis. Quaint and picturesque, the center of art and music, she was also the cradle of modern munitions industries and twentieth-century mass production. There, already, could be seen all of the evils of standardization which were present in her later history. Miss Beard has underscored the fact that in this "land of machines" Nuremberg "held first place for mechanical ingenuity. Since it made the best musical instruments, the music trade was centered there, just as the presence of fine printers brought the book trade to Frankfort; here also the pocket watch was invented, the first globe made for a geographer, and compasses turned out in quantity for *conquistadores*." In Nuremberg, too, a method of calibrating firearms was developed about 1540 which, together with the already highly organized mass production of body armor, gave the merchants of this "sleepy" town both the prestige and the point of view of the Krupps of Essen. It tempted them to plot against the emperor in favor of the Valois kings with the de Wendels of an earlier and even more disorganized France. Other Nuremberg inventions inspired by Wotan were a water mill to grind gunpowder, sawmills and diamond cutters as well as devices for casting cannon to break down the heaviest fortifications, and a method of using sea coal instead of wood for the preparation of iron.*

* * * * *

There is poetic justice in the fact that the country which produced the dullest chapters in the history of taste should have been the one to produce the most lavish and highly documented commentaries on them. Germany in the two centuries following the Renaissance was the outpost of conservatism, the center of hard money; it became the repertory theater for small stock companies of feudal princes who played as amateurs the tragedies and comedies of the great courts of Europe behind their own overbrilliant footlights. The politicians, the theologians and the bankers of Germany produced a society that aped all the formalities and empty gestures of the great men of the Renaissance and Baroque. They contributed, however, little to the world except their material success, which, in its turn, raised to new heights their own personal standards of living.

The two most competent sources for our knowledge of the seventeenth century are the *Teutsche Academie* of Joachim von Sandrart, a painter and author who traveled all over Europe, publishing his notes in 1679, and Caspar F. Neickel, who produced the first general book on museography in 1727. In the foreword of his book Neickel distinguishes between the various types of cabinets which the collectors of Germany had brought together, and the following definitions are useful to record simply as evidences that the tidiness of the German mind was not alone the product of our own day. It is interesting to note how closely the pattern of the *Wunderkammer* of the hereditary prince was followed, yet at the same time how much freer

* Beard, *op. cit.*, 220.

the merchant felt in exploiting the scientific curiosity of his time.

The *Schatzkammer* contains, says Neickel, "precious things but not art or natural history specimens." The *Raritätenkammer*, on the other hand, is a collection of all things rare and "not generally to be seen." The *Gallerien*, he explains, are really long, narrow halls which occasionally serve to hold useful cabinets and closets containing curiosities above which are placed valuable paintings. And, he adds, especially in Italy these cases are occupied by relics and statuettes. The fourth category, the *Studio-Museum*, is in essence what the Germans mean by study room, in which there is not only a cabinet and a repository of rarities of various kinds but also a library filled with books in bookcases. The *Naturalienkammer*, or *Naturalienkabinett*, is devoted to the three kingdoms of nature, animal, vegetable and mineral, and is, as its name implies, strictly a reference room for the study of natural history.

All of these were the natural outgrowth of the medieval *Wunderkammer*, which was, obviously, the indiscriminate hodgepodge embracing at random all of the classifications previously mentioned.

It is the two last categories which are most interesting for the study of taste, for they comprise the *Kunstkammer* and the *Antiquitätenkabinett*. The *Kunstkammer* contains things made of earth and plaster, metals and other materials, such as glass. It includes instruments of precision, telescopes, microscopes, all kinds of optical and scientific apparatus and curiosities fashioned from combinations of natural materials, such as ivory, mother-of-pearl, glass and china. Here, too, are medals and coins and paintings by the most famous masters of Italy, Michelangelo, Raphael, Titian, as well as Rubens. A work by Dürer is a positive necessity in every one of these collections. In regard to the works of art themselves, Neickel observes, they must be originals and not copies, they must have been created by the most famous masters and they must reflect in some way the fancy of the person who collects them. "To my mind," he says, "the following is to be observed, that for paintings a location should be chosen which is not damp and where the light falls into the room so that they may be presented with the greatest clarity and without a dazzling glare." The *Antiquitätenkabinett* seems to have been reserved for the evidences of death, for burial urns and the receptacles of ashes of cremated heathen; tear bottles, idols and heathen gods, burial lamps and the usual type of tomb furniture that was being constantly unearthed in Roman and tribal graves within the German cities.

Although Sandrart never visited the *Kunstkammer* in Berlin, he speaks of it as the most important in Germany, filled with "all the world famous paintings of Italian and Dutch masters, old ones as well as those of modern times." This, of course, was a palpable exaggeration, for Berlin at that time was a village of 10,000 inhabitants and the cabinets of the Elector of Brandenburg naturally could not compare with the more ancient collections in Bavaria and Austria; but the Elector Joachim II at least made an earnest effort. He visited Holland and returned with a library which was opened to scholars.* And the close connection between the Houses of Orange and Brandenburg were expressed in the palace at Oranienburg.

In the collections at Dresden and Munich Sandrart admitted that he had at last seen "what art can achieve." And even more than at Munich, he was filled with admiration for the picture gallery formed at Schleissheim by Maximilian II of Bavaria. His visit to Vienna was equally momentous and he has left a marvelous account of the things which he saw in the *Schatz-* and *Kunstkammern.*† But the private collections of the merchants and industrialists at Nuremberg were what most attracted the attention of these museographers. While they were typical in character and content with the other private collections of

* Hendrik de Fromantiou, the Amsterdam art dealer, became his adviser and agent. He was later succeeded by another Amsterdam dealer, Johannes de Renialme, in the latter part of the century, who furnished to the Elector of that day other valuable Dutch pictures to replace those from the original *Kunstkammer* which had been dispersed during the Thirty Years' War. Renialme attended the auction in London in 1682 of the famous collection of Sir Peter Lely, at which he bought for his patron some £20,000 of works of art.

† Among the many strange things which attracted him were "a large piece of white linen cloth made of stone which Ferdinand III had bought for 18,000 gulden. This stone cloth was the same as that into which the ancient Romans had tied up the ashes of their dead, together with the dead bodies, and had then laid them on the fire to burn until the whole had turned to ashes; then the ashes which were found in the cloth, pure and unmixed, were taken out and enclosed in white marble urns made for that purpose and buried in the burial place with the usual ceremonies." Donath believes that Sandrart was referring to the Roman *linum vivum* recorded by Pliny and valued by him as much as pearls, which was none other than the original Greek asbestos.

Germany, they were, because of Nuremberg's position as the center of the munitions industry of Europe, probably richer and more costly.

The cabinet of Carl Welser had a complete run of Dürer's prints, together with the finest impressions of Lucas van Leyden and of the other German and Netherlandish engravers. Besides the fanciers of prints there were others who went deeply into medals and coins. Two collections in this city stand out, as to both quality and quantity, each of them going back into the middle of the sixteenth century. They were the Praun and the Imhof collections; the former was especially rich in bronzes, and there were some 2000 gems and a large series of coins. Paulus Praun (1548–1616) was an ardent collector of drawings, many of which he had acquired on his Italian journeys, including examples of the work of Raphael, Michelangelo and Correggio. His group of Dürer drawings was considered the best of its day.

The Imhof *Kunstkammer* boasted paintings by Palma Vecchio, Veronese, Dürer and Titian. There were other cabinets belonging to the Ebermayer, Volkmar and Birkenheim families which Neickel has described minutely in his *Museographie*. There also he gives accounts of the principal cabinets in Brunswick, in Frankfurt-am-Main, in Breslau and in Halle, as well as at Dresden and Weimar. He takes especial pleasure in the cabinets of his own home town, Hamburg, saying, "A connoisseur will find complete satisfaction in viewing the excellent cabinets of some of the famous native merchants."

Filled with expensive works of art, furnished by the best dealers, these various German collections are no more distinguishable from one another than were the countless private collections on Fifth Avenue and Park Avenue in the late 1920's before death and taxes had caught up with the profiteers of the First World War. They were the pale reflection made by a comfortable and rich bourgeoisie of the great monarchical patterns which were being laid down to form the future national museums of the leading European powers. Few, if any, of these collections survived in their entirety. They were dispersed and broken up. Some of them were to be reassembled in the nineteenth century to flatter the spirit of Pan-Germanism and to provide clinical cadavers for the experimenters of *Kunstwissenschaft*.

* * * * *

Augsburg, on the other hand, dominated to such an extent by the Fuggers and their associates, differed from the rest of Germany. She knew only one loyalty, that to the Emperor and the Roman Church. This did not mean, however, that the banking house stood for any nonsense from either of them, as may be seen from a letter of 1523 by Jakob Fugger addressed to Charles V:

> It is evident and clear as day, that Your Majesty could not have secured the Roman Crown without me, and I can show documents to prove it with the signatures of all Your Majesty's agents. In this I have not pursued selfish interests. Had I drawn back from the Austrian House and chosen to further France, I should have attained large estates and gold, which were offered to me. What a disadvantage this would have been to Your Majesty and the House of Austria, may easily be judged by Your Majesty on due and reasonable reflection.
>
> Accordingly, I humbly request Your Majesty graciously to recollect my loyal and humble services which have been advanced to the welfare of Your Majesty, and to command that my outstanding sum of money together with the interest for the same be returned and paid out to me without any further delay.

Only a banker who knew that God was on his side could dare to bully his sovereign in such fashion, and Charles knew that without the Fugger brains and organization he was powerless to exploit the natural wealth of his dominions. It was as necessary for him to rely upon the moving genius of this house as it was for him to maintain his armies or the faith of his ancestors.

Augsburg was first and last a mining town, although like Florence her earlier prosperity had been based on trade between the Germanies and Venice, and fustian weaving. She was accustomed to authoritarian rule, having been, long ago, *Augusta Vindelicorum*, the capital of the Roman Empire of the West under Hadrian. But rich as her tradition may have been her minerals were more precious. In the words of Jakob Fugger, "it was the mines which were the greatest gift and source of profit which Almighty God had vouchsafed the German lands." In the year of Jakob's death, 1525, the yearly production of the mines of the Holy Roman Empire was estimated, and Strieder thinks the figure far too low, at a minimum of 2,000,000 gold gulden

($40,000,000), and the mining and smelting industries provided employment for well over 100,000 laborers. The principal achievement of the Fugger house lay not so much in the actual operation of the mines and bringing into the market the vast mineral resources and raw material of the Hapsburg dominions, but "in organizing and regulating mining production and the trade in the products of the mine on a scale corresponding to the needs of contemporary economic life."

To command the unprecedented sums of working capital necessary for these enterprises, and to secure both firm and investor against the awful risks of sixteenth-century life, capitalism required a measure of economic freedom which the medieval system of business ethics, formulated three hundred years earlier by Saint Thomas Aquinas, did not allow. The Christian doctrine of "sufficient livelihood," and the belief that "the individual should strive for an income appropriate to his class, but not much more," did not offer the temptation demanded by the Renaissance men of action. The canonical prohibition of usury had placed an almost insuperable obstacle in the way of all extension of credit. Some new theory had to be developed to meet the needs of new conditions. Jakob Fugger, having established a new form of German capitalism, wished to give it the dignity of statute. He turned to his friend and counselor, Dr. Conrad Peutinger, the humanist and authority on juristic and canonical law. "Peutinger," says Strieder, "more than any other worked for the freedom of trading companies, for making of prices, and for the toleration of capitalistic monopolies or cartels. 'Every merchant,' he claimed, 'is free to sell his wares as dear as he can and chooses. In so doing, he does not sin against canonical law; neither is he guilty of antisocial conduct. For it often happens that merchants, to their injury, are forced to sell their wares cheaper than they bought them.' " Nevertheless, Strieder concludes, "it was because Augsburg in some measure anticipated the philosophy of economic individualism which reached its maturity only in the nineteenth century that Jakob Fugger was able to take on, at least in outline, the character of a modern entrepreneur."*

It is only natural that the Italian Renaissance should have entered Germany by way of Augsburg since the temper of her bankers was

* Jacob Strieder, *Jacob Fugger the Rich*. The Adelphi Co., 1931, pp. 48–50.

surely Florentine. Luther, who had fought the Fuggers as the main bulwark of the Church against the surging tide of Reformation, was forced to admire "a man who could deliver three tons of gold in a single hour," a gesture of which no European prince was capable. Even Lorenzo the Magnificent had never entertained such a notion.

The Chapel of Saint Anne, which Jakob built in 1512, was the first break with the Gothic past and from then on the architecture of the city was transformed with decorations in the style of the Renaissance by Burgkmair, Amberger, Altdorfer and Rottenhammer. Jakob founded the Fugger Library, which his nephews were to enlarge to 15,000 volumes and which a century later, together with the Fugger archives, was to be floated down the Danube on five barges to Vienna to become the core of the Hofbibliothek. He also collected in a small way statues and coins and paintings by German and Italian masters. His nephew Raymond had more time for culture and brought together in his gardens the first collection of Greek and Roman antiquities in Germany. He had also fine bronzes which passed to Albrecht of Bavaria during the depression of 1556–1557. He was an intimate of Erasmus of Rotterdam and he endowed his sons, Johann Jakob, who later became Albrecht's adviser and librarian, and Ulrich, the Protestant patron of the great printer Étienne, with a truly professional interest in the humanities. Raymond's brother, Anton, was a friend of Titian's and amateur of contemporary painting.

Not, however, until Hans Fugger of the third generation did the family name become synonymous with the great tradition of art collecting. A dandy, educated in Italian universities and well traveled in all the principal courts of the peninsula, he cared more for art than for the family business. He started collecting seriously in 1566 and employed an agent in Venice, David Ott, who was in the employ of his rival Albrecht. The competition between these two for a sarcophagus and other trophies reads like the correspondence of Duveen and Knoedler and their patrons J. P. Morgan and Henry Clay Frick. But Hans, whose catholic tastes sought everything of beauty, will probably best be remembered for his influence on German patrons and collectors. As Georg Lill wrote in 1908, "The Munich which we know today, the Michaelskirche, the most powerful creation of the

German Renaissance and the rich artistic monuments around the Wittelsbach court owe their inspiration to Hans Fugger and the influence which he exerted upon his friend Duke William of Bavaria."

While the power and influence of the Fugger house gradually declined as a result of the successive bankruptcies of the Spanish Hapsburgs, their way of living did not diminish and there was no sign of retrenchment for several generations. A pleasant account of Augsburg hospitality is given in one of the Fugger news letters under the date of February 25, 1599.

Last Saturday evening His Serene Highness the Archduke Maximilian together with the reigning prince of Bavaria and about 300 members of his retinue and a stately following of noble dames, arrived here and took lodging in the house of Herr Marx Fugger. On the following Sunday and Monday there was held in the presence of His Serene Highness and his spouse a most magnificent and splendid tourney and tilting at the Ring by the Herren Antonius and Christophe Fugger as *Mantenatores* and the other gentlemen as *Aventuriers* in exquisite ornaments and raiment. Curious processions were also witnessed. In particular a Bavarian peasant wedding at which the peasants were entertained with food and drink in the open wine market. Thereupon these peasants danced and sang and feinted and skirmished with their daggers; all this which was most pleasant to behold contributing to the entertainment of His Serene Highness. On the Tuesday following the Magistrate of the Town gave a sumptuous banquet in the Town Hall to His Serene Highness and to his spouse and to other men and women of high rank; moreover a wonderously beautiful ball in the dancing hall above the wine market was ornamented most pleasingly with branches of fir and a black velvet dais and beautiful hangings. When the dance came to an end at seven at night, two little sham castles and a mighty firework were set alight with innumerable explosions and high flying rockets. Thanks be to the Lord that all passed safely and well. May God grant that this may lead to content on both sides and good neighborly relations.*

* *The Fugger News Letters* (ed. by Victor von Klarwill). John Lane, 1924. Letter 195.

CHAPTER III

The Governess and the Emperor

WHEN Charles V was crowned at Bologna in 1536, Europe at last saw the beginning of the end of a thousand-year struggle between pope and emperor, and between the Germanies and Italy. Nursing his wounds from the Sack of Rome nine years earlier, Clement VII had refused to place the iron crown upon Charles's head in Saint Peter's. The compromise of Bologna thus served notice to an increasingly Protestant world of a fact which Voltaire was to put into words some two hundred years later, that the Holy Roman Empire was "neither holy, nor Roman, nor yet an empire." Yet in his person, which derived its dignity from his Austrian blood and its sagacity from his Burgundian and Spanish inheritance, Charles carried the Hapsburg dynasty to the height of its greatness – "a greatness that has been attributed to the ancient historic forces which were concentrated in him and which moulded inherited ideas of power, belief and behaviour into new forms. He united and completed its possessions," adds Brandi, "mingling old Burgundian ideas of chivalry with the conscientious piety of the Netherlands, with Spanish self-restraint and the universal traditions of the Romano-German Empire, he created the attitude which was in future to be typical of his dynasty. At the same time, out of the mass of his inherited possessions he formed a new European and, in a sense, a new overseas imperialism – a world Empire dependent for the first time in history not on conquest, still less on geographical interdependence, but on dynastic theory and the unity of faith."*

In the later Middle Ages Germany was composed of a congeries of semi-independent feudal states, lay and ecclesiastical principalities

* Karl Brandi, *The Emperor Charles V*. Translated from the German by C. V. Wedgwood. Alfred A. Knopf, 1939, p. 13.

in which there was no order but a great show of precedence. The emperor retained the titular dignities which had been heaped upon him during the preceding centuries. Although his regalian rights had gone together with his imperial domains, he still ranked first among the princes of Europe, using the prestige of his elective office wherever he could to further the dynastic aspirations of his own house. No little part of his outward magnificence was dependent upon the objects accumulated from one generation to the next in his *Wunderkammer;* the more obscure and superstitious the objects, the more they were revered because of their association with the supreme and God-given power of the emperor.

Although the status of the emperor was derived first from God, and secondarily, if one is willing to accept the claims of the Papacy, from his Vicar, the real power of election was vested in a group of seven princes: the Archbishops of Mainz, Trier and Cologne, the King of Bohemia, the Duke of Saxony, the Count Palatine of the Rhine and the Margrave of Brandenburg (later to become the Kingdom of Prussia). The Golden Bull of the Emperor Charles IV had fixed in 1356 the procedures and rights of these princes. A Reichstag or Diet was nominally empowered to review the actions of the emperor and to give the most aimless lip service to the demands of the free cities and the rising middle class. The fall of the House of Hohenstaufen, however, had left Germany without any strong territorial powers. While the Hundred Years' War was being waged by France and England, central Europe was plunged into a similar century of petty strife and squabbles between second-rate princes over "territorialism." Generally speaking, these factions resolved themselves upon geographical lines; the more ambitious territorial powers arose in northern, eastern and southeastern German lands, while the strongholds of the prince-bishops, imperial knights and free cities were centered in the west.

From this welter of conflicting principalities the great houses emerged at about the same time; they were to dominate the German scene more or less until the time of Bismarck. First were the Dukes of Luxembourg, who ruled the Kingdom of Bohemia, Moravia and Silesia and from whom the Hohenzollerns wrested Brandenburg in

1417. Next came the Wittelsbachs, who retained Bavaria until 1918 and were the chief contenders with the Hohenzollerns for the control of the Rhineland and western Germany. The House of Wettin dominated Saxony and the ancient Thuringian lands and, as electors, were more politically important for their influence than by reason of their actual power. The House of Hohenzollern did not, however, come into its own until the rise of Prussia upon the wreckage of the Thirty Years' War.

It is to Austria that we must turn to find the central theme, the one unifying, traditional authority which was to condition the history of Europe in the sixteenth and seventeenth centuries. Originally of Swabian origin, the fortunes of the Hapsburgs were founded by Rudolph I, who had acquired the Austrian duchies in 1278. Gradually taking possession of Switzerland, Swabia and the Tyrol, he soon aspired to the lordship of all upper Germany. With only an occasional interruption in the fourteenth century the Hapsburgs continued as emperors from 1410 until the time of Napoleon. By 1500 they were the leading dynastic power in Europe.

Charles V's grandfather, the Emperor Maximilian I, has already been described in the setting in which, historically, he belongs – in his *Wunderkammer*, as the author of *Der Weisskönig* – a dreamer, a philosopher, a spendthrift, tied hand and foot to the bankers of Augsburg. He was of no political importance as a ruler, contributing nothing but vacillation and exasperation. But his value to history cannot be underestimated for he was both *chevaleresque* and a *cheval de race*. Inordinately ambitious, he managed by astute breeding to hand on to his grandchildren not only the ancient dominions of the Hapsburg house in Austria, Germany and Hungary, but also the Duchy of Burgundy – then the most powerful state in western Europe – and by the further selective breeding of his children, the Spanish monarchy.

Maximilian and his wife, Mary of Burgundy, had one son, the Archduke Philip, who married the mad Joanna, daughter of Ferdinand and Isabella of Spain. Philip died before his father and the fruit of this marriage was the young Charles V, born in 1500. The heritage of Austria and Spain was thus to revert to him. Charles, deprived of any normal relation with a mother shut up for life in a cloister at Burgos, was placed by his grandfather in the care of his widowed aunt, Margaret of Austria, who governed the Netherlands from her court at Malines. She was one of the keenest art collectors of Europe, and it was to her that the future Emperor owed his taste and discrimination in the arts.

Margaret's life was not a happy one. Married at the age of three to the French Dauphin, later King Charles VIII, she spent her childhood in the court of France. The marriage was never consummated as Charles repudiated her in favor of Anne of Brittany. Maximilian then wed her at seventeen to the Prince of the Asturias, Don Juan, the only son of Ferdinand and Isabella, whose tragic death within the year was to be so fateful for Spanish history. A third marriage, to Philibert, Duke of Savoy, came to an end as the result of a hunting accident in 1504. Margaret, a lovely, heartbroken young girl of twenty-four, cut off her golden hair and vowed to devote herself to the affairs of state and to the upbringing of her nephew, the future Emperor Charles V. From these arduous duties, which she performed so competently as to be the admiration of all the statesmen of Europe, she allowed herself two avenues of escape, the development of her art collections and the writing of verse. The culmination of all her efforts, however, was the Church at Brou en Bresse near the border of Savoy, which she built as a tomb for Philibert and where she too was finally laid to rest. So great an undertaking was this church at Brou that her Minister, Mecurin de Gattinare, advised the Regent "*de vendre jusqu'à sa dernière chemise*" in order to pay for it.

Under the Governess of the Netherlands architecture made enormous strides and music, painting and literature emerged from the late medieval flowering of Burgundy into the heyday of the Renaissance. Her palace at Malines, as we know from a most thorough and complete inventory, showed that Margaret was a collector of the first rank. In addition to the priceless tapestries hung on the walls, it mentioned "statuettes, gold and silver caskets and mirrors, crystal, chalcedony and jasper goblets and vases, carved ivories, amber, corals, and curiously wrought chessmen, beautiful fans, medallions, clocks of rare workmanship which struck the hour and the half-hour, magnificent plate, sometimes inlaid with precious stones, glass and pottery, suits of armor, ivory hunting horns and various relics of the chase."* Her library, which was probably the finest outside of Italy, was rich in manuscripts selected not only for their literary quality but for their intrinsic beauty. Many of them are preserved today at Brussels in the Bibliothèque Royale and bear witness to the wide variety of her tastes: "Froissart, the *Fables* of Aesop and of Ovid, several editions of Aristotle, Livy, the *Letters of Seneca* and the *Commentaries of Julius Caesar*, Saint Augustine's *City of God*, of which she had four copies, and Boethius' *On Consolation*. Besides these, there were *The Golden Legend*, *The Round Table*, *Launcelot of the Lake*, *Merlin*, *The Story of Jason and the Golden Fleece*, etc." The library likewise included books on chess, on the interpretation of dreams, on the nature of birds and on manners and customs, such as the *Mirroir du Monde* and the *Mirroir des Dames*. Boccaccio appeared side by side with the lives and legends of the saints; books on hunting and hawking were crowded in with missals and breviaries.

Throughout the many poems which she composed, some of them quite long, there runs a constant strain of sadness, the title of one of the best known being *La complainte de dame Marguerite d'Autriche, fille de Maximilian, Roy des Romans*. Her early and repeated widowhood, her responsibilities to the provinces which she governed so well and to the young Charles whom she adored, and upon whom she poured the devotion of a mother, found an expression and release in words as well as images.

Her versatility went beyond the written word for she drew and painted skillfully, a most uncommon accomplishment for a princess at that time. Paints and brushes are listed among her most intimate possessions, and she is said to have drawn part of the plans for a church at Bruges. Bernard van Orley and Jacopo dei Barbari were her court painters and constant companions, the men who had most influenced her taste, which, indeed, had been formed during her childhood in France and at the Burgundian court.

She apparently had no interest in German art for no German manu-

* Eleanor Tremayne, *The First Governess of the Netherlands, Margaret of Austria.* G. P. Putnam's Sons, 1908, p. 273.

script is listed in her inventory and, much to Albrecht Dürer's annoyance, no German painting. In his *Reisebriefen*, under the date of June 7 and 8, 1521, Dürer records his visit to Malines:

And I went to Lady Margaret's and showed her my Emperor * and would have presented it to her, but she so disliked it that I took it away with me. . . . And on Friday Lady Margaret showed me all her beautiful things; amongst them I saw about 40 oil pictures, the like of which for precision and excellence I have never beheld. There also I saw good works by Jan (de Mabuse) and Jacob Walch (Jacopo dei Barbari). I asked my Lady for Jacob's little book, but she said she had already promised it to her painter. Then I saw many other costly things and a precious library.

In this same visit Dürer describes having seen the treasure of Montezuma brought back by Cortes from Mexico (it subsequently languished in the basement of the Vienna Museum until recent years). It is the first reference to pre-Columbian art by any European, and it was probably the first showing of American art ever held. But interesting as are these aspects of Margaret's collection, it is the picture gallery itself which was the center of attention for it included more than a hundred paintings by the principal artists of the Netherlands – Van Eyck, Van der Weyden, Memling, Van Orley, Michel van Coxie, Mabuse, Bouts, Jacopo dei Barbari, Juan de Flandes and Jerome Bosch.

Most celebrated of all her pictures was the painting of the Tuscan merchant at Bruges, John Arnolfini of Lucca and his wife Joan, by Jan van Eyck. Hanging now in the National Gallery, London, it was recorded in Margaret's catalogue of 1516:

ung grant tableau qu'on appelle Hernoul-le-Fin avec sa femme dedens une chambre, qui fut donné à Madame par Don Diego, les armes duquel sont en la couverte dudit tableaul. Fait du painctre Johannes.†

* Doubtless Dürer's portrait of Maximilian, now in the gallery at Vienna, dated 1519.

† Its history is peculiarly interesting and throws an important light on the subsequent history of prices and values. The painting was commissioned from Van Eyck in 1430. By 1490 it had passed "to Don Diego de Guevara, one of Maximilian's Councillors, who added shutters to it, on the outer side of which were painted his arms and motto. Don Diego presented the picture to Margaret. After her death it came into the possession of a barber-surgeon of Bruges from whom Mary, Queen of Hungary, bought it in exchange for a place worth a hundred florins a year. The picture is mentioned in an inventory of the Queen's effects in 1556. Later it was taken to Spain, and in 1789 was in Charles III's collection at Madrid, but afterwards

If Margaret did much for painters and sculptors, she no less favored the musicians and writers of the Low Countries – Maître Agricola and Josquin des Prés were among her court composers and the reputation of her Flemish singers reached to Rome itself, where the Vatican recruited them for its polyphonic choirs. In literature her reign was made famous by such men as Jean Molinet, Erasmus, Adrian of Utrecht and her historian, Jean Lemaire des Belges, who immortalized the Regent in his *Illustrations de Gaule et Singularitez de Troye, avec la couronne Margaritique*, as well as in his other works. To Margaret also must be given the credit of having pushed tapestry weaving to its fullest accomplishment both as an art and as an industry. After the fall of Arras in 1477, the workmen of that town settled in Bruges, Brussels and Tournai. Amongst the greatest tapestry workers were Étienne Brumbergher, John Ronbrouck, Perquin d'Ervine, Pieter van Oppenem, Jean van den Brugghe, and so on; but the prince of tapestry makers was Pieter van Aelst, who for thirty years turned out innumerable tapestries from his workshops, the most celebrated being *The Acts of the Apostles.* All of the artists of repute were employed in designing cartoons for master weavers who were endeavoring to meet the new taste which, tired of the rigid subject matter of the Middle Ages, was ready to pay any price for the most labored commentary on classic fable and Christian story.

Margaret reigned for twenty-three years, one of the most respected monarchs of her time. She had reached the age of fifty in 1530, the year in which the Iron Crown of Lombardy was placed upon her

fell into the hands of one of the French generals. In 1815 Major General Hay, who had been wounded at Waterloo, found it in the house to which he was removed in Brussels, and after his recovery purchased it and brought it back to England, where in 1842 it was bought by the National Gallery for £730." In the past century the value of Van Eyck has steadily increased. John G. Johnson paid over $25,000 for his *Saint Francis* in 1893. The Ince-Blundell *Madonna* went to the National Gallery of Victoria at Melbourne for £100,000 in 1930. Two Van Eycks recently on the market, both from the Hermitage, were acquired from the Soviet Government; the Metropolitan Museum of Art paid $210,000 for the *Last Judgment,* Mr. Mellon paid $500,000 for the Washington *Annunciation.* More recently still, Marshal Hermann Goering capped the climax by stealing the Ghent altarpiece and taking it with him to Neuschwanstein, where both the picture and the Marshal's person were overtaken by General Patton's Third American Army. It has since been returned by the American Army to Saint Bavon's. The last Van Eyck reported sold was the *Three Maries at the Tomb* from the Cook Collection, Doughty House, Richmond Park, for a reputed price of $450,000.

nephew's head by the Pope at Bologna. Her great mission had been fulfilled. Awakening early on the morning of the fifteenth of November, Margaret asked one of her ladies, Magdalen of Rochester, for a glass of water. "The maid of honor brought her the drink in a crystal goblet, but in taking it back Magdalen unluckily let it fall near the bed, where it broke in several pieces. She carefully picked up all the fragments she could see, but one piece lay hidden in Margaret's embroidered high-heeled slipper. When the princess got up a few hours later, she put her bare feet into the slippers, and tried to walk to the fire, but immediately felt a sharp pain in the sole of her left foot. On examination it was found that a piece of broken glass was in the foot; this was at once extracted, but the wound remained, and bled very little." However, gangrene set in and the Regent died fifteen days later of an overdose of opium which her surgeons had given her before amputating her leg. Her last thoughts were for the House of Burgundy that it might continue undivided by the children of Charles V. She disposed of a few personal effects – one of her best rings to her brother Ferdinand, legacies to servants; she wrote to her nephew:

> I have made you my universal and sole heir, recommending you your countries over here, which, during your absence, I have not only kept as you left them, and restore to you the Government of the same, of which I believe to have loyally acquitted myself, in such a way as I hope for divine reward, satisfaction from you, Monseigneur, and the goodwill of your subjects; particularly recommending to you peace, especially with the Kings of France and England. And to end, Monseigneur, I beg of you for the love you have been pleased to bear this poor body, that you will remember the salvation of the soul, and the recommendation of my poor vassals and servants. Bidding you the last adieu, to whom I pray, Monseigneur, to give you prosperity and a long life.
>
> From Malignes, the last day of November 1530. Your very humble aunt,
>
> MARGARET.*

* * * * *

While Charles lacked the taste and enthusiasm of his aunt, he fully recognized the usefulness of art in maintaining his dynastic preten-

* Tremayne, *op. cit.*

sions and of glorifying his prestige as Emperor. His education, like that of any young prince of the Renaissance, required a familiarity with the arts and artists, but Margaret, so intent on preparing her adored orphan for the grave responsibilities ahead of him, insisted on his studying history, languages and science as well as the manly arts. The more subtle tastes were merely what he acquired informally about the palace or at the dinner table. William de Croy and Adrian of Utrecht, later to become the reform Pope Adrian VI, were his tutors and companions. From de Croy he learned manners, a stately bearing and a reserve which attached him to the Spanish heart; from Adrian he acquired the easy-going simple ways which made him so beloved by the Flemings.

The chief political objectives of Charles's reign, despite the good advice Margaret had given him, were the defeat of Francis I in the imperial election, and in the long wars in Italy over the title to the Duchy of Milan. He also had two other main desires – to hold back the Turks under Suliman II, a constant threat to Christian Europe, and to keep the Protestant Lutheran knights in check and thus prevent the spread of the Reformation. These were the foundation stones upon which his career was built, political foundations which in turn explain the Emperor's attitude regarding all cultural and artistic matters. So Charles's devotion to the Burgundian tradition resulted in his continuing his family's lavish patronage of the Brussels tapestry looms where fantastic cycles of hangings were woven illustrating his victories. Jan Vermeyen, who painted Charles at the age of thirty-three,* became his court painter in this early period.

From his Spanish grandparents, Ferdinand of Aragon and Isabella of Castile, the young Emperor had inherited no small part of his large artistic holdings. Prior to the unification of Aragon and Castile, the collecting of art in the Iberian peninsula had followed a strictly medieval pattern. The Renaissance had barely penetrated Spain although the close connections between Catalonia, Naples and Sicily

* The portrait, formerly in the collection of Lord Northbrook, now in the Worcester Art Museum, has been thought to be by him.

had brought her a constant stream of works of art from Italy. The Moors, who were finally expelled from Granada in 1492, the year of America's discovery, had also left their stamp upon the Spanish taste. In a sense Spain never had a Renaissance; in fact she never needed one since the Visigothic and Gothic heritage was being constantly replenished by new Oriental ideas that kept seeping in by way of Cordova. The art of Italy was likewise an importation, like the Flemish primitives which appeared in chapels and churches throughout the fifteenth century. But whereas the Spaniard understood instinctively the piety and mysticism of Flemish painting, the humanistic works of the Italian Renaissance in the reign of Ferdinand and Isabella were always articles of a foreign philosophy of taste.

The tradition of court painters had been a commonplace since the time of Alfonso the Wise in the thirteenth century, and Isabella, flush with the riches that were pouring in from military conquests in the New World, pulled all of the stops out of the organ and played fortissimo upon a familiar theme. She erected public buildings, built and endowed churches and decorated royal residences. The tomb of her son Juan, Prince of Asturias, as well as the other royal tombs at Granada, the Royal Hospice for pilgrims at Santiago, the monastery of San Juan de los Reyes at Toledo and San Tomás at Avila were all her creations. At Seville she completed the cathedral and endowed a chapel for the Alcazar. But the culmination of the Flemish taste, and its happiest marriage with Gothic Spain, may be seen in the Carthusian Convent of Miraflores near Burgos. It was in this church, the masterpiece of Gil de Siloe, that Joanna the Mad kept her constant vigil by the body of her Burgundian husband.

According to Don Pedro de Madrazo* Isabella left about 460 paintings, most of which Charles ultimately inherited. Joanna's will, in addition to those left by her mother, increased the total by another 36. Certain of the importations date from the embassy of Jan van Eyck to Valencia in 1428, such as, for instance, the *Fountain of the*

* *Viaje Artistico de Tres Siglos par las Colecciones de Cuadros de los Reyes de España.* An excellent summary may be found in Miss Enriqueta Harris's *The Prado: Treasure House of the Spanish Royal Collections.* The Studio Publishers, 1940.

Living Water, but for the most part they were works by the official artists of the court, Michel Situm, Juan de Flandes, as well as certain Spaniards. Francisco Chacón of Toledo, appointed first painter in 1480, also served as Censor of Painting and was required "to prevent any Jew or Moor from daring to paint the form of the glorious Holy Virgin or of any other Saint whatsoever."

CHAPTER IV

Many Caesars

If Charles had developed a passing taste for art in his boyhood at the Flemish court, his real education did not commence until his campaigns in Italy, where, as in the case of so many Germans before and after him, the prodigality of the Renaissance soon transformed his point of view. Until his death a quarter of a century later Titian was to be the dominating cultural influence in his life and one of the few close friends to whom the taciturn warrior could unbend; he did so with an intimacy and pathos that baffled the protocol-ridden Spanish and Burgundian courtiers who surrounded him. Always jealous of any outsider, their anger was aroused particularly when the Emperor bade the painter ride beside him in a state procession at Bologna, and Charles was forced, on another occasion, to remonstrate with them when they objected to his picking up from the studio floor a brush with which Titian was painting the Emperor's portrait, saying to them, "Titian deserves to be served by Caesar – there are many princes but only one Titian."

They first met in 1532 at Bologna when Charles was conferring with the Pope. Through the intervention of Pietro Aretino the artist had been invited by Cardinal Ippolito dei Medici and had made, according to Vasari, "a magnificent portrait of the Emperor. This gave so much satisfaction that the artist received a present of a thousand crowns for the same." Whether or not there was any truth to Aretino's claim of having brought Titian to the notice of the Emperor it is difficult to say, but at all events Aretino never permitted the painter (who was his closest friend) to forget this debt of gratitude. Certainly Charles had independently made up his own mind; for, after visiting the Gonzaga galleries at Mantua, he reached the decision that Titian was to become his court painter. In fact, Titian so pleased the

Emperor that he begged the artist to accompany him on his campaign to Tunis and to return with him to Spain. But Titian refused, and their active association was deferred until Charles returned to Italy. In 1547 Aretino wrote to Titian, who was at Augsburg with the Emperor:

> Neither Apelles nor Praxiteles nor any others who have carved images or painted portraits of kings or princes, can boast of rewards in gold and jewels that can equal in value the honor which your excellent genius has received from His August Majesty in deigning to call you to his court: demonstrating thereby how great a part you occupy in his mind even at the moment when he is framing laws for all the world, and at a time, too, when he is perplexed and thwarted by tumults and by plots. And it would be true, also, as asserted by envious tongues, that he who treats with contempt the being handed down in sculpture or painting as a hero or even the companion of the gods, and desires only to be engraved in the hearts and painted in the memories of good and prudent men – I say, if you believe these reports, then how great a mark of distinction does he pay to your extraordinary merit, when he submits to be represented in a picture by you, thus acknowledging the power of your inimitable hand! Go to him; and when you are at his feet adore him not only in your own name but in mine also.*

Already after his first visit to Italy Charles had issued a patent dated May 10, 1533, in which he declared that he only followed the example of his predecessors Alexander the Great and Octavian in selecting Titian to be his painter; "Alexander having sat to none but Apelles, and Octavian having employed the best of all draftsmen lest his glory should be tarnished by the monstrous failures of inexperienced designers." He thereupon created Titian a Count of the Lateran Palace, of the Aulic Council and of the Consistory, with the title of Count Palatine. He acquired, in addition to the advantages attached to those dignities, "the faculty of reporting notaries and ordinary judges, and the power to legitimize the illegitimate offspring of persons beneath the station of prince, count or baron." His children were raised to the rank of nobles of the Empire with all the honors pertain-

* Samuel Putnam, *The Works of* [*Pietro*] *Aretino* (Trans. into English). 2 Vols., P. Covici, 1926.

ing to families with four generations of ancestors. Charles further created Titian a Knight of the Golden Spur, conferring upon him all the privileges of knighthood: the sword, the chain and the Golden Spur, and the right to entrance at court, a privilege which Titian very frequently exercised. In addition to several grants which yielded him an income that varied between one and four hundred ducats a year (but which because of the dilatory negligence of Charles's ministers was very slow in payment), Titian was to receive a thousand scudi in gold every time he painted a portrait of the Emperor.* How many times he took the Emperor's portrait is not definitely recorded, but there are today in the Prado alone forty-three portraits of the Hapsburg house, portraits of the Emperor and of his family which were done at Augsburg and in Vienna on the several occasions of Titian's visits to the court. The palace of the Pardo, destroyed by fire in the seventeenth century, contained, according to Gronau, no less than seventy-six paintings by Titian, those done for the Emperor and his son Philip II of Spain. Whatever the accurate number may have been, certainly no other monarch was painted so frequently and with so much satisfaction by an artist of such stature.

But aside from this intimacy and faith in the Venetian painter, Charles was not completely devoid of an intellectual life of his own. He lived simply and, after a first flush of extravagance in his extreme youth, dressed as simply – rather as a rebuke to the members of his court. It was said that he would "spend lavishly on great objects but grudged a ducat for superfluity." In Germany he wore a simple fustian cap and a woolen costume worth about a crown in all. He never spent more than two hundred crowns for a fur and according to Navagero his clothes were always mended and he knew when a shirt or handkerchief was missing. His court both in Spain and in Germany was very cheaply run and his household was often without pay for a year. His pages so rarely had new liveries that they were in rags, but he had a fine taste in art and in books. Before he had ever set foot in Italy he had called Italian architects and sculptors to Spain for the embellishment of the great elliptical palace at Granada which was

* J. A. Crowe and Cavalcaselle, *The Life and Times of Titian.* John Murray, 1881 (4 vols.), I, 371.

never finished. On his military travels he took the time to study the monasteries and churches of Italy.

Charles was an insatiable reader and according to Van Male his original bent was for romances, chivalry and chronicles. Monstrelet's *History* was an early companion – he called Commine's *Mémoires* his breviary, and in the troubled years from 1550 on his reading became more and more theological. He read the Vulgate – Maccabees, Esdras, Daniel and any prophecies about the end of the world. He would tell his reader to write for copies of Philo and Josephus. Van Male used to ease the Emperor's insomnia by reading him to sleep although his asthma at times kept him up all night; to these years also belonged his greatest literary labors. In his boat on the Rhine Charles composed his *Commentaries* which Van Male prepared to translate into the Latin "of Livy, Caesar, Suetonius and Tacitus combined." He also translated his favorite book, the *Chevalier Déliberé* by Olivier de la Marche, into Spanish. Thirty volumes went with the Emperor to Yuste for his retirement. They included Caesar's *Commentaries* in Italian, the *War in Germany* by Luis de Avila, the *Chevalier Déliberé*, Boethius in French, Italian and Spanish, and part of the manuscript of Ocampo, the court historian, and several books of meditations and commentaries on the Psalms.*

Charles was an enthusiast in matters of commerce and international finance (had he been alive today, he would have been called an amateur economist), and he was likewise an expert in cartography and mapping. It was his enthusiasm in this direction which gave such support to the mapping of the Western Hemisphere and of the voyages of discovery in the Atlantic and Pacific Oceans.

Although in his youth he was ranked as one of the first horsemen in Europe and delighted in hunting and steeplechasing, he grew to be less and less fond of exercise. His besetting sin was gluttony. He was said to eat at every hour of the day. His courtiers, speaking of his devotion to the table and to meditation, used to say "*dalla messa àlla mensa.*" And Luis de Quijada, on seeing his disobedient master eat oysters, said, "Surely kings must think that their stomachs are not

* For a full account of Charles's private life cf. E. Armstrong, *The Emperor Charles V*, The Macmillan Co., 1910.

made as other men's." He was, however, not a drunkard, and it was rather to the distress of his courtiers that his table was so restricted in its alcoholic beverages. Shortly after his fortieth year Charles began to suffer horribly from gout and it was this increasing infirmity, affecting his entire body, that precipitated his retirement and abdication. Although the chronicles have called it gout (and the biographers of the nineteenth and twentieth centuries have not seen fit to change the diagnosis), the most amateur clinical observation of the record leads to the inevitable conclusion that Charles suffered from a cancer which eventually consumed his whole system. Sir Richard Morison, the British envoy, was admitted to audience in 1552 when Charles was ill of a sore lip. "He had," he says, "no adventitious trappings to give him presence. He was sitting at a bare table without carpet or anything else upon it save his cloak, his brush, his spectacles and his pick-tooth. He could only speak with difficulty, for his lower lip was broken in two places and at his tongue's end he had a green leaf, a remedy against his dryness as in his talk did increase upon it." The envoy was received with exquisite courtesy, "the Emperor concluding with the phrases that old amities which had been long tried and found good were to be much made of. And this reported, said Morison, 'he spake a little louder than he did the rest, as though he would indeed have me think that he did earnestly mean what he said; and yet he had a face unwont to disclose any hid affection of his heart, as any face that I ever met with in all my life; for where all white colors, which in changing themselves, are wont in others to bring a man certain word how his errand is liked or misliked, have no place in his countenance, his eyes only do betray as much as can be picked out of it. He oft maketh me think of Solomon's saying, Heaven is high; the earth is deep; a king's heart is unsearchable.' " *

By 1550 the Emperor had reached the great paradox of his career. He was conqueror of the world, he had subdued his enemies in Italy, he was the most powerful sovereign alive and yet he knew that what

* Armstrong, *op. cit.* Another piece of evidence that Charles suffered from a cancer of the lip is deduced from the popular legend in Spain that the Castilian "lisp" was not native to the Spanish tongue but was adopted as a fashion by the Court as a courtesy to Charles V, who lisped very markedly, possibly because of this physical difficulty.

he had so powerfully consolidated could not continue after him. The Council of Trent which he had initiated in 1545 to reform the Roman Church from within had already been sitting for five of its eighteen futile years. Charles saw that the tide of Reformation, while it might be retarded, could not be indefinitely constrained. He knew, moreover, that he himself was dying of a mortal illness and that the time had come to prepare himself for God, and his dominions for the type of rule which might be carried on beyond his death. While he had tried in vain to secure Austria and the Empire for his son Philip, he saw that he must bow to necessity and divide this Empire, most of which he had inherited, and which he himself had consolidated and brought to such extravagant heights. After several years of struggle and indecision the abdication took place with much ceremonial and sorrow in Brussels in 1556. To Philip II were given the Kingdom of Spain and the Netherlands; to his brother, Ferdinand I, the traditional German lands of the Holy Roman Empire.

The spot which Charles had selected for his retirement was the Hieronymite Cloister at Yuste, situated in a lovely green mountain valley of Estremadura, where he had hunted in his younger days. He arrived there in the fall of 1557 after a ceremonial progress from Ghent by sea to England where he visited his daughter, and then again by sea to Spain, stopping in many places and receiving his former subjects in audience.

The house which he had had fitted up for him was neither a palace nor a monkish cell. He moved in with a retinue of some hundred persons determined to lead the austere life of the cloister. The chroniclers of the time were deeply impressed and rather shocked at the Emperor's simplicity. "When he rode into the towns," says a contemporary, "amid brilliant escort of courtiers and cavaliers, the Emperor's person was easily to be distinguished among the crowd, by the plainness of his attire." Roger Ascham, who was admitted to an audience in the privy chamber some five years before his abdication, had said of the Emperor, "He had on a gown of black taffety, and looked somewhat like the parson at Epurstone." His parsimony seemed to be instinctive, for on one of his campaigns when he was overtaken by a rainstorm, the Emperor took off his new velvet cap and remained uncovered while he sent into town for an old one. "Poor Emperor," said one of his soldiers, "spending tons of gold on his wars and standing bareheaded in the rain for the sake of his velvet bonnet!" But Prescott, from his examination of the inventory of the Emperor's effects prepared by Quijada and Gazetlu soon after their master's death, shows that the accounts of the Emperor's simplicity must have been greatly exaggerated. "Among the items we find carpets from Turkey, Alcaraz, canopies of velvet and other stuffs, hangings of fine black cloth, which since his mother's death he had always chosen for his own bedrooms; while the remaining apartments were provided with no less than twenty-five suits of tapestry, from the looms of Flanders, richly embroidered with figures of animals and with landscapes. Instead of the 'crazy seat' that is spoken of, we find, besides a number of sofas and chairs of carved walnut, half a dozen arm chairs covered with black velvet and two others of a more elaborate workmanship for the Emperor's special use."*

The living apartments were furnished with the most sumptuous gold and silver plate, washbasins and toilet articles of every description; the whole amount of plate was estimated "between twelve and thirteen thousand ounces in weight." He had what for a great sovereign of his day was a mediocre display of jewels; they were chiefly trinkets, mounted caskets of gold and silver and enamel in which there were incrustations of precious gems, and a considerable number of reliquaries containing pieces of the True Cross and other objects of devotion. But the chief decoration which the abdicated monarch brought with him to Yuste was worth far more than either his plate or his jewels, it was a collection of pictures, more than six hundred in number. "There were among them some of the noblest masterpieces of the Prado, pictures that were variously painted, on canvas, wood, and stone, mostly of the size of life and were hung in rich frames around the walls of his apartment." Some were in miniature and among these were no less than three of the Empress; while an elaborate altarpiece showing pictures of the Virgin and Child was ornamented with gold medallions and contained likenesses of the different

* William H. Prescott, *The History of the Reign of the Emperor Charles the Fifth*. Phillips and Sampson, 1857. Vol. III, Book II, p. 384.

members of the imperial family. "But the gems of the collection," continues Prescott, "were eight paintings from the pencil of Titian." There was the *Ecce Homo* for which Buckingham was later to refuse the Earl of Arundel's offer of seven thousand pounds, and the *Mater Dolorosa.* Above all was the celebrated *Gloria* in which he appears with the Empress in the midst of the heavenly host supported by angels, in an attitude of solemn adoration. This superb picture, which after the monarch's death accompanied his remains to the Escorial, was reported by tradition to have been placed over the great altar in the church of Yuste. That this was the case is rendered probable, says Prescott, by the size of the painting, which made it better suited to a church than to a private apartment. In the space above the altar, Charles could, moreover, readily see it through the window of his chamber; and from his sickbed his eyes might still rest on the features of the sainted being who had been dearest to him on earth.

Titian had commenced the painting in 1550 at the moment Charles V began to contemplate his abdication, and there must have been many conversations between the two friends upon the subject of this piece. It was certainly one of the most grandiose conceptions ever undertaken by the master. Aretino wrote of it, "I have heard that in the case of the *Trinity*, the religion and the most sacred faith of Your Majesty is pleased, and that in the *Venus* your gentleness and love. Wherefore Titian has achieved what is the miracle of his style in satisfying at the same time the body and soul of the stupendous Emperor."

It seems strange that we are able to form a better picture of the taste and character of Charles V from the two years which preceded his death at Yuste than we can for all the other fifty-six years of his life. This is because he was a warrior always on the move, going from one capital to the next, and usually associating himself with the moods and the customs of any city in which he found himself. To be sure, he was surrounded by his Burgundian and Spanish courtiers, but it seems that Charles had always before him the vision of a large design and that during his younger days he was willing to sacrifice to it his personal comfort and his interests.

But if the court at Yuste was simple, it nevertheless lacked none of the regularity and protocol of Burgundy which was so much in Charles's blood. A great portion of the day was devoted to the table, where he ate unrestrained and mammoth meals, washed down by quantities of beer and hock. Apparently, knowing that death was upon him, the Emperor decided to indulge himself to the bitter end. Next to his pleasure at the table and his strict devotion to the attentions of his confessor, Charles amused himself with one of several occupations, generally of a mechanical kind, for which he had a considerable taste. His constant companion was Torriano, one of the most ingenious artists and mechanics of his day. They worked together framing models of useful machines and making all types of mechanical experiments, particularly in clocks and watches which, by the structure of internal springs, mimicked the gestures and actions of men to the astonishment of the ignorant monks in the monastery, who, says Prescott, "could not comprehend the movements and sometimes distrusted their own senses, suspecting Charles and Torriano of being in contact with invisible powers." Torriano had early distinguished himself as a hydraulic engineer so that his experiments with the Emperor were largely astronomical and mechanical. They showed, in fact, that the Emperor was capable of a considerable understanding in the mathematical sciences and in physics.

The Emperor would rise at ten o'clock and receive the Gentlemen of the Chamber of the first and second class. At noon he heard Mass and it was then that he indulged his lifelong taste and fondness for music. His polyphonic choir was considered the first in Europe and was the training school for the choir of the Vatican. After Mass, the principal meal of the day, the Emperor dined alone or occasionally invited his confessor to sit with him. At times Van Male, the chamberlain, would read aloud to him, usually from Pliny or from one of the classical authors, and it was followed by the reading of one of the monks of appropriate passages from Saint Bernard and Saint Jerome. He was completely withdrawn from the business of the kingdom and the concerns of government, so entirely abstracted in fact that one of his contemporaries said that "neither the arrival of the treasures brought in his fleets from the Indies nor the sounds of arms, amongst which his life hitherto had been passed, had any power to disturb his tranquility."

Charles V quitted this regular and tranquil life on an August afternoon in 1558, holding in his hand a picture by Titian of the *Last Judgment*. He was not a great collector, nor yet could it be said that he was a great patron of the arts. It was a mere accident of history that he and Titian were alive at the same moment and that he had had the wit to select this man to be his friend and his court painter. The other artists who had worked for the Emperor were persons of quite another class. It is not, therefore, surprising that Charles, so wrapped up in his intimacy with Titian, should never have personally commissioned anything by the hand of his other great contemporary, Michelangelo. "No reasonable person ever said that the imperial dignity did not befit the Emperor. Charles V, if not a highly dramatic personality, was yet by no means a lay figure, nor even the inevitable stage king. He was not quite a great man, nor quite a good man, but all deductions made, an honorable Christian gentleman, striving in spite of physical defects, moral temptations and political impossibilities, to do his duty in that state of life to which an unkind Providence had called him." *

* Armstrong, *op. cit.*, II, 387.

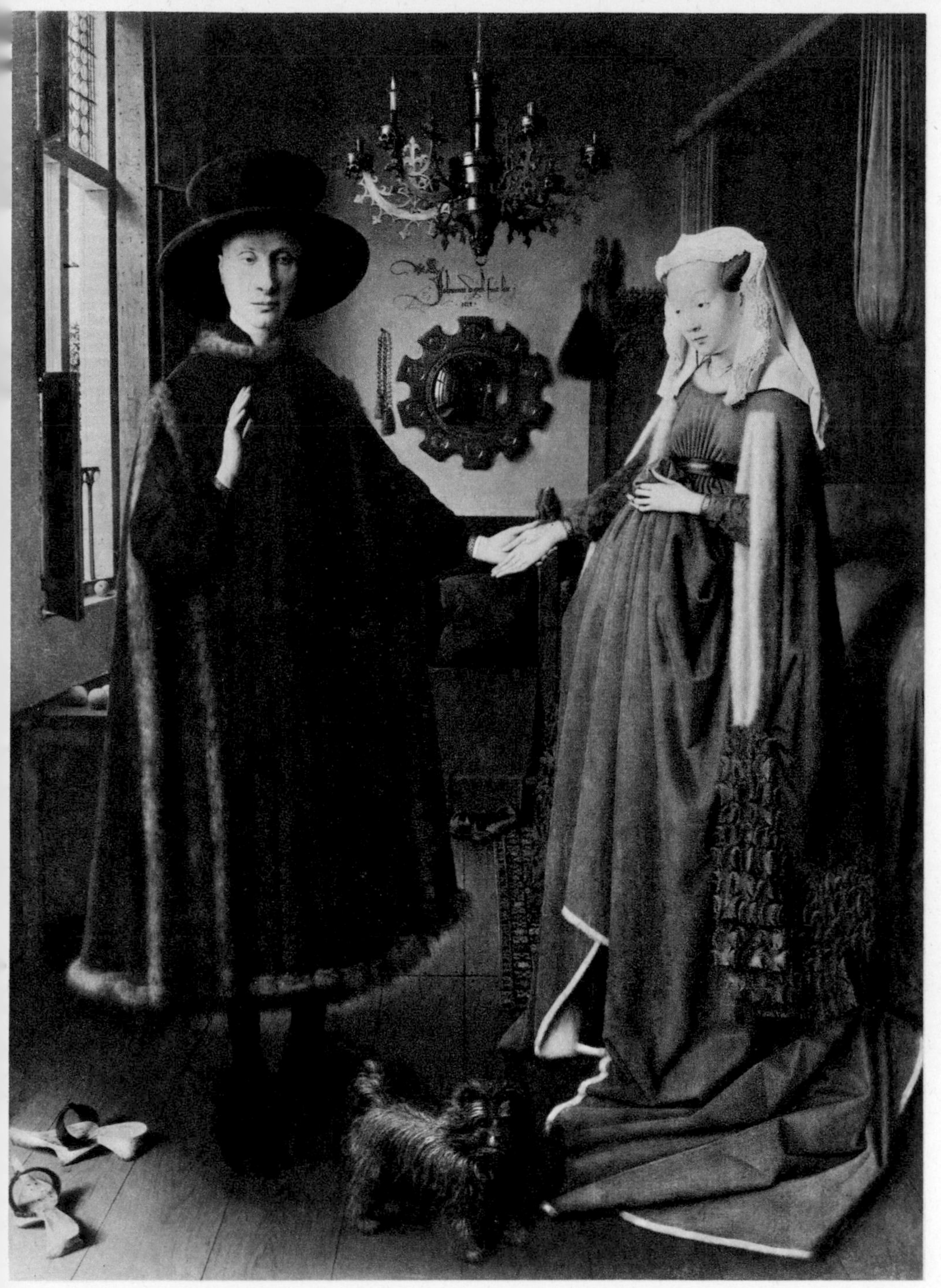

GIOVANNI ARNOLFINI AND HIS WIFE

By Jan Van Eyck. From the collection of Margaret of Austria
London, National Gallery

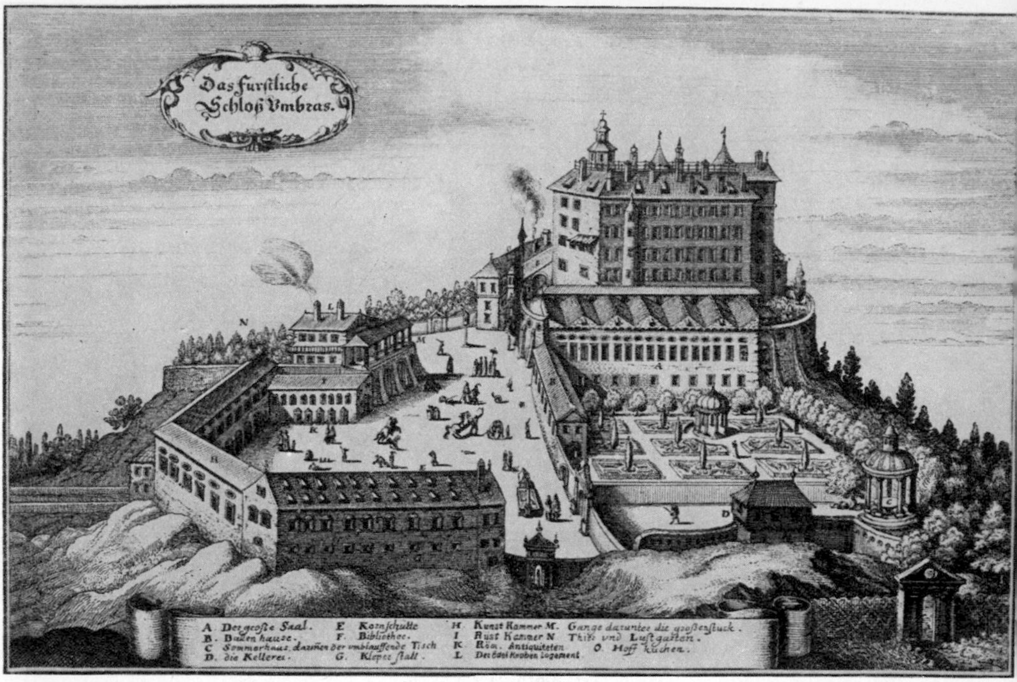

SCHLOSS AMBRAS – CRADLE OF HAPSBURG COLLECTING

EMPEROR LEOPOLD I VISITS THE HOFBIBLIOTHEK

CHAPTER V

The Archducal Collectors

THE act of abdication, so portentous for the political destiny of Europe, was, at the same time, equally prophetic for the history of art. For just as Charles had divided the Hapsburg dominions between his son Philip II, King of Spain, and his brother Ferdinand I of Austria, so was the division made between the personal possessions of the Austrian and Spanish branches. The collections of Margaret of Austria for the most part had passed at her death in 1530 to the Spanish succession; to these Charles added his pictures, particularly those by Titian which he had himself commissioned, and the collections of the Spanish crown which he had inherited from his grandparents, Ferdinand and Isabella. At the time of Charles's death, Philip, in order to pay his father's debts, put up all of these collections at auction but bought back again for himself most of the finer pictures. They form today, together with the later paintings by Velasquez, Greco and Goya, the basis of the royal Spanish collections. Although the inventories of the Escorial and the royal palaces in other cities have been lost, Don Pedro de Madrazo's account placed 357 paintings in the palace of Madrid alone. This is, presumably, but a fraction of the whole; for thus adding to his inheritance Philip encouraged the production of art on the grand scale.

A portion of Margaret of Austria's collections had, however, found its way to Vienna, including Dürer's portrait of her father, Maximilian I. The latter had collected family portraits and owned a curio and art cabinet. These he had bequeathed, together with his antiquities and coins, to Maximilian II, the rest of his collections going to the Archduke Ferdinand of Tyrol and to Carl of Steiermark. The latter's works of art were finally brought from Graz to Vienna in 1765.

Of the earlier sixteenth-century Hapsburgs, Ferdinand of Tyrol was the most picturesque and quite the most original. Although the quality of many of the works of art he had brought together in his romantic Castle Ambras was equal to that of the best collections of the day in Italy or England, the extent of his curiosity showed him nevertheless to be a feudal prince of the German Renaissance, still sharing the interests and superstitions of his predecessors, Albrecht of Bavaria and the Elector of Saxony. He was a very rich man, for, in addition to the fortune which he had inherited, he had married Philippine Welser, a daughter of the Augsburg banking house of that name. His principal hobby was the study of architecture and he drew the plans for the Schloss zum Sterne near Prague. Montaigne called him "*grand bâtisseur et deviseur*" and was enthralled with the workshops for woodcarving and wrought iron he had established, and with the glass blowers he had imported from Murano. "Bohemian glass," so coveted in later centuries as an article of export, had found its origin in these factories.

Ferdinand was also passionately fond of music and the theater; he was the author of a comedy printed in Innsbruck in 1584. His court musician, Giovanni Buontempo, compiled a *Parnassus Musicus Ferdinandicus* including compositions by his master and by Monteverdi. The Archduke assembled his collections at Ambras, which became a Mecca not only for the artists and scholars of Europe but for all the travelers of that day. His armor collection later was the nucleus of the incomparable *Waffensammlung* in Vienna.* The library at Ambras boasted over four thousand volumes and the art collection was known as the *Grosse Kunstkammer*. There were relatively few paintings, mostly portraits after historical subjects in the Giovian manner, and a gallery of the beautiful women to whose charms Ferdinand was always susceptible. His collection of *Handsteine*, small carved minerals — a typical product of the Tyrol, of which some excellent examples are in the Pierpont Morgan Library — was as celebrated as his collection of musical instruments. He shared also the Germanic passion of his cousins for instruments of precision, filling his collection with mathe-

* It was described in a luxurious catalogue published at Innsbruck in 1601 by Johannes Agricola. The illustrations were engraved by Dominick Custos after drawings by Giovanni Fontana.

matical and optical gadgets, including fantastic clocks which showed the movements of the planets as well as the hours of the day, intricate locks so powerful that "*Man mit keinem Schlissel aufthuen kann.*" There were besides ethnographical curiosities of every description.

After Ferdinand's death in 1605, his son, Markgraf Karl von Burgau, sold the entire collections to Rudolph II for 170,000 gulden, with the stipulation that they should remain forever at Ambras. But as in the case of most wills, the centuries withered the dead hand, and after many vicissitudes these collections joined those of Leopold Wilhelm and the Emperor at Vienna.

Of all the Austrian branch, the Emperor Rudolph II (1552–1612) was closest in spirit and in taste to his great uncle Philip II at whose Spanish court he had spent his boyhood. Whereas Philip's religious zeal expressed itself in a fanatical personal austerity, Rudolph abandoned himself to a life of scholarship and to the extension of his medieval *Wunderkammer*. He had a sure eye for pictures, developed largely through his admiration for Titian, and he was an enthusiastic collector of the works of Dürer and Hieronymus Bosch. Rudolph was to be the link between the Vienna Museum and the Prado and he seemed to unite in himself several complex strains of the ancient Hapsburg heritage. Leaving Spain at nineteen, he retired to Prague, where he closed himself up in the Hradschin, refusing to attend to affairs of state and spending his time and fortune on his collections. He lived among his scientists and astrologers, who included Tycho de Brahe and Keppler, his women, his painters, his adventurers and wild animals. There he employed the best goldsmiths and artisans in Europe to create the most complicated instruments imaginable, taking a profound and daily interest in their progress and ingenuity.

Rudolph's collection of works of art was estimated to be worth more than 17,000,000 gulden and was probably one of the greatest ever assembled. It fell victim, alas, to the Thirty Years' War, during which it was broken up and carried away by the Czechs, the Saxons and above all by the Swedes under Königsmark. Fortunately, prior to the siege of Prague, some of the finer things had been removed to hiding and eventually found their way to Vienna. But the great bulk was dispersed, the antiquities ultimately coming to rest in Munich; several bargeloads of pictures were floated down the Elbe to become the treasures of the Mad Christina of Sweden.*

While across Europe at Madrid the three Philips were building up the royal collections of Spain, and Rudolph was occupied with filling the palaces of the Hapsburgs in Vienna, in another corner of their vast dominions the Archduke Leopold Wilhelm was Regent of the Netherlands. During the ten years of his governorship, 1646–1656, he had shown the way and had brought together collections of works of art which seemed to overshadow those of even the other members of his family.

Already there was a great tradition of collecting in Flanders. At Besançon in the Franche-Comté Charles V's two ministers, Charles Perrenot de Granvelle and his son Cardinal Antoine de Granvelle, had set the fashion of collecting and high living in a way that beggared the efforts of the court and rivaled in its sumptuousness another member of the Sacred College, Cardinal Wolsey. The Flemish mind was thus thoroughly accustomed to the rapacity of the connoisseur.

Leopold Wilhelm was the great-great-great-nephew of Margaret of Austria, who had ruled the Netherlands before him; he was, in fact, only twenty years younger than his uncle, Archduke Ferdinand of Tyrol. He had started collecting some time before arriving at Brussels, whither he had gone for a change of climate, and it is known that he acquired certain of his best works of art along the journey from Vienna. He was a sickly person, probably tubercular, with that strain of sadness, bitterness and pride so characteristic of his line. Yet no effort seemed too great a tax upon his strength if it was towards the expansion of his art collection. An inventory taken in 1659 (shortly after his return to Vienna) shows that he had amassed 1397 paintings, 343 master drawings and 542 sculptures. In addition to these was a great quantity of *objets d'art* of every kind. His tapestry collection was one of the finest in the world and his jewels, plate and furniture were in keeping with the pictures.

* These we shall meet again in Rome in Queen Christina's palace, where, following her death, they were sold by her heir, Cardinal Assolini, and his nephews to Prince Odescalchi, who in turn sold them to the Prince Regent of France, the Duke of Orleans. After a sojourn of nearly a century at the Palais-Royal they were sold in London in 1792.

At first the Archduke was guided in his taste by the flower painter Jan Anton van der Baren, who was also his court chaplain. But in Brussels the chaplain was soon supplanted by Teniers, who became the director of the gallery and who has commemorated it with a series of pictures depicting the Archduke and his entourage admiring groups of pictures in the company of artists and personages of the court. That in the Vienna Museum is the most celebrated of the series and shows Teniers exhibiting the works of Catena, Palma and Annibale Carracci to his patron while several artists are examining the drawings and other works of art. Most of the pictures are clearly identified as belonging today to the Viennese collection.

In addition to the "painted Galleries" Teniers used to make small copies or *pastiches* of the individual pictures. These served as models for the copper-plate engravings which he made of the entire collection and which were bound together in the first illustrated catalogue ever made of the contents of an art museum. Some 1246 of these engravings figure in this work entitled the *Theatrum Pictorum*, published in 1660.*

Leopold Wilhelm's short governorship of the Netherlands was, of course, a half century after the death of Philip II. He covered the reigns of Philip III and Philip IV of Spain. He was governor during the dispersal of the great Stuart collections – of Charles I, of Buckingham and Arundel. The two latter collections were disposed of in Belgium and Holland and the Archduke had also agents in England, France and Spain. He lost no time in putting forward the fabulous offers which his personal fortune permitted him. His own portrait was taken no less than thirty-four times and he gave some sixty-five commissions for pictures to artists in the Provinces. No wonder that the artists whom he thus patronized eagerly sought out works of art by the older masters and presented them for his consideration.

Rubens had died shortly before his arrival in the Netherlands but certain of his pupils were employed by the court of whom Gonzales

* Other publications which made this gallery celebrated throughout Europe were the *Theatrum Artis Pictoriae* by Prenner, and the *Prodromus* by Stampart and Prenner, both of which appeared in the eighteenth century. Not only the engravings have survived, but many of the models themselves, some 200 of the *pastiches* being listed in the collection of the Duke of Marlborough at Blenheim Palace as late as 1886.

Coques, "the little Van Dyck," was the dean. Italian painting was brilliantly represented, especially by the great exponents of the Venetian School – Bellini, Giorgione, Titian. Frimmel points out that there were also admirable portraits by Lorenzo Lotto, Paolo Veronese and Tintoretto. His Spanish cousins, too, presented him with works by Ribera and by Velasquez and his school, although he adds that, "unlike the Emperor, Leopold Wilhelm was not given the very finest works of these masters." The brilliant pictures of the Spanish School in the Vienna Gallery did not reach that city until the seventeenth century had run its course and the intermarriage between the Austrian and Spanish Hapsburgs brought about an exchange of family portraits.

It was, however, in the Netherlandish schools of the fifteenth and sixteenth centuries that the connoisseurship of this prince excelled that of most of his contemporaries. Almost all of the important works of this type now in the Austrian collections are derived from this one source – Van Eyck's *Portrait of Cardinal della Croce*, and the paintings by Hugo Van der Goes, Rogier Van der Weyden, Memling and their followers. The panels by Geertgen tot Sint Jans, the *Pietà*, and *Julian the Apostate Burning the Bones of Saint John the Baptist*, were acquired from the collection of Charles I of England. But, like a true Hapsburg, Leopold Wilhelm eschewed the Protestant painters of the Dutch Republic, and while he occupied his palace in Brussels at the very heyday of Rembrandt's career, he did not choose to sully his walls with the works of the Protestant. Only one small picture by this heretic, *Philosopher in His Study*, crept into the inventory. Wouwerman was tolerated in the usual hunting pictures, Ostade by genre; but Frans Hals, Ter Borch and the other giants of the Low Countries, whose greatest pictures lay within a stone's throw of the Archduke's fabulous gallery, remained an undisclosed pleasure until they were rediscovered by later generations of his family.

Leopold Wilhelm returned to Vienna in 1656 taking with him his collections, which at his death he left to his nephew, the Emperor Leopold I. They became the principal attraction of the Hofburg, where they remained until the eighteenth century when they were distributed between the Belvedere and other imperial palaces. To these collections were added those that had come directly down the line from Maximilian II, and those portions of Rudolph II's treasures that had escaped the ravages of the Thirty Years' War.

Fabulous as are the imperial collections of Vienna which descended directly through the Hapsburg line, not the least of her distinction is derived from the Albertina – that most prized and coveted collection of Old Master drawings. Having weathered the successive storms of revolution and war, and now of Russian occupation, it stands in its original palace on the Augustiner Bastei a symbol of the imperturbability of art. It was the creation of Albert Casimir of Sachsen-Teschen (1738–1822), son of Augustus the Strong of Poland. He married the daughter of Maria Theresa, the lovely and companionable Archduchess Maria Christina. Together they devoted their lives and fortunes to gathering drawings and prints of an almost unbelievable quality. Visiting Italy together, Hungary and the Low Countries, where he served as governor, their opportunities were infinite at a moment when the death of Mariette and the French Revolution produced a lull before the English drawing collectors of the Regency got started. By a shrewd exchange with the Emperor Francis II in 1796, the Albertina acquired the incomparable series of Dürers from Schloss Ambras which Rudolph II had bought from the grandson of Willibald Pirkheimer, who in turn had them from Dürer's widow. Other drawings by Dürer came from the heirs of Cardinal Granvella. The work of the Albertina was carried on by Albert's heirs, the Archdukes Karl and Albrecht, and finally by its last proprietor, the Archduke Friedrich. Today it is the proud possession of the State and is known principally to art students through the writings of the late director Dr. Josef Meder, whose book on drawings has become the classic textbook for their study.

The Austrian nobility, because of the wide ramifications of the Hapsburg dominions, had been given, perhaps, a better opportunity than any other Germans of keeping abreast with the foreign and domestic output in the arts. Their contacts with Italy, particularly Venice, were constant, as was their intercourse with the Low Countries and with Spain. But they were so overshadowed by the patronage and endless tradition of the Hapsburg family that only in a few instances did they attempt to collect on the grand scale. There were the Harrachs, the Schwarzenbergs, the Czernins, but above all the Liechtensteins, whose collections of works of art both at Liechtenstein and in their palace at Vienna have survived to have a market value nearly as great as the net worth of the principality itself. That the collections were already famous at the end of the sixteenth century may be seen from the fact that on September 1, 1597, the Emperor Rudolph II wrote from Prague to the first Prince Liechtenstein complimenting him upon the excellent and rare masterpieces of art and paintings which he was supposed to own, and saying that he was sending to him his representative, Count Schliack, whom Prince Carl could trust implicitly; he begged him therefore to "co-operate in every way" with the wishes of the Emperor. Unquestionably, as Donath has pointed out, the Emperor was suspected of covetous designs, but it would seem that when the Count arrived in Vienna, his mission was no more sinister than that of commissioning a series of copies of the Prince's finest works.

The second Prince Liechtenstein, Carl Eusebius, was the true dynamic spirit in making the collection. He was a splendid amateur and connoisseur and his book *Werk von der Architektur* contains a discriminating treatise on the art of collecting. In fact, from the bills which this Viennese prince paid for works of art (and which have been preserved and published) one can obtain one of the best pictures of the international art dealings of the seventeenth century. In 1643 Carl Eusebius was offered a collection of pictures by the brothers Forchoudt in Antwerp which included Pieter Breugel's *Triumph of Death*, valued at 1000 guilders, a *Madonna and Child* by Van Cleef at 300 guilders, and Lucas's *Adoration of the Kings* for 150 guilders. This same firm at a later date sold the celebrated Rubens cycle of *Decius Mus* to Carl Eusebius's descendants. The prices paid by the Prince were fully recorded; among the pictures were two Heads by Albrecht Dürer, *Ecce Homo* and *Unser Liebe Frau*, for 100 taler, and two small portraits by Lucas Cranach, thirty taler each. The *Liebe Frau* by Raphael "in his most perfect and best manner" cost 1500 reichstaler, whereas a painting by Parmigianino, *The Alchemist*, was priced at 2000 reichstaler.

These same account books offer us one of the few remaining records of contemporary Austrian collections; Carl Eusebius bought the cabinet of Wolf Wilhelm Praemer, Imperial Chamberlain, and of the court painter, Christoph Lauch, in 1673; each of these, together with other purchases made *en bloc*, contained many of the most prized examples of the present-day collection. While capital works were added constantly in the eighteenth and nineteenth centuries, it was Carl Eusebius who had laid the foundation and the structure of what is perhaps, even at this time, the greatest single family collection in the world.

With Leopold Wilhelm and Carl Eusebius of Liechtenstein the Austrian genius suddenly subsided. While Joseph II, Maria Theresa, Prince Eugene and their subjects in the eighteenth century were to revive quite brilliantly the flagging spirit of collecting, the Renaissance tradition was over and the passion of this house was spent. It was only in the Spanish peninsula that the Hapsburg torch of connoisseurship was carried on until it went to France and became an appanage of the Bourbon monarchy.

CHAPTER VI

Philip II – Medici or Inquisitor

PHILIP II, the most Spanish of princes, yet through whose veins flowed so much Burgundian and Austrian blood, presented, according to Brandi, "a curious contrast to the richly clad, solid-looking Netherlanders. He had no natural gaiety, nothing of the freshness of youth. Wine made him sick and he fainted during a tournament. On the other hand he could not have his fill of religious ceremonies and walking in processions." * Philip seems to have inherited none of the balanced judgment of his father, Charles V, and Carl Justi has described him as "half Medici, half Inquisitor." A fanatic, whose chief aim in life was to establish the universal supremacy of the Catholic Church not only in Spain itself but in all his external dominions, he was the embodiment in his frail person of that union of driving, biting realism with visionary piety which Unamuno has called so well the "*Sentimiento tragico de la vida.*" That he was interested in art at all was due in large measure to the loneliness which the rigorous etiquette of the Spanish court imposed upon him and to the mystical inner existence which found such a sinister expression in the architecture of the Escorial.

Philip was certainly the most Spanish of all the Hapsburg rulers. He was an autocrat, hard working and able. He carried the destiny of Spain to its highest pinnacle and then plunged it into bankruptcy and the inglorious defeat of the Armada. The Netherlands, Franche-Comté, Naples and Milan were his responsibility besides the Spanish possessions in the New World. The costly intervention in European affairs had not only drained the resources of the Spanish Empire but left the King at the mercy of Italian (particularly Genoese) bankers like the Grimaldi, who made Spain a battleground upon which they

* Brandi, *op. cit.*, 592.

fought the even more powerful Augsburg Fuggers for the financial domination of Europe, America and the Indies. This was the more serious because the expulsion of the Jews and Moors by Ferdinand and Isabella in 1492 had stripped Spain of her financial brains; during the Middle Ages, in fact, the economy of both Castile and Aragon had been almost exclusively in their hands.

Another factor which contributed to financial problems of Philip's reign was the fact that the rise of modern capitalism occurred at the precise moment when the importation of gold and silver from America threatened to destroy the economy of Europe – an economy which had managed for several centuries to maintain a fairly balanced ratio between gold and silver, based largely on the mines in Austria and Germany.

No other period in history, says Hamilton, "has witnessed so great a proportional increase in the production of the precious metals as occurred in the wake of the Mexican and Peruvian conquests. A modicum of treasure was obtained in the Antilles before 1520, but not until the fabulous mines were discovered on the mainland – in New Spain, Peru and New Granada – did the harvest of the precious metals transcend the wildest dreams of the *conquistadores*. Pouring into Europe in a mammoth stream, American gold and silver precipitated the Price Revolution, which in turn played a significant role in the transformation of the social and economic institutions in the first two centuries of the modern era." *

During the period 1503 to 1660 there passed officially through the India House of Seville (*Casa de Contratación*), upon which the Hapsburgs had bestowed the monopoly of American trade and navigation, bullion brought across the seas in galleons and warships in the value of 447,820,932 pesos, not counting, of course, booty and the output of free-lance mining, ventures which were universal practices. "The resultant material prosperity," adds Hamilton, "together with the effect of the specie on national psychology, played a part in the passage of Spain through her golden age of art and literature.† But

* Earl J. Hamilton, *American Treasure and the Price Revolution in Spain,* in Harvard Economic Studies 43. Chap. II ff. Harvard University Press, 1934.

† Cervantes illustrates this fact in his use of treasure and treasure fleets in *Rinconete y Cortadillo* and *El Celaso Extremeno.*

ultimately the importation of treasure in exchange for goods sapped the economic vitality of the country and augmented the Price Revolution, handicapping the entire export industry. Historians have generally agreed that American gold and silver fanned the flames of Hapsburg imperialism, added to the zeal with which Spanish rulers defended the Catholic faith against Protestant and Mohammedan, furnished sinews of war and, in short, constituted an important factor in Spain's aggressive foreign policy. . . . So gold and silver from the Indies were a factor in the shedding of the blood of Spain – sacrificed on the altars of imperialism and religious fanaticism – on distant European battlefields. Other men, lured by the El Dorados of New Spain and the then Peru, emigrated at their most productive age. American treasure doubtless created the illusion of prosperity and thus fostered extravagance and vagrancy. One cannot escape the conclusion that the gold and silver drawn from the Indies ultimately had baneful effects on the mother country." This is brought home most forcibly in the *Fugger News Letters.**

Madrid October 1, 1569

News has just come from Seville that the fleet of eight sails arrived safely from the Spanish Main at St. Lucar on September 28th. These eight ships are supposed to be bringing 340,000 ducats for the King and over 1,500,000 in gold for merchants and private individuals. It is hoped that an additional fleet will arrive next April, as many vessels which have made the Indian voyage are still due. The two fleets which came from New Spain and Peru this year brought in more than three millions, and this is good news, for in these times every penny is badly wanted. This is all I have heard up to the present except that Peru is quite quiet. God grant this may be true.

* The following extracts from the *Fugger News Letters* (first and second series edited and translated into English by Victor von Klarwill) give a convincing picture of the insolvencies during the reign of Philip II and of the effect of gold and silver from America upon the economy of Europe. In the days before printed daily newspapers these were the precursor of the *Wall Street Journal.* These letters were edited at Augsburg, to which they came from the branch banking houses and correspondents in every city in Europe. They were issued in Latin, French, Italian, Spanish and German and distributed to all the other correspondents in the same way that the various Washington *News Letters* are sent to subscribers today. Published from 1568 to 1605, they filled 28 closely printed volumes in the Court Library at Vienna. Subscription was at the rate of 30 florins a year.

from Madrid the 26th day
of September, 1583

The fleet from Spanish India, praise be to God, arrived upon the 13th day of this month without mishap. It carries a shipment of about 15,000,-000's. It is said that they unloaded and left a million in Havana, because the ships were too heavily laden. This is a pretty penny, which will give new life to commerce.

from Venice 12th day
of January, 1590

News reaches us from Lyons that letters from Lisbon of the 18th day of December of the past year report the arrival in Seville from New Spain of the fleet with eight millions in gold. More ships are expected to arrive shortly, which had to remain behind on account of storms. They are bringing a further four millions. This cause for the delay in the arrival of the first ships is the fact that they took their course several degrees higher than is their wont in order to escape the English cruisers who were waiting for them on the usual degree. The other ships have probably taken their course along other degrees for the same reason.

Venice July 8, 1594

We hear from Spain that the King of India is dead and has left His Sacred Majesty of Spain forty millions in gold. The Indian fleet would seem to be bringing more wealth than ever before, to wit: 25 millions in gold of which twelve millions are for His Majesty and thirteen for private individuals.

from Antwerp the 15th day
of October, 1594

This week there have arrived here two couriers who were dispatched hither in great haste from Seville. They bring letters of the 20th day of September in which there is written that a Spaniard Pedro Perez Pardo has failed for 100,000 some aver 150,000 ducats. He is said to have drawn large sums on Martin Perez Barron and on Antonio Gallo of Salamanca in promissory notes. They have been informed that they are not to accept the bills of exchange which are accepted daily by the ordinary in Spain. Such insolvencies and difficulties are to be expected considering these ruinous days of war. The same letters contain news from Seville, that the fleet from New Spain and Peru is expected there within 18 or 20 days. It is said to carry 17 millions of silver; and it is unknown how much gold, as well as 1300 *arobas* of carmine and all kinds of other wares. 170 ships there be in all. May the Lord permit that this fleet land in happiness and safety. This will be of much comfort to the traders of Spain and other places, for the prospects are poor and fraught with peril for the merchants.

from Rome the 8th day
of April, 1596

Letters from the Spanish Court dated the 8th day of March report the arrival in Seville of three galleons laden with two million gold pieces and 500 casks of crimson lake, which the year before remained behind in Porto Rico on their way from India. In Porto Rico 5 Spanish ships have run against two English vessels and captured one of these. When informed by the sailors that Drake with the rest of his fleet was not far away, two of the five Spanish ships again returned to Porto Rico. The other three were overtaken by Drake and burnt whereupon he made bold to land near that spot. The inhabitants, however, put up resistance and killed about 400 of his men, the famous buccaneer Zacaria being among the number. Drake thereupon sailed for the Indies.

from Rome the 29th day
of March 1597

It is written from Madrid on the fourth day of the month that the King has published a decree whereby no silver coins are to be exported from the realm. He has also ordered that the reals which before were worth 30 maravedi, are henceforward to be changed for 40 maravedi. The King has also signed with his own hand the deed of the loan of Herr Fugger and confirmed it by a decree. But for the other merchants the situation is still unfavorable.

The relation of this glut of metal and its attendant price revolution to the history of art and art collecting cannot be overlooked. For there gradually emerged from it a new and totally different point of view concerning works of art than had been known in the Middle Ages and the Renaissance. During those centuries the collector, except where he possessed a humanistic interest in gathering the antiquities of Greece and Rome, was primarily a patron. His relation to the artist was, to a great extent, that of master to servant. There was seldom a broker or dealer or other middleman to stand between them. The artist was attached to the household of the prince and received in return for the execution of works of art commissioned by the patron a substantial wage, his living and certain perquisites which varied according to the estimation in which he was held and the liberality of his host. Rarely was a monetary value placed upon the completed work of art itself. The early contracts invariably provided for compensation for the artist, payment likewise at a fixed rate per day or week for his assistants, and a schedule of costs, particularly for the more precious minerals from which the colors were ground and for the gold leaf applied to the background of the panel. Faces and hands were usually paid for at a higher rate than draped figures; framing and mounting were also specified.

This attitude had so long prevailed, and was, to be sure, continued in Spain well into the reign of Philip II. The continued wars of Charles V and of his son had impoverished not only the court but the nobility of most of Europe. The new middle-class millionaire or profiteer offered a ready market to the princes who had inherited over several generations the cream of the artistic production of the Renaissance. Moreover, the inflation of credit during the first half of the sixteenth century, through the operations of the free Bourse at Antwerp, demanded new and more mobile collateral than the cumbersome and obsolete mortgages on real property then current. Quite suddenly the third and fourth generations of Renaissance patrons found themselves obliged to put a value on the pictures and other objects of art which they had inherited and to sell them as dearly as possible to replenish the family fortunes.

Thus it is safe to say that modern collecting as we know it today dates from the crash in 1557 which followed the frenzied stock market boom of the mid-century. For the first time since the days of ancient Rome do we see in operation the law that high prices are paid for works of art in inflationary periods and collections are liquidated in deflationary periods. Spain under Philip II had reached the point at which the United States has now arrived – of having cornered the gold supply of the earth. But then, since navigation was too primitive to reship it to America and put it back in the mine (for the idea of burying gold and forgetting it at Fort Knox had not yet been thought of), there was nothing to do with it but plaster it on the altars of churches and upon the screens and ceilings of private chapels. It is not by chance that the style of architecture of Spain and Portugal in the later sixteenth century derived its name of *plateresque* from *plata*, the Spanish word for plate.

Philip as heir apparent had visited Italy in 1548, where he summoned Titian "most peremptorily" to meet him in Milan. Four years later they met again at Augsburg, where the painter was working upon a number of portraits and commissions for Charles V. Titian was seventy-five, Philip a youth of twenty-three, and his admiration for the artist knew no bounds. While Titian was employed on the *Gloria* and the *Mater Dolorosa* of the Prado for his father, Philip commissioned a series of mythological compositions for his private cabinet which he had planned in emulation of the palaces of the Doria and Borromeo where he had visited. These included the *Danaë*, the celebrated pendants of *Diana and Actaeon* and *Diana and Callisto* in Bridgewater House, and the *Rape of Europa* in Mrs. Jack Gardner's collection at Fenway Court in Boston, the loveliest and most perfectly preserved Titian in America.*

In addition to these pagan themes, Philip ordered from the Venetian a number of religious compositions illustrating, among other things, the *Martyrdom of Saint Lawrence* and the deeply moving *Christ Carrying the Cross with Simon of Cyrene* of the Prado. Also among the famous canvases from Titian's brush is the *Jupiter and Antiope*, the so-called *Venus del Pardo* of the Louvre which hung originally in the Pardo Palace in the outskirts of Madrid in Philip II's day.†

That Philip was not always prompt in his rewards to his favorite artists is indicated in a letter addressed to the King by the aged Titian six months before the latter's death, in which he reminds him of the long service he had rendered:

Twenty-five years have elapsed, in which I have never received anything at all in recompense for the many paintings I have sent to your

* These pictures were later given by Philip IV to Charles I on his visit to Spain as Prince of Wales to sue for the hand of the Infanta. When the marriage fell through the pictures remained in Spain until Philip V sent them to France.

† His grandson, Philip IV, gave it to Charles I of England from whose collection it was sold by Parliament in 1653. It was purchased by the Cologne banker, Jabach, for £500 for the account of Cardinal Mazarin and has since remained in France as one of the greatest treasures of the Louvre.

PIETER BREUGEL THE ELDER: THE HARVESTERS (DETAIL)

Painted in 1565 for Nicholas Jonghelinc of Antwerp, the picture was recorded in the inventory of Archduke Leopold Wilhelm (1659, no. 586), who brought it from Brussels to Vienna. It was listed in the Belvedere as late as 1809. During the nineteenth century it turned up in Paris in the Doucet collection and in the Jean Paul Cels collection in Brussels. The Metropolitan Museum of Art acquired it in New York in 1919 for $3370.

Majesty on various occasions . . . and having reached a great old age, not without great privations, I now beg with all humility that your Majesty will, with your usual compassion, deign to give your ministers such directions as may seem to you most expedient to relieve my want; so that, since Charles V, your Majesty's father (of glorious memory), numbered me amongst his familiar, nay most faithful servants, by honoring me beyond my deserts with the title of *Cavaliere*, I may be able, with the favor and protection of your Majesty — true image of that immortal Emperor — to uphold as it deserves the name of *Cavaliere*, which is so honored and esteemed by the world; and so that it may be known at the same time that my labors during so many years for the most serene House of Austria have been appreciated, thus causing me, with more joyful heart, to spend the rest of my days in the service of your Catholic Majesty.*

Despite his instinctive parsimony, the traditional formality and splendor of the court of Burgundy was carried on by Philip in the most minute detail. Simple, even frugal, in his own tastes, he nevertheless demanded magnificence and prodigality in his entourage; his household numbered more than fifteen hundred persons, its officers were nobles of the highest rank. His bodyguard consisted of three hundred men — one hundred Spaniards, one hundred Flemings, one hundred Germans. There were forty pages, sons of the most illustrious families in Castile. The Queen, when there was one, and Philip was married four times, had her own establishment on the same scale. Traditionally the court painters served the King as palace functionaries and even at this late date, as in the days of Philip's ancestors at Bruges, were attached as members of the royal household. Their workshops were in the Treasury, adjoining the palace and connected to it by a secret passage to which the King possessed the key.† Antonio Mor (Sir Antonio More as he was known in England), whose still and formal, but nonetheless elegant, style endeared itself to the protocol of the Spanish court, held the position of court painter for a number of years, enjoying until his disgrace the unusual confidence and intimacy of the King. Cumberland, in his *Anecdotes of Eminent Painters in Spain*, gives an account, taken from Palomino, of Mor's relations with Philip that sheds a pleasant light on both their characters:

* Harris, *op. cit.*, 22.

† Harris, *op. cit.*, 23.

He [Mor] was next despatched by the emperor to England, to the court of Mary to take the portrait of that princess previous to her espousal with Philip. Mor employed all the flattering aids of his art in this portrait, and so captivated the courtiers of Spain with the charms of Mary's person, that he was required to make copies of his picture. . . . Having enriched himself in England, he returned to Spain, and entered into the service of Philip II who made slaves of his friends, and friends of his painters; and treated Mor with great familiarity. This great artist wanted discretion, and he met the King's advances with the same ease that they were made; so that, one day whilst he was at his work, and Philip looking on, Mor dipped his pencil in carmine, and with it smeared the hand of the King, who was resting his arm on his shoulder. The jest was rash, and the character to which it was applied, not to be played upon with impunity. The hand of the King of Spain (which even the fair sex kneel down to salute) was never so treated since the foundation of the monarchy. The King surveyed it seriously awhile, and in that perilous moment of suspense, the fate of Mor balanced on a hair; the courtiers who were in awful attendance, revolted from the sight with horror and amazement. Caprice, or perhaps pity, turned the scale; and Philip passed the silly action off with a smile of complacency. The painter, dropping on his knee, eagerly seized those of the King and kissed his feet, in humble atonement for the offence, and all was well, or seemed to be so; but the person of the King was too sacred in the consideration of those times, and the act too daring to escape the notice of the awful Office of the Inquisition; and they learnedly concluded that Antonio Mor, being a foreigner and a traveller, had either learned the art magic, or more probably obtained, in England, some spell or charm wherewith he had bewitched the King.

Mor fled to Belgium, leaving to his pupil Sanchez Coello the task of completing the royal portrait gallery, by then consisting of forty-seven pictures in all, including eleven by Titian (primarily those of the Hapsburg family painted at Hapsburg and Vienna) and fifteen by Mor. The appearance of the gallery of the Pardo Palace (destroyed by fire in 1605) has been reconstructed by Miss Harris,* based upon the contemporary accounts of Argoto de Molino. The portraits were all of the same size and three-quarter length, revealing a little less than

* Harris, *op. cit.*, 23.

down to the knees, encompassing the whole hall, "so that the room is of the greatest beauty and dignity that his Majesty possesses." Titian's portraits of the Emperor and the Empress occupied the principal position and below the frieze of portraits hung Vermeyen's views of Charles's campaigns as well as paintings of the principal cities of his empire. In another room the *Venus del Pardo* hung above a door, and possibly for this reason escaped the fire that destroyed the portrait gallery. The corridors were filled with landscapes and hunting scenes including a series of eight fantasies (*disparates*) by Bosch and the *Descent from the Cross* by Van der Weyden, now in the Escorial, of which the two panels of the *Crucifixion* in Philadelphia in the Johnson Collection are possibly companion pieces.

But it is in the Escorial, that massive and sinister monument to royal prerogative and Catholic mysticism, part monastery, part fortress, which contained a palace, a college, a church, a library and sepulcher, that Philip's tormented soul, torn in the eternal conflict between grandeur and simplicity, found its fullest expression. It took him three years to find a suitable location and in 1563 he laid the first stone with his own hands. For nearly forty years he poured into it "such a combination of breadth of vision and spiritual limitation, of magnificence and severe austerity, as to produce a work on which opinions are as divided between admiration and censure, as they are about its author himself. The Escorial was built in fulfillment of a vow, and the plan of the building is that of a grill, the symbol of Saint Lawrence's martyrdom."

The cement had hardly dried upon the cornerstone before the King put his ambassadors and agents to work to furnish these buildings which Juan Bautista of Toledo and Juan de Herrera had designed. The garrets and cellars of Italy and Flanders were ransacked for works of art — tapestries, sculpture, painting, ironwork, as well as masterpieces of goldsmith's work for the chapels and church vestments. But aside from the problem of purchasing works of art with Philip's new American gold, the ambassadors were charged with finding, particularly in Rome, in Florence, in Genoa and Venice, artists who would come to Spain to attach themselves to the royal household.

Among these were Federigo Zuccaro, Luca Cambiaso, Pellegrino Tibaldi, as well as many others of mediocre talents. Paolo Veronese refused to come and certain of the better artists stayed only for a brief visit. Zuccari, who had been too extravagantly recommended, was allowed to return after three years. Although the King, whose parsimony was steadily increasing, gave him a reward of 2000 gold scudi as well as a pension of 400, he ordered his paintings to be destroyed, or moved to less conspicuous surroundings. "It is not," said Philip, "his fault." And José de Sigüenza, in explaining El Greco's failure to please the King, wrote of the *Theban Legion*, commissioned for an altar in the church of the Escorial, that it "did not please his Majesty – it is not much – for it pleases few, although they say it is a great art, and that its author knows a lot, and there are excellent things to be seen by his hand. In this there are many opinions and tastes. . . ."

As Justi has quite properly observed, the failure of Philip to achieve a full measure of success in the pictorial decoration of the Escorial was more the fault of the period in which he lived than a shortcoming in his own taste. When he was able to acquire fine things he did so without regard to price, and his disposition for the works of Bosch – he had acquired a number from the collection of Felipe de Guevara, whose father had presented Philip's great-aunt Margaret with Van Eyck's *Arnolfini* portrait – proved the independence and discernment of his eye. When he visited the convent of Miraflores and saw the tomb by Gil de Siloe, he was ready to admit, "We have not accomplished anything in the Escorial." It is curious to what extent frustration pursued the monarch, in little things as well as in affairs of state. Although he tried persistently, he was never able to purchase the Ghent altarpiece of the *Adoration of the Lamb* by the Van Eycks and was obliged to have a copy made of it by Michiel Coxie. In his dealings with Spanish artists Philip showed his preferences and his prejudices. Sanchez Coello, Juan Fernandez, the Dumb Painter of Pamplona, and Carbajal were among his favorites; Morales he could not suffer because of his conceit. And it is curious to note that although Philip lived at the moment when the art of *estofado* was at its height, the polychrome sculpture for which the Museum of

Valladolid is so justly famous, not a single piece is mentioned in his inventories.

Philip's last days were passed in the agony of a horrible disease (probably he had inherited a tendency to cancer from his father) which he bore with the resignation and fortitude of the monk he longed to be. Lying on his bed he looked through the aperture in the wall of his room into the chapel and, like Robert Browning's Bishop of Saint Praxed's, was able to

> . . . hear the blessed mutter of the Mass
> And see God made and eaten all day long.

Philip II had fulfilled the destiny of Charles V and, more than that, had lived to witness the inevitable bursting of the bubble whose premonition had unquestionably driven his father to the point of abdication and retirement from the world at Yuste. The Spanish Empire crumbled almost as quickly as it had arisen. From his deathbed Philip could look upon the wreckage of his magnificence. The country was bankrupt, oppressed, corrupted and all but ruined. Both agriculture and craftsmanship had suffered from the expulsion of the Moriscos. Fishing had been ruined by the commandeering of all boats for warfare. The Invincible Armada was no more. Manufactures had ceased from pure inertia. The population, already drained by the Americas (where the Spanish soldiery was decimated by malaria and yellow fever), was thinned still further by war, disease and exile, though it was not until some time later that the seriousness of its decline became apparent. Nor were social classes any better. Excess of luxury in the upper classes contrasted with miserable poverty in the lower. "The King's religious fanaticism bred hypocrisy in his Court and people, and testimonies of every kind speak of a moral tone that sank continually lower." *

On the thirteenth of September, 1598, this Most Catholic King, whose curiously grudging prodigality had set the pattern for the collecting and patronage of art by all future monarchs, was laid to rest in a simple coffin made of wood from one of the ships which

* Henry John Chaytor, "Spanish History to 1492," in *Spain*, ed. by E. A. Peers, Dodd, Mead & Co., 1929.

had fought the heretics. Whether from meanness or from love of art, he had directed that his catafalque not be raised too high lest the smoke from the candles blacken the ceiling of his favorite church. The Venetian ambassador, announcing Philip's death to the Doge, wrote:

Ha abborrito la vanità in tutte le cose.

BOOK FOUR

The Spread of Italian Culture and Finance in France, England and the Netherlands

CHAPTER I

The School of Fontainebleau

STRANGELY enough, French taste, like *le style français* which it inspired, reached its most conscious maturity not in the Middle Ages but in the Renaissance under the tutelage of Italian and Flemish masters brought to France for the express purpose of creating a national art. Although the Romanesque and Gothic, particularly in the Île-de-France and in the great duchies, always betrayed by their purity an essentially French character, it still remained a product of communal religious inspiration that recognized no border. National consciousness had been awakened no more in the intellectual life of the people than it had been in the political mind of Europe. The arts, as well as the economy of France, bore allegiance to the feudal system, dependent upon the Church for authority, and upon the whim of the repentant warrior for patronage. It was, nevertheless, a satisfactory system for the time since it gave value to one currency of opinion and taste based upon a unifying religious belief. Moreover, it was destined to serve an international Christian society, ordained by God, in which the occupations and rewards were prescribed in advance and happily accepted by persons in all walks of life.

Personal individuality was the supreme gift of the Italian peninsula to the modern world. Except in the case of François Villon it was virtually as unknown in France in the early fifteenth century as was the concept of the national state. But the chaos of the Hundred Years' War and the miserable failure of the rival princes to acknowledge the obligations of nobility – although these obligations had none the less been clearly set forth by codes of chivalry and oaths of fealty to which they had long sworn – brought about in the closing years of the century a unification of political purposes. A new set of loyalties permitted the rise of the individual and a receptivity to new ideas; hitherto this had been impossible until Louis XI, the "Spider King," had first broken the back of the nobles by defeating Burgundy at the Battle of Nancy in 1477. Louis's orders for tearing down their fortified castles, the *châteaux forts* which for many centuries had been secure behind moats and battlemented towers, produced immediately upon their ruins the gracious, open, garden villas of Touraine. These became known as the *châteaux de plaisance*. The courtiers of Charles VIII and Louis XII when they descended upon the plains of Lombardy were immediately seduced and conquered by the humanism and antique glory of an imperial and papal Italy. Not since the days of the Crusades had the French mind succumbed so completely to foreign influence.

Naples was the seaport from which the Renaissance was shipped to northern Europe. The booty, which comprised every type of antiquity and work of art, entered France by Marseilles and Montpellier. Provence, having entertained the papal court for seventy long years, had never found it difficult to adapt the graceful manner of Italian life to the smiling terraces of the Côte d'Azur or of the Rhone Valley. René of Anjou, the uncrowned King of Naples and Sicily (whose lifelong struggle with Aragon for control of southern Italy was defeated by his passion for the arts), must be credited with introducing the Renaissance into France. Poet, painter and musician, this romantic and highly civilized monarch employed Francesco Laurana and countless other artists of the *quattrocento*. Being also Count of Provence, he was the liaison between the cultivated, easy-going nobility of the south and his Valois and Orléans relations in the Île-de-France and Burgundy. Though he had little or no part in the actual development of a new French style (for he was first and last a product of a feudalism which merely indulged its fantasy with the fruits of the new learning), René, like the Duc de Berry and Matthias Corvinus, King of Hungary, was one of the last standard-bearers of flamboyant, High Gothic patronage to whom the idea of a national style, as a necessary instrument in maintaining the prestige of the State, had not yet occurred.

It is nevertheless an interesting paradox that it was René, together with another Angevin supporter, Jacques Coeur, who established the framework upon which the royal collections in France were to be imposed. This merchant of Bourges, the epitome of French championship of the middle classes, played a role which, although less romantic, was, to be sure, no less important than that of Joan of Arc. For in putting his business experience and acumen at the disposal of the French crown, he, like the Maid, contributed to the downfall of Burgundy and the expulsion of the British from the Continent. In doing this, however, he lost no opportunity to gratify an appetite for art that was both Gothic in its flavor and Medicean in its rapacity.

Political events in the first quarter of the sixteenth century were shaping for something new. The growing menace of the Hapsburg power, the struggle between Francis I and Charles V for the imperial election and the domination of Italy, had captured the attention of French art and letters. From this newly developed consciousness of the destiny of France in Europe was born *le style français*. This was to be the primary concern of all artistic and literary endeavor from Francis I to Colbert and even to Napoleon: how to absorb, refine and clarify the intellectual discoveries of the Renaissance both in Italy and in the northern countries, and to blend them into a single, vigorous art, built upon the framework of an instinctive logic, and stamped with a good taste that was to be one of the nation's principal assets in later centuries.

The crucible in which were fused and blended the various essences of the French style – Tuscan, Flemish, Lombard – was the court of Francis I and his son Henri II, at Fontainebleau, to which were called the leading painters, sculptors and decorators of the time. The *chefs d'ateliers* in painting were the Italians, Primaticcio and Niccolò dell'-Abbate. Jean Goujon, a Norman, was employed for many important commissions. Andrea del Sarto and Benvenuto Cellini, the Florentine goldsmith and professional philanderer, were brought to France, while the aged Leonardo left Milan only to die, according to legend, in the arms of the King at Amboise. The marriage of the Dauphin, the future Henri II, to Catherine de Medici had further established a taste in favor of the Italians; but, though the structure of the Fontainebleau tradition is built upon an Italianate plan, it is always tempered by French logic and Flemish color.

For the first time in northern Europe court life, as it was to be lived and enjoyed until the fall of the Bastille, came into its own. There was a definite departure from the chivalric code of the Middle Ages, a code dependent upon a chain of fealty ascending to the monarch through a hierarchical succession of nobles and courtiers. The French court now wished to accomplish two things: it sought to put the courtier directly in touch with the monarch, cutting through the hierarchy of nobility, and to cast the spotlight directly upon the person of the king. Thus the sovereign held a much tighter grip upon the members of his household. At the same time, he had to give them in return both bread and circuses. Catherine de Medici wrote to her son, Charles IX, "I have heard your grandfather, Francis I, say that to live peaceably with the French and have them love their King, he must keep them amused for two days in the week, otherwise they would find themselves more dangerous employment."

Perhaps Francis's love of art was partially inspired by the double desire to put on a good show for his subjects and to prove to the foreign embassies that France could hold her head among the most civilized peoples of the earth. Certainly if this was the King's purpose he spared no effort or expense in achieving it. His court, unquestionably the most brilliant gathering of lords and ladies that Europe had ever seen, was always *en fête* and always splendidly dressed. Women, of course, completely dominated court life, monopolizing the interests of the King, because he was the first to recognize the truth of Brantôme's epigram that "a court without ladies is a garden without flowers." Luxury was carried into every department of life from the jewels and silk worn by the King himself to the furnishings and appointments of his apartments. The King's revenue amounted to roughly some 3,000,000 crowns, while the schedule of expenditures included "50,000 crowns for dress and current expenses; 50,000 crowns for his petty pleasures [*menus plaisirs*]; 200,000 for the upkeep of the guards; 70,000 for the Queen and her household; 300,000 for the Dauphin; 40,000 for sport." But the extravagance and liberality of the King, particularly to his mistresses, brought him into debt within a year of his accession to the tune of nearly 1,300,000 pounds.*

* Louis Batiffol, *The Century of the Renaissance*. G. P. Putnam's Sons, 1916, p. 98.

Yet this pleasure-loving monarch was not without his serious side and he gave unstinted support to the coterie of humanists who, under the leadership of Guillaume Budé, brought about the creation of the King's Library and the foundation of the Collège de France. According to Louis Batiffol, "Francis threw himself heart and soul into the scheme." Venice was at this time the great market for manuscripts from Greece and Italy. Guillaume Pellicier, the French ambassador to the Republic, was charged with the task of collecting as many of these manuscripts as possible; money was apparently to be no object. In 1541 Pellicier dispatched four boxes of Greek manuscripts to Fontainebleau. Guillaume Postel went for the same purpose to the Near East, to Constantinople, Syria and Egypt, reaping a rich harvest. A host of others were employed both abroad and in the Palace of Fontainebleau, where, under the roof in a little room above the gallery painted by Il Rosso, Budé laid the cornerstone of the present Bibliothèque Nationale. To this nucleus Francis added the other libraries which he had inherited; the late medieval books from Blois comprising, in addition to the traditional patrimony of the French crown, the collections of the House of Orléans, the Visconti-Sforza library brought back from Milan by Louis XII, and the books assembled by his own ancestors of the House of Angoulême.

The wealth which Francis lavished upon his palaces at Chambord, at Fontainebleau, and in Paris at the Louvre, Saint-Germain and the Château de Madrid, opened the way for French predominance in architecture and decoration. And from the combined efforts of the Flemings and Italians whom he had brought to France emerged the eclectic and elegant style of the French Renaissance. But the decoration by these artists alone was not enough. Francis, having tasted the blood of patronage, determined to outshine his hated rival Charles V and left no stone unturned in bringing to his court the best that the Golden Age had to offer. To him, besides the credit for the creation of the National Library, must also be given the credit of having brought together the core of the national art collections of the Louvre which in later centuries were to be so greatly amplified by Richelieu, Mazarin, Colbert and Vivant-Denon. The private cabinet in the top story of the Pavillon Saint-Louis at Fontainebleau contained his vases, medals, statuettes and drawings; the walls and formal apartments of the palace were lined with the tapestries and sculptures acquired for him by his agents in Italy and in the Levant.

The picture collection of Francis I has been the subject of a recent study by Jean Adhémar of the Bibliothèque Nationale, who shows that when he ascended the throne in 1517 there were already some fine pictures in the collection of his predecessor Louis XII, including the *Madonna of the Rocks* by Leonardo. The year previous, 1516, Leonardo had come to Paris bringing with him the other works in the Louvre: the *Mona Lisa*, and the *Virgin and Saint Anne*, which the King took over in 1520 upon the artist's death. Raphael, too, was urged to come to France but his duties at the papal court prevented his accepting repeated flattering proposals. Nevertheless during his lifetime several of his pictures found their way to Fontainebleau. A *Saint Margaret*, painted for the King's sister, Queen Marguerite of Navarre, was recorded there in 1540; the large *Holy Family* and the *Saint Michael* of the Louvre, commissioned by Pope Leo X, were given by Cardinal Lorenzo de Medici to his aunt, the future Queen of France. Cardinal Bibiena, for whom Raphael had painted in 1518 *Jeanne d'Aragon*, in all probability presented the portrait to the King while he was Papal Legate in France. Le Père Dan also cited in his inventory other works by Raphael in the palace at Fontainebleau.*

* Jean Adhémar, "The Collection of Francis the First" in *Gazette des Beaux-Arts*, July 1946. The same writer has generously communicated in a letter the following notes concerning the beginnings of the royal collections:

"*Le cabinet de curiosités du Roi.*
À Fontainebleau, où il remplace vers 1562 le 'trésor des bagues' envoyé alors à la Bastille. Au dernier étage de la tour du Donjon. Des armoires tendues de velours vert fermées par des rideaux de taffetas de même couleur. Singularités reçues par François Ier et Henri II: hydre à 7 têtes envoyée par la République de Venise; antiquités et inscriptions du Midi de la France (Nîmes, Fréjus, Vienne, Arles); camée de St. Sernin de Toulouse; 'Jules César en cuivre' offert par la ville de St. Quentin; 'médailles antiques, argenterie, animaux, vêtements et ouvrages des Indes et pays étrangers.' Vêtements et instruments ramenés par J. Cartier du Canada, 'bourses, chausses et aiguillettes de Barbarye,' objets rapportés d'Orient par Viller, Belon etc. Le Ier garde est Thevet, sous Charles IX. Thevet, grand voyageur, y joint les curiosités recueillies dans ses voyages en Orient et en Amérique: des plantes rares séchées, des animaux exotiques empaillés, des médailles anciennes, des fragments de sculpture antiques, des pieds de momie d'Egypte, des 'robes de plumages des sauvages d'Amérique.'"

The Cabinet remained in approximately this form until the seventeenth century when it was described by le Père Dan. The bulk of it was kept at the Tuileries in Paris. In 1666 it was removed to the *Bibliothèque Nationale*. (*Cf. Archives de l'art français*, 1853, III, p. 35, and *ibid.*, 1907, pp. 330–336.)

Andrea del Sarto likewise came to France in the year of Francis's accession and during his brief sojourn painted a number of pictures, including the *Charity* of the Louvre. According to Vasari he had first attracted the attention of the King with a *Christ Supported by Two Angels* (known today only through an indifferent engraving by Agostino Veneziano) which was sold to Francis by a dealer for a sum four times that which the artist had originally received. It may have been the rankling injustice of this transaction which took the artist suddenly back to Tuscany, where he spent upon himself the money which the King had given him to buy pictures and sculptures for the royal collection. This is the incident celebrated so charmingly by Alfred de Musset in his play *André del Sarto*. The *Bacchus* of the Louvre, long considered a *John the Baptist* by Leonardo, is possibly one of the pictures which he later made for the King of France as an act of retribution. Salviati, another Tuscan, painted several pictures for the King. Michelangelo had been urged to come to France and had even accepted Francis's invitation. But he was too absorbed with his work ever to leave Rome. Among the other artists who were represented at Fontainebleau were Fra Bartolommeo, Sebastiano del Piombo and Bronzino. Venetian art was conspicuously absent. The antagonism between France and the Venetian Republic had dampened the French monarch's ardor for pictures of this school. A portrait of the King by Titian, done on the order of Aretino from a medal, was, in fact, the only work by this master in the royal collection until the time of Colbert.

Francis's interests were not confined to the Italian School. His fancy for the Flemings, particularly for the droll works of Bosch and the elder Breugel, was quite marked, and these he kept in his more intimate apartments together with the small family portraits, painted on panel, which had come down with the royal succession.

The most precious works in the collection, it seems, were gathered together at Fontainebleau in the *appartement des bains* beneath the *Galerie François Ier*, but while various accounts of it exist, no one of them agrees with any of the others. It is a safe assumption, however, that the pattern of decoration and presentation was deeply influenced by the palace on the right bank of the Arno which the Grand

Duke of Tuscany was bringing at this time to such unprecedented heights of luxury. In this Florentine palace (the Pitti) most of the King's agents and artists had spent long weeks and, since it was the avowed purpose of the King of France to create a setting for his authority equal to or even surpassing that of any prince of Europe, it was quite natural that the household of the Medici, who had by this time been in the business longer than any other family of Maecenas, should be the model.

The King's interest in antique sculpture was equal to his taste for pictures; in 1540 Primaticcio and Jean Goujon were dispatched to Rome to make plaster casts of the great statues of Greece and Rome, particularly those newly discovered figures which were being unearthed through the budding zeal of the archaeologists attached to the Apostolic Household. Among the 133 cases sent back to France were reproductions of the *Laocoon*, the *Apollo Belvedere*, the famous *Ariadne* and *Cnidian Venus* of the Vatican and the group of the *Nile*.

The spread of Italian ideas in France was due in the largest measure to the influence of Catherine de Medici. She was the wife of Francis's son, Henri II, and mother of three kings of France, Francis II, Charles IX and Henri III. To this daughter of the Florentine banking house a love of beautiful things was instinctive and all-absorbing, though her motives in indulging her tastes were partly political. Suffering untold humiliation and indignities at the hand of the King's mistress, Diane de Poitiers (whose patronage of French and Flemish craftsmen for the decoration of her fabulous Château d'Anet had already become almost legendary), Catherine determined to show the superiority of Italian culture at the expense of her husband's countrymen. France at this time had been torn asunder by the religious wars and Catherine symbolized both the power and the authority of her pontifical cousins, Leo X and Clement VII. It was, moreover, to the advantage of the Italian financiers (whose gradual absorption of French commerce and industry ultimately resulted two generations later in the revolt of the Fronde against Cardinal Mazarin) to have this Florentine Queen of France set the fashions of Italy in the new ripe markets of western Europe. "Your Court," she wrote to her son Charles IX, "must acquire the dignity and decorum I formerly found there."

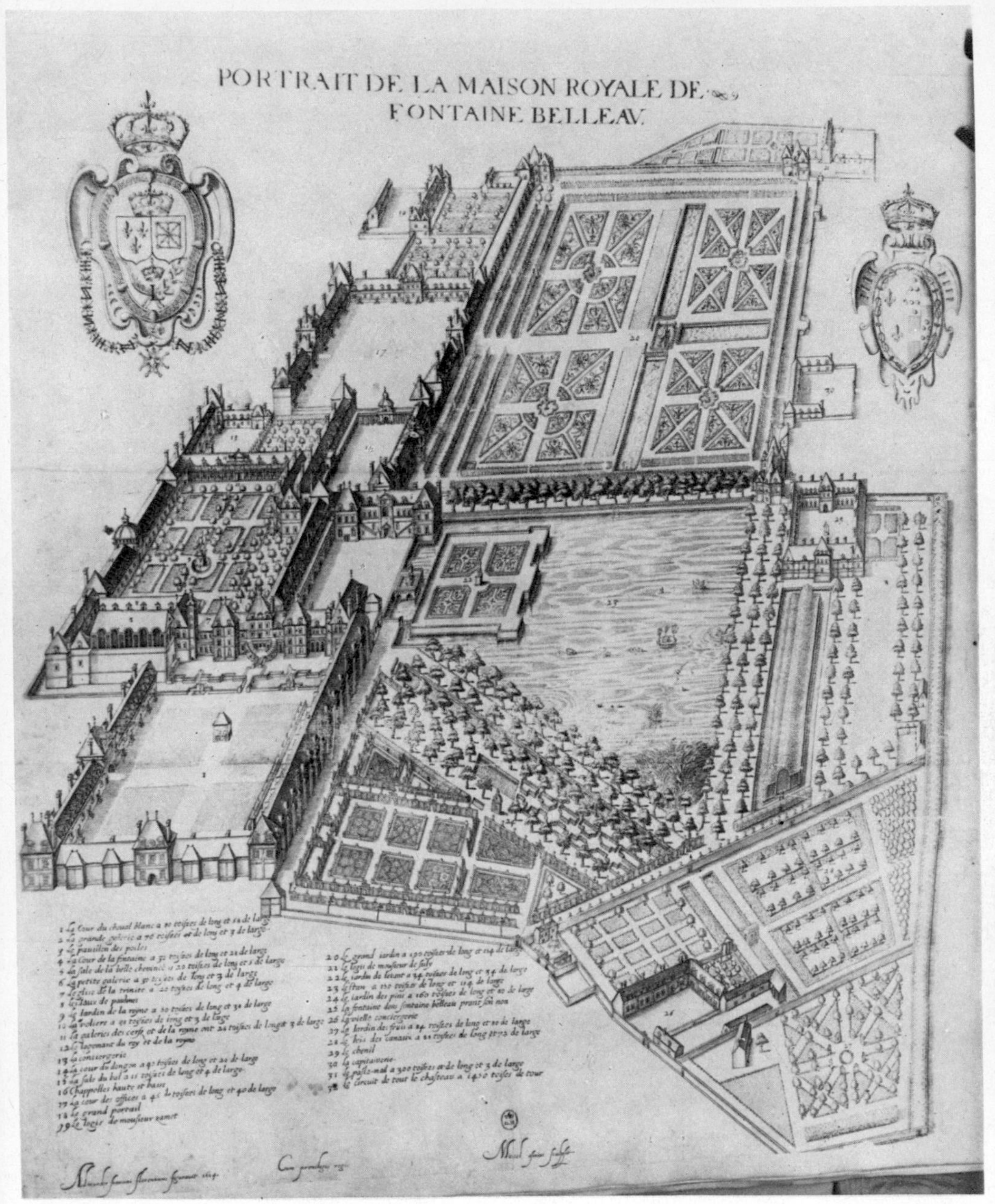

THE PALACE AT FONTAINEBLEAU, c. 1590

After an engraving in the Bibliothèque Nationale

"A PIECE OF ARRAS OF THE JUDGEMENT"

Woven after cartoons by Hugo van der Goes to celebrate the marriage of Charles the Bold and Margaret of York, who are portrayed. Formerly in collections of Richard II, Cardinal Wolsey and Manoel I of Portugal. Worcester Art Museum

By means of splendor and magnificence, by the imposition of a rigorous and stilted *etiquette* which prescribed the minutest details of the King's existence, she ingrained in her sons the sense of absolutism which the Hapsburg and Stuart dynasties were afterwards to share with the Bourbons in the Augustan period of the seventeenth century.

Catherine's "town house," the Hôtel de Soissons, occupying the site of the present Paris Bourse, was a perfect setting for this Italian princess. De Thou described her as *femina superbi luxus*, "a woman of superb luxury." This is, indeed, confirmed by the inventory taken at the time of her death, which shows that she was deeply in debt. Her tapestry collection was proverbial: Flemish, French and Italian, some 129 pieces in all, illustrating the histories of Hannibal, of Vulcan and the more popular pagan and Christian legends. They were rotated, for the hôtel could not accommodate them all at one time; certain panels hung for special occasions while their places on the walls were occupied with other examples or with stamped and painted Cordovan leather of which the Queen had more than 130 pieces. Forty-four Oriental carpets – an almost unheard-of luxury for those times – covered the floors. The house itself was a marvel of the cabinetmaker's art: fine woodcarving, and panels with enamels and Venetian mirrors were set into the walls. One room, the *Mirror Cabinet*, had more than a hundred glasses set in this way, and in the *Enamel Cabinet* were featured 74 portrait medallions of princes, lords and ladies over a foot in height as well as allegories from classical mythology and the lives of the Saints. The popularity of enamels, chiefly from the manufactory at Limoges, was very great. A famous set of such enamel portraits from Diane de Poitiers's Château d'Anet was removed in the French Revolution and has been since preserved in the Church of Saint Pierre at Chartres.*

The furniture and draperies which the Queen lavished upon her palace were equally magnificent, reflecting the rather flamboyant Baroque taste that was gradually creeping into the palaces of the Grand Duke of Tuscany. Ebony chairs inlaid with ivory and mother-of-

* Splendid examples may be seen in this country at the Metropolitan Museum, the Frick Collection in New York, the Walters Gallery, Baltimore, and in the Taft Museum in Cincinnati. It is not unlikely that in these American institutions are many of the 259 enamels, listed in Catherine's inventory, which were dispersed in later years.

pearl, tables and mantels of onyx and black and white marble, vied with satins and velvet; brocades trimmed with crêpe and gold braid served to accentuate the mourning from which the Queen never was willing to emerge after the death of her husband. Her taste in painting was more in the direction of the *bibelôt* and miniature than in the nobler canvases collected by Francis I. Yet she possessed, none the less, 476 paintings of which more than two thirds were portraits. Many of these, painted on commission by Clouet and Corneille de Lyon, are part of the incomparable collection of French paintings of the Louvre, and in her private cabinet were listed "twenty genre pictures and landscapes." The Queen's fancy for porcelain and *objets de vertu* led to the forming of a group of objects now the glory of the *Galerie d'Apollon:* ewers, goblets, *flacons*, gondolas of carved rock crystal and *pietra dura*, Chinese lacquers – among the earliest of these importations to Europe from the Orient – bronzes, ivories, busts and antique medals, fans and Venetian glass. "All of the latest treasures of the most enlightened taste of the day were to be found in her possession." * Of the celebrated ware of Bernard Palissy, the Queen's cabinets held 141 examples, ornaments, bowls and dishes. "There was nothing precious," says Batiffol in summarizing the inventory, "even to books and manuscripts, of which she did not covet a valuable collection. She left 4500 volumes and 776 manuscripts, bearing witness, not to her erudition – the manuscripts were in Latin and treated of austere subjects, and she never read them – but to her eclecticism. We have said nothing of her jewelry and gold and silver plate."

* * * * *

While the court favored the taste of Catherine, it must not be supposed that French nationalism in scholarship, encouraged to a great extent by the Calvinist scholars and the Protestant nobility of Provence and Languedoc, did not manifest itself in the large number of collections which were being formed outside the inner circle at Fontainebleau. French humanism was as characteristically French as it was unlike the Italian variety, and the collections themselves, their general contours and their contents, differed from those of Renais-

* Batiffol, *op. cit.*, 334.

sance Italy as widely as French literature differed from that of Tuscany.

The works of Erasmus and the humanists of the German Reformation had entered France through Geneva and Basel, bringing in their train a point of view and a curiosity in regard to science and the natural world quite foreign to the southern mind, which had accepted the world and its pleasures for what they were worth without particular reference to conscience. In fact the French, who have always filtered morality through a fine screen of logic (thus enabling them to codify and order their emotions and their intellectual processes), placed a particular stamp upon the thinking of the sixteenth century which affected the Catholic writers of the religious wars almost as greatly as it did the Protestants. There were really two separate movements within the French Renaissance. The one attempted to look for knowledge and the liberation of the spirit from the empirical and religious tradition of the Middle Ages through a recovery of the classics; the other proclaimed for the first time the dignity of art by which the architects and poets, as well as painters and sculptors, "no longer regarded themselves as mere craftsmen but as creators and scholars of a high order."

Three years after the accession of Henri II, that is by 1550, Marot, Rabelais and Margaret of Navarre had died and with them the lingering medievalism of late Gothic France. It was at this point that the French passion for methodology, and for the *plan général et définitif*, was allowed to gratify itself to the full. For in the short span of a single generation Joachim du Bellay's *Défense et illustration de la langue française*, Calvin's French edition of the *Institution Chrétienne*, Jacques Amyot's *Plutarch's Lives* and Étienne Pasquier's *Recherches de la France*, the first scientific history of France based on source material, saw the light of day. It was moreover the period of the *Pléiade*, that brilliant constellation of poets who, under the leadership of Ronsard, formed the *Académie du Palais*. It was also the age of Michel de Montaigne, in whose essays and travel diaries are to be found the fullest picture not only of the mind and soul of his day but of the general ambience in which the French intellect developed as a specially bred product of the human race.

Such society became naturally enough a breeding place for bibliophiles. The tradition had, in fact, already been long established; the early Valois kings and in particular Louis XII, Diane de Poitiers, Catherine de Medici, Francis's charming young Protestant sister, Margaret Queen of Navarre, Amyot, Ramus, the Constable of Bourbon, d'Urfé and de Thou had all followed in the footsteps of the great abbots of Luxeuil, Fleury, Cîteaux and Cluny, in their untiring zeal to bring together the finest libraries possible of manuscripts and printed books. But the king of all book collectors, one who has been immortalized through the centuries and who moved so surely and so silently through the reigns of Louis XII, Francis I, Henri II and Charles IX, was Jean Grolier. In 1510, he succeeded his father to the post of Treasurer of the Duchy of Milan, in 1534 he was ambassador to Rome and later served as Minister of Finances. But despite the burden of public office, his life and his fortune were centered in his beautifully bound books. Possibly no other Frenchman of the sixteenth century had the advantages or the opportunity to indulge his tastes so fruitfully. Certainly none has survived so deep in the affection of the collectors of odd volumes of the present day.

The private art collections of the French Renaissance stand midway, like their humanist collectors, between the princely galleries of Florence and Urbino and the *Wunderkammern* of the German Empire. As Bonnaffé points out, the cabinet was the obligatory ornament of every fine and elegant abode. No more than the scholar or the reigning sovereign could the private gentleman refrain from expressing his interest in *la curiosité*. Henri Estienne in his *Apologie pour Hérodote* defined *la curiosité* as "*le sens de l'entendement. Je vous laisse penser,*" he adds, "*ce qu'il diroit des acheteurs d'antiquailles desquels le monde est plein aujourd'huy.*" And in a poem of 1539 Gilles Corrozet describes a cabinet which might have been any one of several hundred of the epoch:

Cabinet rempli de richesses

. . . . .

Cabinet sur tous bien choisi,
Paré de veloux cramoisi,
De drap d'or et de taffetas,
Où sont les ioyaulx à grandz tas

Et les bagues très gracieuses
Pleine de pierres précieuses.

. . . . .

Cabinet de tout accomply,
Cabinet de tableaux remply
Et de maintes belles ymages
De grandz et petis personnages,
Cabinet paré de médailles
Et curieuses antiquailles
De marbre, de iaphe, et porphyre.

. . . . .

Cabinet où est le buffect
D'or et d'argent du tout parfaict,
Cabinet garny de ceinctures *
De Dorures et de Bordures
De fers d'or, d'estocz, de tableaulx,
De chaines, de boutons très beaulx,
De mancherons, de braceletz,
De gorgerins et de colletz,
De perles d'Orient semez,
De gants lamez et parfumez,
De museq, plus cher qu'or de ducat,
D'ambre fin, de savon muscat,

. . . . .

Et parmi tant diuers ioyaulx,
Sont les riches et gros signeaulx,
Les patenostres cristallines
De perles et de fin rubis.

. . . . .

Puis les mignons et bons cousteaulx,
Les forcettes, et les ciseaulx,
Le mirroir, la gente escriptoire,
Le chappeau, l'eschiquier d'yvoire,
Les heures pour servir à Dieu,
Brief en ce beau et petit lieu,
Sont tant d'aultres choses ensembles
Qu'impossible le dire il semble.†

* Belts or tiers of objects about a room.

† Gilles Corrozet, *Blasons domestiques* [*pour la décoration d'une maisons honneste*]. Nouvelles éditions, Paris. Société des bibliophiles françois, 1865.

Throughout France these cabinets appeared; at Rouen, Lyons, Tours, Dijon, Troyes, Rodez (and again at Besançon, where the more elaborate palace of Cardinal Granvella was situated) could be seen these collections of good, bad and indifferent – collections in which a fierce and growing French nationalism was in endless conflict with the official Italianism of the court at Fontainebleau and Paris. Who these collectors were and what they each possessed are relatively unimportant, for while they contributed immensely to the ultimate crystallization of the French intellect and taste in the *Grand Siècle* of Louis XIV, they were sufficiently far removed from the main currents of Italian culture and finance to have left little impression on the future history of collecting or of the composition of our present-day museum.* To be sure, certain individuals stand out in high relief against the general uniformity of these cabinets: Guillebert de Metz has the distinction of being the first private collector not connected with the court in the city of Paris in the fifteenth century. Florimond Robertet, Finance Minister under Charles VIII, Louis XII and Francis I, whose inventory was drawn by his widow in 1532, was a man of great taste and owned a large bronze of Michelangelo's *David,* commissioned originally by the Signoria of Florence. The statue has disappeared although Michelangelo's drawing of it is in the Louvre. Rascas de Bagarris's fine cabinet of medals and antiquities was coveted by Gabrielle d'Estrées and was acquired by her royal lover Henri IV, who shared her passion for medals and engraved gems. They now form part of the Cabinet des Médailles of the Bibliothèque Nationale. Claude de Peiresc, the great scholar and antiquary of Aix, devoted his life to study and travel, giving equal attention to archaeology and art, to numismatics and natural history. He was the close friend of Rubens and of most of the savants and artists of his time. In 1598 the King gave him the Abbey of Notre-Dame de Guistre, near Bordeaux. He was looked upon as the oracle of all matters concerning archaeology or the arts. "*Aucun navire,*" wrote Dom Jacob, "*n'entrait dans un port français sans amener pour son cabinet quelque*

* Adhémar has cited the collection of Tiragneau, a friend of Rabelais, where "*les habits de sauvages composés dextrement de petits coquillages, de racines d'escorce, et leurs velus chapeaux, leurs brayes, leurs tapis et leurs panaches beaux, que tu as arrangés en ceste chambre ornée où tu tiens, Tiragneau, et Péron et Guinée.*"

rareté d'historie naturelle, des marbres antiques, des manuscrits coptes, arabes, hébreux, chinois, grecs, des fragments trouvés dans les fouilles de l'Asie et du Péloponnèse."

But the pattern is generally the same. Two chroniclers of these collections have left us, in addition to the copious inventories, several of which were again published by Parisian antiquaries in the 1860's, fairly glowing accounts of their contents. A German humanist, Zinzerling, writing under the pseudonym *Jodocus Sincerus*, visited with characteristic Teutonic thoroughness all of the collections of which he had heard in France, and they were legion. These he noted and rated according to the principle later made famous by Karl Baedeker. Among those which especially pleased his fancy were the cabinets of an apothecary at Montpellier, Laurent Catelan, and of le Sieur Agard, a goldsmith at Arles, to whom he gives the triple star. Agard's principal claim to fame, however, does not seem to lie in the quality of his collection, though it must be admitted that his Greek and Roman antiquities from the region of Arles and Nîmes, of which he had several hundred, were very fine, but rather in fact that he published in 1611 a catalogue of his collection. Agard must have been a very pompous and tiresome man whose counterpart is met with today in any city of the world, for he was convinced that among his masterpieces he had found, right under the noses of his more professional colleagues, a Cupid in alabaster "*bien poly de la main et artifice de Michael l'Ange où son nom est gravé au dessous la teste.*" * Unlike most collectors, however, he must have suspected that he was a bore for he added, at the end of his detailed descriptions, the remark that he had omitted describing "*milles autres galanteries pour éviter trop grande Prolixité.*" †

* *Discours et Roole des medailles et autrez antiquitez tant en pierreries, gravures, qu'en relief, et autres pierres naturelles admirables, plusieurs figures et statues de bronzes antiques, avec autres statues de terres cuites à l'Egyptienne, et plusieurs rares antiquitez qui ont este receuillies, et à présent rangées dans le cabinet du Sieur ANTOINE AGARD en Provence. A Paris, 1611.*

† By the time that the second chronicler, Dom Jacob, had published his *Traité des Bibliothèques* in 1644 there were more than a hundred private libraries in Paris worthy of recording. Jacob Spon listed 80 "principal cabinets" in 1673 and twenty years later de Bléguy, in his *Livre Commode*, names 134 *fameux curieux.*

CHAPTER II

The Rise of Collecting under the Tudors

ROGER FRY once observed that "three English kings have shown an appreciation of the arts. Two, Richard II and Charles I, were put to death, and George IV, living in less brutal times, only had the windows of his state coach broken by an infuriated mob. A taste for art is clearly dangerous for a wearer of the British crown." However this may be, Their Majesties' most loyal subjects have proved themselves over and over again to be among the most sensitive and astute collectors of art the world has ever seen. And even to this day the country houses of England are the richest mines remaining to tempt both dealer and connoisseur. The record of a single day's turnover at Sotheby's or Christie's, taken at random in any season of any year, bears more than ample testimony to the British genius for discerning acquisition.

The Renaissance, it is true, arrived late in England, which had had little time for the luxuries of the mind during the Hundred Years' War. Then, hard upon their expulsion from France in 1453, the English were plunged for a generation into civil strife between the White Rose of York and the Red Rose of Lancaster. The old nobility who had terrorized Plantagenet England lost their lands and power and thus made way for the new gentry created by the Tudors. They had raised their fortunes and their fabulous country houses upon the ruins of the feudal castles and monasteries which Henry VIII, in a fit of anger at the marital obstructions placed in his path by the Pope of Rome, suppressed. When the King, in addition to the priory of Christchurch, Aldgate, bestowed upon his Chancellor, Thomas Audley, the Abbey of Walden, later known as the Palace of Audley End, Fuller quaintly called it the "first cut in the feast of abbey lands and a dainty morsel – an excellent receipt to clear the Speaker's voice and made him speak clear and well for his master." These country abodes that preceded and heralded the Age of Elizabeth were essentially the last generous outpouring of medievalism – a medievalism which in Italy had already disappeared and in France and Spain was rapidly being transformed into an international style. But the internationalism was not to take hold of Britain for another hundred years when Sir Christopher Wren grafted Palladian architecture upon the Gothic heritage of this island people. A cursory examination of the great houses of the period – Knole House, Hatfield, Penshurst Place, the Leicester buildings at Kenilworth, Longleat and Haddon Hall – reveals that for all their magnificence and prodigality the Italian ornament imposed upon the Anglo-Saxon brick had no more value than a graceful Latin epigram in the poems of Spenser, Ben Jonson or Sir Philip Sidney.

When the peace and plenty of Elizabeth came and the English were at last able to taste the fruits of Italian culture, they had already digested a different type of humanism, that of the Protestants of northern Europe. However, in the eloquent words of Trevelyan, "the Elizabethan system, the grand finale of Tudor triumph, was as much a triumph of the Renaissance as of the Reformation. The two became one, and partly for that reason Shakespeare's England had a charm and lightness of heart, a free aspiring of mind and spirit not to be found elsewhere in the harsh Jesuit-Calvinist Europe of that day. And at the same auspicious moment England's old song of the sea became a new ocean song. The Elizabethan adventurers – Drake, Frobisher, Hawkins, Raleigh and the rest – were sailing the wide world, discovering 'islands far away,' opening to their countrymen at home new realms of hope and fancy – committing indeed crimes in Ireland and in the slave-trade but without knowing that they were crimes or what the dreadful consequences were to be in the deep of time. The music of the Elizabethan madrigal and the lyric poetry to which it was wedded, expressed the reasonable joy in life of a people freed from medieval and not yet oppressed by Puritan complexes and fears; rejoicing in nature and the countryside in whose lap they had the felicity to live; moving forward to a healthy agricultural and mercantile prosperity, and not yet overwhelmed by the weight of industrial materialism." *

* G. M. Trevelyan, *English Social History*. Longmans, Green, 1944 (2nd ed.), p. 97.

It was upon the growing prosperity of the sixteenth century that the great art collections of the time of Charles I were built. If Horace Walpole was able to censure the Good Queen's grandfather because he had left England in a semibarbarous state, one must at least thank the royal miser for having filled the coffers which his descendants later emptied so brilliantly for the arts.

Henry VII seems never to have laid out any money so willingly as on what he could never enjoy, his tomb – on that he was profuse; but the very service for which it was intended, probably comforted him with the thought that it would not be paid for till after his death. Being neither ostentatious nor liberal, genius had no favour from him: he reigned as an attorney would have reigned, and would have preferred a conveyancer to Praxiteles. Though painting in his age had reached its brightest epoch, no taste reached this country. Why should it have sought us? The king penurious, the nobles humbled, what encouragement was there for abilities? What theme for the arts! barbarous executions, chicane, processes and mercenary treaties, were all a painter, a poet, or a statuary had to record – accordingly not one that deserved the title (I mean natives) arose in that reign.*

The courtiers were formed in the image of their sovereign and Sir Thomas Gresham, perhaps, symbolizes the type of businessman who was to conduct the destiny of the British Empire for several centuries to come. Like his father before him, he was Royal Agent to Queen Elizabeth, a successful trader, and in combining the many fiscal and promotional functions of the crown acted "as liaison officer between the mercantile and royal interests." But both Greshams, whose influence and authority at court covered the reigns of Henry VIII, Edward VI, Mary and Elizabeth, built upon the financial genius of the founder of the Tudor line in whom strains of both Lancaster and York were joined. Their policy was to establish the greatness of the nation upon world trade and they were content to leave the embroidery of art and fashion to the courtiers of a later age. Fortunate indeed it was for England that this militant spirit of economy prevailed, for the country, torn apart by the tribulations of the fifteenth century,

* Horace Walpole, *Anecdotes of Painting in England*. Henry G. Bohn, 1862. 3 vols. I, 48.

underwent a period of transition as the Middle Ages ended and the Renaissance began. English trade in the sixteenth century, says Trevelyan, "though again on the increase after a period of relative stagnation, still ran in its medieval channels along the coasts of Northern Europe, with a new thrust into the Mediterranean, for vent of cloth. In spite of Cabot's voyage from Bristol to Newfoundland in the reign of Henry VII, the wider outlook across the Atlantic did not greatly affect Englishmen before Elizabeth was on the throne." But when it did, England experienced a series of economic crises similar to those of Spain. Although England was not involved in the reigns of Henry VIII and of Edward and Mary in great international wars to the extent that Spain was in the time of Charles V and Philip, internal circumstances such as the steady advance in the birth rate, and the hunger for land caused by overpopulation in relation to concentration of large acreage in the hands of a few landlords, brought about a situation of high rents with a corresponding inflation of the general price structure. Between 1500 and 1560 prices generally had doubled and the cost of food had nearly trebled.*

The ability of the English to adapt themselves to the new social and economic conditions of the sixteenth century was probably a factor which contributed very greatly to the form in which Anglo-Saxon democracy was later to express itself. The gentry, from early Tudor times, spread out into the professions and into trade – "the old school tie" not being worn until well on into the nineteenth century when the new aristocracy of the Industrial Revolution required something more than a university accent to distinguish them from their fellow commoners. From the gentry emerged that unique product of this island culture – the British civil servant, the backbone of a governing class. Thus, since the English gentleman was not necessarily

* Trevelyan, *op. cit.*, 119, points out that "there were three stages of the price rise under the Tudors: (1) 1510–1540. Owing to production of silver in Germany, and the dispersal of Henry VII's hoarded treasure by Henry VIII, prices of food stuff go up 30 per cent. Other prices less. (2) 1541–1561. Owing to Henry VIII's debasement of the coin (and a little later to American silver mines beginning to take effect) prices of all kinds rush up about 100 per cent more. (3) 1561–1582. Owing to Mary's better finance and Elizabeth's recoinage, prices are stabilized and rise more slowly. Then in early Stuart times American silver mines again raise prices to peak 1643–1652; after that prices fall."

confined to the protocol and limitations of a courtier's existence to which the *petite noblesse* of the Continent were automatically condemned, he was able to roam the world at will and to take his education in far places. Very early in the development of modern England we see the grand tour becoming part of the acknowledged procedure, not merely for the titled "swells" who later were to take their seats in the House of Lords, but for the sons of notaries and Anglican clergy as well as merchants. Italy quite naturally was the chief object of their pilgrimage and there they came to know the culture of the Renaissance and were in fact a part of it. Padua and Bologna at times were considered to be virtually English universities. So strongly did the Italians feel upon the point that Roger Ascham, Queen Elizabeth's tutor, quotes in his *Schoolmaster*, published in 1563, a proverb current throughout Europe, "*Inglese italianato e un diavolo incarnato.*"

With Bluff King Hal the arts took a turn for the better and Horace Walpole was able to declare:

> The accession of this sumptuous prince brought along with it the establishment of the arts. He was opulent, grand, and liberal – how many invitations to artists! A man of taste encourages abilities; a man of expense, any performers; but when a king is magnificent, whether he has taste or not, the influence is so extensive, and the example so catching, that even merit has a chance of getting bread. Though Henry had no genius to strike out the improvements of latter ages, he had parts enough to choose the best of what the then world exhibited to his option. He was gallant as far as the rusticity of his country and the boisterous indelicacy of his own complexion would admit. . . . Francis I was the standard which these princely champions (of the Field of the Cloth of Gold) copied. While he contended with Charles V for empire, he rivaled our Henry in pomp and protection of the arts. Francis handled the pencil himself. I do not recall that Henry pushed his imitation so far; but though at last he woefully unravelled most of the pursuits of his early age (for at least it was a great violation of gallantry to cut off the heads of the fair damsels whose true knight he had been, and there is no forgiving him that destruction of ancient monuments, and Gothic piles, and painted glass by the suppression of monasteries; a reformation, as he called it, which we antiquaries almost devoutly lament), yet he had countenanced the arts so long, and they acquired such solid foundation here, that they were scarce

eradicated by that second storm which broke upon them during the Civil War, – an era we antiquaries lament with no less devotion than the former.*

Walpole to the contrary, Henry VIII produced but a poor imitation of the artistic patronage of his contemporaries, Charles V and Francis I. Holbein was the only first-class painter whom he attracted to his court and the royal collection, consisting of 150 pictures, mostly portraits by this German master who had been introduced by Erasmus, was certainly the most mediocre royal cabinet in Europe. No giants of Italy are recorded there either by their presence or by their works save Pietro Torregiano, the stormy Florentine sculptor who had fled to Spain after breaking Michelangelo's nose in a studio brawl, and who was imported to work on the unfinished tomb of Henry's father.

The admirable catalogue to the Exhibition of the King's Pictures at Burlington House (1946–1947) † sheds much needed light upon our knowledge of Tudor collections. There is little that survives to tell the story – the *Wilton Diptych* in the National Gallery painted for Richard II and the latter's portrait in Westminster Abbey. In the National Gallery of Scotland in Edinburgh is a large altarpiece by Hugo van der Goes with portraits of James III and his Queen. For the rest we must reconstruct our idea of the earliest royal collections of Edward III and his successors from what remains of the Palace of Westminster, the Abbey itself, King's College, Cambridge, and the chapels of Eton and Windsor. Raphael's *St. George* ‡ was brought to England by "the Perfect Courtier," Baldassare Castiglione, when he came to receive the Order of the Garter for his patron, Guidobaldo, Duke of Urbino.

For the cabinet of Henry VIII the inventories published recently by the Courtauld Institute § show that he had, in addition to the Mabuse *Adam and Eve* and Holbein's *Noli me tangere*, a variety of

* Walpole, *op. cit.*, I, 57.

† *Catalogue of the Exhibition of the King's Pictures* (1946–1947), Royal Academy of Arts, London. Pub. by H. M. Stationery Office.

‡ Now in the National Gallery, Washington.

§ *Three Inventories of Pictures in the Collections of Henry VIII and Edward VI*, ed. by W. A. Shaw, London. Allen and Unwin, 1937.

religious pictures "executed at the command of the king, illustrating themes of Protestant propaganda, one of which represented the *Pope Stoned by the Four Evangelists*." Holbein's chief commission, the portrait of the King, perished in the fire at Whitehall in 1698. "But his art is splendidly represented," the catalogue continues, "in the series of drawings in the Royal Library at Windsor and by fine portraits acquired by later Kings, from Charles I to George IV. The famous portrait of Christina of Denmark, later Duchess of Milan, painted by Holbein for Henry VIII when he was seeking her hand in marriage, was apparently given to Lord Arundel soon after the King's death, and is now in the National Gallery."

Cardinal Wolsey, on the other hand, whose pride hastened the anticlerical revolution that accompanied his fall, was the only collector on the continental scale. To be sure, certain of the great nobles and bishops such as John Fisher, Bishop of Rochester, the Archbishops of Canterbury, Cranmer, Parker and Laud, Lord Burghley, the Earl of Leicester and Sir Robert Bruce Cotton were soon to go down in history among the most distinguished of bibliophiles. But in the broader field of art collecting there was no one of the front rank between Wolsey and the accession of the Stuarts. The Cardinal's household consisted of nearly a thousand persons and "he marched in state with silver pillars and pole-axes borne before him. . . . Here was a prince indeed," says Trevelyan, "of the cosmopolitan hierarchy of Europe before which men had bowed for centuries." His visits to the Holy See had inoculated him with the contagion of its Medicean occupants. It was an age of building, not so much of churches but of princely dwellings and public buildings. Harrison, in his *Description of England*, styled Henry VIII as "the onlie phoenix of his time, for fine and curious masonrie." If this is true of Windsor, of Hampton Court and Saint James's, how much more truly could it be said of the colleges at Oxford and Ipswich which were the recipients of the Chancellor's endowments. There was no article of beauty or of luxury that the Midas finger of Wolsey did not touch.

The reigns of Edward, Mary and Elizabeth, save for the continued progress of architecture and the decorative arts to furnish the splendid houses of the new nobility, were singularly lacking in that grandeur of taste which the Stuarts were to usher in. Even Walpole, combing the notebooks containing the lifelong researches of George Vertue in the records and archives of the crown, was unable to list more than a handful of imported Hollanders and Flemings, together with a group of portrait and miniature painters, like Nicholas Hilliard and Isaac Oliver, who were to give a moderate distinction to the beginnings of the British School.

The chief employment of these portraitists seems to have been the taking of likenesses of the Queen. "There is no evidence," says Walpole, "that Elizabeth had much taste for painting; but she loved pictures of herself. In them she could appear really handsome; and yet to do the profession justice they seem to have flattered her the least of all her dependents. There is not a single portrait of her that one can call beautiful. The profusion of ornaments with which they are loaded are marks of her continual fondness for dress, while they exclude all grace, and leave no more room for a painter's genius than if he had been employed to copy an Indian idol, totally composed of hands and necklaces. A pale Roman nose, a head of hair loaded with crowns and powdered with diamonds, a vast ruffle, a vaster fardingale, and a bushel of pearls, are the features by which everybody knows the pictures of Queen Elizabeth. Besides many of her majesty," Walpole concludes on a less apologetic and disdainful note, "we are so lucky as to possess the portraits of almost all the great men of her reign; and though the generality of painters at that time were not equal to the subjects on which they were employed, yet they were close imitators of nature, and have perhaps transmitted more faithful representations than we could have expected from men of brighter imagination." *

Strange it is that while some of the greatest literature the world has ever known was being produced, the plays of Shakespeare and the King James version of the Bible, the visual response of this great creative people should seem to have been on such a minor key. But the yeast was already working; the fifty years following the death of Elizabeth were to bring to her shores, if only temporarily, the greatest galaxy of masterpieces that a cultivated taste has ever witnessed.

* Walpole, *op. cit.*, I, 150.

CHAPTER III

The Glorious Sunburst of the Stuarts – Charles, Buckingham and Arundel

"THE trumpet of art blows louder through time and space than any other trumpet." If Charles I never so consciously expressed this opinion as did French Louis, he was none the less aware of it, for no other monarch has supported the absolutism of his authority so completely upon the all too brittle framework of a great collection. The Reverend Mr. Dallaway, who edited Horace Walpole's *Anecdotes*, quotes Mr. Gilpin as follows:

. . . if Charles had acted with as much discernment as he read, and had shewn as much discernment in life as he had taste in the arts, he might have figured among the greatest princes. Every lover of picturesque beauty, however, must respect this amiable prince, notwithstanding his political weaknesses. We never had a prince in England, whose genius and taste were more elevated and exact. He saw the arts in a very enlarged point of view. The amusements of his court were a model of elegance to all Europe; and his cabinets were the receptacles only of what was exquisite in sculpture and painting. None but men of the first merit in their profession found encouragement from him, and these abundantly. Jones was his architect and Vandyck his painter. Charles was a scholar, a man of taste, a gentleman and a Christian; he was everything but a king. The art of reigning was the only art of which he was ignorant.*

Perinchief, the King's biographer, further attested that

his soul was stored with a full knowledge of the nature of things; and easily comprehended almost all kinds of arts that either were for delight or of a public use. . . . He was skilled in things of antiquity, could judge of medals whether they had the number of years they pre-

* Walpole, *op. cit.*, I, 261.

tended unto; his libraries and cabinets were full of those things on which length of time put the value of rarities. In painting he had so excellent a fancy, that he would supply the defect of art in the workman, and suddenly draw those lines, give those airs and lights, which experience and practice had not taught the painter. . . . He encouraged all parts of learning, and he delighted to talk with all kinds of artists, and with so great a facility did apprehend the mysteries of their professions, that he did sometimes say, "He thought he could get his living, if necessitated, by any trade he knew of, but making of hangings"; although of these understood much, and was greatly delighted in them, for he brought some of the most curious workmen from foreign parts to make them here in England.*

The King had shared his interests with his elder brother, Prince Henry, who died young, leaving to Charles a fine collection of works of art and the uneasy task of wearing a crown intended for another. Their father, James I, had no taste whatever except, possibly, the same bad taste of which Walpole accused him in literature. His court painters, and he had a procession of them, were men whose talents endear them only to archivists and antiquaries. How came his sons to have so much discernment and passion for the arts is unexplained and it is, indeed, impossible to separate out their several treasures, for the inventories compiled both before and after Charles's execution merely list the royal collections together, though the King and his favorite, Buckingham, whose own collections were outdistanced only by those of Charles and Arundel, were always grateful to Prince Henry's memory. *A Catalogue and Description of King Charles the First's Capital Collection of Pictures, etc.*,† is based primarily upon a faulty list by Vanderdort, a Dutch portraitist and medalist originally in the service of Prince Henry, who had succeeded as Surveyor of the King's Pictures. The document, confused by Vanderdort's ignorance both of the English tongue and of the subject of his responsibility, is interesting more for the general view which it gives of the artistic glory of the reign than for accuracy of its information. The collections of the

* Walpole, *op. cit.*, I, 262.

† From an original MS. in the Ashmolean Museum, Oxford, prepared for the press by Mr. Vertue and printed by W. Bathoe, 1757. With an advertisement by Horace Walpole, Esq.

King, which at high-water mark had reached the astounding total of 1387 pictures and 399 sculptures, were amassed by the greatest industry on the part of the monarch (and his agents and ambassadors abroad) from many sources.*

Cross, whom Carducci refers to as Michael de la Crux, was the King's agent in Spain. Already, upon the occasion of his visit as Prince of Wales to Madrid with Buckingham, Charles had spent nearly half a year amusing himself at the Spanish court and sitting to Velasquez; he devoted most of his waking hours to the enlargement of his cabinet. Here it was, according to Stirling-Maxwell, that "his ambition was awakened to form a gallery worthy of the British crown – the only object of his ambition which it ever was his fortune to attain." † While in the Spanish capital he purchased the collections of the Count of Villamediana and of the sculptor Pompeo Leoni which were sold at auction there during his residence. "He offered Don Andreas Velasquez 1000 crowns for a small picture on copper by Correggio, but was refused it; and he met with like ill success in his attempts to obtain the precious volumes of Da Vinci's drawings and manuscripts, from Don Juan de Espina, who excused himself on the plea that he intended to bequeath this collection to the King, his master." Many fine pictures were, however, presented to him by the King and the courtiers. Philip gave him the famous *Antiope* by Titian, his father's favorite picture, a truly royal gift; *Diana Bathing*, *Europa* and *Danaë*, works of the same master, which, although packed up, were left behind when the negotiations for the Prince's marriage with the Infanta were broken off, were included in the gift.‡

Upon his return to England and his accession to the throne, ministers, courtiers and the ambassadors of foreign powers, knowing the

* An important study, as yet unpublished, has been made of the documents in the Royal Library at Windsor by Brian Reade of the Victoria and Albert Museum, South Kensington. It is hoped that these researches, which throw a new light upon the collecting habits of Prince Henry and Charles I, will soon be made available to the public.

† William Stirling-Maxwell, *Velasquez and His Works.* J. W. Parker & Son, 1855. P. 80.

‡ The *Cain and Abel* by John of Bologna, also given Charles at this time and later bestowed by him upon Buckingham, is probably none other than the marble group now called *Samson* in the collection of Sir Thomas Worsley, Bn., in Yorkshire.

King's pleasure in these things, made constant presents from their private cabinets and in their turn employed agents to scour the continental palaces for works of art. Whitlocke relates the story that "in December the Queen was brought to bed of a second daughter named Elizabeth. To congratulate her Majesty's safe delivery, the Hollanders sent hither a solemn ambassy and a noble present, a large piece of ambergrease, two fair china basons almost transparent, a curious clock, and four rare pieces of Tintoret's and Titian's painting. Some supposed that they did it to ingratiate the more with our King, in regard his fleet was so powerful at sea, and they saw him resolved to maintain his right and dominion there." Winston Churchill thus had ample precedent for lavishing the finest craftsmanship of the United Kingdom upon the Sword of Stalingrad.

Charles's principal acquisition, the greatest single coup in the history of collecting by any purchaser, prince or patron, was the fabulous hereditary collections of the Dukes of Mantua. These collections, purchased *en bloc* in two separate transactions, were finally acquired by the King's agents Daniel Nys and Nicholas Lanier for a reputed total of £80,000 in 1627 and the Mantegna *Triumphs* in 1629. The precise year is in doubt and the records show that Charles was buying heavily from other agents – twenty-three pictures of prime importance being acquired by one Froseley. * Nicholas Lanier, Master of His Majesty's Music, and a great lover of pictures, was dispatched to Italy in 1625 "to provide for him some choice Pictures." He must have made large purchases, says Sainsbury, for we find Burlamacchi, the King's banker, and the Rothschild of the day, "complaining that he is called upon to provide 'the great somme' of £15,000 to pay for these works of art." Probably Lanier related to the King the wonders of the Mantuan cabinet for he was again in Venice in 1627 and Sir Isaac Wake, the ambassador, was commanded to give Lanier "his best advice and assistance" and later to "obtain free transportation for such pictures, paintings, statues and other rarityes as had been provided in

* Brian Reade, "William Frizell and the Royal Collection" in *The Burlington Magazine*, vol. LXXXIX (March 1947), pp. 70 ff. throws an interesting light upon these early purchases of Charles I.

these parts for ye adorning of his Ma[tes] Cabinet." Next follows a series of letters from the dealer Daniel Nys * which continue faithfully the great tradition of the picture dealer's correspondence and tarnish to some extent the spontaneous glitter of the late Lord Duveen of Millbank:

Daniel Nys to Endymion Porter

Venice, April $\frac{17}{27}$–*May* $\frac{2}{12}$
1628

Illustrious Sir and most esteemed Patron:

Signior Lanier, who is the bearer of this letter, has used every care and diligence to repair and trim up the pictures procured from the young Duke of Mantua, and has caused them to be encased and conveyed, by the ship *Margaret*, in a way in which his Majesty will be greatly pleased to see them; and he will understand from him the course I have taken to obtain them. Since I came into the world, I have made various contracts, but never a more difficult one than this, and which has succeeded so happily. In the first place the City of Mantua, and then all the Princes of Christendom, both great and small, were struck with astonishment that we could induce the Duke Vicenzo to dispose of them. The people of Mantua made so much noise about it, that if Duke Vicenzo could have had them back again, he would readily have paid double, and his people would have been willing to supply the money. The Prince of Guastallo proffered half the gain, I believe, to make them a present to the Emperor (Rudolph II). The Grand Duke of Tuscany, and same of Genoa, have done the same. It seems as though some fatality had favoured me, not for myself, but for the sake of him for whom I negotiated, I mean the King of Britain. Pray God they may arrive safe in port and that his Majesty may receive a lasting enjoyment from them. In treating for them, I used every artifice to obtain them at a moderate price; as, had it been known that I was acting for his Majesty, they would have demanded so much more. At present I am in treaty at Rome to procure the picture of St. Catherine of Correggio, and hope to succeed. These wars against Monferrat are the cause of the Duke of Nevers pledging many of his jewels, but I doubt whether he will dispose of the marble statues, the list of which

* This correspondence is given in Sainsbury, Hervey and Michaelis. Cf. Bibliography.

you have had before. In case his Majesty should desire to have them, will you please to let me know, so that others may not carry them off, and I will then do all I can to procure them to the best advantage. Moreover, I beg you will be pleased to assure his Majesty, that I will speedily give him advice of all that is fine that may fall into my hands, in order that he may become the master of it; having entirely dedicated myself to his service, in all that he may judge me worthy of. Sigr. Lanier departed this evening with two pictures of Correggio, the finest in the world, and which alone are worth the money paid for the whole, God grant him a favorable voyage. I have provided him on all sides with good letters of credit. And so ending, I recommend myself to your good favour, and beg you will retain me in his Majesty's favour.

To the same:

Most Illustrious Sir:

It is now the 12th of May. The above is a copy of my last; and this serves to confirm the departure of Sig. Lanier, from whom I have letters from Bergamo of the 2nd May. He departed *via* the Grisons for Basle in good health, and with fine horses, God accompanying him throughout. He carries with him two pictures of Correggio, in tempera, and one of Raffaelle, the finest pictures in the world, and well worth the money paid for the whole, both on account of their rarity and exquisite beauty. The ship *Margaret* must now be far advanced on her voyage. I have not as yet heard that she has arrived at London, so that his Majesty may see so many beautiful and exquisite pictures. Among them is the Madonna of Raffaelle del Cannozzo, for which the Duke of Mantua gave a Marquisite worth 50,000 scudi, and the late Duke of Florence would have given the Duke of Mantua 25,000 ducatoni in ready money: the man who negotiated the matter is still alive. Then there are the twelve Emperors of Titian, a large picture of Andrea del Sarto, a picture of Michelangelo di Caravaggio; other pictures of Titian, Correggio, Giulio Romano, Tintoretto and Guido Reni, all of the greatest beauty. In short, so glorious and wonderful a collection, that the like will never again be met with; they are truly worthy of so great a king as his Majesty of Great Britain. In this negotiation I have been aided by divine assistance, without which success would have been impossible; to Him then be the glory, etc.

This letter is confirmed by the ambassador to Venice, Sir Isaac Wake, to Lord Conway, who inspected the shipment aboard the

"*Margaret* of London whereof Thomas Browne of London is master . . . indeed a tall ship, very strong & well manned with 37 mariners."

In another letter to Lord Dorchester (formerly Sir Dudley Carleton), Nys reviews what he has already done and sheds much interesting light upon the second part of the negotiations.

Your Excellency knows that I was in treaty to induce the Duke Ferdinand of Mantua to sell his pictures, who bit at it, and the Duke Vicenzo having assented, he sold them to me for 68,000 scudi, to the great astonishment of all Italy, and the extreme disgust of the inhabitants of the city of Mantua. I performed this action solely to acquire the favour of his Majesty, without having the least interest in that contract, nay, I have lost five or six months' time in negotiating, and in going backwards and forwards, and I kept Sig. Nich. Lanier in my house all that time without receiving anything. It is true that he wished to give me 500 scudi, but I would not accept them, nor do I intend to now; all that I have done is for a single object, to acquire the good favour of the King, which I value more than all things in the world. Now in treating with the Duke Vicenzo, he had reserved to himself nine large pictures of the *Triumph of Julius Caesar*, by Andrea Mantegna, and had two new chambers built in which he had arranged them.* He demanded 20,000 Spanish doubloons for them, an evident sign that he did not wish to sell them. The best informed persons told me that I had left the most beautiful behind, and that not having the *Triumph of Julius Caesar*, I had nothing at all; this touched me to the core; I did not dare say anything for fear, his Majesty knowing it might feel aggrieved; and I in part dissembled with Sig. Lanier, who, before his departure hence had treated for the marbles and statues of the Duke, with some pictures which had been discovered in certain secret chambers. They demanded for these pictures 10,000 half doubloons of Spain, and for the statues 50,000 half doubloons, but it did not appear to Sig. Lanier, or to myself, that we could give £10,000 sterling. So the matter rested. Now the Duke Vicenzo being dead, the Duke of Nevers has come into possession of them; and finding himself straitened by war, he was obliged to sell and pledge his furniture. While the Grand Duke, and the Queen Mother of France, were treating for the marbles, a messenger arrived post from Mantua to advise me of it, but I would not then make any stir about these statues and pictures which I had viewed and

* These pictures are now in the Orangery at Hampton Court.

reviewed with Sig. Lanier; not because they were not worth or sufficient, but solely because I had received no orders from his Majesty. I declined them two or three times. Signor Jiulio Caesare Zaccarello, chief minister of the Duke, who holds all his customs and his revenues, then came to Venice. He said to me, "You commit a great error in not taking the Duke's statues and pictures; they will be carried off by the Grand Duke or the Queen Mother of France." I answered. "Let them take who will, I will not." He replied, "I could get you the nine pieces of Andrea Mantegna, that is the *Triumph of Julius Caesar;* will you not determine, because I know that the Duke Vicenzo would part with them"; then I answered, "Yes, I will take them, but I will not spend more than £10,000 sterling for all the marbles and pictures, including those nine pieces of the *Triumph of Julius Caesar.*" The Duke not knowing the importance of those nine pieces was satisfied, and the Jiulio Cesare Zaccarello returned with an agreement drawn out for £10,500 sterling. There were no means of gaining time to advise his Majesty, but I knowing the worth of the statues, that all the pictures were originals, and besides that, the *Triumph of Julius Caesar* of Mantegna was a thing rare and unique, and its value beyond estimation, I thought to do his Majesty a great service and to gain his gracious favor by the transaction. I had not the least idea of any interest either in this or in the first purchase. I sought only the goodwill of the King. . . .

With this monumental and heart-rending display of altruism the greatest deal of art history was concluded. Nothing comparable to it was seen again until the purchase by the late Andrew W. Mellon of thirty-three paintings from the Hermitage, many of which, acquired by Catherine the Great from the collection of Sir Robert Walpole at Houghton, had once graced this cabinet of Charles I and the House of Mantua. Mr. Mellon paid $19,000,000 to the Soviet Government — in fact he paid for a single item more than Daniel Nys had paid to the Duke on behalf of his sovereign for the entire lot.

It would be futile to enumerate all of the pictures which the King amassed at Whitehall and in his other palaces. A partial table is given below, prepared by Dallaway for his edition of Walpole's *Anecdotes:* "In the palace of Whitehall were 460 pictures disposed in various apartments, including 102 in the Long Gallery. Those only of the more celebrated masters are here noticed."

LIMNINGS

Holbein	4	Hoskins	7
Janet	4	A. More	1
J. Oliver	13	The Princess Louisa	1
P. Oliver	14	Giovanna Garzovi	1
Hilliard	13	By unknown hands	14
Sir J. Palmer	1	Frossley	1

PAINTINGS

Albert Dürer	3	Poelenburg	4
M. Angelo da Carav.	2	Polidoro	9
Bassano	5	Pordenone	4
Annibale Carracci	2	Raphael	9
Correggio	11	Rubens	7
Guido	4	Rembrandt	3
Holbein	11	Tintoretto	7
Honthorst	9	Titian	28
Julio Romano	16	Van Dyck	16
Miervelt	6	Vansomer	2
Ant. More	5	P. Veronese	4
D. Mytens	10	Leonardo da Vinci	2
Parmegiano	7		

This table is obviously what it purports to be, a rough summary prepared in the first years of the nineteenth century without careful reference to the sources. To collate and verify the three existing lists of Charles's collections would take years of patient labor with little or no reward — for the taste of the compilers, reflecting the prejudices of their day, does not see fit to identify the "primitives" of the *quattrocento* in which (as we know from earlier accounts in Italy) the Gonzaga collections were so rich. Missing, too, is mention of that other stroke of genius, the purchase upon the advice of Rubens of the Raphael cartoons now in South Kensington. These cartoons had been sent by Leo X to Flanders as designs for tapestries in the Vatican. * Nor does it take account of the vast holdings in sculpture, and in

* The Pope paid Raphael £150 for the cartoons of the tapestries for which he later was charged £7000. Upon delivery of the hangings the Vatican lost interest in the original designs, which Rubens later found stored in the manufactory.

drawings and medals, to which casual references give but the merest suggestion of their fantastic wealth. Nor, too, does it include the classical antiquities, particularly those from the Temple of Apollo at Delphi, obtained in the Levant by Sir Kenelm Digby in the amount of £17,989, which lined the halls and galleries of Greenwich and Somerset House. The *Catalogue of the King's Pictures* today gives the following summary:

It is only in imagination that the collection of Charles I can be reconstructed, but a mere list of some of the great masterpieces which it contained and which are now scattered will in itself give an impression of its quality. Of all the painters Titian was the most magnificently represented, and it is not too much to say that almost all the best works of that master now in the Louvre, as well as many fine ones in Vienna and Madrid, were in the possession of Charles I. The list of the most important ones runs as follows: the twelve Emperors (now destroyed); the *Entombment*, the *Supper at Emmaus*, the so-called *Alfonso d'Este with Laura de' Dianti*, the *Jupiter and Antiope* (the *Venere del Pardo*), the Davalos *Allegory*, the *Man with a Glove*, another portrait and a *Holy Family*, as well as probably the *Vièrge au Lapin* (all in the Louvre); the *Saint Margaret*, the portrait of Charles V, the *Venus with an Organ Player* (in the Prado); probably the *Girl in a Fur* in the Museum at Vienna and the *Doge Andrea Gritti* in the Czernin collection; *Alexander VI before Saint Peter*, at Antwerp. To these must be added many paintings which cannot now be traced and the two Titians still in the Royal Collection, the portrait called *Sannazaro* (No. 199) and the *Lucretia* (No. 212).

Round this astonishing nucleus were grouped other works scarcely less important. Giorgione's *Concert Champêtre* (Louvre) and Mantegna's *Dead Christ* (Brera, Milan); Raphael's *La Perla* (Prado), several works by Correggio, the *Education of Cupid* (National Gallery), *Jupiter and Antiope*, and two allegories (Louvre), as well as the *Holy Family* and *Saint Catherine* (still in the Royal Collection); Andrea del Sarto's *Holy Family* in the Prado, the two great Tintorettos at Hampton Court and works by Veronese, Jacopo Bassano, Parmigianino and many other Italian artists: Gentileschi, whom the King had brought to England to decorate the Queen's House at Greenwich further brought the artists of the Seicento to his notice.*

* *Catalogue of the King's Pictures*, p. x.

The King's interest in the art of the northern countries was hardly less enthusiastic, although he acquired no such single haul as the Mantuan collection, which was, of course, primarily Italian. The nucleus comprised the Holbeins which he had inherited. He exchanged the *Erasmus* and a *Holy Family* by Titian with Louis XIII for Leonardo's *Saint John the Baptist* (later returned to the Louvre). He gave the Holbein drawings, which Queen Caroline later found in a table drawer, to the Earl of Pembroke for the Raphael *St. George* which had somehow left the Royal Collection temporarily during the intervening years. He was the patron of Rubens and Van Dyck. The former was the friend of Buckingham; the latter became the favorite of the King, residing in England from 1632 until his death in 1641. The incomparable series of royal portraits reveal the skill with which he "invested Charles himself, his Queen, and the members of the court with a restrained elegance and a dignified distinction which to posterity has become an integral part of the vision which is conjured up by this Court. How far the King and his courtiers really possessed these qualities and how far they were due to the adroit and subtle flattery of the artist it is now impossible to say, but no portraits can convey as intensely as Van Dyck's the peculiar characteristics of the English gentleman."

CHAPTER IV

George Francis Villiers—Duke of Buckingham

THE tomb of George Villiers in Westminster Abbey is engraved with the words, "The Enigma of the World." Sir Henry Wotton determined "to write the Life and the End, the Nature and the Fortunes of George Villiers, late Duke of Buckingham (esteeming him worthy to be Registered among the great examples of Time and Fortune)." Sir Dudley Carleton, one of the wittiest connoisseurs of art and ambassador at The Hague, called him "an Englishman, a Gentleman, a Soldier, and a Protestant." Lord Clarendon said of him:

> His ascent was so quick that it seemed rather a flight than a growth; and he was such a darling of fortune that he was at the top before he was seen at the bottom – as if he had been born a favorite, he was supreme the first month he came to Court.

Madame de Motteville, who met him in Paris in 1625, spread the general opinion of those who, like Sir John Oglander, considered him "one of the handsomest men in the whole world." "*Il était bien fait, beau de visage; il avait l'âme grande; il était magnifique, libéral, & Favori d'un grand Roi. Il avait tous ses trésors à dépenser, & toutes les pierreries de la Couronne d'Angleterre à se parer.*" In Spain, whither he went with the Prince of Wales in 1623, he was equally successful with the ladies. "He was," wrote Bishop Hackett, "a person whose like was not to be seen among the swarthy and low-growthed Castilians. . . . From the Nails of his Fingers – nay from the Sole of his Foot to the Crown of his Head, there was no Blemish in him. And yet his Carriage and every stoop of his Deportment, more than his excellent Form, were the Beauty of his Beauty . . . the Setting of his Looks, every Motion, every Bending of his Body was admirable. . . . No wonder if such a Gallant drew Affections to him at Home and Abroad, especially at Madrid which was a Court of Princes."

To Alexandre Dumas, *père,* most of us today owe our knowledge of the great Duke of Buckingham. But the biographies of the time recording his amours are scarcely less glamorous than *The Three Musketeers.* In 1625, Buckingham was sent as ambassador to France to bring away the future Queen of England, Princess Henrietta Maria, to be the wife of Charles I. Anne of Austria, the Queen of Louis XIII, was in the fullness of her blond beauty; she was twenty-four and tragically unhappy yet ripe for the love she did not have. The sequel was inevitable; in the words of Lord Clarendon

> [Buckingham] in his Embassy in France, where his Person and Presence was wonderfully admired, and esteem'd (and in truth it was a Wonder in the eyes of all Men), and in which he appeared with all the Lustre the Wealth of England could adorn him with, and Outshin'd all the bravery that Court could dress itself in, and Overacted the whole Nation in their most peculiar Vanities: he had the ambition to fix his Eyes upon, and dedicate his most violent Affections to a Lady of a very sublime Quality, and to pursue it with most importune Addresses; Insomuch as when the King (of France) had brought the Queen his Sister as far as he meant to do, and deliver'd her into the hands of the Duke to be by him conducted into England; the Duke in his Journey, after the departure of that Court, took a Resolution once more to make a Visit to that great Lady, which he believed he might do with privacy. But it was so easily discover'd, that provision was made for his Reception . . . he swore that he would see, and speak with that Lady, in spite of the Strength and Power of France.*

Despite the efforts of the court to prevent him, Buckingham visited the Queen. Conjecture has existed to this day as to the exact nature of their relations, yet it remains one of the most romantic and hotheaded pages of Stuart history. Certain it is that Buckingham, whatever his affections for Anne of Austria, was determined to "offend in his wantonness." He successfully achieved the mortal and lasting enmity of Richelieu – an enmity that was to affect the course of Franco-British history for two hundred years.

The great portrait of the Villiers family at Hampton Court Palace by Gerard van Honthorst presents, indeed, another aspect of the

* Charles Richard Cammell, *The Great Duke of Buckingham.* Collins, 1939, p. 257.

Duke's private life. Despite his roving eye he was a kind husband and a good father. Gardiner, the contemporary historian, wrote at the time of Buckingham's death at the age of thirty-six:

> The Duchess [Lady Katherine Manners], in truth, had no doubt of her lost husband's perfections. In the inscription which she caused to be affix'd to the monument, she spoke with sweet remembrance of his gifts of mind and body, of his liberality, and above all of his singular humanity and incomparable gentleness of disposition. To her he was still the enigma of the world, who had been styled at one time the parent, at another time the enemy of his country. She, at least, herself cherishing in her heart a warm attachment for the ancient forms of religion, could speak with wonderment, if not perhaps with half-concealed sarcasm, of the strange fate which caused him to be charged with attachment to the Papacy whilst he was making war against Papists, and be slain by a Protestant whilst he was doing what he could to give assistance to Protestants.*

* * * * *

Buckingham, although he had already reached full stature as a favorite with James I, was a man, so to speak, after Charles's own heart whom the latter emulated and supported both in taste and in liberality. Charles Richard Cammell, his most recent biographer, has claimed that "the beauty of their friendship, like its deathless devotion, has few parallels in history. In the higher fields of human progress, its fruits were the most glorious and enduring. Charles and Buckingham — or, more properly, in this admirable concomitance of culture, Buckingham and Charles — vied with one another in affectionate rivalry alike in their connoisseurship and in their acquisition of whatever was great or exquisite in art. In this, as in all else, Buckingham, the elder of the two, the stronger, the more inspired, was the moving spirit; he was the original; Charles was the emulator and perfector. But if Buckingham was the first architect of Charles's culture and the high priest of his initiation into the Mysteries of the Beautiful, it must be confessed that his disciple was a twin-spirit, his intellectual complement." † When they were in Spain together, Buckingham advanced the Prince £12,000 from the fortune King James had given him.

* Cammell, *op. cit.*, 336. † Cammell, *op. cit.*, 336.

This courtesy Charles amply repaid by turning over to him the Gianbologna *Cain and Abel* which Philip had presented to him. It was Buckingham who introduced Rubens to the English court, releasing him from his service to the King and opening the way to the great commissions for the Banqueting Hall at Whitehall Palace.

Buckingham's collections were brought together principally at York House, which he had wrested from Bacon when the latter fell from power. He used it exclusively for entertaining, although his other residences were scarcely less magnificent. "The Galleries and Roomes," wrote Peacham, "are ennobled with the possession of those Romane Heads and Statues, which lately belonged to Sir Peter Paul Rubens, Knight, that exquisit painter of Antwerp." These antiquities which Rubens had obtained from Sir Dudley Carleton in exchange for thirteen of his own pictures were only a fraction of the larger art collection Buckingham had bought from Rubens on the occasion of his visit to Antwerp in 1625.* Seven years after the Duke's assassination (by a disgruntled courtier) in 1635, an inventory was taken for his unlucky heir who, in 1649, was to see the whole "embezzled" by the Parliament. Horace Walpole's *Catalogue of Pictures belonging to the Duke of Buckingham* (published in 1758) was a revision of this document. The inventory represents only part of the collection,† listing 19 pictures by Titian, 17 by Tintoretto, 15 by Paolo Veronese, 13 by Palma Vecchio, 20 by Bassano, 6 by Holbein, 4 by Andrea del Sarto, 6 by Domenico Feti, 3 by Guido, 2 each by Leonardo da Vinci and Raphael, 4 by Mytens, 2 each by Breugel and Mabuse, and no fewer than 30 by Rubens; Michelangelo, Giorgione and Van Dyck were represented along with a score of other artists of quality, too numerous to mention here.

A feature of this inventory and well worth recording here is the room by room description of York House, the whole hung with tapestries and mirrors and lined with statuary. The full luxury of the Stuart court may be reconstructed from a summary of this tour (which Cammell has paraphrased from the original document):

* A voluminous and illuminating correspondence exists regarding these transactions.

† At the first Duke's death a number of canvases were sold to the Earl of Northumberland and to the Montagues, ancestors of the present Duke of Buccleuch.

In the Hall – Van Dyck's *Scipio* and by Titian, "one great Piece of the Emperor Charles, a copy called Titian's Glory being the principal in Spain, now in the Escurial."

In the coming in above: 22 pictures by Rubens, Guido, Bassano, Tintoret, Quentyn Metsys, van Somer, Palma, etc.

In the Great Chamber – 10 paintings by Rubens including "A Great Piece of Ceiling for My Lord's Closett" and "My Lord on Horseback." (These appear to be the *Apotheosis* pictures at Osterley Park.) Also Titian's *Diana and Calisto.*

In the Vaulted Room – 3 Bassanos, a "Hans Holbein" and a Tintoretto.

In the Sumpter Room – "the Venetians are challenged by Mabuse and by 'A Picture by the Life' of 'Raphael or Peter Aretino.' "

In the Passage by the Ladies Closet – 12 paintings by Rubens, Palma's *Jupiter and Danae*, etc.

In the King's Withdrawing Chamber, the *King's bedchamber*, *my Lord's closett* with the Giorgione and Titian's *Ecce Homo.*

In the Gallery – In all 58 pictures among which are *A Naked Man in Chaines and Tortures* by Mich. Angelo or a copy of his.

The visit concludes with the private apartments and indicates the smaller, more intimate devotional pictures.

A new note had been struck, one not met with in the history of collecting to this date – a note that blared across the Channel to arouse the envy of Richelieu and Mazarin. And yet, in reading through these lists, one wonders whether Charles was not the more sensitive and the greater collector of the two. Buckingham's contemporaries were so dazzled by the man and his magnificence that they yielded him first place. Be that as it may, another titanic figure looms into view – one who as collector and connoisseur as well as archaeologist eclipsed them both. He was called "The Father of *Virtù* in England."

CHAPTER V

The Father of *Virtù* in England

RUBENS's portrait of Thomas Howard, Earl of Arundel, from Warwick Castle, now hanging in the Isabella Stewart Gardner Museum in Boston, not only shows Rubens the portrait painter at his best but proves the sympathy which he must have felt for this extraordinary sitter. In the handsome, thoughtful face which contrasts so boldly with the shining armor which he wears, Rubens has found the pride of race and security of intellect which, despite the sadness and ill-health from which he suffered all his life, Arundel alone of the great Stuart connoisseurs possessed. Edward Walker, the secretary who accompanied Arundel to Germany in 1636, has given us another vivid portrait of him:

> He was tall of stature, and of Shape and Proportion rather goodly than neat; his countenance was Majestical and grave, his Visage long, his Eyes large, black and piercing; he had a hooked Nose, and some Warts or Moles on his Cheeks; his Countenance was brown, his Hair thin both on his Head and Beard; he was of a stately Presence and Gate, so that any Man that saw him though in never so ordinary Habit, could not but conclude him to be a great Person, his Garb and Fashion drawing more Observation than did the rich Apparel of others; so that it was a common Saying of the late Earl of Carlisle, "Here comes the Earl of Arundel in his plain Stuff and trunk Hose, and his Beard in his teeth, that looks more like a Noble Man than any of us.". . .

And again he wrote:

> All Persons strived to outvie each other in the Bravery and Riches of their Apparel and Entertainment; but this Earl kept his old Plainness, and yet wanted not the Honour and Esteem due to his Person and his Quality.

HENRY VIII

London, National Portrait Gallery

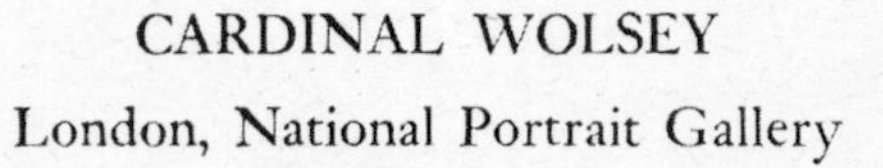

CARDINAL WOLSEY

London, National Portrait Gallery

FRANCIS I

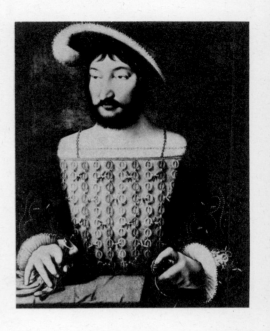

Philadelphia, Johnson Collection

QUEEN ELIZABETH

By an unknown artist. Metropolitan Museum of Art

THOMAS HOWARD, EARL OF ARUNDEL

By Rubens. Boston, Isabella Stewart Gardner Museum

MANTEGNA: THE TRIUMPHS OF JULIUS CAESAR

From the collection of Charles I. Hampton Court Palace

He was born in 1585, the sixty-one years of his life bringing him almost to the close of Charles's career upon the scaffold, though the greater part of his activity had been spent in the service of James I. Being deprived, because of his grandfather's attachment to Mary, Queen of Scots, of his rightful claim to the Duchy of Norfolk, for the restitution of which he struggled in vain all his life, Arundel became a bitter introspective man, independent and remote, yet at the same time a lover of all that was beautiful both of the mind and of the hand of man. He none the less served the King loyally both at home and abroad, where he was charged with many embassies; but his heart lay always in Italy where in his youth he had taken his bride and to which he returned to die. He was a profound and natural humanist and was, according to his librarian, Franciscus Junius, "the epitome in England of Castiglione's 'Perfect Courtier.' " *

The nucleus of his collection was a few pictures inherited along with Arundel House from the Fitz-Alans, but with consummate patience and determination the original cabinet was amplified until it held front rank – yielding in no degree in scholarship and connoisseurship to those of his two great rivals.

Arundel increased these original possessions by purchasing *en bloc* several cabinets abroad and in England, using them as a skeleton upon which to build the collection as a whole and to which he would add newly found masterpieces whenever opportunity arose. As a collector of drawings of the Old Masters he was particularly systematic and thorough, buying portfolios from his correspondents in Italy. His happiest strike was when he purchased the cabinet of Daniel Nys in Venice into which had been amalgamated the drawing collections of Mantua at the time when Nys was negotiating the sale of the Mantuan pictures for the King of England. Nys had apparently kept the drawings for himself.†

While Buckingham may have had a quicker eye for the fine thing

* M. F. S. Hervey, *The Life, Correspondence and Collections of Thomas Howard, Earl of Arundel.* Cambridge, University Press, and The Macmillan Company, New York, 1921, pp. 225 ff.

† An admirable account of these transactions has recently been given by Denys Sutton, "Thomas Howard, Earl of Arundel as a Collector of Drawings," in the *Burlington Magazine,* Vol. LXXXIX (January, February, March, 1947).

and Charles a craftsman's appreciation, it is to Arundel, their senior, that we must look for the fully rounded collector. Their rivalry was friendly enough but the competition between the three was always keen. No one of them would yield an object voluntarily to the other two. In Arundel, too, is the beginning of that great line of archaeologists and antiquaries who have brought such distinction to the English universities and to the Civil Service. When Arundel went to Italy in 1606, where he remained for several years, he took with him the King's Surveyor of Works, Inigo Jones, as a member of his household. At Rome they became enamored with the classic world and Arundel assembled a fine collection of antiquities, which, however, he was forbidden to export. But here his taste was crystallized; he began to cast his eye beyond the Seven Hills to the greater antiquity of Greece. Henry Peacham, whose *Compleat Gentleman* was published in 1634, observed the early archaeological interests that were stirring and credits Arundel with their advancement.

> In Greece and other parts of the Grand Signor's Dominions (where sometimes there were more Statues than men living, so much had Art out-stripped Nature in those dayes) they may be had for digging and carrying. For by reason of the barbarous religion of the Turks, which alloweth not the likeness or representation of any living thing, they have been for the most part buryed in ruins or broken to pieces; so it is a hard matter to light on any there, that are not headlesse or lame, yet most of them venerable for antiquitye and elegancy. And here I cannot but with much reverence, mention the every way Right honourable Thomas Howard, Lord high Marshall of England, as great for his noble Patronage of Arts and ancient learning, as for his birth and place. To whose liberall charges and magnificence this angle of the world oweth the first sight of Greek and Romane Statues, with whose admired presence he began to honour the Gardens and Galleries of Arundel House about twentie yeeres agoe, and hath ever since continued to transplant old Greece into England.

Joachim Sandrart, the first of that procession of arid German scholars to inventory the artistic riches of the British Isles, confirmed Peacham's opinion in describing a visit to the collection in 1632 when Arundel House was at its prime.

Foremost amongst the objects worthy to be seen, stood the beautiful garden of that most famous lover of art, the Earl of Arundel; resplendent with the finest ancient statues in marble, of Greek and Roman workmanship. Here were to be seen, firstly, the portrait of a Roman Consul, in long and graceful drapery, through which the form and proportion of the body could be readily perceived. Then there was a statue of Paris; and many others, some full-length, some busts only; with an almost innumerable quantity of heads and reliefs, all in marble and very rare.

From the garden one passed into the long gallery of the house; where the superlative excellence of the works of Hans Holbein of Basel, held the master's place. Of these the most important was the Triumph of Riches. . . . Near this appeared also the Triumph of Poverty. In the same gallery were some of Holbein's best portraits; to wit, those of Erasmus of Rotterdam, Thomas More, Chancellor of Henry VIII; the great English monarch and the incomparable Princess of Lorraine, beloved of that monarch. . . . Other portraits were there also; some by old German and Dutch masters; some by Raphael of Urbino, by Leonardo da Vinci, by Titian, Tintoretto, and Paul Veronese. In the acquisition of these works the Earl had made numerous and prolonged journeys into Italy, Germany and Holland, in order to collect, from various sources, original works of these renowned artists.

Arundel, who had access to the King's ministers and ambassadors in foreign parts, employed them as well as countless other agents, particularly painters, to inform him of anything good that might be on the market. The inventory made in Amsterdam in 1655 is published with valuable commentaries by Miss Hervey in her *Life.** It is an absorbing document in contrast to the listings of the property belonging to the King and Buckingham, for in it we see fewer princely pedigrees and a greater spirit of adventure. That Arundel was a born collector is attested by the independence and maturity of his taste. The inventory has 799 listed items of which 200 are *objets d'art* including sculpture, but not counting the classical antiquities. Of the remainder, nearly 600 are pictures. Few of the great masters from Michelangelo down the scale, indeed, are lacking, but what is far more interesting, equal attention seems to have been lavished upon

* Hervey, *op. cit.*, 473 ff.

the 200 or more paintings to which no hand is ascribed. Arundel thus appears to be among the first who admired the work of art for its own merit and he was profoundly unconcerned by what the dealer and the critic thought of it.

His first love was for antiquity and in his exploitation of the classics, both in art and in literature, his gardens became the rendezvous for the scholars and men of letters of his day. Francis Bacon, a frequent visitor, died in Arundel House on Easter Sunday, 1626; Tenison relates that Bacon, "coming into the Earl of Arundel's garden, where there were a great number of ancient statues of naked men and women, made a stand and as astonished cried out: 'The resurrection.' " And even Lord Clarendon, whose account of Arundel's life is a compound of envy and malice, said, probably quite truly, "His expenses were without any measure, and always exceed very much his revenue." No obstacle was allowed to stand in the way of an important purchase and it was only the difficulty of transportation which prevented his bringing from Rome the obelisk then lying broken in four pieces in the Circus of Maxentius. Bernini thereupon stepped in and took it to crown his fantastic fountain in the Piazza Navona.

After ransacking Italy and carrying off what he could, Arundel looked with longing on the shores of Greece and Asia Minor and on the Aegean Islands. The appointment in 1621 of Sir Thomas Roe as ambassador to the Sublime Porte brought about a collaboration which is recorded fully in one of the most amusing correspondences of the Renaissance. Roe was a scholar and connoisseur of no mean distinction who declared his willingness "to look back upon antiquity." He was no less careful, however, to keep one eye looking back over his shoulder to the interests of his patron, the Duke of Buckingham, who did not himself care so much for antiquities but who, as Favorite, could not afford to be eclipsed by the Earl Marshal. Roe was given every opportunity and every entrée. He anticipated Dr. Schliemann by nearly two hundred years in acquiring "a stone taken out of the old Palace of Priam, in Troy, cut in hornèd shape."

Many other antiquities were on their way to Arundel House when Buckingham brought pressure to bear upon the ambassador, requiring a division of the spoils. Arundel retaliated by sending out the Reverend

William Petty, a Cambridge scholar whose knowledge and appreciation of classical works of art was exceeded only by the subtlety of his wit and his indifference to ordinary ethics. Roe and Petty worked up a scheme together which for its boldness is one of the great stories of archaeology and, had it succeeded, would have reduced Ponsonby's dream of removing the reliefs of the Mausoleum of Halicarnassus to a minor operation. "They proposed nothing less than to get into their power six out of the twelve large reliefs which adorned the so-called 'Porta Aurea,' the finest of the gates of Constantinople, erected by Theodosius the Great." Through it the Byzantine emperors used to make their solemn entry into the city. Since the Turkish conquest it had not been opened but was walled up and built into the fortifications known as the Seven Towers. Though it had consequently become inaccessible, it was still regarded as the principal gate. For about a year this quixotic plan cuts a grand figure in the correspondence. To get the Sultan to consent to the entire demolition of the Golden Gate proved to be as difficult for the agents as the idea of reaching their object by corruption of state officials. Sir Thomas wrote to Buckingham in May 1625:

> There is only one way left by corruption of some churchmen, to dislike them as agaynst their law; and under that pretence, to take them down to bee brought to some privat place; from whence, after the matter is cold and unsuspected, they may be conveyed. I have practised this for the foure, and am offered to have it done for 600 crownes. To send them home chested, and freighted with some other bribes att the water syde, may cost 100 more. This is a great price but I rather despayre of obteyning them.

Again in October the Ambassador writes to the Favorite:

> The vizier dares not, for his head, offer to deface the chiefest port, so many will clamour against him; the capteyne of the castle, nor the overseer of the walls, cannot doe it without a speciall command from the grand signor; the solders cannot steale them, being 30 foot, and 40 foot high, made fast to the wall with iron pins; and must bee let downe with scaffolds and the help of at least 50 men; for if they fall they will breake to dust, the ground being so thinne and worne with age. There is then but one way left in the world, which I will practise; and if I can procure

them, your lordship shall know my service by the part I send you, without Mr. Petty or any other helpe. Within the castle, and on that gate, is a continuall watch of 20 soldioures: it is the king's prison; and how hard it were to take downe such things, of at least a tonne weight apiece, from the Tower-gate of London, your lordship will easily judge. And if I gett them not, I will pronounce, no man, nor ambassador, shall ever be able to doe it; except also the grand signor, for want will sell the castle.

Their failure to loot the Sublime Porte through the fear of the Grand Treasurer or local superstition in no way dampened the ardor of these agents. Mr. Petty was dispatched to Asia Minor where, according to another letter in October from Roe to Arundel

. . . hee had gotten many things, going to Ephesus by sea, hee made shippwrack in a great storme upon the coast of Asia; and saving his owne life, lost both all his collection of that voyadge, and his commands and letters [of credit] by mee procured; desiring mee to send him others, or else, that he can proceed no further. Hee was putt in prison for a spy, having lost in the sea all his testimonyes; but was released by the witness of Turks that knew him. From thence hee recovered Scio, where he furnished himself againe; and is gone to the place where he left his boate to fish for the marbles, in hope to find them, and from thence to Ephesus, and this is the last news I heard from him.

The following spring in another letter to Arundel Roe gives a vivid account of the problems which beset all archaeologists both past and present:

My Lord,

My last letters brought your lordship the advice of Mr. Pettyes shippwracke, and losses upon the coast of Asya, returning from Samos: his commands and letters of recommendation, and his labors, together there perished. The first I presently renewed, and sent them to Smyrna; and the other, I thincke, he hath by great industry, since recovered. From that tyme, what adventures hee hath passed, his owne enclosed will give best satisfaction; and it shall suffice me to say in grosse, that although hee will not boast to mee, yett I am informed hee hath gotten many things rare and antient. Ther never was a man so fitted to an employment, that encounters all accidents with so unwearied patience; eates with Greakes on their worst dayes, lyes with fishermen on plancks, at the best; is all things to all men, that he may obteyne his ends, which are your lordship's service. He is gone to Athens, whither also I have sent; and from thence promiseth mee to visitt this citty where, I shalbee glad to enterteyne him, and to know the history of his labors.

I have in my endeavour bad success, by ignorance of those that I am forced to employ, who send me heavy stones at great chardge, that proove newe images, wher I seeke old idolls; for such also were the Roman statues of their emperors. From Angory, I had a half-woman, brought 18 dayes by land, upon change of mules, which wants a hand, a nose, a lip; and is so deformed that shee makes me remember an hospital. Yet the malicious Turkes brought trouble on the buyers, by a false command, accusing them of a great wealth stollen out of the castle; it hath cost mee mony to punish them, and that is all I have for my labor. I have sent three servants togither to Tassas, Cavalla, Philippi, and all the coast of Thrace; followed Mr. Petty to Pergamo, and Troy; am digging in Asya; and to fulfill the proverb, turning of all stones. Somewhat I hope to gett, to save my creditt; but I dare not write to his grace until I am in possession; so often I have beene by Greekish promise deceived.

Those on Porta Aurea stand up, ready to fall, in spight of all my arts and offers; the tymes are so dangerous that I dare not venture to entreague others; but there is an opportunity attended to make them stoope. The glorye of taking them from the gate of Constantinople inciteth mee farther then any bewtye I see in ruines, that only showe there was once bewtye; good emblemes of one that had beene a handsome woman, if an old woman were not a better; yet few love them.

When I have made my collection, I will not forgett that I was engaged by your Lordship's commands; as I am assured your Lordship will not grudge mee to performe the service I owe the duke of Buckingham, betweene whom, and your Lordship, if ther had beene an union, ther had nothing beene difficult to us both here, and many things much cheaper. . . . So humbly kyssing your Lordship's hands, I commit you to the heavenly protection.

Your Lordship's most ready servant
THO. ROE

Constantinople, 28 March, old stile, 1626

* * * * *

During his long career many honors and changes came to Arundel. The King in 1641 appointed him Lord High Steward of the Royal

Household – a post which carried heavy duties not only in the War Council and administration of the naval forces but also in dealing with the House of Commons. But the clouds, thick with rebellion, were gathering on the horizon, and the turbulence of general discontent, becoming concentrated on one person, was about to burst over his head. Lord Stafford was destined to be the first victim of the popular fury; Charles, in a futile effort to hold back the tide and save his own neck, betrayed him. It was Arundel's misfortune as Lord High Steward to preside over the trial. The spectacle was too much for the loyalty of the Earl to stomach, particularly when the King refused once more Arundel's petition signed by eighteen peers to restore to him the Duchy of Norfolk. He resigned his position and begged leave to travel; his health was breaking and he needed the change. King Charles availed himself of this pretext to appoint him in attendance to Queen Marie de Medici, who was leaving England for the Low Countries, and he was commanded, together with the Countess of Arundel, to escort her abroad.

This was the signal for Arundel's self-imposed exile. In February 1642, with the major part of the pictures and works of art of his cabinet (excepting the Arundelian marbles which were to play such an important role in the future direction of British taste), he embarked for Antwerp. As the shores of England receded from view, Arundel, leaning over the gunwale of the ship, was heard to exclaim: "May it never have need of me." Indeed he never returned to his native land. Sojourning in the Netherlands, he soon went on to Italy. There it was that he drew up for John Evelyn those charming memoranda – "Remembrances for Things Worth Seeing in England and in Italy" – which Evelyn used as a "Baedeker" for his Italian tour. Although Arundel's fortune was exhausted and he had been obliged to sell many objects of art and jewels – the 1655 inventory lacks many capital items he was known to have possessed – he went on with his researches and continued to satisfy the itching fingers of the true collector that he was. Evelyn visited him for the last time in Padua in 1645:

This morning, the Earl of Arundel, now in this city, a famous collector of paintings and antiquities invited me to go with him to see the garden of Mantua, where as one enters, stands a huge colosse of Hercules. From hence to a place where was a room covered with a noble cupola, built purposely for music; the fillings up, or cave betwixt the walls, were of urns and earthern pots, for the better sounding; it was also well painted. After dinner, we walked to the Palace Foscari all'Arena, there remaining yet some appearances of a theatre, though serving now for a court only before the house. There was now kept in it two eagles, a crane, a Mauritanian sheep, a stag, and sundry fowls, as in a vivary.*

Although he had taken with him to the Netherlands the bulk of his treasures, the house in London was not entirely denuded of its works of art. Marbles still remained, though neglected. The collections abroad were gradually dispersed after the Earl's death. The celebrated inventory of 1655 was not, however, drawn up until a year after the death of the Countess at The Hague.

The liquidation of the property in London, which was willed by the Earl to Countess Alethea for her absolute disposal, led to the breaking up of the collections that were left. Part fell to her eldest son, Henry Frederick, the new Earl, another share falling to William Howard, Viscount Stafford, was removed to Tart Hall near Buckingham Gate. This latter group formed part of the sale in 1720 at which Dr. Mead purchased his bronze head of Homer.† Those antiquities and the library which had remained with the title at Arundel House suffered seriously in the Civil War. The entire property was laid under attachment by the Parliament, for in 1651 an inventory of the "severall goodes, picktures, and statues at Arundel House in the Strand" was made. Though several of the pictures seem to have disappeared at this time, the antiquities were spared, only to be neglected in turn by the new Earl, the profligate and uncultured Lord Maltravers, later Duke of Norfolk. The latter's divorced wife sold the statues to the Earl of Pomfret's father and they were later given by the Countess of Pomfret to Oxford University. As to the inscriptions, Evelyn in 1677 records:

I obtained the gift of his Arundelian Marbles, those celebrated and famous inscriptions Greek and Latin gathered with so much cost and in-

* *The Diary of John Evelyn.* E. P. Dutton & Co., *Everyman Edition.* I, 209.
† Later presented to the British Museum by the Earl of Exeter.

dustry by his illustrious grandfather, the magnificent Earl of Arundel, my noble friend whilst he lived. When I saw these precious monuments miserably neglected, and scattered up and down the garden, and other parts of Arundel House, and how exceedingly the corrosive air of London impaired them, I procured him to bestow them on the University of Oxford. This he was pleased to grant me; and now gave me the key of the gallery, with leave to mark all those stones, urns, altars, etc., and whatever I found had inscriptions on them, that were not statues. This I did; and getting them removed and piled together, with those which were encrusted in the garden walls, I sent immediately letters to the Vice-Chancellor of what I had procured, and that if they esteemed it a service to the University (of which I had been a member), they should take order for the transportation.*

The following year Evelyn was again called to London to wait upon the Duke of Norfolk,

who . . . at my sole request bestowed the Arundelian Library on the Royal Society. . . . I procured beside printed books, near one hundred Mss., some in Greek of great concernement. The printed books being of the oldest impressions, are not the less valuable. I esteem them almost equal to Mss. Amongst them, are most of the Fathers, printed at Basil, before the Jesuits abused them with their expurgatory Indexes; there is a noble Ms. of Vitruvius. Many of these books had been presented by Popes, Cardinals, and great persons, to the Earls of Arundel and Dukes of Norfolk; and the late magnificent Earl of Arundel bought a noble library in Germany (those of the Kings of Hungary and of Dr. Willibald Pirkheimer the patron of Dürer), which is in this collection. I should not, for the honour I bear the family, have persuaded the Duke to part with these, had I not seen how negligent he was of them, suffering the priests and everybody to carry away and dispose of what they pleased; so that abundance of rare things are irrecoverably gone.†

At a distance of three centuries we begin to understand how much the scholarship of the English speaking world owes to Thomas Howard, the "Father of *Virtù* in England."

* Evelyn, *op. cit.*, II, 31–32.
† *Ibid.*, II, 126–127.

CHAPTER VI

The Tragic Dispersal by the Parliament

THE blazing artistic sun of the Stuarts which had ridden so high in the heavens, and which had promised so well for the future of the arts in Britain, was suddenly darkened by the total eclipse of Civil War and Regicide. The Puritans, drunk with power and with vengeance, set out to prove the barbarousness of their divine mission. "In all ages," Walpole observed, "the mob have vented their hatred to tyrants on the pomp of tyranny. The magnificence the people have envied, they grow to detest, and mistaking consequences for causes, the first objects of their fury are the palaces of their masters. If religion is thrown into the quarrel, the most innocent are catalogued with sins. This was the case in the contests between Charles and his parliament. As he had blended affection to the sciences with a lust of power, nonsense and ignorance were adopted into the liberties of the subject. Painting became idolatry; monuments were deemed carnal pride, and a venerable cathedral seemed equally contradictory to Magna Charta and the Bible. Learning and wit were construed to be so heathen, that one would have thought the Holy Ghost could endure nothing above a pun. What the fury of Henry VIII had spared, was condemned by the Puritans: ruin was their harvest, and they gleaned after the reformers. Had they countenanced any of the softer arts, what could those arts have represented? How picturesque was the figure of an Anabaptist? But sectaries have no ostensible enjoyments; their pleasures are private, comfortable, and gross. The arts that civilize society are not calculated for men who mean to rise on the ruins of established order."

As early as 1645 the Parliament began to sell the pictures at York House, sequestered from the second Duke of Buckingham, and also the property belonging to the King. To cloak their "embezzlement" with some semblance of legality and divine authority the following orders were issued on July 23 of that year:

Ordered, that all such pictures and statues there (York House), as are without any superstition, shall be forthwith sold, for the benefit of Ireland and the North.

Ordered, that all such pictures there as have the representation of the Second Person of the Trinity upon them shall be forthwith burnt.

Ordered, that all such pictures there as having representation of the Virgin Mary upon them, shall be forthwith burnt.

From this it was an easy step to the decrees confiscating the collections of the King immediately upon his execution. Theoretically the proceeds of the sale of such property would be used for the maintenance of the fleet. A few months after the monarch's death in July inventories were taken and reserve prices established for the works of art. The dispersal, which was made chiefly by private sale as well as by auction, dragged on until 1652–1653. The King's private property was held at £49,903.2.6. The pictures, next to the jewels in value, were disposed of in two lots in 1650 and 1653. They realized, in spite of prices so low that the Venetian ambassador, Giovanni Sugredo, reported them to the Doge as "*prezzi vilissimi*," the unheard-of total of £118,080.10.2. Never before, since Roman times, had collections of works of art fetched a sum equal to what indeed it was, a king's ransom, but a ransom that was paid too late. An excellent if somewhat romantic account of the sale is given in Walpole's *Anecdotes*. More thorough examination of the various documents has been made in recent years.* All the evidence, however, leans more and more to the belief that the Protector himself was not so bad as he was painted and took what steps he dared to prevent the Roundheads from carrying out their worst intentions. It was he who saved the Raphael cartoons and the Mantegna series of the *Triumph of Julius Caesar* for the nation. A partial list of prices taken from Walpole's *Anecdotes*, is revealing:

* Extracts of the inventories with notes are printed in the *Nineteenth Century*, Aug. 1890, pp. 211–217; also cf. *Hist. Mss. Comm.*, Seventh Report (1879), pp. 88 ff.; also, W. G. Burn-Murdoch, *The Royal Stuarts in their Connection with Art and Letters*, Edinburgh, 1908; and H. N. Nixon, "Cromwell's Artistic Taste" in *Rutland Magazine*, Vol. I, 1903, p. 100.

Raphael – *Cartoons*	£ 300.
Mantegna – *Triumphs of Julius Caesar*	1000.
Van Dyck – *Royal Family*	150.
Van Dyck – *The King on Horseback*	200.
Titian – *The Twelve Caesars*	1200.
Titian – *Alexander VI & Caesare Borgia*	100.
Tintorett – *The Muses*	100.
Julio Romano – *Triumph of Vespasian & Titus*	150.
Julio Romano – *The Nativity*	500.
Correggio – *The Sleeping Venus*	1000.
Titian – *The Venus del Pardo*	600.
Raphael – *The Little Madonna*	800.
Raphael – *St. George*	150.
Raphael – *La Perla*	2000.

Of equal interest with the prices of these pictures in the auction room three hundred years ago are the personalities who descended like vultures upon the carcass of the King's treasure. They were persons all of them destined to play an important role in the development of continental taste during the *Grand Siècle*. How shrewd, too, they were as bidders, for even then the prices were absurd. Were these same items to be put today upon the block in London, even after six years of war, most of the items listed above would fetch, surely, £100,000. Those who came were prepared to pay any price and were dumfounded at their opportunities. Don Alonzo de Cardenas, the Spanish ambassador, bought so many pictures for Philip IV that "eighteen mules were required to carry them from Coruña to Madrid." Among these were Raphael's *Madonna della Perla*, Mantegna's *Dormition of the Virgin*, and Titian's *Portrait of the Emperor Charles V with a Dog*, which today are considered three of the principal masterpieces of the Prado.

The next buyer of apparently inexhaustible means was the celebrated banker of Cologne and agent of Cardinal Mazarin, Evrard Jabach, whose collection later was acquired by Colbert for the Louvre. A contemporary account says that "the sale of the collection of the King Charles I gave his bold intellect and safe judgment a unique opportunity." He bought not only paintings and drawings for his own account but also tapestries, *objets d'art* and antiquities for the Cardinal. Tradition states that when Jabach returned from the sale he entered Paris at the head of a convoy of wagons "loaded with artistic conquests, like a Roman victor at the head of a triumphal procession." That erratic and passionate collector, Queen Christina of Sweden, purchased the chief rarities in medals and jewels for her cabinet. This group, one of the few units of her vast collections to remain reasonably intact, is preserved today, and is divided between the Paris Cabinet des Médailles and the Museum at Stockholm. The agents of the great Archduke, Leopold Wilhelm, Governor of the Netherlands, one of the fabulous collectors of all time, bought heavily for the Picture Gallery in Vienna; particularly pictures by Titian, Veronese and other members of the Venetian School. A group of painters acting either for themselves or as agents of other princes were De Critz, Wright, Baptist and Leemput. Chief among this group was that able but unsavory character, Sir Balthazar Gerbier, whose family has been immortalized in the large *Family Group* by Rubens at Windsor Castle. Gerbier was employed not for his artistic talents alone but as spy and confidential agent; his sycophantic correspondence with the Duke of Buckingham, the history of his many shady activities in nearly every European city, the hold which he exerted upon Rubens and the chief artistic personalities of his time, and the private art academy which he had founded in London – all of these evidences of his charm and wickedness give him, though on a much fainter note, something of the place in the north held earlier at Venice by Pietro Aretino.

Last but not least were the banker-dealers from the Low Countries who swarmed to the sale. Of these the brothers Reynst distinguished themselves by adding superb pictures to their already celebrated cabinet in Amsterdam. It was to these brothers that Ridolfi somewhat bombastically dedicated in 1646 his work on the Venetian painters, *Le Meraviglie d'arte*. One of the brothers had spent most of his life in Italy at the head of his business. "Both were typical, enlightened amateurs," says Frits Lugt, "gifted, with flair, and not afraid of big prices. Owing to the splitting up of the famous Vendramin collection at Venice and to several other opportunities they seized, they were able to set up a gallery of Italian pictures and antique sculptures such as was never again seen in Holland. Its memory is handed down, unfortunately in an incomplete fashion, in a series of engravings reproducing its best pieces. This publication, well-known to print collectors, was one of the first of its kind, anticipating by more than half a century the Cabinet Crozat and the Cabinet du Roy. Unfortunately the splendor of this collection was shortlived. The two brothers died in their prime and, after the death of the second, their collection found itself without a guiding spirit." * Subsequently politics intervened; the widow of the brother who had lived at Amsterdam agreed to part with 24 pictures and 12 pieces of sculpture, "worth three barrels of gold," which the States-General, in a conciliatory gesture to the rising power of Britain, presented to Charles II on the occasion of the Restoration. These works of art, now at Hampton Court, are among the few remnants of the Stuart collection belonging to the Crown.

But as Walpole pointed out, "the restoration of royalty brought back the arts, not taste. Charles II had a turn for mechanics, none to the politer sciences. He had learned to draw in his youth . . . but he was too indolent even to amuse himself. He introduced the fashions of the Court of France, without its elegance. He had seen Louis XIV countenance Corneille, Molière, Boileau, Le Soeur, who, forming themselves on the models of the ancients, seemed by the purity of their writings to have studied only in Sparta. Charles found as much genius at home; but how licentious, how indelicate was the style he permitted or demanded! Dryden's tragedies are a compound of bombast and heroic obscenity, enclosed in the most beautiful numbers. If Wycherly had nature, it is nature stark naked. The painters of that time veiled it but little more; Sir Peter Lely scarce saves appearances but by a bit of fringe or drapery. His nymphs, generally reposed on the turf, are too wanton and too magnificent to be taken for anything but maids of honour." †

If Lely, like Le Brun, was conspicuous for his want of genius and originality as a creative artist, he added a considerable distinction to

* Quoted from a personal communication of Mr. Lugt to the writer.

† Walpole, *op. cit.*, II, 427. Two years before the artist's death a Puritan tract against Lely's ladies at Hampton Court was published under the title *Cooke's Just and Reasonable Reprehensions of Naked Breasts and Shoulders.*

the reign as its foremost connoisseur and collector. His collection of pictures and drawings was magnificent, acquired to a large extent from the second Duke of Buckingham – what was left of the masterpieces of York House. He lived grandly and boasted that since he was too occupied with commissions from the King to travel and visit other cabinets and galleries, he must perforce surround himself with the best models of the past at home. He bought heavily – as much as his rich wife's means permitted – from the dispersal of the late King's and Arundel's collections, and he acquired from Van Dyck's widow the very fine group of works of art which that artist had brought together. It was his portfolios of drawings by the masters which held particular attention and which finally helped to bring the total realized by his heirs to the enormous sum of £26,000. Among them were drawings by Veronese, Titian, Claude, Giorgione, Michelangelo, and four even by Van Eyck.

While it may be supposed that Lely spared no pains to provide himself with the best he could afford, the accusations of dishonesty later laid at this doorstep seem exaggerated even for those times. Under his tutelage Charles II, starting virtually with the Mantegna *Triumphs* and the Raphael cartoons – almost all that the Roundheads had left him of his father's cabinet – increased the royal collections to something above 1100 pictures and 100 sculptures. These were distributed about the various palaces of Saint James's, Whitehall, Hampton Court and Windsor. To this group a meager handful of unimportant canvases were added by James II, whose four stormy years upon the throne, in Walpole's words, "crowded with insurrections, prosecutions, innovations, were not likely to make a figure in a history of painting."

The Stuart House had sought to recapture, if not the actual works of art which had given such luster to the reign of Charles I, at least its former prestige of patronage and connoisseurship. But calamity pursued them to the end. William of Orange had barely settled himself upon the English throne when Whitehall, in which no less than seven hundred pictures were exposed, was consumed by fire. Only the Banqueting Hall remains. Waagen gives the record of the ghastly toll: "Of the three by Leonardo da Vinci, three by Raphael, twelve

EL GRECO: VIEW OF TOLEDO (DETAIL)

Formerly in the Oñate Palace in Madrid. Bequeathed by Mrs. H. O. Havemeyer to the Metropolitan Museum of Art

by Giulio Romano, eighteen by Giorgione, eighteen by Titian, six by Palma Vecchio, six by Correggio, seven by Parmigianino, twenty-seven by Holbein, four by Rubens, thirteen by Van Dyck, fourteen by William Van de Velde, which were in that palace, and of which a very considerable part were evidently genuine, the greater part were destroyed on that occasion." *

Perhaps it is to the everlasting glory of the Puritans that by their fury in sending out of England to the Continent so many masterpieces a small fraction of the Stuart Gallery had been saved from the hand of God.

* Waagen, *Treasures of Art in Great Britain.* John Murray, 1854. I, 15 f.

BOOK FIVE

Collecting in Spain and the Low Countries in the Seventeenth Century

CHAPTER I

Antwerp and the Burgundian Heritage

GUICCIARDINI, the Florentine historian and chronicler, visiting Antwerp in 1560, recorded that there were in the city 300 artists, 169 bakers and 78 butchers. It is not to be supposed from this that the prosperous burghers of Flanders were more interested in feasting their eyes than their stomachs. But the popularity of art had been a matter of long standing; artists for two hundred years or more had received the active support of the Counts of Flanders and Brabant and, more particularly, of the Dukes of Burgundy. It was in the court of Philip the Good, who had established the Order of the Golden Fleece in 1429, that chivalry came to its ultimate and most luxurious flowering. In the late fourteenth and early fifteenth centuries the capital was at Bruges, although Ghent and Ypres were possibly the richer centers of Flemish industry. But after the defeat and death of Charles the Bold in 1477, Antwerp rose upon the ashes of Burgundo-French culture to a place of absolute supremacy.

What distinguishes the Renaissance of the Low Countries from that of Italy is the difference in point of view toward subject matter, and of the artist to society. There had been in the north no comparable monumental tradition of a classical past. Such art as there was in the Middle Ages was the product of religious enthusiasm and a taste for luxury – a courtly life in which "the extremes of mysticism and of gross materialism meet." The brothers Van Eyck may be said to have closed the period of medievalism in art, rather than have opened a doorway to the Renaissance. Most of what was produced was applied art valued only for its decorative aspects. A portrait by Rogier van der Weyden, for example, differs from one by Piero della Francesco in its approach to the problem of reality. Piero's realism is universal and generic. The portrait of Federigo da Montefeltro is more than the likeness of the *condottiere* of Urbino; it is the collective classical portrait (and here classical is used in the sense of Greek and Roman antiquity) of the prince, and bears the same relation in the visual arts that Castiglione's *Perfect Courtier* or Machiavelli's *Prince* bears to given individuals in history. Not so with Rogier, whose portraits haunt one down the centuries as the record of an intimate knowledge and analysis of the character and person of the sitter. He cannot be confused with any other prince or merchant. His name and rank, the diseases which have left their impress on his countenance, the evil which he has done his fellow men together with the deep piety in his soul, are there for men to see so long as the material fabric of the portrait lasts.

The same differences in temperament between north and south are observable in religious art, for, to the Italian painter, a religious picture was a commission to express primarily through the means of a formal composition a philosophic truth or teaching of the Church. To the Fleming, on the other hand, the religious picture was a vehicle for sharing with the spectator some inner mystical experience.

In Flanders, too, the persistence of feudalism, long after it had been forgotten in the Mediterranean countries, greatly affected the social position of the artist, who considered himself no better than a craftsman and was therefore ready to be called upon for any task within the royal household. Such a relationship as that which existed between Mantegna and Isabella d'Este was virtually unknown in the court of Burgundy, where the patronage of art was to a large extent a monopoly of the State. The artists were employed not only on the decoration of churches and palaces, but they gilded chairs, designed posters for important events and decorated the figureheads of royal ships. The workshops of Van Eyck and Hugo van der Goes produced decorations for wedding festivities and funeral ceremonies. When the Archduke Maximilian was a prisoner at Bruges in 1488, Gerard David painted pictures on the wickets and shutters of his prison. The cartoons of the celebrated series of tapestries representing the *Conflict of the Virtues and Vices* (leading to the grand climax of the *Last Judgment* tapestry, now in the Worcester Art Museum) are taken from painted hangings which lined the streets of Bruges in 1468 for the marriage of Charles the Bold and Margaret of York. The *entremets* for this occasion, designed by Hugo van der Goes, Rogier van der Weyden and Dierec Bouts, consisted of "gigantic pies enclosing complete orchestras, full rigged vessels, castles, monkeys and whales, giants and dwarfs, and all the boring absurdities of allegory." This taste for popular expression finally outdid itself in the productions of the liturgical theater and in mysteries performed upon the steps of the cathedrals.

But with all its profusion and magnificence, the art of Flanders at the end of the fifteenth and in the early years of the sixteenth centuries was essentially an art of decay – a dry rot which ate into every phase of intellectual life. It was a period of transition from the scholasticism of the Middle Ages to the free Humanism of the Renaissance. Quite naturally the art of the Netherlands reflected the political and economic revolution that was taking place; while the Hollanders clung to ancient symbols and traditions, these same traditional attitudes had already lost their meaning and were repeated as if by memory in an effort to recall the security of an earlier age. This "craving to give form to every idea," says Huizinga, "and the overcrowding of the mind with figures and forms systematically arranged – all this reappears in art. There, too, we find the tendency to leave nothing without form, without figure, without ornament. The flamboyant style of architecture is like the postlude of an organist who cannot conclude. It decomposes all of the formal elements endlessly; it interlaces all the details, – there is not a line that has not its counter line. The form develops at the expense of the idea, the ornament grows rank, hiding all the lines and all the surfaces. A *horror vacui* reigns, always a symptom of artistic decline." *

Perhaps a clue to the Burgundian attitude may be seen in the use of the word "donor" as applied to Flemish art in contrast to the idea of "patron" which was the Florentine convention. Aside from the members of the court, there were few collectors, although, paradoxically, ownership of works of art by middle-class persons was more widespread than it was in Italy. People who could afford pictures or statues acquired them as a matter of course. But the great men of the

* Johan Huizinga, *The Waning of the Middle Ages*. E. Arnold, 1924, p. 227.

court, with a natural piety unlike that of most Italians, sought to immortalize themselves with liberal donations to convents and hospitals where their portraits might be perpetuated in the chapel altarpiece.*

The Flemings never felt that they dared openly challenge the authority of the Duke by excelling him in the magnificence of their own surroundings. The gift to churches and hospitals offered a way out. Jean Chevrot, Bishop of Tournai, was the donor of the incomparable *Seven Sacraments* by Van der Weyden now in the museum at Antwerp; Pierre Bladelin, the financial minister of the Duke, is seen in the Middelburg altarpiece in Berlin. Among other notable donors whose names appeared frequently in the history of Flemish painting were Jodocus Vydt, the Canon van der Paele and Chancellor Rolin.

This taste for pageantry, imposed from above by the dukes themselves, had produced a popular interest in art which had taken firm hold of the people. As early as 1463 Willem Groestelinc of Grammont held a public exhibition of religious pictures at Ghent, where works of art had even then been accepted in payment of rent and groceries. Lotteries of pictures were held with substantial prizes, Jan van Eyck's widow participating in one of the earliest in 1445.

How the artist's studios looked at this time may be learned from Rogier van der Weyden's picture of *Saint Luke Painting the Blessed Virgin*, of which one of the variants is in the Museum of Fine Arts in Boston. It represents the Evangelist kneeling before the Madonna, who is seated at a window opening on a balcony, drawing her portrait on a piece of parchment with a silver pencil. To be sure, the architecture is idealized but, even so, something of the studio atmosphere appears.

Floerke has shown that all of artistic production, as well as the buying and selling of art, was under the absolute control of the Guild of Saint Luke. It was to this Guild that the painter applied for apprenticeship and from which he received his papers as journeyman and master craftsman. The Guild's authority extended to the point of controlling the Friday markets, and without its permission secondhand

* The Medici, Portinari and Sassetti families of Florence, and the Arnolfini of Lucca, are of course the notable exception and must indeed have been inspired during their constant business connections with Bruges.

dealers were forbidden to sell works of art. It even imposed its rule over the liquidation of the effects in a deceased artist's studio.*

Gradually Bruges, which for a century had shared with Ghent the favors of the court, was eclipsed by Antwerp, and the latter, now entering upon a half century of frantic boom-town prosperity, became also the cultural center of the Low Countries. The knight in armor had yielded to the burgher, who naturally enough wished to reflect about him all of the magnificence which money could buy. It was the center of the export trade and of Italian finance, and the Antwerp Bourse became notorious as a center of wildcat speculation. The presence, too, of so many bankers and businessmen from Italy and the Levant opened new and profitable ventures in the four corners of the globe. Not the least of these was the new and rapidly growing business of importing and exporting works of art – a business which required the same methods of exhibition, examination and financing that we know today.

The first of these exhibitions for the purpose of selling pictures of which we have any record was held in Antwerp in 1540, although it is presumed that they had been held by congresses of the various branches of the painters' guild for many years previously. At this time the square courtyard of the Exchange, which had been created in 1531 "*in usum negotiarum cuiusque nationis ac linguae urbisque*," was transformed into a series of small shops sublet to art dealers. This was known as the *Schilders-Pand*, in which was held a permanent yet constantly changing exhibition. It must have been a very profitable affair, for Floerke tells us that the *Pand* was rented in 1565 to Bartholomew de Momper for the enormous sum of 1258 florins per year. Here it was that the Antwerp dealers filled the demands from abroad for Flemish art and in turn acted as importers and brokers in Italian masterpieces. Tapestries from Arras, miniatures from Limburg, polychrome figures from Bruges found their way, together with the portraits and religious pictures of Memling, Gerard David, and the Breugels, to Padua, Milan and particularly to Naples and to Venice.

* H. Floerke, "*Studien zur niederländischen Kunst- und Kulturgeschichte; Die Formen des Kunsthandels, das Atelier und die Sammler in den Niederländen vom 15–18. Jahrhundert.*" Georg Müller, 1905. These researches have been of invaluable assistance for the material in this chapter and the following.

Many of the Florentine banking houses maintained their own establishments in Antwerp so that these could commission directly from the artists, several of whom, like Van der Weyden, traveled to Italy for study and employment.

The art dealers in Antwerp usually joined the Guild of Saint Luke, to which also the jewelers, pawnbrokers, gilders and picture framers clamored for admittance. In Amsterdam, on the other hand, they joined the booksellers' guild and publishers' associations.

Notwithstanding the traffic with Italy, Spain and Portugal still offered the largest market for Flemish art. The inventories of Ferdinand and Isabella are swollen with Netherlandish names, and the Hanseatic cities likewise offered rich and fertile markets. But the crash finally came with the collapse of the Antwerp Bourse in the late 1550's and the art business suffered with every other; it was merely another type of commodity financing which had overextended its credit. Paradoxically, during this century when the middle class finally came to flower, the Hapsburgs had achieved their greatest glory and had endowed the future generations of Europe with some of the noblest collections of works of art ever assembled.

CHAPTER II

Middle-Class Art in the Dutch Republic

After the death of Charles I, patronage of art moved to the Continent, at first to France and Spain. But gradually, as the long reign of Louis XIV moved inexorably through the century, Holland became the art market of the world, which it was destined to remain for the next two hundred years. The absence of a royal court, with its conventions of etiquette and protocol, gave an opportunity for "free enterprise" to the capitalist which was soon reflected in his houses and his works of art.

In considering the art of the Low Countries during the sixteenth and seventeenth centuries, we must guard against the tendency to speak of the Netherlands as we do today in a single breath. Holland and the Spanish Provinces – Flanders and Belgium – were separated by a deep abyss of temperament and faith; it was a dividing line, sharper and far more impenetrable than the barrier of the Pyrenees, which cut off France from Spain. By the turn of the century the north had freed itself from foreign rule but Spain remained in complete occupation of the southern areas. There was virtually no communication between what had so long been a united congeries of medieval duchies and principalities. Any visitor between the two was looked upon with suspicion as a spy or saboteur. Even Rubens had the greatest difficulty in obtaining a passport to visit Holland. The hostility continued well into the eighteenth century when the southern provinces passed from Spanish to Austrian domination. Belgium remained Catholic but did not achieve political liberty until after the Napoleonic Wars.

The Dutch business empire of the seventeenth century was built largely upon the principles of trade and mercantilism established a hundred years earlier in Antwerp. Gradually the younger port of Amsterdam was developed as the Hollanders showed their ability to navigate larger and deeper bottoms than did the early Flemings; this permitted a broader exploration of their East Indian trade. Wealth and power moved north; Flanders, sadly deflated by the Spanish bankruptcies, was torn with religious conflict, and England, absorbed by Civil War, proved to be, until Pepys reorganized the navy for Charles II, no match for the maritime power of Holland. In fact, the carrying trade of Europe was temporarily in the hands of the Dutch burghers who introduced new practices and theories of trade; for the idea of mercantilism was a radical departure from the Italian financial doctrine which had dominated the Renaissance, and through it were developed monopolies for the protection of "infant industries" by subsidies, tariff walls and various forms of tax exemption. The Dutch believed implicitly that, to survive, a state must always have a favorable balance of trade.

This point of view required a new type of character and personality and with it emerged the captain of industry on the grand scale. For the first time do we see the American businessman – the corporation president and "tycoon" move across the pages of history. We must not forget that New York has never totally abandoned the traditions and manners of New Amsterdam, and possibly the natural antipathy existing even to this day between the commercial metropolis at the mouth of the Hudson and the more English colonies of New England and the South arises from these divergencies of mind and spirit which existed three hundred years ago. Already do we see the blind belief in the power of money. The absolutism of the oligarch, of course, was the logical and natural corollary to the absolutism of the king, and where there was no king to set the pace, the businessman created standards in his own image to please no one in particular except himself. In the spirit of the Sons of the American Revolution and the D.A.R., the patricians of Old and New Amsterdam crashed the gates of the petty nobility, allying themselves by marriage, and by the purchase of questionable patents, to fortunes a little better than their own. The battles of the bears and bulls on the Amsterdam Exchange produced a pattern of financial warfare which ever since has dominated the stock markets of both continents and which even the naïve idealism of the Securities Exchange Commission in Washington has been powerless to control. What Amsterdam set out to be, and would ultimately have been had not Pepys and Colbert intervened, New York has since become both in spirit and in fact.

Colbert looked with disdain upon the Hollanders, whom he described as "*remplit de vent et de vengeance*," and Voltaire spoke of Holland as a "lethargic Hell." Taine, with the discernment and perspective of two centuries, was filled with wonder and admiration of the Dutch people, whom he called "*Un petit peuple de marchands perdu sur un tas de boue*." But the Anglo-Saxon and Dutch characters have become so blended and interwoven that the Netherlands have remained for most Americans a second spiritual home.

If Amsterdam was American in tempo, we in this country have inherited the virtues and tolerances of the Dutch as well as their intellectual curiosities. For although the city on the Zuider Zee was a paradise for the Protestant merchant, she welcomed at the same time every religious dissenter and every refugee: Huguenot and Catholic, Jew and heretic, Puritan and political exile. Her printing presses were open to philosophers of all beliefs, almost no doctrine or theory of government or economics was too radical; she seemed to delight in pointing the finger of scorn at the Inquisition. Paradoxically enough, and like her American successor, Amsterdam, while she gave asylum to any artist, was instinctively conservative in taste. She was concerned with the world of actuality and appreciated that intimate reality which best expressed itself in pictures of interiors, of still-life and the pleasures of the table. Her interest in the past was academic and when, as a gesture of piety, at times she grudgingly preserved the monuments of her Gothic past, she had little or no desire to revive its earlier culture. Amsterdam likewise ignored the Renaissance and all its implications; she was, except for a small and precious circle of antiquarians, absorbed by the present and determined to make the most of the modern world on which she thrived.

Such an attitude was favorable to a popular interest in art where the contemporary scene, faithfully rendered, achieved a validity in itself. The small interior, easily heated, lent itself to pictures more readily than the vast open rooms of the Italian villa, and the Dutchman liked to surround himself with reminders of the commonplace.

Physical comfort and the satisfaction of natural appetites were more important to his daily existence than, for example, mythology or the lives of the saints. A work of art, he thought, should be judged upon its merits and should require no special training or knowledge of the classics to understand it; it was a commodity that aimed to please and, measured by the success of its appeal, could be considered as a safe investment for the middle class. Consequently almost everyone owned and bought pictures as a matter of course. John Evelyn, who visited Holland in 1641, reported that "the peasants were so rich that they were looking for investments and often spent 2000–3000 florins for pictures." Bredius observed that "in the seventeenth century it was quite natural for a Dutchman to possess a small picture gallery; the nobleman as well as the plainest and most modest burgher had a house full of pictures and there was nothing unusual about finding from 100–200 pictures in a modest home."

There was of course, despite this broad popular market, collecting on a larger and more important scale. The capitalist collector was proverbially shrewd, a good buyer as to both price and quality. While in some instances his connoisseurship seemed to lack the intellectual refinements of his contemporaries in France, Italy and England, the Dutchman had "a flair for the turn of the market." Like our own, his collections were safe – remarkable assemblages of "gilt-edged" securities, bought on the sound advice of practicing artists and brought together for the most part without style and little humanistic curiosity. The formation of these collections, moreover, coincided with the crisis in gold which, amassed a generation earlier in foreign trade, was lying idle and uninvested, glutting the markets of Amsterdam throughout the Thirty Years' War. Thus in the middle of the seventeenth century this city became the liquidating market for Europe's princely collections, just as London was to be after the French Revolution and Napoleonic Wars, and New York following the World War of 1914–1918. The bankers invested heavily and their children and grandchildren reaped their reward in the eighteenth century by selling their works of art to the *curieux* of France and England.

Holland in the seventeenth century was the envy of Europe. Prosperity abounded, prosperity built upon trade and colonies. There was money enough to sustain and protect at first a native art and handicraft. But with the development of Dutch industry by 1650 these products had become a major factor in the export business. Pictures, prints and Delftware no longer catered exclusively to the rich and comfortable burghers at home but acquired an international flavor. Wouvermans, Ter Borch, Metsu and de Hoogh were really a century in advance of French taste. Italians visiting Holland, like the Grand Duke of Tuscany, Cosimo III, fell in love with the art of Vermeer and Willem Van de Velde. The English, who were alternately political antagonists or allies of the Dutch, began systematically to drain Holland of its best pictures; so assiduous were they that in many instances, such as Albert Cuyp, for example, only a handful of the artist's works remained in the country.

The Southern Netherlands on the other hand declined during the second half of the century, as did its art. The earlier impetus of Rubens and Van Dyck had created a desire upon the part of those with already established fortunes to fill their houses and private galleries with works of art. Moreover, the Catholic connections with Spain and Italy, to say nothing of the closer contacts with the France of Louis XIV, had inspired a mass production which, if it failed to attain the quality of the group of artists working at The Hague, at Amsterdam and Delft, was at least impressive in its dimensions. This trade has been the subject of recent investigation by Jan Denucé, who has combed the inventories of Antwerp and the documents and records of many of the leading picture merchants.* The art market of Holland was no less turbulent, and, since it commanded more money, it became the target for both speculator and charlatan. Jan Pieterz Zoomer, the most influential dealer in Amsterdam, was lampooned as a "John the Baptist of the arts," and in the next generation the moralist Justus van Effen wrote a series of letters in *De Hollandsche Spectator* (nos. 267 and 277) in 1734, in which he decried the tricks of the trade, the imaginary values placed on works of art and the credulity of the amateur:

* Cf. Jan Denucé, *Kunstuitvoer in 17e eeuw te Antwerpen*, 1930, and *The Antwerp Galleries, Inventories of the Art Collections of Antwerp in the 16th & 17th Centuries*, The Hague, 1932.

Godfried Schalken's paintings were highly esteemed in London and were sold there at high prices by the art dealers, who bought them from the artist in Holland. Schalken determined to cross to England with some of his best pictures in hope of an ample return far exceeding his travel expenses. He went and obtained an introduction to a great Lord, to whom he sold a painting, greatly to his satisfaction. This annoyed one of the gang who used to make big money with his pictures. For there as here these fellows begrudge the poor painters whom they do not hold under tribute the very light in their eyes. He did not rest until he had brought that excellent artist under suspicion and in disfavor not only with his Lordship but also, through the latter, among all connoisseurs. In order to accomplish his scheme he went to visit his Lordship and asked to have the picture shown to him. The request was granted. He gave it much praise and inquired how much had been paid for it. The owner told him. "You have been scandalously overcharged," the dealer exclaimed. "That much money! That much money! I undertake to supply your Lordship with its counterpart at much smaller cost; and then you will realize that it is much cheaper to buy through us than to let yourself be cheated by the painters." His Lordship, being a good economist and at the same time a good patriot, reasoned that he ought not to neglect his own advantage and that he should help his countrymen to turn an honest penny; he commissioned this crafty knave to buy the picture for him if it had not yet been sold. The impostor went straight to the artist, inspected all he had, amongst other things the painting he was looking for. He showed a willingness to buy it, promised him piles of money and his favor and support in the future if he would let him have it at a moderate price. Schalken let himself be imposed upon; he sold it to him for a song in the hope of later promotion with the fellow's aid. But he reckoned without his host, for the other took the picture straight to his Lordship, to whom he sold it for the price he had paid Schalken, pretending that he still made a fair profit out of the transaction. His Lordship believing that he had been swindled, spread the news around; and very soon hardly anyone in London would buy anything from Schalken.

* * * * *

A painter from a neighboring town arranged at Rotterdam an auction of pictures, mostly copies done by himself. He had a catalogue printed and distributed, in which a picture by Jan Steen was listed under No. 1. An art dealer who knew what is what but who was not averse to perpetrat-

PRINT SALE AND EXHIBITION AT PRAGUE, c. 1580
After an engraving in the Bibliothèque Nationale

DE Curateur over den Insolventen Boedel van Rembrant van Rijn / konstigh Schilder / sal / als by de E.E Heeren Commissarissen der Desolate Boedelen hier ter Stede daer toe geauthoriseert / by Executie verkopen de vordere Papier Kunst onder den selven Boedel als noch berustende / bestaende inde Konst van verscheyden der voornaemste so Italiaensche / Fransche / Duytsche ende Nederlandtsche Meesters / ende by den selven Rembrant van Rijn met een groote curieusheyt te samen versamelt.

Gelijck dan mede een goede partye van Teeckeningen ende Schetsen vanden selven Rembrant van Rijn selven

De verkopinge sal wesen ten daeghe / ure ende Jaere als boven / ten huyse van Barent Jansz Schuurman / Waert in de Keysers Kroon / inde Kalver straet / daer de verkopinge voor desen is geweest.

Segget voort.

NOTICE OF REMBRANDT'S BANKRUPTCY

"The Trustee of the insolvent estate of Rembrandt van Rijn, painter, shall, as authorized by the Commissaries of the Chamber of Bankruptcy, by execution sell the prints still included in the estate, consisting of the art of various of the most eminent Italian, French, German and Netherlandish masters, and collected by the said Rembrandt van Rijn with great discrimination. Also a large parcel of drawings and sketches by Rembrandt van Rijn himself.

The sales shall be on the days, hours and year as above, at the house of Barent Jansz Schuurman, keeper of the Keysers Kroon in the Kalverstraet . . . where sales have been held before. Tell it to others."

A ROYAL VISIT TO AN ANTWERP COLLECTION, 1615

The Infanta Isabella and the Archduke Albert visit Cornelis van der Geest in company with Rubens, Gerard Seghers, Jordaens and other personalities. By Willem van Haecht. New York, S. van Berg Collection

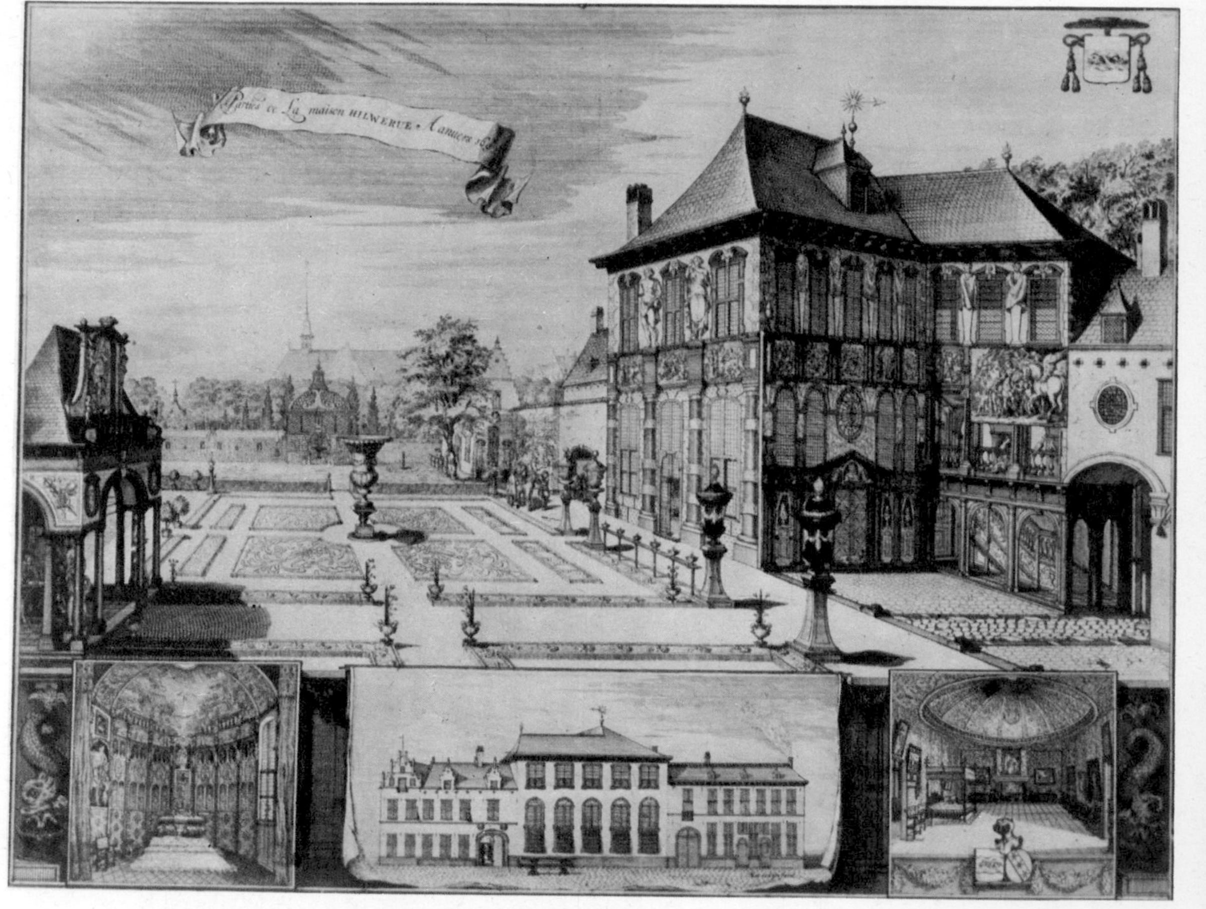

THE RESIDENCE OF SIR PETER PAUL RUBENS AT ANTWERP

After an engraving in the Metropolitan Museum of Art

ing a little deceit, went to the inn where the artist was staying and found him copying the prize picture of the forthcoming show, which he mistook for the original. He asked the artist to sell it to him underhand; for there was time enough to finish the copy before the show opened, and he could auction off the copy instead of the original. At first the painter refused to do it; he was an honest man, he said, and would not engage in such knavish tricks. But when he was offered enough money, the bargain was struck, and the latest Jan Steen replaced the old bastard at the auction. The dealer, meanwhile, secretly warned all his acquaintances that No. 1 was a copy, of which he possessed the original. However, he bought it himself for very little, lest anyone else, he said, should be duped into buying a fake. A few days later he sent his supposed original to another city to have it offered for sale to the connoisseurs. There it was found to be a fake, and the dealer was told where the original was to be seen, and that the first copy that had been made of it served somewhere as a chimney piece. The original, therefore, was already a great-grandfather, for each bastard had produced another bastard.

"An art dealer sent his wife to The Hague with a copy after Wouwerman; for it is with copies of the most famous masters that people are most easily duped if they have not a thorough knowledge of their manner and brushwork. She offered it to art dealers, pretending that it had been in the same family for generations, but that she did not know whose work it was. One of them bought it for a Wouwerman. Others saw it some time later and proved to the buyer that it was a copy by confronting him with the original. The woman happening to be in The Hague one day, was threatened with court action. 'For what?' she asked with a show of innocence. 'For selling me a copy.' 'Impossible,' she replied in self-defense. 'For although I do not know the name of the artist, I know for certain that his name is not Copy.'

"If that sort of swindle is happening with native art," I observed, "how then do they juggle people with foreign paintings, especially with Italian ones?"

"I will tell you a story about that," cried the painter. "I saw it happen myself at my master's house. A crafty fox of an art dealer had him copy an Italian picture. When it was finished he came to look at it and was asked whether he liked it. It had a slight blemish, he replied, but that could be remedied in a few hours. My master promised to correct it if he would show him what was wrong with it. Thereupon the other took a knife, cut a hole in the canvas, ordered him to patch it up at the back, and to restore it in front as well as he could. Then, he said, it will pass for an original, for most Italian paintings have suffered much damage." *

Throughout his many commentaries on the art world, says Lugt, "Van Effen refers to art dealers of southern origin (Brabanders) who had chosen Holland as their hunting ground. But there must also have been many serious experts and collectors in the seventeenth and eighteenth centuries who needed no advice. One may say that, considering the enormous reserve of fine pictures, an occasional mistake did not matter, and the real connoisseurs certainly kept their eyes open. With their sense for quality they distinguished the copies and imitations from the originals of their countrymen. As to Italian pictures, they must wisely have taken all attributions with a grain of salt. In the north every Venetian picture of around 1500 was called a Giorgione, just as the contemporary Dutch pictures were invariably called Luca de Olanda (Lucas van Leyden) in Italy." †

To return a moment to the Golden Age, the most spectacular collecting was that which centered about Rembrandt and his friends and patrons. Typical among them were Constantine Huygens at The Hague, secretary to the Prince of Orange and father of the celebrated physician, and Jan Six, the Amsterdam aristocrat, who many years after Rembrandt's death became Burgomaster. The latter was portrayed twice by the artist in the etching of 1647 and in the painting of 1654. Other family portraits by Rembrandt, Hals and Potter remained together in the family and were bequeathed to the Dutch Government in 1936 by the archaeologist and art historian, Professor Jan Six. Another Six collection formed in the eighteenth century by collateral descendants was dispersed in recent years.

Rembrandt was himself an omnivorous collector whose eyes and appetites were, unfortunately, larger than his pocketbook. The inventories taken at the time of his bankruptcy, ironically enough the very moment when he was at the height of those majestic powers of his later paintings, so sought after today at any price, are the docu-

* The passages quoted above were generously translated from the Dutch by Adrian J. Barnouw, Queen Wilhelmina Professor of Dutch History and Literature, Columbia University.

† From a private communication of Mr. Lugt to the author.

ments which tell us most about his personal taste. Not only was he a collector of paintings and drawings by the old masters – particularly the Italians, some of whom he collected while others he knew only by reputation – but his collection of prints contained a working library of ideas and iconographical suggestions. Moreover, his passion for antique busts * was rivaled only by his interest in weapons and ethnological specimens from America and the Indies. His paintings further show that he kept a vast costumery; among these were the magnificent vestments of the Ghetto which appear in his studies of Jewish rabbis and in the Biblical scenes of his religious prints. Everything which he saw or touched became a "stage property" to be put aside for documentation or the posing of a model.†

Vosmaer has put together from various documents a room-by-room description of Rembrandt's house at its most brilliant epoch, immediately prior to the bankruptcy sale of 1656. It is a charming account, in French, to which in recent years other scholars, particularly Valentiner, have made additions and corrections. But since no account of it exists in English, the following summary of Vosmaer's mid-Victorian comments has seemed worth while:

The house was a vast one on the Jodenbreedstraet in the Quarter of Saint Anthony. It was built in the so-called Dutch Renaissance style in brick and trimmed with dressed stone. . . . With the aid of the inventory, let us step into this house which we may still enter at the present time. We first arrive in the vestibule which in the bourgeois house of the seventeenth century had its characteristic furnishings. It was the type of entrance hall that Pieter de Hooch so often painted. Over by the window the stone tiles were covered by a section of deal flooring on which were arranged six Spanish chairs covered with black cushions. Twenty-four pictures covered the walls giving a preparatory glimpse of the taste of the master of the house. There were, together with several antique heads in plaster, four paintings by Brouwer, four by Lievens, a small landscape by Hercules Seghers, and fourteen pictures by Rembrandt him-

* He possessed a splendid *Socrates* and a head of the blind Greek poet, both of which he painted into his "*Aristotle and the Head of Homer*" in Mrs. Erickson's collection.

† The inventory is given with critical commentary in C. Hofstede de Groot, *Die Urkunden über Rembrandt*, Martinus Nijhoff, 1906, p. 189; and in Charles Blanc, *L'Œuvre Complet de Rembrandt*. Paris [1859–1861].

self; among these were several still-lifes, some *Vanitas,* a group of landscapes and one of those beautiful lion hunts so much admired in his etchings, and, finally, a *Saint Jerome,* perhaps one of his earliest known works painted in 1629.

Once admitted in the antechamber, the visitor, if he was obliged to wait, had plenty with which to occupy his time. It was a veritable salon. The walls were hung with pictures, many of them enclosed in elaborate gilt frames. There one saw sixteen pictures by Rembrandt, mostly landscapes, several studies of houses, a *Descent from the Cross,* a large *Raising of Lazarus,* a *Flagellation* et cetera. There were also canvases by Pinas, a *Tobias* of Pieter Lastman, some things by Lievens, Seghers, Brouwer, Simon de Vlieger and even Lucas van Leyden. But what captured the attention were the Italians; a Palma Vecchio, a painting by the elder Bassano and a head by Raphael. This antechamber was furnished with a great walnut table, covered with a Tournais carpet, large Spanish arm chairs with green velvet cushions, a large mirror in an ebony frame and a marble-topped *rafraîchissoir.* Admitted now as friends of the house, we enter the adjoining room and find ourselves no longer in the dwelling of a simple painter but in a museum. Always the walls are overloaded with pictures; those by Rembrandt are in profusion, a *Virgin and Child,* a sketch for the *Crucifixion,* a Female Nude, figure pieces by Brouwer, more landscapes of Seghers', and very rare items by Porcellis and Aertgen van Leyden; the head of an old man by Jan van Eyck and two copies after Annibale Carracci. Here and there were certain utensils which indicated that Rembrandt was in the habit of using this room when he did his etching and engraving, and pulled the impressions of his immortal prints.

The hall or room immediately behind this proclaimed itself as the "*centre du ménage.*" It had a large mirror, a table across which was thrown an embroidered shawl; the chairs were upholstered in blue like the bed; there was a great linen press of cedar wood and a smaller wardrobe of the same material. But the man who lived in this room was an artist and even here surrounded himself with works of art. The walls were filled with his own pictures, among which were a *Concorde du pays* (?),* a *Resurrection,* a sketch of the *Entombment,* and an *Ecce Homo* in grisaille; there were pieces again by Seghers, Lievens, Lastman, Aertgen

* It has been suggested that *Concorde du Pays* refers to an allegorical painting by Rembrandt, known only from the documents, celebrating the *Union of the Ten Provinces.*

van Leyden and two Italians, a *Madonna* by Raphael and *The Good Samaritan* by Giorgione.

On the first floor, the master had his studios and his museum. First there was the art cabinet (*de kunstkamer*). It was more than one could take in at a single visit; every corner was filled to overflowing with statuettes in porcelain and plaster; his classic marbles included the portrait busts of Homer, Aristotle and Socrates and the Roman emperors. Globes, minerals, sea-shells, stood side by side with stuffed and mounted birds and animals; here there were Chinese and Japanese porcelains, curios and esoteric arms and weapons, suits of armor, a painted shield attributed to Quentin Massys; there, casts taken from nature, life masks, particularly that of Maurice Prince of Orange, Venetian glasses, fans and precious books. Finally there were some sixty portfolios in leather containing his drawings and prints, a collection rich not alone in his own work but illustrating the principal Italian, German and Netherlands schools.*

Adjoining this museum there was a smaller cabinet, followed by a suite of rooms which repeated in detail the contents of the larger and more formal rooms. Oriental arms and armor as well as musical instruments were a constant source of delight and inspiration to Rembrandt as his own work bears witness. And his selection of casts proved his deep interest in the art of sculpture; he possessed a cast of the *Laocoon*, one of the earliest of such casts to reach the north of Europe, and several reproductions of Michelangelo's greatest works.

Rembrandt, who never hesitated to put a proper value on his own production, was too shrewd to bargain for the finest objects of his collection. He bought on the instant and was always ready to pay the top price for anything he really wanted. Hofstede de Groot cites the record prices paid by Rembrandt in the auction room for prints—ironically it was he who created the first bull market in this field, particularly for the Italians and early Germans. A document dated March 19, 1659, by the appraisers Lodewyck van Ludick and Adrian de Wees, establishing the rights of the young Titus, put the value of Rembrandt's collections in the years 1640–1650 at 11,000 florins for the prints, drawings, medals and antiquities as well as the marine speci-

* Carel Vosmaer, *Rembrandt Harmens van Rijn, sa vie et ses œuvres.* 2nd ed., The Hague, 1877.

mens; the pictures by the old masters were valued separately at 6400 florins. He sold his own prints as dearly as he could, but when the opportunity arose he seized upon a group of etchings by Lucas van Leyden for 80 reichstaler. "We know," says Valentiner, "that Rembrandt thought highly of Lucas van Leyden . . . through Hoogstraeten and Sandrart we are told that he paid a large sum for his etchings by Lucas, the *Ecce Homo*, the *Entombment*, the *Danaë* and others. His pupil Leendeet Corneliz later bought his Lucas sketch book for the enormous sum of 637 gulden. Even after the auction Rembrandt obtained a loan of 600 gulden giving as security the prints and drawings by Lucas which remained in his possession." Valentiner likewise deduced that among his Italian prints Rembrandt had examples of Marc Antonio, and that he purchased whenever he could engravings of paintings of the Venetian School.* While neither Holbein nor Dürer is specifically mentioned in the inventories, there are fragmentary references which confirm his interest in and possession of their works.

In the purchase and resale of pictures he was no less acute. The Rubens *Hero and Leander* that he bought for 425 gulden borrowed from his "Magistrate" ("referee in bankruptcy" to use the modern term) he sold to another magistrate for 530 gulden. Frequently he paid his taxes by selling some of his own pictures. And, what is most endearing, the documents show that Rembrandt frequently encouraged his own pupils by buying their works from them and thus created a market for the younger men. But except for that of those associated with him he did not buy much contemporary work.

At the time of the death of his first wife, Saskia van Ulenborch, in 1642, Rembrandt was at the height of his career. He was rich and famous. But he was bored. His experience in dealing with committees for the so-called *Night-Watch*, the *Sortie of the Banning Cock Company*, had confirmed in him a growing distaste for the official art which the Hollanders of the day were willing to pay for. Rembrandt retired within himself, devoting his energies to creating the mature and free masterpieces which mean so much to us today. He took up with his

* W. R. Valentiner, "Rembrandt und seine Umgebung" in *Zur Kunstgeschichte des Auslandes*. Vol. XXIX, Munich, Strassburg, J. H. Ed. Heitz, 1905, pp. 64 ff.

model, the peasant girl, Hendrickje Stoffels. He could not marry her because the property had been left in trust by Saskia for their young son Titus. The stern rock-ribbed Protestant community could not look with favor upon a life of sin. Rembrandt was deserted by his friends and pursued by his creditors. Hurt and angry, he painted more and more to please himself and employed his genius in opening up, like a surgeon dissecting a cadaver, the society which he had learned to despise. But as he grew away from those who had been his patrons, he came closer to the poor, particularly to the miserable inhabitants of the Ghetto among whom he had lived; in his prints and drawings he showed himself to be one of the greatest masters of human tragedy. The bankruptcy proceedings of 1656 were all that was needed for the final separation of Rembrandt from the official Holland that today claims him so wholeheartedly. The last ten years of his life were spent in the most abject material poverty, redeemed by a richness of the spirit which the world has rarely seen equaled at any other time.

* * * * *

To a greater or lesser degree the other cabinets of Amsterdam, The Hague and Delft reflected the tastes and appetites of which Rembrandt's collection was the epitome. These galleries and works of art were considered a sort of communal property for the instruction of rising Dutch artists. When Constantine Huygens, the poet and secretary of the Prince of Orange, remonstrated with Rembrandt and Lievens for not going to Italy to pursue their studies face to face with the works of Raphael and Michelangelo, in order to avoid the "narrowmindedness of their contemporaries," Rembrandt replied, "We are in the flower of our youth and have no time for travel; moreover, the princes are so fond of the art of painting that the best works can be found outside Italy, and things one would have to look for in different places over there can be found here massed together and in great abundance."

When Rembrandt replied in this vein, Lugt insists, he was not belittling the wonders of Italy but expressing the general opinion of his time. For not only in the collections of the princes, but in those of the merchants and the art dealers of Amsterdam he felt that he was in daily communication with the best that the southern artists had produced. And even before his own reputation as a painter was secure, Rembrandt, through his cousin, the art dealer Ulenborch, had had access to any house or gallery he wished to see. The two most famous Flemish painters, Rubens and Van Dyck, both slightly Rembrandt's seniors, Lugt points out, "had an important share in the activities of contemporary collectors. Both of them prized Titian above all and their enthusiasm was contagious. Their relations with the grandees of the period greatly contributed to the spreading of Titian's reputation. Having been eclipsed in the North during the sixteenth century by the great qualities of draughtsmanship of the schools of Rome and Bologna (Raphael and the Carracci), the Venetian was at last recognized there as *the* great master of color and composition, thanks to the enthusiasm of his devoted admirers Rubens and Van Dyck. The latter were not content to sing his praises but set the example as collectors." *

Rubens left ten pictures by Titian in his estate at the time of his death, in addition to thirty-two copies he had made of Titian's work when he was at Madrid. Nor do these include the Venetian pictures which he had sold in 1625 to Buckingham. And Van Dyck was scarcely less active as a collector than either Rubens or Rembrandt. Although Marie de Medicis's secretary, who visited Van Dyck's house in Antwerp with the Queen in 1631, wrote that he had seen there "the Titian cabinet, that is to say all the best works of this great master," very little has been known about this collection. No inventory has come down to us and Van Dyck's correspondence has told as little of it as his biographers. But a few years ago, according to Lugt, a list in Italian of the pictures in Van Dyck's possession was found by accident in the unlikely Viennese archives of the Ministry of War. "This catalogue," he says, "compared with some of the master's sketches and corroborated by other references, has made it possible to establish that he was the fortunate owner of the great picture known as the *Cornaro Family* (which in reality is the Vendramin

* Quite aside from the information contained in his monumental *Marques de Collections*, Mr. Lugt has given the writer valuable advice and references. He has moreover generously made available the notes of a lecture on Dutch Collectors of Italian Art given at the Metropolitan Museum. Cf. also Lugt in *Oud-Holland*, 1936, pp. 97–131.

Family), acquired some fifteen years ago by the National Gallery in London for £125,000, also the famous picture in the Louvre of *Laura Dianti and Alfonso de Ferrara* (*'una corteggiana con un specchio ed un huomo'*), and of the magnificent portrait, wrongly called *Ariosto*, again at the National Gallery acquired in 1904." In all, Van Dyck was said to have owned no less than nineteen pictures by Titian alone.

The Altman Collection at the Metropolitan Museum has a portrait by Van Dyck of one of the great collectors of the Netherlands, Lucas van Uffelen. De Piles considered Uffelen, in fact, "one of the keenest collectors that ever existed." Van Dyck was often a visitor at the merchant's house in Venice where he was engaged in the trade between the Netherlands and the Adriatic. The sale at Amsterdam of his property, April 9, 1639, was one of the celebrated events of the day. Unfortunately no catalogue is known but contemporary accounts have given some idea of its richness; the total fetched was nearly 60,000 florins, an almost unheard-of sum for the period. Rembrandt was present and made a rapid sketch of the picture, which Lugt says was "the sensation of the sale; it was Raphael's portrait of *Castiglione* now in the Louvre, sold to a French collector for 3500 florins. Another picture owned by van Uffelen was Titian's *Flora*, one of the glories of the Uffizi which, after many vicissitudes in England, France and Austria, was returned to Italy in the eighteenth century."

Possibly the most picturesque figure in the art world of Amsterdam was Alfonzo Lopez, Louis XIII's agent whom Richelieu sent to Holland to buy guns, warships and munitions. There for many years this diplomat, jeweler and art dealer, who claimed to be descended from the Moors of Granada, ingratiated himself by buying pictures on his own account and acting as agent for his two Cardinal patrons, Richelieu and Mazarin. Upon his return to France, where he adopted both the citizenship and the religion of his sponsors, *le Seigneur Hébreu*, as Richelieu called him, became a councilor of state and outdid himself in magnificence, driving about Paris in a carriage drawn by six horses, hoping to be mistaken, as he often was, for the ambassador of the King of Spain. At Amsterdam he bought on the same grand scale on which he lived, always with an eye to the future sale of his effects in Paris which was to take place in 1641 in his house on the rue des Petits-Champs. Tallement des Réaux reported the occasion, saying that "there was a special crier. It was a smaller version of the *Foire de Saint-Germain*, continually frequented by the best people." The painter Claude Vignon, writing to Langlois the print seller and publisher in London, telling him that Lopez's sale was to take place in December, sent his greetings to Van Dyck and said that he had just seen Titian's *Ariosto* at Lopez's house.*

It must be recalled also that the Earl of Arundel's collection was moved to the Netherlands in 1643 and that soon after there followed many of Charles I's pictures as well as many items of the Duke of Buckingham's that had been confiscated by the Parliament. These assemblages provided for the first time an opportunity for the people of the Low Countries to see early Italian pictures of the *cinquecento*. For Arundel had in addition to 34 Titians, 12 Giorgiones, 10 Tintorettos, 12 Correggios, 32 Raphaels and 25 Veroneses – to name but a few items in the inventory drawn up for his widow in 1655 – a group of early pictures and drawings by Antonello da Messina, the Bellinis and other Venetian and Florentine masters.

Daniel Nys, who had negotiated the sale of the Duke of Mantua's collection to Charles I in 1629, and whose cabinet of drawings had been purchased by Arundel in 1637, was an Antwerp merchant residing for many years in Venice, practicing the art business on the side. Unquestionably he must have acquired a taste for the early pictures in which the hereditary collections of the Gonzaga were so rich. And it is reasonable to suppose that at the time of his negotiation there were many pictures, not conforming to the high Renaissance taste of Venice, which never reached the British Isles; for while their existence was known in the palace at Mantua, they do not appear in the subsequent letters or inventories. The cellars and attics of the art dealers in Belgium and Holland, where the international traffic was at its peak, must indeed have been filled with this type of unwanted

* In this same letter Vignon asks Langlois to give his most cordial greetings to Sieur Rembrandt and to tell him that he is going to sell the latter's picture of *Balaam's Ass*. The picture is now in Paris in the collection of the Musée Cognac-Jay.

and unsalable residue, and it is in the collections of the well-to-do artists rather than in the cabinets of princes that these pictures, acquired for their artistic merit and not for their prestige, were more likely to turn up.

The list of auctions in Amsterdam between 1600 and 1800 only serves to emphasize the full importance of this movement. There were not only the amateurs of Italian art but those as well who fancied the home-grown product. Amongst these it suffices to mention but a handful of names: Jacob Engbrechtsz Rauwaert, whose collection was sold for 14,411 florins in 1612, was said to have owned the best group of pictures by the Fleming, Pieter Aertsen. He had sold several pictures to Count von Tippi, agent for the Emperor Rudolph, for 1000 Flemish pounds. Martin Kretzer collected over a period of twenty years, specializing in the works of Titian, Bassano and Andrea del Sarto. He was also noted for the pictures by the Italianate Dutchmen whom he admired – works by Lastman, Poelenburgh, Pinas, Honthorst, Terbruggen, Both and de Laar. His catalogue for a sale in 1670 included pictures by Rubens, Van Dyck, Rembrandt, Lievens and Fabritius.

Another type of collector, the precursor of Durand-Ruel and Ambroise Vollard, was Hermann Becker, who had brought together a stupendous collection by advancing and lending money to artists who paid him back in pictures. Rembrandt was deeply in debt to him and paid him, we know, with at least two canvases, the *Diana* and the *Juno*. And another collector, Antoon van Leyen, employed painters for the daily wage of four florins. He took Immenraat with him to France, Italy and Germany on a journey of two and a half years "to sketch and draw every thing he was told to." Van Leyen was to pay all traveling expenses and in case he were to die on the trip, Immenraat's estate was to receive 300 florins as indemnity. He was also entitled to make copies of any of the pictures and drawings for himself.*

The pattern of these collections varies. That of the brothers Reynst, whose collection of Italian masters was the greatest Holland has ever seen before or since – composed of masterpieces from the Vendramin

* Cf. Floerke, *op. cit.*

Palace in Venice and from Charles I — was probably from the point of view of quality one of the most important next to Rembrandt's in the city. However, the entity of the collection was short-lived, for the pictures were dispersed in 1660 when Gerrit's widow sold those pictures which had been acquired from the sale of Charles I to the States-General. These paintings, now at Hampton Court Palace, were presented by the people of Holland to Charles II. Other collections were formed, partly as investment, partly as a matter of pride. No doubt greed, too, played a role, as in the case of Philip van Valckenisse, who left upon his death in 1614 a collection of several hundred pictures.*

* * * * *

The art business, which had assumed an unprecedented importance in this period, followed the paths laid out a century or two earlier in Antwerp. Exhibitions were held with regularity and the art dealers were obliged to adhere strictly to the rules laid down by the Guild of Saint Luke. There was, however, a certain restiveness, for in 1639 a group of painters obtained the large hall of a convent in Utrecht for an independent sales and exhibition gallery, while at The Hague the painters separated from the Guild and founded an association known as the *Pictura*.†

To the art dealers of Amsterdam we owe most of the conventions and customs of the present-day art business. Looking over the records and Floerke's admirable researches, there seems to be, indeed, very little that is new under the sun. A body of competence was built up from which the art galleries of Paris and London, and later New York, took their cues. There is scarcely a firm today of international significance that does not directly or indirectly trace its beginnings to this Holland market. Duveen Brothers entered England by way of Amsterdam, and if one scratches the surface of Bond Street or the

* Cf. Tancred Borenius, *The Picture Gallery of Andrea Vendramin.* London, 1923. Cf. also J. Denucé, *The Antwerp Galleries, Inventories, etc.*, The Hague, 1932.

† According to Floerke, "Articles 19 and 21 of their constitution provided for a permanent exhibition. About a century later this exhibition was extended to include pictures by non members and by giving each member the right of exhibiting as many pictures as he would like and offering them for sale. The exhibition was open every Tuesday from 11–1, and an attendant was ready to serve the visitors with catalogues and prices."

rue de la Boétie it may generally be said that the thing which distinguishes the fine art dealer from the *petit antiquaire* is some training or atavistic connection with Amsterdam of the seventeenth and eighteenth centuries.

Even then a code of ethics imposed itself upon the art business, infractions of which were heavily dealt with. Gerrit Ulenborch, who in 1670 was considered not only the finest connoisseur of Italian art but also the wealthiest and most upright dealer in Holland, was caught up in a scandal involving the sale of 13 famous Italian pictures to the Prince Elector of Brandenburg for 30,000 florins. Hendrick van Fromentiou declared them to be forgeries. The court asked fifty-one artists to render their opinions; thirty-one supported Ulenborch, twenty voted against him. He was obliged to leave Amsterdam a broken man and to find refuge in London, where he eked out a living by painting landscapes and backgrounds for Sir Peter Lely, whom he had known in better days.

Floerke considered that the most prominent art dealer of the seventeenth century was Johannes de Renialme. An inventory taken when he was obliged to pawn a part of his stock in 1640 provides an almost unique record of prices. It included 30 landscapes by Hercules Seghers (today one of the very rarest and most expensive masters of the Dutch School) at 30 florins each. Rembrandt's *The Priest* is listed at 100 florins. When Renialme died in 1659 he left about 400 pictures in his estate valued at 36,573 florins, among which was Rembrandt's *The Adulteress Before Christ*, now in the National Gallery, London. (The estimated value of the picture to the estate was 1500 florins; it was acquired by Angerstein at an auction sale in London in 1807 for £1250.)

Amsterdam's supremacy as the capital of art long survived her greatness as a world power. Not in fact until long after the Napoleonic Wars did she yield her place to London and to Paris. Throughout the eighteenth century the princes of northern Europe, who were emulating the Kings of France and England in supporting their brittle regimes with a truly royal patronage of art, sent their agents to Holland in the hope of buying works of art worthy of their pretensions. Catherine the Great and the Duc de Choiseul were among this number who tried in vain to purchase the celebrated cabinet of Govert van Slingeland. The latter, a notorious stickler for quality, never admitted more than forty pictures to his cabinet at any one time. He frequently would buy an entire collection, keeping one or two items for himself, then selling the rest at auction. When Slingeland died in 1767 he ordered his collection to be sold. The catalogues were already printed when the Prince of Orange, William V, Stadtholder of the Netherlands, intervened and purchased it *en bloc* for 50,000 florins. Thus was established the nucleus of the royal collections of Holland, the glory of the Mauritshuis at The Hague.

CHAPTER III

Art and Diplomacy in Spain and the Low Countries

THE seventeenth century was one of high diplomacy and late Baroque art. No one perhaps epitomizes this world so well as Peter Paul Rubens, ambassador extraordinary of the Archduchess Isabella of the Netherlands to Charles I of England, Philip IV of Spain, to Marie de Medicis, Queen of France, and to Holland. Both officially and unofficially, his was the deciding voice in many affairs of commerce and of state. Part of his success in the great world of his day was due to his personal charm and ability to deal with people. But this was not enough – Rubens was something more; in addition to the momentary allegiance which he gave to the sovereign who employed him for a specific mission, he embodied an attitude towards art and towards the cultivation of the mind for which Europe at that time was ripe and eager. An intellectual curiosity was fermenting in the minds of a highly educated elite, and was making increasing and constant demands upon it. The choice of Rubens as a negotiator between princes who were struggling for prestige and precedence upon the gaming tables of authoritarianism and Divine Right was predicated above all things upon an instinctive knowledge that the Flemish painter was expert in the one currency which was generally acceptable to persons of all walks of life, of all faiths and all nationalities.

At a moment when gold and silver from the New World had merely added to the complexities of modern life, art was accepted *faute de mieux* as a language of expression – a form of intellectual and political Esperanto – and these same princes, who knew that their houses of cards were falling about their ears, clutched madly, like drowning men, to whatever straws the artists would hold out to them. The Kings of England turned first to Rubens, then to Van Dyck and after that to Lely; the Kings of France depended upon Le Brun, Bernini and Poussin for matters extending far beyond the decoration of their palaces, and to Velasquez more than to any other man belongs the credit for that final brilliance of Philip IV before the setting of the Hapsburg sun.

These painters, to be sure, were men of extraordinary talent, and since it has become the custom in recent times to look with growing horror upon the encroachments of the Age of Specialization, the "universal genius," the man who could adapt himself to any task, has consequently been considered as one of the lost creatures of antiquity. Tomes have been written about the universality of Leonardo, his interest in science, in the laws of physics and mechanics; of the wonders of Michelangelo, who was architect, engineer, and one of the greatest painters and sculptors of modern times. But such writing has always seemed to ignore the fact that it is society rather than the individual which establishes the universality of any single genius. Society alone must create the ambience in which this type of universal genius must operate. To the absolute monarch the artist was gradually replacing the confessor of the Middle Ages, for he held in his hands the new key to those generalities of mind and spirit without whose knowledge no ruler can be in contact with his people. The artist played, indeed, a peculiar role in general affairs, one which today, if played by anyone at all, is that of the publisher-editors of our great newspapers and magazines who were quite unknown three hundred years ago. An analogy between the role of Rubens in his time and Lord Beaverbrook's relation to the government of Winston Churchill is not so remote and farfetched as it might seem.

One must not suppose, however, that Rubens – or any one of the artist-diplomatists of which he was the archetype – sprang from the head of Jove fully prepared to carry out his missions. At first these artists, too, were looked at with practiced and jaundiced eyes by career soldiers and courtiers. The fact that in almost every instance it was necessary to ennoble them is evidence of the treachery of the paths which they trod so skillfully.

It was due in large measure to the rigorous training which Rubens

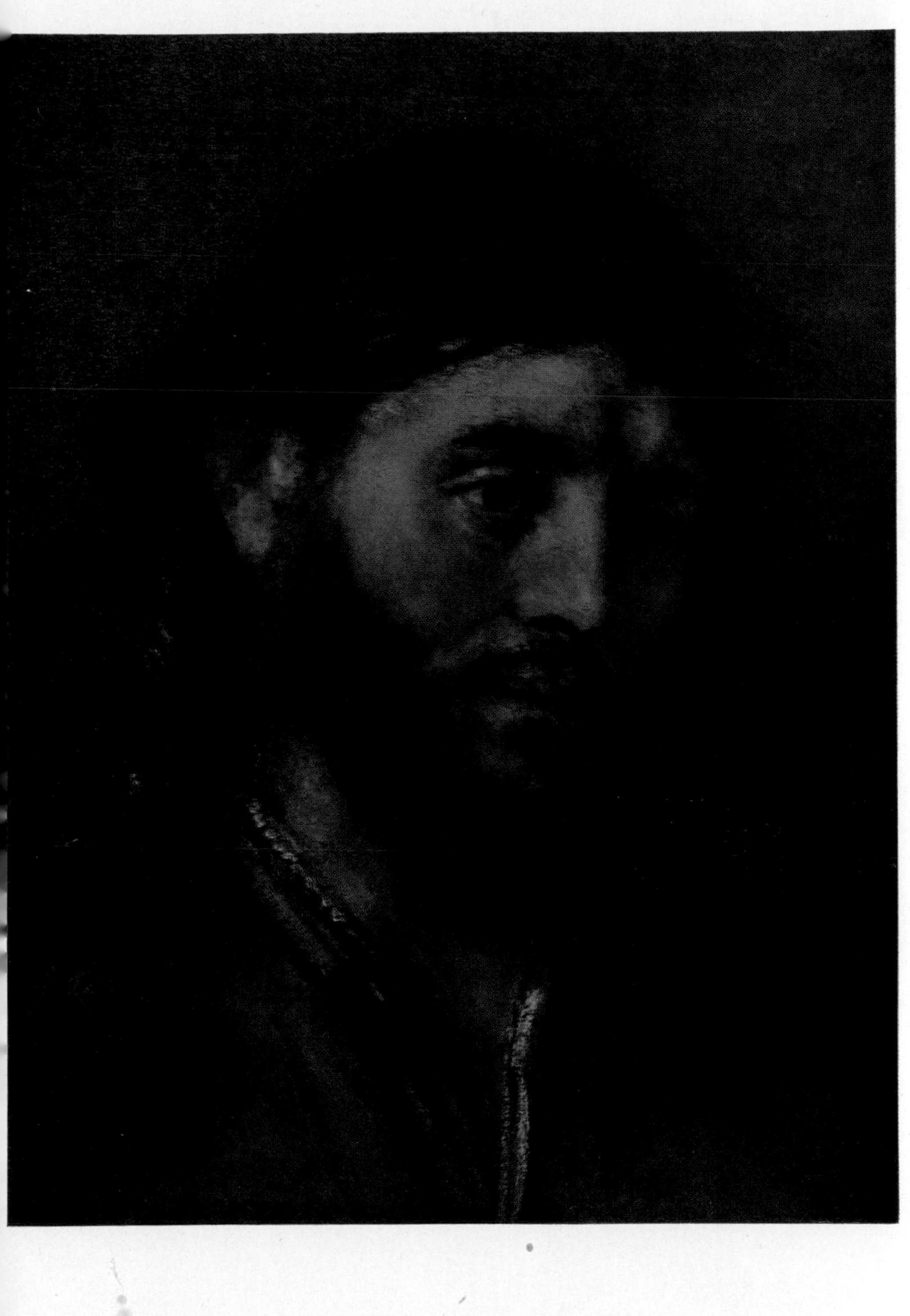

REMBRANDT: HEAD OF CHRIST (DETAIL)

This picture was sold from the J. Wandelaer collection in Amsterdam on September 4, 1759, for 5 florins 10. Passing through several notable collections in the eighteenth and nineteenth centuries, it was bequeathed to the Metropolitan Museum of Art in 1917 by Isaac D. Fletcher, whose estate valued it at $65,000.

as a young man had received at the court of Mantua that he was able to meet the world so knowingly. The Duke Vincenzo had recognized in him not only his extraordinary talents as a painter but also the more sober qualities of scholar and businessman. In sending Rubens to Spain for the first time in 1603, with presents of pictures and horses for Philip III, the Duke contributed to that fund of worldly experience which a later King of Spain was to capitalize. But Rubens initially was rude, and in these early days at the court of Philip III not overly impressed. He kept aloof from the Spanish painters and confined himself to studying the old masters, particularly the Raphaels and Titians in the royal collection.

The stage across which Rubens, and soon the young Velasquez, were to move with such versatility was the political stage of all Europe. It was the eve of the Thirty Years' War which was to end so disastrously for Austria and Germany in 1648. Rome, abandoning the Renaissance, was plunged into an era of nepotism, Inquisition and Baroque art; the crown of Spain was being worn magnificently but inconsequentially by the two Philips, III and IV, who, while they contributed unstintingly to the glories of the Prado, continued the rapid dissipation of their Hapsburg inheritance. The English Stuarts were sowing the seeds of regicide and Civil War. In a France exhausted by religious conflict, the power of the king was strengthened through the cleverness and discipline of two Cardinal Prime Ministers. Sweden, under Gustavus Adolphus, was menacing the imperial authority by pushing the influence of Scandinavia to its farthest limits and clearing the stage for the abdication of Queen Christina, later to be queen of collectors and amateurs in the papal capital. Holland was tasting the fruits of oligarchy and quietly stealing away from England and from France the trade of the New World. To Flanders, curiously enough, fell the task of holding, for better or for worse, the balance of power during the early and middle years of the seventeenth century.

Rubens completed his first mission to Spain and returned to Mantua, where for four years he served the Duke and devoted himself to painting and the pursuits of his humanistic interests as scholar and collector. Visiting Venice, Rome and Genoa, and the court of the Grand Duke of Tuscany, he acquired a fabulous group of pictures and statues for which he paid not in coin but by exchange of his own works. Already his reputation was such that he was able to drive whatever bargain he might wish.

In 1608 he returned to Antwerp to enter into one of the most productive periods of his career. The following year he married the beautiful Isabella Brandt and built himself an Italian palace of which a description, made some forty years after Rubens's death (when it had passed into the family of Canon Hillewerve), has been preserved. Max Rooses has published it together with some engravings which give at least a partial idea of its luxury.

> Once past the threshold of the entrance gate a magnificent effect became visible. The vestibule with its colonnade and its richly sculptured staircase, the courtyard with its lavish sculpture and painting on a façade of imposing proportions and distribution, the majestic style of the portico, with its prospect of the garden and pavilion, and the vases and the statues that crowned it, all recalled rather a mansion in a land where the orange-tree bloomed, than a dwelling in our rude northern countries. Prince or tradesman, no one could enter without being struck by the luxury and good taste of the master of this abode.*

The fame of this palace spread abroad; de Piles, writing about it from hearsay, adds that

> between the courtyard and the garden he built a room round in shape, like the Pantheon temple at Rome, which was lighted only from the top through a single opening in the center of the dome. This room was full of busts, antique statues, and precious pictures which he had brought from Italy, and of other things very rare and curious.

Just what these collections were, it is difficult to say since no list now exists. We do know that he had bought from Sir Dudley Carleton a great collection of antique marbles for which he had given him eighteen pictures painted by his own hand. The extended correspondence over these negotiations has been preserved intact. But for the clearest impression of what Rubens collected we must turn to York House. The Duke of Buckingham in 1627 purchased for £10,000 the greater portion of this cabinet, which he had admired two years

* Max Rooses, *Rubens*. Duckworth, 1904, pp. 149, 151.

previously at Antwerp. Certain things Rubens retained, as he later wrote to his friend the scholar Peiresc, among them the engraved gems. However, the greatest part of Buckingham's fine things surely came from this source, as we may deduce from the voluminous correspondence between the Duke and his agent, Sir Balthazar Gerbier.

One is not surprised to find that a painter of Rubens's ability should have a sure and sensitive taste for the greatest works. Artistic judgment would, after all, seem to be a natural corollary to success and creative talent. What is surprising, though, particularly among artists, is to find scholarship and scientific interest in archaeology. Both of these Rubens had to a marked degree. Much of his private correspondence was in Latin, abounding with allusions to Cicero, Homer and Plato, adorned with classical "tags" and epigrams that would have endeared him to an Oxford don of the nineteenth century. "By the light of this correspondence," writes Stevenson of Rubens's early manhood, "one sees him in the midst of a circle of superior young men who pat each other on the back (in Latin) and pride themselves on belonging to an exclusive intellectual society. The coarser, baser, more natural roots of life in Flanders do not sprout spontaneously in the pretentious efforts at refinement of this coterie of select young men." *

Upon his return from Spain and Italy, Peter Paul Rubens was a man of the world, rich, happily married to a woman of great beauty. He was under no obligation to associate himself either with his boisterous fellow artists at the Brussels court or with the precious *Romanistes* of Antwerp. He had, moreover, from this time on more orders for work at hand than he could possibly fill. "With his excellent sense," continues Stevenson, "he ordered his life upon a very prudent system. In the morning he rose very early, and while he painted someone read aloud Livy, Plutarch, Cicero, Virgil or other poets. Then he would stroll in his gallery to stimulate his taste by the sight of the works of art he had brought from Italy. On other occasions he would study science, in which he always retained an active interest. Although he lived splendidly, he ate and drank moderately; and the gout from which he suffered in later life was certainly undeserved.

* R. A. M. Stevenson, *Peter Paul Rubens*. Oxford University Press, 1939, p. 17.

He painted in the afternoon till towards evening, when he mounted a horse and rode out of the town." * As prosperity came to him more abundantly he added to his collections, corresponding regularly with the learned men of his day, Gevaerts, Lipsius and Peiresc. To the latter he addressed a letter on the use and origin of antique tripods: Sir Peter Paul Rubens to N. C. Fabri De Peiresc.†

Antwerp, July 31 1630
August 10

Most Illustrious & Esteemed Sir:

Your much desired packet has at length reached me, with the very accurate drawings of your tripod and many other curiosities, for which I send you the accustomed payment of a thousand thanks. . . . I have not however had time in two days, viz., yesterday and to-day, to read your discourse on the Tripod, which without doubt, on that matter, must touch all that falls under the human intellect; but I will not omit, for all that, to state, according to my accustomed temerity, my views on this subject, which I am sure you will, with your usual candour, take in the best part. In the first place; all the utensils which rested on three feet, were anciently called tripods, although they served for most varied purposes, as tables, seats, candelabra, baskets, &c. And amongst others they had an instrument to place on the fire under the crocks (*chaudrons* in French) for cooking meat, as used still at the present day in many parts of Europe, then they made a combination of the crock and the tripod, as we know by our pipkins of iron and bronze with three feet; but the ancients had made them with the most beautiful proportions, and, to my mind, this was the true tripod mentioned in Homer and other Greek poets and historians, which they adopted *in re Culenaria*, to cook their meats; and with respect to the viscerations used in the sacrifices, they began to have "*inter Sacram suppelectilem ad eundem usum.*" But the Delphic Tripod I do not believe they derived from this kind, but that it was a sort of seat placed on three feet, as they still use commonly throughout Europe, which had not the basin concave, or if it were concave, to preserve within it the spoils of the Python, (we find in the antique monuments seats with four feet, as the *Sella Jovis* (seat of Jupiter), but still some stools or seats have three feet, as our own stools,) it was

* *Ibid.*, 22.

† W. Noel Sainsbury, ed. *Original Unpublished Papers illustrative of the life of Sir Peter Paul Rubens*. Bradbury and Evans, 1859, pp. 150–153.

covered on the top, and upon this the Pythoness could seat herself with some hole underneath, but that she sate with her thighs in the depth of the concavity does not appear to me likely, from the inconvenience and cutting of the brim of the basin. It may still be, that upon this cup was distended, as upon a drum, the skin of the Python, and for that reason called the curtain, and that it was pierced, together with the crock. Certain it is, that in Rome they find divers tripods of marble which have not any concavity, and they are accustomed still, as you will see in several places cited underneath, to place often the statues dedicated to different gods on the same tripods, which could not be, if not on a solid and level bottom; and we must believe that, in imitation of the Delphic tripod, they applied it to other gods, and that the tripod denoted every kind of oracle or sacred mystery, whence we see it still in the Mimae of Marcus Lepidus, P.M. But what is more to our purpose I will state with more care, that is, that the ancients used a certain kind of warming dish or *réchaud* (as they say in French) made of bronze, (there are two *réchauds* of silver made in Paris of this kind, these they adopted in every part,) to resist the fire, and in the form of a tripod, of which they made use in their sacrifices, and perhaps even in their banquets. There is no doubt, however, that this was the brazen tripod so frequently mentioned in the Ecclesiastical History of Eusebius and others, which served for the burning sacrifices to their idols, as you will see in the places cited underneath. . . .

We are all surprised that you, Sir, in so great a public calamity, should remain with your mind so well in repose, that you can, with your usual taste, continue your most noble study in the observation *rerum antiquarum; Specimen animi bene Compositi et vera Philosophia imbuti.* I hope, however, that on the arrival of this the evil will have ceased, and that you are already on your return to your sacred museum, that it will please God may be with you all happiness and contentment for many years, as this your devoted servant desires with all his heart, and kisses the hands of your most illustrious Lordship.

Your affectionate Servant,

PETER PAUL RUBENS.

This happy period of tranquillity was to be interrupted by diplomacy for in 1622 Rubens was called to Paris by the Queen Mother, Marie de Medicis, to decorate her favorite residence, the Palais du Luxembourg. These large decorations, now in the Louvre, depicting the most glorious scenes from her life and that of her late husband,

Henri IV, were undertaken for 20,000 *écus*. Rubens remained in Paris several months and returned again from Antwerp on other occasions to complete this famous cycle. In the end he was never paid for them and found himself in the position of so many artists, of having to raise money for the person who employed him. During these visits he became friendly with the dashing Duke of Buckingham, who gave him important commissions, lavished presents upon him and deliberately embroiled him deeper and deeper in international affairs.

Rubens, whose first loyalty was always to the Governess of the Spanish Netherlands, the Archduchess Isabella, became a special ambassador in turn to Holland, to England, to France and to Spain. No one in the provinces had access to so many important ears or was in a position to be the confidant and recipient of so many intimacies. The policy of Flanders at this time was to keep England friendly with Spain and apart from France; it was also important for her to remain at peace with Holland. The situation was extremely delicate. Spain was a declining power but James I, and his son Charles I, refused to see the writing on the wall and insisted upon an alliance with her. Richelieu, on the other hand, knew that Spain was finished and set little store by her friendship and support. Moreover, the Cardinal had so embittered Buckingham by separating him from Anne of Austria that even his resentment against the Spanish Minister, the Conde-Duque de Olivares, paled beside his burning hatred for the French. Buckingham, Rubens and Olivares might well have succeeded in reconciling France and Spain had not the English Favorite tried to persuade the Most Catholic King to aid the Huguenots at La Rochelle against Richelieu. Such a proposal was of course ridiculous and Rubens at this point was dispatched to Spain in the summer of 1628 to learn the true feelings of the King. Hardly had he set foot on Spanish soil when news came of Buckingham's assassination and Richelieu's capture of La Rochelle. Rubens's diplomatic mission therefore came to nothing. But since he had brought eight pictures with him as a gift for the King, this visit, which was to be spent in the constant companionship of Velasquez, proved to be one of the great and providential accidents of the history of art.

* * * * *

The Madrid to which Rubens came for the second time could boast, according to Stirling-Maxwell, "finer galleries of art and a greater number of amateur artists than any other city, Rome only excepted. . . . The palace of the admiral of Castile was adorned with many fine specimens of Raphael, Titian, Correggio, and Antonio Mor, curious armor and exquisite sculptures in bronze and marble; and that of the Prince of Esquilache, Francisco de Borgia, one of the nine poets who are called the Castillian Muses – was also famous for the pictures which adorned its great hall." * The Conde-Duque de Olivares, Don Gaspar de Guzman, had one of the finest libraries in Spain, particularly rich in manuscripts and incunabula. He was the friend and patron of Velasquez, whose loyalty and continued friendship to him in the years following Olivares's disgrace shed a pleasant light on the character of the Spanish painter; and he was likewise a protector of Rubens and a collector of his works. Other collectors of importance were the favorites of Olivares, the Marques de Legañes and the Count of Monterey, the notorious "thieves of Milan"; Monterey boasted owning a famous series of sketches by Michelangelo known as *The Swimmers* and Don Juan de Espiña claimed to have two volumes of sketches and manuscripts by Leonardo da Vinci.

Despite the indifference of Philip III to art in any form (he had obligingly allowed his portrait to be taken on several occasions), the impetus given collecting by his father was not entirely exhausted by the latter part of the sixteenth century. Throughout Spain a series of important cabinets had been brought together. At Alba de Tormes, the famous Duke of Alba, "the Scourge of Flanders," hero of Mühlberg and conqueror of Portugal, had filled his palace, as he did another one, La Abadia in Estremadura, with pictures and statuary, bringing a Florentine, Tommaso, to do murals of his military exploits. The house of Mendoza, equally famous in arms, diplomacy and letters, had established a fine library and museum at Guadalajara. In Zaragossa the palace of the Aragonese Duke of Villahermosa had been painted by a pupil of Titian, Paolo Esquarto, who was brought from Venice especially to record the history of this family. Similar histories had been painted at Mirabel, the seat of Luis de Avila, Grand Commander

* Sir William Stirling-Maxwell, *Velasquez and His Works.* London, 1855, p. 12.

of Alcantara, a faithful soldier of Charles V. The castles of the Silvas at Buitrage, of the Sandovals at Denia, the Beltrans de la Cueva at Cuellar, and the Pimentels at Benevente were "rich in adornments and trophies of the chisels and pencils of Italy." Town houses such as that of the Secretary Antonio Perez in Madrid and the palaces of the Velascos at Burgos and of the Riberas in Seville were equally resplendent.

Although Madrid was the capital of the kingdom, Seville at this time was the most prosperous and cultivated city of Spain. It was into this milieu that Diego Rodriquez de Silva y Velasquez was born in 1599, the same year in which Rubens's other great pupil, Van Dyck, first saw the light of day at Antwerp. Velasquez's family, like that of Rubens, were people of position and substance and the young artist never wanted for the proper introductions. His early apprenticeship was spent with the Sevillian painter Francisco Herrera the Elder, studying with him the collections of the Ribera Palace. He passed on from him to another painter, Pacheco, whose daughter he married five years later. Velasquez's familiarity with art was in the collections and churches of his native city, since it was the Church – and particularly the cathedral chapters – which was the great art patron of the day, far exceeding in many ways the patronage of the crown itself. "The chroniclers dilate," continues Stirling-Maxwell, "with unction and with pride on the splendor of their sacred palaces, and the plate and jewels which blaze around their honored shrines." * One may rest assured that any pupil of Pacheco was familiar with these ecclesiastical treasures for he proclaimed loudly that "the chief end of the works of Christian art, is to persuade men to piety, and to bring them to God."

The year 1622 brought the young Velasquez to Madrid, where, through the favors of Don Juan Fonseca, he had access to the royal galleries. His sojourn there was purely a voyage of study, in which he applied himself to copying the old masters, but Fonseca took his measure. Shortly after his return to Seville he was called to Madrid to be attached as painter to the royal household. There began the intimacy with the King which was to last unbroken throughout his life.

* Stirling-Maxwell, *op. cit.*, 14, 15.

Philip IV, had he not been King of Spain, might yet be remembered as one of the leading literary figures of his day. He wrote an exquisite and lucid Spanish prose, produced a series of comedies in verse, translated admirably from the Italian. His talents as a painter were competent if uninspired, receiving eulogies from the court as the herald of a new Golden Age, "*Para animar la lassitud de Hesperia.*" He was above all *Rey por ceremonia,* to which he gave himself in the footsteps of his grandfather. But unlike Philip II he also abandoned himself to the pleasures of the flesh. His attraction to and for women was his undoing, and consequently his ministers, Olivares and (finally) Luis de Haro, had a free hand to misrule the state, reaping the whirlwind of oppression and rapacity at home, declining commerce and revolt in the colonies and distant provinces. Bloody and disastrous wars occupied most of the forty-four years of his reign, closed by the inglorious Treaty of the Pyrenees.

But however irresponsible a ruler he may have been, Philip IV will go down in history as one of the most passionate connoisseurs and patrons of art that ever sat upon a throne. Unlike most royal personages, such as Charles I of England or Louis XIV, who acted only upon advice of agents, Philip, himself an artist, entered into an intimacy with his court painter which animated his whole being and which today reflects itself so indisputably in the collections of the Prado. "The liberality and affability with which he [Velasquez] is treated by so great a monarch is unbelievable," wrote Pacheco. "He has a workshop in his gallery and his Majesty has a key to it, and a chair so that he can watch him painting at leisure nearly every day."

When Rubens arrived in Madrid in August 1628 he and Velasquez, who was twenty years his junior, had already exchanged letters and were disposed to become friends. Immediately they took to one another, the elder recognizing the genius of the younger man, the younger anxious to get all that he could from an artist he had long admired. Rubens was also, according to Pacheco, more suave and less arrogant than he had been on his first visit to Spain.

> He [Rubens] associated little with painters, only with my son-in-law did he make friends, and he praised his works very highly, because of their simplicity; they went together to visit the Escorial.

He brought his Majesty, our Catholic king Philip IV, eight pictures of different subjects and sizes, which are placed in the new room amongst other famous paintings. In the nine months that he spent in Madrid, without neglecting the important business on which he came and although he was indisposed some days with the gout, he painted many things, as we shall see, so great was his skill and dexterity. First of all he portrayed the King and Queen and the Infantes, in half-length, to take back to Flanders; of his Majesty he made five portraits, including one on horseback, with other figures – very excellent. He portrayed the Infanta in the Convent of the Descalzas Reales more than half length, and made copies of it; of private persons he made five or six portraits. He copied all the works of Titian in the King's possession . . . including the portraits of the Landgrave, the Dukes of Saxony, of Alba, and of Lobos, and a Venetian Doge, and many other works besides those belonging to the King. He copied the portrait of Philip II full-length and in armor. . . . It seems incredible that he could have painted so much in so short a time and with so many occupations. . . . And all the time he was at the Court his Majesty and the chief ministers showed great appreciation of his person and talent. His Majesty bestowed on him the office of Secretary to the Privy Council at the Brussels court for his lifetime and that of his son Albert, with a yearly stipend of one thousand ducats. His business finished, when he took leave of his Majesty the Conde Duque gave him, on behalf of the King a ring worth two thousand ducats.*

The following year Rubens returned to Flanders hoping to spend the rest of his days working for the Spanish crown and taking with him many uncompleted sketches and studies for work which he later executed and sent back to Spain. After the appointment of his brother, the Cardinal Infante Ferdinand, as Governor of the Netherlands in 1634, the King appointed Rubens as his principal agent for the acquisition of paintings. Through him Rubens was commissioned in 1636 to paint a series of mythological pictures to decorate the Torre de la Parada and the Palace of Buen Retiro – 112 pictures were shipped to Spain – many of them were destroyed in the eighteenth century when the Torre de la Parada was sacked by the Austrian Pretender.

Philip also bought 32 works by Rubens and his school, 17 of them original compositions by Rubens himself, 10 of them copies he made

* Pacheco, *Arte de la Pintura.* Madrid, 1866. Eng. trans. by E. Harris, *op. cit.,* 32.

after Titian. Later, in 1648, after Rubens's death, "part of the large cartoons representing the *Triumph of Faith,* painted in Rubens's atelier for the Infanta Isabel, were sent to Madrid at Philip's request and placed in the Carmelite Church at Lorches. The tapestries previously made from them in Brussels had already been sent to Madrid.*

Upon his return from Spain, Rubens was sent for the better part of a year as ambassador to England. There Charles I commissioned him to do the banqueting saloon at Whitehall. He also painted in England the *Peace and War* in the National Gallery and the *Saint George* in Buckingham Palace. For these he was knighted by the King and he returned to Flanders with "an increased reputation, a gold chain and hopes of peace." While in London he had visited York House, where he saw once more the collections which he had sold to Buckingham, murdered only the year before. His emotions and his impressions of England are recorded in a letter to Pierre Dupuy:

I console myself by thinking with joy on all the beautiful things I have met with on my journey. This island, for example, seems to me worthy the consideration of a man of taste, not only because of the charm of the countryside, and the beauty of the people, not only because of the outward show, which appears to me most choice and to announce a people rich and happy in the bosom of peace, but also by the incredible quantity of excellent pictures, statues and ancient inscriptions which are in this Court.†

And in a letter to his old friend Peiresc he says very much the same:

My only pleasure is to see, during my pilgrimages, so many various countries, so many cities, so many peoples following different customs. I am far from finding in this island the barbarous ways which its climate might warrant, since it is so different from gracious Italy, and I must confess that, from the point of view of painting, I have never seen such a quantity of pictures by the great masters as in the Palace of the King of England and in the gallery of the late Duke of Buckingham. The Earl of Arundel possesses an enormous number of antique statues and of Greek and Latin inscriptions, which you have seen since they have been pub-

* Only some sketches remain today in the Prado, for the cartoons were taken from Spain in the French invasion in 1808.

† Stevenson, *op. cit.,* 37.

lished by John Selden, with the learned commentaries which one might have expected from that talented and cultivated author.

* * * * *

The last ten years of Rubens's life were again comparatively tranquil and free from the interruptions of diplomacy. Upon his return from England he married, for the second time, the luscious, full-blown beauty, Hélène Fourment, a child of sixteen, the youngest daughter of his friend and kinsman, Daniel Fourment. "Her appearance pleased Rubens," writes Stevenson, "indeed women of her type had always haunted the painter's canvases, and now from this time she herself, the incarnation of the Rubens ideal of Venus, sat for many of the personages in her husband's pictures." Rubens himself was a handsome, famous, rich and somewhat gouty widower of fifty-three. His new wife, his commissions for the King of Spain and his interest in archaeology became the all-absorbing passions of his later life.

His visit to his former treasures at York House had perhaps filled Rubens with the restless nostalgia which lies endemic beneath the surface of every born collector; for at the time of his death in 1640, his Antwerp palace was once again filled with masterpieces, although the quality of this second collection, despite Rubens's increased wealth and power, does not appear to have compared with that which he sold Buckingham and was to a large extent a gallery of his own works. It comprised 314 numbered items and 15 not numbered, of which 319 are pictures, and 10 statues or objects of *virtù*. There were 46 pictures by Rubens after Italian masters – including the copies of the Venetians he had made at Madrid – 94 original pictures, 7 pictures in which the figures were by Rubens, a large number of portraits from life by Rubens or Van Dyck, a quantity of drawings and sketches for his principal works, and numerous copies of his pictures. The presence of so many duplicates in the inventory of Rubens's studio indicates that he used to keep at the disposal of collectors an assortment of portraits of contemporary princes, of landscapes, and of pleasing and attractive subjects.*

* * * * *

* Rubens was buried on June 2, 1640, and six days later the notary Guyot began to draw up the inventory, and set to work at the same time to catalogue the pictures. By

The decade following Rubens's departure from Madrid was even more fruitful and rewarding for Velasquez, who, at the age of thirty, had now reached the full stature of his art. Although he never held the formal titles of ambassador, nor was he ever specifically entrusted with political affairs, the Spanish painter by virtue of his friendship with the King who had made him court painter, with the monopoly of painting the royal portraits, and also *Aposentador* of the palace, was in fact a plenipotentiary even more powerful than Rubens had ever been. The increase and enrichment of the royal collections was one of the chief policies of Philip's reign, and Velasquez was charged with its execution.

On the eve of his departure Rubens is said to have convinced the King of the necessity of Velasquez's going to Italy, where he had never been. The King gave his painter leave of absence for two years without loss of salary, 4000 ducats, quarters and free medical service for his household, and a gift of 400 ducats. Olivares added to this a purse of 200 ducats and many letters of introduction, arranging for the painter and his indentured Negro servant to accompany the great Spinola, who was about to sail from Barcelona for Venice, en route to govern the Duchy of Milan.

Everywhere Velasquez received honors befitting the emissary of the King and resided in state at the Spanish Embassy. Venice was enjoying the relaxation of her "silver age" and Velasquez, eschewing the society of the rather mediocre artists of the day, plunged himself into the study of the great colorists of a century before and assiduously applied himself, following the example of Rubens at Madrid, to copying the works of Giorgione, Titian, Veronese and Tintoretto.

After several months he set out for Rome, passing by Ferrara and Bologna. The account of his approach to Rome and of the condition of the city upon whose acquaintance Velasquez had so long set his heart is one of the memorable chapters of Stirling-Maxwell's biog-

---

July 14 it was completed in Flemish, French and English. It was not printed till later, by Jan van Meurs, and then only in French. Out of the whole edition only one copy has survived (now in the National Library in Paris; reproduced by Paul Lacroix in the *Revue Universelle des Arts*, I, 268 [1855]. An English text has been published three times; cf. note on p. 620). The title of the catalogue is: *Specifications des peintures trouvées à la maison mortuaire de feu Messire Pierre Paul Rubens, chevalier etc.*

raphy, which after a span of nearly a hundred years, remains, like Symonds's *Renaissance*, an imperishable landmark in the literature of art:

He was advancing towards the eternal city amidst the monuments of her ancient and modern glory. . . . Velasquez, happily, was in a condition to enjoy these things; to indulge all the emotions of an accomplished mind, as the landmarks, new and yet familiar, appeared, and as the dome of the Great Basilica, rising above the classic heights around, harbingered the mother-city of his art and his faith. Unlike most painters, he entered these sacred precincts with a name and a position already established, but with no fears of failure to disturb his serenity, no visions of penury –

"To freeze the genial current of his soul."

In far different circumstances, and with different feelings, that road had been traversed, but a few years before, by two brethren of his craft, who were to become his equals in renown, Nicolas Poussin, an adventurer fresh from his Norman village, and Claude Gellée, a pastry-cook's runaway apprentice from Lorraine.

The Papal chair was at that time filled by Urban VIII, Maffeo Barberini, a pontiff chiefly remarkable for his long incumbency of that splendid preferment, his elegant Latin verses, and two works executed at his cost from the designs of Bernini, the grand high altar of St. Peter's, and the Barberini palace, for which the Coliseum served as a quarry. He and his Cardinal-nephew, Francesco Barberini, received Velasquez very graciously and offered him a suite of apartments in the Vatican; which the artist humbly declined, contenting himself with less magnificent lodgings, and the right of access, granted as soon as asked, at his own hours to the papal galleries. Then he applied himself with great diligence to study, and with his crayon or colors, culled some flowers from the new world of painting which now burst upon his gaze. Michelangelo's *Last Judgment*, in the Sistine Chapel, scarce ninety years old, was yet undimmed by the morning and evening incense of centuries. Of this he copied many portions, as well as the *Prophets* and the *Sybils;* and he copied also, the *Parnassus, Theology*, *Burning of the Borgo*, and other frescoes of Raphael.

Happier than Venice, Rome at this epoch could boast more artistic talent than had been found within her walls at one time since the days of Michelangelo. Many of the Bolognese masters were sojourning for a season, or had fixed their abode in the capital. Domenichino and Guercino were now engaged on some of their best works, the *Communion of St. Jerome* and the *Finding of the Body of St. Petronilla;* the Grottaferrata, and the Ludovisi frescoes. Guido Reni alternated between the excitements of the gaming table, and the sweet creations of his smooth-flowing pencil. Albani, the Anacreon of painting, was adorning the halls of the Borghese and the Aldobrandini with cool forest glades, peopled with sportive loves and graces. The great landscape painters of France, Poussin and Claude, were laying the foundations of their delightful and fertile schools. Beautiful fountains, palaces, and churches, rising in all quarters of the city, displayed the architectural genius of Bernini, the friend of popes, the favorite of princes, and the most busy and versatile of men.*

Living quietly at the Villa Medici, from which the magnificent collections of Cardinal Leopoldo had not yet been removed to Florence, Velasquez was able to withdraw from the artistic controversies which raged in the capital at this time. And it was probably here that he matured his ideas for the development of the King's collections. After a bout of fever, he went to Naples, where his father's friend and patron, the Duke of Alcalà, was Viceroy, and finally embarked for Spain, reaching Madrid in the spring of 1631.

The next eight years were spent at court and were years of enormous productivity. Velasquez took charge of the decoration of the Palace of *Buen Retiro* on the site of the present *Palacio Real.* The *Salón de los Reinos,* now the Artillery Museum, is all that remains today of the palace and still retains the ceiling decorations which he painted. For this room he likewise completed the equestrian portraits of Philip III and his Queen which hung on either side of the throne. At the opposite end of the room were the portraits of Philip IV, and Queen Isabella and the Infante Don Balthazar Carlos. On the long walls were the large battle pieces including the *Surrender of Breda,* and a series of smaller pictures by Zurbaran representing the *Labors of Hercules.*†

In 1649 Velasquez went again to Italy "to find and to purchase the best paintings to be found by Titian, Paolo Veronese, Bassano, Raphael, Parmigianino and the like. For there are few princes who

* Stirling-Maxwell, *op. cit.,* 112–115.
† Harris, *op. cit.,* 30.

possess pictures by these masters, and least of all in the quantity that your Majesty shall have them through my zeal." Palomino reported that he was only partially successful, bringing back "a series of ceiling decorations by Tintoretto, the *Venus and Adonis* and some portraits by Veronese." It was on this occasion that he made his brilliant portraits of Innocent X for which, Horace Walpole relates, "When the Pope sent his Chamberlain to pay the artist he would not receive the money, saying that the King, his master, always paid him with his own hand. The Pope humored him." * While in Rome Velasquez exhibited his *Forge of Vulcan* (Prado) to the ecstatic admiration of the artist colony.

The King had remarried during Velasquez's absence and upon his return in 1651, the artist was immediately assigned the task of painting the new faces in the royal family. The most famous are the *Portrait of Queen Marianna*, and *Las Meninas* (finished some years later), in which the King himself is said to have painted the cross of the Knights of Santiago upon the breast of Velasquez, who is shown standing before the easel. Velasquez, however, was no less occupied with his functions of *Aposentador*, Marshal of the Palace, for he was responsible for the sanitation, the furnishing and decoration of all the royal residences and was likewise Keeper of the King's collections. Santos, in his *Descripción*, wrote, "The royal palace, so far as regards its endowment of paintings, has become one of the greatest in the world." And indeed it had, since there were assembled within it the accumulated treasures of a dynasty, the Hapsburg, which had had at its beck and call, for several centuries, the greatest artists of the whole of Europe. To these were added not only Philip's purchases in Italy and Flanders but also the eighteen muleloads of pictures which his ambassador Cardenas, at London, had bought from the sale of Charles I of England. "*La Perla*," Raphael's *Holy Family*, Philip placed above the high altar in the sacristy of the Pantheon at the Escorial because he considered it the gem of his collection.

This fascination which the Hapsburg princes of Spain shared with

* One of these portraits has remained in the Doria Palace in Rome. The smaller version was acquired by Sir Robert Walpole and passed to the Hermitage in Russia. It is now in the Mellon Collection in Washington.

VELASQUEZ: *LAS MENINAS*

The artist stands before the easel, Philip IV appears in the doorway.
The Prado

Veduta dell'insigne Basilica Vaticana coll'ampio Portico, e Piazza adjacente

PIRANESI: THE NEW SAINT PETER'S

The foundation stone of the new basilica was laid by Pope Julius II in 1506. Bramante designed the building in the form of a Greek Cross with a hexastyle portico, and an immense cupola supported on four colossal piers. After Bramante's death, Leo X appointed Giuliano di Sangallo, Gioconda da Verona, and Raphael, who altered the plan to a Latin Cross. When Raphael died in 1520, Leo X appointed Baldassare Peruzzi, who returned to Bramante's plan. Little progress was made until Michelangelo took over the work (1546–1564). He adopted the Greek Cross but began the dome on his own plan. He lived to complete only the drum of the dome. Giacomo della Porta, following Michelangelo's plan, completed the dome in 1590. Finally in 1605 Maderna once more adopted the form of the Latin Cross, lengthening the nave and destroying all the eastern section of the old basilica. He also designed the present façade. The colonnade was the work of Bernini. The present-day Saint Peter's is virtually what we see in this engraving of the eighteenth century.

THE VATICAN, 1593, AFTER TEMPESTA

VATICAN CITY TODAY

THE APOTHEOSIS OF THE *WUNDERKAMMER*

Father Kircher's museum in the Jesuit Collegio Romano

their cousins in the north for the great art of the Renaissance subsided simultaneously, and almost as quickly in the Iberian peninsula as it did in Austria and the Low Countries. With Philip IV the curtain fell, almost symbolically, when the latter gave his daughter in marriage to the young Louis XIV of France. The preparation of the Isle of Pheasants in the Bidassoa River (the neutral point on the border for the meeting between the Kings of France and Spain) was Velasquez's last official act. Not since the Field of the Cloth of Gold had Europe known anything more magnificent or more prodigal. A splendid account, gleaned from contemporary sources, is given by Stirling-Maxwell:

The Pheasants' Isle was at this time about 500 feet long by 70 broad. The *Aposentador's* new building, extending from west to east, consisted of a range of pavilions, one story high, and upwards of 300 feet in length. In the centre rose the hall of conference, flanked by wings, each containing a suite of four chambers, in which equal measure of accommodation was meted with the nicest justice to France and to Spain. Along each front of the edifice ran an entrance portico, communicating, by means of a covered gallery, with a bridge of boats, whereby the monarchs were to make their approach, each from his own territory. Within, the apartments were as gorgeous as gildings and rich arras could make them. Velasquez, it appears, superintended the decorations on the Spanish side only, as far as the centre of the hall of conference. The same style of adornment, however, prevailed throughout; the walls being covered with tissues of silk and gold, and with five tapestries, representing histories sacred and profane, the building of the ark of Noah and the city of Romulus, or the adventures of Orpheus and Saint Paul. The French decorators had a leaning to the lays and legends of Greece and Rome, and the tapestries on the side of the great hall recorded the feats of Scipio and Hannibal, and the Metamorphoses of Ovid; while the hangings of the graver Spaniards revealed the mysteries of the Apocalypse.

During the week which the courts of Spain and France passed on the frontier of the kingdoms, the banks of the Bidassoa furnished scenes worthy of the pencil of Titian and the pen of Scott, and its island pavilion historical groups such as romance has rarely assembled. There was Philip IV, forty years a king, with regal port, which neither infirmity, nor grief, nor misfortune, had been able to subdue; and Louis XIV in the dawn of his fame and the flower of his beauty. There were two queens, both daughters of Austria, in whom also grey experience was contrasted with the innocence of youth, and whose lives exemplify the vicissitudes of high place; Anne, by turns a neglected consort, an imperious regent, and a forgotten exile; and Maria Teresa, the most amiable of Austrian princesses, who though eclipsed in her own court, and in her husband's affections aspired in an age of universal gallantry to no higher praise than the name of a loving mother and a true and gentle wife. The Italian Cardinal (Mazarin) was there, upon whom the mantle of Richelieu had fallen, with his broken form but keen eye that read in the new alliance the future glory of France and Mazarin; the cool, wily Haro, in his new honors as Prince of the Peace, Turenne, the old Maréchal de Villeroy, the young Duke of Créqui, Median de las Torres and a host of others.*

Spain had at long last played into the hands of Richelieu and his successors; the artistic as well as political supremacy of Europe was handed over the Pyrenees to create the *Grand Siècle.*

* Stirling-Maxwell, *op. cit.*, 183 ff.

BOOK SIX

Rome in the Augustan Afterglow

CHAPTER I

Nepotism and Baroque Art

THE Holy Year 1600 was something more than a jubilee for the Church; it marked, indeed, the full triumph of Roman Catholicism. Three million pilgrims pressed about the tombs of the Apostles and, so that nothing might be lacking to the glory of the Papacy, an auto-da-fé was held on the Campo dei Fiori and Giordano Bruno, the Dominican philosopher, was solemnly burned at the stake. Rome had entered upon a new era; the Renaissance, which had lingered on after the Sack, was a relic of the dead past. Mythology was chased from the papal palaces; the nude figures above the high altars which Aretino had cited in his attack on Michelangelo were banished, and the Jesuits were free to impose their dogma and their Baroque art. Rome in her frantic efforts to assume temporal domination of Europe had seemed to lose her hold upon the faithful through the scandals of the Borgia and the Medici. But the Council of Trent had achieved the separation from Rome of the Protestant communities; she was free once more to confirm the Papacy as the absolute empire of Catholicism. From the ashes of the Golden Age emerged a more awful and majestic capital, *urbs aeterna*, supported by the savage discipline of the Inquisition and the atavistic veneration of the entire Christian world.*

An important vehicle for the imposition of the new authoritarianism was the revolutionary architecture of Vignola's Church of the Gesù, built in 1586.† The Society of Jesus had been formally approved by Paul III in 1540, thirteen years after the Sack, and they had set up their headquarters in Rome. They had spread their influence abroad as far as Paraguay and China. At home, during the plague and pesti-

* The writer is particularly indebted to the seventeenth-century chapters of Emile Bertaux's *Rome de Jules II à nos jours* (H. Laurens, 1905) and to the histories of Ranke and Pastor.

† The façade was designed by Giacomo della Porta.

lence that followed the looting of the city, they had developed a considerable popularity which they capitalized and invested in the building of their Mother Church. Upon it they lavished not only the multicolored marbles of the antique world, pillaged from the ruined monuments of the Caesars, but also the gold and silver of the New World that came to them from their houses in Spain and Portugal. This church, built in the form of a Latin Cross, followed to a point Giovanni Battista Alberti's Church of Sant' Andrea at Mantua, but there were novelties of architecture which became standard practice for the Jesuit Order and which confirmed Vignola's interpretation of Vitruvius as the rule for mission establishments in both hemispheres.

The nave was deep and broad to permit larger congregations to hear their eloquent and persuasive preachers, the side aisles were honeycombed with small chapels, and the chancel, now considerably shortened, received the high altar at the deepest point of the apse. Decoration followed a strict employment of the Orders, and a classicism, into which had already crept the severity and mysticism of the Escorial, was played with contrapuntal accents against the more prodigal conceits of Baroque and Rococo. Architecture had struck a new mood, a new attitude; the "lightness and cheerful freedom distinguishing the early part of the century were abandoned for pompous solemnity and religious magnificence." This was reflected not only in the building of the Gesù but throughout the ecclesiastical and secular buildings which the Popes of the Counter Reformation and their families were to build.

The century that separated the two Sistine pontiffs (Sixtus IV, 1471–1484, and Sixtus V, 1585–1590) had wrought many changes in the outer aspects of Rome. The lower city which had withdrawn to the banks of the Tiber was entirely restored under Julius II; Saint Peter's was rising in great majesty. Julius had also restored in part the ancient palace of the Vatican and "across from the declivity that separated the old buildings from the Villa of Innocent VIII, called the Belvedere, he laid the foundations of the *Loggie*." Raphael and Michelangelo had contributed their immeasurable share to the glory of the Christian capital; private palaces, too, like the Farnese and the Farnesina, were monuments to them and to the artists who followed in their footsteps. The Medici were filling their palaces with works of art and manuscripts of every variety, and the Orsini were likewise enriching their palace on the Campo dei Fiori. The banker Agostino Chigi, Julius's treasurer, had set an example of personal magnificence which up to that time had been unparalleled.

But for fifty years following the capture of the city, when Rome had lost a large portion of her population, public building had come almost to a standstill. Pius IV had made some minor additions to the Vatican and had built the Palazzo dei Conservatori, and Gregory XIII had added another wing to the Vatican. Aside from that, Renaissance Rome had barely moved forward. Suddenly, in the five years of the pontificate of Sixtus V, the city increased in population and extent by one third and became a vast contractor's depot. These five years saw the completion of the dome of Saint Peter's, the continuation of the *Loggie* and the closing in of the missing wings that form the hollow square of the Vatican; the erection of the palaces of the Lateran and the Quirinal, for which the Papacy had no real need at that time, and a second Sistine Chapel in the flank of the Church of Santa Maria Maggiore. But in addition to these monuments Sixtus V will best be remembered for his physical changes to the city proper; he restored the two great aqueducts, the *Acqua Marcia* and the *Acqua Claudia*, bringing water a distance of more than twenty miles for the fountains with which he and his successors were to embellish the *piazze*. He built an entire new quarter to which he gave the name of Borgo Felice and he extended the broad Via Felice (now Via Sistina) from the Trinità dei Monti to Santa Maria Maggiore. The erection in the Piazza San Pietro of the obelisk taken from the Circus of Caligula was one of the great ceremonial events of his reign.

This frenzy for building, for pulling down the monuments of the past to make room for the new, had in it more of method than of madness. Having been shorn of their temporal authority, the Popes wished to show that the religious capital which had been restored to the Catholic faith was even more splendid, and above all more authentic than ever before. "How complete," says Ranke, "was the revolution which took place in the relation of the age to antiquity! As in former times men emulated the ancients, so did they now, but their earlier efforts were directed towards an approach to their beauty of grace and form; now they sought only to vie with, or exceed them, in extent and magnitude. Formerly the slightest trace of the antique spirit was revered in however trifling a monument; now the disposition seemed rather to destroy these traces. One sole idea held predominance among the men of the day; they would acknowledge no other. It was the same that had gained ascendancy in the Church – the same that had succeeded in making the State a mere instrument of the Church. This ruling idea of modern Catholicism had penetrated throughout the being of society, and pervaded its most diversified institutions." *

Nowhere did this desire for prestige and the high opinion of posterity reveal itself more clearly than in the frank and unblushing nepotism by which the Popes strove to perpetuate their rank and their family fortunes. An ambassador at Rome in the time of Urban VIII wrote home about him, "*Il savait que la possession seule de l'argent distingue de la foule, et il jugeait qu'il n'était pas convenable que le parent d'un pape pût se trouver, à la mort de celui-ci, dans une position restreinte.*" From the time of Sixtus V on, the reigning Pope chose from his family two men – the one became cardinal-nephew, a prince of the Church, the other became a Roman prince, the founder of a dynasty. The dignities of the cardinal, a celibate priest, died, of course, with him, whereas the Roman prince transmitted his preferments, titles and estates, together with the huge sums of money given him from the revenues of the Church, to his family and to posterity. Thus a new aristocracy arose, each pontiff leaving behind him a line of princes; after the Farnese the Aldobrandini, the Borghese, the Ludovisi, the Pamfili, the Odescalchi, the Chigi and so on. New families came to power from pontificate to pontificate, obtaining hereditary wealth and, more often than not, using it against one another; they took their places immediately among the high aristocracy of the country, a rank which was readily accorded them.

The sums of money, lands and works of art lavished upon the papal nephews produced an afterglow of the Golden Age – a little Renaissance – that later endowed the galleries and museums of Europe

* Ranke, *op. cit.*, I, 385.

and America as liberally as did the revival of Leo X. Sixtus V gave his cardinal-nephew, whom he entrusted with large political authority, an ecclesiastical income of 100,000 scudi.* To his other nephew, whom he married to a princess of large fortune, he was no less liberal. The Aldobrandini Pope, Clement VIII, over a period of thirteen years bestowed upon his kinsmen 1,000,000 scudi in hard money as well as many valuable estates. Paul V's generosity to the Borghese, Ranke points out, made them the richest family in Rome. During the twenty years of his pontificate, Urban VIII passed on to the Barberini the incredible sum of 105,000,000 scudi. "The palace of this family," said a contemporary chronicler, "that of the Quattro Fontane, is a royal work; the vineyards, the pictures and statues, the wrought silver and gold and precious stones, that were heaped upon that house, are of more value than can be believed or expressed."

Since they could not themselves transmit to their heirs the Holy See, Ranke observes, the Popes "were the more in earnest to secure hereditary dignity to their families by conferring on them large possessions both in money and land. . . . They were careful to provide themselves with arguments for their own justification. They proceeded from the principle (later formally approved by the Jesuits) that they were bound by no vow of poverty, and having decided that they might fairly consider the surplus proceeds of the spiritual office as their property, they likewise inferred that they possessed the right of bestowing this superfluity on their kindred." †

Competition between these princely houses produced a life of splendor such as had not been seen since the Medici had occupied the throne of Peter. "*C'est le temps héroïque des fêtes et des spectacles, des bals, de la comédie ballet, de l'opéra à machines; ce sont les belles années du carnival romain.*" Not only were the town houses transformed into royal palaces but their environments were altered to provide the proper ambience and approaches; *piazze*, avenues and *corsos*, *borghi*, and *tempietti*, fountains and cascades abounded everywhere; the edges of the Campagna bordering upon the walls were

* The scudo or ducat, the approximate equivalent of the French *écu*, had an equivalent gold value of twenty dollars.

† Ranke, *op. cit.*, I, 385.

cleared of slums and planted with beautiful parks, the villas and summer palaces "formed a shady belt of trees and parterres around the city." Jacques Spon of Lyons, who visited Rome in 1675, wrote, "*Les beaux jardins et maisons de Rome, attirent tout ce qu'il y a de curieux, et ce sont de vrais paradis terrestres et comme des lieux enchantés que les vignes Borghese, Pamfili, Montalti, Ludovisci, aussi bien que les jardins du Vatican, Monte Cavallo et de Medicis.*"

The Roman palaces of the seventeenth century differ only in detail from the great palaces of the sixteenth. They are enormous, sturdy edifices with vast halls to accommodate the many guests at princely festivals, and having quantities of rooms in which to lodge the hangers-on and parasites, the lackeys, and the ruffians whom the master was obliged to keep at hand in order to unleash them in the street during a conclave or a quarrel over precedence. The walls were capable of withstanding siege, the ground floor exterior often being rusticated to give the appearance of a citadel. But the openings were ample and the doorways, formerly narrow at a time when the nobility and the clergy went on horseback and on mules, were now wide enough to permit the passage of gala coaches and state carriages. The cornices usually were more or less fanciful imitations of Michelangelo's cornice on the Farnese Palace. The decoration of the interiors emulated the murals and stuccos of the Farnesina. The façades, generally bare, without pilasters or carved ornament, were severe and majestic. The villas and casinos copied and modified the various plans which the architects of the sixteenth century had invented for their country places. "The palaces and villas of Rome," adds Bertaux, "did not go searching for new ideas, new fantasies; they remained during the Baroque centuries the gravest of monuments, the most correct and the least profane."

Another consequence of nepotism was a complete change in the pattern of Roman collecting. Hitherto, ever since their return from Avignon, the Popes had collected primarily for the Holy See. The Vatican itself was the center of humanism; archaeology was a monopoly of the Church, and any antiquities found within her territories became immediately her property. These finds were brought together at the Vatican, where, late in the fifteenth century, Sixtus IV had already established the Library and the Belvedere and also Rome's earliest museum on the Capitol. There were in addition many private collections comprising chiefly the monuments unearthed by accidental or methodical excavation in the estates of the older Roman families, particularly in those areas of the city which had been rich in imperial monuments. Ulisse Aldrovandi in 1550 cited more than a hundred such collections, many of which had been drawn by Martin van Heemskerk and have been studied more recently by Hübner. Throughout the sixteenth century the collections of the Vatican were being replenished from these sources by purchase and by gift. Among the more important were those of the Cesi, the Giustiniani, the Strozzi and Massimo, the Maffei, the Mattei, the Valli, as well as those of the Colonna and Orsini.

While the enormous wealth of Rome in antique statuary has frequently been stressed in the earlier chapters of this book, it would not be out of place to quote here from Augustus Hare,* who speaks of the enormous number of pagan ruins which existed in Rome right down to modern times. "A monumental record of A.D. 540, published by Cardinal Mai, mentions 324 streets, 2 capitols – the Tarpeian and that on the Quirinal – 80 gilt statues of the gods (only the Hercules remains), 66 ivory statues of the gods, 46,608 houses, 17,097 palaces, 13,052 fountains, 3,785 statues of emperors and generals in bronze, 22 great equestrian statues of bronze (only the Marcus Aurelius remains), 2 *colossi* (Marcus Aurelius and Trajan), 9,026 baths, 31 theatres, and 8 amphitheatres." It must be pointed out that this document was written subsequent to the first sack of the city by the Goths in A.D. 410. How much greater must have been the quantity of antiquities buried in the centuries immediately preceding!

Starting with Sixtus V, the Vatican temporarily lost its importance when the papal nephews entered the field; gradually each Roman palace became a museum competing with the papal collections for the finest works of art. Every palace, too, had a gallery of paintings in which the Bolognese masters held first place, and, in addition, every oratory and chapel was provided with suitable works of art, executed by the artists who currently were receiving large official commissions

* Augustus Hare, *Walks in Rome*. David McKay, Philadelphia. I, 12.

from the reigning pontiff. This was considered neither graft nor genteel blackmail; it was merely one of the many perquisites of a high and sacred office. Sculptors were employed to adorn the courts, arcades and vestibules, as well as the occasional architectural inventions of the palaces, with statues and reliefs. All of these embellishments followed implicitly and without question the prevailing taste of the day.

Another factor which wrought profound changes in the character of the later collections was the gradual decline of humanism. By 1600 it was said that "there did not exist one Hellenist of reputation in all Italy." Ranke claims that this in a sense was the inevitable result of the progress of science which hitherto had sought primarily "to fill up the chasms left by the ancients. . . . A more profound and searching spirit of investigation had arisen; men were conducted to more extensive observations even while seeking to pursue the light offered by the ancients, the mind of the student became free from their tutelage. Discoveries were made that led beyond the circle prescribed by them, and these again opened up further inquiries." * There were limits, of course, beyond which it was dangerous to go, for the Holy Office determined at what point the human mind must cease to speculate upon the miracles of philosophy and natural science. The pursuit of truth and freedom of personal belief were no more tolerated than they are today in Russia and, as a consequence, a heavy pall of dogma hung low over every form of creative expression. The nation would seem, Ranke observed, in speaking of Italian literature, "to have worked out and used up the whole amount of the poetical conceptions descending to it from its bygone history, and the ideas proper to the Middle Ages; it had even lost the power of comprehending them. Something new was sought for, but the creative genius would not come forth, nor did the life of the day present any fresh material. Up to the middle of the century, Italian prose, though from its nature didactic, was yet imaginative, lifelike, flexible and graceful. Gradually prose also became rigid and cold." †

When we gaze upon the broad canvases of the Bolognese School, painted at a time when Venice was immortalizing her past glory on

* Ranke, *op. cit.*, I, 387.
† Ranke, *op. cit.*, I, 389–390.

the walls of the Doges Palace through the genius of Tintoretto and Veronese, we realize the empty bombast of the Baroque idiom. The painter's craft had possibly never reached a higher state of perfection; the knowledge of anatomy derived from the medical schools of Padua and Bologna had developed a fidelity of drawing and execution that was as tedious as it was learned. It was an art not only of propaganda but of "the Propaganda." The Church had obtained complete mastery over the minds of men and fantasy was reduced to a series of accepted conventions based upon the teachings and experiences of others.

Thus Roman collecting, which bulks so large both in quality and in quantity of the objects housed in the palaces of the princely families, is at once a colorless and unimaginative affair. We know these collections mostly by their later histories — after their dispersal from the places of their origin. In the eighteenth century they each achieve personality by virtue of the dynamic qualities of their new owners: Catherine the Great, Walpole, Frederick of Prussia, Ludwig of Bavaria. In Rome they form an aggregate, an average of rich accumulations brought together, not by people of real flesh and blood, but by a system, the nepotal system. It is not because these treasures were dispersed by sale and purchase, or later by the looting of Napoleon, that they fail to stir the imagination, but because we know so little, and care less, about the people who brought them together. Incredibly valuable as were these collections in works of art, not until the advent of the erratic Queen of Sweden do we find a collector of the stature of an Arundel, a Mazarin or a Philip IV, in the palaces and *borghi* of the Eternal City.

CHAPTER II

Christina of Sweden – Convert, Cavalier and Collector

THE half century that preceded Christina's arrival in Rome in 1650 followed the brilliant pattern of the latter years of the sixteenth. The fame of the city, the wealth and lavish patronage of its ruling families, attracted to it from everywhere in Europe the finest talents in architecture, painting and sculpture. The foreign colony, which later was to become legitimized through the establishment of official academies of art, had already made it obligatory for any artist of repute to have studied there at some period of his career. The prophet could no longer be without honor of Rome in his own country. It was not only the century of Bernini, of Caravaggio and the Carracci, of Domenichino and Guido Reni, it was more properly the century of Poussin, of Claude, of Velasquez, and of those ardent, boisterous Flemings, members of the "Bentvogels," a society for mutual assistance to whose cavalier existence the *vie de Bohème* of more recent times owes its origins.

During this period the Papacy was passed around among the great Roman families. Paul V, a Borghese, followed the Aldobrandini Clement VIII.* The Barberini Urban VIII reigned from 1623 to 1644, succeeded for ten years by Innocent X of the Pamfili. The Pope during Christina's active years in Rome was a Chigi, Alexander VII, who ruled until 1667, to be followed at the end of the century by the short pontificates of Rospigliosi, Altieri, Odescalchi, Pignatelli and Albani. The pattern laid down by Sixtus V was scarcely altered: nepotism, palaces and public works, lavish commissions to contempo-

* Upon the death of Clement VIII, a Medici, Leo XI, was Pope for a few months in 1605 and the Ludovisi Pope, Gregory XV, reigned only from 1621 to 1623.

rary artists. The collections in these palaces became larger, richer and more learned. The program for the beautification of the city continued in full force, culminating in Bernini's colonnade for Alexander VII in front of Saint Peter's. This ornamental but highly useless enterprise, destroying a large section of the medieval city, pleased only the Holy Father's sense of symmetry and cost over 7,000,000 scudi; 284 columns, 88 pilasters, he said, "to serve as a shelter for carriages from the sun and rain."

The discovery of an ancient Roman fresco, "The Aldobrandini Wedding," gave authority to a spirit of classicism which was espoused by Poussin and which, with the assistance of the pedants and the pundits who gathered there to criticize and classify the contents of the various palaces, was destined to develop into a doctrine of which Winckelmann in the eighteenth century was to be High Priest. Poussin copied this painting several times; one copy exists today in the Doria Gallery. In the Ludovisi collections he saw the incomparable canvases illustrating the *Amores* of Philostratus, painted by Titian originally for the Alabaster Chamber of the Duke of Ferrara. They profoundly influenced all his later work.* Everywhere that he went "correcting nature," Poussin absorbed and reinterpreted the continuing power and tradition of Rome as revealed through her man-made monuments.

Not so with Claude, for to him was vouchsafed another understanding, another poetry. Far more poignantly than those who came after him, Fragonard, Hubert Robert, or even Corot, he caught the low-lying, opalescent atmosphere of the Tiber. He saw the natural beauty of Rome and dared to call attention to it in the face of all the Augustan severity of his contemporaries. Perhaps it is through the conflicting moods of these two Frenchmen that we can better see the city and Campagna of the seventeenth century than through the eyes of the Italians themselves. For the cult of Rome has always been a cult of those who came to scoff and remained to pray. Spoiled by the overwhelming richness of their endless past, the Romans seem to have

* Two of these pictures, the *Worship of Venus* and the *Bacchanal*, were given shortly afterwards by Cardinal Ludovisi to Philip IV and are now in the Prado. The third, *Bacchus and Ariadne*, is in the National Gallery, London. Cf. Philostratus, *Imagines*, I, 6.

become immunized against the revelation of the beauties they possess.

Into this world capital of art, religion and power politics, the mad, erratic daughter of Gustavus Adolphus blew like a violent gust of the north wind. Her early years – she was born in 1626 – were spent in the barbaric fastnesses of the Baltic and she was determined to bring the foreign culture which she worshiped to her people, whom she actually despised. Swedish life, measured by that of other countries, was very primitive indeed. There were not more than ten brick houses in Upsala, the center of learning, and most of the dwellings were "built of the bodies of great fir trees, covered with turf." According to a contemporary "there was in Sweden one king, one religion and one doctor." The ambassadors of France and Spain lent a ready ear to her ambitions, thus paving the way for her conversion to Catholicism and putting an end to the menacing Scandinavian power in Europe. She ascended the throne at eighteen and her first act was to end the Thirty Years' War by the Peace of Westphalia; immediately she set about transforming Stockholm into the "Athens of the North."

Christina's efforts to found an Academy of Sciences were nearly as fruitless as her labors to introduce art and artists to her country. The aged Descartes, who was the star of her crown, died of pneumonia after a few short months at her court. The Queen, seeing in his death a symbol of her failure to create an intellectual center, wrote, "If I were superstitious, I should weep like a child over his death, and I should repent having drawn this bright star from its course. His death depresses me: it will always fill me with justified but useless regret."

When Christina ascended the throne only one picture, and that by a Swedish painter, could be found in the palace at Stockholm. The Queen summoned at once Sebastian Bourdon, one of the founders of the French Academy, and a Dutchman, David Beck, who later was to tour Europe making copies of the Old Masters for her. Bourdon painted a few portraits, five of which finally landed with her collections in the Palais Royal in Paris. A few Flemish tapestries and some book collections which her agents acquired abroad were the nucleus of the possessions of the Swedish crown until the fortunes of war brought her the incomparable treasures of the Emperor Rudolph II.

VERONESE: MARS AND VENUS UNITED BY LOVE (DETAIL)

This painting, signed *Paulus Veronensis. F.*, is first listed in 1648 in the inventory at Prague of the Emperor Rudolph II. Looted by the Swedes, it was recorded in the Roman inventories of Queen Christina, who bequeathed it to Cardinal Azzolino. The latter's nephew, Marchese Pompeo Azzolino, sold it to Prince Baldassare Odescalchi, who in turn sold it in 1721 to the Duke of Orléans. It appears in the inventories of the Palais Royal in Paris at a valuation of 15,000 livres, was sold in London in 1798 for 300 guineas and again in 1903 for £6300 at the Wimborne sale. It was acquired by the Metropolitan Museum of Art in 1910 for £8000.

These collections, valued at 17,000,000 gulden, which Arundel had visited and admired at Prague a decade earlier, were captured by Königsmark when he occupied the city a few months before the Peace of Westphalia. The town was plundered by the soldiery but the contents of the palace were reserved for the Queen. Königsmark, in fact, feared that peace might be proclaimed before he could send the booty home. Eusebius Miseron, a noted sculptor and keeper of the collections, refused to give up the keys and was indeed keen enough to send away to Vienna some of the finest pictures before the Swedes arrived. But notwithstanding, in November 1648, five barges loaded with works of art were floated northward on the Elbe to Stockholm where the Queen was impatiently awaiting their arrival. The catalogue, prepared by the French critic du Fresne and completed four years later, a few weeks before Christina's abdication when the collection was once again packed up to resume its travels, listed nearly 500 pictures, about 100 statuettes in bronze, marble and alabaster, celebrated codices including the *Argentius of Ulfilas,* clocks, instruments of precision, jewels "and a living lion."

The Queen's taste at this period was limited to the art of the southern countries. She cared nothing for German painting and was only too glad to give the Spanish ambassador as a gift for Philip IV the Cranach *Adam and Eve* of the Prado. And to the Duke of Bracciano she wrote, "*Il y a un nombre infini de pièces, mais en dehors de trente ou quarante que sont des originaux italiens, je ne tiens aucun comte des autres. Il y en a d'autres maîtres allemands, dont je ne sais pas les noms. Tout autre que moi les estimerai beaucoup, mais je vous jure que je les donnerai tous pour une paire de tableaux de Raphael, et je crois de leur faire encore trop d'honneur.*" It was this intolerance of any thing or idea manufactured in the north that caused her to leave behind when she abdicated a hundred or more Dutch and German pictures which became the nucleus of the present National Museum at Stockholm.

Christina's restlessness and intolerance were gradually getting the better of her. Continually embattled with her ministers of state and the dominating hierarchy of the Lutheran communion, she turned her eyes and her thoughts to Rome. Through the confessor of the

Portuguese ambassador, who always required his presence at their interviews, since the envoy spoke no language but his own, Christina carried on underneath his nose a series of theological discussions which resulted in the arrival in Stockholm, in 1652, of two Jesuits to give her instruction in Catholicism. "The charm of this affair to Christina," observed Ranke, "was principally in the certainty that no one had the slightest suspicion of her proceedings." For some time she had seen the handwriting on the wall and knew that as the leader of a foreign party, wishing to embrace the hated Popish religion, in her refusal to marry, and in her insistence upon appointing her cousin, Charles Augustus, her successor, the only course left open was to relinquish the throne. "*Je me serois sans doute mariée*," she says in her autobiography, "*si je n'eusse reconnu en moi la force de me passer de l'amour*." "It is a far greater happiness to obey no one, than to rule the whole world." When she rode out of Stockholm dressed as a man under the name of Count Dohna, she was met at the Danish border by a courier of the King asking her for the last time whether she would marry him. "Tell his Majesty," she replied, "that had I wanted to marry, it would have been more suitable for me to have chosen a husband myself when I was a ruling sovereign than to have myself chosen as a wife now that I have given up my crown."

Before leaving Sweden Christina had ordered a medal struck to commemorate her abdication. On the face of it is an indifferent portrait of herself; the reverse shows a labyrinth surrounded by an inscription from Vergil, "*Fata viam invenient*."

At this period no distinction was made between crown property and the personal possessions of the sovereign. Christina took with her, in consequence, collections valued at 2,000,000 riksdaler (30,000,000 gold francs), and stripped the country of its works of art, particularly those won at Prague. The first year was spent at the lavish Brussels court of the Archduke Leopold, in whose palace she was privately received into the Roman Church. Here amidst the treasures of this great collector, Christina, who had never before left her country, was in her element, feasting her eyes, broadening her tastes, and diminishing her purse by the purchase of many pictures from Buckingham's collection then being sold at Antwerp. From the Netherlands the cavalcade of 220 persons proceeded to Rome by way of Innsbruck, where she was publicly proclaimed a Catholic. The rest of the journey was a triumph; wherever she stopped on the way flags and banners were broken out, princes met her in state, banquets and games were held in her honor. Finally on the outskirts of Rome Pope Alexander VII met his royal convert beneath a *baldacchino* specially designed for the occasion by Bernini. When she knelt before him, the Pope raised her up, seating her at his right hand, and drove her into Rome to the entrance of the Farnese Palace which she was to occupy.

The Palazzo Farnese at this time was often placed by its owner, the Duke of Parma, at the disposition of distinguished visitors whose favor he wished to cultivate. Possibly the most beautiful private house in all of Rome, it still contained the collections of Paul III and those of his commissioner of public works, Mario Maccharone, and to these the Duke Ottaviano Farnese had added in 1546 the celebrated antiquities of the Sassi Palace which he had bought for 1000 scudi. Then again in 1600 the Orsini collection entered the palace. This included 400 cameos, 113 pictures and cartoons, 150 historical inscriptions, 58 portrait busts and 1500 coins. All of these objects were valued by the testator, Fulvio Orsini, at 13,595 scudi.* The pictures, including works by Raphael, Titian, Leonardo, Dürer and Cranach, were valued separately at 1789 scudi, the Cranach *St. Jerome* being set down at 10 scudi! Most of these works in the late eighteenth century followed the rest of the Farnese collections to Naples where they formed the basis of the National Museum.

Christina's seven months of residence in these surroundings were hardly rewarding to the courtesies of the Duke of Parma. Immediately the Queen removed with her own hands the white draperies with which the nude statues had been decorously swathed, while her servants robbed and pillaged. Gold and silver galloon was torn from the furniture. Priceless pieces of silver were removed and plated copper substituted. The coach of the Spanish ambassador, Pimentelli, was ravaged while he was calling on the Queen. Beautiful marquetry doors were torn down, stripped of their gilding and used for firewood. The Marchese Giandemaria, whom the Duke of Parma had

* Cf. inventory discovered by Nolhac in the Biblioteca Ambrosiana at Milan.

deputized to do the honors of the palace, was in despair and refused to allow the Queen to enter the Orsini museum without his being present to watch her.

Herein lay the basis of the reputation which preceded Christina's arrival in Paris, whither she went on a fruitless errand to persuade Mazarin to put her on the throne of Naples. "*Je ne vois pas par ce recit*," the Cardinal wrote to Colbert after she had visited the royal collections, "*que la Regne aye vue mon appartement du Louvre; mais en cas qu'elle demande à le voir, je vous prie de prendre garde que la folle n'entre pas dans mes cabinets, car on pourrait prendre de mes petits tableaus*."

Not until her return to Rome in 1662 to occupy the Palazzo Riario did Christina start to collect in earnest. She bought *en bloc* the Carlo Imperiali collection from Genoa and ardently undertook excavations in every part of Rome wherever the presence of antiquities in the soil was suspected. So great was her success that at her death the inventory listed 122 sculptures, among them the group of the *Muses* found at Hadrian's Villa, the *Faun* discovered near the Chiesa Nuova and a *Venus* which she herself unearthed. All of these statues, together with many more busts and reliefs, remained in Rome with her heirs until they were purchased by Philip V of Spain for 50,000 scudi and taken to the Palace of Saint Ildefonso. They are today in the Prado.

This amazing woman amateur, *literata*, archaeologist, was at the same time something of an ascetic in her private tastes. "She was free from all vanity," Ranke writes; "she never sought to conceal that one of her shoulders was higher than the other; she had been told that her principal beauty was the rich profusion of her hair, yet she did not bestow upon it the most ordinary attention. To all the more minute cares of life she was wholly a stranger; utterly regardless of what appeared on her table, she never expressed disapprobation of any kind of food that was set before her, and drank nothing but water. She never acquired or understood any sort of womanly works, but on the contrary delighted to be told that at birth she had been supposed to be a boy. . . . She was a very bold horse-woman; with one foot in the stirrup she scarcely waited to be in her saddle before she started at full speed. In the chase, she would bring down her game with the first shot. She studied Tacitus and Plato, and not unfrequently expounded the meaning of those authors more clearly than professional philologists." * She also took a lively interest in science and in the cultivation, while at Rome, of a pure Italian style in literature, founding in 1680 an academy for the simplification of the turgid style then prevailing. She loved all of the diversions of the mind, attending concerts, carnivals and dramatic entertainments for which she wrote informal comedies. Scarlatti was her concertmaster and her singers and players were considered the best in Rome. Wherever intrigue, wit and scandal were discussed, Christina, in the midst of all her other pursuits, was always to be found.

Yet the Queen's letters to her friend and heir, Cardinal Azzolini, are filled with sadness and a sense of failure. "I have lost everything that could make life pleasant for me," she wrote, "and after such a loss I am no longer able to cherish my life nor do I wish to do so, and I think that the day of my death will be the happiest day of my life, as it will be the last day on which I shall be alive." The death for which she longed came to her in 1689. Her last request was that her simple gravestone should bear the following inscription:

D. O. M.
VIXIT CHRISTINA
ANNOS LXIII

Posterity has differed in its estimate of this woman; countless explanations of her life, political, Freudian and pious, have been offered. The most amusing, and most vicious, is that given by Horace Walpole, perhaps a little jealous of her superiority as a collector, in describing a hundred years later her posing for her portrait:

As he (Dahl) worked on Queen Christina's picture, she asked what he intended she should hold in her hand. He replied, "A fan." Her Majesty, whose ejaculations were rarely delicate, vented a very gross one, and added: "A fan! Give me a lion; that is fitter for the Queen of Sweden." I repeat this, without any intention of approving it. It was a pedantic affectation of spirit in a woman who had quitted a crown to ramble over Europe in a motley kind of masculine masquerade, assuming a right of

* Ranke, *op. cit.*, II, 392.

assassinating her gallants, as if tyranny as well as the priesthood were an indelible character, and throwing herself for protection into the bosom of a church she laughed at, for the comfortable enjoyment of talking indecently with learned men, and of living so with any other men. Contemptible in her ambition by abandoning the happiest of performing good and great actions, to hunt for venal praises from those parasites, the literati, she attained, or deserved to attain, the sole renown which necessarily accompanied great crimes or great follies in persons of superior rank. Her letters discover no genius or parts, and do not even wear that now trite mantle of the learned, the affectation of philosophy. Her womanish passions and anger display themselves without reserve, and she is ever mistaking herself for a queen, after having done everything she could do to relinquish and disgrace the character.*

The verdict of history regarding Christina's character and her place in the political arena of her day is still uncertain; but she has unquestionably offered us one of the most brilliant and penetrating chapters in the history of art. "*La peinture, la sculpture et tous les autres arts qui en dépendent sont des impostures innocentes, qui plaisent et qui doivent plaire aux gens d'esprit. C'est un défaut à un honneste homme que de ne les aymer pas, mais il faut les aymer raisonnablement.*" With these words Christina dismissed her own activity in the arts although no collection save that of Charles I of England has had louder or more recurrent repercussions. Across three centuries these collections have enriched the greatest galleries of the world and left her mark upon them. It was her superior connoisseurship which Horace Walpole, prig that he was, could neither forget nor forgive. With her closed the Renaissance of Italy. Collecting in Rome from that time on returned its functions to the State and to the Church, and was guided in its course by a new spirit of learning, that of the classical ideal.

Cardinal Azzolini, Christina's closest friend, was her executor and universal legatee but he survived her by only a few weeks. His nephew, Marchese Pompeo Azzolini, who, inheriting very little money with the works of art, could not afford to keep them, sold the bulk of the collections to Prince Livio Odescalchi for 123,000 scudi. Two hundred and forty pictures, of which at least 66 had come from

* Walpole, *op. cit.*, II, 648–649.

Rudolph's gallery in Prague, were included in the sale. The Odescalchi had been active as bankers since early in the sixteenth century. Paolo Odescalchi, secretary to Pope Paul IV, had brought the family to the front rank and had laid the foundations for a museum that might hold its head up with those of the proudest nephews of the Papacy, by purchasing a collection of statues from Giuseppe della Porta. These marbles passed with Christina's to Spain in 1724. Christina's library was bought by Cardinal Ottoboni, who later became Pope Alexander VIII and gave it to the Vatican. Her medals and coins, of which she had more than 6000, included those that her father, Gustavus Adolphus, had taken at Munich; to these were added those belonging to Rudolph II, a collection from Nuremberg presented to her by Charles Gustavus, as well as the cabinets of Charles I, and other collections in Germany and Italy picked up for her by her antiquarian, Francesco Gottifredi.

But the Odescalchi were to fall on evil days. In 1714 Pierre Crozat arrived in Rome as the agent of the Regent, the Duc d'Orléans, with an offer of 110,000 *écus* for the entire collection; the Odescalchi were asking 200,000. Crozat left Rome disgruntled. Six years later he returned with an offer of 93,000 *écus* for the pictures alone. The offer was accepted, the medals and numismatics being sold to Pope Pius VI for 20,000 in 1794. They remained at the Vatican, however, for only a few years, the Pope being obliged to cede them to Napoleon by the Treaty of Tolentino; they have been ever since the glory of the Cabinet des Médailles of the Bibliothèque Nationale in Paris. The drawings, of which there were many thousand, the Regent gave to Crozat for his pains; many of these were acquired for the royal collections of France at the Crozat sale in 1742 and are now in the Louvre. The pictures acquired by the Regent arrived in Paris in 1722 and included some of the most famous canvases that we admire today.

CHAPTER III

The Formation of the Vatican Museums

IF the seventeenth was the century of the Roman *nipoti*, the eighteenth was that of the dilettanti who flocked to the capital from everywhere in Europe. Italy, no longer a power in world politics, had subsided into the role of being a vast academy dedicated to the study of the past. The eighteenth-century Popes, reacting against the domination of the Jesuits, finally suppressed them and put an end to the terror which they exercised over the minds of men; freedom of thought and action again was tolerated. Moreover, the extravagances of their predecessors had drained the treasury of the Popes to a considerable extent and a general debt had been piled up which brought ruin in its wake to many of the princely houses established by them during the hundred and fifty years preceding. The purses of the Kings of France and Britain were long and easily replenished from the empires they were building overseas. They could meet any price and afford almost any luxury. The courts of Germany, particularly of Prussia, Bavaria and Saxony, were anxious to emulate the larger powers and to reflect the magnificence of their newly found sovereignty in collections of antiquities and galleries of art. Far larger portions of their revenues were diverted to this purpose than were either justified or reasonable, and they were encouraged in these extravagances by a new class of scholar-gentleman who was emerging from the status of household secretary-servant, which he had enjoyed for centuries, into the role of courtier, savant, diplomat and man of letters.

The Roman nobility welcomed these foreign scholars with open arms and upraised palms, hoping that they might be instrumental in helping them redeem their art collections and turn them into hard cash. Seldom has the scholar been more in vogue, more petted and sought after. The antiquarian abbé seemed to move through brick walls without ever having to go over them; he was ubiquitous, humble, malicious and usually a first-class man of business. His activities were cloaked with a fine screen of learning; he might be the author of a book on the topography of Rome or the commentator on the travels of a Greek or Latin antiquary; he was sometimes a philologist with eyes only for inscriptions, at other times a student and connoisseur of engraved gems – a form of art especially popular since they were easily pocketed and could be minutely classified more readily than larger statuary which required establishments beyond his means. We see among these dilettanti the beginnings of specialization; some fancied terra cottas, lamps and vases, others preferred, like the Jesuit Athanasius Kircher, to study the obelisks and other fragments of Egyptian art which had crept into Rome over the centuries. There were Hellenists, Romanists and Etrurians, and those who devoted themselves to the study of manuscripts of the Old Testament. They were the friends of artists, particularly sculptors and engravers, who illustrated their learned volumes with pictures of lost monuments and imaginary reconstructions of the temples and gardens of antiquity.

Usually they were members or correspondents of one of the many academies and scientific societies which flourished at this time not only in Rome but throughout the cities of Italy; they all had one thing in common: each was beholden to some prince or patron for whom he was finding suitable works of art, frequenting the dealers like the Englishman Jenkins or the studios of the restorers, of whom the most famous was Cavaceppi, offering advice on the reconstruction of a nose or an arm, and picking up scraps of information which he might send home relative to the antique market.

The liquidation of the Roman collections was a matter of deep concern to the Vatican, which sat by watching the treasures lavished by the Popes upon their nephews leave Italy to become the pride and glory of foreign monarchs and, alas too often, of princes of the Protestant faiths. Arundel in the seventeenth century had already taken what he could; part of his antiquities were given by the Countess of Pomfret to Oxford University, the other major portion going to enrich the country seat of the Earl of Pembroke, Wilton House, where in 1720 more than 1300 busts and other sculptures were added from the Roman palace of the Giustiniani, a large quantity of objects from the sale of Mazarin's collections and other pieces from the impoverished Neapolitan family of the Valetta. Pembroke had earned the reputation of being unwilling to let any of his portraits be nameless and was designated by Winckelmann as "the audacious priest." "An ancient virtuoso," Horace Walpole remarked, "indeed would be a little surprised to find so many of his acquaintances new baptized. Earl Thomas did not, like the Popes, convert Pagan chiefs into Christian; but many an emperor acts the part at Wilton of scarcer Caesars." In 1724 Queen Christina's marbles were sold by the Odescalchi to Spain. Four years later Ficoroni negotiated the sale of the Chigi collection for 34,000 scudi to the King of Poland at Dresden; and even Cardinal Alessandro Albani, who was a most enthusiastic collector, was obliged to part with thirty statues to the same monarch for 20,000 scudi. These events caused great excitement in Rome. It was said as in ancient times, *Romae omnia venalia*, and an effort was made to save as much as possible for the Eternal City. Cardinal Albani's incomparable collection of portrait busts was bought, not by a foreign amateur, but by the Pope, in the year 1734, and the founding of the Capitoline Museum seemed to provide the most effectual means of obviating the dispersal of antique sculptures.*

This Alessandro Albani, the friend and patron of Winckelmann, shared with Camillo Borghese the honors of being the most spectacular collector and spendthrift of the eighteenth century. Immediately upon selling his second collection to the Pope, he started a new one; this was of somewhat different character for the blindness of his later years developed keenly his sense of touch for antique bronzes. This third cabinet (he had already sold the first to the King of Poland) was composed of statues from Tivoli, the Villa d'Este and Hadrian's Villa, and was subsequently pillaged by the French to be sold later in Paris to King Ludwig of Bavaria. What fragments remained in Rome were inherited by Count Castelbarco of Milan, who eventually sold them to the Torlonia for their villa in Rome.

The Borghese collections likewise go back into the early years of the seventeenth century when Scipio Borghese, the favorite of Paul V,

* Michaelis, *op. cit.*, gives a detailed account of these transactions.

received from his uncle (in addition to a yearly income of 250,000 scudi) a collection of a hundred pictures which the Pope had confiscated from the Cavaliere d'Arpino. Included in this lot was a Raphael, now in the Louvre, from the Baglione Chapel of the Church of San Francesco, which the Pope stole from the people of Perugia and later declared to be a gift from them to the Cardinal, "*per sua devotione.*" To these were added in 1619 quantities of works of art taken from the papal storehouses.

This state of things which, if the pillaging of the capital of Christianity was not arrested, would have resulted in its decline as a center of pilgrimage and study, brought decisive action from the Popes, who ordered strict prohibitions against the exportation of antiquities, and financed elaborate excavations to replace the collections which had already gone. This was indeed imperative for, in addition to the collections sold abroad, Rome was to receive another body blow in the dispatch of the Farnese collections to Naples and those of the Medici Palace to Florence.

Yet despite these losses it was still the Rome of Piranesi and Edward Gibbon, an age of scholarship, tempered with the romantic vision of ancient ruin; it was a city torn apart by the pick of the excavator, not as it had been a century before, for the purpose of erecting new and more spacious palaces and churches, but for the conscious exploitation of history and art. As the Popes of the seventeenth century had collected primarily for the *palazzi* and villas of their families, their successors once more returned to a systematic development of the museums and galleries of the Church.

Papal encouragement of archaeology was already a very ancient tradition although each pontiff had followed a pattern of his own. Pomponius Laetus had created as early as 1478 the Academy of the Antiquarii on the Quirinal; here presided distinguished antiquarians who, like Andrea Fulvio Sabino, had been instrumental in persuading Sixtus IV della Rovere to give his collections to the Museum of the City of Rome on the Capitoline Hill. Julius II, on the other hand, placed his antiquities, together with those of the Vatican itself, in the Belvedere, a villa then adjacent to the palace. Their successors added from time to time to these beginnings with newly excavated pieces.

Julius III possibly set a bad example by removing his collections to the distant Villa Giulia.

The Reformation had cited these collections as "shameless" proof of the corruption and pagan idolatry of the Papacy. The Council of Trent in the face of puritanical attacks had tried feebly to defend the collecting of ancient art. Perhaps it may have been this questioning of motive which caused the interruption of official archaeology in favor of the development of the private collections of the papal families. But not until the Albani Clement XI, who reigned during the first twenty years of the eighteenth century, do we find any plans for the development of the papal collections on a large scale. Under the scientific influence of scholars like Bianchini, provision was made for the care of coins and inscriptions, as well as of Oriental and Christian antiquities. The Museum of the Capitol opposite the Palazzo dei Conservatori was built to house them. The next Pope, Clement XII Corsini, added to these the collections purchased from Cardinal Albani. Benedict XIV enriched them with many important monuments, among them the Capitoline *Venus*, and he gave for the first time official papal sanction to the inclusion of objects of Egyptian art.

Then a lull occurred, particularly in the pontificate of Clement XIII, whose interest in art, says Michaelis, "had limited itself to providing the naked angels in his pictures with clothes, and the antique statues in the Belvedere with tin fig-leaves." Fortunately the cultured Cardinal Ganganelli came to the papal throne in 1769 and the situation was completely changed. A new wave, like that at the beginning of the century, of excavation and exportation, particularly by Englishmen, was beginning to threaten Rome. "The Pope," says Michaelis, "decided to follow the example of Clement XII and Benedict XIV by starting as a collector himself; he received the most ardent cooperation from his treasurer, Monsignor Braschi, who in the year 1775 succeeded Clement in the chair of Saint Peter as Pius VI, and carried out on a much extended scale the plans of his predecessor. Instead of enlarging the Capitoline Museum, it was soon thought more expedient to append a new museum, the Museo Pio-Clementino, to the already long-illustrious collection of statues in the Belvedere of the Vatican Palace."

The superintendence and publication of this collection were entrusted to Giambattista Visconti, and after his death to his son, the great Ennio-Quirino. The right of the government to forbid the export of valuable specimens, which now resembled a right of pre-emption, was more strongly exercised, and a severe rivalry maintained against foreign amateurs for the acquisition of high-class marbles. On the other hand, enterprising spirits were encouraged to begin fresh excavations, the government waiving certain onerous preliminary rights. Moreover the government itself, in emulation of private individuals, undertook, for the benefit of the new museum, several excavations that proved highly productive. The rooms of the museum increased yearly in space and magnificence and when about ten years had passed, although by no means completed, it was considered "the first museum in Rome and in all the world."

To these pontiffs we are indebted for the museums that we know today. Further additions were made during the nineteenth century. The *Pinacoteca* founded by Pius VII comprises the pictures stolen by Napoleon which were returned from France. He likewise added the *Braccio Nuovo* in 1817. Gregory XVI in the middle of the century added the Etruscan and Egyptian museums at the Vatican and transformed the Palace of the Lateran into a public gallery. His successor, Pius IX, established within it the Museum of Christian Art. Thus after many centuries the Popes of Rome had brought together into a group of carefully co-ordinated galleries the most comprehensive museum of the past ever known to man.

BOOK SEVEN

Art and Absolutism in France

THE BARBERINI PALACE – ROME

After a drawing by Martin van Heemskerck, c. 1550

THE VILLA BORGHESE ON THE PINCIO

By Guglielmo Bauer, c. 1630

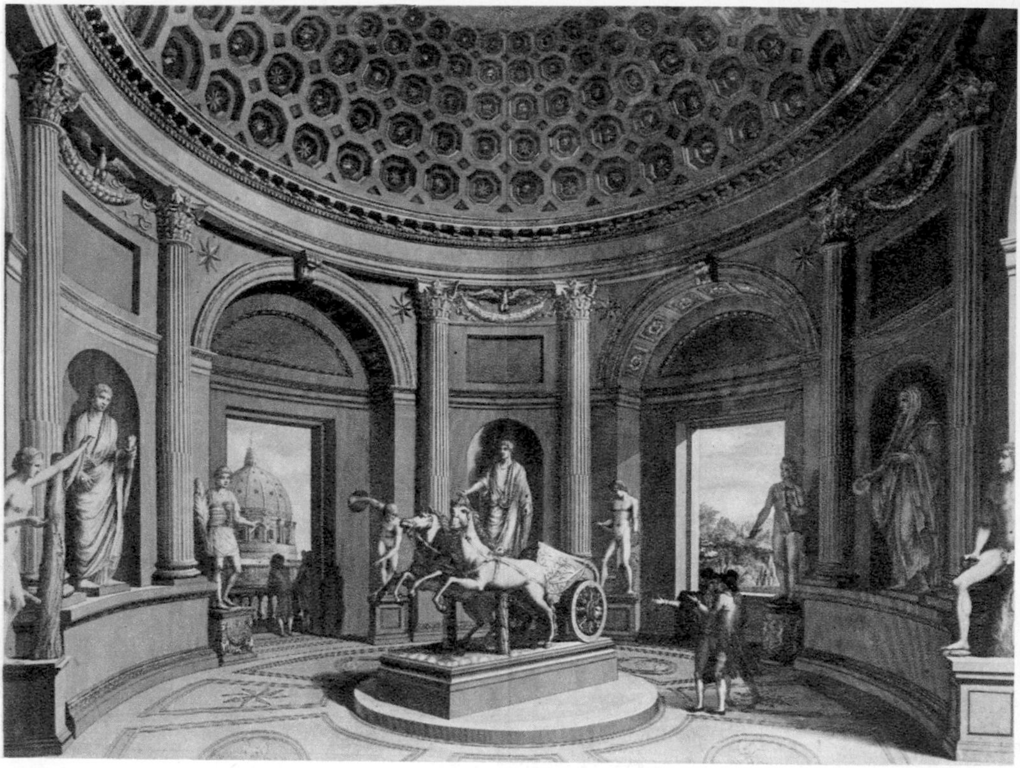

THE VATICAN MUSEUM: SALA DELLA BIGA

After an eighteenth-century engraving in the Vatican Library

PANNINI'S IMAGINARY GALLERY

After the painting in the Boston Athenaeum

CHAPTER I

The Academic Ideal

THE growth of absolutism from Francis I to Louis XIV may be divided into four stages: the first, that of Francis and Henri II (1515–1559), was the period of popular acclaim for the monarchy, and one in which the first fruits of the Italian Renaissance were given to the French people; the second, during the reign of Henri IV (1598–1610), consolidated a country torn by religious and civil strife. It required nothing less than the personal popularity of the King to compensate the Protestant peoples of Languedoc for their betrayal (through his conversion to Rome) and for the loss of their traditional liberties. The third and fourth stages cover the deliberate program of authoritarianism, developed by Richelieu during the minority of Louis XIII and continued by Mazarin. A crescendo finally was reached in the court of the *Grand Monarque*. One policy was common to all of these stages, that of fostering through the sale of offices a new class of nobles who in theory would be loyal to the crown which had created them. This is the origin of the *noblesse de la robe* and of the *bourgeois gentilhomme*. By the time of Louis XIV, they in turn had become so powerful that, despite the comic view taken of them by Molière, they constituted a new and serious threat to the royal authority. The importance of these parvenus to the history of art is incalculable, since the history of seventeenth-century patronage and collecting in France is primarily the history of the rivalry between the King, made more and more magnificent through the extravagances of his ministers of state, and the new millionaires who by the ostentation of their personal expenditures wished to humiliate him. Nothing less than the Château de Versailles, Colbert well understood, could put these upstarts in their proper places.

Not until the expulsion of the English in the mid-fifteenth century, and the unification of the Valois power by Louis XI, may France be said to have become a nation. Prior to that time she had been an agglomeration of feudal territories held together by common language, customs and religion. With the growth of the monarchy's prestige during the Renaissance the person of the sovereign became more elevated. He ceased to be *princeps inter pares* as he had been throughout the Middle Ages – a leader among other nobles – but became absolute, untouchable (almost in an Oriental sense), arrogating to himself an authority which he believed to be divine. It was the necessary instrument for imposing a central government upon a people to whom personal liberty had always been more important than constitutional prerogative; it was, moreover, a means of reaching those same people, peasants and artisans, shopkeepers and soldiery, directly and intimately, without the filter of the traditional nobility. Thus two purposes were served; the power of the nobles against the person of the king was permanently broken and the king in turn spoke for the nation rather than for his peers.

Cardinal Richelieu was quick to recognize the value of authoritarian doctrine. "Kings," he said, "are the living images of divinity." Despite Richelieu's complete ascendancy over Louis XIII, it none the less required a "lifelong and continuous effort to maintain it unimpaired over an apathetic and indifferent prince, who admired but had no affection for his minister." The precariousness of Richelieu's position thus made him quick to flatter the monarch by every possible device. He grafted onto the doctrine of absolute monarchy those doctrines of classical authority which the artists and critics of the Renaissance had formulated, and which provided a logical and legalistic basis for a true royal patronage of the arts.

The foundation of the Académie Française in 1635 was the first step in the establishment of the intellectual despotism of the *Grand Siècle*. This was followed by Colbert's creation of the Académie des Beaux-Arts in 1648 – ruthlessly directed by Le Brun – the Academy in Rome in 1666, and the Academy of Architecture in 1671.

The academy system was an intellectual ideal, and yet at the same time a practical framework upon which could be built a program for the glorification of the French monarchy. This framework was to become the envy of Europe and to serve until the end of the Romantic movement as the accepted pattern for governmental patronage and subsidy. Mazarin, Colbert and Le Brun built upon the foundations of Richelieu, and the artist, antique-ridden, and torn by the controversies of aesthetic theory, "willingly surrendered himself to the despotism of one monarchy and one aesthetics." The Italian Renaissance, bogged down by conflict and too much expert knowledge, became in France a well-ordered doctrine whereby the Academy "prescribed the very subjects of its pictures, and insisted upon the morality and nobility of the arts. The conception of the Great Style exalted the importance of the arts . . . history and classical mythology were usually awarded the palm of nobility." * "It was an ideal," wrote Chambers, "the ideal of the Ideal. It held up impossible abstractions, the unities of the drama, the Orders of architecture, beautiful nature and the antique. No sooner did it rise to power than it opened itself to dangerous attacks by the very reason of the impossibility of its abstractions. It suppressed passion and individuality. *Et sur mes passions ma raison souveraine*. But the academic idea did not deny to genius its proper exercise within prescribed laws – any more than mathematics, the ideal science, has at any time excluded true genius – and it threw a very significant doubt on the too common supposition that passion and individuality are good for men. The academic idea was a grand exhibition of human will and human legislation. It was the very intellectual peak of the Renaissance. Not Leonardo, not Michelangelo, not Raphael, not Titian, but Le Brun, is the consummation of the aesthetic consciousness of Western Europe; to him European taste theoretically converges and from him recedes. But it was the accident of history that the consummation coincided with the life of an inferior artist." † Le Brun became the interpreter of the political and intellectual ambitions of the three great ministers of the *Grand Siècle* – Richelieu, Mazarin and Colbert – upon whom the artistic supremacy of the French nation in the name of the king was founded.

* Chambers, *op. cit.*, 96, 100.
† Chambers, *op. cit.*, 101, 102.

CHAPTER II

Le Cabinet du Roy

WHEN Louis XIV came to the throne, the royal picture collection did not exceed more than 200 items. Le Père Dan – in his *Trésor des Merveilles de Fontainebleau*, published in 1642 – listed only 47 paintings, among them works by Leonardo, Titian, Raphael and del Sarto. The engraved stones, the medals and bronzes, as well as the antique statues brought together by Francis I, were scattered throughout the royal palaces and little care was given to them. Catherine de Medici's collections had, of course, come into the possession of the crown but her two sons were little interested. Henri IV and his mistress, Gabrielle d'Éstrées, were addicted to antique gems, cameos and intaglios, and formed cabinets which now are an important part of the Cabinet des Médailles. Queen Marie de Medicis, while she loved splendor and exchanged lavish gifts with the other courts of Europe, as a collector is not to be mentioned in the same breath with the other members of her family; her particular claim to fame lay in her patronage and employment of Rubens.

The arts were truly in a desultory state and certainly not worthy of the greatest monarchy in Europe. While there are lists and records of collections in France in the closing years of the sixteenth and the turn of the next century, they still reflected *la curiosité princière*, that backwash of medievalism more characteristic of Germany than of Italy. The collectors were interested in their possessions for their own private enlightenment and amusement; they saw in them no political or doctrinal importance.

Not so with Richelieu, who, passionately fond of art himself, saw the value of collecting as an expression of royal authority. His activity and philosophy were, therefore, directed to this purpose, even when he acquired works of art for his own palaces which he later bequeathed to the crown. He was in constant communication with his agents in Germany and Italy, urging them to buy all the great masterpieces they could find. An incurable collector, he readily understood the problems and responsibilities of ownership and he employed the leading architects of France to build great palaces in which to house his treasures. These, he hoped, in time would become the nucleus of a French national museum and library. At first these collections occupied the Arsenal, then a house on the Place Royale. Marie de Medicis gave him the Petit Luxembourg which the Cardinal had had rebuilt and decorated by Jean (Le Gros) Le Maire. But the Petit Luxembourg proved to be too far away; he wished to be closer to the Louvre where he could sense the intrigue of the court. In 1624 he bought a group of houses in the old Quartier Saint-Honoré – the site of the present Palais Royal – and had Le Mercier start the construction of the Palais Cardinal. This palace – not completed until 1636 – was several times enlarged to meet the requirements of the Cardinal's expanding fortunes and ambitions.

The palace was one of the most sumptuous in Paris. When it was completed and suitably furnished, the Cardinal gave it to the King, whose Queen, Anne of Austria, occupied it during the Regency. Richelieu was infected by the Italian passion for the portrait gallery. The *Galerie des hommes illustres* contained 26 portraits, over life size, of historic personages from Suger, the medieval Abbot of Saint Denis, to Louis XIII. The Cardinal established a similar gallery of sculpture in the Bibliothèque, where was lodged a series of Roman portrait busts of emperors and famous men, acquired in Italy by Mazarin, who at that time was the Cardinal's secretary.

Richelieu's library, which with the possible exception of the Vatican and the Laurentian in Florence was the vastest and most superb library in the world up to the time of Mazarin, was lodged in an adjoining building. More than 900 manuscripts, bound for the most part in red morocco, stamped with the arms of the Cardinal, had been gathered for him by agents in every corner of the globe. Louis XIII had permitted him to acquire the great Huguenot library of La Rochelle, and to these fabulous collections were soon added those of the crown which Francis I and Guillaume Budé had so laboriously brought together at Fontainebleau in the middle of the sixteenth century. François Savary de Brèves, who was French ambassador at the Sublime Porte for nearly a quarter of a century, had provided more than 100 manuscripts – the nucleus of the glorious *fonds oriental* of the Bibliothèque Nationale. This library, together with the building that housed it, Richelieu finally willed to the King of France "*pour qu'elle puisse servir non seulement à sa famille, mais au public.*"

The apartments of the Palais Cardinal were equally magnificent. The *Appartements du Roy et de la Reine* were filled with pictures of first quality. Le Grand Cabinet was considered "*la merveille et le miracle de Paris*" with its pictures by Andrea del Sarto and Poussin, and Leonardo's *Saint Anne.* The Chapel contained not only the Cardinal's incredible collection of jewels but a most magnificent series of religious plate – monstrances, crucifixes and chalices. Lopez, the lapidary and antiquarian who resided so long in Amsterdam, was the Cardinal's confidential agent and, because he was a Spanish Jew, was often the butt of the churchman's savage humor and vicious practical jokes.

The inventory of the Palais Cardinal published by de Boislisle lists 500 pictures including the names of Raphael, Titian, Leonardo, Solario, Giulio Romano, Luini, Giovanni Bellini, Niccolò dell'-Abbate, Correggio, Albano, Poussin and Claude, Rubens, Philippe de Champaigne, and examples of the Bolognese and Lombard Schools. In addition, there were 50 statues, 100 portrait busts and a great quantity of small bronzes, "antique or after the antique." A lavish suite of historical tapestries led the list of textiles, which included embroideries, velvets and Persian rugs. Furniture was of the highest order and included many encrusted tables of mosaic and porphyry made in Florence, the specialty of the private workshops of the Grand Dukes of Tuscany. What is more remarkable, considering the date, is the mention of a quantity of Chinese lacquers and more than 400 pieces of Chinese ceramic.

No sooner was the palace given to the crown in 1636 than Anne of Austria remodeled it, transferring most of the pictures to Fontainebleau and replacing them with copies. Fortunate it was that she did this, for while it was given over to Henrietta Maria, widow of Charles

I, and her suite of English courtiers, who had fled to Paris from the fury of the Regicides, the palace was ransacked. Evelyn visited the exiled Queen there in 1657 and tells how the courtiers broke up the furniture and paneling, selling the gilding to be melted down for gold and breaking out the windowpanes in order to sell the lead. Finally the palace was given by Louis XIV to his nephew, Philippe d'Orléans, who remodeled it extensively and added to it. It was by this circuitous history that Richelieu's palace became the Palais Royal and finally the Palais d'Orléans.

Richelieu's prodigality, so lavish when he was collecting for the crown, was no less extravagant when it came to acquiring objects for himself. In 1633 he bought the charming but comparatively modest "*château et maison seigneuriale du Val de Rueil en Parisis*" for 47,000 livres, and spent four times that amount in laying out its brooks and gardens. Here it was that the Cardinal retired to work in consultation with his ministers, and to rest from his continual bouts of ill-health. But Rueil was too modest and the Palais Cardinal too scattered a complex of palaces and galleries. The Cardinal had always dreamed of the great well-ordered Renaissance villas in the Roman Campagna. He ordered Le Mercier to pull down his ancient family seat of the du Plessis at Richelieu, near Chinon in the Poitou, and build a palace on a grandiose scale, suitable to the dignity and position of the King's First Minister.

The Château de Richelieu was more than a château; it was, in fact, a complete town in the style of Louis XIII as perfect in its way and for its date as Versailles or Nancy for the time of Louis XIV and Louis XV.* The principal street of the town was composed of twenty-eight *hôtels particuliers* flanking the forecourt – a plan preserved in the Bibliothèque Nationale indicates the persons in the Cardinal's entourage who were to occupy each house. There were in addition a college for the education of the sons of the nobility, a

* The château is described by Jean Desmarets, *Promenades de Richelieu ou les Vertus Chrétiennes* (Paris, 1653), also in prose and verse by Vicquier, the florist and chief gardener, *Château de Richelieu ou l'Histoire des dieux et des héros de l'antiquité, avec réflexions morales* (Saumur, 1676). Jean Marot published the plans and elevations of the château in twenty-eight plates in 1660 under the title *Le Magnifique Château de Richelieu*, Paris.

market place and a tribunal. Crossing a series of courts and forecourts, the various establishments spread out – stables, storehouses, service buildings of all kinds. Finally, as at Versailles, the approach culminates at the main gate of the château, a magnificent affair ornamented with antique statues, pyramids and columns. Berthelot's bronze figure of *Fame* surmounted the archway and, immediately above the gate itself, was placed his heroic marble statue of Louis XIII. The interior Court of Honor was flanked by pavilions on three sides; into the fourth or main façade was incorporated the principal entrance, above which were placed in niches the marble *Slaves* by Michelangelo, two of the greatest sculptures the Louvre today possesses.

How these marbles came to Richelieu is one of the fascinating digressions in the history of collecting. Originally designed for the tomb of Pope Julius II in Rome, they were given by Michelangelo to Roberto Strozzi.* The latter presented them to the King of France, Francis I (no doubt under duress), and he in turn presented them to the Connétable Anne de Montmorency, who placed them in the façade of the Château d'Ecouen where they are indicated in an engraving by Ducerceau. There they remained until Richelieu cast loving eyes upon them. The Duc de Montmorency, condemned to death for treason and hoping in vain on the scaffold for last-minute clemency, gave them to the Cardinal together with Annibale Carracci's *Saint Sebastian.*

In the same Court of Honor were disposed the Cardinal's finest antique sculptures, including the sixty statues which the Holy See had permitted him to remove from Rome. Among these was a marble *Venus* discovered at Pozzuoli which Bernini and Poussin described as "finer than the *Medici Venus.*"

From this principal entrance the great porphyry staircase rose in double convolutions leading to the state apartments. The ceiling of the Appartement du Roi, painted by Nicolas Prévost, depicted the *Story of Achilles* and the walls were hung with gold-thread Brussels hangings of the *Trojan War*. The *Adoration*, *Nativity* and the *Flight into Egypt*, a triptych by Dürer, was the principal attraction of the

* When the money gave out it became necessary to redesign the tomb on a more modest scale. The *Slaves* could not be accommodated.

royal chapel. In the Cabinet du Roi were those favorite treasures from the *Studiolo* of Isabella d'Este which were taken by Richelieu from the Ducal Palace at Mantua when it was sacked in 1630: Mantegna's *Parnassus* and the *Triumph of Minerva*, a mythological scene by Lorenzo Costa and Perugino's *Combat of Love and Chastity*.* These pictures are now in the Louvre: a fourth in this same series of Poussin's glorious *Bacchanales* is the *Triumph of Neptune*, so long in the Hermitage, was acquired by the Philadelphia Museum in 1936 from the Soviet Government. The other apartments were equally magnificent. The Chambre du Cardinal boasted Carracci's *Saint Sebastian* and the *Saint Francis* as a contrast to a full-length portrait of *Son Eminence* by Philippe de Champaigne. The Grand Galerie had twenty murals, ten on each side, representing the *Conquests of Louis XIII under the Ministry of Richelieu*, and was surmounted by a ceiling of the *Labors of Ulysses*. In front of each mural was an antique portrait bust in marble; that of Julius Caesar in the center was of porphyry, and at either extremity of the gallery were equestrian portraits of Louis XIII and the Cardinal. "*Toute la sculpture*," said an eyewitness, "*tant du plafonds que du lambris, est dorée d'or bruni, mêlé de blanc poly, ce qui donne un brillant incomparable à cette galerie.*"

Richelieu, who, by his own magnificence, had presumed more daringly than had ever any royal subject in humiliating the King, ironically never set foot in the palace he created. Ill-health and political affairs kept him continuously in Paris. But even in its ruined state today the Château de Richelieu is a symbol of the Cardinal's lust for power and glory, and his belief in the divine authority of the King and of the King's Minister. It is the curtain raiser to Versailles; by 1640 art had become not only the servant of the State, but also the symbol of royal prerogative. This vehicle of monarchical expression was yet to be organized and codified in the ministries of Mazarin and Colbert through the administrative genius of the latter and the classical absolutism of Le Brun.

* According to the catalogues of the Louvre these pictures had been purchased prior to 1627, but this is a debated point.

CHAPTER III

The Rise and Fall of Mazarin

When Richelieu died in 1642 he left the conduct of France to his secretary. Temperamentally they were very different. In their art collecting these differences of temperament are manifest, for while Richelieu, the visionary architect of the French monarchy, loved art personally, his acquisitions were programmatic and in conformity with his theories of government. Mazarin, on the other hand, the wily diplomat, was also the sleek and cynical *marchand amateur*, the perfect courtier with an avarice for riches that was surpassed only by his knowledge and connoisseurship of art. Possibly no other collector, before or since, has ever had a finer sense of value or a surer eye; his taste, like himself, was pompous, that of a Prince of the Church, a Minister of France, yet of one who always retained something of the qualities of the *condottiere* and the *commedia dell'arte.*

He was born at Piscina in the Abruzzi in the second year of the seventeenth century and was educated at Rome, where, prior to entering the service of Richelieu, whom he met there in 1630, he had served in succession as secretary to the Cardinals Bentivoglio, Sacchetti and Barberini. The basis of his fortune was a rosary which he had bought from a priest for 10,000 ducats and sold as emeralds and diamonds for 60,000 livres. This he augmented on his arrival in France by selling his Italian collections for many times their worth.

Under Richelieu he prospered until, at the age of forty-one, he became the Prime Minister of Anne of Austria, moving into the Louvre and later to the Palais Cardinal to be next the Queen. From 1640 to 1645 he rose rapidly in power and fortune; his growing collections constantly requiring greater space, he took over a group of *hôtels particuliers* on the rue de Richelieu, where he built his palace, the present Bibliothèque Nationale.

Mazarin collected only that which was beautiful; he gave no thought to the curiosities which still haunted the great cabinets of Europe. But his taste was no less catholic as a consequence – sculpture, paintings, tapestries, rugs, jewels, magnificent furniture. Bernardino Daineo was the curator of the *garda roba* where the rock crystals and goldsmith's work were kept. Lescot, his jeweler, went to Portugal to buy jewels and tapestries. The agents of France were everywhere instructed to miss no opportunity to buy for the Cardinal, who himself wrote to Cardinal Grimaldi asking him to supervise the entry of the French army into Milan and to procure for him all of the finest pictures, manuscripts and other works of art. It was in fact well known throughout the chancelleries of Europe that the Prime Minister of France could always be bribed with an art object provided the quality were good enough.

The years 1640–1648 marked the peak of Mazarin's activities as a collector and of his rising unpopularity with the French, who were embattled against the Italian financiers. The manipulations of the latter, spreading out fanwise from Lyons under the tacit protection of the Cardinal, had brought French business completely within their power. The *Fronde* was growing into open revolt and in August 1648 the court fled to Saint-Germain. The following January Parliament ordered the sale of Mazarin's belongings. The decree was delayed by a temporary lull due to the activities of the *Fronde*.* Two years later Mazarin fled into exile to the estates of the Elector of Cologne. Situated first at Brühl, he still kept his finger on state affairs and wrote his agent Ordodei "*de voir ce qu'il pourra faire de mieux avec Jabach et Bernardino pour mettre mes hordes en sûreté contre quelque accident qu'il puisse arriver.*"

This period of eighteen months of Mazarin's exile in Cologne corresponds with that of the liquidation of the collections of Charles I of England by the Parliament. Whatever dangers may have existed, and they were real indeed, for Mazarin's property in Paris, he still persisted in acquiring the best that could be obtained. He sent the

* The *Fronde* (a name derived from the word for "sling" with which the mob broke the windows of the Cardinal's palace) became a party in revolt against the financial policies of Mazarin.

Cologne banker, Jabach, who likewise was one of the very first connoisseurs of his day, to London where the latter acted not only for his patron but also for himself. Among the principal pictures he acquired for the Cardinal's account, now in the Louvre, were Titian's *Venus del Pardo*, one of the great treasures which Philip II loved so deeply and which his grandson, Philip IV, had presented to Charles I; Correggio's *Antiope; The Deluge* by Carracci; and three famous Raphaels, the *Portrait of Baldassare Castiglione*, the *Saint George*, now in the Mellon Collection at Washington, and the *Saint Michael.* George Vertue's notebooks give an account of the sale and list a quantity of precious vases, statues and tapestries also purchased for the account of the French Minister.

The "accident" foreseen by Mazarin soon took place. While he was building up his collections in exile, Parliament was seeking to destroy his power and wealth. An *Arrêt* dated December 29, 1651, ordered the public sale of the "*meubles et bibliothèque du Cardinal Mazarin*" and that from the proceeds the sum of 150,000 livres be given to his prosecutors. The young King Louis XIV intervened a month later and forbade the execution of this decree. He immediately ordered the sale of the books stopped, for they had already started with the library. This was confirmed by a *lettre de cachet* and he instructed Foucquet to intervene. Parliament, however, was in full revolt; the sale continued, and they issued a decree on July 24, 1652, to the effect that "all of the furnishings yet remaining in the Palais Mazarin were to be sold forthwith, etc." The King's Council again protested, revoking the decision of the Parliament and annulling the decree. The Counselor-Commissioners for the sale were held responsible "*en leur personnes, biens et posterité, de tout ce qui pourroit estre fait et entrepris au préjudice de l'intention de Sa Majesté.*"

Once more the Commissioners attempted to defy the King and immediately posted a public notice of the sale to be held in Paris.*

* *De par le Roy,*
et nos seigneurs les Commissaires députés par arrest de la Cour du Parlement, pour la vente des meubles du Cardinal Mazarin on faict à scavoir: Qu'à la requeste du Procureur général du Roy, il sera Vendredy prochain, deuxième iour d'aoust, deux heures de relevée, au logis dudit Cardinal Mazarin, procédé pardevant lesdits sieurs Commissaires à la vente des Statues, Bustes, Figures, Tables, Peintures, et autres meubles trouvés audict logis, au plus offrant et dernier enchérisseur, en la manière

But the back of the *Fronde* was already broken. How far the sale took place, who made the catalogue, who attended, who was the auctioneer, the chroniclers do not say. Two weeks later, August 10, Parliament petitioned the King "in order to bring peace to his subjects" to separate from Mazarin. At the same time it asked to be dissolved. Only this latter request was granted; two days later a further decree was given against the continuation of the sale of Mazarin's effects. This time the King was obeyed and the revolt was at an end.*

Louis XIV returned triumphantly to Paris in October and the following February Mazarin, after two years of exile, was welcomed back, "*attendu, désiré, acclamé par tous les partis, maître du Roy, maître de la France, plus omnipotent que Richelieu.*" Quickly reconciled, Mazarin bore no ill will against those who two years previously had sought to take his life. He devoted himself with untiring zeal to the consolidation of his political authority and to the recovery of his lost property. He turned to Colbert, who was then Intendant to the Minister, and ordered him to make an inventory. The chapter head-

---

accoutumée. Et sera la présente Ordonnance publiée à son de trompe et cry public, et scellée, affichée aux carrefours de cette ville, et à la barre de ladicte Cour. Donné par nous Conseillers et Commissaires susdits, le 31e jour de juillet 1652. Aussi signé: PORTAIL BINART, PITHOU.

* On August 25 Loret published in the *Muse Historique* the following verses on the affair:

Monsieur Pitou, Monsieur Portail,
Qui tous deux vendoient en détail
Les meubles de son Eminence,
Par une royale défence
Ont céssé leur commission
Touchant cette vendition
Qui déplait fort à notre Sire.
Et me suis mesme laissé dire
Qu'a fin de les mortifier,
On leur a fait signifier
Que des biens dudit inventaire
Le Roi se dit propriétaire
Par un don dudit Mazarin
Qu'il luy fict au retour du Rhin,
Et que jusques aux moindres pièces,
Fussent les gands de ses trois nièces,
Pour sa Majesté contenter,
Il fallait tout pour representer,
Savoir: pourcelaines, peinctures,
Bijoux: cabinets et sculpturés,
Et mesme a peine, en cas de non,
D'en répondre en leur propre nom.

ings of this document alone * stagger the imagination and give some small clue to the overwhelming wealth of the Cardinal. His palace became the wonder and envy of all Europe, the library containing more than 30,000 volumes and several thousand manuscripts. Among the many notables who came to visit his collections was Queen Christina of Sweden, who examined everything from cellar to attic and whose presence inspired such fear of theft on the part of the Cardinal.

Mazarin's entertainments, which he provided to distract the King, were unparalleled and surpassed anything which even the Renaissance Popes had offered to their courts. A lottery held in 1658 in honor of the King and Queen of England is described in the diary of the Grande Mademoiselle and also in Loret's poem. Other equally lavish receptions were held, such as that on the occasion of the treaty of the Pyrenees for which Velasquez had done the Spanish decorations, and for the marriage of the Cardinal's niece, Hortense Mancini, to the Duc de la Meilleraye.

Mazarin died in 1661; he was only fifty-nine but he was already exhausted by his power and riches. All of the passion for art, the disillusionment and cynicism of this extraordinary prelate, whom many believed to be at heart an atheist, are summed up by the Duc de Brienne in his *Mémoires*, where he describes the Cardinal a day or so before his death taking leave of his treasures – the only friends for whom he cared. It is a remarkable document, unique in the history of collecting, to show to what extent possessions can take possession of the possessor:

I was strolling through the new apartments of the palace. I stopped in the small gallery where one sees the woolen tapestry representing Scipio executed from the cartoons of Giulio Romano; it had belonged to the Maréchal de Saint André. The Cardinal did not possess a finer one. . . . I heard him coming from the shuffling of his slippers which he dragged along the floor like a man who is very weak. I hid behind the tapestry and I heard him saying, "I must leave all that." He stopped and paused at every step because he was very feeble, turning first to one side and then to the other and casting his eyes upon the objects which appeared before him. He said from the depths of his heart, "I must leave all that," and turning around he added, "And also that. What terrible efforts it has

* Published by the Duc d'Aumale in *Les richesses du Palais Mazarin*, Paris, 187?.

cost me to acquire those things. Can I leave them? Can I abandon them without regret? . . . I shan't see them any more where I am going." I heard his words very distinctly, they touched me, possibly more than they might have touched the Cardinal himself. . . . I gave a deep sigh and he heard me. "Who is that?" "It is I, Mon Seigneur, who am awaiting Your Eminence with a letter of great importance which I have just received." "Come closer, come closer," he said in a sad voice. He was undressed, wearing a wrapper of camel's hair trimmed with fur and his nightcap. He said, "Give me your arm, I am feeble. I can no longer do anything." "Your Eminence would do well to sit down," I said and was about to take him a chair. "No," he said, "I am better off walking. I have things to do in my library." I gave him my arm and he leaned against me. He did not want me to speak to him of business. "I am no longer," he said, "in a condition to listen to those things. Talk to the King and do whatever he tells you. I have many other things in my head at the present time." And coming back to his original thought, "Look, my friend," he said, "at that beautiful picture of Correggio and again at that *Venus* of Titian's and at Carracci's incomparable *Deluge* for I know that you like pictures and that you understand them well. Good bye, dear pictures that I have loved so well and which have cost me so very much." *

* * * * *

* *Je me promenais dans les appartements neufs de son palais. J'étais dans la petite galerie, où l'on voyait une tapisserie tout en laine qui représentait Scipion, éxécutée sur les dessins de Jules Romain; elle avait appartenu au maréchal de Saint-André: le cardinal n'en avait pas de plus belle. . . . Je l'entendis venir au bruit que faisait ses pantoufles, qu'il traînait comme un homme fort languissant. Je me cachai derrière la tapisserie, et je l'entendis qui disait "Il faut quitter tout cela!" Il s'arrêtait à chaque pas, car il était fort faible, et se tenait tantôt d'un côté, tantôt de l'autre; et jetant les yeux sur l'objet qui lui frappait la vue, il disait du profond du coeur: "Il faut quitter tout cela!", et se tournant, il ajoutait, "et encore cela! Que j'ai eu de peine à acquerir ces choses! Puis-je les abandonner sans regret? . . . Je ne les verrai plus où je vais." J'entendis ces paroles très distinctement. Elles me touchèrent peut-être plus qu'il n'en était touché lui-même. . . . Je fis un grand soupir, et il m'entendit. "Qui est là?" dit-il, "qui est là?"—"C'est moi, Monseigneur, qui attendais de parler à Votre Éminence d'une lettre fort importante que je viens de reçevoir."—"Approchez, approchez," me dit-il d'un ton dolent. Il était nu, dans sa robe de chambre de camelot fourée de petit-gris, et avait son bonnet de nuit sur la tête; il me dit: "Donnez-mois la main, je suis bien faible, je n'en puis plus." "Votre Éminence ferait bien de s'asseoir" et je voulus lui porter une chaise—"Non," dit-il, "je suis bien aise de me promener, et j'ai affairs dans ma bibliothèque." Je lui présentai le bras, et il s'appuya dessus. Il ne voulait point que je lui parlasse d'affaires. "Je ne suis plus," me dit-il, "en état de les entendre; parlez-en au Roi, et faites ce qu'il vous dira: j'ai bien d'autres choses maintenant dans la tête"; et revenant à sa pensée, "Voyez vous, mon ami, ce beau tableau du Corrège, et encore cette* Venus *du Titien, et cet incomparable* Déluge *d'Antoine Carrache, car je sais que vous aimez les tableaux et que vous vous y connaissez très bien. Ah! mon pauvre ami, il faut quitter tout cela! Adieu chers tableaux que j'ai tant aimés et qui m'ont tant couté."*

Just as Richelieu had willed the reins of government to his secretary, Mazarin, the latter's dying recommendation to the King was to elevate his intendant, Colbert, to be his successor. In accepting the task, Colbert faced difficulties which Richelieu and Mazarin had not known, and to which, indeed, each one had contributed in no small way. The prodigality of the *Grand Siècle* had so overtaxed the financial resources of the kingdom that he was obliged to find new policies and new sources of revenue. Yet at the same time the flattery to which Louis XIV had become committed demanded ceaseless expenditures to enhance and maintain at its zenith the glory of the monarchy. Colbert's policies, although they provided certain temporary funds and thus put off the day of reckoning, were destined in the long run to failure. The impending disaster of the French Revolution was still a century away but nevertheless loomed like a threatening cloud above the exaggerated brilliance of the Roi Soleil.

Paradoxically, it is to Colbert, who had only a moderate polite interest in collecting, and who of the three great ministers was the least acute in aesthetic sense, that France owes her supremacy in the world of art. In his administration were created or fully reorganized the Academies of Art, the Palace of Versailles, the continuation of the building of the Palace of the Louvre, and all of the functions of the present-day Ministry of Public Instruction and Fine Arts. This pattern, which was followed implicitly by nearly all of the governments of Europe, culminated in the Museum of the Louvre, an achievement that bored the monarch in whose name it was founded and for which the rightful credit is seldom given to the King's Minister.

Colbert was unquestionably the most efficient organizer the art world has ever seen. When he came to power, the Cabinet du Roy contained scarcely more than 200 pictures. At his death they numbered 2000, nearly all of the very finest quality. His first act was to buy the cream of Mazarin's collection for the crown. The Cardinal had intended to make his will in favor of the King, leaving him all his property and his palaces. The King, however, very graciously refused, and accepted from the Cardinal only eighteen precious stones which Clement de Ris believed to be the eighteen great diamonds in the crown of France. Within a month of taking office Colbert ordered

Christine peut donner des Loix
Aux Cœurs des Vainqueurs les plus braues,
Mais la Terre a t'elle des Rois
Qui soient dignes d'en estre Esclaues.
De Scuderi.
Bourdon Pin.
Nanteuil sculpebat 1654.

QUEEN CHRISTINA OF SWEDEN

Engraved by Nanteuil after the portrait by Sébastien Bourdon

ABBE WINCKELMANN
After Raphael Mengs

PHILIPP VON STOSCH
After P. E. Ghezzi

THE CORTILE OF THE BELVEDERE
Showing the *Laocoon* and the *Apollo Belvedere*
After an eighteenth-century engraving in the Vatican Library

CARDINAL RICHELIEU

By Philippe de Champaigne. London, National Gallery

CARDINAL MAZARIN AMIDST HIS COLLECTION
After the engraving by Nanteuil

another inventory in order that the King might purchase what he wanted from the heirs. Aside from innumerable objects of art of every description, particularly tapestries and jewels, the following were the gross valuations accepted by the Minister:

546 original paintings valued at 224,573 livres
283 pictures of the Italian School
77 " " " Dutch "
77 " " " French "
109 of various schools, including drawings, miniatures and mosaics
92 paintings, copies after old masters, estimated at 2,571 livres
241 portraits of Popes from Saint Peter to Mazarin — 723 livres

The experts for the pictures were André Podestà, Pierre Mignard and du Fresnoy; those for sculpture were Valpergues and Beaudouin who "bought 130 statues (now for the most part in the Louvre) and 196 busts, antique and modern. For the statues Colbert paid 50,000 livres, for the busts 46,920 livres. In addition, 1,955 livres were paid for *diverses matières pour mettre sur tables et cabinets*." The collection includes 46 Persian carpets, and the group of Flemish tapestries was the largest ever assembled outside that of the Spanish royal family. The rest of Mazarin's property, which quantitatively exceeded the above list many times, was divided among the heirs, the lion's share going to Hortense Mancini and her husband, the Duc de la Meilleraye. (The latter in a fit of prudery mutilated with an axe all the male statues he inherited.) The library became the nucleus of the Bibliothèque Nationale. The Duc de Brienne laments the dispersal of this great palace which he knew so well, and closes his account with the remark:

> *La belle mule de don Louis de Haro, après avoir servi de monture aux deux premiers ministres, a porté un médecin crotté sur le pavé de Paris; et les chars de triomphe du Cardinal, après qu'on eut vendu les velours et la broderie, ont été métamorphosés en carrosses à cinq sous.* *

* For a summary of the Mazarin estate cf. Edmond Bonnaffé, *Dictionnaire des amateurs français au dix-septième siècle*. Paris, 1884. (Mazarin.)

CHAPTER IV

The *Grand Dessein* and the Sunset of the *Grand Monarque*

L'ÉTAT *c'est moi; le Roi gouverne par lui-même.*" Louis XIV, always jealous of his prerogatives, never gave Colbert the title which Richelieu and Mazarin had borne. Consequently Colbert found it necessary to spend his life flattering the King into believing that in the majesty of his person he, Louis, was the actual ruler of France. At the time Colbert came to power the insolence of the monopolist, of the banker, the *bourgeois gentilhomme*, had reached a point which thoroughly aroused the jealousy of the King. The Superintendent Foucquet had splurged with such extravagance at his Château of Vaux-le-Vicomte that he had dared to humiliate His Majesty even to the point of looking with too much favor upon the royal mistress. The *bourgeois gentilhomme*, that constant target of the satirist and pamphleteer, thus constituted a serious threat to the sovereign authority. Colbert's first objective as *Contrôleur-Général des Finances* was to humble this new nobility and bring them to heel. He called the attention of the King to Foucquet's malfeasance of office; Foucquet was disgraced and his property confiscated.

Immediately, Colbert set about making the King the focal center of court life and directed all of the energies of the State towards producing that outward magnificence which stamped its character on his reign. This was accomplished by such pageants as the *fêtes du Carrousel* and by a variety of entertainments of the court in which the King himself became the principal actor playing before the footlights of the world.

Requiring additional titles to bolster his authority as *Contrôleur des Finances*, Colbert had bought for his own account from Madame de

Rataban the traditional office of *Surintendant des Bâtiments.* This gave him complete and direct authority over all architectural and decorative projects of the crown. The parallel in our own times, of course, was the case of the late Andrew W. Mellon, who, in the capacity of Secretary of the Treasury, was at the same time director of the building projects of the government. One cannot but wonder how consciously Mr. Mellon patterned himself on his great predecessor in France; for, while the former collected in the name of the King, the latter collected for the nation. The recent development of the city of Washington, the return and strict adherence to Major l'Enfant's plans, are strangely reminiscent of the organizing genius which created Versailles.

Colbert through these combined offices brought within his orbit all of the artistic production of France. He enlarged the Tuileries and appointed André Le Nôtre *Contrôleur des bâtiments et dessinateurs des jardins du Roi;* the *Manufacture Royale des Tapisseries et Meubles de la Couronne* was placed under the joint direction of Le Brun, Van der Meulen and the *ébéniste*, Charles-André Boulle. The grave mistake of Colbert's life was his ceding to the King on the building of Versailles. He recognized the danger, but the King's heart was set upon it. The monarch could no longer stomach the Château de Saint-Germain because from its windows he could see on the horizon the Abbey Church of Saint Denis where he was destined to be buried, and it recalled "*la vanité des choses de ce monde et la brièveté de la vie.*" For his new summer residence Louis chose the hunting lodge which his predecessor had purchased at Versailles for 20,000 *écus*. Although he was opposed in principle to the building of the Château de Versailles, for he realized the terrific drain it would be on the resources of the whole of France, Colbert recognized the overweening vanity of the King and knew that his desire for flattery demanded his encouraging him in this extravagance. He knew, moreover, that in giving in to the King in this his primary interest he would be free to do as he liked in his own ambitious building program in Paris. Consequently, against his better judgment, Colbert gave the project his full support.

Colbert "shuddered," states his American biographer, Charles Woolsey Cole, "at the sums that were poured out on the *château*, the fountains, the gardens, the canal. But he superintended the work, on which between 30,000,000 and 50,000,000 *livres* were expended. In comparison to this, 7,000,000 spent on Marly and its machine, the 3,000,000 lavished that Madame de Montespan might have Clagny, and the 3,000,000 spent on the Trianons pale into insignificance. Under Colbert some 80,000,000 *livres* were put into royal edifices of one sort or another" (1,000,000 livres on Fontainebleau, 900,000 on Vincennes, 5,500,000 on Saint-Germain, nearly 1,000,000 on Chambord, and lesser amounts on Compiègne, Blois and Monceau).*

The full impact and realization of the extravagances of the King at Versailles, egged on by his rival Louvois, was a blow from which Colbert never recovered and which was to hasten his death some twenty years later.

In addition to the official residences of the King at Versailles and in Paris, there were other royal palaces in which were lodged "the chief of the blood royal, viz. the King, Monsieur the Dauphin and the three grandsons, the Dukes of Burgundy, Anjou, and Berry. Monsieur or the King's brother (the Duke of Orléans), and his son the duke of Chartres and Mademoiselle his daughter." Dr. Martin Lister in his "A Journey to Paris in the Year 1698" gives an account of his visit to the country place of the Duke of Orléans.

St. Cloud is the nearest Paris, and the castle is very magnificent, and most commodious. The great saloon and the gallery are extremely well painted. The gardens are of a vast extent, twelve or fifteen miles in compass.

At the end of the apartments of Monsieur, are a fine set of closets: the first you enter is furnished with great variety of rock crystals, cups, agates upon small stands, and the sides of the rooms are lined with large panes of looking-glass from top to the bottom, with Japan varnish and paintings of equal breadth intermixt; which had a marvellous pretty effect. The other room had in it a vast quantity of bijou, and many of very great price; but the Siam pagods, and other things from thence, were very odd.

* Charles Woolsey Cole, *Colbert and a Century of French Mercantilism.* Columbia University Press, 1939. I, 314. Many writers believe that in terms of our purchasing power today a livre is the equivalent of a dollar. And, of course, both wages and materials for building were many times less than today.

There was also one very small Roman statue of white marble, not ten inches high, which cost 20,000 crowns; one leg of it was a little injured. It seemed a piece of admirable workmanship. It was a boy, who had in the skirt of his tunic a litter of puppies, and the bitch lying at his feet and looking up.*

It was the son of Monsieur, Philippe d'Orléans, who later became Regent upon the death of Louis XIV, who brought together at the Palais Royal the most magnificent private collection ever seen in France. And indeed it was a collection which rivaled that which Colbert was forming for the *Grand Monarque*. Germain Brice in his *Description de la Ville de Paris* † becomes ecstatic in his description of the palace and its contents. He speaks glowingly of the *boiseries*, of the furniture and decoration, the rock crystal chandeliers and the looking glasses. The principal gallery contains "a quantity of select pieces by the masters of the first rank, like Raphael, Julio Romano, Pietro da Cortona, Guido, Titian, Paul Veronese, Tintoretto, Correggio, Albano, the Carracci, Joseph Pin, Paul Rubens, Van Dyck, Rembrandt, Poussin and many others. There are also works by Le Brun; the *Massacre of the Innocents* which was considered the masterpiece of this excellent painter and occupies a place of distinction. One especially observes among the others a great painting by Van Dyck painted after nature which represents the family of Charles I, the King of England, who had his head cut off at London, an execrable event without example, and many other pieces of very great consequence."

According to Waagen, the following collections were acquired by the Regent *en bloc* or in part: those of the three Cardinals Richelieu, Mazarin and Dubois, of the Dukes of Grammont, Noailles, Vendôme, Ménars and Hautefeuille, Lord Mellfort, the Abbé de Maisainville, of Messieurs Deval, de Nosse, de Seignelay (the son of Colbert), Forest de Nancré, Tambonceau, Paillet, Corberon, de Bretonvilliers, de Launay, de la Ravois, du Clier de Lorraine, Dorigny and the Abbé Decamps. He also acquired from the Cathedral of Narbonne the *Raising of Lazarus* by Sebastiano del Piombo which had been painted

* Martin Lister, "A Journey to Paris in the Year 1698," in John Pinkerton, *A General Collection of Voyages and Travels*. London, 1804–1814, XV vols., vol. IV.

† 8th edition, 3 vols., Paris 1725.

as a companion piece for Raphael's *Transfiguration.* His principal acquisition, however, had been a great part of the gallery of Queen Christina in Rome which he bought from Prince Odescalchi. Among them were the celebrated Correggios, the *Leda,* the *Io* (now at Berlin), the *Danaë* of the Borghese Gallery, and *Cupid Sharpening his Bow,* now ascribed to Parmigianino in Vienna. Titian's *Venus with the Mirror* (Cobham Hall), *Venus Rising from the Sea* (Bridgewater House) and the *Venus, Mercury and Cupid* at Stafford House (now ascribed to Schiavone) were also included. These were in a lot of 47 paintings for which alone the Regent had been prepared to offer 20,000 livres.

The story of how the Orléans collection was dispersed in England in the 1790's belongs to another chapter, that of the new collectors under George III and the English Regency; perhaps no single collection has had so great an influence upon the formation of taste during the nineteenth century.

But private collecting was not confined either to the crown or to the members of the royal family. Edmond Bonnaffé * lists over eleven hundred *curieux* who collected works of art, mostly of a very high order. Chief of these was the Surintendant Foucquet, whose magnificence and whose ambition had given Colbert the opportunity to consolidate his power upon Foucquet's ruin. Nicholas Foucquet, who was also financial minister to Louis XIV, was born in 1615 and died in disgrace in 1680, nearly twenty years after his fall from power. He was a passionate collector, a great judge of works of art which he gathered together in his two principal residences, Saint Mandé and Vaux. At Saint Mandé the gallery, the salon, the library, the orangerie and the gardens were filled with pictures, marbles and statues, mostly antique or worked by the hand of Michel Anguier. Foucquet's library, celebrated by Corneille, contained 27,000 volumes, a collection of medals, prints and paintings, rarities from every country, particularly two Egyptian sarcophagi which La Fontaine immortalized in an epistle in verse addressed to the Surintendant. Vaux-le-Vicomte, Foucquet's country place, was the collective masterpiece of Le Vau, Le Brun and Le Nôtre. The apartments were decorated by Le Brun,

* *Dictionnaire des amateurs français au dix-septième siècle.* Paris, 1884.

the statues and furniture and magnificent tapestries, particularly a celebrated series of the Raphael cartoons and another series of Mortlake hangings representing the history of *Vulcan* and the story of *Iphigenia* – all of these works had been produced in the ateliers created by Foucquet and directed by Le Brun. The furniture included tables of porphyry, rock-crystal chandeliers, silver mirrors and a series of beds which had never before been rivaled. One bed alone was said to have cost 14,000 livres. In 1655 Foucquet sent his younger brother, the Abbé Louis Foucquet, to Rome on a political mission, charging him with the purchase of works of art. The Abbé became immediately an intimate of Poussin, who was his principal counselor and who himself made many designs and decorations for Foucquet's palace at Vaux.

The picture collection contained many celebrated works, all of which were dispersed in 1661; a considerable portion was acquired by Colbert for the King and is now in the Louvre. The collections and palaces of Foucquet served both as a model and as a warning to other *curieux* of Paris. For, while it was considered proper to indulge in the collector's fancy, it was not fitting for a subject, other than a member of the royal family, to compete openly with the king in personal magnificence.

In contrast to the latter collections and those of the *nouveau riche* tax collectors or Farmers-General is that of François Roget de Gaignières, one of the most enlightened minds of the seventeenth century. He was tutor to the children of the royal family, governor of the principality of Joinville and equerry to the Duke and Mademoiselle de Guise. Gaignières was the forerunner of the great French archivists and librarians so celebrated in the nineteenth century. He was a man of modest fortunes but these he devoted, as well as all of his waking hours, to bringing together the remnants and relics of French history. Without Gaignières the knowledge of medieval art in France today would indeed be limited. Employing a paleographer and an artist, Gaignières made a systematic collection of all of the historic monuments visited on his constant voyages throughout France. He rummaged in all the attics of the great and formed not only an incredible collection of books, manuscripts and drawings but was the first to bring together the type of object which later made possible Lenoir's Musée des Monumens Français and the later development of the Cluny Museum. Gaignières has, in fact, been called "the French Vasari." But unlike the latter he wrote the history of French art from the documents and objects of art rather than from the lives of the painters. His collection of portraits of historic personages alone numbered more than 27,000. He gave his collections to the King in 1711. The latter accepted them only on the condition that he would pay Gaignières 4000 livres on account and an annuity of 4000 livres for the rest of his life. At his death 20,000 livres would be given by the King to his heirs. Seven years later, after Gaignières's death, the Bibliothèque Royale received 2407 manuscripts, 24 large portfolios filled with drawings of costume, 31 volumes of drawings of tombs made throughout the churches of France, 117 volumes devoted to geography and maps, 100 volumes of engraved portraits, and the portrait of Jean Le Bon which had been given him by Colbert. The balance of the collection, containing early editions, together with 3000 other items of divers nature and some 15,000 drawings and engravings of portraits, was sold at auction. Three thousand of the drawings of the tombs of France were stolen from the Bibliothèque Royale in 1784 and are today part of the Bodleian Library of Oxford. Dr. Lister, who visited Gaignières in 1698, gives a pleasant account of the wealth of curiosity in the Paris of this period:

> I waited upon the Abbot Droine to visit Monsieur Guanières, at his lodgings in the Hostel de Guise. This gentleman is courtesy itself, and one of the most curious and industrious persons in Paris, his memoirs, manuscripts, paintings, and stamps are infinite, but the method in which he disposes them, is very particular and useful. He showed his *portefeuilles in folio* of red Spanish leather finely adorned. In one, for example, he had the general maps of England; then the particular maps of the counties; then the maps of London, and views about it; and so all of the cities in England and places and houses of note of the counties.
>
> In other bookcases he has the stamps of the statesmen of England, nobility of both sexes, soldiers, lawyers, divines, physicians, and men of distinction. And in method he has all Europe by themselves.
>
> His rooms are filled with the heads of a vast number of men of note

in oil paintings and miniatures or water-colours. Among the rest, an original of King John, who was prisoner in England, which he greatly values.

He showed us amongst other curious manuscripts, a capitularie of Charles V, also the gospel of St. Matthew wrote in golden letters on purple vellum. This seemed to me to be later than that manuscript I saw at the Abby of St. Germains; that is, the letters less and more crooked, though indeed, the letters of the title page are exactly square.

One toy I took notice of, which was a collection of playing cards for 300 years. The oldest were three times bigger than are now used, extremely well limned and illuminated with gilt borders, and the pasteboard thick and firm; but there was not a complete set of them.

Among the persons of distinction and fame, I was desirous to see Mademoiselle de Scuderie, now 91 years of age. Her mind is yet vigorous, though her body is in ruins. I confess, this visit was a perfect mortification, to see the sad decays of nature in a woman once so famous. To hear her talk, with her lips hanging about a toothless mouth, and not to be able to command her words from flying abroad at random, puts me in mind of the Sybil's uttering oracles. Old women were employed on this errand, and the infant-world thought nothing so wise as decayed nature, or nature quite out of order, and preferred dreams before reasonable and waking thoughts.

She shewed me the skeletons of two cameleons, which she had kept near four years alive. In winter she lodged them in cotton; and in the fiercest weather she put them under a ball of copper full of hot water.

In her closet she shewed me an original of Madame Maintenon, her old friend and acquaintance, which she affirmed was very like her: and, indeed she was then very beautiful.

The Marquis d'Hopital, one of the Académie de Sciences, whom I found not at home, returned my visit very obligingly. I had a long conversation with him about philosophy and learning; and I perceived the wars had made them altogether strangers to what had been doing in England. Nothing was more pleasing to him than to hear of Mr. Isaac Newton's preferment, and that there were hopes that they might expect something more from him: he expressed a great desire to have the whole set of the *Philosophic Transactions* brought over, and many other books, which he named but had not yet seen.

CHAPTER V

The Beginnings of the Louvre

IT is a curious fact that despite the importance of Versailles for the history of art and architecture (as well as for its imposition of French taste upon all the lesser monarchies of Europe), it played in comparison to the Palace of the Louvre a negligible role in the history of collecting. While the very best craftsmen of France were employed on fittings of the château and the greatest sculptors and painters of Europe lavished their attentions upon its formal works of art, the royal collections, properly speaking, were seldom if ever there. Only for short sojourns at the end of the seventeenth and the early part of the eighteenth centuries were a few treasures, taken from Fontainebleau and Paris, used to embellish the life of the court.

The foundations of the present Museum of the Louvre had already long been laid in the early history of France. According to popular tradition, the site of the fortress erected by Philip Augustus in the thirteenth century had been occupied by a much earlier tower of the time of Pepin, built by the Saracens; others considered it a bulwark against the Norman invasion of the ninth century. Even the name *Louvre* has been a matter of speculation and debate. Possibly it comes from *loever*, the Frankish word for moat, or possibly it is derived from *léproserie*, a leper colony so common in the early Middle Ages; another suggestion has sought to associate the name with *louvrée* or wolf's den where the animals were kept before being released for the royal hunt.

Whatever the origin of the name *Louvre*, and no one can say with certainty what it was, Francis I found the castle sufficiently sinister for it to remind him of his imprisonment in the Alcazar at Madrid, and he resolved to transform it into a palace comparable in size and dignity to those which he had seen in Italy. A year before his death

(1546) he ordered the tower razed and appointed the architect, Pierre Lescot, to rebuild the Louvre. Henry II confirmed the appointment and approved in 1549 the "*grand dessein*" of a rectangular palace about an open court, "*conçu dans le style nouveau.*" The sculptor, Jean Goujon, whose knowledge of architecture was enhanced through having illustrated the French edition of Vitruvius, became the "*chef des ateliers des sculpteurs.*" Lescot died in 1568 but the *grand dessein* was carried forward. Henry IV and Louis XIV had continued to add to the palace. During the time of Richelieu virtually nothing was done to the palace and it languished in the state in which it stood at the end of the sixteenth century; but Mazarin's architect, Le Vau, though preserving the plan, departed from the earlier style in bringing the façade on the Seine into correspondence with his design across the river for the Collège Mazarin, the present home of the Institut de France.

Colbert, full of doubts about the wisdom of Versailles, tried to focus the attention of the King upon this great incompleted palace. "*Cette maison,*" he wrote of Versailles, "*regarde bien d'avantage le divertissement de Votre Majesté, que sa Gloire,*" and he pressed him for a decision on the completion of the Louvre "*qu'à défaut des actions éclatantes de la guerre . . . rien ne marque d'avantage la grandeur et l'esprit des princes que les bâtiments, et toute la postérité les mesure à l'aucune de ces superbes maisons qu'ils ont élevées pendant leur vie.*"

Finally, after many false starts, Colbert declared in 1664 in the name of the King "*la noble ambition de reprendre l'ancien et magnifique dessein.*" But actually Italian taste, which at that moment was in the ascendancy, found the old plan too complex. Colbert, then in the midst of creating the French Academy in Rome, decided to import Bernini, who represented to the French all that was pompous and correct in Italy. Richelieu, who had sat to him for a portrait bust in bronze when the Cardinal went to Rome to receive his red hat, had already tried in vain to bring Bernini to the court of Louis XIII. But through the intermediary of Cardinal Barberini, Pope Alexander XI at last permitted Bernini with his son Paolo, his pupil Matteo da Rossi and a suite of six, to leave Rome at the command of the French court.

He was received at the frontier with royal honors, brought to Paris and presented to the King by Colbert. Scarcely had he rested from his journey before Bernini set out by his arrogance, and his contempt for everything French, to make himself thoroughly detested. A cabal of French architects under the leadership of the critic Charles Perrault, brother of the amateur architect and physician, Claude Perrault (whose plans were later accepted by Colbert), rose against him. Le Brun sided with the French and within a year Bernini's plans were rejected; he left Paris in disgust to return to Rome. French architecture had declared its independence from Rome; it was also the Magna Charta for French chauvinism. The colonnade of the Louvre was continued for a dozen years on the plans of Perrault, associated with Le Brun and Le Vau. Then in 1676 construction stopped abruptly; there was no more money.

The constant drain of wars, the staggering costs of construction at Versailles and the endless expenditures on the frivolous pleasures of the King had crippled the resources of the country. Now completely under the domination of Madame de Maintenon, Louis became morose and introspective and given over to religious excesses. He was appalled at his own extravagances and the financial ruin of his reign. He lost his taste for building on so vast a scale and even thought of abandoning the Louvre altogether and of building another smaller palace at the Invalides.

If the King's enthusiasm for the building of the Louvre was diminishing, Colbert's conception of the palace as an ultimate museum remained unaltered. Member of the Académie Française, patron of all the academies fostered by him – Rome, Beaux-Arts, Sciences, Musique – the *Contrôleur-Général des Finances* during the twenty-two years of his ministry never missed an opportunity to bring within the orbit of the crown whatever artistic wealth lay at hand. Having purchased the cream of the Mazarin collection for the Cabinet du Roy in 1661, ten years later Colbert acquired the collection of the Cologne banker, Evrard Jabach, who had so ably represented Mazarin at the sale of Charles I. Jabach had amassed, in addition to 101 splendid pictures, some 5600 master drawings and these became the nucleus of the Cabinet des Dessins of the Louvre. Jabach knew that his was probably the finest private cabinet in Europe at that time and valued it at 463,425 livres, but Colbert drove a terrible bargain, so sharp indeed that Jabach besought him to treat him "*en Chrestien et non en More.*"

Four years previously Colbert had already founded the King's Print Cabinet by purchasing some 250,000 prints which Michel de Marolles, Abbé de Villeloin, had brought together over a period of twenty years. It was a labor of scholarship and love, the first print collection on the grand scale and one which appealed to Colbert, who in a small way had amused himself with illustrated books. Marolles, whose yearly income from benefices was not more than 7000–8000 livres, was among the first of the private collectors in history to sacrifice his life and fortune to his passion. He may truly be called the "Father of Print Collecting," for while earlier collections, indeed, had been formed, by the very scope of his activity, and his interest in separating his many thousands of pieces of paper into artistic schools, Marolles lifted the printed picture from a bypath of typography to being one of the major prizes of the born collector.

The *Correspondance Administrative sous le règne de Louis XIV* * is filled with the constant exchanges between Colbert and his agents abroad. Abbé Benedetti was buying antiques for him in Rome. The ambassador, the Duc de Crécqui, was instructed to buy the *Farnese Bull* (now in the Naples Museum) from the Duke of Parma but it was too heavy to transport. He entered into long negotiations for erecting a monumental staircase in Rome ascending the Trinità dei Monti, and he attempted to purchase the Villa Ludovisi together with its huge collections for the French Academy. The Bishop of Béziers, Louis XIV's ambassador to Venice, after many long delays succeeded in obtaining the august permission of the Venetian Senate to buy the two great Veroneses now in the Louvre. He negotiated as well for Titian's *Virgin with the Twelve Apostles.* The ambassador in London nearly succeeded in buying the Raphael cartoons which Cromwell had saved from the effects of Charles I. The offer, about to be accepted, was finally refused by pressure from the Earl of Danby, who was determined they should not leave England. Equally unsuccessful

* Vol. IV.

were the efforts to acquire from the King of Spain the pictures which Philip IV had bought from Charles I.

Nevertheless Colbert (who had the unrestricted taxing power of France at his disposal) at no time deviated from his purpose and never hesitated to buy when occasion offered. Piece by piece, lot by lot, Colbert had in the space of twenty-two years increased the collections of the crown from some 200 paintings to more than 2000, and had added more than 10,000 drawings and a quarter million prints — to say nothing of countless acquisitions in tapestry, sculpture and *objets d'art.*

From Richelieu Colbert had originally inherited the idea of bringing together the treasures of the crown into a museum for delectation of members of the Academy, and for the instruction of young artists. Hitherto the royal collections had been scattered throughout the various palaces. Colbert in collaboration with Le Brun revived the idea of transforming the Grande Galerie of the Louvre into a picture gallery. The decoration of the Galerie d'Apollon was entrusted to Le Brun, who outdid himself with allegories of the King in the role of the Greek god. Other galleries were decorated under his direction. Finally, on December 6, 1681, the gallery was inaugurated by a visit of the King. The Museum of the Louvre, not to become public until after the Revolution, was thus created. The following account in the *Mercure de France,* probably the first account in history of a museum opening, is, in spite of the quaintness of the language, not unlike the journalistic efforts of the present day.

On Friday, the fifth of this month, the King honored Paris with his presence and came to the old Louvre to see his cabinet of pictures. It is in a new apartment on the side of the superb Gallery of Apollo. The gold one sees shining from every corner is the very least of its rarities. The gallery is a masterpiece of painting and sculpture and contains among other ornaments several pictures of an accomplished beauty by M. Le Brun. Everything is admirable, even to the hardware on the doors and windows, finely chiselled and gilded with incomparable workmanship. The gallery which was formerly in this place was burned shortly after the marriage of the King, and His Majesty ordered the new gallery to be built. Some of the pictures were saved from the fire, several representing the French kings. They are now preserved with the others at the Louvre. What is called the Cabinet of the King's Pictures in the old Louvre contains seven large galleries, very high, and of which several are more than fifty feet in length. There are in addition to these four galleries in the old Hôtel de Grammont which adjoins the Louvre. You may well judge that one cannot see so many places filled with the King's pictures without their number appearing to be infinite. The highest apartments are hung with them right up to the cornices. One sees, moreover, in several places a sort of screen or shutter covered on both sides in such a manner that, closed back against the wall, it makes possible three additional rows of pictures.

Here is approximately the number of those greatest masters which are in the eleven galleries. There are sixteen by Raphael of Urbino; he is the most highly esteemed of all modern painters. As he was only 36 when he died, the number of his works cannot be large; thus it is fair to say that the King has the greatest part of them. Among the pictures of this great master there are three that are without price: one represents *The Transfiguration* which is in Rome; His Majesty owns the two others which are the *St. Michael*, life-size, and *The Holy Family*. The last is the most highly esteemed of them all; it is painted on cedar wood and for this reason it is better preserved than all the others. Raphael painted it for King Francis I in the year 1518. This learned man who died two years afterwards, and to whom the Pope who governed the Church in those times wished to wed to his niece, was then in the vigor of his age and his genius was beginning to come to full flower. This painting is five feet, six inches high and four feet, three inches wide, containing five life-sized figures and two smaller ones. I will not comment further on this masterpiece of art; it is by Raphael, that is all that one needs to say. The other paintings are: six by Correggio, five by Giulio Romano, ten by Leonardo da Vinci, eight by Giorgione, four by Palma Vecchio, twenty-three by Titian, nineteen by Carracci, eight by Domenichino, twelve by Guido, six by Tintoretto, eighteen by Paul Veronese, fourteen by Van Dyck, seventeen by Poussin, six by M. Le Brun, among which there are some forty feet in length.

These paintings are accompanied by a quantity of others, how many I do not know; I know only that they are by Rubens, Albano, Valentino, Antonio More and other masters equally well known. Besides these pictures there are in the old Hôtel de Grammont several groups of figures and bas-reliefs in bronze, marble and ivory. It is difficult to persuade oneself in seeing so many masterpieces where art seems in several places to have surpassed even nature, that the greater part of them have been assembled during a time when the King had upheld his advantages with such brilliance in the face of a Europe united against him. It is true that His Majesty has acquired several of them since peace has been made; but one can say that this time of peace has been a more severe drain upon his finances than the war itself because of the great fortifications that the prudence and the foresight of the Estates General have ordered to be built in order to guarantee His Majesty's invincibility against the enemies of the whole world. Notwithstanding everything goes ahead at an equal pace since he has himself taken charge of the affairs of State. The finances are in good hands; he enjoys everything which belongs to him and it is because of that, and being in a state in which he can uphold at all times these various expenses, that he has had the ease to see pass into his cabinet the greater part of those objects which the "*curieux*" of Italy and of all of Europe find most beautiful. It is no longer necessary to travel in order to see the greatest rarities. The King's love for the arts and the vigilance of those who cause them to bloom beneath him have brought together practically everything of consequence in these superb houses. His Majesty found everything in splendid order under the direction of his first painter, M. Le Brun of whom I have spoken several times. He is the Director of his cabinet of pictures and of the manufactury of the Gobelins, and Chancellor and principal Rector of the Academy of Painting and Sculpture of which I hope to inform you at an early opportunity. One ought not to be astonished that everything was in such splendid condition despite the number of years and the humidity which ordinarily ruin this class of work. M. Le Brun knows the way in which paintings should be conserved and employs only the most able technicians. Although the King has, beside this large number of pictures, twenty-six at Versailles by the learned masters that I have just named, he chose an additional fifteen to decorate his apartments and gave the order to have them transported from his cabinet in the Louvre. They are by Paul Veronese, Guido, Poussin and M. Le Brun. His Majesty examined for a while the works of the latter and seeing them in the midst of such illustrious examples, said to him obligingly, "How well they hold up amidst those of the great masters. After his death may they be as greatly sought after but that he hoped that this would not happen soon because he had great need of him." One cannot too much laud the taste of the King. His Majesty having seen the paintings in the seven great galleries of the Louvre then proceeded to visit four rooms in the adjoining old Hôtel de Grammont. His Majesty left

PARIS SEEN FROM THE PONT ROUGE

After an engraving by Perelle

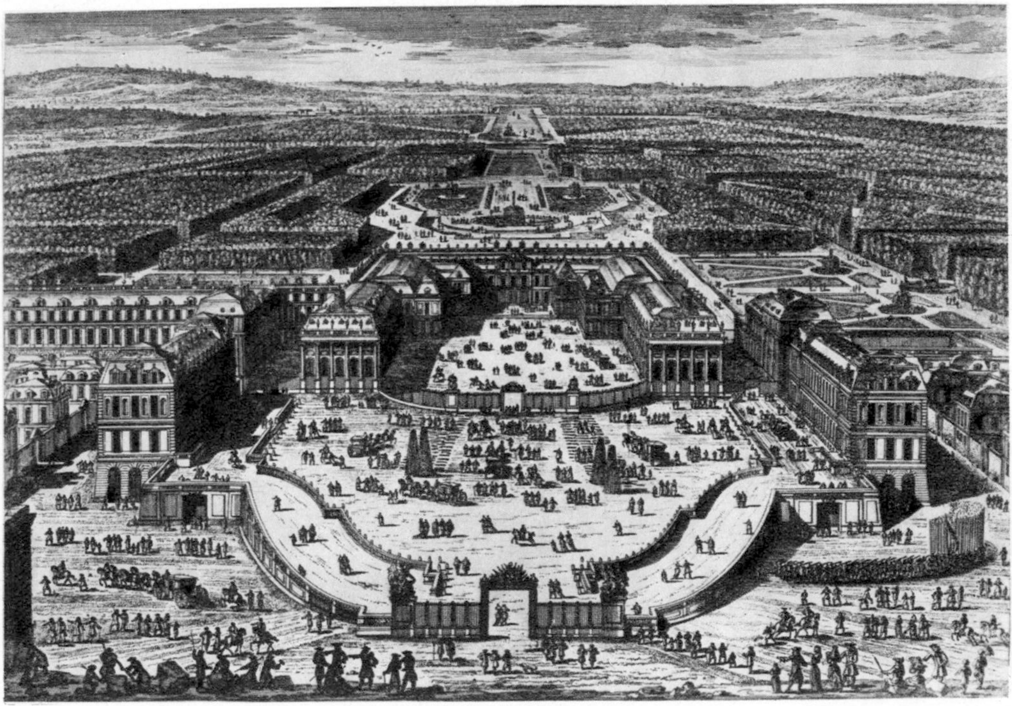

THE CHÂTEAU DE VERSAILLES

After an engraving by Perelle

LOUIS XIV, ACCOMPANIED BY THE GRAND DAUPHIN AND COLBERT, VISITS THE GOBELINS

From the drawing by Le Brun for the tapestry commemorating the visit deeply satisfied at having seen all of his pictures in such good condition. The oldest ones and the rarest are closed in boxes with shutters of which the surfaces are gilded and painted; one might almost say that they are in themselves pictures which hide the others. It is necessary to take special precautions for those which were made a great many years ago and can be very easily spoiled.

* * * * *

Two years after the opening of the Louvre, Colbert, who was rapidly losing the favor of the King (now completely under the thumb of the Minister of War, Louvois), died of a stroke. An era of petty economy set in; Louvois succeeded as *Surintendant des Bâtiments* and a new administration appeared. The brothers Perrault were dismissed in 1690 and Le Brun was replaced by Mignard, perhaps a painter but a man of little force. The *Grand Siècle* was over.

The old Louis XIV lived on until 1715. While collecting continued among the fashionable *curieux*, it was no longer done in the name of the king. Court life, which had become so restricted and stereotyped, had provoked a new restlessness. The court, accustomed to spending the better part of the year in small attic rooms at Versailles, dancing attendance on the king, transplanted this life of small apartments to Paris. The great *hôtels particuliers* gave way to a new kind of *immeuble*, the large apartment house of the *faubourg*. The scale of life of the nobility was very much reduced. Formal living took on another aspect which required a new type of decoration; the *bibelôt* came into its own and, as the old aristocracy gradually were obliged to sell the major works of art acquired by their ancestors, a vogue was established for the lighter and less pompous styles of the later Louis.

But it was the economic disaster caused in 1720 by the bursting of John Law's "Bubble" which more than any other factor set the seal upon French fashion. For in this speculative orgy virtually the entire court was ruined. Once more the nobility were forced to sell their works of art abroad and when, at last, under the reckless encouragement of Madame de Pompadour, they again turned to the pleasures of collecting, it was to the frivolous productions of their contemporaries rather than to the pompous old masters so highly prized by their parents and grandparents. The furniture of the *ébéniste* and *ciseleur*, the *bric-à-brac*, the porcelain decorations from the monopolistic factories of the crown, took the place of the more solid financial investments of Renaissance art; it was so to speak an inflation of the paper currency of art against an ever-thinning gold reserve. A *garçonnière* could after all be furnished by the Beauvais factory for the price of a Titian or a Tintoretto and could indeed provoke an amatory response that was perhaps more bucolic than that of the graver Arcadian shepherdesses of a century before, but no less intimate. John Law had taught the French to look for dividends wherever they could find them.

The history of the Compagnie des Indes is inextricably bound up with the history of taste, for since it sought to bring into its giant maw every asset of the King of France, it not only paid the piper but it also called the tune. French taste was only one of its myriad monopolies; the company had grown steadily more demanding as the Scottish financier increased his influence over the Regent, the Duc d'Orléans. Law, who was an early advocate of a state bank supported by paper notes, had settled in Paris in 1715 and had formed in the following year, with his brother William, a private bank, chartered by the government. It was so highly successful that the Regent adopted Law's scheme for a national bank. The new institution issued prodigious quantities of bank notes and at first enjoyed perfect credit. (The old national bonds meanwhile remained, as they had long been, at a price far below their face value.) Within another year Law had so dazzled the Regent that he encouraged him to embark upon the "Mississippi Scheme" for the purpose of raising money to replenish the exhausted treasury of France. The Compagnie d'Occident was established with a capitalization of 100,000,000 livres; 200,000 shares were offered and quickly bought up. In return the company was granted for twenty-five years exclusive privileges of trading in Louisiana and the Mississippi area. The colony so fabulously rich in natural resources was also believed to abound in gold and silver and other precious metals. The company had the right to farm taxes and coin money. The company, soon taking over the Banque Royale and the French East India Company, obtained similar privileges regarding trade with China, the East Indies and the South Seas. It guaranteed, on its part, the national debt. The name of the entire affair was changed to Compagnie des Indes; 50,000 new shares were competed for by 300,000 applicants. Law was made Comptroller of Finances and a Councilor of State.

The frenzy of speculation far exceeded that of any other boom in history. While the day's turnover in shares was of course unequal to that of the New York Stock Exchange in 1929, in relation to population and the per capita wealth of Europe the results were even more devastating and widespread. Fictitious values rose on every commodity; the price of living skyrocketed; manufactured goods increased 400 per cent. Rich and poor alike, who had a few sous to rub together, rushed to Paris to take any lodgings whatever in garrets or in cellars in order to be able to play the market.

Then came the crash. The Regent had increased the paper circulation of the Banque Royale to the unheard-of figure of 2,700,000,000 livres. Wary speculators sold short and secretly converting their stocks to gold and silver shipped the bullion to England and to Belgium for security. In February 1720 there was a general run on the bank and by decree the government reduced the value of the shares 50 per cent. Restrictions were placed on the ownership and exportation of metal. But the shares steadily declined to a low of 24 livres each and Law prudently fled to Brussels, then to England, and finally spent the declining years of his life gambling in the cafés and casinos of Venice.

The *Grand Siècle*, which had drained the resources of the country with wars and the extravagances of Versailles, left to the two Louis a heritage of bankruptcy not only in the financial structure of the kingdom but also of the intellect. The *philosophes*, belonging to the world of the future and building their new capital upon the liberal ideas of the English Revolution of the preceding century, departed from the old gold standard of the *Grand Monarque*. There was an attendant flight from France of everything of negotiable value: gold and silver, jewels, works of art. Despite the elegance of Pompadour and the mirage of Napoleon, France was not to know real prosperity again until the *bourgeois* prosperity of Louis-Philippe.

CHAPTER VI

The Fashionable *Curieux:* Madame de Verrue

THE return of the court from Versailles brought back to Paris a certain sovereignty of taste which had been submerged in the vaster conceptions of Colbert and Le Brun. Official styles invariably breed their own reaction and in this case there was a violent and explosive desire for lightness and fresh air. Patronage at first clung to the heavier conventions of the *Grand Siècle* although private collecting, so long subordinated to the governmental buying of the court of Louis XIV, had been tempered by the new fashions and tastes seeping in from Amsterdam, the current art market of the world, and from Venice, which prided itself on being the center of the international "café society" of the eighteenth century.

Court life had changed; released from the rigors of etiquette at Versailles, the nobles fled to their country places, where they soon found that they were even more bored than they had been in waiting on the aged King. They returned to town, to relatively small apartments in the *faubourgs*, spending the nights in gambling and dancing, lavishing small attentions on beautiful women, writing comedies on love and giving birth to epigrams with the same careless abandon with which on their country estates they reaped the harvests of their *droits du seigneur*.

It was the age of frivolity; the lid of absolutism was off. A century had been spent in trying to please the King, and although the courts of the two succeeding Louis did not share, nor could they approve, the liberalism or the constantly sharpening knife of Jacobinism which was so literally to sever their proud necks in the "Terror," the spirit which was abroad, and with which they were inevitably infected, resulted in a cynicism and barbed wit which dominated the arts and also literature and love. Daintiness and elegance were the order of the day; life was in most respects merely a rehearsal for one's *mémoires* in which style and malice were to be the measure of intelligence and any moral value sacrificed to the neat turning of a phrase. It was also the age of the *philosophes* but it was characteristic of a decaying aristocracy that they understood only the sophistry of the latter and none of their essential wisdom.

The changes in domestic architecture were the product of a long-felt need in the art of living. As early as the reign of Henri IV, Mrs. Putnam has pointed out, "the Marquise de Rambouillet had built for herself a new *hôtel* in the rue Saint Thomas du Louvre and placed her staircase in a corner of the building instead of in the middle where all the world had supposed a staircase must be. . . . The central staircase had cut the house in two, with an enormous drawing-room on one side and an enormous bedroom on the other. No one had conceived a less naïve distribution. Mme. de Rambouillet took the first step toward the humanization of the *hôtel*. . . . Having recovered from the staircase the central section of her house, she could arrange the whole floor in a suite of communicating rooms, throwing them together or separating them at will by a system of folding doors, symmetrically arranged. In working out her main idea she added highly agreeable details, loftier ceilings, larger windows and a livelier scheme of decoration. Before her day no one had thought of painting walls with any other color than red or tan; she invented her famous blue room. So much of the tradition of the *donjon* and its furniture remained that the chief mobile feature of the blue room was the great bed in its alcove which the lady occupied to receive her guests – the *lit paré* of a hundred contes of the middle ages." *

Mrs. Putnam continues to show that "throughout the reign of Louis XIV this theory prevailed," only to be modified again in the eighteenth century when woman finally emerged the victor in the age-long struggle between the sexes. Pierre Patti, an architect of Louis XV, wrote:

* Emily James Putnam, *The Lady*. Sturgis and Walton, 1910, p. 211.

Nothing does us so much honor as the invention of the art of distributing apartments. Before us the one consideration was the exterior and its magnificence; the interiors were vast and inconvenient. There were drawing-rooms two stories high and spacious reception rooms. All these were placed end to end without detachment. Houses were solely for publicity, not for private comfort. All the pleasant arrangements that we admire today in the new hôtels, the artful detachment of rooms, the concealed staircases so convenient for hiding an intrigue or avoiding importunate visitors, those contrivances that lighten the labor of servants and make our houses delightful and enchanted dwellings, all these are the invention of our day.

As the ponderous disappeared from the architecture so did it lose its appeal in the furnishings and works of art that accompanied it. Heavy timbers and rafters were concealed by ceilings and paneling.

The colossal was replaced by the little. The statues, the columns, the great canvases made way for china figurines, for carven garlands and for mirrors. If the gentlemen of France breathed more freely when Louis XIV was dead, the lady's emancipation needs a stronger figure. She was herself again; powers had been accumulating for her as money accumulates for an heir during his minority; her great century was before her; and the first outward result of her action was to diminish the scale. Her furniture was not henceforward to make her look dwarfed; she was tired of the rôle of an ill-executed caryatid. The grandiose and the symmetrical had never become her; her ardent wish was to be surrounded with small objects and to get rid, as far as possible, of things with two sides alike.

The very thoughtlessness of eighteenth-century art was what appealed to her, for it was an art which any rich person can put upon the walls of the dining room without risking the ulcers of actuality or the concern of where the next meal was coming from.

In 1730 the collectors of France were a house divided. On the one hand there was the court group of whom the Regent and Madame de Verrue were the acknowledged leaders. The great number of titled amateurs who bought and sold are listed together with the catalogues of their sales in Charles Blanc's *Trésor de la Curiosité*. Most of these collections disappeared before the Revolution and turned up again in Germany and Russia, some of the fine things going to the new group of collectors in England. As opposed to these were the "scholar-collectors," the historians of art and catalogue writers, who emulated at the same time the academicians with whom they corresponded in Italy and the swelling number of encyclopedists in France. New curiosities and appetites led the latter into many phases of criticism never before explored.

If the eighteenth was the century of the dilettanti in Italy and England, it became in France that of the *amateur* and *curieux* who expressed themselves in luxurious catalogues *in-folio*, profusely illustrated and dedicated with permission, and for the usual consideration, to this or that *Monseigneur*.

But the art historian in the eighteenth century was no less compromising in the matter of the contemporary product than he is today. Mariette, who was generally acknowledged as their dean, fulminated against the decline which had steadily taken place since the great masters of the Renaissance. "They strive only to please," he said, "and they become, so to speak, the slaves of the dominating taste. That which reigns today is the pretty (*joly, graziozo*). They look only for subjects that are graceful, and which are pleasing, more for what they represent, than for the depth of knowledge they display — a knowledge peculiar to the true connoisseur. It is like a general plague." *

As in love, so in collecting, Frenchwomen of the eighteenth century led the field; their salons became the forum and to some extent the salesroom for both antique and modern. Here was decreed the

* How deeply this frivolity had taken root may be seen in the instructions and specifications for a painting given to Lancret by the Duc d'Antin, *Surintendant des Bâtiments* for Louis XV, for whom the picture was commissioned: *Dans le voyage de la reine Maria Lecsinska, de Strasbourg à Fontainebleau, il est arrivé plusieurs accidents, mais surtout de Provins à Montéreau, où le second carrosse de dames s'ambourba, de façon qu'on ne put le retirer. Six dames du palais furent obligées de se mettre dans un fourgon, avec beaucoup de paille, quoiqu'en grand habit et coifées. Il faut représenter les six dames, le plus grotesquement qu'on pourra, et dans le goût qu'on porte les veaux au marché, et l'équipage le plus dépenaillé que faire se pourra. Il faut une autre dame sur un cheval de charrette, harnaché comme ils le sont ordinairement, bien maigre et bien harassé, et une autre en travers, sur un autre cheval de charrette, comme un sac, et que le panier relève, de façon qu'on voie jusqu'à la jarretière; le tout, accompagné de quelques cavaliers culbutés dans les crottes, et des galopins qui éclairent avec des brandons de paille. Il faut aussi que le carrosse resté paraisse embourbé dans l'éloignement, enfin tout ce que le peintre pourra mêttre de plus grotesque et de plus dépenaillé.*

taste of the epoch; the furniture was changed to meet the lightness of the conversation and the fragility of dress and high coiffure. Decoration was reduced to the intimacy of the *affaire clandestine;* the *bibelôt* and the porcelain came into their own and provided the *ébéniste* and cabinetmaker with pretty trivialities to lighten the severity of classic lines; already the discoveries of Pompeii and Herculaneum were gradually beckoning the artist. Most important of all was the relatively low cost of modern decoration, produced in the heavily subsidized factories of the crown. The aristocracy, which had gambled its inheritance in the parlors of Versailles, and again in the small boiseried chambers of the rue de l'Université and Saint-Germain, no longer had the means to compete with the Kings of Prussia and of Saxony, or with the Great Catherine, for the masterpieces of the Renaissance. Having invested all too heavily in the enterprises of John Law, they welcomed a style which gave them elegance and luxury at a time when it was fashionable to be restrained.*

* * * * *

* An illuminating view of the opinions of the opposition is found in *Tableaux, Dessins, Estampes, Etc.* (Chapter CCCVIII), Louis Sébastien Mercier, *Tableau de Paris*, vol. IV, Amsterdam, 1782:

La manie coûteuse & insensée des tableaux & des dessins que l'on achete à des prix foux, est bien inconcevable. Il n'y a point de luxe, après celui des diamans & des porcelaines, plus petit & plus déraisonnable: non qu'un tableau ne vaille son prix; mais parce qu'il est bizarre, ridicule, indécent de couvrir d'or des peintures dont l'utilité & la jouissance sont également bornées.

Que des princes forment des cabinets, ils se doivent à tous les arts. Mais qu'un particulier entreprenne une collection toujours incomplete, ces dépenses énormes l'empêcheront, à coup sûr, d'être un bon parent, un bon ami, un obligeant citoyen: il n'aura plus d'argent que pour des toiles peintes. Plus il possédera, plus il voudra encore posséder: sa maison, sa famille, tout ce qui l'environne, se sentira des prodigieux sacrifices qu'il offrira sans cesse à une manie dont la nature est de ne jamais contenter celui qu'elle tourmente.

Les méprises étant faciles & les erreurs ordinaires, nouvelle source de chagrins & de contrariétés: l'entêtement prend la place du goût, & la fureur de la possession empêche la paisible jouissance.

Je n'ai jamais pu concevoir comment on ne se contentoit pas d'une belle copie au défaut de l'original. Souvent l'oeil le plus exercé hésite entre les deux peintures; & quand on pourroit avoir par ce moyen trente beaux tableaux pour le prix qu'on met à un seul, comment se ruine-t-on pour un tableau unique?

Tel homme a vendu ses maisons & ses terres, pour faire une collection d'estampes renfermées dans des porte-feuilles invisibles, & qu'il n'ouvre pas quatre fois l'année. Il se traîne encore aux ventes; crie à l'huissier, d'une voix éteinte, un sol; *dit tout haut qu'il est un fou, emporte l'objet; & il lui faut de fortes lunettes pour contempler son acquisition. A sa mort, tout cela sera dispersé en différentes mains, & l'*oeuvre *tant poursuivie ne sera jamais complete.*

The contrast between the seventeenth and eighteenth centuries is best seen in the tastes and fortunes of two royal mistresses whose charm and feeling for the arts were as gay and easy as their virtue, two of the most fascinating women in the entire history of collecting – Jeanne d'Albert de Luynes, Comtesse de Verrue, and Jeanne-Antoinette Poisson, Marquise de Pompadour.

Madame de Verrue was the most serious rival with whom the Regent Philippe d'Orléans had to compete in the salesroom, but it does not seem that their paths too often crossed. He was absorbed with acquiring pictures from Italy. His passion for Correggio had resulted in his buying Queen Christina's pictures from Prince Odescalchi. The Palais Royal was filled with magnificent canvases and became the official residence of the arts. Madame de Verrue played in other fields – she was an experimenter in the northern schools, particularly of Holland, and those of her French contemporaries. Her catholicity, her desire and curiosity for objects of *virtù* of every type, and her extravagances recalled the prodigality of Mazarin and testified to her long residence at an Italian court.

Married as a child of fourteen to the Comte de Verrue, she was taken to Turin, where her mother-in-law was lady in waiting to the Dowager Duchess of Savoy. Her beauty and her soft French charm aroused the passions of the Duke, Victor Amadeus, who proceeded, by conniving with the avaricious parents of her husband, to batter down the resistance of the ravishing young bride. Virtue, alas, was on the point of conquering when, happily, the lecherous importunities of her husband's uncle, the aged Abbé de Verrue, threw her in disgust into the waiting and jealous arms of the Duke. The latter, being also King of Sardinia and deeply envious of the brilliant excesses of the court of France, lavished upon his mistress the tremendous fortune

Un vieux tableau à moitié peint & effacé, dont on ne distingue plus rien, sera préféré, parce qu'il est original, à un tableau moderne & intéressant, dont la couleur est fraîche & agréable. Quel est donc le défaut de ce dernier? Le peintre est vivant.

Il faut que les particuliers laissent aux princes ou aux grands, dont l'opulence est excessive, le privilege de mettre de grosses sommes en tableaux & en statues. C'est une folie de consumer son patrimoine en curiosités; c'est un vice d'oublier ses parens & ses amis pour des peintures ou des gravures. Ces arts sont faits pour figurer dans des sallons publics, & non dans des cabinets. L'amateur immodéré n'est qu'un maniaque.

On n'a point encore ridiculisé sur notre scene cette folie ruineuse: elle mériteroit bien les pinceaux d'un auteur comique.

which he had inherited. Jeanne d'Albert de Luynes for six years reaped the harvest of love and servitude. She was under the constant surveillance of a jealous lover and of the Austrian partisans at court who thought less than nothing of the Duke's being dominated by a Frenchwoman. "Since she was obliged to live her life in a cage," says Clement de Ris, "she determined to gild its bars," and thus threw herself with passion into the one pastime the Duke allowed her – buying works of art and jewels, and enlarging her interests among her books and manuscripts.

Six years of this imprisonment in an atmosphere so hostile that she barely escaped death in a plot to poison her, foiled by the promptness of an antidote administered by the Duke himself, was more than she could tolerate. While her royal lover was absent from Turin she packed up her art treasures and escaped across the border with her brother into France. Her husband, now in the service of Louis XIV, was less reasonable than the Duke, who had recognized their children and settled a fortune upon her. But the Comte de Verrue, already a power at the French court, saw to it that his wife, who had never been anything to him except a rich source of revenue, was placed once more under surveillance, this time by the Benedictine nuns of the rue du Cherche-Midi, at whose house in Paris she was required to live. She spent another year under duress but was able to supervise the building of her *hôtel particulier* next door, into which she quickly moved with new liberty and new abandon.

It was in this abode, where her *salon* became one of the most brilliant of all Paris, that she earned the sobriquet of *la dame de volupté*. Her fortunes increased in proportion with the attentions lavished upon her. Her most devoted lover was the Comte de Lassay, to whom she bequeathed some of her finest pictures, "*tous les tableaux qui garnissent un des côtés de la galerie sur le terrain des Carmes . . . 46,000 frs.*" Her most intimate friends included the Duchesse de Bourbon (daughter of Louis XIV and Madame de Montespan) and many other persons highly placed at court, but her preference was for the society of scholars, painters and connoisseurs. It must have been a very advanced and very rebel group, judging by her possessions; her collection boasted pictures by Claude, Lancret, Pater and Watteau, and included three by Chardin, whose talent was then scarcely recognized. Not one of the official group surrounding Le Brun or Mignard was represented. Two of the Claudes were purchased by Godefroy for an English collector and are in the National Gallery, London; another is at the Louvre. Her Italian pictures showed her apparent lack of interest in that art; of the dozen or so names listed only those of Pietro da Cortona and Carlo Maratti would pass muster today. But in the Dutch and Flemish fields she was adventurous and whimsical: Rembrandt and Van Dyck, neither of whom was up to then generally well known in France, Karel Dujardin, Wouvermans, Metsu, all of these artists passed through her hands in pictures which have since enriched the Louvre and many other public collections.

No portrait of the Comtesse de Verrue seems to have survived, but Clement de Ris, who searched diligently both in Paris and in Turin, has reconstructed from fragmentary remarks of her contemporaries some impression of her appearance in early middle age:

> I describe her as she was about 1715, small, plump and bright-eyed, brown beneath her powder, with a touch of rouge upon the cheeks. Her dress is of dove-colored silk; from beneath the skirt escapes a foam of white of lingerie in which her inventory was so prodigal. She is seated in the middle of the gallery beneath the shadows of the Carmelite convent, in an arm-chair covered with a flowered Chinese silk mentioned in the inventory. Her gold-headed cane is at her side and the café-au-lait lap dog lies sleeping, nudging her feet with his black muzzle. In her left hand she plays with a snuff box filled with the tobacco that we know and in her right hand she holds some novel from her library, *Daumalinde, the Queen of Lusitania*, *The Heroine Musketeer*, *Almanzaide*, or *L'Amour sans Faiblesse* which she reads distractedly and with frequent interruptions. A light scent of powder *à la Maréchale* or of cream of Benjamin bathes her with a lightly perfumed atmosphere. The carefully closed curtains give a freshness to the apartment, yet at the same time protect from the sunlight the Van Dycks, the Wouwermans, the Berghems and the Bolognas. Alas, the door opens and one of her intimates comes in, a brother or M. de Chauvelin, or the Duchesse de Bourbon or M. de Lassay, or her daughter the Abbess of the Abbaye aux Bois.

This lovely creature who had warmed the hearts of men and understood the other arts so well lived on until 1736. She marked the transition from the *Grand Siècle* to the eighteenth century, and in her catholic possessions the differences of the tastes of both ages were manifest. She died as she had lived, with wit and elegance, composing for her epitaph the frankest apology for the collector that has ever been written:

Ci-gît dans une paix profonde
Cette dame de volupté
Qui, pour plus grande sûreté
*Fit son paradis dans ce monde.**

* Clement de Ris, *Les Amateurs d'Autrefois.* E. Plon, 1877, p. 181. The sale of Madame de Verrue's collection occurred March 27, 1737. An inexact list of prices is given by C. Blanc, *Trésor de la Curiosité,* p. 1. According to Lugt the catalogue appears rarely and only in manuscript copies. (Cf. Lugt, *Répertoire des Catalogues de Ventes,* Vol. I, 1938.) Here he discusses at length the importance of the sales catalogue for estimating the taste of the eighteenth century.

CHAPTER VII

The Reign of Pompadour

ABSOLUTISM dies hard; in fact it took the storming of the Bastille and the razor edge of the guillotine to put an end to it. With the country exhausted by the wars of Louis XIV, its resources drained by his extravagances at Versailles and the aristocracy bankrupt from gambling and bad investment, Jeanne-Antoinette Poisson's appearance on the stage of France provides something of a shock and at the same time the comic relief of bread and circuses which the times demanded. In the twenty-one years that she was *Maîtresse en Titre du Roi de France,* Louis XV squandered about 72,000,000 livres upon her. She was to all intents and purpose "The State," the most powerful person at court, making and unmaking ministers, disposing of public offices, honors and pensions. The court party were always at her throat; Maurepas mobilized the street urchins of Paris against her by putting in their mouths the foulest and wittiest of epigrams. But in the two objectives of her life she was an unqualified success: being the charming and diverting mistress of a bored and royal moron, and the Colbert of her day, the great influence and organizing genius of the arts which, apart from her gay surrender to sexual diversion, were her one and all-consuming passion.

She was born in Paris in 1720, the daughter of a civil servant, and married quite young to Monsieur Le Normand d'Étioles, nephew of the *Fermier-Général,* Le Normand de Tournehem. Not too much is known of her early life, though Berbier said that she received "all the education possible." "*On lui fit apprendre la gravure à l'eau-forte, le chant et le clavecin.*"

An admirer of French art and artists almost to the point of chauvinism, the young and wealthy bride immediately surrounded herself with celebrities like Voltaire, Boucher and Rameau, who were only too glad to be sought out by her. Voltaire wrote at this time: "*Madame Le Normand d'Étioles était bien élévee, sage, aimable, remplie de grâces et de talents, née avec du bons sens et un bon coeur. Je la connaissais assez; je fus même le confident de son amour. Elle m'avoua qu'elle avait toujours eut un secret sentiment qu'elle serait aimée du roi, et qu'elle s'était sentie une violente inclination pour lui. Enfin, quand elle eut tenu le roi entres ses bras, elle me dit qu'elle croyait fermement à la destinée, et elle avait raison.*"

One of her first moves was to establish a little theater in her private apartments. Here the nobility of France competed with each other for the smallest parts; the Prince de Dombec played the bassoon in the orchestra, the Duc de Chartres was proud to be an extra; one courtier promised the Pompadour's maid a commission in the army for her lover if she would get him the part of the policeman in Molière's *Tartuffe*. Boucher was her designer and stage director for sixteen years. He was, in fact, her court painter, producing decorations for her many châteaux and palaces, constantly discussing with her and advising her on the most intimate questions. It was he who, at a critical moment in her relations with the King, produced the erotic pictures in the *cabinet secret* which regained the good humor of His Majesty. These pictures, originally in her boudoir at the Arsénal where she received the King, were done in the best tradition of the *menus plaisirs* of the Renaissance; they were later denounced by Louis XVI in a fit of moral indignation and ordered to be destroyed. Happily de Maupéon, to whom the order was given, hid them, and only some of them are now preserved.

Her ability as an etcher and engraver went far beyond the limits of a polite accomplishment. Some of her work exists today and shows an almost professional sureness of her craft. Boucher and Vien collaborated with her in making designs for the principal events of the reign of Louis XV, for which she executed the plates and which Voltaire apostrophized:

Pompadour, ton crayon divin
Devrait dessiner ton visage;
Jamais une plus belle main
N'aurait fait un plus bel ouvrage.

Hardly had she become established as the royal favorite when she set out upon her career of directing and organizing the arts. In 1746 Le Normand de Tournehem, her husband's uncle, was made *Ordonnateur-général des Bâtiments du Roi,* a post similar to that held by Colbert under Louis XIV. Already she had received the marquisate de Pompadour and a property at Versailles from the King. Her younger brother, Abel Poisson, then only twenty years old and known as the Marquis d'Avanthier (from the title of Marquis de Vaudières conferred upon him by the King), became his uncle's titular assistant and active agent, taking his orders directly from his sister. Poisson's appointment and his further elevation to be Marquis de Marigny created a furor at the court, which failed to recognize that this quiet, shy and handsome lad possessed many of the qualities of taste and intelligence of the Pompadour. In order to divert public attention he was shipped to Rome on a grand tour under the chaperonage of the architect Soufflot and Cochin the archaeologist-engraver and friend of Caylus. In Italy and particularly in Rome, where he enlivened official circles by stealing the mistress of old de Troy, Director of the French Academy, Marigny became a profound and accomplished student of art and archaeology, receiving the type of training and experience which, together with his sister's wit and sagacity, brought about the purifying of taste and simplification of the *Rocaille* in the *style Pompadour* or *Louis XV*. Upon his return from Rome and the death of Tournehem in 1751, Marigny succeeded to the directorship both in fact as well as in title, and one of his first official acts was to name Boucher to succeed Coypel as *Premier Peintre du Roi* with a handsome pension and an apartment in the Louvre.

It was this triumvirate of Pompadour, Boucher and Marigny who were to transform French taste and to give the necessary royal assent to the prevailing classicism. Boucher, who personally had little sympathy with classicism, began to play the role for his day that Watteau had played a generation earlier; but whereas the latter peopled his pictures with *fêtes galantes* and with actors from the Italian *commedia dell'arte*, Boucher filled his canvases with the gods and goddesses of Olympus and the Arcadian shepherdesses of the opera. He lavished his talents upon the Pompadour, to whom he was deeply attached, and his portraits of her as a consequence, particularly those of the Wallace and the Rothschild collections, have a warmth of feeling and a height of psychological perception which this tactile painter of the luscious female nude seldom reached.

The interests of the Pompadour in the new styles grew more and more intense as the wealth of the King was visited upon her. Always intent on some new conceit of art or architecture to while away his increasing boredom, she developed a veritable mania for building châteaux and pavilions in the country and little intimate *garçonnières* in town. In 1746 she built the Ermitage in the park at Versailles; three years later the Château de la Celle at the Porte de Versailles and a villa at Fontainebleau. The Hôtel d'Évreux in Paris, in which she never lived, built by Molet for the Comte d'Évreux at the meeting of the Faubourg Saint-Honoré with the Champs Élysées, was altered for her at the cost of 100,000 livres. Other places were built for her at Crécy, Aunay and Ménars. But her favorite of all was Bellevue on the slopes of the Seine between Sèvres and Meudon, completed by the architect Lassurance in 1750. In a period of six years she spent 3,000,000 livres on the furnishings alone; it was the great show place of the epoch. Boucher was her decorator, devising, in addition to a miniature theater, a Chinese boudoir, a painted bedroom, bathroom and picture gallery of gods and goddesses *en galanterie*. Caffieri did the plaster work; only the best *ébénistes* were employed. The paintings, mostly of the contemporary French School, were valued alone at 60,000 livres; Venetian mirrors, Gobelin tapestries, porcelains, both Chinese and from her factory at Sèvres, crystals and bronzes filled the house. Coustou and the leading sculptors and painters of the day were employed by Boucher on the decoration; Bouchardon, Pigalle and Falconnet, Joseph Vernet and Van Loo. The King's Mistress was never too occupied by affairs of state to attend to the smallest details of her personal luxury. With a very fine sense of the fitness of things, on the twelfth of May, 1749, she granted a pension of 1000 *écus* to the *ébéniste* Migeon, of the Faubourg Saint-Antoine, for having made her an exquisite *chaise percée*.

"The Pompadour's tastes," says Trenchard Cox, "inclined towards fine workmanship rather than to florid detail, and at times her inclina-

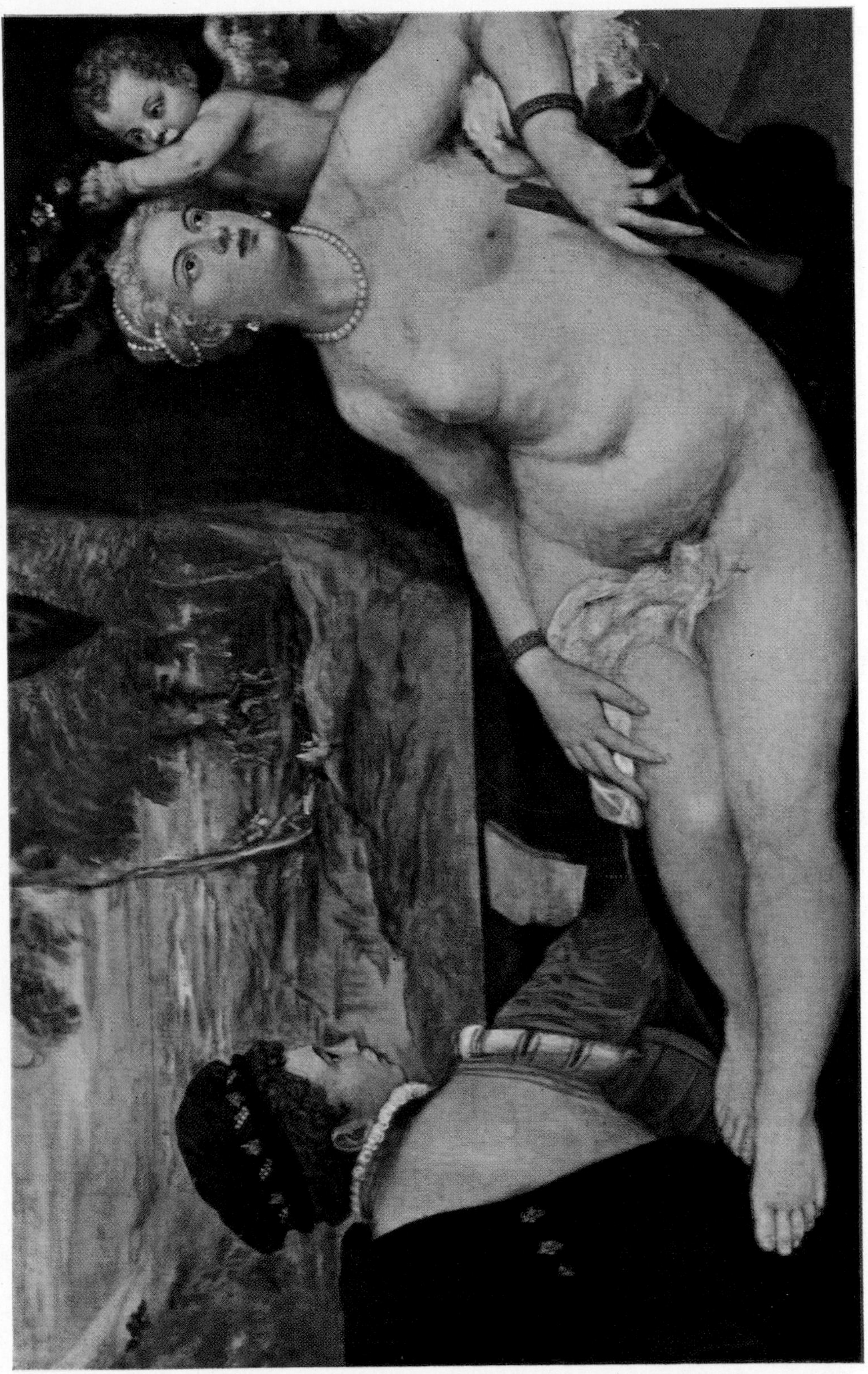

TITIAN: THE "HOLKHAM VENUS" (DETAIL)

This version of *Venus and the Lute Player* was recorded in an eighteenth-century guidebook as having belonged to Prince Pio. Margaret, Countess of Leicester, listed it in her inventory of Holkham in 1765. It remained there until 1931 when it was acquired by the Metropolitan Museum.

tions strayed to the antique. She delighted in reproducing antique intaglios with the etching needle, and used to consult upon this matter the eminent archaeologist and engraver Cochin, one of the great opponents of the *Rocaille*. It was Cochin, indeed, who led the reaction against the florid style. In 1754 he published in the *Mercure de France* an impassioned tirade against the senseless contortions of the *Rocailleurs*, beseeching goldsmiths, chisellers and sculptors in wood to submit to the eternal laws of reason, not to the transient follies of fashion. He begged his contemporary craftsmen when making a chandelier 'to make the stem straight and not twisted as if some mischievous person had been bending it. We will not ask,' he said, 'for the suppression of the palm trees which are cultivated so profusely in our apartments, on chimney-pieces, around mirrors and long walls; that would be to deprive our decorators of their dearest resource. But may we not at least hope that, when a thing is square without offence, they will leave it so and not torment it into an absurd design!' "*

The admonitions of Cochin did not fall on deaf or unsympathetic ears. Pompadour's friendship with Caylus and the influence of the severe Soufflot upon his young ward Marigny had brought about a welcome for more sober classic lines. The discoveries of Pompeii and Herculaneum, whose influence upon collecting and on scholarship had already been so very great, had now penetrated the world of fashion. Ladies began to wear their hair *à la grecque*, their waistlines rose as abruptly as their bosoms; hoops and heavy taffetas gave way to diaphanous silks and muslins, and wigs, particularly those of the actresses and *salonnières*, were relegated to the closet. To resemble a painted Tanagra figurine was the great conceit and ambition of the moment. The so-called *style Louis Seize*, Cox insists, "was crystallized about the year 1760, fourteen years before the accession of the sovereign from whom it takes its name."

But her love of personal luxury and display did not diminish the largeness of the Pompadour's ideas for the furtherance of the arts by the State. She had the great ambition, observed Dumesnil, "of mark-

* Trenchard Cox, *A General Guide to the Wallace Collection.* London, H. M.'s Stationery Office, 1933, p. 72.

ing her passage with monuments and institutions which might carry her name down through posterity." These ambitions found their widest expression in the porcelain factory at Sèvres, in her plans for the completion of the Louvre and in her vain efforts for the improvement of the city of Paris.

The rage for soft-paste porcelain had been introduced from the Orient. The Duchesse de Maine had already established a royal faïence industry to give employment to local artisans and to meet the growing demand for tableware among the rapidly increasing bourgeoisie. In 1740 two brothers Dubois, one a modeler, the other a painter, proposed to sell the secret of the *pâte tendre*, which they claimed to have learned at Saint-Cloud, to the Marquis Orry de Fulvy, brother of the *Contrôleur Général des Finances*. The interest of the King resulted in their being given the riding stables at Vincennes as a factory. The Dubois failed, and a new company was formed under the title of *Manufacture royale de porcelaine de France*.

In 1756 at the instigation of Pompadour the works were moved to a pavilion that had formerly belonged to the musician Lulli at Sèvres, where they could be under her close and constant supervision and where she herself could work with the factory as a designer and artisan. The vogue for the various wares, both the earlier Vincennes and the products of the Sèvres works, spread all over Europe. The newly discovered unglazed *biscuit*, developed by Bachelier, was pushed by Pompadour and gave the sculptors of France a new and easily salable medium. Artificial it may have been, but the rage for porcelain at the court of France was none the less valid; one of the reasons, in fact, why there is so little good silver of the seventeenth and eighteenth centuries left in the country is that the courtiers, following the example of the King, sent their table silver to be melted at the mint and had it replaced by porcelain. Possibly a more pressing argument than fashion was the flight of capital from France, where already the murmurs of revolution were reaching polite society. The cult of porcelain permitted the exportation of one's silver plate to England without comment. Ambassadors and rulers throughout the world received presents of Sèvres from Louis XV, shipments going to China and to Turkey; and among the large orders which poured in from foreign countries was that of Catherine the Great, who ordered a service in *bleu turquoise* of 744 pieces for which the bill amounted to 328,000 livres.

Although, at the Pompadour's suggestion, an exhibition of some of the King's pictures was held at the Palais du Luxembourg from October 1750 through 1761, the first *free public* exhibition of them to be made, she was unable to revive Richelieu's idea of transforming the *grande galerie* of the Louvre into a museum of the principal paintings of the royal collection. This was thwarted by her enemies at court who, not wishing to give her the least loophole for popularity, objected that it would denude Versailles and that it would be an unhealthy concession to the public to permit them to see the royal pictures which hitherto had been reserved for the King and the nobility. Similarly her efforts to complete the Louvre – for the large additions built by Colbert on the plans of Perrault still remained unroofed and the Cour Jean-Goujon had been filled with builder's litter for nearly a century – were defeated by the court which joined the clergy in opposing her desire to transform Paris into a series of garden squares like Mayfair and Westminster. This would have necessitated taking over many rich Church lands and convent gardens, and the violence of the opposition was naturally in direct ratio to her reputation for sin to which her life of easy virtue had committed her. One plan of Pompadour's which was never realized was that of cutting a wide avenue along the present rue de Tournon from the Luxembourg to the Collège Mazarin. Happily this was not done, for it would have deprived recent generations of epicures and *bon vivants* from gorging themselves at Foyot's and watching with glazed stupefaction the senators playing croquet across the street after lunch.

But Pompadour consoled herself, and re-established her position in the eyes of the Church by ordering the erection of the Madeleine as a tomb for herself and a gesture of atonement to posterity. This she hardly need have done for her great monument, indeed, was eighteenth-century Paris, the Paris that Baron Haussmann was to tear down – that unique creation for which Hitler, like Napoleon before him, was willing to grant a plenary indulgence. Jeanne-Antoinette Poisson, this child of destiny, left her mark not only on her city and on her country but on her century as well. But in the words of d'Argenson her greatest force lay in her subtlety:

> To the most touching graces of her person seconded by everything most charming that education is capable of giving, she joined an art so necessary at Versailles: the art of flippancy towards the King, a *badinage* hitherto unknown at Court. Her address never failed to put a premium on the least *bagatelle*. No one had so much grace as she in telling a story or an anecdote of the Court or of the city. She was particularly talented in the distribution of her favors, always *à propos*, never letting them show themselves until the occasion was presented at which they most successfully might be appreciated. Her penetration went to the point of discovering the very moment when each of these would be most agreeable; and she did not often have to wait. The curtain (of her conversation) was lowered and the scene was changed so rapidly that one scarcely had time to recover from the surprise and admiration of the last act.*

La Pompadour, despite the wide variety of her cares and interests, remains one of the greatest art patrons and collectors of her period. It may be true that her extravagances gave the *coup de grâce* to an already expiring monarchy; certain it is that the Seven Years' War with England and Prussia was generally laid at her doorstep and with it the loss of France's possessions in India and North America. It was, however, her worst enemies who best appreciated her many talents. In the *Chroniques secrètes* of the Abbé Baudeau there is recorded a speech of Duclos in a serious political discussion of the *philosophes:* "*Aux choses nouvelles, il faut un mot nouveau. Nous avons une nouvelle espèce de gouvernement; c'est à moi, comme historiographe de France et secrétaire de l'Académie, à trouver le mot: je l'ai trouvé; ceci est une 'conocratie'!*"

Faced with remorse at continual reverses she nevertheless retained

* *Aux grâces les plus touchantes de la personne, secondées de tout ce que l'éducation peut donner de plus charmant, elle joignit un art, si nécessaire à Versailles: l'art de badiner dans un ton inconnu au roi et à la cour. Son adresse ne manquait pas de donner du prix aux moindres bagatelles. Personne n'avait autant de grâce qu'elle à raconter une histoire ou des anecdotes de la cour et de la ville. Elle excellait surtout dans l'art de déployer, toujours à propos, ses gentillesses et de ne les faire paraître qu'au moment favorable où elles pouvaient être le mieux senties. Sa pénétration allait jusqu'à découvrir le moment où chacune d'elles cesserait d'être agréable: elle ne l'attendait pas. Déjà la décoration était changée qu'on n'était pas encore revenu de la surprise et de l'admiration qu'elle avait excitée.*

to the very end her great vitality and strength of will. "When she could no longer retain the King's love," Cox remarked, "she was a match for his companionship and stoically regarded his transferred attentions as the irrevocable fulfilment of natural laws. Even on her death-bed she would not give way. When the priest, who had given her a hurried viaticum, made a movement as if to depart, Pompadour, the courtesan, prematurely old at forty-two, said with her accustomed imperiousness, defiance, courtesy and wit: 'One moment, please, Monsieur le Curé, we will go out together.' "

CHAPTER VIII

The *Curieux* and the *Philosophes*

By the eighteenth century the private collector had become a rather complex personality, reflecting not merely the ephemeral tastes of the courts through which he moved, but also the new intellectual curiosities which were manifested in the type of objects he collected. The latter reveal for the first time a conscious effort on his part to understand the changing economic and political conditions of his day. Suddenly the curtain had been rung up on the modern world; the rational basis of existence which, with all its materialism and frenzied search for abstract virtues, is a commonplace today had been achieved only by a divorce from a medieval world that had spent itself in the extravagances and exaggerations of the Renaissance and Baroque.

These changes were due not only to a more liberal spirit of inquiry which permitted a new attitude towards science and technical invention, but to the expansion of commerce which these inventions, and particularly the printing press, had made possible. The *savant* had, in fact, taken possession of the court; for, as the Augustan authority of the *Grand Siècle* gradually relaxed and it became less dangerous for the courtier to investigate the world of philosophy, conversation was no longer restricted to the gossip of the attic hallways of Versailles. Suddenly we see the man of letters stalk through the drawing rooms and gardens, scattering his favors with a promiscuous enthusiasm which reduced *la galanterie* to a mere pedestrian amusement.

But the scholar was not always looked upon with reverence by everyone. There was a healthy and knowledgeable skepticism towards his intellectual pretensions, his ability to dispose of every subject and his fashionable tastes. The comedies of Molière had early taken his full measure. The *curieux* were beginning to give way to the *phi-*

losophes. And in a court so heavily burdened with the Augustan importations from Italy it is not surprising that the worm turned with the century. A natural resentment had been built up against any official expression of the intellect. About 1700 Charles Perrault, who a few years earlier had so completely routed the Italian architect and sculptor Bernini on the plans for completing the Louvre, threw down the gauntlet of French chauvinism when he said:

La belle antiquité fut toujours vénérable,
Mais je ne crus jamais qu'elle fut adorable.
Je vois les Anciens, sans plier les genoux,
Ils sont des grands, il est vrai, mais hommes commes nous.
Et l'on peut comparer, sans craindre d'être injuste,
Le Siècle de Louis au beau Siècle d'Auguste.

There were those, too, to whom not even chauvinism offered a way of life. La Bruyère was equally scornful of the scholar, the statesman and the prelate. The collector, however, and the *curieux* drew his particular fire and in the thirteenth chapter of his *Caractères* he denounces him in terms which are familiar enough in the present day.*

Curiosity is not an Inclination for what is good or beautiful, but for what is rare and singular; things which another can't match. 'Tis not an affection for those things which are best, but for those which are most sought after, and most in the Fashion. 'Tis not an amusement, but a passion and often so violent, that it yields to Love and Ambition only in the meanness of its Object. 'Tis not a passion for everything scarce and in vogue but only for some particular thing rare, and yet in Fashion . . .

Diognetes, . . . endeavours to inform himself by Medals; that he esteems them the speaking Evidences of past Transactions, and fix'd unquestionable Monuments of Ancient History, nothing less: you guess perhaps, that all the pains he takes to recover a Head, proceeds from the pleasure he enjoys in seeing an uninterrupted series of the Emperors, 'tis yet less: *Diognetes* knows nicely all the parts of a Medal; has a case full of Medals, except one place; and 'tis this vacuity which makes him so uneasy, that truly and literally to fill this, he spends Estate and Life.

* Jean de La Bruyère, *The Characters: or the Manners of the Present Age*. London, 1713. It is generally supposed that this was a personal attack on the great print collector, Michel de Marolles, Abbé de Villeloin, whose collection was purchased by Colbert for the crown. Cf. p. 349.

Will you see my Prints, adds *Democedes?* And presently he draws them out, and shews them you; you find one neither finely printed, neatly grav'd, nor well design'd, and therefore more fit to hang upon the Walls of the most publick Places on Holy-days, than to be preserv'd in a Cabinet: he allows it to be ill grav'd and worse design'd, but assures you it was done by an Italian, of whom there's little extant; that 'tis the only one in France of his hand; he bought it very dear, and would not part with it for a much better. I labour under a sensible Affliction, continues he, which will oblige me to leave off troubling myself with Prints the rest of my Life; I have all *Calot*, except one Print, indeed so far from being the best, 'tis the worst he ever did: But how shall I compleat my *Calot?* I have hunted this Print these twenty years, and now I despair of ever getting it: This is very hard!

Another satyrizes those who make long Voyages, either thro Uneasiness or Curiosity, who keep no Journal; furnish us with no Relations or Memoirs; who go to see what they have seen; who desire only to remember new Towers or new Steeples, and to pass rivers only because they are unknown; who go out of their own Country purely to return again; who love to be absent, fond of having it said that they have been a great way off. And this Satyrist talks well and gains attention.

But when he adds, that Books are more instructive than Travelling, and gives me to understand he has a Library, I desire to see it; I visit this Gentleman, he receives me at his House; where at the foot of the Stairs, I am struck with the scent of *Russia* Leather, which all his Books are bound with. In vain he encourages me, by telling me they are gilt on the Backs and Leaves, of the best Editions, and by naming some of the best of them: in vain he tells me, his Gallery is full of 'em, except a few Shelves painted so like books, that the fallacy is not to be discern'd: And adds that he never reads nor sets foot in this Gallery, but would do it to oblige me. I thank him for his Complaisance, but would as soon visit a Tan-Pit as what he calls his Library.

Some People by an intemperate desire of Knowledge, and unwillingness to be ignorant of anything, are greedy of all sorts of Learning, and Masters none; fonder of knowing much than knowing well, and had rather be superficial Smatterers in several Sciences, than to dive profoundly into any one alone: They everywhere meet with Masters to reclaim them; Bubbles to their own Curiosity, and often by very painful efforts, can but just extricate themselves from the grossest Ignorance.

Others have the Key of the Sciences, but never enter themselves; they spend their Lives in learning the *Eastern* and the *Northern* languages, those of both *Indies,* those of the two Poles; nay that of the World in the Moon itself. The most useless idioms, the most ridiculous and magical Characters, employ their Minds and excite their Industry; they pity those who content themselves with their own Language, or at most Latin and Greek. These Men read all Historians, and know nothing of History; run thro all Books, but are not the wiser for any; their defect is a barren Ignorance of Things and Principles; but their best Collection, their greatest Riches conflict in abundance of Words and Phrases, which they huddle together, and load their Memory withal, whilst their Understandings are empty.

* * * * *

The political changes were even more profound; French hegemony had been symbolically brought to a close by the Revocation of the Edict of Nantes in 1685. The English Revolution, ending the Stuart dynasty three years later, ushered in a new freedom under the parliamentary supervision of the House of Hanover. It had been a revolution of the spirit of which Newton and Locke were the leaders, and of which the adventurers who sailed the Seven Seas in search of colonial wealth and the enrichment of natural science were the disciples. Britain emerged the conqueror of the world, politically, materially, but above all morally, because her code was based upon science and the free exchange of knowledge between free men. The philosophical regeneration of the Continent, won with such tragic consequences in France, was the result of English freedom, conceived at home but carried to perfection in her rebellious colonies. The final essence of democracy was distilled not in the House of Commons or in the laboratory of Dr. Franklin, nor was it expounded by the Committee of Public Safety, but in the writings of Thomas Jefferson, in the Declaration of Independence and the Constitution of the United States.

Man's progress along the pathway of Enlightenment was not accomplished, however, without bloodshed and without violent political distortions and economic upheavals. Power was not relinquished everywhere with grace and, although the century marks in general the rise of the bourgeoisie and the lower orders at the expense of the nobles, absolutism, despite carefully watered philosophical exchanges (such as those to come later between Frederick II and Voltaire and of Catherine the Great with Diderot), continued unabated in the Germanies and Russias. The consolidation of the Austro-Hungarian dominions in 1687, the vast expansion of Russia as a world power under Peter the Great and Catherine, and the transfer of Spain from Hapsburg to Bourbon in 1700, marked simultaneously the emergence of a new power in the north. Germany, which hitherto had been but a geographical expression, a group of states with common language and customs loosely held together by the confederation of the Holy Roman Empire, became, through the transformation of Brandenburg into the Kingdom of Prussia, a challenge to the growing authority of Russia in the east and to the declining power of France in the west. England, upon whose throne the Elector of Hanover was to sit until 1837, and to whom Sir Robert Walpole gave a half century of peace, was concerned with her dominions overseas and was not to feel the threat of Germany in Europe until the consequences of Industrial Revolution had forced her to seek a larger continental market for her manufactured goods.

The minor states, now totally eclipsed, compensated for their loss of sovereignty by imitating (at Potsdam, Cassel and Schönbrunn, to name but three) so far as their means would permit, and by the use of less costly materials such as stucco and plaster, the Château de Versailles; the latter remained until the time of Napoleon the symbol of royal prestige and of divine right. Holland, caught between the French army and the British navy, contented herself with being a modest republic, a cultural outpost of France and of French fashions. Poland was partitioned and Sweden, reduced in power, was no longer able to enjoy the fruits of her expansion a century earlier. The middle of the century saw also the decadence of the Latin countries; Spain remained a backwater of Catholic reaction opposed in principle to the philosophy of enlightenment and living uncertainly on the wealth of colonies abroad which were growing steadily away from her. Portugal passed from the Hispanic orbit to that of England; she has to a large extent remained a political colony of Britain until the present day, drawing her wealth for the most part from Brazil and Macao. Italy enjoyed a popularity in western Europe that chose to overlook her deep political and economic decay, for she was still the objective of the grand tour without which no gentleman's education was complete. The theories of art, the science and the literature created in her Renaissance were no less sought after than the masterpieces which filled her palaces and churches, or the antiquities that lay buried in her ageless soil. But as a political entity she had virtually ceased to exist. The Kingdom of Naples, the Grand Duchy of Tuscany and the Republic of Venice were the successive pawns in the great game of European politics and the Papacy, "depressed to the nadir of her historical orbit," was unable to prevent the hostility to the Church to which rationalism now joined forces along with "Jansenism, Gallicanism and State absolutism."

The "Enlightenment" saw a new world view and established a new intellectual order. This view was more compatible with the political and economic map of Europe and compared with other spiritual revolutions in history. "Like the Greek Sophists," Preserved Smith has said, "the philosophers of the Enlightenment found in the comparison of their standards with those of other races and in the mutual contradictions of the wise, reason for doubting the validity of the accepted religious and ethical systems. Like the humanists of the Renaissance they turned eagerly from an other-worldly and pessimistic, to a secular and optimistic mood. Like the Reformers they appealed to the ornamental, or the voluptuous, or the moralistic. Perspicuity became the queen of literary virtues; clarity, neatness, wit, readability, were cultivated at the expense of eloquence, emotion, and profundity. Poetry declined the dangerous ardors of the sublime to cultivate the pretty graces of the drawing-room." *

Such an intellectual climate naturally gave encouragement for the pursuit of archaeology and the history of art. Although Vasari in his *Lives of the Painters* had blazed the trail which most of the art historians of the next three centuries were to follow, his approach was more frankly biographical than critical. There remained the necessity of establishing the rhetoric and discipline of art history. The lead was taken by the archaeologists for they were dealing, after all, with

* Preserved Smith, *A History of Modern Culture*. Henry Holt and Co., 1934, p. 17.

measurable and tangible relics of the safe past, whereas the critic was still subject to the partisan stresses and strains of the disputes of the Academy. The two great controversies, drawing *versus* color, and the ideal *versus* the real, had absorbed the waking hours of painter and critic alike since the days of Poussin. Far from being resolved in the eighteenth century, they were nevertheless summed up by De Piles in his declaration, "I love the celebrated schools, I love Raphael, Titian and Rubens, and I seek always to discern the rare qualities of those great painters; but whatever qualities they may have, I love truth more." As the artist moved deeper and deeper into the era of Enlightenment his observation of, and fidelity to, nature constantly increased; he became imbued with the scientific spirit of the times and the influence of the Academy was felt less and less until, finally, under the guidance of Rousseau and Diderot, Romanticism became an established fact.

But taste was subjected to the same laws which governed all forms of intellectual activity. It was held that art, like science, "is derived from the study of nature and therefore is susceptible of geometrical formulation." The beautiful and the true are the products of reason and can be deduced by clinical observation on the one hand, and by *a priori* mathematical formulae on the other. As a substitute for the study of nature the classics offered the next best opportunity for the development of taste because of their dependence upon the true observation of nature, particularly of the human form. Junius had even contended that "a picture is nothing else in itself but a delusion of our eyes." * He also recognized that even in nature it is seldom possible to find the perfection which antiquity claimed for the ideal beauty; distilled "out of the fairest bodies. . . . The ancients studied rather to produce a perfect pulchritude according to the true law and rule of symmetrie; aspiring to that same grace of comeliness and beauty, which as it cannot be found in any particular bodie, so may it be gathered out of many bodies." Color, he added, must be sacrificed

* Franciscus Junius, the librarian of Thomas Howard, Earl of Arundel, in his treatise *De Pictura Veterum*, published at Oxford in 1637, had anticipated many of these arguments, taken up later in the poem of Du Fresnoy, *De Arte Graphica*, and in the works of De Piles. Cf. Chambers, *op. cit.*

to good drawing and the whole subjected to what was "most commonly called the aire of the picture."

* * * * *

The general principles laid down for archaeology and the fine arts emanated, as always, from Rome, where the Villa Albani had become famous as the Mecca for all serious students of classical antiquity. There Cardinal Albani and his secretary-librarian Winckelmann presided over the scholars who had attached themselves to the Holy See. But the Vatican itself with its collections of antiquities was the actual pivot about which the archaeological world revolved; the study of the past now gave, in fact, a new direction to the Apostolic Household. Baroque Rome, which had bowed for well over a century to the Jesuits, was seeking a greater degree of intellectual freedom. By their open and violent conflict with the Enlightenment of the eighteenth century, and by their interference in political and financial affairs, as much as by the abuses of the Holy Office of the Inquisition, the Jesuits had aroused such fury that by the middle of the century they were expelled, first from Portugal, then from France. Spain abolished the Order and drove 6000 priests from her dominions. This was followed in 1773 by the suppression of the Jesuits by Pope Clement XIV. The Counter Reformation had virtually come to a close and the Papacy, which a generation earlier under the philosopher Pope Benedict XIV had even welcomed the ideas of Voltaire and Montesquieu, sought to show that the Vatican was as enlightened as any of the courts of Europe.

The antique wealth hidden in the soil of Rome proved to be the most eloquent witness to the great tradition to which the Papacy had fallen heir, and the Popes of the eighteenth century recognized that in the monuments and works of art comprehended in their collections lay the key to respectability in a more liberal age. Gradually the antiquities which lay scattered upon the Seven Hills of Rome were brought together within the complex of the Vatican. Clement XI, an Albani, was the first to contribute his large collections of coins, inscriptions, busts and Christian antiquities to the Papacy. The Museum of the Capitol, opposite the Palazzo dei Conservatori, was created. Clement XII, his successor, acquired the collection of the latter's nephew, Cardinal Albani. The work of reorganizing the collections was carried to completion by Benedict XIV and his treasurer, Cardinal Braschi, who later became Pope Pius VI. The Museo Pio-Clementino was completed and the Vatican collection which we know today became the principal museum of Europe. It seemed only proper that a kind Providence should send from the north a Protestant convert to care for them in the shape of Winckelmann.

Johann Joachim Winckelmann was born December 9, 1717, in Stendal in the Altmark. He was the son of a poor shoemaker and succeeded only with the greatest difficulty in being admitted to the Latin classes of the town school. As a Lutheran choirboy he won the support of the blind rector, who understood his great capacity and musical appreciation; and it was to this Protestant clergyman that Winckelmann owed his early interest in the classics and to whom he returned after a bitter, poverty-stricken period in Berlin. In 1738 he went to the University of Halle where he studied theology, the law, Hebrew, and attended the early lectures on aesthetics by Baumgarten. Two years later he took a position as tutor at Osterburg in a household which had a splendid library of French and English literature which he read omnivorously; and it also was at this time that he pursued his studies in mathematics and in medicine. He was deeply influenced, too, by Newton's physics and by his lessons in anatomy. And it was at this time that he developed his own personal philosophy and his great interest in the Grecian Platonic idea of youth. From these philosophic studies emerged a preoccupation with the Greek Ephebus which might, in a more subjective age, be mistaken for another type of curiosity. It was manifest in all of Winckelmann's activities and writing, and it was, perhaps, the very quality that endeared him so to the group of English men of letters of the later nineteenth century who surrounded his biographer, Walter Pater. After a brief passage as schoolmaster in Seehausen and as third librarian to Count Heinrich von Bunau at his country estates in Saxony, Winckelmann finally arrived at the court of the King of Poland at Dresden. The latter post gave him the leisure that he had so long wanted and brought him into contact with the collectors and scholars of the Saxon capital.

Winckelmann's introduction to antique sculpture was the collection of marbles in the gardens of the Marstallgebaude. "The purest springs of art," he said, "have been opened; happy the one who seeks and finds them. To search for these springs means to go at last to Athens, and Dresden is becoming more and more an Athens for the artists." His years in Dresden were, in fact, merely a preparation for those years in Rome from which alone he counted his real existence. At Dresden Winckelmann came under the influence of two Italians, the court physician Bianconi and the Papal Nuncio, Archinto, who was later to befriend him and to give him the necessary entrées in Rome. It was also Archinto who converted him to Roman Catholicism in the summer of 1754.

The following year Winckelmann published the first of his great books, *Thoughts on the Imitation of Greek Works in Painting and Sculpture*, in which he sought to explain "the noble simplicity and the calm greatness of Greek statues." The purpose of this work was, frankly, to bring about a reformation within the pictorial arts and a renewal of good taste in contemporary work. The Greeks, he contended, were the only true supporters of good taste, and accepting this premise as an axiom he went on to show that imitation of the Greeks was therefore more rewarding than the direct imitation of nature; for, he maintained, "Ideal beauty is conceived only in the human mind. . . . The brush of the painter should be dipped in understanding. . . . History is the greatest model that a painter could choose, mere imitation will not raise a work of art to the height of a tragedy or of an epic poem." And he counseled the artist of the present to turn to the great models, the stones, the coins and the utensils of antiquity to find therein the lessons on which the subject matter of modern art might be established.

From Dresden it was but a step to Rome, whither he went in the fall of 1755. "Rome," he cried ecstatically, "is the greatest school of all the world and I also have been purified and tested. I believed that I had solved everything and now since I have come here I see that I knew nothing." He was immediately presented to the Pope,

Benedict XIV. His old friend from Dresden, Cardinal Archinto, had become the new Papal Secretary of State and Winckelmann was first lodged in the Chancellery as its librarian, and then in 1759 he became attached to the household of the art-loving Cardinal Albani, the greatest collector in Rome, with whom he lived. Honors followed quickly. He became attached in various capacities to the Apostolic Household, a member of the Academy of Saint Luke, an antiquarian of the Apostolic Chamber and Prefect of all the antiquities in Rome. Winckelmann thus became officially the keeper and director of all archaeological activities and, by custom, the dean of the archaeologists in Europe. At Rome also he became a friend of the German painter Raphael Mengs, likewise a product of the Saxon court at Dresden, whose "dry, correct and lifeless pictures" were the rage of the classicists of his day and which later set the dismal tone for the painters of the Spanish Academy who brought him to Madrid.

It was the enthralling years amid the collections of the Vatican and those of his friend and patron, Cardinal Albani, that transformed Winckelmann, according to Justi, from a man of letters writing about art according to hearsay into a true philosopher actively using his five senses. The "Abbate Winckelmann" lived his days amid the statues of antiquity in the Museum of the Capitol, in the Belvedere, in the villas and palaces of the Ludovisi and the Mattei, and at night he dreamed long dreams of the classic past and formulated his ideas for *The History of Ancient Art*. This great work was to become the cornerstone for modern archaeology and art history. For here he departed from the two previously accepted methods, the biographical and the controversial, and produced works in the spirit of the new history and historiography. "The history of ancient art that I have undertaken to write," he says, "is no mere chronicle of the epochs and vicissitudes of the same; but I have taken the word history in the wider significance that it has in the Greek language; and my purpose is to offer an essay towards a systematic body of doctrine . . . the nature of art is the principal end; and over this the history of artists has little influence. . . . The history of art should therefore teach the origin, growth, change, and decadence of the same, together with the various styles of the peoples, ages, and artists, and should prove its theses,

THE MUSE OF PAINTING INSTALLS THE
CABINET DU ROY

From an unidentified engraving in the Bibliothèque Nationale

THE VERNISSAGE OF THE CABINET DU ROY
(1669 or 1681?)

From an unidentified engraving in the Bibliothèque Nationale

WATTEAU: *L'ENSEIGNE DE GERSAINT* (DETAIL)

Formerly in the collection of Frederick the Great. Berlin

THE EDUCATION OF BACCHUS
Engraved by Madame de Pompadour

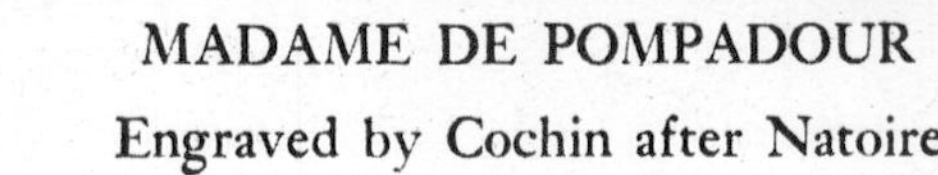

MADAME DE POMPADOUR
Engraved by Cochin after Natoire

CAYLUS

MARIETTE

CROZAT

THE *CURIEUX* AND THE *PHILOSOPHES*

Miniature engravings from a scrapbook in the Bibliothèque Nationale

as far as possible, by reference to the extant works of antiquity."*

In the first part of this monumental history he took up aesthetic questions and treated the conflicting origins and forms of art among the various nations and peoples of the earth. According to him the first and most important point in a work of art is the idea which it embodies and whether that idea is original or partly borrowed; the second point is beauty – that is, the variety and simplicity of it; the third is its technique. In the second part of the history, Greek art alone is discussed and its evolution is brought down to the time of the Emperor Severus and Constantinople. In his successive treatments of the art of Egypt, Phoenicia, Persia, Etruria, Greece and Rome, Winckelmann gave for the first time a connected account of the "unconscious evolution of style, in obedience to the pressure of social forces and not as the sport of individual caprice. . . . Each age, each school, each manner, succeeds its precursor logically, and each is connected with the current political and intellectual forces. . . . He turned archaeology into a science."†

In addition to these large, monumental publications, Winckelmann occupied himself with other work. He produced the sumptuous *Monumenti Antichi Inediti* (with 216 engraved plates, chiefly from the collections of Cardinal Albani) and devoted much time to the study of ancient gems. He prepared the luxurious descriptive catalogue of the gem collection of Baron Philip von Stosch, the son of a physician in Kustrin who had abandoned his patents of nobility and had wanted a clerical career for his son. But Stosch preferred to become an adventurer; he restored the *von* to his name and went abroad. Arriving in Florence, Philip von Stosch was employed by Horace Mann, the Resident of the English King, to spy upon the Stuart pretenders. At Rome he was admitted immediately to the intimate circle of Clement XI and Cardinal Albani. Through Count Flemming he had been introduced at the court of Saxony and was made a Royal Counselor to the King of Poland and took part on the latter's behalf in the Congress of Cambray. After 1721 he decided to abandon politics and spent his life at Rome and in Florence in the role of courtier and

* J. J. Winckelmann, *The History of Ancient Art*. 1764.
† Preserved Smith, *History of Modern Culture*. II, 621.

dealer. He also enjoyed the role of man of mystery. He was a passionate collector of engraved gems, forming what was probably the most important collection of his day. It consisted of some 3000 gems of which 253 bore inscriptions and was valued at 11,000 zecchini. No one before or since has brought together a single collection of such quality and scope. He had published a preliminary catalogue dedicated to the King of Poland, but it was not until after his death in 1757 that his nephew, Münzel-Stosch, gave the task to Winckelmann, whose descriptive and definitive catalogue remains one of the monumental works upon the subject. It was upon the basis of this catalogue that Frederick II of Prussia, seven years after Stosch's death, acquired the collection, which until recently was one of the greatest treasures of the Altes Museum in Berlin.

In addition to this collection of gems, Stosch had assembled a cabinet of idols and sacrificial utensils, of coins, and a great archaeological library. It contained Greek and Roman manuscripts and a considerable variety of busts and bronzes; he also had acquired a series of medieval chronicles, a collection of diplomas and paintings by his contemporaries as well as drawings and prints. He compiled a geographic and topographic atlas in 334 volumes, employing a staff of scholars and assistants. Winckelmann considered the museum assembled by Stosch the richest one in the world, surpassing even the art cabinet of the Kings of France. It was indeed one of the more brilliant anachronisms and phenomena of his day.

But neither Stosch nor Winckelmann was alone in his spirit of adventure. Casanova had already exhibited a profound knowledge of ancient art and included an essay on beauty in his *Mémoires*. Cagliostro and Pollnitz, too, recognized the usefulness of the arts as an entrée into polite society. Baron d'Hancarville (alias Han or Comte de Graffney) was responsible for the standard work on the Greek vases in Hamilton's possession. Edward Wortley Montagu, the son of the bluestocking Lady Mary, lived as a Moslem in Venice and at the Porte, studying languages and other more refined forms of Oriental intercourse, while a member of the English Parliament, John Wilkes, a notorious demagogue and debauché, translated the *Anacreon* and edited the works of *Catullus* and *Theophrastus*. Then as now, to pursue the Muse of archaeology was to live dangerously. A thin veneer of scholarship appeared to cover a multitude of sins; Winckelmann remains, however, the only archaeologist on record upon whom, despite the many professional temptations, murder has ever been successfully carried out. He was assassinated by an acquaintance, Arcangeli, to whom he had been showing some ancient coins in the bedroom of an inn at Trieste on his return from Germany to Rome. It is ironical that the motive in his case was simple robbery, and the murderer was not a long-suffering colleague, but a common thief. "Like an unencumbered pedestrian," said Goethe, "Winckelmann departed with a joyous countenance from this world as poor as he came into it."

* * * * *

To use the words of Laurence Sterne, "They order this matter better in France." Whereas archaeology proved to be one of the consuming passions of the *curieux* and the new discoveries of Pompeii and Herculaneum were avidly being studied together with the *Voyages Pittoresques* to Greece and the Levant (that were coming off the presses more rapidly than they could be digested), it was tempered by a perspective and an understanding of the classical past unknown to the scholars of Germany. The latter, cut off from Rome for a century and a half by the Reformation, now approached archaeology with an uncontrolled and naïve appetite. The constant exchanges, on the other hand, between Paris and the Eternal City, through the establishment of the French Academy in Rome as early as 1666, had developed a worldly ease and tolerance among both artists and scholars that was certainly more graceful – even if it lacked the profundity of the philologically minded pundits from across the Alps. This, combined with a national wit and native culture, made it possible for the Frenchman to venerate the past without doing so at the expense of the contemporary artist. And consequently, during the last years of Louis XIV's endless reign, during the Regency and the reign of Louis XV, Paris produced the most brilliant group of scholar-collectors and amateurs the world had seen up to that time. These men were not necessarily *grands seigneurs;* they were recruited from various social groups: Crozat and Randon de Boisset were financiers; La Roque was editor and publisher of the *Mercure de France*, the leading journalist of his day; Mariette came from a family of tradesmen, printers and engravers; Caylus was a nobleman and a soldier, the man who acted as liaison between the archaeologists of Rome and Paris.

Twenty-five years Winckelmann's senior, Count Caylus was a most distinguished, as well as a most versatile, antiquarian, a notorious ladies' man and a person of great fortune. Born in 1692, he had served with distinction in the later campaigns of Louis XIV. After the Peace of Rastadt he resigned his commission to devote himself to his chief interest of archaeology, traveling in Italy, Greece, Egypt and the Levant, afterwards going to England and to Germany, studying, collecting and writing upon the antiquities of the respective countries. An early Egyptologist, he also became an authority on numismatics and engraved gems. He wrote the *Lives of the Painters* (which he illustrated with his own engravings) while his romances, fairy tales and scabrous comedies, which formed the lighter side of his literary efforts, enlivened the Thursdays of Mademoiselle de Lespinasse. His learning, often in error, was nevertheless proclaimed with loud and determined finality. The *Receuils d'Antiquité* (published in quarto, filling seven volumes) are devoted to describing the collections which he bequeathed to the King; and his house, according to Le Beau, "offered the appearance of a museum of antiquities; a large Egyptian god stood guard at the entrance; medals, curiosities from America and China were hung upon the walls of the staircase. His apartments were at one and the same time an Olympus, a temple, a Senate, a *champ de Mars;* on all sides one was surrounded by gods, priests, magistrates, soldiers, exhumed from the soil of Egypt, Etruria, Italy and Gaul." He was in constant correspondence with scholars in Italy and, at the time when Pope Clement XIV was taking steps to prevent the exportation of antiquities from Rome, Caylus seemed to be the one Frenchman with money to compete with the English in the bootleg market.*

The contrast between Caylus and Winckelmann may be seen in their respective approaches to the Academies; Caylus lavished his

* Pacciaudi wrote Caylus on January 23, 1760: "*Je suis étonné qu'à Paris il n'y est point d'amateurs. . . . Je crois que c'est comme chez nous, personne ne fait plus de cabinet. . . . Je suis vraiment fâché que ces diables d'Anglais emportent dans leur pays ces belles antiquités.*"

fortune upon them while the German exploited them to his own ends. Unlike Winckelmann and Raphael Mengs, Caylus worshiped the antique but did not try to force upon contemporary artists the antique style, for he realized more than any of his contemporaries that the antique had once been modern in its own day. He anticipated to some extent the neoclassic revival of the nineteenth century and in his appreciation of nature was not too far removed from the ideas of Rousseau which were then beginning to germinate. When he founded in the Academy a prize for expression, that is the expression of the passions, he provided as a prerequisite: "This study is to be made through nature and not otherwise (*par le naturel et non autrement*)." "And to one young painter, newly gone to Rome to continue his training, Caylus wrote, 'You must at your age follow your own taste, let your sentiment lay hold of you, and seek to charge your memory with beautiful things, that is to say, with things that affect you, — it matters not what things they are; but you should mind their beauty as you study them, accounting for the reason that they appeal to you rather than copying them slavishly.' " *

Caylus died in 1765 and was buried in a porphyry sarcophagus. (He had bought it against the inevitable occasion, believing it to be Roman; the Louvre, where it now rests, proclaims it a fine example of Egyptian art!) Not all of Paris, however, shared the affection felt for him by his friends. Yet Grimm, in his *Correspondance littéraire*, writes kindly and understandingly of Caylus as he was at the end of his life:

> It was said of him, with a certain truth, that he was the protector of the arts and the scourge of artists, because in encouraging them, and helping them with his purse, he exacted a blind deference to his counsels, and, after having set out in the rôle of benefactor, he ended up, often enough, in that of tyrant. But if his character held disadvantages for the artists, the good which he did for the arts more than overbalanced his shortcomings. The Comte de Caylus enjoyed an income of at least 60,000 livres; but he did not spend as much as 10,000 on his own person. Heavy woolen stockings, stout shoes, a suit of coarse brown cloth with leather buttons, a broad hat on his head, that was his customary outfit, which surely was not ruinous. A rented carriage from a livery stable was the

* Chambers, *op. cit.*, 118–119.

largest item of his expenditures. Everything else he used for doing good and for the encouragement of talent. If a young man of happy dispositions and without bread presented himself, as so often happens with a nurseling of the Muse, the Comte de Caylus set him up in the studio of a good master of the Academy, payed his pension, presided over his education, and looked out for everything. The public owes to him, in this way, the talents of Vassé and several other young artists of the Academy of Painting and Sculpture.

What is moreover singular in a man who has devoted himself so completely to the arts, he gave the impression of a boor with his rough manners, although at heart he was essentially good natured. What is no less strange is that with his tastes, which usually presuppose so much delicacy and warmth of spirit, he seemed insensible; *il écrivait platement, sans imagination, et sans grâce.*

Diderot, whom Caylus cordially detested and who was amused by the conceit of his sarcophagus, thus consigned him to posterity:

Ci-gît un antiquaire, acariâtre et brusque,
Oh! qu'il est bien logé dans cette cruche étrusque.

On the other hand, to Pierre-Jean Mariette, his warmest friend, is ascribed the following quatrain:

Misanthrope par volupté
Il cultiva les arts en philosophe aimable,
Et vit trop en homme estimable
Pour n'être pas taxé d'originalité. Par son meilleur ami.

* * * * *

Seldom in the history of collecting has there occurred a more formidable partnership than that which existed between the Comte de Caylus, Pierre de Crozat and Pierre-Jean Mariette. Caylus was the classicist, Crozat the Maecenas, a man of taste, of almost unlimited means and an almost equally unlimited capacity for kindnesses and friendship. Mariette, the scholar, was the least attractive of the group, embodying all the petty irritations and avarices of the learned man whose horizon is limited by the books piled high upon his desk. All three were collectors of the first water who, by virtue of their knowledge and discrimination, opened up fields of interest which their royal predecessors of the *Grand Siècle* never knew existed. Thus the *amateur-savant* so familiar in Paris during the Second Empire and the early days of the Third Republic was born out of the ennui and exhaustion of the court during the senescence of the *Grand Monarque.*

There was a brief moment of two or three decades when official France lost interest, and before England and the princes of Germany and Russia seriously entered into the fray. Ironically enough, although the treasures amassed by this brilliant group (who preceded and pointed the way for the more highly organized Society of the Dilettanti in England) were among the most important collections ever to be brought together on French soil, they did not long remain there. In the decades ushering in the Revolution they were dispersed to Prussia, to Saxony, to Denmark and to Sweden, but above all to Russia where the Great Catherine, who was never known to curb any of her appetites, swept all the crumbs from the tables of the masters of western Europe into her ample bosom.

The brothers Crozat arrived in Paris in the earliest years of the eighteenth century from Toulouse where they had jointly held the unofficial office of ministers of finance and tax collectors for Languedoc. They were engaged at the same time most profitably, according to the bland custom of the day, in private banking, and were among the earliest investors in the Louisiana Company in which Antoine, the elder, finally won monopolistic control. Pierre, the collector, known as *Crozat le pauvre* to distinguish him from his brother, withdrew from finance to devote his already considerable millionaire's fortune to acquiring works of art. Each brother built himself a splendid house in town and Pierre also bought and altered a charming little château or *maison seigneuriale* at Montmorency. What started as an avocation became with him virtually a professional career. Between his first trip to Italy in 1714 and his death in 1740 Pierre de Crozat had gathered together no less than 19,000 drawings of the Old Masters, 400 pictures – mostly the finest paintings which Jabach, the great Cologne banker, had concealed from Colbert and kept for himself – 400 sculptures and a great and famous library. What was indeed more remarkable for the epoch was his advanced taste in porcelains which included several hundred pieces of Chinese and Japanese wares and the first group of Italian faïence and majolica brought to France.*

Germain Brice in his *Description de Paris* (2nd edition, 1752) gives an account of the low two-storied palace on the Place Louis-le-Grand (at the end of the Rue de Richelieu and the present Boulevard des Italiens – the site of the Opéra-Comique) which Pierre Crozat built to house his collections. The house was famous later in the eighteenth century as the residence of another collector, the Duc de Choiseul.

The prodigious quantity of curiosities of every kind which fill the interior is above all the thing which makes this considerable house worthy of being visited. Two large apartments on the ground floor, one to the right, the other to the left, hung with excellent pictures and in one of which one sees a very beautiful antique *Bacchus* restored by François Flamand, lead into a great gallery which occupies the entire depth of the house on the garden side; . . . this has a very fine proportion and is richly decorated in the male taste without affectation or superfluity of ornament. . . . The apartments of the attic storey are similarly distributed . . . and it is here that the amateurs of painting and sculpture find plenty to satisfy their curiosity. The master of the house has long vaunted his interest in beautiful things and has had the good fortune to see an infinity of other famous cabinets pass successively into his own: it is that which comprises today the ample collections of pictures, busts, bronzes, models by the most excellent sculptors, engraved stones, both *cameo* and *intaglio*, prints, and especially of drawings of the great masters, of which he is the possessor and which he finds his pleasure in showing to the amateurs of art who come to visit him. The place where the most rare and precious objects are conserved is the octagon cabinet, lighted (from above) in the Italian manner, and disposed in a similar way as that famous gallery of the Grand Duke of Florence, called the *Tribuna*, which likewise contains such a quantity of precious pieces.

Crozat, whose collection of drawings by the Old Masters was probably the greatest ever brought together, spared no pains and no expense, buying them piece by piece or in job lots – in whichever way gave him the best advantage.†

* Other than such pieces which the Medici queens may have brought as part of their personal baggage.

† Among the more celebrated cabinets he acquired were those of Monsieur de la Noue, a famous antiquary; of Mademoiselle de Stella, who had herself added to the

WATTEAU: LE MEZZETIN

This picture, originally in the celebrated Parisian collection of Jean de Jullienne, was sold at auction (March 30, 1767) to the Empress Catherine II of Russia for 708 livres 1 sou. It remained in the Hermitage until the Metropolitan Museum purchased it in 1934 from the Soviet Government, through a New York art dealer, for $150,000.

Mariette presided over the collection and it was to Crozat's house that Caylus and all the distinguished collectors and artists of Paris came with an ease and independence that made it more a scholars' club than a private residence. Here they studied the Old Masters, particularly through their drawings, lovingly comparing one style with another and becoming familiar, not so much with the major works on canvas of the Renaissance and Baroque, but rather with those intimate sketches and tentative suggestions which their predecessors had committed to paper and which revealed their original intentions and their most elusive flights of fancy. Watteau, wide-eyed, sad and tubercular, the dreamer, who attracted Crozat's sympathy and friendship, long resided in this house and while there painted the decorations of the Seasons for the dining room. It was indeed at Crozat's house that Watteau, who never visited Italy, first became familiar with the drawings of Titian and of Rubens upon which he patterned his own style. The Venetian pastelist, fiery Rosalba Carriera, who quickened the pulse of the stern Mariette, also lived there two years with her mother and two sisters, enchanting the elegant *cognoscenti* as much with her beauty, her violin and her carnival wit as with her art.

---

very rich nucleus bequeathed to her by an uncle; he bought the collections of Montarsis, de Piles, Girardon. Cornelis van Meulen, the painter, was his agent in Antwerp and obtained for him the famous drawings by Rubens belonging to Antoine Triest, the Bishop of Ghent. Other agents bought for him at the sales in Holland and in England, including the best of Lord Somers's collection (which included many of Sir Peter Lely's finest things), and that of van der Schelling in Amsterdam, although Crozat lost out to the Duke of Devonshire in the case of the Flinck cabinet in Rotterdam. But it was in the field of Italian drawings that Crozat's possessions were incomparable. His Giulio Romano drawings came from the debris of Vasari's collection which the Abbé Quesnel bought from the Bishop of Séez; he likewise bought the two volumes of Caraccis which Pierre Mignard as a student had brought back from Rome. The principal drawings belonging to Queen Christina the Duke of Orléans had already given him as a commission for having negotiated the purchase of the Correggios from Prince Odescalchi. On his trip to Italy in 1714 Crozat had bought everything upon which he could lay his hands: at Bologna the cabinet originally in the possession of the celebrated critic and connoisseur, Count Malvasia; at Venice a quantity of pastels by Barrocchio; at Rome he bought the collections of drawings belonging to Carlo degli Occhiali and of Agostino Scilla, a Sicilian painter who had a great number of drawings by Polidoro Caravaggio, and also from a Spaniard, Vittoria, a former pupil and friend of Carlo Maratti who had the finest group of drawings from the latter's studio. But Crozat's greatest coup in Italy was at Urbino when he purchased from the descendants of Timoteo Viti, one of Raphael's assistants, a quantity of that master's finest drawings virtually in the condition in which they had left his studio. Cf. Lugt, *Marques*, no. 2951.

The Louvre today has retained a happy souvenir of the *soirées chez Crozat* in a drawing long attributed to Watteau from the collection of Mariette. In the foreground are seated Caylus, Mariette, Madame de Julienne, Watteau and the Abbé de Marolles, while the players were Rosalba, Rebel, Paccini, Madame d'Argenon and the Papal Nuncio who, appropriately, played the "*archiluth.*" And the de Goncourts recall that one evening Le Bas, who was the greatest improviser on the violin of his day, was a guest of Crozat at a concert. The violinist was late and in his absence Le Bas amused himself with his instrument. Crozat ran up to him and kissed him. "Ah, Monsieur le Bas," he said, "I am delighted to make this discovery. You must take the place of my first violin." Le Bas accepted. Since the music room was on the ground floor, he plotted his escape by planning to jump out the window at the last moment. But the violinist arrived in time and Le Bas was saved.

In 1779 appeared the first volume of the *Receuil d'estampes d'après les tableaux et les dessins du Cabinet du Roi, de celui du duc d'Orléans et d'autres cabinets.* It was an ambitious proposal, financed by Crozat and directed by Mariette, to make public for the first time through reproductions the greatest masterpieces of the French capital. Two volumes were originally planned, each divided into two parts, and the plates were distributed among the principal engravers of the city. But the publication languished. Mariette was occupied with other labors, and although many years later other sections of it appeared, it was not until a year after Crozat's death, that his own splendid works were fully known through Mariette's great catalogue.*

Crozat in his will had named Mariette as the person to prepare this catalogue and he instructed the executors that his collections be sold, the proceeds to be given to charity. The sale realized a total of nearly 300,000 livres. A large part of the collection passed to his nephew, Baron Thiers, who later sold it through the Empress's agent, Diderot,

* This catalogue appeared under the following long and cumbersome title: *Reflexions sur la manière de dessiner des principaux peintres, par P. J. Mariette – Tirées de la description sommaire des dessins des grands maîtres d'Italie, des Pays-Bas et de la France, du cabinet du feu M. de Crozat (Paris chez Pierre-Jean Mariette, rue Saint-Jacques, aux Colonne d'Hercules, 1741).*

to Catherine of Russia for the Hermitage. Full accounts of the sale and the principal buyers are given, of course, by Lugt, by Charles Blanc, by Dumesnil and by Clément de Ris. Mariette, who by this time was a man of considerable fortune, acquired the finest drawings for himself. In this he was accused by his competitors, and perhaps not unjustly, of concealing the most exquisite examples of Raphael and Michelangelo in groups of less important drawings, then of offering the several parcels in job lots which he himself promptly bought in before other buyers had had an opportunity of going through them. This type of shrewdness is not entirely unknown today in the world of scholars and Mariette, who was both critic and financier, merely pointed the way to future generations. By such skillful operations he amassed a collection which, though not so large, was no less important or fine in quality than that of his friend and patron Crozat.

The Crozat catalogue and sale were not, of course, Mariette's first ventures into scholarship and art dealing. His grandfather and his father before him had both been engravers, printers and publishers. Mariette, who had continued the family business (until he retired in 1753 to devote himself to scholarship), had merely carried on a long and honorable tradition. At twenty-six he had been called to Vienna by Prince Eugene to put in order the famous print cabinet of the Emperor Charles VI, to be incorporated later in collections of the Albertina. There he remained for two years, sorting, estimating and classifying prints, preparing notes and documents which a hundred or more years later were to be the basis of Adam Bartsch's monumental work.

From Vienna he went on to Rome, his sticky fingers gathering up drawings and prints of inestimable value all along the way. While in Italy he formed those lifelong friendships with academicians and scholars that are revealed in his voluminous correspondence: with Antonio-Maria Zanetti, who for forty-two years was *custode* of the library of San Marco in Venice; in Bologna he became attached to Zanotti and to Luigi Crispi, at Florence to Bottari, the engineer and scholar whom Clement XII appointed *custode* of the Vatican Library, and whose works, besides publications on the antiquities at the Holy

See, included a ponderous, critical edition of Vasari. It was in Rome that Mariette laid the foundations for those future works of collaboration with Caylus and Winckelmann. The *Lettere pittoriche* between Bottari and himself belong also to this period and give a discerning and meticulous, if rather dull, account of the art world of Rome and Paris.

These were the days of lavish and prolific publication, and Mariette, never one to withdraw modestly into the background, was the champion catalogue writer and commentator of Europe. His early works included, among others, commentaries on Leonardo and on Michelangelo, and his election to the Florentine Academy only served to underscore his predilection for the Italian Schools. Spurred on by Caylus, he turned his attention momentarily to classical antiquity, publishing jointly with him Caylus's collection of engraved stones. They wrote an equally important history of ancient painting based upon the frescoes found a century earlier on the Via Flaminia and upon those of the Villa Albani subsequently unearthed in the Farnese gardens on the Palatine. His preference for Greek art over Roman embroiled him in a controversy with Piranesi, who was in the midst of bringing out his plates for his *Della magnificenza ed architettura dei Romani.* Mariette's lifetime of research, his countless prefaces, his critical commentaries on the several schools, his biographies often more caustic than profound, were finally brought together in the middle of the nineteenth century.* Without Mariette's pioneer work in the history of the art of Renaissance and Baroque times (a counterpart to the trail blazed by Winckelmann through the ancient world) the present state of criticism would be very different indeed.

Only in his old age did the austere Mariette show any sign of mellowing. At seventy he wrote to Bottari (August 3, 1764):

> I have been amusing myself by translating [Horace Walpole's *Anecdotes of English Painting*] and am already at the third volume. But this work will certainly be for myself alone, since I do not find in it anything of sufficient importance to warrant it being given to the public in our tongue.

* *Abécedario de P. J. Mariette et autres notes inédites,* edited by de Chennevrières and de Montaiglon, filling six volumes of the *Archives de l'art français.*

I could wish, at least, that this work might have done honor to the English nation; but suppressing all that concerns the artists abroad, the rest deals with almost nothing other than with painters of little reputation, and nearly all are portraitists. The author, nevertheless, is a man of great wit, and who has put into his book all of the wit at his command. It is Mr. Horace Walpole, son of the Minister who for so long governed England: this work is enriched with about a hundred portraits and the printing is really quite magnificent. It would make you laugh if I told you that the Church of Saint Peter's is not to his taste and that he finds it too surcharged with ornament and thus not fitting a temple worthy of the Majesty of the Supreme Being who inhabits it. He finds the embellishments, sown with such profusion, are placed there to support the superstition of which he so maliciously accuses our Roman Church. And what edifice do you think he gives in preference to Saint Peter's? A church built in the Gothic style in which the walls are bare: *raisonnement qui fait pitié.*

Ironically, while Mariette was soon forgotten as a historian, his collection of drawings and prints lived on, and, by their dispersal, became woven into the fabric of the major print cabinets of the world. It was his wish that the entire lot be purchased for the Cabinet du Roi and he offered it in his will *en bloc* to the crown for 100,000 livres. Already he had refused offers for it from the Empress of Austria, Maria Theresa, Catherine the Great of Russia, the Elector of Saxony and the Kings of Poland, Prussia and England. Joly (the director of the *Cabinet des planches gravées et estampes de la Bibliothèque du Roi*), who realized the value of the collections, made a gallant effort to procure them. He opened a letter to Malesherbes, the King's minister, "The cabinet of the late M. Mariette is composed of two unique parts, which should and can belong only to a great King." He then went on to recite its contents and its qualities; the drawings, of which there were some two thousand, were, among many others, those that Mariette had acquired from Crozat, who, in turn, had bought them from the heirs of Jabach. The other part, the prints, in far greater number, were those which throughout his life he had patiently and reverently brought together. With superlative examples he could show the entire development of that art from 1470 to the time of his death. The paintings, terra cottas, bronzes and engraved gems were negligible and merely the pleasant furnishings with which he lived. But the prophet was without sufficient honor in his own country.

Mariette died in 1774 but died too late. La Pompadour, who had understood these things in her day and who would unquestionably have pressed the matter at court, had died ten years before. There was no one to champion the cause. The sale, the various sessions of which took place in 1775 and 1776, with a catalogue elaborately prepared by Basan, realized a total of something over 300,000 livres, which went to charity. Three days before the sale d'Angivilliers, the Minister of Fine Arts, because of public clamor offered through the intermediary of the art dealer Lempereur to buy the collection from the estate for 300,000 livres, just three times the price for which Mariette had offered to sell it to the King. The offer was refused and Lempereur was thereupon commissioned to bid at the sale to the extent of 120,000 livres. He bought well and the results today may be seen at the Louvre and at the Bibliothèque Nationale. The rest was dispersed far and wide. One has only to read the full account of it * to realize that this sale was no less significant for the history of art than that of Sir Peter Lely a hundred years before. Possession today of a drawing or a print that bears the stamp of Crozat or of Mariette corresponds in no small degree to the thrill of finding a painting or statue which once passed through the hands of the Dukes of Mantua or of the Medici.

The purchases made by Lempereur at the sale of Mariette were the last acts of an expiring monarchy. The Revolution was advancing with inexorable speed and, except for the final splurge of Madame de Pompadour – twenty years of prodigality and reckless patronage of the arts in a society which no longer cared for bread but spent itself in refining the icing on the cake – the eighteenth century, from the collapse of John Law's Bubble in 1720, was a period of gradual liquidation in the arts. Only those artists really prospered who were favored by the royal mistress. Upon her death in 1764, the vacuum which was

* Frits Lugt, *Les Marques de Collections de Dessins et d'Estampes.* Amsterdam, 1921. Cf. Mariette.

to last until the conquests of Napoleon set in. One by one the collections of the *curieux* were sold and left the country; the salons of the bluestockings and the *philosophes* were fast becoming salesrooms from which the more provident and farsighted *émigrés* were planning their escape and placing their funds abroad. Even the very great were bent on establishing connections that might cover their retreat; Voltaire became the darling of the King of Prussia, and Diderot, the most celebrated, and certainly the ablest, critic of his day, whose reportage of the annual *Salons* of sculpture and painting remain among the imperishable pages written on French art, entered the service of the Russian Empress; to him, together with her ambassador, Prince Demidoff, she gave *carte blanche* to purchase anything that might give glamour and prestige to her upstart Baltic capital. The trend was to reach its climax by the sale of the Orléans collection in England in 1792.

If Caylus, Crozat and Mariette were the archetypes of the eighteenth-century *curieux*, it does not mean that by the brilliance of their performance they discouraged the lesser luminaries from shining in their own light. It was expected that men of means would collect, buy and sell, and according to the direction of their individual tastes they patterned themselves upon one or the other of the accepted divinities. The catalytic of this group, who invariably beat their paths at some time of their careers to the door of Crozat and Mariette, was Gersaint, the charming and plausible art dealer who had befriended Watteau. A fine connoisseur and knowledgeable critic, Gersaint had the added gifts of great personal charm and a noted wit. Blondel de Gagny, Jean de Julienne, the great industrialist and director of the Gobelins, put themselves in his hands. La Rocque, the editor of the *Mercure*, was more independent in judgment and more limited in his means but held his own with any of them. The Duc de Choiseul, Lalive de Jully, Randon de Boisset, all of these men belonged to the fraternity of the *curieux*. They appear in Charles Blanc's *Trésor de la Curiosité*, together with the catalogues of their sales, the records of prices fetched by each item and the total values of the sales. The more recent work by Frits Lugt will give perhaps a less colorful impression but more accurate information regarding the ultimate fate of these collections which represented the last and final flowering of taste under the French monarchy.*

* Charles Sterling has been kind enough to call to the writer's attention a guide to the Parisian cabinets in the mid-eighteenth century (Dezallier d'Argenville fils, *Voyage pittoresque de Paris; ou indication de tout ce qu'il y a de plus beau dans cette grande ville en peinture, sculpture, et architecture.* 2nd ed., Paris, 1752. Chez de Bure, *ainé*). This book not only contains a list of the artists in residence in the city but also describes the contents of the principal cabinets. One is surprised at the catholicity of the taste: the Spanish School is represented by the works of Velasquez, Louis de Vargas, Ribera, Murillo and Pietro Candido; the Low Countries by Jan van Eyck, Rembrandt, Lucas van Leyden, the two Breugels. Lely is the only English artist mentioned but the Germans are better known: Dürer, Holbein, Rottenhammer, Elsheimer and several minor masters. While the royal collectors and the Duc d'Orléans were concentrating on the Venetians of the High Renaissance, certain of the *curieux* were introducing the primitives of the Bellinis, Francia and Perugino. The Flemings, Rubens, Jordaens, Brouwer and Van Dyck, were among the most commonly listed.

BOOK EIGHT

English Collectors in the Age of Reason

CHAPTER I

Georgian Taste and Expanding Fortune

THE English political revolution of 1688 marked both the end of absolutism and the triumph of constitutional government. At a time when every effort was being made in France to build up the prestige and personal power of the monarch, there was a tendency in England to minimize the importance of the court. A half-century of civil war, of regicide and religious conflict, had given the Parliament the right to make laws, to levy taxes and to provide for the army; above all society recognized not so much the landholders of the old nobility as the new capitalist investor who derived his wealth from Britain's Empire overseas. Democracy was accelerated by the increase in population both at home and in the colonies abroad, for the British Empire, like the United States in the nineteenth century, was looked upon as the land of opportunity. It was the political and commercial revolution which paved the way for the industrial revolution that was to take place a century later. Strangely enough, this growth of political liberty took its fullest expression in the American Revolution and in the Constitution of the United States.

This new wealth and power resulted in two phenomena – the English country house which created the country gentleman, and the country gentleman who in turn created the country house. They tended to promote a new type of snobbery which differed from that of the Continent. In France the *bourgeois gentilhomme* and the *noblesse de la robe* had derived their wealth exclusively from the patronage of the king. In England, on the other hand, there was a snobbery of landed interests, of persons not necessarily received at court, but whose security depended upon the nature and importance of their estates in the country. From this very fact emerged that still unsettled conflict between Mayfair and "county" families. It was a social system which, although based upon hereditary privilege, permitted at the same time a receptivity to new ideas, and the putting of those ideas into execution; and it was a social system which also permitted men of comparatively humble birth to rise to the top and become part of the gentry and the landed aristocracy.

When Voltaire visited England between 1726 and 1729 he was amazed at the young English nobles and their capacity as patrons of letters and of science. He was filled with admiration of their "great rural palaces filled with pictures brought from Italy and furniture from France, of the editions of Italian, French and Latin authors that lined their bookcases." He cultivated philosopher lords like the third Earl of Shaftesbury and scholar statesmen like Somers and Montagu, for it was here that he found that true republic of letters upon which the modern world was built, a republic exemplified by the science, philosophy and religion of such leaders as Newton, Locke and Bishop Berkeley. It was a republic, however, like that of Greece, dependent upon the luxury of an aristocratic tradition and the leisure and independence which wealth alone might provide.

This aristocratic spirit went through the entire structure of the British upper classes. "At the top of the hierarchy were the dukes, who in any other country at that time would have been called princes. At the lower end was the squire, the man with an income of £200 to £300 a year, farming his own land and speaking the broadest provincial dialect. He was distinguished," continues Trevelyan, "from the yeoman by a coat of arms and by the respect that was paid him as a gentleman. If once in his life he went to London on business, he was noticeable in the city crowd for his horsehair periwig, his jockey belt and his old-fashioned coat without sleeves. His library, traditionally at least, consisted of the *Bible*, Baker's *Chronicles*, *Hudibras*, and Fox's *Book of Martyrs* and, whether he read these works or not, his views on Puritans and Papists usually coincided with those expressed in the last two." * But whatever were his politics or his religion, his principal preoccupation was rebuilding his estates, for the time had come when the money (made through the development of the British Empire in the days of Elizabeth) at last permitted a replenishing and

* Trevelyan, *op. cit.*, 306.

rebuilding of the estates at home; consequently architecture became his principal preoccupation whether he was a duke with an income of £100,000 a year or a poor country squire.

To the gentleman's passion for altering his country seat to meet the new architectural fashions was added the necessity of rebuilding his house in town. London had been destroyed in the great fire of 1666 and the Palace at Whitehall had endured a similar calamity a few years later. The rebuilding of the city proper was entrusted to a group of architects under the leadership of Sir Christopher Wren; but the residential quarters of Westminster, Chelsea, Mayfair and Regent's Park followed the new and somewhat simpler Georgian tastes. Since most of these properties belonged to the landed aristocracy and to the gentry, it is not surprising that they were personally concerned in the architectural appearance of their new investments. After the Restoration, architecture, through the interest of the country gentleman, became therefore the elegant accomplishment and the diversion of the man of fashion. It appeared to be the one outlet in which the young débutant, back from the grand tour, could put into practice the ideas which he had absorbed in Italy, in France and in the other countries he had visited. The drawing board thus became the polite tool of the young man about town; and since the English always had maintained that architecture was the most logical of all arts, a knowledge of the rules of the game, particularly of the high Renaissance and of Palladio, was considered a harmless way for him to develop his taste and his enthusiasms.

Richard Boyle, third Earl of Burlington, was the most ardent and accomplished of these amateur architects, and through his collaboration with William Kent continued to dominate the scene until his death in 1753. But classicism, indeed, had not been unknown in Elizabethan and Jacobean building; there had long existed a tradition of borrowing from the antique. The publication of Palladio's *Antiquities of Rome* and Colin Campbell's *Vitruvius Brittanicus* merely put a new and more learned aspect on borrowed forms. These lavish publications were paid for by Burlington, Lord Pembroke and their friends. Further works appeared during the first half of the eighteenth century, such as Knyff's *Noblemen's Seats,* Kent's *Designs of Inigo Jones,*

Batty Langley's *Treasury of Design* and, a little later, James Paine's *Plans and Elevations of Noblemen's Houses*. During this same period individual books were devoted to the publication of each of the great houses, such as Matthew Brettingham's plans for Holkham, and Ware's engravings of the plans and decorations by Campbell, Ripley and Kent for Sir Robert Walpole's Houghton Hall. Even among the great names, architects who have left their mark upon the palaces of London and the country seats scattered far and wide over the English landscape, do we find the quality of determined and unprofessional irresponsibility peculiar to the amateur. Inigo Jones was the product of the theater and remained at heart a stage designer; Sir Christopher Wren, after graduating from Oxford, became its Savillian Professor of Mathematics, and Sir John Vanbrugh, who has left us those "still-births of memory," Blenheim Palace and Castle Howard in Yorkshire, was a dramatist and playwright.

The Palladian ideal was to achieve "Strength coupled with Politeness, Ornament with Simplicity and Beauty with Majesty." It was the complete denial of those progressive steps by which for more than a hundred and fifty years the architects of Britain had sought to reconcile their handiwork with the pearly light and cool, green, damp climate of their island. The great bays and oriels were suppressed, and the amusing freedom of the brickwork was abandoned for the severity and accuracy of classic lines. Chimneys gave way to horizontal skylines; dormers were cut into the roof and were no longer an integral part of the walls of the house. Floor plans were governed by the strict rules of symmetry and "no longer went adventuring according to their own sweet will." The Palladian great house, after the custom at Vicenza, formed a large symmetrical block of which the lower story was sometimes rusticated.* The *piano nobile*, raised up a short flight of steps, was dedicated to formal living and to entertainment. Horace Walpole, describing one of the more typical country seats, wrote:

The situation is delightful. The house is very spacious. It is built in the form of an H; both fronts pretty much alike. The hall, the dining-parlour,

* Antoinette Perrett, "Amateur Architects of the Eighteenth Century," in *Country Life* (New York), April 1937.

two drawing-rooms, one adjoining to the study, the other to the dining-parlour . . . are handsome, and furnished in an elegant, but not sumptuous taste; the hangings of some of them beautiful paper only. There is, adjoining to the study, a room called the Music-Parlour, so called in Sir Thomas's time and furnished with several fine musical instruments. . . . The dining-room is noble and well proportioned; it goes over the hall and dining-parlour. It is hung with crimson damask, adorned with valuable pictures. . . . The best bed-chamber adjoining is hung with fine tapestry. The bed is of crimson velvet, lined with white silk; chairs and curtains of the same. . . . The suite of rooms on the first floor are each dominated from the colour of the hangings, which are generally of damask. Mrs. Curzon tells us, that, on occasion, they make fifteen beds, within the house, in which the best Lord of the land need not disdain to repose. . . . The offices are said to be exceedingly convenient.

This was the beau ideal of the nobleman's country seat; a compact mass, bare of decoration save for a classical order, "free or engaged," running through several stories. A lofty, projecting columnar portico was not uncommon, and a balustrade and attic story usually surmounted the whole. A frequent arrangement for these great houses was to place the stables and similar offices in two detached blocks and to connect them by curved colonnades with the main building. Sometimes there were four wings, one at each corner, usually lower than the main house and often complete entities in miniature of the great house itself.*

The gentleman's town house (because of the fact that the higher value of land placed a premium on compactness) merely emphasized and compressed into a smaller space the luxury and formality of his country seat; it differed from it very little in theory or detail. As in our American cities the lots were usually deep and narrow, and this compelled an evolution of the state apartments from the entrance hall towards the rear of the building instead of branching out on either side of it as was possible in the country house. But in each instance both architect and occupant were enslaved to a certain standard of Italian living and were not allowed to deviate by so much as a hairs-

* Antoinette Perrett, "Eighteenth Century Architecture: An Elegant Hobby for Gentlemen," in *Country Life* (New York), September 1937.

breadth from the conventions of the sophisticate and Italianate young men for whose favor they went to such extremes.

Naturally this sycophantic attitude to foreign styles aroused the hostility and scorn of the irreverent. Alexander Pope in his *Moral Essays* addressed the fourth epistle to the Earl of Burlington:

> 'Tis strange, the miser should his cares employ
> To gain these riches he can ne'er enjoy,
> Is it less strange, the prodigal should waste
> His wealth to purchase what he ne'er can taste?
> Not for himself he sees, or hears or eats;
> Artists must choose his pictures, music, meats;
> He buys for Topham, drawings and designs,
> For Pembroke, statues, dirty gods and coins;
> Rare monkish manuscripts for Hearne alone,
> And books for Mead, and butterflies for Sloane.
> Think we all these are for himself? no more
> Than his fine wife, alas! or finer w—
> For what has Virro painted, built, and planted?
> Only to show how many tastes he wanted.
> What brought Sir Visto's ill got wealth to waste?
> Some demon whispered, "Visto has a taste."
> Heav'n visits with a taste the wealthy fool
> And needs no rod but Ripley with a rule.

Elsewhere in this same essay Pope continues:

> You shew us Rome was glorious, not profuse,
> And pompous buildings once were things of Use;
> Yet shall (my Lord) your just, your noble rules
> Fill half the land with imitating fools;
> Who random drawings from your sheets shall take
> And of one beauty many blunders make
> Load some old Church with vain Theatric state
> Turn Arcs of Triumph to a garden-gate. . . .

A modern critic, John Steegmann, has at long last come to Burlington's defense. "It may be right," he says, "that the opinion of a wealthy and aristocratic amateur should not carry weight if it be not supported by any qualification other than wealth or birth, but in the society of the first two Georges, when the arts depended even more than they do today upon the rich patron, that patron considered it a part of the obligations of his rank to have a working knowledge of what he was patronizing. It was much more than the mere desire of him who pays the piper to call the tune; it was the desire of the man to whom actual creation is denied to be associated as closely as possible with the articulate, creative artist." *

To be sure the Burlingtonian canon could not last; for human beings sooner or later rebel at discomfort which merely satisfies the intellectual interests of another. The sacrifices of proper heating, the stately emptiness of these big houses and the vast retinue of servants required to run them, were bound to bring about a reaction against the "sublime and picturesque" in favor of a house easier to live in. But nevertheless the very fact that a house was built in the period between 1700 and 1770, adds Steegmann, "implies an excellence which we can be sure is there even before we see the house." For we know that it subscribed to a fixed canon of taste and was executed according to the prevailing rule.†

To the amateur architects of the Georgian period we owe that eclecticism from which grew the exotic delights of Sir William Chambers at Kew, Strawberry Hill, William Beckford's Fonthill Abbey and Kent's villa for Pelham at Esher. It opened the door to the new classical taste of the brothers Adam, and later exponents of the taste of George III's long reign like Nash, whose thirst for the exotic culminated in the Royal Pavilion at Brighton, that final curtain raiser to the splendid horrors of Queen Victoria and the Albert Memorial.

* John Steegmann, *The Rule of Taste*. London, The Macmillan Co., 1936, p. 28.

† Possibly at no other time in history has the style of domestic architecture played so conscious a role in the political and intellectual life of the day. The reader is referred to the articles on "Taste, Architecture and Gardens," and "The Interior of the House" in the second volume of Turberville's *Johnson's England*. Geoffrey Webb has there summed up most brilliantly the changes which took place in the middle of the century and the causes which brought them about.

CHAPTER II

The Scientific Interests

THE most important innovation of the natural scientists of the eighteenth century was the separation of man from the general body of zoology. Voyages of exploration over the entire globe and narratives of travelers had brought in an immense amount of unsuspected material for the comparative study of man. These observations, indeed, were distorted, idealized and romanticized to meet the needs of political and philosophical propaganda during the third quarter of the seventeenth century. It was this curiosity which gave rise to the various scientific academies of which the earliest were the Royal Society in London and the Académie des Sciences in Paris. From the middle of the seventeenth century on, there also appeared throughout the continent of Europe a wide variety of learned and scientific publications, and in their pages it is possible to see the gradual welding together of the occult and the scientific, of the mysterious and the rare, which became the basis for modern scientific thought. By a gradual process of evolution we see the *Wunderkammer* of the German princes transformed into the scientific laboratory and specimen collection of the English physician and naturalist. John Evelyn, as he tells us in his journal, scarcely let a week pass in which he did not visit some cabinet of curiosities in the possession of men of learning or of science, either at home or abroad.*

As early as the reign of James I the tendency toward scientific collecting had been clearly marked in the cabinet of Arundel's contemporary, Sir Robert Bruce Cotton. It was he who had founded the Society of Antiquaries, and who had begged Queen Elizabeth to establish a state library in which documents of national interest might be preserved. Unsuccessful in this latter attempt, he set to work him-

* John Evelyn, *Diary* (1620–1665).

self to acquire as many of the documents as possible; not only those to which he had access in the Public Records Office, but more particularly those documents of the English monasteries which had been suppressed at the time of Henvy VIII.* All of this material, together with his extraordinary collection of manuscripts, was turned over by his heirs to the nation and has since become one of the important units of the British Museum. Robert Harley, the first Lord of Oxford, who followed in Cotton's footsteps and became a trustee of the Cottonian Library, left a collection of printed material running into many thousands of volumes, and a large cabinet of coins and medals.

In 1686 appeared the first edition of *The Collected Works of Sir Thomas Brown, Knight, Doctor of Physick, Late of Norwich.* In this volume was contained his *Religio Medici* and other writings. There are included in it also certain "tracts . . . all which commending themselves by their Learning, Curiosity and *Brevity* . . . seemeth to be distempered with such a niceness of Imagination." One of these tracts, the *Musaeum Clausum,* is the imaginary catalogue of a collection and library "containing some remarkable Books, Antiquities, Pictures, and Rarities of several kinds scarce or never seen by any Man now living." The catalogue is divided into three parts – the first dealing with imaginary authors, or rather with the imaginary works of the great writers of antiquity, with subjects left unanswered by the chronicles of the past, the solutions to which, written in their own hands, Sir Thomas, who had both humor and curiosity, would have liked to find. Among these items are, for example, "The Letter of Quintus Cicero which he wrote in answer to that of his brother, Marcus Tullius, desiring an account of Britany wherein are described the country, state, and manner of the Britains of that age." And again, "A punctual relation of Hannibal's march out of *Spain* to *Italy*, and far more particular than that of *Livy* where he passed the River, *Rhodanus* or *Rhosne;* at what place he crossed the *Isura* or *L'Isère;* when he marched up toward the confluence of the *Sone* and the *Rhone,* or the place where the City *Lyons* was afterwards built; how wisely he decided the difference between King *Broncus* and his Brother; at what place he passed the *Alpes,* what Vinegar he used and

* Rigby, *op. cit.*

where he obtained such quantity to break and calcine the Rocks made hot with Fire." Sir Thomas also sought for his library the "Manuscripts and Rarities brought to the Libraries of *Aethiopia* by *Zaga Zaba*, and afterwards transported to *Rome*, and scattered by the Souldiers of the Duke of *Bourbon*, when they barbarously attacked the City."

Browne's interest in natural history heavily weighted the library in that direction; it included a "sub-marine Herbal describing the several Vegetables found on the Rocks, Hills, Valleys, Meadows, at the Bottom of the Sea"; and "an exact account of the Life and Death of *Avicenna* confirming the account of his Death by taking nine Clysters together in a fit of the Colick." Other works included writings by Aristotle and King Alfred, a commentary by Josephus in Hebrew written by himself and "a Commentary of Galen upon the plague of Athens described by Thucydides," and two books attributed to Julius Caesar which the Cardinal of Liège said were in an old library of that city.

The pictures in Sir Thomas Browne's imaginary cabinet were no less fanciful and no less filled with the unrecorded exploits of antiquity. They included "a Picture of the great Fire which happened at *Constantinople* in the reign of *Sultan Achmet.* The Janizaries in the meantime plundring the best houses, Nassa Bassa, the Vizier riding about with a Cimitre in one hand and a Janizary's Head in the other to deter them; and Priests attempting to quench the Fire by pieces of *Mahomet's* Shirt dipped in holy Water and thrown into it." Other pictures included "Draughts of three passionate Looks; of Thysetes when he was told at the Table that he had eaten a piece of his own Son, of *Bajazet* when he went into the Iron Cage; of Oedipus when he first came to know that he had killed his Father and married his own Mother." In addition the catalogue lists "a Portrait of a fair English Lady drawn *al Negro*, or in the Aethiopian hue, excelling original White and Red Beauty, with this Subscription, "*sed quandam volo nicti Nigriorem*"; and "other Pieces and Draughts *in caricatura* of Princes, Cardinals, and famous Men; wherein among others the Painter had singularly hit the signatures of a Lion and a Fox, the face of Pope Leo X." Finally the collection contained some "rare chance

Pieces" that would delight the surrealist of today, "which either drawn at random, and happening to be like some person, or drawn for some, and happening to be more like another; while the Face mistaken by the Painter; proves a tolerable Picture of one he never saw."

The antiquities and rarities of several sorts recorded in the *Musaeum Clausum* follow more the interest of natural history and science. They include "the Skin of a Snake bred out of the Spinal Marrow of a Man; Vegetable Horns mentioned by Linschoten which set in the ground grow up like Plants about Goa; Spirits and Salt of Sargasso made in the Western Ocean covered with that Vegetable; excellent against the Scurvy." Other curiosities are "a Ring found in a Fishes Belly taken about Gorro, seemed to be the same wherewith the Duke of Venice had wedded the Sea; a neat Crucifix made out of the cross Bone of a Frog's Head and a Glass of Spirits made out of Aethereal Salt, Hermetically sealed up, kept continually in Quicksilver of so volatile a nature that it will scarce endure the Light, and therefore only to be shown in Winter or by the light of a Carbuncle or Bononian Stone."

As a concession to the fashionable taste with which, in general, he was so little concerned, Sir Thomas listed a number of curiosities of an archaeological nature: "Certain ancient Medals with Greek and Roman Inscriptions, found about *Crim Tartary;* conceived to be left in those parts by the Souldiers of *Mithridates*, when overcome by Pompey, he marched about the North of the *Euxine* to come about into *Thracia.*" These formed a counterpart to the "ancient Ivory and Copper Crosses found with many others in *China;* conceived to have been brought and left there by the Greek Souldieres who served under Tamerlane in his Expedition and Conquest of that Country." Byzantium and Renaissance Italy were neither of them absent from his thoughtful curiosity: "Some handsome Engraveries and Medals, of *Justinus* and *Justinianus*, found in the custody of a Bannyan in the remote parts of India, conjectured to have been left there by the Friers mentioned in Procopius, who traveled in those parts in the Reign of Justinianus and brought back into Europe the discovery of Silk and Silk Worms." But perhaps Sir Thomas was having the most fun of all conjuring up "an original Medal of *Petrus Aretinus*, who was called

Flagellum Principum, wherein he made his own Figure on the Obverse part with this Inscription.

Il Divino Aretino

"On the Reverse sitting on a Throne, and at his Feet Ambassadors of Kings and Princes bringing Presents unto him, with this Inscription,

I Principi tributati dei Popoli tributano il Servetor loro."

"He who knows where all this treasure now is is a great Apollo. I'm sure I am not he." With these words Sir Thomas concludes his catalogue. It is, indeed, an amazing paradox that this flight of fancy mixed with the whimsey of the humanist and physician should have come off the press within a year of the appearance of Sir Isaac Newton's *Principia Mathematica*. Despite the humor and satire of Sir Thomas Browne's museum, this imaginary cabinet is nevertheless not too far removed from those actually in existence and which later brought about the great museums of the present day.

* * * * *

The first museum catalogue had already appeared in England in 1656 and listed the contents of the "*Museum Tradescantium* or a Collection of Rarities preserved at South Lambeth near London, by John Tradescant of London." This *accumulation* of the oddments of art and natural history was the result of a two-generation interest in a family of travelers, explorers and adventurers. The elder Tradescant, a gentleman of fortune and a volunteer against the Algerian Corsairs, had, as early as 1618, traveled deep into Russia in search of rare plants. The Duke of Buckingham later sent him to America, and instructed his agent, Edward Nicholas, that it was the Duke's pleasure that Tradescant should "deal with all merchants from all places, but especially from Virginia, Bermuda, Newfoundland, Guinea, Binney, the Amazon, and the East Indies, for all manner of rare beasts, fowl and birds, shells and stones." The table of contents of the collection, abbreviated by the Rigbys, divides exhibits into the following groups:

1. Birds with their eggs, beaks, feathers, clawes, spurres.
2. Four-footed beasts with some of their hides, hornes and hoofs.
3. Diverse sorts of strange Fishes.

4. Shell-creatures, whereof some are called *Mollia*, some Crustacea, others Testacea, of these, are both *univalvia* and *bivalvia*.
5. Severall sorts of Insects, terrestriall – { anelytra, coleoptera, aptera, apoda }
6. Mineralls, and those of neare nature with them, as Earths, Coralls, Salts, Bitumens, Petrified things, choicer Stones, Gemmes.
7. Outlandish Fruits from both the *Indies*, with Seeds, Gemmes, Roots, Woods, and diverse Ingredients Medicinall, and for the Art of Dying.
8. Mechanicks, choice pieces in Carvings, Turnings, Paintings.
9. Other Variety of Rarities.
10. Warlike Instruments – European, Indian, etc.
11. Garments, Habits, Vests, Ornaments.
12. Utensils and Householdstuffe.
13. *Numismata coynes*, antient and modern, both gold and silver and copper.

    Hebrew, Greeke, Roman both – { Imperiall and Consular }
14. Medalls – gold and silver, copper, lead.*

Items 15 and 16 deal with the *Hortus Tradescantius* and enumerate the "Plants, Shrubs, and Trees both in English and Latine," and, finally, item 16 is "A Catalogue of his Benefactors." Among the more singular items in this collection were "blood that rained in the Isle of Wight, attested by Sir John Oglander, a Dodo bird, and a Bird sitting on a pearch naturall, together with several drafts and pieces of paintings of sundry excellent masters."

The Rigbys have charmingly told of the vicissitudes of this collection after Tradescant's death – of his intimate connections with Elias Ashmole, the antiquary, whose own collections were enormous, how Tradescant's widow later fell under the hypnotism of Ashmole, the litigations and the lawsuits, and, finally, how in 1683 the Ashmolean Museum, into which Elias had welded the collections of the

* Rigby, *op. cit.*, p. 233.

Tradescant family awarded him by the courts, was opened to students. In the words of John Evelyn, this was the "first public institution for the reception of rarities in art or nature established in England," and it has remained one of the chief ornaments of the University of Oxford.

Samuel Pepys, Secretary of the Board of the Admiralty, was an indefatigable collector, particularly of rare and precious books, recording in his *Diary* how willingly he would accept fine books as bribes in return for public favors. He had a passion for neatness and order and developed a system of cataloguing his library which he passed on with tight restrictions for its care and use and which still obtain today at Magdalene College, Cambridge, where it ultimately came to rest. The gentlemen who formed these cabinets and special libraries were in constant correspondence with other collectors on the Continent.*

Such museums, says Preserved Smith, "did far more than furnish materials for scholars. They became one of the great instruments of the education of the public and of the propaganda of the scientific spirit. Of the large crowds that came to gaze at exotic animals and plants, rare gems and Greek vases, Roman coins and Chinese weapons, two-headed calves, freaks, mermaids, unicorns, and basilisks, most sightseers found little but an afternoon's pastime, but a considerable number won a general insight into the world of nature and of history, and a respect for the explorers of it. Among the wealthy it became the rage to make a collection of fossils or of insects, or of dried plants as well as of manuscripts, pictures, and coins." † The very absurdities into which the dabblers in science fell proved the wide profusion of taste. Many of the writers of the age, Smith continues, "testified to their study of science. Montesquieu applied himself to geology and physiology; Rousseau to anatomy and chemistry; Diderot to anatomy and physiology; Thomas Gray to entomology on which he wrote a Latin poem; Goethe made himself an electric machine out of an old

* Chief among them were King Christian V of Denmark, Dr. Albert Seba, whose Amsterdam cabinet was purchased by Peter the Great of Russia in 1716, Buffon in Paris, and the keepers of the Natural History Cabinets of the King of France and of the University of Leyden.

† Smith, *A History of Modern Culture*, II, 141.

JOHN ZOFFANY: THE TRIBUNA AT THE UFFIZI

Sir Horace Mann showing the Medici collections to English noblemen. London, Royal Collection

STRAWBERRY HILL

From the manuscript of the *Aedes Walpolianae*
Metropolitan Museum of Art

THE GALLERY AT STRAWBERRY HILL

Farmington, Connecticut, W. S. Lewis Collection

A

COLLECTION of fine *PICTURES*,

Brought from ABROAD by

Mr *ANDREW HAY.*

Will be Sold by AUCTION, at Mr. *Cock's* New-Auction Room in *Poland-street*, the Corner of *Broad-street* near *Golden-Square*, on *Saturday* the 19*th* of this *Inst. February*, 1725-6. The Pictures may be view'd on *Wednesday* the 16*th*, and every Day after till the Hour of *SALE*, which will begin at a 11 o'Clock in the Forenoon precisely.

CATALOGUES to be had at the Place of Sale, and at Mr Hay's *in* Monmouth-Court *near* Suffolk-street.

NOTICE OF A PICTURE SALE

THE SPECIOUS ORATOR.
WILL YOUR LADYSHIP DO ME THE HONOR TO SAY £50-000
—A MERE TRIFLE —A BRILLIANT of the FIRST WATER
an unheard of price for such a lot, surely.

MR. CHRISTIE, THE GREAT AUCTIONEER

THE ART TRADE IN LONDON

THE FOUNDLING HOSPITAL

Hogarth shows how children were admitted

A FOP WATERING THREE DEAD PLANTS

Hogarth's protest against the Old Masters in the catalogue of 1761

spinning wheel and some medicine phials. Those sciences, said Diderot, 'least common in the past century become more common from day to day,' and Voltaire at the dedication of his tragedy, *Alzire*, wrote, 'We live in an age, I venture to say, where the poet must be a philosopher and when a woman may dare to be one openly.' Bettinelli in a dialogue called *Love and Fashion* described the woman of the world in which 'natural history, chemistry, and astronomy are her daily recreation; here you would see her collection of butterflies or of snails or of plants or of minerals, there a small furnace and alembics, and, yonder, microscopes and telescopes with which she observes the stars, especially Venus.'' *

The culmination of this general movement was the creation of the British Museum by Act of Parliament in 1753. It was brought about primarily by the collaboration of two men, William Courten, descendant of a very wealthy family of East Indian traders and colonizers in the West Indies, and Dr. Hans Sloane. The latter, a collector and scientist of far greater capacities, eventually incorporated both the collections which William Courten had inherited from his grandfather, and those which he had amassed himself, and joined them to his own already extraordinary cabinet.

Courten, whose ambition, says Edwards, † was "to collect a Museum which should eclipse everything of its kind heretofore known in England," became embroiled in financial difficulties which forced him to leave the country. He met Sloane at Montpellier; both were deeply interested in every expression of natural science and formed a lifelong intimacy based on their congenial tastes. John Evelyn describes visiting Courten's house in London in December 1686, after the latter had returned to England under the assumed name of Mr. Charlton:

I carried the Countess of Sunderland to see the rarities of one, Mr. Charlton, in the Middle Temple, who showed us such a collection as I had never seen in all my travels abroad either of private gentlemen or princes. It consisted of miniatures, drawings, shells, insects, metals, natural things, animals (of which divers, I think 100, were kept in glasses of spirits of

* *Ibid.*, II, 9.
† *Lives of the Founders of the British Museum.* Trübner, 1870. I, 259 ff.

wine), minerals, precious stones, vessels, curiosities in amber, crystals, agate, etc. all being very perfect and rare of their kind especially his books of birds, fish, flowers, and shells drawn in miniature to the life. He told us that one book stood him in £300; it was painted by that excellent workman whom the late Gaston, Duke of Orleans, employed. This gentleman's whole collection, gathered by himself, traveling over most parts of Europe, is estimated at £8,000. He appeared to be a modest and obliging person.*

While still a young man of twenty-seven Sloane had journeyed to the West Indies as physician to the Duke of Albemarle, then Governor of Jamaica, and during his fifteen-month stay in the Islands had collected over 800 species of plants which he brought back with him to London. From that time on he prospered, becoming physician to the royal family, and in 1727 he succeeded Sir Isaac Newton as President of the Royal Society. In addition to these honors he was knighted and elected President of the Royal College of Physicians. A man of large wealth, he had by 1727, "partly by travel and partly by the purchase of large private collections, brought together no less than 5,497 mineral specimens, 804 corals, 8,426 vegetable specimens, 3,824 insects, 3,753 shells, 568 birds, 54 mathematical instruments, 20,288 coins and medals, 2,666 manuscripts and other objects amounting in all to 53,000 items." †

By the middle of the century Sir Hans Sloane's collection had increased very greatly in value and was worth, in his estimation, £50,000. In his will in 1753, in which he offered the collection to the nation at what he believed to be the nominal price of £20,000, he wrote that the items in it were things "tending in many ways to the manifestation of the glory of God, the Confutation of Atheism and its consequences, the Uses and Improvement of the Arts and Sciences and benefit of Mankind." It was his further hope that these things might "remain together and not be separated, and that chiefly in or about the City of London, whence they may by the great influence of people be of most use." For several months the future of the collection hung in the balance. The Reverend John Jeffreys in a letter

* Evelyn, *op. cit.*, II, 163.
† Cf. Lugt, *Marques*. (Sloane, no. 1363.)

from Paris expressed the general fear that Parliament might not act favorably in regard to this purchase:

> I hope the Speaker's scheme for purchasing Sir Hans Sloane's collection will not meet with opposition. I have had some conversation with Abbé Sallier about the collection and I gave him the catalogue you were so good as to send me. If it is offered to the French king, the Abbé will use all his interests with Monsieur d'Argenson that it may be bought, but I most sincerely hope we shall prevent it going out of our country.

But Parliament did act within a year of Sloane's death and appropriated the necessary money, not only for the Sloane collection, but for the purchase of the Harleian and Cottonian libraries of manuscripts. The act founding the British Museum states its purpose in the following words: "whereas all arts and sciences have a connection with each other, and discoveries in natural philosophy and other branches of speculative knowledge for the advancement and improvement whereof said collection was intended, do, or may in many instances, give help and success to the most useful experiments and undertakings."

Six years later, the British Museum was formally opened to the public on January 15, 1759.

CHAPTER III

Horace Walpole and the Rule of Many Tastes

AT the time of the founding of the British Museum, Horace Walpole was thirty-five years old. He wrote to his friend Horace Mann, the King's Resident in Florence, in February of that year: "You will scarce guess how I employ my time; chiefly at present in the guardianship of embryos and cockle shells. Sir Hans Sloane is dead and has made me one of the trustees to his museum, which is to be offered for £20,000 to the King, the Parliament, the Royal Academies of Petersburg, Berlin, Paris, and Madrid. He valued it at fourscore thousand; and so would anybody who loves hippopotamuses, sharks with one ear, and spiders as big as geese! It is a rent charge, to keep the foetuses in spirits! You may believe that those who think money the most valuable of all curiosities will not be purchasers. The King has excused himself saying he did not believe that there are £20,000 in the Treasury. We are a charming wise set, all philosophers, botanists, antiquarians, and mathematicians. . . . One of our number is a Moravian who signs himself Henry XXVIII, Count de Reus. The Moravians have settled a colony at Chelsea, in Sir Hans' neighborhood, and I believe he intended to beg Count Henry XXVIII's skeleton for his museum."

The person of Horace Walpole was the natural meeting ground of the tastes and tendencies of the *cognoscenti* of eighteenth-century England. He was the son of Sir Robert Walpole, the great Prime Minister to George I and George II, and was later in life to inherit, upon the death of his eldest brother's son, the title of fourth Earl of Orford.

Miss Laetitia-Matilda Hawkins (daughter of Sir John Hawkins,

Dr. Johnson's executor and biographer), who was his neighbor at Twickenham, has described him at about the time when he was embarking on his plans for Strawberry Hill:

> His figure was as has been told, and everyone knows, not merely tall, but more properly long and slender to excess; his complexion and particularly his hands, of a most unhealthy paleness. His eyes were remarkably bright and penetrating, very dark and lively: – his voice was not strong, but his tones were extremely pleasant, and if I may say so highly gentlemanly. I do not remember his common gait; he always entered a room in that style of affected delicacy, which fashion had then made almost natural; *chapeau bras*, between his hands as if he wished to compress it, or under his arms – knees bent, and feet on tiptoe, as if afraid of a wet floor.
>
> His dress in visiting was most usually, in summer when I saw him a lavender suit, the waistcoat embroidered with a little silver or of white silk worked in the tambour, partridge silk stockings, and gold buckles, ruffles and frills generally lace. I remember when a child thinking him very much under dressed, if at any time except in mourning, he wore hemmed cambric. In summer no powder, but his wig combed straight and showing his very smooth pale forehead, and queued behind, in winter powder.*

"Few writers," says Wilmarth S. Lewis, the American editor of his letters and a distinguished collector of Walpoliana, "have fluctuated more in critical esteem than Horace Walpole. To his own age he was a brilliant essayist and historian (the eighteenth century in general knew nothing of his letter writing). In the nineteenth century, Byron stated that he was a greater writer than any living man 'be he who he may.' Crocker and Lord Liverpool, on the other hand, agreed that no more evil man had ever lived, because, they said, he had poisoned history at its source. Carlyle saw him as a light shining in the darkness; to Macaulay he was a *pâté de foie gras* produced by an effete society. . . . [He] was witty and shrewd but he was not a courtier; he was something of a fop; he was thin-skinned and abnormally self-conscious, but he was not trivial. He had an unworthy fear of ridicule and was prone to ridicule people he feared, but no

* Laetitia-Matilda Hawkins, *Anecdotes, Biographical Sketches and Memoirs.* 1822–1824. 3 vols. I, 105–106.

account seemed to have been taken of his generosity. Saintsbury said Walpole was the key to the society of his time. Saintsbury meant that portion of society which ruled England from St. James's Street and Whitehall; but as I continued to read it seemed to me that Walpole was the key to more than that. I began collecting everything which had to do with him; and these objects – his works, letters, and the books of prints formerly in his library – disclosed the grand project of his life which was nothing less than the deliberate and carefully planned transmission to posterity of a true picture of his time.

"Horace Walpole felt the preoccupation with the future which was characteristic of many eighteenth century men. He was determined to be remembered by posterity, to have a reputation independent to that of his father, Sir Robert. He knew that he was not suited to an important political career. He saw from the beginning that he could best gain his end by writing." *

His education was the conventional and suitable one for the son of a wealthy Prime Minister. Upon finishing at Eton, where he had established a historic friendship with the poets Thomas Gray and the young Richard West, he went on to Cambridge for a year or so, where he was more concerned with literary affectations than he was with opportunities for learning. The years 1739 to 1741 were occupied by the grand tour. Accompanied by Gray, and armed with letters from his illustrious father to the embassies abroad, he spent the first year in France, the one foreign country to which he returned in later life.

The year in Italy, however, was the more effective for the formation of his interests and his style. He divided his time between Rome, where, as a Whig and a Protestant, he moved uneasily in the Catholic society of the Vatican and of the exiled Stuart Pretenders, and in Florence, where he lived for more than a year with Horace Mann, the King's Resident at the Court of Tuscany. In Mann Walpole found a friend with sympathetic tastes, and thus began that weekly correspondence between the two which, although they never met again, lasted for more than forty-five years. The picture of young Walpole moving triumphantly through the fashionable world of Italy, offering criticism in the arts to one group and political advice to another, act-

* *Atlantic Monthly*, July 1945, pp. 48–51.

ing as a diplomatic spy for his father upon the activities of the Pretenders, and as the *cicisbeo* of a beautiful and ardent Florentine *signora*, has been beautifully painted by W. R. Ketton-Cremer in his recent biography.

Walpole, who at this time had just turned twenty, was an exception; but he was, in fact, the exceptional development of a type which followed the established rule. His contemporaries were at home in the architecture of Palladio and had come to know by heart the principal palaces and churches of Italy; they were equally well informed in regard to the prevailing theories of painting and sculpture which illumined the last flickering of the Baroque.* They had all read Richardson's *Theory of Painting*, issued in 1715; this, and his guidebook to the art treasures of Europe published seven years later, were the eighteenth century's textbooks in the arts. These works in fact received the approbation of Winckelmann and formed to a large extent the basis for the famous *Discourses* which Sir Joshua Reynolds gave before the Royal Academy from 1769 to 1791. Whether or not Walpole was a profound student of Richardson, or whether he personally had influenced Sir Joshua, cannot easily be determined. We do know, however, from the catalogue of the fine library at Strawberry Hill that Walpole owned the works of Richardson and Algarotti. We also know that Richardson took Horace Walpole's portrait the year before the latter went abroad on the grand tour, and it is reasonable to suppose that they talked during the sittings about the monuments the young traveler was to see. Walpole enjoyed something of the same experience with Sir Joshua Reynolds, who painted his portrait in 1757.

The whole tenor of Walpole's criticism and the point of view of the *Aedes Walpolianae*, which he produced upon his return from Italy, indicate that he had absorbed in the cafés and salons of Rome and Florence a dilettante's knowledge and appreciation of these questions. Moreover, he was constantly on the lookout for fine pictures and statues to be added to his father's growing collection at Houghton

* The most accepted theories were those based largely upon the didactic poem of Dufresnoy (of which the first English edition appeared in 1695) which had summed up the controversies of the time, and upon the theories expounded by Poussin, who was forever altering the Roman landscape to fit the classical formulae of his compositions.

Hall; he had access to all the private palaces and collections and must have been constantly in the company of art dealers, painters and critics who were only too glad to tutor a young Englishman of such prominence and wealth.

* * * * *

Walpole returned from Italy scarcely more than a year before his father fell from power. He returned to find an England barren of the cultivation which his own generation were to bring to it in time. Collecting, which had been so brilliant a century earlier in the reign of Charles I, excepting in the field of scientific curiosities, had almost come to a complete stop with Cromwell's Roundheads. The dispersal of the splendid collections of Charles I, of Buckingham and Arundel in the 1650's had been the signal for despair; the collector and the man of taste had been engulfed in the tidal wave of Puritanism which had swept over England. Although, to be sure, in the reign of James II some 1100 pictures had been salvaged and brought together again at Whitehall and Hampton Court, the fire at Whitehall, when so many of these great works of art perished in flames, had appeared to give the *coup de grâce* to the Royal Collection.

No better picture of the desolation of the arts at this time has been painted than that by Walpole himself in his *Anecdotes of English Painting*. Of King William he says, "This prince, like most of those in our annals, contributed nothing to the advancement of the Arts. He was born in a country where taste never flourished, and nature had not given it to him as an embellishment to his great qualities. He courted fame, but none of her ministers. Holland owed its preservation to his heroic virtue, England its liberty to his ambition, Europe its independence to his competition with Louis XIV; for, however unsuccessful in the contest, the very struggle was salutary. Being obliged to draw all his resources from himself, and not content to acquire glory by proxy, he had no leisure, like his rival, to preside over the registers of his fame. He fought his own battles, instead of choosing mottoes for the medals that recorded them; and though my Lord Halifax promised him that his wound in the Battle of the Boyne 'should run for ever purple in our looms,' his Majesty certainly did not bespeak a single suit of tapestry in memory of the action. In England he met with nothing but disgusts. He understood too little of the nation, and seems to have acted too much upon a plan formed before he came over, and, however necessary to his early situation, little adapted to so peculiar a people as the English. He thought that valor and taciturnity would conquer or govern the world; and vainly imagining that his new subjects loved liberty better than party, he trusted to their feeling gratitude for a blessing which they could not help seeing was conferred a little for his own sake. Reserved, unsociable, ill in his health, and soured by his situation, he sought none of those amusements that make the hours much happier. If we must accept the Palace at Hampton Court, at least it is no monument of his taste; it seems erected in emulation of, what it certainly was meant to imitate, the pompous edifices of the French monarch. We are told that,

> Great Nassau to Kneller's hand decreed
> To fix him graceful on the bounding steed.

. . . In general I believe his Majesty patronized neither painters nor poets, though he was happy in the latter; but the case is different; a great prince may have a Garth, a Prior, a Montague, but no Titians and Van Dycks, if he encourages neither. You must address yourself to a painter if you wish to be flattered – a poet brings his incense to you. Mary seems to have had little more propensity to the arts than the King: the good Queen loved to work and talk, and contented herself with praying to God that her husband might be a great hero, since he did not choose to be a fond husband." *

The twelve years of Queen Anne fared little better: "The reign of Anne, so illustrated by heroes, poets, and authors, was not equally fortunate in artists. Except Kneller, scarce a painter of note. Westminster Abbey testifies there were no eminent statuaries. One man there was who disgraced this period by his architecture as much as he enlivened it by his wit. Formed to please both Augustus and an Egyptian monarch, who thought nothing preserved fame like a solid mass of stone, he produced the *Relapse* and Blenheim!" †

* Walpole, *op. cit.*, II, 585–586. † *Ibid.*, 627.

That Horace Walpole should feel so bitterly about Sir John Vanbrugh, the witty dramatist and architect of Castle Howard and Blenheim, may have been due in part to the fact that Blenheim Palace and its vast collection were amongst the very few formidable rivals to the supremacy of the Walpole taste at Houghton. Blenheim Palace, one of the great extravagances of the age, was built by Queen Anne as a gift to her favorite general and statesman, the Duke of Marlborough, following his smashing victory in the little German village. His Duchess, Sarah, was the favorite at court – Queen Anne's most intimate friend and adviser. The building of this huge palace was something of a scandal for it was generally supposed that it was paid for by money voted by the Parliament. On the contrary, it has since proved to have been paid out of the privy purse, and at the death of Queen Anne, the Duke of Marlborough denying all responsibility for the payment, Vanbrugh himself was obliged to advance the money to the workmen, who gladly accepted one third of the debt.

"He wanted," said Walpole of the architect, "all ideas of proportion, convenience, propriety. He undertook vast designs, and composed heaps of littleness. The style of no age, no country, appears in his works; he broke through all rule and compensated for it by no imagination. He seems to have hollowed quarries rather than to have built houses; and should his edifices, as they seem formed to do, outlast all record, what architecture will posterity think was that of their ancestors? The laughers, his co-temporaries, said that having been confined in the Bastille, he had drawn his notions of building from that fortified dungeon. That a single man should have been capricious, should have wanted taste, is not extraordinary. That he should have been selected to raise a palace, built at the public expense for the hero of his country, surprises one. Whose thought it was to load every avenue to that palace with inscriptions, I do not know; altogether they form an edition of the acts of Parliament in stone. However partial the Court was to Vanbrugh everybody was not so blind to his defects. Swift ridiculed both his own diminutive house at Whitehall, and the stupendous pile at Blenheim." *

The palace was commenced in 1702 and the Duke soon filled it

* Walpole, *op. cit.*, 638–639.

with pictures and other collections. The German Emperor and the cities of the Netherlands, Brussels, Antwerp and Ghent vied with one another in presenting the art-loving general with works by Rubens, who was his favorite master. One of them was the Metropolitan Museum's *Meleager and Atalanta*. Among the more spectacular pictures in the collection was the equestrian portrait of Charles I by Van Dyck, sold for 150 pounds at the great sale in 1649, and rediscovered by Marlborough in Munich. Also he had a lovely family portrait of Rubens with his wife and child in their garden, and he had the good fortune to receive as a gift from his brother, Lord Spencer, a painting which Gavin Hamilton had bought for him in Italy. It was none other than Raphael's *Madonna of the Ansidei*. There were 120 small pictures by Teniers which were copies of paintings included in the collection of the Archduke Leopold Wilhelm. The Duke was not always fortunate, for nine Titians which were given him by Victor Amadeus, King of Savoy and lover of *la dame de volupté*, Madame de Verrue, turned out to be copies after the engravings of Caraglio Padovanino.

The Duke's collection was considered far into the nineteenth century as the most celebrated and conspicuous one in England and merited the approbation of no less a critic than Waagen. It was dispersed in 1885 when more than 360 pictures were put up at auction. The National Gallery in London bought the *Ansidei Madonna* and the *Charles I* for £70,000 and £17,500 respectively. Alphonse de Rothschild paid £55,000 for the *Helena Fourment* and the *Family Portrait* by Rubens. Edmund Rothschild bought *The Three Graces* by the same master. The *Venus and Adonis* and the *Anne of Austria*, both in the Metropolitan Museum in New York, fetched £23,389. The total for the entire sale was over £350,000.*

* Castle Howard, that other monument to Vanbrugh's "ghastly good taste," does not properly belong to this discussion, for the collections which have made the House so famous were not formed until the end of the eighteenth century when the Earl of Carlisle became the great patron of Canaletto and acquired in 1793, at the sale of the collection of the Prince Regent, the Duke of Orléans, his most celebrated masterpieces. In fact, the gallery of classical sculpture and the picture gallery were not added until after 1800.

CHAPTER IV

Houghton and Strawberry Hill

It remained for the Walpoles, father and son, first at Houghton and then at Strawberry Hill, to show the world the prowess of their taste. In the dedicatory epistle prefacing the catalogue of his father's collection the young Horace opens his description of Houghton with the following words: "Your Power and your Wealth speak themselves in the Grandeur of the whole Building. And give me leave to say, Sir, your enjoying the latter after losing the former is the brightest proof of how honest were the foundations of both. Could the virtuous men, your Father and Grandfather, arise from yonder Church, how would they be amazed to see this noble edifice and spacious plantations, where once stood their plain homely dwelling! How would they be satisfied to find only the Mansion House not the Morals of the Family altered!"

If Houghton Hall, consciously or unconsciously, followed the pattern of Richelieu's great palace in the country near Tours, it was no less than the latter the crowning achievement of the statesman, the politician and the man of wealth.* It contained the collection of a man who supported his own insecure culture upon the opinions of others, but who seldom failed in his objective because of his extraordinary knowledge of mankind. Walpole's collection, which it is said in the beginning cost him less than £40,000, became the greatest in England since the time of Charles I simply because of his superior ability to judge the judgment of others. Although the Tories who finally brought about his downfall constantly implied that his collection was the result of peculation and bribery while in office, it has nevertheless been since proved that his wealth was almost exclusively derived

* Designed originally by Colin Campbell, completed by Ripley and decorated by William Kent it may be compared with Holkham and the other great palaces of the Palladian revival.

from successful speculation in the South Seas companies from which he prudently sold out. All of this wealth he poured into Houghton during the score of years (1722–1745) which were required to complete it. He had frequently to borrow during the building period and he died £40,000 in debt.*

"Houghton," says Ketton-Cremer, "is a magnificent house; but it is quite unjust to condemn it for ostentation. Beside the stupendous palaces of Vanbrugh, or the vast Palladian structures raised later in the century, its scale might almost be described as modest. There is nothing in the design to mark it as the fulfilled ambition of a wealthy parvenu; it is simple, massive, dignified, and every foot of its surface is remarkable for its sober perfection of detail and finish. In its spacious magnificence, it was the perfect expression of Sir Robert; and it is hard to believe that he could have ever wished it smaller by a single foot. The house matched the man. There was something of his personality in all its pictures and in all its furnishings — in the solemn massive east front; in the more ornate west front which faced the gardens; in the astonishing hall and its famous lantern, which was so often ridiculed in *The Craftsman;* in the Marble Parlor, with its cool alcoves and granite cistern, refinements to aid deep drinking and heavy dining on a hot day; in the bedchambers with their superb tapestries and marvelous embroidered bed hangings; in the velvet, the gilding, the friezes and doors and chimney pieces; and above all in room after room filled with pictures from floor to ceiling, the Gallery, the Salon, the Carlo Maratt Room and all the other rooms with their profusion of pleasant family portraits, indifferent hunting scenes, and unrivalled masterpieces by every painter whose work was admired by the *cognoscenti* in the reign of George II." † The whole house in fact breathed

* The South Seas Company, organized in 1711 by Lord Treasurer Harley for the purpose of wiping out the national debt (then amounting to £10,000,000), was the English counterpart to John Law's Compagnie des Indes. The company assumed the debt in return for a monopoly of trade in the South Seas. It followed a parallel course of speculation and manipulation to that of the French Company. By August 1720, the month following the bursting of the "Mississippi Bubble," shares were being offered at £1000. The chairman and some of the principal directors sold out. In the crash that followed, although thousands of innocent stockholders were ruined, about a third of the original capital was saved. A parliamentary investigation revealed a scandalous complicity of the Cabinet.

† R. W. Ketton-Cremer, *Horace Walpole.* Longmans, Green & Co., 1940, pp. 46–48.

the air of security and sureness of position and when, in 1742, his twenty-three years as Prime Minister were ended, and he went to the House of Lords as the Earl of Orford, his spirit was not in the least dampened. He simply transformed a room intended for a greenhouse into the picture gallery in which he hung the pictures from his collection that had theretofore decorated the walls of No. 10 Downing Street.

Macaulay, writing a hundred years later and cordially despising both of the Walpoles, conceded that Sir Robert "had undoubtedly, great talents and great virtues. He was not indeed like the leaders of the party which opposed his government a brilliant orator. He was not a profound scholar like Carteret or a wit and a fine gentleman like Chesterfield. In all these respects his deficiencies were remarkable. His literature consisted of a scrap or two of Horace, and an anecdote or two from the end of the dictionary. His knowledge of history was limited. . . . His manners were a little too coarse and boisterous. . . . When he ceased to talk of politics, he could talk of nothing but women; and dilated on his favorite theme with a freedom which shocked even that plain spoken generation and which was quite unsuited to his age and station. The noisy revelry of his summer festivities at Houghton gave much scandal to grave people, and annually drove his kinsman and colleague, Lord Townshend, from the neighboring mansion of Rainham.*

"But, however ignorant he might be of general history and of general literature, he was better acquainted than any man of his day with what it concerned him most to know; mankind, the English nation, the Court, the House of Commons and his own office. . . . He retired after more than twenty years of power with a temper not soured, with a heart not hardened, with simple tastes, with frank manners, and a capacity for friendship."

It was in these twilight years of retirement, between the return of his son, Horace, from the grand tour in 1741 and Sir Robert's death in 1745, that they lived in London and at Houghton, growing to know one another really for the first time; and it was during this period that

* Thomas Babington Macaulay, "Essays on Walpole," *Edinburgh Review*, October 1833.

Horace produced the *Aedes Walpolianae*, the description of Houghton Hall and its contents. It is a remarkable work, the outstanding piece of English art criticism of the eighteenth century before Sir Joshua, and except for the prejudices of youth, no less penetrating than the *Discourses*. To the reader of the present day it is amazing to see the independence of judgment which this young man exercised, and yet at the same time how readily he subscribed to the traditional absurdities of the generation or two that preceded him. So far as style and language are concerned there has seldom been written, even counting the more exact knowledge we have today, more readable or more attractive criticism. The original manuscript is in the Metropolitan Museum in New York. It is a large folio scrapbook, written in Horace Walpole's own hand, in which he pasted the engravings made by Ware and by others of the plans for Houghton and of the pictures in the collection. It is a most revealing document, for it shows the work to have been entirely done by Horace Walpole himself. But also by the changes and the corrections in the text, it is possible to see the way his ideas developed in the course of preparing the publication.

His introduction is worth examining in detail for it not only contains a synopsis of the major schools of European painting, but is prefaced by an apologia for collecting and a very shrewd and knowledgeable account of the practices then current:

> In Italy the native soil of almost all Vertù, descriptions of great collections are much more common and much more ample. The Princes and Noblemen there, who loved and countenanced the arts, were fond of letting the world know the Curiosities in their possession. There is scarce a large collection of Medals but is in print. Their Gems, their Statues of Antiquities, are all published. But the most pompous works of this sort are the *Aedes Barbarinae* and *Giustinianae*, the latter of which are now extremely scarce and dear.
>
> Commerce, which carries along with it the Curiosities and Arts of Countries, as well as the Riches, daily brings us something from Italy. How many valuable Collections of Pictures are there established in England on the frequent ruins and dispersion of the finest Galleries in Rome and other Cities! Most of the famous Pallavicini Collection have been brought over; many of them are actually at Houghton. . . . Statues are

not so numerous and consequently they come seldomer, besides that the chief are prohibited from being sold out of Rome: a silent proof, that the sums sent thither for purchase are not thrown away, since the prohibition arose from profits flowing into the City by the concourse of Strangers who travel to visit them. For however common and more reasonable the pretext, I believe, ten travel to see the Curiosities of a Country, for One who makes a journey to acquaint himself with the Manners, Customs and Policy of the Inhabitants.

There are not many Collections left in Italy more worth seeing than this at Houghton; in the preservation of the Pictures, it certainly excels most of them. That noble one in the Borghese Palace at Rome, is almost destroyed by the damps of the apartment where it is kept.

Then follows a passage which is refreshingly modern and will gladden the hearts of those who live today under the tyranny of the German historians of art:

The numerous volumes wrote on this Art [that is, the art of painting] have only serv'd to perplex it. No Science has had so much jargon introduced into it as Painting: the bombast expression of the Italians, and the prejudices of the French, joined to the vanity of the Professors, and the interested Mysteriousnesses of Picture-merchants, have altogether compiled a new language. . . .

As great as are the prices of fine Pictures, there is no judging from them of the several merits of the Painters; there does not seem to be any standard of estimation. You hear a Virtuoso talk in raptures of Raphael, of Correggio's grace, and Titian's coloring; and yet the same Man in the same breath will talk as enthusiastically of any of the first Masters, who wanted all the excellencies of all of the Three. You will perhaps see more paid for a Picture of Andrea del Sarto whose Coloring was a mixture of mist and tawdry, whose Drawing hard and forced, than for the most graceful air of a Madonna that ever flowed from the pencil of Guido. And as for the Dutch Painters, those grudging Mimicks of Nature's most uncomely coarsenesses, don't their earthen pots and brass kettles carry away prices only due to the sweet neatness of Albano and to the attractive delicacy of Carlo Maratti?

The latter painter, who was at the height of his fashion, and to whom was devoted an entire drawing room with nearly a dozen of his pictures at Houghton, is scarcely known today. Walpole pays a

RUBENS: VENUS AND ADONIS (DETAIL)

Painted for a member of the Hapsburg family, the picture descended to the Emperor Joseph II, who presented it to John Churchill, First Duke of Marlborough. It remained at Blenheim Palace until 1886 when it was sold at auction for £7560. Acquired by Colonel Oliver H. Payne, it was given to the Metropolitan Museum of Art in 1937 by his nephew, Harry Payne Bingham.

passing tribute to Cimabue and to Mantegna as the founders of Italian painting. The Roman School he admires, particularly "for Drawing, Taste, and Great Ideas." But he finds that Michelangelo is "as much too fond of Muscles as Rubens was afterwards of Flesh." The Venetians he found "as renowned for their Colouring as for their Drawing."

Titian, Giorgione, Pordenone, Paul Veronese, Tintoret, the Basssans, Paris Bourdon, Andrea Schiavoni, and the Palmas were chief Masters of it: Titian and Veronese are by far the best. The landscapes of the former and the architecture of the latter were equal to their Carnations. Giorgione had great ideas. Pordenone and Tintoret were dark and ungraceful. The Palmas were stiff and the Bassans particular.

He admits Leonardo da Vinci to be a universal Genius and feels that his "Colouring of Flesh does not yield in roundness to Titian's; nor his skill in Anatomy to Michael Angelo; his judgment in it was far greater." He did not care for the Neapolitans, who "produced little good," although he admitted that Luca Jordano did well but owed everything to his master, Pietro Cortona. "There cannot be," he says, "three manners more unlike, than in the *Cyclops*, the *Judgment of Paris*, and the two small ones in the Carlo Maratt Room, all by him. His genius was like Ovid's, flowing, abundant, various, and incorrect."

Walpole speaks with all the enthusiasm of his generation of Salvator Rosa, of his landscapes, of his knowledge of the force of shade and his masterly arrangement of horror and distress.

In Lord Orford's *Prodigal* is represented the extremity of Misery and low Nature; not foul and burlesque like Michelangelo Caravaggio; nor minute, circumstantial and laborious like the Dutch Painters. One of them would have painted eating Broth with a wooden Spoon, and have employed three days in finishing up the Bowl that held it. In the *Story of the Old Man and His Sons* one sees Drawing and a taste of Draperies equal to the best collected from the Antique. Salvator was a Poet and excellent Satirist.

His remarks upon the Spanish School are the conventional ones which one might expect and he accepts without comment the great portrait head of *Pope Innocent X* by Velasquez which hung in the room called the Cabinet; the ceiling of this same room was the original sketch by Rubens for the banqueting hall at Whitehall depicting the *Apotheosis of James I.* Of the French School he had more to say:

> One Character runs through all their Works, in close imitation of the Antique, unassisted by Colouring. Poussin was a perfect Master of Expression and Drawing, though the proportion of his Figures is rather too long. Le Soeur his Disciple, to the style of his Master and the study of the Antique, joined an imitation of Raphael which had his life been longer would have raised him above Poussin. . . . Sebastian Bourdon was liker Poussin, only that as Poussin's Figures are apt to be too long, his are generally too short, and consequently want the Grace which often consists in overlengthened Proportions.

And then he adds an observation very advanced and brave for the Englishman of 1740. "Le Brun's colouring was better than any of the French but his Compositions are generally confused and crowded." He accepted Claude as the "Raphael of landscape painting." Of the Flemings he accepted only Rubens and his scholar, Van Dyck, who "contracted a much genteeler taste in his portraits." But true to the teachings of du Fresnoy and Richardson he reserved his greatest admiration for the Bolognese School, the school which had dominated the taste of the earlier Englishman in Rome.

> This was the School that to the dignity of the Antique, joined all the beauty of living Nature. There was no Perfection in the others, which was not assembled here. In Annibal Caracci one sees the ancient Strength of Drawing. In his Farnese Gallery, the naked Figures supporting the Ceiling are equal to the exerted Skill of Michelangelo, superiorly coloured.

Finally at the end of the introduction Horace Walpole sums up the fashionable taste of his day:

> I shall conclude with these few Recapitulations. I can admire Correggio's Grace and exquisite Finishing; but I cannot overlook his wretched drawing and Distortions. I admire Parmegiano's more majestic Grace, and with the length of Limbs and Necks, which forms those graceful Airs, were natural. Titian wanted to have seen the Antique; Poussin to have seen Titian. Le Soeur, whom I think in Drawing and Expression equal to Poussin, and in the great Ideas of his Heads and Attitude second to

Raphael, like the first wanted Colouring and had not the fine Draperies of the latter. Albano never painted a Picture but some of the Figures were stiff and wanted Grace; and then his scarce ever succeeding in large Subjects will throw him out of the list of perfect Painters. Dominichini, whose *Communion of Saint Jerome* is allowed to be the second Picture in the world, was generally raw in his Colouring, hard in his Colouring, hard in his Contours, and wanted clearness in his Carnations and a knowledge of the Chiaro Oscuro. In short, in my opinion, all the qualities of a perfect Painter never met but in Raphael, Guido and Annibal Carracci.

The main body of the text of the *Aedes Walpolianae* is, of course, devoted to an accurate room-by-room description of Houghton Hall and its contents. "The Great Hall is a Cube of forty [feet]," the stone gallery around three sides, the ceiling in frieze *al bois* by Altari, the bas-reliefs on the chimney and doors are from the antique; the great staircase was painted in *chiaro oscuro* by Kent; in the middle were four Doric pillars which rose to support a fine cast in bronze of *The Gladiator*, by John of Bologna, which was presented to Sir Robert by Thomas, Earl of Pembroke. Opening out from the hall were the small breakfast room filled with English and Dutch works and an Italian picture by Pordenone of *The Prodigal Son* which was formerly in the collection of the Duke of Buckingham; the Supping Parlor was devoted to Julio Romano's *Battle of Constantine and Maxentius*, a copy of Raphael's picture at the Vatican and a series of portraits of the Walpole family by various artists. In the Common Parlor were Rembrandt's *Portrait of His Wife* and that of *Sir Thomas Gresham* by Antonio Mor, as well as a splendid *Bacchanalian* by Rubens. The Library boasted the only portrait in existence of *George I*, painted by Kneller, and in the Drawing Room were the principal Van Dycks, those of *Charles I*, his wife, *Henrietta Maria*, and *Archbishop Laud*. The Saloon was hung in crimson flowered velvet, its furniture by Kent, in black and gold, and contained many famous paintings and sculptures of the Renaissance. The Carlo-Maratt Room was hung in green velvet and illuminated by magnificent silver sconces. The tables were of lapis lazuli; the pictures by Maratti came for the most part from the Pallavicini Collection and had been bought for Walpole by

Jervase from the Arnaldi Palace at Florence. They included the celebrated portrait of *Pope Clement IX Rospigliosi*, the *Judgment of Paris*, *Galatea*, *The Holy Family*, the *Virgin Teaching the Child Jesus to Read*, the *Saint Cecelia* and an *Assumption of the Virgin.* There was also a series of classical scenes by Maratti and Luca Giordano.

The great triumph of the house was achieved in the Gallery, or Men's Room, 73 feet long and 21 feet high. It had originally been designed as a greenhouse but was altered after Sir Robert's fall from power.

The middle rises 8 Feet higher with Windows all around; the Ceiling is a design of Serlio's and the inner Library of Saint Mark's at Venice and was brought from thence by Mr. Horace Walpole, Jr.; the Frieze is taken from the Sybil's temple at Tivoli. There are two Chimnies and the whole Room is hung with Norwich Damask. . . . On the farthest Chimney is that capital picture and the first in this collection, *The Doctors of the Church:* they are consulting under the Immaculateness of the Virgin who is above in the Clouds. . . . In this Picture which is by Guido in his brightest Manner and perfectly preserved, there are six old Men as large as Life. The Expression, Drawing, Design and Colouring, wonderfully fine. In the Clouds is a beautiful Virgin, all in White, and before her a sweet little Angel flying. Eight Feet eleven inches high by six Feet wide. After Sir Robert had bought this Picture and it was gone to Civita Vecchia to be shipt to England, Innocent XIII, then Pope, remanded it back, as being too fine to be let out of Rome; but on hearing who had bought it, he gave Permission for its being sent away. It was in the Collection of the Marquis Angeli.

This gallery also contained two important pictures which seem to have been lost.* The first was *The Last Supper* by Raphael, said to have been in the collection of the Earl of Arundel and described in the catalogue of his pictures. From there it went into the possession of the Earl of Yarmouth and from him to Sir John Holland, of whom Lord Orford bought it. The other picture, representing the *Eagle and*

* They do not appear in the catalogues of the Hermitage in Saint Petersburg nor were they printed in the de luxe catalogue of pictures bought by the Empress of Russia at the time of the sale.

Ganymede, by Michelangelo, was one of a group which he often repeated but with alterations. One was in the possession of the King (George II); another belonged to the Queen of Hungary; one is printed in the "Teniers Gallery" and another was said to be in the Altieri Palace at Rome. Possibly these pictures were sold later from the collection by the second Lord Orford, who was constantly in debt, or more likely they proved to be inferior examples. One picture that attracted Walpole enormously but is no longer considered by the hand of Leonardo da Vinci was "the Joconda, a Smith's Wife reckoned the handsomest Woman of her Time: she was the Mistress to Francis I, King of France. She would often sit half-naked with Musick for several hours to be drawn by him. Mézeray calls her *la Ferronière*, and says, 'her Husband being enraged at the King's taking her, caught on purpose a very violent Distemper, which he communicated thro' her to the King who never recovered it.' The same Story is told of Lord Southesk and King James II, when Duke of York."

* * * * *

But however conventional the *Description* of Houghton, we find the culmination of Horace's taste in the Gothic extravaganza of Strawberry Hill. Critics have been baffled by it for many years – the current sensibility so sympathetic to the Gothic Revival and its implications has found in it an ineffable beauty. The more sober and ponderous opinion of the generation that preceded us has looked upon it with polite and restrained horror as the legitimate eccentricity of a man of letters to whom beauty was, perhaps, a rhetorical accomplishment but certainly not a necessity of life. Yet to Walpole it became the expression of his restlessness and the realization of his imaginary *Castle of Otranto*. Macaulay spoke of Walpole's ingenuity, his facility and inventiveness in everything he touched, in his building, his writing and his gardening – even to the upholstery and gimcrackery of his furnishings. Walpole's love of detail, his passion for the minute and the unimportant, his infinite capacity to reduce artistic forms to literary niceties, which too often could be appreciated only by himself and his Committee on Taste, were at once the strength and weakness of the man. As a collector, in such violent contrast to his father, it would be fair to say that he was a mid-Victorian a century ahead of his time. Although his journals and other writings show that he was letter-perfect in the collectors' lore of the day, he had none of the rationalism and suavity of the Augustan Age. He collected emotionally and then submerged what he had acquired beneath a veneer of such perfection of polish that his criticism seemed graver and less whimsical than it really was.

Horace Walpole not only revived but actually relived the monkish mag-piety of Gothic England whose austerity he was never fully able to resist; he yielded, too, to the constant battering of Renaissance humanism (in which he had been grounded) and the enlightenment of his own age. And it is safe to say that without his outrageous disregard for the accepted canons of the eighteenth century, that strange quality of undisciplined intellectual curiosity, eagerly imitated by his contemporaries and which later gave such impetus to the British Museum, would have been seriously retarded. For he was the first to embody in one person the role of antiquary and connoisseur; and in so doing he became the symbol and archetype of the antiprofessional English amateur; in no other time or place has the cultivation of the Philistine been carried to such extravagant heights.

Quite aside from the wide catholic interests which his collecting and criticism of art always displayed, one senses a deep passion on the part of Horace Walpole to find in England a climate for the reception of the arts and a cultivation of private taste. Mr. Lewis has suggested that Walpole, after his return from the grand tour, and deeply hurt by the political decline of his father, smarted under the comparative barbarism of his own country. The years of building Strawberry Hill were not a period of mere self-indulgence. They were part of a larger plan of which the *Anecdotes of English Painting* were the culmination. His preoccupation with the Gothic past, his taste for the British landscape, which he subjected to the most rigorous examination, and his treatise on the *Art of Gardening*, all contributed to the formation of an elaborate and patriotic sense of a mission to be fulfilled. The mission was to put into proper perspective the greatness of England's past and to show that not only had she called upon the Continent in order to achieve her present eminence, but had contributed so much from her own history. It was, moreover, a medievalism not without vanity, for he justified his antiquarianism by tracing his own ancestry back beyond Chaucer to the Welsh kings.

The antiquarian of the 1740's, Ketton-Cremer has shown, was of necessity something of an explorer:

> He had a remarkably open field; he was enthusiastic, ignorant, full of amateurish and improbable theories: vistas of exciting discoveries stretched out before him. All over England stood the ruined monasteries and castles, neglected, crumbling, turned into cottages and cowsheds and quarries for building. One pushed through the nettles and skirted the duckponds, thrust aside a hurdle and entered the chapel or refectory of a great monastic house. One rode or drove through almost impassable lanes, and came upon historic mansions tumbling in ruin, with paint still visible on their carvings, painted glass in their windows, and perhaps a farm laborer's family shivering in one of the towers. One traced forgotten cloisters, detected the site of kitchens and high altars, stood in great undercrofts whose forests of pillars glistened with water; one found the castle well and the castle privies, and made unlikely speculations about the tilt-yard and the ladye's bower; and returned to the inn inspired with the romance of the past. And the parish churches were equally fruitful of interest and romance. In disused chancels, in recesses behind the squire's smart pew with its cushioned arm-chairs, were hidden the dusty and crumbling effigies of the Mowbrays and the de Veres, the gilding thin upon the alabaster, the rusted helms hanging above, paint flaking from the coats which perhaps one was entitled to quarter with one's own. In the windows might be unbroken figures of saints, portraits of kings and queens; the sexton would often be glad to sell a few armorial quarries or some carving or a brass, the patron might give away whole windows of painted glass to an antiquarian friend. So Walpole, on his way to stay with Nugent at Gosfield or with Rigby at Mistley, would turn aside his chaise to explore some dilapidated castle or forgotten church. From these small beginnings came the elaborate tours with Chute, the "Gothic pilgrimages" which he described so brilliantly in his letters. His passion for Gothic, the passion which influenced the taste of a century, began in this quiet way, with genealogies, with visits to a few churches and castles: then, fed by Ashmole, Dugdale, county histories, the deeper knowledge of Chute and Gray, but above all by the beauties of spire and arch and tracery which he now began to observe and to appreciate, it in-

creased day by day, until his house and his writings were irrevocably destined to follow Gothic forms.*

If the Elizabethan historian Harrison styled Henry VIII "the onlie phoenix of his time for fine and curious masonrie," how far would he have let his imagination run in describing Horace Walpole! For he too was a phoenix who rose from the ashes of the Baroque tradition of the Continent and mingled with them the embers of his native hearth. The annotated and priced copy of Walpole's *Description of Strawberry Hill* which Mr. Lewis has preserved at Farmington is eloquent with the testimony of these two aspects of Walpole's curiosity. Not only does it record him as a serious judge of pictures, of their quality and monetary value, but it likewise shows how shrewd a buyer of local antiquities he became, and, comparatively speaking, what trifling sums he paid for his excursions into English history. Yet it was the accumulation of these apparent trivialities which has led to his indifferent reputation as a collector of art. Charles Blanc, the celebrated critic who founded the *Gazette des Beaux-Arts* in 1859, led the list of those who ridiculed him.

> *Il était un excentrique prétentieux, un faux original, non pas à la façon anglaise, mais à la mode française. . . . Il devint l'homme le plus artificiel, le plus difficile et le plus capricieux que puisse créer la satisfaction sans limites de tous les goûts qui traversent l'esprit. Son imagination se promenait des tripotages de la comédie parlementaire, et des futiles cancans des boudoirs de la cour, aux salles de ventes où il poursuivait avec acharnement les plus pauvres reliques de la curiosité, le peigne de la reine Marie, le chapeau rouge du cardinal Wolsey, la pipe que l'amiral Tromp avait fumée dans son dernier combat. Il avait l'enthousiasme du futile, du mesquin et de l'inutile. Imbu de tous les préjugés de l'aristocratie et enchainé par toute son existence au respect de la royauté, il faisait l'esprit rebelle en fait de politique.*†

But the picture which we get from his letters and from Walpole's own account books shows him to have been anything but a fool. He remains not only the foremost art critic in the English tongue up to his day – the Richardsons and Reynolds not excepted – but a collector

* Ketton-Cremer, *op. cit.*, 135.
† Blanc, *op. cit.*, 129–130.

who, if not able to disburse the fortunes or realize the opportunities of his father and his father's generation, brought together, rationally or irrationally, one of the most widely catholic collections ever formed. He had a sure eye for quality and seemed to know instinctively where real worth began and when association should be suppressed. The Gallery was the largest room in the house and contained his finest pictures, the most splendid porcelains, bronzes and marbles. The windows shone with colored glass, much of it designed for the room with the quarterings of the Walpoles painted on them; other windows contained a veritable museum of stained glass gathered up from among the abbeys and churches of England and Flanders. On the other side of the room were five deep canopied recesses containing a chimneypiece designed by Chute and Pitt – members of the Committee on Taste. The furniture, Ketton-Cremer continues, was "covered with the same crimson damask as the walls; its woodwork was painted black and gold. The walls were loaded with pictures, the recesses were filled with them – portraits of relations and friends, portraits of the celebrities of the sixteenth and seventeenth centuries, the painting by Mabuse of the *Marriage of Henry VII*, landscapes and subject pieces by an endless variety of artists. There was work by Cornelis Jansen, Rubens, Lely, Rosalba, Liotard, Reynolds – an extraordinary medley of periods and styles. On a sepulchral altar stood the famous Boccapadugli eagle which had been dug up in the Baths of Caracalla in 1742, and which Walpole liked to think had inspired Gray with the line about the 'ruffled plumes and flagging wing.' " *

The Chapel contained the smaller and more precious trinkets of his cabinet. Here Walpole let himself go in crowding his shelves and showcases with *personalia* and objects of literary rather than artistic importance – although, to be sure, his silver, jewels, enamels and illuminated manuscripts included items of the first water. "In the niches were placed casts or bronzes of the *Venus de Medici*, an *Antinous*, the *Apollo Belvedere*, the *Farnese Flora* and his own mother. Above the altar was a cabinet which contained his marvelous collection of miniatures – the Olivers, the Coopers, the Hoskins. . . . In two glass cases were some of his supreme treasures – the bust of Caligula in bronze with

* Ketton-Cremer, *op. cit.*, 199–200.

silver eyes; the missal 'with miniatures by Raphael and his scholars'; the silver bell carved with miraculous ornament by Benvenuto Cellini. Jostling these were such curiosities as Henry VIII's dagger, a mourning ring of Charles I, the great seal of Theodore, King of Corsica, and the cravat carved in wood by Grinling Gibbons. The entire room was an indescribable display of pictures, bronzes, carvings, ivories, enamels, faïence, *pot-pourri* jars, snuff-boxes, kettles, tea-pots, cups and saucers, seals and rings." *

Today only the houses stand as reminders of the artistic greatness of the two Walpoles. Sir Robert's great collection of pictures was sold in 1777 to the Empress of Russia by his wastrel son, the third Lord Orford. The present owners have restored the house itself.†

Strawberry Hill has become Saint Mary's College, a Roman Catholic college for boys. The trumpery has long vanished, the chapel has been shorn of all its ridiculous conceits and "Mass is now said daily beneath Horace Walpole's golden star."

* Ketton-Cremer, *op. cit.*, 202.

† Cf. *Country Life*, London, July 1924, p. 19.

CHAPTER V

Hanoverian Pretenders to the Throne of Art

If Houghton and Horace Walpole were exceptional, they nevertheless were the exceptions that proved the rule. Where they did not follow the pattern of the Age of Queen Anne, they set the example for the newer age of Dr. Johnson; for in Houghton Hall, and in Horace's description of it, we see a complete documentary record of fashionable taste and artistic theory in the middle of the eighteenth century. It was only natural that the Whig aristocracy, that unique product of English civilization, should provide a setting that was both suitable and attractive to a governing class. Their party was in power during the greater part of the eighteenth century. They produced more ambassadors and officers of state than the rest of England put together and they lived on a scale that was appropriate to their power. A man, it was said, "can jog along on £40,000 a year and jog very well he did." It was a life of luxury, of vast retinues of servants, of hangers-on and open hospitality. He divided his time between his house in town and his country seat. There he spent more than half the year recovering from the rigors and excesses of the London season, following out the pattern of existence prescribed by the fashionable authors whom he had read at Oxford or at Cambridge, composing neat letters dripping with Latin tags he had learned at Eton and at Westminster, filling them "with gossip of people whom he had met on the Grand Tour, in the clubs on St. James Street and in the foreign embassies at which at least in one of them he had served at some moment of his career." He usually, as a constituent of one of his own boroughs, if he stood for Parliament, voted a strict adherence to the foreign policy of his party, yet at the same time supported the immediate demands of the farmer tenants upon whose labor his fortunes were established. His allegiances, his sense of responsibility and his politics were not unlike those of the young Athenian in the Age of Pericles; for he, too, believed in a democracy which recognized only its own class, yet at the same time made due allowance for the lower orders who provided the sinews of preferment.

But Lord David Cecil has shown that his interests were not exclusively confined to politics:

> Parliament sat only for a few months in the year; and even during the session debates did not start until the late afternoon. The Whigs had the rest of their time to devote to other things. If they were sporting, they raced and hunted; if interested in agriculture, they farmed on an ambitious scale; if artistic, they collected marbles and medals; if intellectual, they read history and philosophy; if literary, they composed compliments in verse and sonorous, platitudinous orations. But the chief of their spare time was given up to social life, they gave balls; they founded clubs; they played cards; they got up private theatricals: they cultivated friendship and every variety, platonic and less platonic, of the art of love. Their ideal was the Renaissance ideal of the whole man whose aspiration it is to make the most of every advantage, intellectual and sensual, that life has to offer.*

It was an age that preferred rhetoric to philosophy and that wore taste with the same easy and well-tailored confidence with which the *macaroni* wore an embroidered silk waistcoat.

While the French salons were embattled over the rights of man, English society had put aside momentarily the spirit of enquiry which had made the end of the seventeenth century and the first years of the eighteenth so distinguished and so exciting. The material successes of the manufacturers at home, and the exporters in the colonies abroad, had put a premium upon superficiality, a premium that bore, none the less, the stamp of good breeding. Never was the currency of the professional in any field more basely depreciated. Elegance, pleasantness and style were all that mattered. It was a state of mind which naturally enough produced the portraits of Sir Joshua Reynolds, of Gainsborough and of Romney. While profundity may have been acceptable on the floor of the House of Commons, it was not acceptable

* David Cecil, *The Young Melbourne*. Bobbs Merrill, 1939, p. 7.

in society, nor was it either admired or encouraged in the middle classes. The very insignificance of the court of the first two Georges had of necessity thrown the fashionable world back on its own resources and produced instead of a single court, as in France, a myriad of courts which seemed to center around the life peculiar to every English country house.

Until the third quarter of the eighteenth century whatever encouragement was given to the arts was given in spite of the House of Hanover rather than because of it. George I, whom we have already looked upon through Horace Walpole's eyes, confined his attention to music, for which he had the sentimental ear of his German ancestors. His son George II, observed Steegmann, "the last of England's soldier-monarchs," did little better. His oft-quoted remark, "I hate bainting and boetry," elicited the lash from Pope. In the *Dunciad* the mighty mother thundered:

> You by whose care in vain he curs'd
> Still Dunce the Second reigns like Dunce the First.

His Queen, Caroline of Ansbach, was, however, a person of considerable taste, and it was she who discovered, in the drawer of a table rescued from the fire at Whitehall, the incomparable series of Holbein drawings which had been in the royal collection and which today are the pride of the Royal Library at Windsor. Their son, Frederick Lewis, Prince of Wales, the father of George III, was, however, an active factor in the artistic life of his day. Frequently encouraging artists in secret and buying their works, he also knew by heart the contents of the royal collections and spent much time at Whitehall and at Hampton Court, cataloguing and studying the pictures which had come down among the various possessions of the crown. "I have something of every kind," he said to Vertue, "because I love the arts and curious things." *

* Careful and critical descriptions of the royal palaces and their contents at Hampton Court, Kew, Saint James's, the Queen's house in Saint James's, in the late 1750's and the early 1760's, are given by Horace Walpole in his *Journals of Visits to Country Seats, etc.* and by Vertue in his *Notebooks*. Among the pictures acquired by Frederick Lewis which have remained in the royal collection are the Rubens *Winter*, the *Gerbier Family* and Van Dyck's *Saint Martin*. He bought excellent Italian and French pictures, particularly by Claude, and a volume of sketches and drawings by Poussin which had belonged to Dr. Mead.

Something of Frederick Lewis's taste and connoisseurship must have passed on to his son George III and to his grandson George IV for, ironically, these two monarchs, among the most feckless ever to sit upon the English throne, were to be, after Charles I, the greatest augmenters of the royal collections. This does not necessarily imply that either of them had a particular taste or knowledge of pictures. It was rather that they were so bored with their official life that they listened to good advice in art in order to avoid listening to it in politics. George III had as his adviser the librarian Richard Dalton, who scoured Italy on his behalf and acquired for him in 1762 the collection of Joseph Smith, a painter and His Majesty's Consul in Venice. George IV made his most spectacular acquisitions during the long period of his Regency when his father's mental condition did not permit him to function normally. Sir Thomas Lawrence at home, and a group of painters living in Italy and in the Low Countries, were the collaborators of the Prince Regent – who did not become King George IV until 1820 – in building up the royal collections on the wreckage of the French Revolution and the Napoleonic Wars.

Among the portrait painters who had attracted the particular attention of George III were Zoffany, Gainsborough and Ramsay. Reynolds was less generally the recipient of favors from the Prince of Wales, although he exercised a considerable influence over the King. Gainsborough, on the other hand, was the author of a variety of full-length and other smaller portraits of George III and Queen Charlotte. But of all the artists who won ascendancy over the King the foremost was the Philadelphia Quaker, Benjamin West, whose tiresome and correct historical canvases seemed to fill a gap in an otherwise vacant royal mind. Later, as President of the Royal Academy, West became the arbiter of a taste which he was rarely thought to possess and embarked upon a career that was destined to seal forever a lack of sympathy between the artists of the two English-speaking lands.

Consul Smith was the link between the London clubs and the coffeehouses of eighteenth-century Venice. He had settled there, at first in business, about 1700 and was soon appointed consular officer. The Consulate in those days was the bank and registry office for young

Englishmen on the grand tour; and it became a convenient way for the milord and dilettante to acknowledge the Consul's services by buying a picture from him. It solved, moreover, the ubiquitous and difficult question of tipping. Smith's first wife, Catherine Tofts, was a well-known singer, much admired by the Italians. It was through her that Smith first had entrée to the inner circle of contemporary artists. His second wife, Elizabeth Murray, was the sister of the King's Resident, so that those English noblemen that he did not meet in the banking rooms of the Consulate, he met at dinner at the Residence. The connection was profitable for Joseph Smith and indispensable for the royal collections – for Venice was at that particular brief moment even more than Antwerp or Amsterdam the art market of the world.

The *Memoirs* of Casanova de Seingalt recount the exploits of Smith, who maintained a fine palace on the Grand Canal as well as a gracious villa at Mogliano, between Mestre and Treviso. Horace Walpole in his letters is apt to sneer at Smith's pretensions as a patron of art. He was also the friend and patron of Canaletto, for whom he acted for nearly twenty-five years as business manager. Smith introduced him to English handlers and arranged the painter's visit to England. George III acquired from Smith 53 paintings by Canaletto – among the most superb of his romantic landscapes – and 100 drawings, most of which have remained in the royal collections. Nowhere can this artist be studied to better advantage. Smith also had acquired a fine cabinet of engraved gems and the collection of drawings and engravings belonging to Cardinal Alessandro Albani which was almost unrivaled in its representation of the seventeenth-century masters – particularly the Carracci, Domenichino, Poussin, Bernini and Maratta. To these he added the following pictures which his widow likewise sold to George III: 38 by Rosalba Carriera, 28 by Zuccarelli, 7 by Piazzetta, "21 flower pieces by Monsieur Baptiste," * 4 by Longhi and a group of miscellaneous paintings by Bellini, Veronese, Titian, Castiglione and many others.

But astute as he was as a collector of pictures, Smith's heart was above all in the library which he had formed slowly, piece by piece,

* Jean Baptiste Monnoyer – French seventeenth-century flower painter.

over thirty years and which he described so lovingly in his will.* It is evident that the Royal Purchaser for the Library mentioned by Consul Smith was George, Prince of Wales, who succeeded in 1760 to the throne as George III.

The inducement to the young prince to be in the fashion as a collector of books, pictures, and articles of *virtù* may be explained conjecturally in the following way. The Prince of Wales was, as is well known, very much under the influence of John Stuart, Earl of Bute, especially since the death of Frederick, Prince of Wales, in 1751. Bute was an enlightened amateur and dilettante, who formed a valuable library at Luton Hoo, and also had a good collection of pictures and engravings. This example, and that of other leading personages in high society, was likely to recommend itself to the young prince, if the materials were available. An agent for this purpose was forthcoming in Richard Dalton, who in 1750 accompanied the Earl of Charlemont on his tour to Greece and the East, and was one of the first to make drawings of the monuments of classical archaeology. Through the influence of Bute, Dalton became librarian to the Prince of Wales, and it can hardly be doubted that it was Dalton who negotiated with Consul Smith for the purchase of the latter's library and collection of works of art.†

After the accession of George III, Dalton was appointed not only Librarian, but also Keeper of Pictures and Antiquary in His Majesty's Household. He was among the first in England to draw and engrave classical antiquities and to engrave the portrait drawings by Holbein, then at Kensington Palace. He was also an early advocate for the establishment of a Royal Academy of Fine Arts. Dalton was likewise instrumental in bringing Bartolozzi, the engraver, to England. Be this as it may, George III purchased the Library and the collection of gems and cameos formed by Consul Smith, and a considerable portion, if not all, of the pictures and drawings.

While Smith's collections were primarily Italian he was responsible for introducing a number of Netherlandish pictures into the royal collections. Among those he acquired – and they were for the most part indifferent examples of the little Dutch masters – were three of

* The full text of the will is given by L. Cust, "Notes on Pictures in the Royal Collection," in the *Burlington Magazine*, vol. XXIII, pp. 150 ff.

† Lionel Cust, *Notes on Pictures in the Royal Collections*. Chatto and Windus, 1911.

MR. TOWNLEY'S COLLECTION

Engraved by Worthington after John Zoffany

LORD ELGIN

By G. P. Harding after Anton Graff. British Museum

great importance: two portraits by Rembrandt, *Young Man in a Turban* and *Rabbi with a Flat Cap*, and the heavenly *Lady at the Virginals* by Vermeer, one of the greatest Dutch pictures extant which was bought as a van Mieris for less than £100.

George III, probably the greatest liability to the British crown since King John, had managed to blunder happily into the Elysian fields of eighteenth-century collecting. May the pictures he acquired be a consolation for the colonies he lost in the opaque centuries that lie ahead.

CHAPTER VI

The Golden Age of the Dilettanti

By the middle of the century collecting had reached the same height of fashion which it had achieved in France a generation earlier. Not only had the court begun to take a faltering leadership, but the vogue extended far beyond the coterie of the nobility and included many commoners as well. A Frenchman wrote home from London, "A taste for pictures makes an article of their luxury; they sacrifice to this taste in proportion to their fortune." It was common knowledge among the dealers and private owners on the Continent that the Englishman would pay the top price for anything that took his fancy; nor was it overlooked that his knowledge was generally less than his enthusiasm. Many of the canvases which hung so triumphantly upon the walls of the great houses masqueraded under names to which they bore no possible allegiance.

So great had the vogue become that in 1766, scarcely five years after George III had ascended the throne, the professor of botany in the University of Cambridge, Thomas Martyn, published two volumes entitled *The English Connoisseur; Containing An Account Of Whatever Is Curious In Painting, Sculpture, Etc., In The Palaces And Seats Of The Nobility And Principal Gentry Of England.* Of the twenty-eight cabinets listed, four are parts of the royal collection distributed between Hampton Court, Kensington Palace, Saint James's Palace and Windsor Castle. Five of them are at the University of Oxford, in All Souls College, the Ashmolean Museum, the Bodleian Library, Christ Church College, New College, and the cabinet of General Guise. Among the other fine collections were those of the Dukes of Devonshire in his several places at Chatsworth, Hardwick Hall, Chiswick and Devonshire House in Piccadilly, of Marlborough at Blenheim Palace, and of Northumberland in Northumberland

House; the already world-famous cabinets of Sir Robert Walpole at Houghton Hall, of Earl Temple in Stowe House in Buckinghamshire, and the Earl of Pembroke at Wilton House in Wiltshire. There were also some minor cabinets that belonged to various knights and gentlemen, all of which reflected spottily and dimly the pattern set at Houghton by the Walpoles. Later in the century were added to this list the Dukes of Bedford and Hamilton, the Marquises of Lansdowne and Bute, the Earls of Exeter, Leicester, Warwick, Spencer, Burlington, Radnor and Egremont. Among the cabinets of the gentry those of Paul Methuen and Welbore Agar Ellis were destined to make future history.

More recently there has been found another list which sheds a new light upon the state of collecting in England in the middle of the century. Mr. Wilmarth S. Lewis discovered among his treasures at Farmington, Connecticut, a list written in Horace Walpole's own hand entitled *Collections Now in England, 1757* which he has generously allowed to be published here for the first time. It was written by Walpole on the flyleaf of one of the books he bought at Vertue's sale, *A Description of the Earl of Pembroke's Pictures*, published at Westminster in 1731. It is the most authentic record that exists of the extent of English collecting of the period and, taken in conjunction with the already well-known *Journals of Visits to Country Seats, etc.*, rounds out the picture which Walpole painted of the possessions of his contemporaries.

"COLLECTIONS NOW IN ENGLAND, 1757"

[It will be noted that he made subsequent additions.]

The King's, the chief at Kensington and Hampton Court.
The late Prince of Wales's, at Leicesterhouse.
The Earl of Orford's, at Houghton.
The Duke of Devonshire's, in Piccadilly: and miniatures, gems, andc.
Earl of Pembroke's, at Wilton, and great number of statues.
Sir Paul Methuen's, in Grosvenor Street.
Countess of Burlington's, at Chiswick, and in Piccadilly. She left them to the Duke of Devonshire.

Mr. Gideon's, in Kent.

General Guise's, now in Oxford.

Sir Gregory Page's, at Blackheath.

Lord Duncannon's, in Cavendish Square; and antique gems.

Lord Royston's (late Duke of Kent's) in Grosvenor Square (Changed by HW to St. James's).

Mr. Cleeve's, pewterer, in Kent.

Lord Harrington's, at Petersham.

Duke of Bedford, has a few.

Mr. Ward, the Chymist, at Whitehall. Sold.

Viscountess Dow. Cobham, a few, in Hanover Square. Sold.

Lord Westmorland, a few, at Mereworth.

General Campbell, at Somerset House and in Kent, and curiosities.*

Lord Carlisle, a few, and antique gems, china, marble, &c.

Countess of Cardigan, at Whitehall, a few, and many miniatures, &c.

Duchess of Portland, fine miniatures and curiosities, and shells.

Earl of Leicester, some pictures, and fine statues and drawings, at Holkham in Norfolk.

Lady Elizabeth Germayn, some fine pictures, magnificent cabinet of antique gems from the Arundel collection &c. sold by auction.

Horace Walpole, in Arlington Street, fine cabinet of miniatures, some pictures, antiques, medals, shells, china, prints, &c.

James West, Esq., coins, prints, curiosities. Sold by auction.

At the late Sir Andrew Fountain's at Narford, in Norfolk, a few pictures, antiques, and fine closet of Fayence.

Charles Hamilton, at Cobham, antique statues and busts.

Monsr. Harang, in Albemarle Street, pictures. Sold.

Sir Luke Schaub, in Dover Street, do [Sold by auction in 1758 at extravagant prices, for near £8000s].

Charles Frederick, in Berkeley Square, coins and antiquities.

Dr. Ducarel, coins.

Dr. Chauncy, prints and antiquities.

Various other persons have collections, particularly of coins and prints, and of a few pictures.

The Earl of Exeter has great quantities of pictures at Burleigh, but they are chiefly of Luca Jordano and the scholars of Carlo Maratti.

Earl of Bristol has pictures and bronzes, in St. James's Square.

* The best pictures and all the drawings were kept by his son Lord Fred. Campbell; the rest of the collection was sold. [H. W.]

Mrs. Cavendish of little Burlington Street has some pictures and a fine collection of agates, precious stones &c. that were her father's, Lord James Cavendish.

Within a few years have been sold and dispersed the great library of Sclater Bacon of Cambridgeshire, the noble collection of antiquities, pictures, prints, books and pamphlets of Edward Harley Earl of Oxford, the valuable collections of coins of Mr. Fairfax and Martin Folkes, the numerous library of Dr. Rawlinson, the collection of various sorts of Mr. Sadler, and above all the well chosen and rich collection of pictures, books and antiquities of Dr. Meade.

The fine collections of drawings of Mr. Richardson and Mr. Pond are sold.

Duke of Marlborough at Blenheim has some fine pictures, particularly of Rubens bought by the old Duchess, and the fine Sunderland library, collected by his father.

Earl Waldegrave has one room of pictures, of which about a dozen are very fine. They were collected by his father while Ambassador at Paris. The capital one is a Madonna and Child by Raphael in his second manner, very clear and well preserved, and was given to him by Prince Charles. Sold by auction.

Mr. Spenser has some fine pictures and drawings.

Earl of Cholmondeley and Mr. Trevor Hampden, drawings.

Earl of Egremont and Mr. Hans Stanley have a few good pictures.

Captain William Hamilton, pictures.
Mrs. Dunch at Whitehall has a very few pictures, but fine. } [Sold 1761]

Lord Viscount Folkstone at Longford near Salisbury has about a dozen good pictures – one of his Clauds is inferior to no picture of that Master.

Mr. Hum. Morrice has a few fine pictures that were Sir. William Morrice's.

[Earl of Waldegrave's collection was sold in 1763 for £2800s.]

* * * * *

The cabinet of Dr. Mead, which Walpole lists only in passing, illustrates the persistence of the Augustan taste in the first half of the eighteenth century and epitomizes the ideal of the gentleman's collections. It was, of course, more learned and less amusing than Horace Walpole's, but perhaps its unique quality was that it was formed and kept in London where it became a rendezvous for cultivated society; it did not serve, as did the contemporary cabinets in the country seats, as a framework for the prestige of the nobility.

Dr. Mead exemplified the growing prestige of the physician and the new place which he occupied in society, characteristic of the middle of the eighteenth century. He was no longer the barber-surgeon of Molière's comedies; he was the recognized man of science who was at the same time conversant with the humanities. Dr. Johnson, who knew the famous physician intimately, declared that "Dr. Mead lived more in the broad sunshine of life than almost any man." His collection stands midway between that of Sir Hans Sloane and that of the Earl of Orford, to both of whom he was by a few years junior.

The fashion for collecting among physicians was not new; but in the eighteenth century it became them to surround themselves with something more decorative than bottled specimens in spirits. Rouquet, the Swiss-French enameler, has drawn a rather ironic picture of the doctor. After enlarging upon his costume, his sword, his ample and well-combed periwig, his chariot, his vanity and his erudition, the author goes on to note that he had, almost invariably, a hobby: "One, busies himself with paintings, antiquities or prints; the next, with natural curiosities in general, or with particular departments of them; some preserve in bottles all the *lusus naturae* that are discovered or invented; others devote their energies to objects more agreeable, and are 'gallants.' " And he continues maliciously: "This apparent inattention with which the English practitioners exercised their calling is sometimes of inestimable value to the patient. Nature, it is suggested, frequently takes advantage of their negligence to exert all her own efforts in effecting a cure." *

But Dr. Mead's stature carried him far beyond the danger of Rouquet's barbs. His friend Dr. Maty wrote of him: "No foreigner of any learning, taste, or even curiosity ever came to England without being introduced to Dr. Mead; as it would have been a matter of reproach to have returned without seeing him. On these occasions his table was

* William T. Whitley, *Artists and Their Friends in England 1700–1799*. Medici, 1928, p. 28.

always open, where, what seldom happens, the magnificence of princes was united with the pleasure of philosophers."

His early training was obtained in Holland whither his father had fled because of the suspicion of Puritan sympathies. Having completed his medical studies he went to Italy, and while he was looking in an attic for something which he required for the continuation of his medical experiments, he discovered the first antique to enter his collection. On his return to England, his experiments with snake poison and other aspects of the new toxicology earned him sufficient fame to be called by the court to the deathbed of Queen Anne. His practice was as great as his popularity and it is estimated that his income was somewhere between five and seven thousand pounds a year. "Clergymen, and in general all men of learning, were welcome to his advice, and his doors were always open every morning to the most indigent, whom he frequently assisted with his purse; so that notwithstanding his great gains he did not die very rich." This same biographer declared that "his large and spacious house in Great Ormond Street was converted into a temple of nature, and a repository of time."

He built a gallery for his favorite furniture, his pictures and his antiquities. His library contained upwards of 10,000 volumes in which he spared no expense for scarce and ancient editions, for copies well chosen and highly preserved, for the richest and most durable bindings. The Latin, Greek and Oriental manuscripts and the collections of antiques, medals, coins, prints and drawings,* were "equaled by nothing in the kingdom in the hands of a private man." Several pieces of ancient painting and among others that of the court of Augustus, found in Rome in 1737, had cost him vast sums. And as for his collection of pictures by the great masters, "they had been chosen with so much judgment, that after his death they were sold for £3,400, that is about six or seven hundred pounds more than the money he gave for them." In addition to his splendid antiquities of

* The Royal Library at Windsor contains a large group of drawings assembled by Dr. Mead which were acquired by Frederick Lewis, Prince of Wales, for the royal collection. Many of the items were by Poussin and also was included the large series of drawings of Roman antiquities by Bartoli which had come from the library of Cardinal Massimo in Rome.

which one was a bronze head of *Homer* from the collection of the Earl of Arundel,* he had a cabinet of bronzes and a collection of coins and gems.

The picture collection, which included nearly all of the names of the artists admired at Houghton Hall, had in addition certain works which reflected the doctor's medical predilections. There was, for example, a painting by Spagnoletto of the *Flaying of St. Bartholomew* which attracted him "by its just anatomical expression of the muscles." And Pannini painted for him *The Landing of Aesculapius at Rome at the Time of the Plague.* Watteau, suffering from consumption, had journeyed to England in 1719 to put himself under Dr. Mead's care and while there painted two pictures for him, *L'Amour Paisible* and the *Comédiens Italiens.* These canvases, which had opened Dr. Mead's door to other French contemporaries, were sold after the latter's death in 1754 for £42 and £52.10, respectively, and the only drawing by Watteau in the collection fetched a guinea, and this at a time when Frederick the Great of Prussia was willing to pay any price for a work of art by this master.

Sir Osbert Sitwell and Margaret Barton † have contributed a valuable analysis of the Mead collection — an analysis that is equally true of all of the cabinets of the day:

> Although it must be kept in mind that this was no casual display of taste but both the life work and the life recreation of a patron of genius and a man in other directions of marked ability, it is interesting to reflect on so noble a collection, and to deduce what we can from the presence and absence of certain objects. It resembled other galleries formed at this period in its scope, which was extremely heterogeneous; for though possessed of a genuinely aesthetic outlook, Dr. Mead had doubtless inherited the traditional point of view of the English connoisseur, and perhaps feeling it his duty, and at the same time inspired by the scientific spirit which had accompanied his profession, had amassed objects of curiosity as much as of beauty. Thus besides books, drawings, prints and statuary it contained fossils, Egyptian mummies and animals preserved in spirits. As for the pictures, the catalogue of the sale enumerates: 45 portraits by

* Now in the British Museum.

† Cf. their essay on "Taste" *in Johnson's England,* ed. by Turberville. Clarendon Press, 1933. II, 19.

Holbein, Titian, Rubens, Rembrandt, Hals, Ramsay, Richardson, Kneller and others; 23 landscapes and sea pieces by Claude, G. Poussin, Rembrandt, Breughel, Salvator Rosa, Vandeveldt and others; 13 architectural and ruin pictures by Canaletto, Pannini, and N. Poussin. 14 Dutch still-lives and animal pictures. 55 historical pictures by Julio Romano, Veronese, V. Carracci, Rubens, Solimena, Van Dyck, Watteau, Bourdon, Guercino, Teniers, N. Poussin, Borgognone, Barrochio, Palma Vecchio, Gerard Dou, G. Poussin, Rembrandt, Carlo Maratti.

Among the remaining pictures were five copies and some sketches by Raphael. The pictures realized together just over £3400. The highest sum given for any one item was £183 paid for a Carlo Maratti, Sir Joshua's favorite painter. Works by Holbein, Rubens and Claude came next in price, and brought in over £100 each. . . .

No primitives are mentioned in the account of the sale. To the eighteenth century the dawn of painting was the Renaissance. No artist earlier than Raphael was admired, because the kingdom of art was entirely limited to the pictures produced since his birth, and to the works of Romans and Greeks, though not of the archaic Greeks. Nothing else existed in it. Then again, there is no representative of the Spanish school of any period; but this was because for many years to come the student was obliged, if he wished to see a single Spanish picture, to visit Spain. The work of the great Spanish artists was the property of the Crown or else belonged to rich convents and grandees. Moreover, exportation was prohibited under severe penalties. But Dr. Mead was not alone in his display of real taste and knowledge. Whatever its absurdities, the Grand Tour was year by year educating the patrons and through them benefiting the arts. English painting was beginning to blossom at last.

The pattern of English collecting had thus been established, a pattern which was to continue until the close of the nineteenth century. The country houses and town houses of the United Kingdom were to become the happy hunting ground for the collectors of the present day. Had the persons on Horace Walpole's list neglected the opportunities lying at their feet, there would not be any National Gallery in London and the very idea of museums in America would never have been born.

* * * * *

In the light of the expenditure on art, the failure of the collector to patronize the home-grown industry resulted inevitably in a popular heresy against the old masters. In the clubs and in the coffeehouses the wits, goaded by their artist friends, lampooned the fashionable English *curieux* and pilloried the dealers who were coining money while the artists starved. It was the same old wicked world that we find today in which virtue went unrewarded and the arts were sacrificed to the worshipers of Baal. Hogarth (who was to show his resentment by his famous tailpiece to the catalogue of the 1761 Exhibition which represented "an Ape Dressed as a Fop assiduously watering three dead plants") felt so bitterly on this point that he wrote an article which appeared in the *London Magazine* * in which he says:

> The picture jobbers from abroad are always ready to raise a cry in the public prints, whenever they think their craft is in danger; and indeed, it is their interest to depreciate every English work as hurtful to their trade of importing, by shiploads, dead Christs, Holy Families, Madonnas, and other dismal dark subjects on which they scrawl the names of Italian masters, and fix on us poor Englishmen the character of universal dupes. If a gentleman with some judgment casts his eyes on one of those pictures, and expresses doubt as to its originality or perfection, the quack answers, "Sir, you are no connoisseur; the picture is I assure you, in Alesso Baldminetto's second and best manner, boldly painted, and truly sublime; the contour gracious; the air of the head in the high Greek taste; and a most divine idea it is." Then, spitting in an obscure place, and rubbing it with a handkerchief, takes a skip to t'other end of the room and screams out in raptures, "There's an amazing touch! A man should have this picture a twelve-month before he can discover all its beauties!" The gentleman, though possessed of judgment, ashamed to be out of the fashion by judging for himself, is struck dumb by this cant, gives a vast sum for the picture, though he modestly confesses that he is indeed quite ignorant of painting, and bestows upon a frightful picture with a hard name, without which it would not be worth a farthing, a frame worth fifty pounds.

The French, and there was a considerable colony of mediocre artists who had settled in London because their talents were not appreciated in Paris, were among the leaders in the revolt. Rouquet,

* As early as 1737.

the critic, devoted pages of his journal to describing the auction rooms to which the fashionable world attended, and the rowdy scenes and fights, the competitions among the bidders for however trifling a fragment of an antique statue or a canvas by the hand of some name accepted by the world of fashion. And Roubiliac, the French sculptor whose ivory soap orators, statesmen and warriors, cluttering up its transepts, have done so much to chill the marrow of Westminster Abbey's exquisite Gothic bones, trumpeted:

Prétendu connoisseur qui sur l'antique glose
Idolotrant le nom sans connaître la chose,
Vrai peste des beaux-arts, sans goût, sans Équité,
Quittez ce ton pédant, ce mépris affecté
Pour tout ce que le temps n'a pas encore gâté.
Ne peux-tu pas, en admirant
Les maîtres de la Grèce et ceux de l'Italie,
Rendre justice également
À ceux qu'a nourris ta Patrie?
Vois ce salon et tu perdras
Cette prévention injuste;
Et bien étonné, conviendras
Qu'il ne faut pas qu'un Mécenas
Pour revoir le Siècle d'Auguste.

The theater, however, offered the most entertaining forum in which to hurl insults at the fashionable taste. Vauxhall and Ranelagh competed for the last bon mot at the expense of the collectors, and in a series of entertainments given by Foote at the Little Theatre in the Haymarket in the 1750's, called *Foote's Giving Tea to His Friends*, was a comedy called *Taste*.

In the preface Foote says, "I was determined to brand those Goths in science who have prostituted the useful study of antiquity to trifling superficial purposes, and who had blasted the progress of the elegant arts among us by unpardonable frauds and absurd prejudices." This farce is so amusing and so characteristic of the art world of the eighteenth century (and of the time-honored practices today on Fifty-seventh Street, on Bond Street and the rue de la Boëtie) that it seems worth while to revive at least a part of it for the modern reader in the pages of this book.

TASTE – A COMEDY BY FOOTE

ACT I SCENE I – *A Painting-Room*

* * * * *

(*Enter* BOY *with* PUFF)

BOY. Mr. Puff, Sir.

CARMINE. Let us be private. What have you there?

PUFF. Two of Rembrandt's etchings by Scrape, in May's Buildings; – a paltry affair – a poor ten-guinea job; however, a small game – you know the proverb – What became of you yesterday?

CARMINE. I was detained by Sir Positive Bubble. How went the pictures? The Guido, what did that fetch?

PUFF. One hundred and thirty.

CARMINE. Hum! four guineas the frame, three the painting; then we divide just one hundred and twenty-three.

PUFF. Hold – not altogether so fast – Varnish had two pieces for bidding against Squander, and Brush five for bringing Sir Tawdry Trifle.

CARMINE. Mighty well. Look ye, Mr. Puff, if these people are eternally quartered on us, I declare off, sir; they eat up the profit. There's that damned Brush – but you'll find him out. I have, upon his old plan, given him copies of all the work I executed upon his recommendation; and what was the consequence? He clandestinely sold the copies, and I have all the originals in my lumber-room.

PUFF. Come, come, Carmine, you are no great loser by that. Ah! that lumber-room! – that lumber-room out of repair is the best-conditioned estate in the county of Middlesex. Why, now, there's your Susannah; it could not have produced you above twenty at most; and, by the addition of your lumber-room dirt, and the salutary application of the 'spaltham-pot, it became a Guido, worth a hundred and thirty pounds; besides, in all traffic of this kind, there must be combinations. Varnish and Brush are our jackals, and it is but fair they should partake of the prey. Courage, my boy! never fear!

Praise be to Folly and Fashion, there are, in this town, dupes enough to gratify the avarice of us all.

* * * * *

ACT II Scene I – *An Auction-Room*

(*Enter* Puff *as* M. le Baron de Groningen, Carmine *as* Canto, *and* Brush. *To them* Lord Dupe, *etc.*)

Lord. Sir, you have obliged me. All these you have marked in the catalogue are originals?

Brush. Undoubted. But, my lord, you need not depend solely on my judgment; here's Mynheer Baron de Groningen, who is come hither to survey and purchase for the Elector of Bavaria, – an indisputable connoisseur; his bidding will be a direction for your lordship. 'Tis a thousand pities that any of these masters should quit England. They were conducted hither at an immense expense; and if they now leave us, what will it be but a public declaration that all taste and liberal knowledge is vanished from amongst us?

Lord. Sir, leave the support of the national credit to my care. Could you introduce me to Mynheer? Does he speak English?

Brush. Not fluently, but so as to be understood. Mynheer, Lord Dupe, the patron of the arts, the Petronius for taste, and for well-timed generosity, the Leo – and the Maecenas – of the present age, desires to know you.

Puff. Sir, you honour me very mightily. I was hear of Lord Dupes in Hollandt. I was tell he was one delatant, one curieuse, one precieuse of his country.

Lord. The Dutch are an obliging, civilised, well-bred, pretty kind of people. But pray, sir, what occasions us the honour of a visit from you?

Puff. I was to come for paints for de Elector of Bavaria.

Lord. Are there any here that deserve your attention?

Puff. Oh! dare are good pieces; but dare is one I likes mightily; the off sky, and home track is fine, and the maister is in it.

Lord. What is the subject?

Canto. It is, my lord, St. Anthony of Padua exorcising the devil out of a ram-cat; it has a companion somewhere – oh! here, which is the same saint in a wilderness, reading his breviary by the light of a glow-worm.

BRUSH. Invaluable pictures, both! and will match your Lordship's Corregio in the saloon.

LORD. I'll have them. What pictures are those, Mr. Canto?

CANTO. They are not in the sale; but I fancy I could procure them for your Lordship.

LORD. This, I presume, might have been a landscape; but the water, and the men, and the trees, and the dogs, and the ducks, and the pigs, they are obliterated – all gone.

BRUSH. An indisputable mark of its antiquity – its very merit; besides, a little varnish will fetch the figures again.

LORD. Set it down for me. The next?

CANTO. That is a *Moses in the Bulrushes.* The blended joy and grief in the figure of the sister in the corner, the distress and anxiety of the mother here, and the beauty and benevolence of Pharaoh's daughter, are circumstances happily imagined, and boldly expressed.

BRUSH. Lack-a-day, 'tis but a modern performance; the master is alive, and an Englishman.

LORD. Oh! then I would not give it house-room.

* * * * *

(*Enter Novice*)

* * * * *

BRUSH. Mr. Canto, the gentleman would be glad to see the busts, medals, and precious reliques of Greece and ancient Rome.

CANTO. Perhaps, sir, we may shew him something of greater antiquity – Bring them forward – The first lot consists of a hand without an arm, the first joint of the forefinger gone, supposed to be a limb of the Apollo Delphos – the second, half a foot, with the toes entire, of the Juno Lucine – the third, the Caduceus of the Mercurius Infernalis – the fourth, the half of the leg of the infant Hercules – all indisputable antiques, and of the Memphian marble.

PUFF. Let me see Juno's half foot. All the toes entire?

CANTO. All.

PUFF. Here is a little swelt by this toe, that looks bad proportion.

ALL. Hey, hey.

PUFF. What's dat?

CANTO. That? pshaw! that? why that's only a corn.

ALL. Oh!

PUFF. Corn! dat was extreme natural; dat is fine, the maister is in it.

ALL. Very fine! invaluable!

* * * * *

CANTO. Bring forward the head from Herculaneum. Now, gentlemen, here is a jewel.

ALL. Ay, ay, let's see.

CANTO. 'Tis not entire, though.

NOV. So much the better.

CANTO. Right, sir; the very mutilations of this piece are worth all the most perfect performances of modern artists. Now, gentlemen, here's a touchstone for your taste!

ALL. Great! great, indeed!

NOV. Great! amazing! divine! Oh, let me embrace the dear, dismembered bust! – a little farther off! I'm ravished! I am transported! What an attitude! But then the locks! How I adore the simplicity of the ancients! How unlike the present priggish, prick-eared puppets! How gracefully they fall all adown the cheek! – so decent, and so grave, and – who the devil do you think it is, Brush? Is it a man or a woman?

CANTO. The connoisseurs differ. Some will have it to be the Jupiter Tonans of Phidias, and others the Venus of Paphos from Praxiteles; but I don't think it fierce enough for the first, nor handsome enough for the last.

NOV. Yes, handsome enough.

ALL. Very handsome, handsome enough.

CANTO. Not quite; therefore I am inclined to join with Signor Julio de Pampedillo, who, in a treatise dedicated to the King of the Two Sicilies, calls it the Serapis of the Egyptians, and supposes it to have been fabricated about eleven hundred and three years before the Mosaic account of the creation.

NOV. Prodigious! and I dare swear true.

ALL. Oh, true; very true!

PUFF. Upon my honour, 'tis a very fine bust; but where is de nose?

NOV. The nose? what care I for the nose? Where is de nose? Why, sir, if it had a nose, I would not give sixpence for it. How the devil should we distinguish the works of the ancients, if they were perfect? The nose, indeed. Why, I don't suppose, now, but, barring the nose, Roubiliac could cut as good a head every whit. Brush, who is this man with his nose? The fellow should know something of something, too, for he speaks broken English.

BRUSH. It is Mynheer Groningen, a great connoisseur in painting.

NOV. That may be; but as to sculpture, I am his very humble servant. A man must know damn little of statuary that dislikes a bust for want of a nose.

CANTO. Right, sir; the nose itself, without the head, nay in another's possession, would be an estate; but here we are behind, gentlemen and ladies, an equestrian statue of Marcus Aurelius without the horse, and a complete statue of the Emperor Trajan, with only the head and legs missing; both from Herculaneum. This way, gentlemen and ladies.

CHAPTER VII

The Royal Academy

THE first attempt at founding an academy of the arts in England had been made by Charles I, who instituted the Museum Minervae in 1636, the eleventh year of his reign. Only gentlemen were to be admitted and they were to be instructed in arts, sciences, languages and sports. The academy fell to nothing when the rest of the King's plans were crushed by the Commonwealth.*

Another plan for an academy of arts had been sketched by John Evelyn in 1662; but it was not until 1711 that the first school for drawing or painting from the life was organized. Its cosmopolitan group of supporters included Sir Godfrey Kneller, Michael Dahl, Antonio Pellegrini, Louis Laguerre, Jonathan Richardson and James Thornhill. A subscription of a guinea each was levied, and suitable premises for the new institution were found in Great Queen Street, which was then, as for the past two centuries, greatly favored by the painters. On Saint Luke's Day, October 18, the subscribers to "the academy met in the ruinous mansion which was to be their home" and unanimously elected Kneller as governor. Among the members of the new academy was James Seymour, the father of the artist and a wealthy collector of the period, as well as Mr. Owen McSwiney, an Irish dramatist and theatrical manager who had lived in Venice and had acted as the intermediary between Canaletto, Rosalba and the other artists and their patrons in England. The father-in-law of Hogarth, Sir James Thornhill, became its second governor in 1715.

The struggle for the recognition of the artists had long been the principal preoccupation of Hogarth's career; but it was not until the exhibition of 1761 that the issue came finally to a head; for, prior to

* Much of the material that follows is taken from John Pye, *Patronage of British Art*. Longman, Brown, Green, and Longman, 1845.

the accession of George III, there had been no spontaneous or consistent patronage and recognition of native talent in the British Isles. At this time Hogarth complained:

> Whilst the wealthy collectors were furnishing their mansions with objects of *virtù* and enriching the dealers, the artists followed their various employments from portrait to sign painting and continued to study at their private academy. They had become more numerous and notwithstanding the discountenance experienced by British art, genius and cultivated intellect had arisen among them. The Turk's Head, Gerrard Street, Soho, had become their rendezvous for transacting matters of business and to many of them it was also a resort for passing their social hours. There, perhaps, some of them occasionally ruminated on their inability to give practical effect to their resolutions of emancipating themselves from the thraldom in which they were held and on those fascinations of art by which they had been seduced to follow it with little countenance or reward in a country where poverty is infamous. For as they possessed neither property nor political power in common, with the exception of the portrait painter, they had no recognized right to respectful consideration.

The abortive efforts to found an academy during the reigns of George I and George II had, in fact, left the artist with very little hope of any kind of patronage or encouragement from the crown. The social position of the artist was not exalted. If he was attached to or protected by a nobleman he was little better than a servant or a tradesman. It would probably have been better for him had he never tried to acquire social status, observed Steegmann, for thereby he gained but little and lost a measure of his independence; "by entering the higher social world he became inevitably subject to the prejudices and snobbery of that world; so there must have been every inducement to escape these positions suggested in a letter written in 1743 by Lady Charlotte Fermor to her mother Lady Pomfret: 'After supper we all danced to our own singing in order to teach Signor Casali (an Italian they have in the house) English country dances; he is a painter, and I fancy as low-born as they generally are, though by means of an order he wears, set in diamonds (which he tells me was given him by the King of Prussia and which very few people can have), and some fine suits of clothes he passes for the most complete fine gentleman in the world, and is treated upon an equal footing with the rest of the company.' " *

At long last, amidst the confusion of the world of fashion, a circular appeared in the coffeehouses of London:

Academy of Painting, Sculpture, etc. St. Martin's Lane 23rd October 1753.

There is a scheme on foot for creating a public academy for the improvement of painting, sculpture and architecture and it is thought necessary to have a certain number of professors, with proper authority, in order to making regulations, taking subscriptions, etc., erecting a building, instructing the students, and concerting all such measures as shall be afterwards thought necessary. Your company is desired at the Turk's Head in Gerrard Street, Soho, on the 13th November at 5 in the evening to proceed with the election of 13 painters, 3 sculptors, 1 chaser, 2 engravers and 2 architects, in all 24 for the purposes aforesaid. (*Signed*)

Francis Milner Newton, Secretary.

A short time later, in 1755, another project was set on foot looking forward to the establishment and the obtaining of a charter for a royal academy. It was signed by some twenty of the leading artists of the day. It proposed "that the establishment should consist of a president, thirty directors, fellows and scholars, and be called the Royal Academy of London for the Improvement of Painting, Sculpture and Architecture." It also carried with it an appeal for funds and this was forwarded to the noblemen and gentlemen who composed the Society of the Dilettanti and who were already doing such Trojan service in the furtherance of classical archaeology and *virtù.* Almost immediately difficulties arose between the artists and the Dilettanti; the latter, finding that they could participate neither in the government of the academy nor in the appropriation of their own funds, broke off negotiations; and "the wealthy English generally to whom the appeal was made, having at that time no interest either in British art or artists, the project of course failed; and the defeated artists retired once more to their habitual obscurity, to contemplate the peculiarity of their new position, their appeal to the country having proclaimed their luckless views and helpless condition."

* Steegmann, *op. cit.*, p. 98.

It is paradoxical that Hogarth, who had fought all his life such a bitter struggle for the recognition of the artist, was himself opposed to the establishment of a royal academy; his principal objection being that "though academies sometimes improve genius, they never create it," and that they tend to create artists, while it was patronage of high art that was wanted and needed in England:

In Holland selfishness is the ruling passion; in England vanity is united with it. Portrait painting, therefore, ever has, and ever will succeed in this country better than in any other. The demand will be as constant as new faces arise; and with this we must be contented, for it will be vain to attempt to force what can never be accomplished, at least by such institutions as Royal Academies on the system now in agitation. If, hereafter, the times alter, the arts, like water, will find their level. Among causes that militate against either painting or sculpture succeeding in this nation, we must place our religion, which, inculcating unadorned simplicity, doth not require, nay, absolutely forbids, images for worship or pictures to excite enthusiasm. Paintings are considered as pieces of furniture, and Europe is already overstocked with the works of other ages. These, with copies countless as the sands on the seashore, are bartered to and fro, and are quite sufficient for the demands of the curious, who naturally prefer scarce, expensive, and far-fetched productions, to those they might have on low terms at home. Who can be expected to give 40 guineas for a modern landscape, though in ever so superior a style, when we can purchase one which, for little more than double the sum named, is warranted original by a solemn-faced connoisseur? This considered, can it excite wonder that the arts have not taken such deep root in this soil as in places where the people cultivate them from a kind of religious necessity, and where proficients have so much more profit in the pursuit? Whether it is to our honor or disgrace, I will not presume to say; but the fact is indisputable, that the public encourage trade in mechanics rather than painting and sculpture. Is it then reasonable to think that the artist, who, to obtain essential excellence in his profession, should have the talents of a Shakespeare, a Milton or a Swift, will follow this tedious and laborious study merely for fame, when his next-door neighbor, perhaps a porter brewer, or haberdasher of small wares, can, without any genius, accumulate an enormous fortune in a few years, become a Lord Mayor, or a Member of Parliament and purchase a title for his heir? Surely no; for as very few painters get even moderately rich, it is not reasonable to expect that they should waste their lives in cultivating the higher branch of the arts, until their country becomes more alive to its importance, and better disposed to reward their labors. These are the true causes that have retarded our progress.

But notwithstanding Hogarth's point of view, the need for a royal academy was in the air. Already another attempt at creating such an institution had been made by the Incorporated Society of Artists in Great Britain in 1765. The latter took a house in Pall Mall and over the door was inscribed "The Royal Academy." Apparently there was some justification for this suggestion of royal patronage. The King had, in some manner or other, approved the scheme and had subscribed £100 to the funds of the society; but dissensions soon arose and the seceding party lost no time in creating an institution of its own.

* * * * *

The opportunity for the artists in London to see works of art at this time was very limited; for even among the private collections (with the exception of that of Dr. Mead, who had opened his house habitually to students), the fees or tips which it was necessary to give the servants were so exorbitant that the average art student could not possibly afford to visit the collections. The Duke of Richmond had opened his gallery of statuary at Whitehall as a studio for young artists in 1760. It was furnished with casts of the most celebrated ancient and modern figures at Rome and at Florence. The invitation given to students was by public advertisement, and the gallery was for some time presided over by Mr. Cipriani, who recorded "that the result was a purer taste among British artists in the drawing of the human figure than that which they had previously displayed."

Curiously enough, the history of the Royal Academy (and the patronage of British art in general) is closely interwoven with that of the Foundling Hospital whose destiny had run parallel with that of the Academy and which was to give such encouragement to British art. The reign of George II had already witnessed the rise of a number of charitable organizations of various kinds, supported by voluntary contribution and later by parliamentary grants. The Foundling Hospital, whose very existence seemed to offend the morality of the day, had attracted the attention of the artists – particularly Hogarth – who found in it a weapon against the society which he was attacking so vigorously in his popular print series such as the *Rake's Progress* and the *Harlot's Progress*. The patronage of art in turn by this hospital by exhibiting contemporary work was a device looking towards a respectability which neither the foundling nor the artist seemed to have in eighteenth-century London.* There is, therefore, a certain irony in the circumstance that the Foundling Hospital was accused of encouraging both the production of bastards and of British artists.

The Foundling Hospital – or as it was then called, the Hospital for the Maintenance and Education of Exposed and Deserted Young Children – had been founded in 1739 by the big-hearted Captain Coram out of the profits of his trading vessel. Immediately it began to fill a need in the charitable life of London and won the instant support of the artists, who could not fail to recognize the tragedy of the deserted children who were brought to its door. A basket was hung at the gate of the hospital for the reception of infants and notice of each arrival was given by the clanging of a great iron bell. So great, indeed, was the demand for admission that between the years 1756 and 1760 14,900 children were admitted. The hospital was unable to accommodate the foundlings presented to it so that the mothers who brought them were all obliged to wait outside the gate while they balloted with balls out of a bag to see which children would be admitted or thrown back on the world.

Unable to make financial contributions, but thoroughly aroused to the conditions which made the hospital so necessary, the artists contributed to it by their works. Handel and Hogarth both became governors. The former gave a benefit performance of the *Firework Music* and composed the "Foundling Hospital Anthem." He later gave annual performances of *The Messiah* for the charity. Hogarth's first gift in 1740 was his portrait of *Captain Coram* and later on he raffled

* Lord Brougham had denounced the hospital in the Lords by saying, "All men are now agreed that such establishments are not charity, but nuisances of an enormous nature, having the direct effect of encouraging immorality and increasing infanticide; and the funds destined to support these hospitals have been otherwise employed, the name alone being maintained."

his large picture, *The March of the Guards*, for the hospital. All but a few tickets were sold; the latter were given to the hospital, including the winning ticket, and the picture, which now hangs in the Court Room, and for which the governors of our own day were to refuse £50,000, became its property.

Other artists followed the example of Hogarth, by giving and promising to give works of art to the establishment. On the thirty-first of December, 1746, a General Court was held at the hospital, and elected a group of artists who had donated their works to be governors, with authority to meet at the Foundling annually on the fifth of November, "to consider what further ornaments may be added to the building without expense to the charity." Thus authorized, "the artist governors commenced holding their annual business meetings there; and, regarding liberty as the parent and friend of the arts, they made themselves convivial by dining together and by drinking claret and punch as was the custom of that time, in commemoration of the landing of King William III, which practice was continued for many years."

"The progressive course of these events," observes Pye, "with the sanction of the King, the Parliament and the aristocracy rendered the Foundling Hospital a place of immense attraction, general resort, and rendezvous, for people of all classes; and the contributions made by the artists, partly portraits of its distinguished patrons, constituting as they did the first collection of British works of art to which the public had the right of admission, contributed to no inconsiderable degree to increase that attraction; and by making certain artists known and talked of by the multitude as lions of their day, acquired for the few some of those advantages which the many had long sought in vain and hence arose the first idea of the whole body of British artists presenting themselves before the world by making a public exhibition of their works."

Finally, in November 1759, a general meeting was held at the Turk's Head in Soho when it was resolved that "once in every year, on a day in the second week in April, at a place that shall be appointed by a committee for carrying the design into execution, to be chosen annually, every painter, sculptor, architect, engraver, chaser, seal cutter and medalist may exhibit their several performances. *That the intention of the meeting is to endeavor to procure a sum of money to be distributed in charity towards the support of those artists whose age and infirmities, or other lawful hindrances, prevent them from being any longer candidates for fame.* And it is resolved that the sum of one shilling be taken daily of each person who may come to visit the said performances." The objection to the society's taking money at the door of the Foundling Hospital was got around by admitting the public free but charging sixpence for each catalogue that was sold. This, then, is the origin of the annual exhibitions of contemporary British art which to this day have been the backbone of the Royal Academy.

But with that capacity for dissension which is part of the artist's genius, the various groups of artists quickly fell to fighting with one another, and from 1760 to the opening of the Royal Academy of Arts on the second day of January, 1769, by royal proclamation, there was held a series of rival exhibitions and competitive entertainments.* By 1770, however, the various rival organizations had been eclipsed and the Royal Academy emerged as the unchallenged body under the leadership of Sir Joshua Reynolds. The primary purpose of the Academy as it was put before the King was a teaching institution and a fellowship for the artists. Sir Joshua Reynolds was chosen for the first president. He was knighted and in the spring of 1769 the first exhibition of the Royal Academy took place. Sir Joshua pronounced the following solemn words:

Gentlemen, – an Academy in which the polite arts may be regularly cultivated is at last opened among us by Royal munificence. This must appear an event in the highest degree interesting, not only to the artists, but to the whole nation. It is indeed difficult to give any other reason why an Empire like that of Britain should so long have wanted an ornament so suitable to its greatness, than that slow progression of things which naturally makes elegance and refinement the last effects of opulence and power. An institution like this has often been recommended upon considerations merely mercantile; but an academy founded upon

* A diploma had been obtained from the King in the last weeks of the preceding year.

such principles can never effect even its own narrow purposes. If it has an origin no higher, no taste can ever be formed, manufactured; but, the higher arts of design flourish, their inferior ends will be answered, of course. We are happy in having a Prince who has conceived the design of such an institution according to its true dignity, and to promote the arts as the head of a great, a learned, a polite, and commercial nation; I can now congratulate you, Gentlemen, on the accomplishment of your long and ardent wishes. The numberless and ineffectual consultations which I have had with many a person to form plans and concert schemes for an academy afford sufficient proof of the improbability of succeeding but by the influence of Majesty. But there have, perhaps, been times when even the influence of Majesty would have been ineffectual; and it is pleasing to reflect we are thus embodied, when every circumstance seems to concur from which honor and prosperity can possibly arrive. . . .

Having killed its rivals, the Academy quickly became the fashion of all London. The King, persuaded first by Reynolds and then by its second president, the American historical painter Benjamin West, had at last through the Academy assured the social position of the artist in England.

To the student the Academy was certainly a blessing. A traveling scholarship enabled the winner to work for a year in Rome. The drawing school had the most eminent anatomist of the day, Dr. William Hunter, as its professor. Four men of different types were employed in the life class, each receiving five shillings a week with a shilling extra for each sitting. Women models, disapproved of by the morality of the day, were paid half a guinea for a sitting of two or three hours. There was a rule that no person under twenty should draw from the female model unless he was married. Further it was decided that no one, "the Royal family excepted, is admitted into the Academy during the time the female model is sitting."

This propriety may be compared with the public outcry against the casts of nudes in a room adjoining the great gallery at Somerset House. They were said to be "the terror of every decent woman in England." One newspaper declared that men and women rather than pass them by had sacrificed the pleasure of seeing the pictures.

* * * * *

In the first of his discourses Sir Joshua states "that the principal advantage of an Academy is, that, besides furnishing able men to direct the student, it will be a repository for the great examples of the Art. These are the materials on which genius is to work, and without which the strongest intellect may be fruitlessly, or deviously, employed." These were indeed brave words for the London of 1769 for there was nowhere that the artist could go excepting to dealers' galleries in Mayfair or to the studios of other artists to see master works of art. There were none of the continuing traditions of the royal collections that existed in Paris, where, even during the great days of Versailles and when the private apartments of the Louvre were used as galleries it was always possible for artists to gain admission by knowing the proper persons. In London there was nothing. All of the magnificent collections of England were dispersed through the fine country seats more than a day's journey by stagecoach from London; to them the artists never gained admittance. Dr. Mead's house, which had been open to all artists and students in Great Ormond Street, was closed. He had died the same year that the British Museum was founded, 1753, and the collection was dispersed at a sale that followed shortly after.

Shortly before Reynolds's death there was much talk in the Academy of purchasing an estate belonging to the Chartered Society of Artists consisting of a number of rooms with a piece of land adjoining, and Sir Joshua offered to lend the whole or any part of his notable collection of Old Masters for the study of students. According to James Barry this scheme was brought to nothing by the violent opposition of the architect, Sir William Chambers. Barry thereupon urged the members of the Royal Academy that some part of their money should be spent on "the purchase of some one or more exemplars of ancient art and a room or rooms to put them in. This beginning, which would come so gracefully and with such peculiar propriety from the Academy would, with a generous public that only wants such an occasion, soon fructify and extend to a National Gallery which, whilst it would complete the views of the Academy with respect to the education of its pupils, would also no less beneficially extend to the improvement and entertainment of the nation at large."

The notion of a national gallery, very much in the air, had again been brought to a head by the sale of the celebrated Walpole collection at Houghton to the Empress of Russia. A debate took place in 1777 in the House of Commons in which John Wilkes, M.P., proposed at a meeting of the Committee of Supply that the annual grant towards the upkeep of the British Museum should be increased from £3000 to £5000. The motion was introduced by Edmund Burke. Wilkes at the same time advocated the establishment of a national gallery to be contained in the British Museum:

I understand that an application is to be made at Parliament that one of the first collections in Europe, that in Houghton, made by Sir Robert Walpole, of acknowledged superiority to most collections in Italy and scarcely inferior even to that of the Duc of Orléans in the Palais Royal at Paris may be sold. I hope it may not be dispersed, but purchased by Parliament and added to the British Museum. I wish, Sir, the eye of painting as fully gratified as the ear of music is in this island, which at last bids fair to become a favorite abode of the polite arts. A noble gallery ought to be built in the garden of the British Museum for the reception of this invaluable collection.

Wilkes underlined his plea by reproving George III for having removed the Raphael cartoons from Hampton Court Palace to Buckingham House. He continues:

Such an important acquisition as the Houghton collection would in some degree alleviate the concern which every man of taste now feels at being deprived of seeing those prodigies of art, the cartoons of the divine Raphael. King William, although a Dutchman, really loved and understood the polite arts. He built the princely suite of apartments at Hampton Court on purpose for the reception of those heavenly guests. The nation at large were then admitted to the rapturous enjoyment of their beauty. They remained there until this reign. At present they are perishing in a late baronet's smoky house at the end of a great smoky town.

They are entirely secluded from the public eye. Yet, Sir, they were purchased with public money before the accession of the Brunswick line, not brought from Herrenhausen. Can there be, Sir, a greater mortification to any gentleman of taste than to be thus deprived of feasting his delighted view with what he most admired, and had always considered the pride of our island, as an invaluable national treasure, as a common blessing, not as private property. The kings of France and Spain permit their subjects the view of all the pictures in their collections.

Nothing came of Wilkes's plans for the encouragement of the arts. The Houghton pictures went to Russia, and his speech in support of Burke's motion indicates that the refusal to enlarge the parliamentary grant was chiefly responsible for the extremely limited facilities for those who wished to examine the treasures of the infant British Museum. At this time only sixty visitors a day were admitted and these were shown through the rooms in parties of ten. An hour was allotted to each party and as no individual was allowed to linger or to lose touch with the guide, the Museum was of little use to the ordinary man in the eighteenth century.

Throughout the period of the Napoleonic Wars the agitation for and against a national gallery continued but Parliament was so absorbed with the execution of the wars and with the great accumulation of national indebtedness that nothing serious was achieved. Farington's *Diary* records an alternative to Barry's plans, namely that the Academicians allow a certain sum each year for the acquisition of pictures and that each member of the Academy should paint one picture for the gallery. But Benjamin West, who had by then succeeded as president, was indifferent from the beginning towards the idea of a national gallery. However, when he went to Paris in 1811 to see the collections brought together by Denon he was converted. He visited the Louvre in company with Fox and Baring, who both promised upon their return to London to open the question in Parliament once more. Back in London an effort was made to gain Pitt's support but Pitt was prevented by the pressure of business, and when Fox at last succeeded him, he died before he could redeem his promise.

The National Gallery was not to become a reality until 1824 when the Regency was over and George IV was seated on the throne. Just as the sale of Sir Hans Sloane's collection had been the spark that set on fire the enthusiasm for the British Museum three quarters of a century earlier, so it was the threat of losing another celebrated collection to the Continent, that of John Julius Angerstein, which at long last forced Parliament into establishing a national picture gallery. England had learned her bitter lesson from the loss of the Walpole pictures to Russia and from the prestige which Napoleon had gained, even in his ultimate defeat, in the creation of the Museum of the Louvre.

The steps leading to the National Gallery, the tides of fashion and snobbery of the Regency, the emergence of the artist collectors, Reynolds, Lawrence and their contemporaries, belong in spirit to the nineteenth century. The collector's tradition of a thousand years was slowly dying from the holocaust of the French Revolution. How it came once more to life – in quite another dress – in the Regency and Napoleonic times belongs not to this book but to its sequel, which will be devoted to the Industrial Revolution and the Romantic movement. For the Regency must be looked upon not as the end of an era but as the beginning of modern times, and it was the impetus of the men of fashion surrounding George IV that showed the pathway to the earliest collectors in America.

CHAPTER VIII

Athenians, Goths and Mandarins

By 1750 the glamour of Augustan Rome had begun to tarnish. Young men of fashion, imbued with classicism and reviewing in the solitude of their country places their discoveries and their gallantries in Italy, began to look for new worlds to conquer. Already in 1738 Charles VII, King of Naples, had excavated Herculaneum, and the uncovering of Pompeii took place ten years later. To those who had returned to England the disclosures of these two buried cities were made known through the publications of the Accademia Ercolanese, containing magnificent plates of many of the treasures that had been unearthed – pictures, bronzes and lamps. Before the middle of the century Piranesi was issuing his engravings of the remains of ancient civilization, engravings which stressed the romantic aspects of ruined antiquity which the English noblemen were to repeat in the garden *allées* of their country places. Abbé Winckelmann, firmly installed as custodian of the Vatican collections, was putting a new premium on pedantry, yet at the same time opening the door to visions of the Greek world which hitherto had been seen only through Italian eyes. As early as 1740 Horace Walpole had written back from Naples to his friend Richard West:

> One hates writing descriptions that are to be found in every book of travels; but we have seen something today that I am sure you've never read of, and perhaps never heard of. Have you ever heard of a subterraneous town? A whole Roman town, with all its edifices, remaining under ground? This underground city is perhaps one of the noblest curiosities that has ever been discovered. There is nothing of the kind known in the world; I mean a Roman city entire of that age, and that has not been corrupted with modern repairs. Besides scrutinizing this very carefully, I should be inclined to search for the remains of other towns that

were partners with this in the general ruin. 'Tis certainly an advantage to the learned world, that this has been laid up so long.

The champions of classicism, always at war with the romantics who were rapidly gaining the ascendancy in literature, were deeply gratified that a new impetus of the classical tradition, revivified by these new finds, would sustain their point of view; and the eager reception given in 1764 to Winckelmann's *History of Ancient Art* and to Lessing's *Laokoon* two years later gave ample indication that the classical empire of the mind would survive at least another century. Their sworn enemies were of course the exponents of the Chinese and Gothic tastes. So deeply, indeed, had these romantic fashions penetrated the great world that critics began to wonder at the sanity of the younger aristocracy. When Robert Wood published in 1753 *The Ruins of Palmyra*, and the subsequent *The Ruins of Balbec*, the *Monthly Review* congratulated the British public on their appearance in the following words:

> It is with peculiar pleasure we observe such a work as this produced at a time when wars seem to have engrossed the attention of mankind. The drawn sword has not yet frightened the Muses from their seats; they have more dangerous enemies in the Chinese and Goths, than in the sons of Mars. Such specimens of architecture as have already been communicated to the public, by the learned and ingenious editor of *The Ruins of Balbec*, with others which are respective of Athens, etc., will, we hope, improve the taste of our countrymen, and expel the littleness and ugliness of the Chinese, and the barbarity of the Goths, that we may see no more useless and expensive trifles; no more dungeons instead of summer houses.

An antidote to romantic restlessness was the formation of the Society of the Dilettanti, a fashionable dining club of the sons of peers and their friends, in 1734. This society, at first a convivial drinking club of the polite young men about town, soon became a most important voice in the future course of classical archaeology. In its earlier and gayer moods the Dilettanti resembled more closely an undergraduate eating club or college fraternity than it did a learned society. The President, while in the chair, was required to wear a scarlet toga, the folds of which were arranged by the Painter to the Society, who for many years was none other than Sir Joshua Reynolds. The Master of Ceremonies was decked out in "a long robe of crimson taffety," full pleated with a rich Hungarian cap and a long Spanish Toledo; the Secretary was dressed in a long black robe after that worn by Machiavelli in one of his portraits. Meeting for dinner the first Sunday of each month from November to May at a tavern – for many years it was the Star and Garter – they would drink bumpers to one another and toasts to "Grecian taste and Roman spirit." They would, in fact, lift their glasses to any intellectual enterprise and the cry "*Viva la Virtù*" was the signal for much Bacchanalian conversation filled with classical allusions and Latin epigrams.

But for the rest, the society provided young men of promise in painting, sculpture or architecture with a means of going to Italy to pursue their studies and, on their return, with commissions which would insure them both a living and a guarantee that their work would become known; and, despite apparent frivolity, the names of most of the great connoisseurs and patrons are found included in the list of its members. Not, indeed, until some generations later were solemnity and intelligence regarded as identical virtues.* Their funds, and the capital of the society, which became quite considerable, were accumulated not so much through gifts and subscriptions, which the young peers could well afford, but by fines levied by the president for their misconduct at the dinners. Such entries in their minutes as "Mr. Langlois being convicted of hob or nobbing with Sir Richard Worsley was fined two shilling and six pence" or again, "Lord Sandwich and Mr. Banks, having called this respectable society by the disrespectful name of club, were fined a bumper each which they drank with all proper humility." But their largest sources of revenue came from a resolution adopted in 1744 that "every member who has any increase of income either by inheritance, legacy, marriage or preferment do pay half of 1% of the first year of his additional income to

* Sitwell and Barton, *op. cit.*, 21. "The reign of the doctors and the professors, the theorists, critics, and earnest-minded was still to come, and without doubt these untoiling butterflies accomplished more for English art than all the laboring stage elephants of the next century because a lot of money, judiciously spent, and not a great amount of advice, is ever that which the artist needs."

BELLOTTO: THE ROYAL PALACE AT DRESDEN

CATHERINE, EMPRESS OF ALL THE RUSSIAS

By Van Loo. Metropolitan Museum of Art

the general fund, but that every member upon payment of £10 shall be released from such obligation." And it is amusing to note how these preferments were levied; for in May of the following year a subsequent resolution was adopted:

All preferment shall be valued according to the subsequent rates viz:

An Arch Bishop	his Blessing
A Duke	his Grace
A Marquis	his Honour
An Earl	nothing
A Viscount	something
A Bishop	12
A Baron	6 pence
A Judge	6s. 8d.
A Knight of the Gate	13s. 4d.
A Knight of the Thistle	10 pounds Scotch
A King at Arms	5 pounds English
His Majesty's Ratcatcher	8 pounds
A Knight of the Bath	9 pounds
A Trumpeter	10 pounds

Lord Charlemont, an eager Dilettante, was one of the first Englishmen to distinguish between Greek and Roman art. In 1746 he had traveled to Greece, accompanied by Richard Dalton in the capacity of draftsman, and on his return to England published the first engravings of the Parthenon and the Erechtheion. Curiously enough the Englishman had paid very little attention to the Levant during the past hundred years. No one seems to have taken up the inquiries of the Reverend William Petty and Sir Thomas Roe, whose faithful work for Arundel and the Duke of Buckingham was one of the brighter chapters of the reign of Charles I.*

English collectors and their agents had almost entirely confined

* The collections of the King and the Duke of Buckingham had been dispersed, and Arundel himself had died in 1646 before the Civil Wars were ended. The Arundel marbles were gradually dispersed and the bulk of the collection finally came to rest at the University of Oxford. Another part went to form the nucleus of the Earl of Pembroke's collection at Wilton House. The Wilton collection soon was enlarged by the acquisition of the antiques which had belonged to Cardinal Mazarin and of numerous busts collected somewhat indiscriminately in Italy. Cf. Sir Lionel Cust and Sir Sidney Colvin, *History of the Society of the Deilettanti*, Macmillan, 1898.

their attention to the acquisition of such works of sculpture and fragments of architecture as were movable and portable within reasonable expense. But, as Sir Lionel Cust points out, a beginning had been made in that other branch of classical research in which the Dilettanti were, by and by, to reap their especial laurels; that is, in the systematic exploration and study of ancient monuments as they were to be found *in situ.*

About 1674 or a little earlier the Marquis Olier de Nointel, French ambassador to the Ottoman Porte, passed through Athens, and was so much struck by the beauty of the sculptures still remaining on the Parthenon that he employed a painter, Jacques Carrey, a pupil of Le Brun, who accompanied him in 1674, to make careful drawings in red chalk of all the sculptures which then survived.* Wars and earthquakes, the ravages of time and man, had left little above ground which was undamaged or entire. "The Turks never a willfully destructive race, had nevertheless allowed, in contemptuous negligence, all the monuments of antiquity which had survived the classical days to perish slowly by reckless usage, decay and ruin." Even in Carrey's day the sculptures of the Parthenon were in a very damaged and mutilated state, but his drawings derive an especial value from the fact of the further destruction which ensued during the Venetian bombardment under Morosini in 1687. A narrative of Olier de Nointel's expedition was published in 1688 by Cornelio Magni, who accompanied it. Shortly after Carrey had commenced his drawings, Sir George Wheler traveled to the Levant and to Greece with the French antiquary and critic of Lyons, Jacob Spon.

The English account of this expedition † had awakened the interest of the more adventurous Englishmen making the grand tour, and particularly the members of the Society of Dilettanti who looked beyond the Seven Hills of Rome. Those who responded instantly to these new opportunities were a group of architects, painters and connoisseurs who had earned their living by selling antiquities to English

* For the controversy over the actual authorship of these drawings, cf. Colignon, *Le Parthénon,* pp. 72 and 73.

† Published in 1678 under the title *A Journey into Greece* by George Wheler, Esquire, in company of Dr. Spon of Lyons, together with other works published in Italy and France.

noblemen visiting the capital. Three names stand out among this group, Matthew Brettingham, the architect of the Earl of Leicester's house at Holkham, and Gavin Hamilton, the painter. The third, Thomas Jenkins, in many ways the most picturesque and attractive of the three, was reputed to be the most notorious falsifier and swindler in the antique business in Rome. All three were friends of Winckelmann and Cardinal Albani and not only had access to many of the private palaces and collections in the city but were highly privileged in the matter of excavations, and for a number of years conducted digs in the most celebrated gardens and villas of antiquity. Winckelmann recommended Jenkins as the agent for the sale of the collection of gems which had belonged to the late Baron Stosch, afterwards purchased by Frederick the Great for Berlin. Jenkins was a consummate actor and gallery player, resorting to tears and other dramatic gestures in order to put over a bargain or a sale, frequently weeping and refusing at first to part with an object that was close to his heart at any price, and always working wherever possible on the emotions and sympathies of the prospective purchaser. Gorani said of him, "He would furnish material for an excellent comedy. Perhaps his emotion is genuine, perhaps he is really attached to his stock in trade. In any case, if this affectation is part and parcel of his business, we must acknowledge that he has brought it to the highest possible degree of perfection."

Michaelis's account of Jenkins is based upon the testimony of Nollekens, the English sculptor who had lived at Rome for nearly ten years learning from Cavaceppi the principles of restoration and the gentle art of faking through the judicious application of "patina" by tea and tobacco juice.

"I got all the first and best of my money by putting antiques together. Hamilton and I and Jenkins generally used to go shares in what we bought; and as I had to match the pieces as well as I could, and clean them, I had the best part of the profits. Gavin Hamilton was a good fellow, but as for Jenkins, he followed the trade of supplying the foreign visitors with intaglios and cameos made by his own people, that he kept in a part of the ruins of the Coliseum fitted up for them to work in slyly by themselves. I saw him at work, though, and Jenkins gave a whole handful of them to me to say nothing about the matter to anybody else but myself. Bless your heart! He sold them as fast as they made them." The history of the Minerva of Newby Hall is one that chills the marrow of the museum curator of the present day and describes the general mode of procedure which has in fact been in vogue in Rome for the past one hundred and fifty years. After he had purchased the beautiful torso of Hamilton for a moderate price, and had it furnished by Cavaceppi with a head that did not belong to it, [Michaelis states] that "the statue was advertised as uninjured; its origin was shrouded in mystery; an extraordinarily high price, about which buyers and sellers were bound to keep silence, was demanded, and then increased on the score of the difficulty of obtaining permission for exportation. By a false announcement that the King of England was the purchaser the Papal Government was cajoled into giving the permission, and finally an exact statement of every restoration was given to the custom house authorities in order to reduce the fees." *

In 1742 the English colony in Rome was augmented by the presence of two men whose lifework, *The Antiquities of Athens*, was to be the cornerstone of nineteenth-century archaeology. The first was James Stuart, the son of a north British sailor, who had started life as a fan painter for Goupy, and who later made his way to Rome on foot, where he became a student of the classics at the College of the Propaganda. He had published there a treatise in Latin on the obelisk of the Campus Martius which had gained him the favorable notice of the Pope. The other, Nicholas Revett, the son of an English squire, had come to Rome to study painting with Benefiale. Six years later, 1748, Brettingham, Stuart, Gavin Hamilton and Revett went on a walking trip to Naples where they visited Herculaneum and the new excavations at Pompeii which had been laid open in that year. It was on this trip that they drew up a prospectus for a scheme entitled *Proposals for Publishing an Accurate Description of the Antiquities of Athens, Etc.* For Stuart and Revett it was to be a labor of love; Gavin Hamilton no doubt was motivated principally by the opportunities that it offered for obtaining objects which could be sold profitably

* The discovery of the late P. T. Barnum was not as revolutionary as we have been led to suppose. Adolf Michaelis, *Ancient Marbles in Great Britain.* Cambridge, The University Press, 1882, p. 77.

in the London market. Two years later Stuart and Revett, fortified with funds from the Earl of Malton and Lord Charlemont, set out for Venice to take ship to Greece.

At Venice they came under the influence of Sir James Gray, the British Resident, an ardent member of the Dilettanti, who was so much impressed by these young men that he proposed them as members to the society, they were duly elected upon their return to England four years later. After many delays, including a rugged but romantic journey through Dalmatia, they finally reached Athens. There they met John Bouverie, James Dawkins and Robert Wood, three English gentlemen who were engaged on a similar mission of their own to Asia Minor. Despite plague and fever, of which Bouverie later died, wars and innumerable difficulties with the Turkish police, it was due to the collaboration of these pioneers in archaeology that the work in Athens was completed. In rapid succession *The Antiquities of Athens* and *The Ionian Antiquities* appeared, as well as other publications of monuments in Asia Minor and the Levant, heretofore unknown to Western Europe. The Dilettanti were so enthusiastic that they immediately undertook to finance the subsequent volumes, II, III and IV, of "Athenian" Stuart's work.

It was inevitable that this new and enlightened study of archaeology should be reflected in architecture and interior decoration. Already in France by the middle of the century the *style Louis Seize* was being exemplified in the apartments of Marie Antoinette at Fontainebleau. Madame de Pompadour and, more or less casually, her successor, Madame du Barry, had welcomed the classical innovations which affected every aspect of decoration and textile design. The patterns of French silk, and the waving floral sprays of the Rococo, were also being straightened and curved by the severity of classical lines. In England a similar transformation was taking place under the direction of a Scottish family of architects and designers.

The brothers Adam, Miss Sackville-West has said, "were elegant and delicate in the extreme. The most surprising thing about them is that they were brothers, not sisters. There were four of them, Robert, James, John and William. Robert (1728–1792) and his brother James, who was associated with him in all his work are the two that count.

They delighted in the lighter classical mode: niches, lunettes, bas-reliefs, chimney-pieces, and furniture designed to match the outside building. Elegant both inside and out, the Adam brothers imposed quite as strongly as Inigo Jones, a new style on the English house. . . . The Grecian gracefulness flowered in rooms finely proportioned, as delicately colored as the egg of a bird, primrose and Wedgwood blue, lemon yellow and cream, pale green and white, it seems strange that this highly original and sophisticated style should have been the product of Scotland and Diocletian's palace at Spalato." *

Robert Adam had spent three years in Italy, where he made the acquaintance of Winckelmann and had become an intimate of Piranesi. Clérisseau, the French archaeologist, accompanied him to Dalmatia to examine and make measured drawings of the public buildings and the Palace of Diocletian. Upon his return to England he put these researches into immediate practice in such great houses as Syon House and Lansdowne House. Portland Place still stands, despite the blitz, as a monument to his genius.

If the Adam style can be accused of triviality and insipidity, one must at least admit that it was a style that was consonant with the taste and learning of its epoch. By discovering for the first time that the Romans themselves, guided by a nice sense of scale, had carefully distinguished between the internal decorations of a public edifice and the smaller apartments for domestic living, "he exploded the theory of the pompous and the ponderous which had dominated the earlier forms of Georgian architecture. Ponderous cornices and entablatures that crowned the walls of apartments were banished in favor of decorative patterns that were light, gay, elegant, whimsical, and even bizarre." What influenced him most in the development of his own style, Sprague Allen has insisted, was "antique stucco-work in delicate relief and Raphael's painted arabesques in the Loggia of the Vatican. He declared that this classical style of ornament was by far the most perfect that had ever appeared for inside decorations and when employed with skill was capable of inimitable beauties." His own mural designs, using as motifs the Sphinx, the Griffon, the Ram's head, the

* V. Sackville-West, "English Country Houses" in *Panorama of Rural England.* Chanticleer Press, 1944, p. 64.

signs of the Zodiac, the over-medallions, the oblong plaque or tablet in festoons of drapery executed in low-relief, were all part of the repertoire of classical conceits which made the new drawing rooms of Whig society so pleasant and yet so spacious.

The rage for Athenian purity did not escape the attacks of the irreverent; one critic wrote that in the rooms of Mr. Adam "the nick-nackery of the Cabinet maker, Toyman, and Pastry cook preside with impunity. Here let the light and elegant ordinance of the bedpost triumph over the clumsy orders of old Greece. Here let Pilasters rival the substance and ornaments of figured ribbons, and the rampant foliage of antiquity, give place to the exquisite prettinesses of casts from the cabinet, the medal case or the seal engravers show glass." And Hogarth, always resentful of any foreign influence, and believing only in the artificial stimulus of the home-grown product, caricatured Stuart's *Antiquities* in an engraving entitled *The Five Orders of Perriwigs*, published in 1761. This engraving he styled "The Five Orders of Perriwigs as they were worn at the late coronation, measured architectonically."

CHAPTER IX

Amateurs and Archaeology

THE last quarter of the eighteenth century saw an activity on the part of the collectors of classical antiquities which was to culminate in 1811 in an atmosphere of acrimony over the acquisition by Act of Parliament of the Elgin marbles. In the meantime, in the persons of Charles Greville, his uncle Sir William Hamilton, Charles Townley and R. Payne Knight, the future supremacy of the British Museum's department of classical antiquities was to be guaranteed. The influence of Sir Joseph Banks, who had given his great library to the British Museum, turned the eyes of the Society of the Dilettanti, of which he was an officer, to the development and encouragement of that newborn institution. Greville, who had discovered the beautiful Emma Lyon, later Lord Nelson's Lady Hamilton, was a collector of coins and medals of some accomplishment. Sir William Hamilton, her obliging husband, was almost professional in his zeal for antiquities; he formed in succession two of the greatest collections of antiquities ever assembled.

Living for twenty-six years in Naples as the British Envoy and Plenipotentiary to that court, Hamilton was in daily communication with the archaeologists at Herculaneum and Pompeii, and was, in fact, "the first man of means on the spot to buy those items which the peasants surreptitiously concealed and brought away from the excavations." Also, his position as a diplomat at court made it possible for him to receive consideration in the partition of the official finds which were being dug up day by day. Passionately interested in any form of antique art, Hamilton's principal contribution was as a collector of "Etruscan" vases of which he had brought together some 730 excellent examples. The catalogue of these vases, made by the romantic and abstruse d'Hancarville, was the first attempt to classify this ancient pottery into various types and groups. "To Hamilton belongs the merit," says Michaelis, "of being the first one to appreciate the severe beauty of their shapes, coloring and drawing, the mingled simplicity and feeling of the designs figured upon them; as it was he who recognized the value of these unpretentious vessels for forming and ennobling modern art taste." * These vases, together with 175 terra cottas, 300 pieces of ancient glass, 627 bronzes, a quantity of armor, 150 objects in ivory, 150 gems and as many gold articles of jewelry, more than 6000 coins, mostly of Magna Graecia, and a miscellaneous collection of marbles, were brought by him to England in 1772 and sold to the British Museum for £8400. This purchase was the first major addition made by public money to the Museum since its foundation, and it laid the groundwork for its future classical collections. Sir William was also instrumental in the development of the collection of the Dowager Duchess of Portland, and it was through him that she had acquired the famous "Portland vase." He returned once more to Naples and started immediately to form another collection; part of it later passed into the collection of Mr. Hope of Deepdene, but the larger part of it was lost in shipwreck.

While Hamilton was busying himself in Naples, another British diplomat at Venice was raking in all the fragments of Greek antiquity that he could find in Greece and along the Adriatic shores. He was Sir Richard Worsley, a passionate amateur archaeologist who published his large collection in two important volumes known as the *Museum Worsleyanum.* Part of his collection is now in the possession of his descendants, the Earls of Yarborough at Brocklesby Park.

But of all the amateurs of the eighteenth century who devoted their lives and their fortunes to the remains of classical antiquity, Charles Townley, of Townley in Lancashire, is the most conspicuous and the most lovable. He was descended on his mother's side from the Earl of Arundel and was both a Catholic and a Jacobite. He had lived in Rome from 1765 to 1772, where he was an intimate friend of Sir William Hamilton, whom he frequently saw in Naples, and also was closely associated with Gavin Hamilton and the equivocal Jenkins, often acting as a silent partner in their excavations and ne-

* Michaelis, *op. cit.*, 110.

gotiations. Despite the prohibitions of the Vatican and the efforts of the Pope and his archaeologists to save the finest things for Rome, Townley seldom lost to his competitors any article which he really wanted. In 1772 he returned to England and brought with him his collections for which he had built a special gallery and house at number seven in Park Street, Westminster. This house became the principal rendezvous of the connoisseurs, artists and literary men of the time. Sir Joshua Reynolds and Zoffany constantly attended "Mr. Townley's famous Sunday dinners," and Nollekens, whom Townley had known in Rome, paid tribute to Townley's excellent table. "I am sure," said he, "to make a good dinner at his house on a Sunday; but there is a little man a great deal less than myself who dines there the name of Devay, a French Abbé; who beats me out and out: he is one of the greatest gormandizers I ever met with though to look at him you would declare him to be in the most deplorable state of starvation."

Zoffany has immortalized Townley in his library surrounded by his friends in a conversation piece which is here reproduced. Nollekens's biographer, J. T. Smith, who knew Townley and was frequently at his house, has said of it, "It was a portrait of the Library, though not strictly correct as to its contents, since all the best of the marbles displayed in various parts of the house were brought into the painting by the artist, who made it up into a picturesque composition according to his own taste. The likeness of Mr. Townley is extremely good. He is seated, and looks like the dignified possessor of such treasures: at his feet lies his favorite dog 'Kam' a native of Kamtschatka, whose mother was one of the dogs yoked to a sledge which had drawn Captain King in that island. Opposite to Mr. Townley is Monsieur d'Hancarville, seated at a table with a book open before him behind whose chair stand two other of his friends, Thomas Astle, Esquire, and the Honorable Charles Greville, conversing."

To this same biographer we are indebted for a description of Townley's residence, a description so important in picturing for us the neoclassicism of the day that it seems well to include it here.

From what I have seen and heard described, in no instance can a private residence be found to equal that of the late Charles Townley, Esquire. . . . As the visitor entered the hall, his attention was arrested by an immense sarcophagus on his left hand, measuring seven feet in length, opposite to which were two heads of lions, the size of life, one on either side of the chimney-piece. His hall was also adorned with bas-reliefs, sepulchral monuments, inscriptions, cinerary urns, etc. from the villas of Fonseca, Montalto, Pullucchi, Antoninus Pius, the Justiniani Palace, etc. The staircase was enriched with sepulchral urns and numerous Roman inscriptions, and a very curious and ancient chair of Pavonazzo marble. In a space over the dining room door was a bas-relief of a mystical marriage. When the marbles were conveyed to the British Museum this space was filled up with a cast of a boar taken from the celebrated one at Florence.

The parlor, or dressing room in Park Street, contained a rich display of votive altars, sepulchral urns, and inscriptions. Among the Marbles was a most spirited statue of a Satyr, the thumb of whose right hand is enclosed between his two fore-fingers; it is now number 24 in the Townley Gallery in the British Museum; and this small but excellent specimen of ancient art was presented to Mr. Townley by his friend Lord Cawdor. The ancient, rare and truly interesting collection of Terracottas, brought from Rome by Nollekens . . . was let into the walls of this room. Of the female figures in these specimens the tasteful Cipriani was so extremely fond, that he has been heard to declare to Mr. Townley that they afforded him so much pleasure that he never knew when to leave them.

The dining parlour, looking over St. James's Park, was a room in which Mr. Townley has entertained personages of the highest rank in this kingdom, as well as visitors from all nations who were eminent for the brilliancy of their wit or their literary acquirements; and contained the greater part of his statues. Here stood those of *Libera*, *Isis*, *Diana*, and the *Discobolus*, a *Drunken Fawn*, and an *Adonis;* but above all, that most magnificent one of *Venus*, which measures 6 feet 4 inches in height. Mr. Nollekens informed me that in the conveyance of this statue to England the following singular stratagem to save the immense duty upon so large and so perfect a figure was resorted to. In consequence of it having been discovered that the figure had been carved from two blocks, and put together at the waist, at the commencement of the drapery it was separated, and sent at different times; so that the duty upon each fragment amounted to a mere trifle. It is now number 14 in the Townley Gallery in the British Museum.

Among the busts was that of *Caracalla,* and one of the most beautiful vases, perhaps in the world; it is embellished with Bacchanalian figures, and was brought from the villa of Antoninus where other treasures of art have been discovered.

Over the chimney-piece in the drawing-room looking into Park Street, was a bas-relief in terra cotta of a marriage ceremony modeled by Mr. Nollekens from the one over the dining room door. This performance was highly esteemed by Mr. Townley, who always spake of Mr. Nollekens as the first sculptor of his day.

The drawing room, commanding a most beautiful view of the park, contained principally the following heads and busts: *Decebalus, Marcus Aurelius, Hadrian, Trajan, Hercules, Antinous,* and *Adonis;* but, of all the others, that of *Isis* upon the *Lotus* was considered by artists to be one of the most perfect and beautiful specimens of sculpture. It was purchased of Prince Laurenzano of Naples in 1772. This bust of *Isis,* which Mr. Nollekens considered to be a portrait of the sculptor's model, was so much admired by him, that he always had a copy of it in marble purposely for sale: the last one was sold, after the collection was purchased by the government, to John Townley, Esquire for one hundred guineas who was delighted to see so exquisite a copy placed in a situation which the original had graced for so many years. . . .

The library was highly interesting; it was lighted from above and was in every respect an excellent room for study. The marbles in it were not so numerous as those in the dining parlor but they consisted of some choice specimens, among the busts were those of *Antoninus Pius, Titus,* Caracalla's wife *Plautilla, Lucius Verus,* and a celebrated one of *Homer* which has been so repeatedly and admirably engraven.* Townley was so enamored with his favorite busts of Isis, Pericles and Homer, the most perfect specimens of ancient art, that he employed the hand of Skelton, Sharpe's favorite pupil, to engrave them upon a small plate which he used as his visiting card. This elegant performance, always considered a great rarity, was left only at the houses of particular persons, so that the possession of it is now greatly coveted by the collectors of such *bijoux.* Here were also the heads of Adonis and that beautiful one of a child with its locks uncut over its right ear; together with the exquisite little statue of Angerona, which is now called a Venus, and numbered 22 in the

* This was the head of Homer which Townley had purchased from the sale of Dr. Mead in 1754 and which had, a century earlier, belonged to Arundel.

gallery of the British Museum. Mr. Nollekens renewed the arms of this figure for which restoration I stood when his pupil.*

It was Townley's intention to bequeath his collection to the British Museum and he so stated in his will, but the complications involving settlement of his estate made it necessary for the executors to sell the collection. It was bought reluctantly by the nation for the British Museum for £20,000. A Townley gallery was arranged, and here these Greek and, alas, for the greater part, Roman marbles maintained undisputed precedence till long after the controversy of the Elgin marbles had been forgotten. Townley must best be remembered, however, by the publication which he undertook for the Society of the Dilettanti in collaboration with Payne Knight. This publication, which did not see the light of day until after Townley's death, was entitled *Select Specimens of Ancient Sculpture Preserved in the Several Collections of Great Britain*. Selection of the pieces to be engraved was made by the authors.†

It is perhaps ironic that the sun of the Society of the Dilettanti which had ridden so high in the heavens for half a century was to set behind a cloud of disfavor brought about by their publication of a book on phallic worship, and their insistence that the sculptures of the Parthenon, brought to England by Lord Elgin, were neither important nor Greek originals. In fact, they supported, under the violent leadership of Payne Knight, a suggestion made in 1680 by Dr. Spon, that they were nothing but Roman copies of the time of Hadrian.

Richard Payne Knight bore all of the complexities and difficulties inherent in the true archaeologist – jealousy, infallibility, coupled with a sense of persecution and a madness for his own subject. His knowledge was exceeded only by his influence and powers of persua-

* John Thomas Smith, *Nollekens and His Times*. Ed. Wilfred Whitten. John Lane, 1920. Vol. I, pp. 213–219.

† "The engravings of the plates occupied eight years, from May 1799 to May 1807. The 63 works of art selected were chiefly taken from the collections of these two gentlemen, 23 being from Mr. Payne Knight's collection and 23 from Mr. Townley's. Of the remainder, 4 came from the Marquis of Lansdowne's collection, 9 from the Earl of Egremont, 2 from Mr. Hope's, and one each from those of the Earl of Yarborough and the Earl of Cork. The volume contained 75 plates and from these we are able to judge the very high quality of collecting in the last half of the eighteenth century." Cf. Michaelis, *op. cit.*

sion, and his taste, so marked in limited fields of specialization, was warped to a degree which bred vindictiveness and intolerance regarding anything which was not the fruit of his personal discovery. As a youth of seventeen he had visited Italy and in 1777 spent a year in Sicily, where he had produced a journal which so deeply moved the German poet Goethe that he translated it into his own tongue under the title *Tagebuch einer Reise nach Sicilien.* As a result Payne Knight posed as the arbiter of taste in London society, delivering his oracular opinions with a finality which finally exploded in his face.

If as a scholar Payne Knight was difficult, as a collector he was really eminent. His cabinet of antiquities included marbles, gems, coins and bronzes; in the latter he had real discrimination, although little in sculpture. He was also an energetic collector of drawings by the Old Masters, especially Claude; these acquisitions formed, in fact, a very important addition to the treasures of the British Museum, to which they were all bequeathed upon his death.

Had Townley lived, possibly Payne Knight might not have fallen into the errors of judgment which he did; for, in many ways, their tastes and interests were complementary. Townley was interested in sculpture and his house, as his collection shows, abounded with marbles of every size and shape. Payne Knight, on the other hand, was interested in the cabinet object, most exquisite gold and silver jewelry and coins, small bronzes, and objects in which perfection of workmanship was the predominating quality. This same attention to minutiae is, of course, characteristic of the *petit maître,* which he undoubtedly was, and which rendered him insensible to larger forms. At the time of his death his collection was valued at between £50,000 and £60,000, a phenomenal figure for those days, which leads us to some idea of his interests and activity.

In 1784, Payne Knight met at Townley's house the fascinating French adventurer, Pierre François Hugues, who had assumed the name of Baron d'Hancarville and had been associated with Sir William Hamilton in the publication of the latter's Greek and Roman vases. His lifework, however, had been compiling his *Recherches sur l'Origine, l'Esprit et les Progrès des Arts de la Grèce* which was finally published in 1785. The latter work, a "fantastic farrago of mystical symbolical revelation and groundless hypothesis," was the imaginative but totally unscientific precursor of Sir James Frazer's *The Golden Bough.* But the eighteenth century had not passed through the evolution of Huxley and Darwin and was not ready for exploration into the symbolism and the meaning of orgiastic excesses. When, therefore, the collaborated work of Payne Knight and Sir William Hamilton, influenced by Hancarville, brought before an avid public the full details of the worship of Priapus, it opened the floodgates of righteousness to a storm not seen since the days of Noah and which was to engulf the Ark of British taste for generations to come.

Posterity and the learned world might indeed have forgiven Payne Knight for this lapse of good breeding; but it is his warfare, conducted for nearly twenty years, against Lord Elgin which has condemned him to walk like a lost spirit forevermore in that select purgatory of the classical archaeologists. In his first volume of the *Specimens,* Payne Knight, without ever having seen the marbles brought back from Athens, went out of his way to condemn them and appropriated Spon's original, but perfectly tentative, suggestion that they were Roman works. While there were a few dissentient voices, Knight's prestige and domination over the members of the Society of the Dilettanti were sufficient for them to sustain his opinions. What Payne Knight's motive in all this really was has been a matter of considerable speculation. Some writers have thought that a connoisseur of such true measure and ability must have taken the position deliberately in order to protect the reputation of the collections of his friends, such as those of Townley and Lord Lansdowne, whose relative inferiority, they claim, he must have sensed. But these arguments have invariably been put forward by other archaeologists who, with a vainly naïve and consistent sweetness, have failed to recognize in Payne Knight's attitude the very essence of the archaeological character and temperament. More probably, it was the pride and stubbornness of the omniscient, for not even a statesman at a peace conference is more unable to repudiate a previously held opinion than the academic potentate who passes as an authority in his particular field.

Until the appearance of the publications of "Athenian" Stuart, the eighteenth century had depended upon the drawings made for Nointel by Carrey a century earlier and upon the notes of Spon and Wheler for their knowledge of the monuments of the Acropolis. During this period the Acropolis had been abandoned to the Venetians, to the Turks and to the builders of modern Athens. The latter had for centuries been burning for lime as many of the marbles as they could lay their hands upon, from which they made mortar for the construction of the medieval city. Finally, the bombardment of Athens in 1687 by the Venetians had been the signal for abandoning what was left of the classical remains to wholesale vandalism.

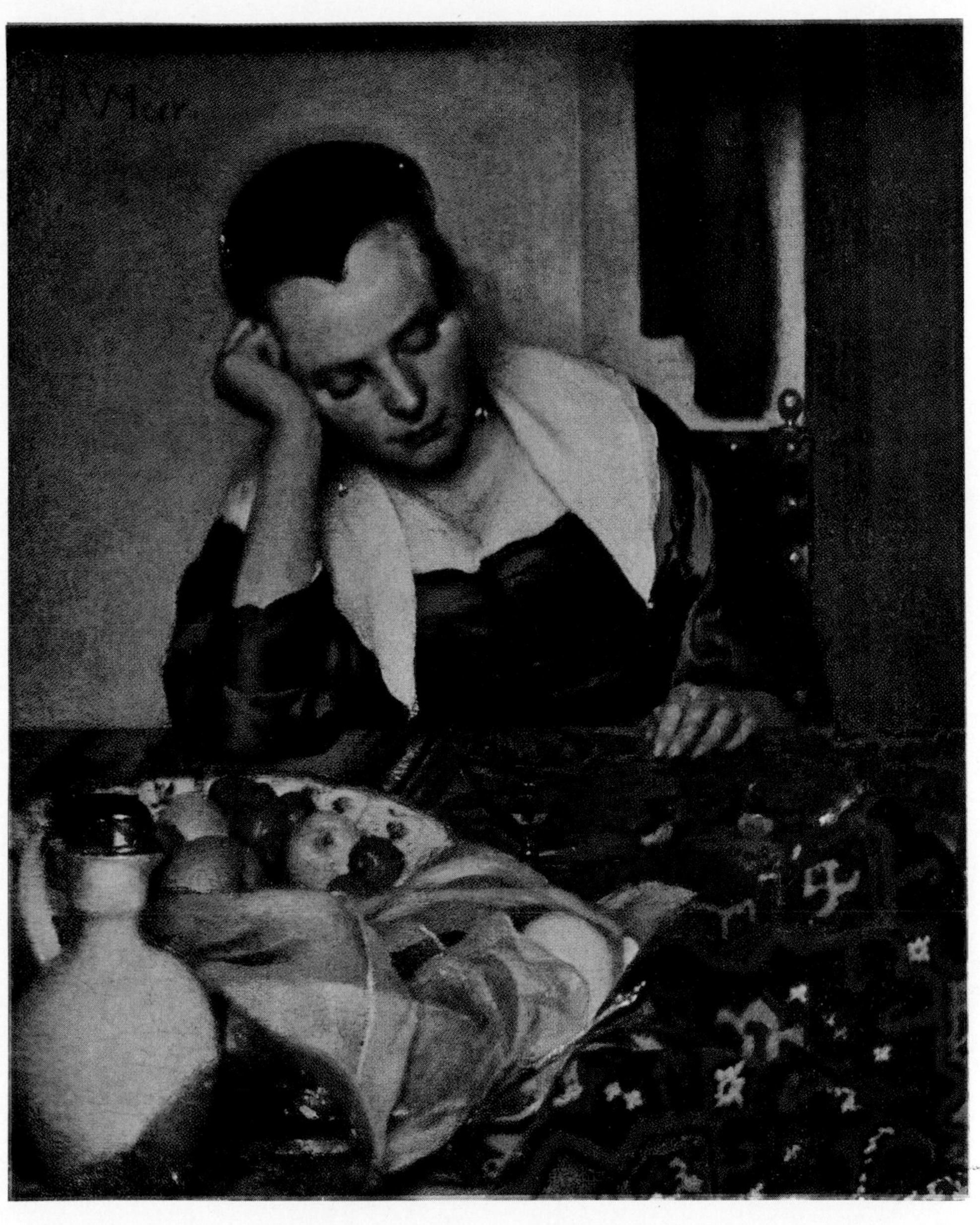

VERMEER: A GIRL ASLEEP (DETAIL)

This picture is recorded in a sales catalogue as having fetched 62 guilders at auction in Amsterdam in 1696; in the John Waterloo Wilson Sale at Paris in 1881 it brought 8500 francs. The late Benjamin Altman, who bequeathed it to the Metropolitan Museum of Art, is reported to have paid $126,620 for it in 1908.

CHAPTER X

The Battle of the Elgin Marbles

"To transplant old Greece into England." This was the ideal that nearly two hundred years earlier Peacham had recommended to Lord Arundel, but its achievement did not take place until the conclusion of the Napoleonic Wars. That it was achieved at all was due to the collaboration between a Yorkshire architect and his employer, Thomas Bruce, the seventh Earl of Elgin, for whom Harrison was building Broom Hall in Fifeshire. Thomas Harrison had studied in Rome and had long been an enthusiastic disciple of "Athenian" Stuart. When in 1799 the Earl of Elgin was appointed ambassador at Constantinople, Harrison suggested to him "the possibility of obtaining casts and drawings of the remains of ancient sculpture at Athens for his new mansion at Broom Hall." Elgin was captivated by the idea and thought at first that the government should finance a careful recording of all the monuments that remained of the Age of Pericles. Pitt was interested, but refused to authorize any additional expense to a government already overburdened with the costs of war. Elgin, therefore, decided to undertake the work at his own cost and, with the advice of Sir William Hamilton, who was then in Sicily, he engaged a draftsman, two architects and two *formatori* to go with him to Athens. With this suite the ambassador proceeded to Constantinople. He did not himself go near Athens but after the necessary preparations had been made he dispatched the little party thither under the direction of Hamilton. In consequence of Bonaparte's successes in Egypt at this time, British influence in Constantinople was very slight, and it was impossible to obtain permission to do more than make drawings. The Athenian authorities, adds Michaelis, "showed themselves most ingenious in intrigues, evasions, and hindrances of all kinds; entrance to the Acropolis for example, cost a daily *douceur* of almost £5."

Accordingly for nine months the undertaking had only very small results.

A change then occurred in Egyptian affairs, and the influence of England, says Michaelis, whose account of the Elgin affair is given here, became again predominant at the Porte. Elgin instantly availed himself of the favorable turn.*

A new *firman* at once permitted the erection of scaffolding and the taking of plaster casts (May 1801). Work began in good earnest on the Acropolis, entrance to which no longer entailed a daily payment, although there were even now no lack of instability and vexations on the part of the garrison. A personal visit paid by Lord Elgin to Athens convinced him of these facts and he consequently applied for further powers. He was soon enabled to arrange for the purchase and demolition of two houses next to the Parthenon. Under one was discovered a rich booty of costly fragments and pediment figures: under the other nothing at all. The Turkish owner pointed with a sardonic smile to the lime in the city wall, which had been made from the sculpture that once stood there! This was not the only experience of the kind. It was impossible to ignore the fact that the ruin of the noblest works of art in the world was progressing with giant steps. Since the drawings of Dalton, Stuart, and Revett had been taken half a century before, much had vanished and much had been destroyed. In the year 1787 the French Vice-Consul, Fauvel, had abstracted a metope and a slab of the frieze from the Parthenon for his ambassador, Count de Choiseul-Gouffier, and the same enterprising agent was accused of cherishing schemes far more extensive. Year after year, also, travelers had been coming in increasing numbers, taking away larger or smaller fragments by way of chips. The saddest fate, it was clear, awaited the buildings of Athens and the sculptures of Phidias: they would be gradually broken up and dispersed to every nook of the world.

The chaplain of the embassy, Dr. Phillip Hunt, was "the life and soul of the undertakings at Athens." It was he who suggested to Lord Elgin that he obtain a further *firman* by the terms of which greater liberty was granted to his working people. It was this *firman*, in fact,

* Michaelis in his *Ancient Marbles in Great Britain* (pp. 133–137) has summarized the evidence given in the *Report from the Select Committee on the Earl of Elgin's Collection of Marbles*, etc. (London, John Munz). A more recent and detailed study is by A. R. Smith, "Lord Elgin and His Collection," in *Journal of Hellenic Studies*, II, 1916.

which Elgin's detractors were to use against him in the House of Commons many years later, for it permitted, through the elasticity of its language, almost any liberty on the part of his expedition "in going in and out of the citadel of Athens; or in fixing scaffolding around the ancient Temple's Idols; or in modeling with chalk or gypsum the ornaments and visible figures thereon, or in measuring the fragments and vestiges of other ruined edifices, or in excavating, when they find it necessary, the foundations, in search of inscriptions among the rubbish." It finally commanded "that they be not molested and that no one meddle with their scaffolding or implements, nor hinder them from taking away any figures of stone (*qualche pezzi di pietra*) with inscriptions or figures." The elastic final clause, continues Michaelis, "of this memorable permit was so luminously expounded by Hunt to the Governor of Athens, the interpretation being backed up by an appropriate present of brilliant cut glass lustres, firearms, and other articles of English manufacture, that the Governor at once gave leave for a metope to be taken from the Parthenon. Hunt was prudent enough to have this forthwith put on board ship and sent off to England. Later in Hunt's report to the committee appointed by the House of Commons to consider the affair he stated that the facility with which this had been obtained had induced Lord Elgin to apply for permission to lower other groups of sculpture from the Parthenon which he did to a considerable extent not only on the Parthenon, but on other edifices in the Acropolis."

The results of these labors, which employed between three and four hundred men for about a year, are well known, and have been summed up by the German archaeologist:

> The principal pedimental figures, fifteen metopes and fifty-six slabs of débris from the Parthenon (without including numerous fragments), one of the sculptured *Korai* from the Erechtheion, four slabs from the frieze of the Temple *Athene Niké*, besides a number of architectural remains and more than a hundred inscribed stones, formed the precious booty. Many of these had not been taken from their original places without difficulty; in particular the removal of several metopes, and of the statue from the Erechtheion had severely injured the surrounding architecture; at the same time the fact must not be forgotten that a great part of the

sculptures had long been severed from their connection, they had been scattered over the whole surface of the fortress, sometimes built over with miserable hovels or else let into walls, and that they now owed their collection and preservation to the zeal of Lord Elgin's agents. It may be doubted whether Lord Elgin was quite discreet in thus using the influence of his official position to further his private undertakings; or whether the interpretation of that *firman*, made with the connivance of the Athenian magistrates was in accordance with the views of the Turkish Government – if indeed the elasticity of the wording had been made altogether clear. But only blind passion could doubt that Lord Elgin's act was an act of preservation, that he took the only possible steps to keep together the remains of the most comprehensive creation of Phidias, and guarded from further disfigurement so much as they had been lucky enough to survive all preceding disasters, from Morosini's bombardment to Fauvel's partial depredation.

Lord Elgin was recalled to London in 1803. He stopped at Athens to see the completion of the work and inspected 200 chests full of marbles which were ready for transportation. Lusieri and his secretary, William Richard Hamilton (not to be confused with the Neapolitan Sir William), stayed behind to superintend the shipping of them. Elgin proceeded to Rome where he showed the drawings of the models to Canova, the first of the European artists to admire them. It is interesting to note that it was Canova himself who persuaded Elgin that the marbles should be left in the condition in which he found them and never to permit the hand of a restorer to touch them. While continuing his journey to England Elgin was taken prisoner by the French in 1805 and confined to Paris for two years. His art treasures "met with misfortunes of another kind."

The majority of them reached England in various ships but in the absence of the owner and his family the chests remained unclaimed in sundry English harbors. About a dozen large chests were shipped in Athens on board the brig, *Mentor*, in which Hamilton, who had returned from his travels, also took ship. Near the island of Cerigo the vessel sprang a leak and struck upon a rock just at the entrance of the harbor and sank. Hamilton's energies succeeded in rescuing in the same year four chests which were brought up by skillful divers, at Kos and Syne. Further costly endeavors to raise the whole ship by the aid of two frigates were unsuccessful; and it was not until two years later, when the vessel had fallen to pieces, the same divers rescued the remaining chests from the bottom of the sea and brought them again to the light of day. This freight could now be brought to England. Meanwhile, Lusieri had to withstand other dangers in Athens. War having been declared against England by the Porte in 1807, he was forced to leave the city. Lord Elgin's marbles which were stored in magazines were seized by the French and taken to the Piraeus where they were threatened with the fate of shipment to France. Thus they seemed likely to be dispersed again. But England held supremacy at sea and so no secure opportunity for their transportation was found. The hostile preparations were closed by a hasty peace, and Lusieri soon found himself again in possession of all the property. Not, however, until 1812 was this vast freight consisting of about 80 chests sent off to England.

Lord Elgin, the moment he was taken prisoner by the French, sent word to the British Government, wishing them to take over the collections which he had gathered together. But already the insidious work of Payne Knight had done its damage. In his introduction to the *Specimens of Ancient Sculpture* he attacked the friezes and metopes of the Parthenon as "merely architectural sculptures, executed from Phidias' designs and under his directions, probably by workmen scarcely ranked among artists, they can throw but little light upon the more important details of his art. They are evidently the works of many different persons, some of whom would not have been entitled to the rank of artists in a much less cultivated and fastidious age." And at the first dinner party at which Payne Knight and Elgin met upon the latter's return to England, Payne Knight cried out in a loud voice, "You have lost your labor, my Lord Elgin, your marbles are overrated; they are not Greek, they are Roman of the time of Hadrian."

But so craven and vindictive was the character of Payne Knight's attack that immediately the artists of the Royal Academy came to Elgin's rescue: Benjamin West, the Philadelphia painter and President of the Royal Academy; the keeper of its collections, the Swiss, Henry Fuseli; but most important of all, Benjamin Robert Haydon. All of these artists, freed from the classical doctrine of an earlier generation, appreciated these sculptures for what they were and declared them to be the most beautiful examples of the true Greek art the world had ever seen.

The marbles were exhibited for a time in what was called "Elgin's Museum," a mews connected with his house on Park Lane. Haydon, who went to see them with Wilkie, the painter, who had a card of admission, described his reaction to them:

> I had no more notion of what I was to see than of anything I had ever heard of and walked in with the utmost nonchalance. . . . To Park Lane then we went, and after passing through the hall and thence into an open yard, entered a damp, dirty penthouse, where lay the marbles, ranged within sight and reach. The first thing I fixed my eyes on, was the wrist of a figure in one of the female groups, in which were visible, though in a feminine form the radius and the ulna. I was astonished, for I had never seen them hinted at in any female wrist in the antique. I darted my eye to the elbow, and saw the outer condyle visibly affecting the shape as in nature. I saw that the arm was in repose and the soft parts in relaxation. That combination of nature and idea, which I had felt was so much wanting for high art, was here displayed to midday conviction. My heart beat! If I had seen nothing else, I had beheld sufficient to keep me to nature for the rest of my life. But when I turned to the Theseus, and saw that every form was altered by action or repose, – when I saw that the two sides of his back varied, one side stretched from the shoulder blade being pulled forward, and the other side being compressed from the shoulder blade being pushed close to the spine, as he rested on his elbow, with the belly flat because the bowels fell into the pelvis as he sat, – and when returning to the Ilyssus, I saw the belly protruded from the figure lying on its side, – and again when in the figure of the fighting metope I saw the muscles shown under the one armpit in that instantaneous action of darting out, and left out in the other armpits because not wanted, – when I saw in fact the most heroic style of art, combined with all the essential detail of actual life, the thing was done at once and forever.
>
> Here were principles which the commonsense of the English people would understand; here were principles which the great Greeks in their finest time established and here was I, the most prominent historical student, perfectly qualified to appreciate all this by my own determined mode of study under the influence of my old friend and watchmaker, – here was the hint of the skin perfectly comprehended by knowing well what was underneath it.

Oh how I inwardly thanked God that I was prepared to understand all this! I felt the future, I foretold that they would prove themselves the finest things on earth, that they would overturn the false beau ideal, where nature was nothing, and would establish the true beau ideal, of which nature alone is the basis.

I shall never forget the horses' heads, the feet in the metopes! I felt as if a divine truth had blazed inwardly upon my mind, and I knew they would at last rouse the art of Europe from its slumber in the darkness.

I do not say this now, when all the world acknowledges it, but I said it then when no one would believe me. I went home in perfect excitement, Wilkie trying to moderate my enthusiasm with his national caution. . . .

I passed the evening in a mixture of torture and hope; all night I dozed and dreamed of the marbles. I rose at five in a fever of excitement, tried to sketch the Theseus from memory, did so and saw that I comprehended it. I worked that day, and another, and another, fearing that I was deluded. At last I got an order for myself; I rushed away to Park Lane; the impression was more vivid than before. I drove off to Fuseli, and fired him to such a degree, that he ran upstairs, put on his coat and away we sallied . . . at last we came to Park Lane. Never shall I forget his uncompromising enthusiasm. He strode about saying, "De Greeks were Godes! De Greeks were Godes!"

And again in a letter to Lord Elgin dated September 23, 1809, Benjamin Haydon wrote:

I can see in those exquisite productions every great principle of art, all that is grand, necessary and beautiful. You have immortalized yourself, my Lord, by bringing them, and if you would but erect a building worthy of them, and admit students, your immortality would be on firmer ground. Michael Angelo was produced from Lorenzo de Medici's gardens. I should have no fear for the art of my country, were they once studied as they ought – they will create excellence wherever they drop – and I prophecy that from their landing in this country posterity will date the commencement of real art; – they are so pure, so uncontaminated, – nothing superfluous. That horse's head is the highest effort of human conception and execution, if the greatest artist the world ever saw did not execute this, I know not who did – look at the eye, the nostril and the mouth; – it is enough to breathe fire, into the marble around it – enough to create a soul, under the ribs of death.

I have intruded my own notions of their excellence, which I hope you my Lord will excuse. I am yet inexperienced, and diffident of all my opinions, but what to relate to the marbles – here I would stand content, until the world was in ruins about me, that I should have been permitted to study those very marbles appears to me when I reflect like a vision – for ever believe me, my dear Lord, Yours gratefully,

B. R. HAYDON

Postscript. The horse's head, the reclining figure and the Theseus, with the two sitting, the two lying women, the Bacchus and the metope of the figure grappling with the Centaur, are quite enough to reform art, or to create it, wherever they appear. Though fifty other things are all equally capable of doing that, in the collection. I again beg pardon my Lord for intruding my opinions.

* * * * *

But the entreaties of Haydon and his fellow artists fell upon deaf ears. The aristocratic circle, the cabinet and the House of Commons were in the pocket of Payne Knight and his friends in the Dilettanti. When Elgin, who had met with many financial reverses as a result of this undertaking, was obliged to offer the sculptures for sale to the British Government, Prime Minister Perceval offered him but a fraction of his price. Meantime the controversy had become so bitter, and the grounds of the Dilettanti for opposing the sculptures so untenable because of the opinions of artists on the Continent, that they turned their guns upon Lord Elgin's character, accusing him of having embarked upon a commercial enterprise of looting Greece under the protection of his diplomatic mission for the purpose of lining his own pockets. He was pilloried as a "marble dealer," and even a "marble stealer," and was described as a modern Pict. Lord Byron jumped into the fray in 1812, always the champion of Greece, and put into the mouth of Childe Harold the lament:

Thy walls defaced, thy mould'ring shrines removed
By British hands, which it had best behoved
To guard those relics ne'er to be restored. . . .

The year previously he had sent from Athens a libelous poem, *The Curse of Minerva*, in which he poured out his venom on both Lord Elgin and Benjamin West:

First on the head of him who did the deed
My curse shall light, – on him and all his seed:
Without one spark of intellectual fire,
Be all the sons as senseless as the sire:
If one with wit the parent brood disgrace,
Believe him bastard of a brighter race;
Still with his hireling artists let him prate,
And folly's praise repay for wisdom's hate
Long of their patron's gusto let them tell,
Whose noblest *native* gusto – is to sell:
To sell, and make (may shame record the day!)
The state receiver of his pilfer'd prey!
Meantime, the flattering, feeble dotard, West,
Europe's worst dauber, and poor Britain's best,
With palsied hand shall turn each model o'er,
And own himself an infant of fourscore:
Be all the bruisers call'd from all St. Giles,
That art and nature may compare their styles;
While brawny brutes in stupid wonder stare,
And marvel at his lordship's *stone-shop* there.
Round the throng'd gate shall sauntering cox-combs creep,
To lounge and lucubrate, to prate and peep,
While many a languid maid, with longing sigh,
On giant statues cast the curious eye;
The room with transient glance appears to skim,
Yet marks the mighty back and length of limb,
Mourns o'er the difference of *now* and *then;*
Exclaims, "these Greeks indeed were proper men";
Draws slight comparisons of *these* and *those*,
And envies Lais all her Attic beaux:
When shall a modern maid have swains like these?
Alas! Sir Harry is no Hercules!
And, last of all, amidst the gaping crew,
Some calm spectator, as he takes his view,
In silent indignation, mix'd with grief,
Admires the plunder but abhors the thief.

The tide was soon to turn in Elgin's favor, however. After the conclusion of the Peace of Paris in 1814, Ludwig, Crown Prince of

Bavaria, visited London with the express purpose of buying if he could the marbles of the Parthenon. He had just recently obtained for Munich the celebrated sculptures from the pediment of the temple at Aegina. He was loud in his praise of the sculpture and discreet in his activities; for he is said to have left £30,000 in the hands of his agent to step into the controversy at the proper moment. Ennio Quirino Visconti, the Director of the Musée Napoléon, likewise arrived in London with the same ideas in mind. Visconti was the son of the great archaeologist who had formed for Clement XIV and Pius VI the Museo Pio-Clementino at the Vatican. Entering into the service of Napoleon, he had supervised the transportation of the Roman monuments to Paris and was considered the foremost authority of his day, but also, in the opinion of many, "an authority whose opinion could be bought for £10."

Elgin still wished to place his marbles permanently in the British Museum. Yet it was not until his former secretary, W. R. Hamilton, had become the Under-Secretary of State for Foreign Affairs that the opinion of the government was finally turned away from the prejudices of the Dilettanti and looked with favor upon the acquisition of these celebrated works. Moreover the Prince Regent, later to become George IV, had in that same year, 1814, acquired for £15,000 the famous reliefs from Phigalia for the British Museum. Payne Knight and his circle perversely were loud in their favor and eulogies of these sculptures.

At long last the arrival in London of Canova produced the necessary action. He cried out that Lord Elgin's marbles "surpassed even the *Apollo Belvedere*." "Oh that I were a young man, and had to begin again, I should work on totally different principles of what I have done and form I hope an entirely new school."

The unkindest cut of all, and the one which took the ground completely from under Payne Knight's feet, was Canova's advice that "if the British government had paid £15,000 for the Phigalia reliefs, certainly the Elgin marbles were worth £100,000." At this suggestion of a bargain the House of Commons began to prick up their ears and express the question latent in everybody's mind – "Since these sculptures had been acquired by Elgin on a diplomatic mission, were they not quite properly the natural property of the British Government?" There was much talk of confiscation and the prerogative of the crown. These doubts had been expressed by Henry Bankes on the floor of the House and there was great dismay on the part of Elgin's friends when the former was appointed chairman of the Select Committee of the House to inquire into the matter. This committee was further charged "to inquire whether it be expedient that the collection should be purchased on behalf of the public, and if so, at what price it may be reasonable to allow for the same."

It was at this point, before the House had an opportunity to act, that the agent of the Crown Prince of Bavaria came forward openly with his offer for £30,000. But Bankes, despite his earlier prejudices, behaved with great propriety and was a thoroughly impartial president. We must again rely upon Michaelis's excellent account of the trial. On the twenty-ninth of February, 1816, the hearing of witnesses began, Lord Elgin being the first. He, Hamilton and Hunt were naturally the chief witnesses for the establishment of the facts, and a second group of travelers was called upon to confirm the condition and neglect of the Acropolis and the degree of danger which threatened the antiquities had they been left there in the hands of the Turks and the Greeks. Then there was a still larger group of artists and connoisseurs of which the most violent antagonist was Payne Knight himself. Haydon was not called upon because of the violence of the sentiments against Payne Knight which he had already expressed. But the testimonies of the artists "have a very different tone, particularly those of the sculptors Flaxman, Chantrey Westmacott and Rossi; the eccentric old Nollekens was less communicative. Different as were their modes of answering this or that separate question – Flaxman gave the committee a set lecture on the history of art – they were unanimous in the opinion that the Elgin marbles belonged to the very highest class of all known antiques, they not only excelled Townley's Greek or Roman sculptures, but deserved to be preferred before the Phigalia reliefs. Such had already been the opinion of Canova. . . . It was a fist battle between the old and the new periods of taste, but the victory of the latter was a foregone conclusion." Haydon, outraged that he had not been called by the committee, fulminated in the press with an article "on the judgment of connoisseurs being preferred to that of professional men." It was an article which created a sensation to which replies and rejoinders were written and which was translated into many languages going the rounds of Europe as a new gospel of art. Then came, just at the twelfth hour, "the two masterly treatises of Visconti which he had read before the Paris Academy the preceding autumn. Lord Elgin received them in time to have them printed, together with a letter from Canova, both in the original language and in English. The book appeared in May. The Earl's skill in thus marshaling in battle array his native troops and his foreign auxiliaries exactly at the right moment elicited no small admiration." Finally on the seventh of June, 1816, the parliamentary debate took place. Although Elgin's bare costs had risen to £51,000 and the interest he laid out on the capital was reckoned at £23,000, a proposal was made to return to Perceval's former offer of £35,000. This was reluctantly accepted. By a vote of 82 to 30 the Elgin marbles were acquired for the British Museum for that sum. By this vote the rule of Rome was ended, and Greek archaeology stepped up to take its rightful place upon the throne.

BOOK NINE

German Absolutism and the Ersatz Versailles

CHAPTER I

Poland and Saxony, An Eighteenth-Century Pattern

THE eighteenth century was the only cosmopolitan century that Germany had ever known. It was the century that gave her her greatest men and her strongest characters: Kant, Frederick II, Goethe – of whom Napoleon said, "*Voilà un homme!*" – and Beethoven. But the eighteenth century also failed to produce a single German artist of importance. Whenever a work of art was wanted, it had to be imported. Although the middle class was satisfied with the pedestrian accomplishments of Chodowiecki and Graff, the princely patrons had to turn to France and Italy. German noblemen seemed to have a horror of the home product. The court of Louis XIV and of his successors was slavishly imitated, and generally badly, not only by the innumerable princelings and the ruthless rulers of Saxony, but even by such an outstanding national figure as Frederick the Great.

The eighteenth century, unlike our own, did not value originality for its own sake. Imitation was by no means something to be avoided; it was the shortest way to attaining a high standard of culture. The German princes were trying frankly to excel each other in the imitation of the French pattern. Corneille, Racine and Molière dominated the stage; Lully prevailed in the opera, to which were also admitted the best of the Italians; palaces were built *à la mode de Versailles*, gardens were modeled after Le Nôtre, and objects of art were not less eagerly collected than by the French kings themselves. The German galleries of the eighteenth century owed their existence and their character neither to a genuine interest in living art nor to a historical tendency, but solely to the princes' wish to enjoy the perquisites of beauty. This explains that eclectic character so well described by a contemporary, who said that like the bees they obtained honey from every flower. Even the art patronage of such an independent personality as Frederick II is characterized by this eclecticism: he erected a Chinese pavilion in the park of Sanssouci and a year later a Gothic tower at Potsdam; he preferred French art, Pesne was his court painter, yet he was also collecting antiques and longing to visit Italy. "*Si de si fortes entraves ne me retenaient pas ici, je ferais cinq cents lieux pour voir une ville antique ressuscitée de dessous les cendres du Vesuve.*" *

Court life, as at Versailles, was a daily pageant with the prince in the leading role. The arts were there to provide the setting, the love of the theater was universal and its unreal character harmonized perfectly with the make-believe time in which they lived. The first building erected by Frederick the Great after his succession to the throne was a theater which bore the inscription *Fredericus Rex Apollini et Musis*. The sums spent on the theater were enormous, frequently exceeding those devoted to the patronage of literature and music. The staff of the Dresden Opera, for example, consisted of 175 persons and a single ballet is reported to have cost 36,000 taler. Talent was paid for its day on the same relative scale as at Hollywood at the present time.

Of all the German princes the rulers of Saxony were for four centuries the most distinguished for their flair as art patrons and collectors. The Elector Frederick the Wise (1486–1525), a follower of Martin Luther, had sought to raise the cultural standards of his country by remodeling his capital upon the pattern of Italian palaces which he had visited in his youth. After founding the University of Wittenberg, he invited Luther, Spolatin and Melanchthon there as professors. But his interest in art was conditioned chiefly by his desire to make his name live forever in its monuments. The Elector Augustus, the first of that name (1553–1586), had formed a remarkable library to which he added the more or less conventional art and curio cabinets of the period. They were no better or no worse than those of their contemporaries at the other German courts. His immediate successors, the two Christians and the four Georges,

* Letter to Algarotti.

THE SALON OF 1787

VENTE
DE
MEUBLES ET EFFETS
DE LA CI-DEVANT REINE,
PROVENANT DU PETIT TRIANON,
EN VERTU DE LA LOI DU DIX JUIN DERNIER,

Le Dimanche 25 Août 1793, l'an deuxième de la République une & indivisible, 10 heures du matin, & 4 heures de relevée, & jours suivans.

SAVOIR:

Tous les matins. BAtterie & ustensiles de cuisine & d'office, ferrailles & meubles communs.
Tous les soirs. Meubles de suite, consistans en Lits avec leurs housses de différentes étoffes; armoires, secrétaires, commodes, tables, consoles, partie à dessus de marbre; feux, chaises longues, fauteuils, canapés, banquettes, chaises à tabourets de damas, lampas, velours de soie d'Utrecht, & moquette; faïence, verrerie, porcelaine d'office & de table.

Les autres Meubles de toute espèce, & en grande quantité, seront annoncés par de nouvelles affiches.

Cette vente se fera en presence des Représentans du Peuple, & des Commissaires du District, au ci-devant Château de Versailles.

N. B. Les Meubles de la ci-devant Liste civile peuvent être transportés à l'étranger, en exemption de tous droits.

Les Commissaires de la Convention Nationale.
CH. DELACROIX, J. M. MUSSET.

DE L'IMPRIMERIE NATIONALE.

NOTICE OF THE SALE OF MARIE ANTOINETTE'S FURNITURE

TRIUMPHAL ENTRY OF ITALIAN ART IN PARIS

NAPOLEON TAKES THE BRONZE HORSES OF SAINT MARK'S

NAPOLEON'S MARRIAGE TO MARIE LOUISE IN THE GRANDE GALERIE OF THE LOUVRE

took good care of the collections and did their best to increase them. The inventory of 1640 shows that all pieces listed in the earlier inventory of 1587 were still there and that many new ones had been added. A report of a group of envoys from Weimar who visited Dresden in 1654, and the *Cedretum* of the *Kunstkammerer*, Tobias Beutel, published in 1671, give copious and detailed accounts of the state of the collections in Dresden before the eighteenth century.

It was on the accession to the throne of the Elector Frederick Augustus II (1670–1733) that Saxon patronage reached its full stature. Augustus the Strong was the very incarnation of the Baroque period. He had acquired the throne of Poland through bribery and conversion to Catholicism after John Sobieski's death in 1696, only to be deposed five years later by the Swedes who had invaded Saxony. Yet he returned to it once more after Charles XII of Sweden had been defeated by Peter the Great at Poltava.

While making the grand tour as a young man he had developed a voracious appetite for art and a determination to put the great collections which he had inherited into more suitable surroundings. A fire in his palace at Dresden in 1701 gave him the necessary excuse and in 1711 the Zwinger – generally considered the finest example of the Rococo in Germany – was commenced and the Royal Physician, Dr. Johann Friedrich von Heucher, appointed to sift out and rearrange the collections. The Zwinger was to unite a series of buildings: an immense banqueting hall, dance halls with baths and grottos, colonnades and pleasure walks. There were to be gardens and waterfalls. It was the masterpiece of that consummate toyman and architect Pöppelmann.

Twenty years later the task had been completed. The prints were catalogued in ten large volumes; there were the cabinet of *Naturalia*, the mathematical salon, the print room, the art cabinet, which contained paintings of the sixteenth and seventeenth centuries and which remained an independent unit until the middle of the nineteenth century. There were also the armory and the Green Vault, or *Grüne Gewölbe*, in which the most priceless jewels and cabinet objects were installed.

There among the precious royal playthings were exhibited an ivory frigate in full sail, Siamese twins in ivory and 142 fallen angels carved out of a single tusk. In the place of honor is a dish with an elaborate representation of the "Scarlet Woman." There are goblets made of ostrich eggs, a silver beaker from Nuremberg in the form of a young lady, and the Bible of Gustavus Adolphus. One may see vessels and trinkets made of every stone mentioned in the Book of Revelations. A "perpetual-motion" clock represents the Tower of Babel, whereon perch eight town pipers blowing four pipes, three trombones, and a waldhorn.*

Augustus II had purchased in 1723 from William I of Prussia the great collection of antiquities which the latter had acquired from the Odescalchi Palace in Rome, chiefly the classical portions of the collections of Queen Christina of Sweden, and of Canon Bellori and of Prince Chigi, together with the 32 celebrated antiquities that he had purchased from Cardinal Albani. The militaristic King of Prussia was content to sell him these antiquities on the condition that payment by the King of Saxony should be made in the form of a group of exceptionally tall Saxon soldiers for the King of Prussia's favorite regiment. But these antiquities never played a very important role in the life of the court at Dresden for they were kept for the most part in a shabby woodshed and those which had been placed about the gardens were used as targets by the Prussian soldiers during the occupation of Dresden in 1759.

It is to Augustus the Strong and to his son Augustus III that we owe the Dresden which we have so long admired and which is today but a memory. The former inaugurated in 1694 the Dresden Picture Gallery with the nucleus he had inherited. He "bought joyously" in the taste of the eighteenth century – Rubens, Jordaens, Teniers, Dou, Metsu, Ter Borch and Wouwermans. He also acquired the first Italians – Giorgione, Albani and Cima. The gallery progressed under the passionate enthusiasm of his son, who neglected the responsibilities of state to satisfy his love of art. Count Brühl, his Minister, was likewise a collector of the first rank and employed the famous connoisseur Heinecken, the "German Mariette," to fill the palace with the most priceless objects of Italy. Whereas his father had increased the royal

* R. H. Schauffler, *Romantic Germany* (N. Y. 1909), p. 291.

collection with 200 pictures, Augustus III in a single year, 1742, acquired by purchase no less than 715. Three years later he bought the world famous cabinet of Duke Francesco III of Modena. Never before had so splendid a collection been seen north of the Alps: Titian's *Tribute Money*, the four great Correggios, the enormous Veroneses, and celebrated pictures by Andrea del Sarto, Carracci, Guido Reni, Dosso Dossi and Garofalo. There were also celebrated canvases by Velasquez, Holbein and Rubens. The gallery of the Duke of Modena was acquired for "twelve barrels of gold." The purchase of the Wallenstein collection followed. This was interlarded with many individual pictures of the Flemish and Dutch Schools and, of course, the French School, which Heinecken had acquired for him in Paris. The peak was reached with the acquisition of the *Sistine Madonna*. Carlo Giovanni of Bologna, like so many other artists in Italy, abandoned painting for the more profitable activity of procuring old masters for the King of Saxony. It was he who negotiated with monks of the Church of San Sisto at Piacenza for the picture. When it arrived in Dresden to take its place in the Throne Room, the King was ready to receive it. With a gesture more Victorian than it was Augustan, he pushed the throne aside, exclaiming, "Make room for the great Raphael!"

By the middle of the eighteenth century the power of the Rococo and of the Baroque had spent itself; in the attempt to revive the classic style, its form was improved, its fascination increased. Winckelmann, who had come to Dresden in 1748, was perhaps the person most responsible for the revolution about to take place in German taste. His name has always been closely associated with that of Augustus III, who sent him to Italy, and he was in constant communication with the Prince during his sojourn in the Holy City. His *Thoughts on the Imitation of Greek Works in Painting and Sculpture* was published in 1755, shortly before his departure for Italy; its main theme being that "the only way for us to become great, even unsurpassable should this be possible, is to imitate the Greeks."

The influence of Winckelmann, emanating from Rome and spreading all over Europe, has already been stressed in the chapters on the growth of the Vatican collections and the dawn of art history in the eighteenth century. His *History of Ancient Art* dedicated to Baron Stosch appeared in 1764, the same year as Kant's *Betrachtungen über das Gefühl des Schönen und Erhabenen;* Lessing's *Laokoon* came off the press two years later. Madame de Staël prophesied that Winckelmann's work would have a greater influence on German literature than upon German art, and this prophecy was amply fulfilled. When he was a young student in Leipzig and taking drawing lessons from Oeser, Goethe was deeply conscious of his debt to Winckelmann. "His ideas," he said, "will influence my whole life. He taught me that simplicity and calm are the ideals of beauty." These ideas concerning classicism took such deep root that the cartoon and the form took precedence over color. It was the drawing, in imitation of the antique, that counted and Schiller even went so far as to say when he visited the Dresden Gallery, "The pictures would be quite nice if only they had not been painted." But while German classicism originated in that citadel of the Rococo, it was in Berlin that the ideas of Winckelmann came to their full fruition and accomplishment. After visiting the collections of Frederick the Great, he wrote, "I saw Athens and Sparta at Potsdam and I am filled with a worshipping devotion for the divine monarch."

CHAPTER II

Frederick the Great and the Rise of Collecting in Prussia

FREDERICK II, who was born in 1712 and died in 1786, experienced the full measure of the eighteenth century; he died just as the storm of the French Revolution was breaking over the heads of the Bourbons. As a philosopher, as a statesman and as a man of letters, he more nearly embodied the ideals of the *philosophes*, into whose company he was admitted by Voltaire, than any other person of royal blood of his day. He had the will and character of a king but at the same time the temperament and sensibility of the artist. Like so many men of the eighteenth century, he was a prodigious letter writer, revealing himself with an amazing frankness. These letters addressed to his brothers, his sister, his friends among the great throughout the world, and to the courtiers of his immediate entourage, seemed to offer an escape to this lonely man from the isolation imposed upon him by his rank.

The formation of Frederick's character was determined by the bitter antagonism that existed between him and his father, the soldier king, Frederick William I of Prussia. The latter had regarded himself as the personification of all Prussian virtues and interpreted his son's intellectual interests and artistic tastes as manifestations of a deplorable degeneration and an exasperating lack of respect to him. The Prince, on the other hand, educated by Huguenot tutors, considered his father a brutal and ignorant tyrant, ignorant both of his family and of his people. The conflict between father and son soon reached such a point that at the age of eighteen Frederick planned an adventurous escape to the court of England, which then seemed to him the cradle of all freedom. But the King, learning of the plan, prevented its execution.

The Crown Prince was stripped of his rank, threatened with death, then imprisoned, and his closest friend and helper, Lieutenant Katte, was executed in his presence.

Sobered by this experience, the romantic and brilliant youth emerged from being a fiery rebel into a sensible, mature man. He gave up his futile resistance against the King and complied with his wishes. He began to take a moderate interest in the army and in 1733 concluded a *mariage de convenance* with Elizabeth Christine of Brunswick-Bayern. Yet he succeeded in reserving for himself the right of shaping his own private life according to his tastes. Settling down to live and work at Rheinsberg, a beautiful estate given him by his father, Frederick devoted himself to his extensive intellectual interests. He spoke and wrote French and sought to be considered among the distinguished writers in that language. At this period he produced his *Considérations sur L'État Présent du Corps Politique de l'Europe* and his *Anti-Machiavel,* carrying on at the same time a lively correspondence with Voltaire. The latter led eventually to the French philosopher's arrival at Frederick's court in 1750, where he became the idol of the group of intellectuals who attended the King's dinner parties.

It was during the peaceful years at Rheinsberg that Frederick started collecting, adorning two rooms with pictures by Lancret and Watteau. After his accession to the throne in 1740 he added to them a great number of other prominent French artists, yet Watteau always remained his favorite. The Prussian King's preference for this master was soon realized by the Paris art dealers, with the result that Watteaus were manufactured by the dozens for the express purpose of selling them to him. If Frederick's collections were not altogether distinguished in the light of present-day criticism, one must stop to consider that there had been previously nothing in Prussia that could be compared with them.*

* Cardinal Albrecht of Brandenburg, in the first half of the sixteenth century, had been the patron of Cranach and Grünewald, but aside from his collection of their works there was little else besides the old-fashioned *Kunstkammer* of the Elector Joachim Friedrich. Sporadic purchases of Netherlandish paintings had been made by the Great Elector and by Frederick I, in addition to the inheritance of the House of Orange.

When Frederick the Great came to the throne he inherited a handful of relatively unimportant works and the confusion which his father's horror for anything that was not practical had made of the crown property. Already in the second year of his reign he embarked upon his collection of sculptures which reached before his death a total of 5000 items. The first purchase was of some 300 pieces in the collection of the Marquis de Polignac for 80,000 livres. These antiquities had nearly all come from Rome, where Polignac had had the ambitious design of diverting the Tiber in order to make possible excavations in the river bed. In 1747 Frederick acquired the splendid *Praying Boy*, a bronze in the best period of Greek art, which had belonged originally to the Surintendant Foucquet. Thirty years previously it had been acquired by Prince Eugene at whose death Prince Liechtenstein in turn had acquired it for 5000 taler. Some years later at the Julienne sale at Paris, Frederick the Great was one of the largest purchasers, acquiring 50,000 livres' worth of works of art including the ancient busts of *Augustus* and *Caesar*. His agents in Rome acquired many items from the collections of the Passionei Cavaseppe and Pietro Natali and over a hundred marbles came to him at the death of his sister, the Margravine of Bayreuth. Frederick placed the bust of *Marcus Aurelius*, whom he regarded as his ideal, in his bedroom and the busts of *Homer*, *Apollo* and *Socrates* in his library. All of these ancient marbles were ultimately removed to the Antike Tempel which he had built in the garden of Sanssouci.

Frederick's taste in painting was for the work of contemporary Frenchmen as it was in contemporary sculpture. He was particularly fond of the works of Adam, Bouchardon, Pigalle and Girardon. Later on he acquired statues by Coustou le Jeune, Lemoyne and Vassé. These modern sculptures were used as decoration for the picture gallery at Potsdam which was erected by the King in 1755. A few years later, while he was away engaged in the Seven Years' War, the Marquis d'Argens wrote to him, "All of the young men of taste here in town are making the voyage from Berlin to Potsdam to see the gallery with as much enthusiasm as the faithful who follow the pilgrimages to Loretto or Saint James of Compostella."

Previous to the formation of this gallery Frederick had been collecting French art almost exclusively for, due to the influence of his court painter, Pesne, this was virtually the only art which he knew. But after a visit to Dresden he seriously grappled with the problem of providing Brandenburg with a culture that was equal to that of Saxony. In a letter to his sister the Margravine of Bayreuth, dated November 30, 1755, the King wrote: "The gallery of pictures which I am making is entirely new; I have taken nothing from the galleries in Berlin; notwithstanding I have already brought together about 100 pictures of which there are two Correggios, two Guidos, two Paul Veroneses, a Tintoretto, a Solimena, twelve Rubenses, eleven Van Dycks, without counting the other masters of high reputation. I still need about 50 pictures which I am expecting from Italy and Flanders and which should, I think, complete my gallery. You see, my dear sister, that philosophy does not always banish folly from the heads of men; the folly of pictures will be of short duration with me; for the moment that there are enough according to the rule which I have laid down, I will not buy anything further."

This pledge, given but not kept by many a collector, was not kept by the King, who continued to collect as long as he lived. When the picture gallery at Sanssouci was filled to capacity, he started decorating the new palace.

It has often been claimed that Frederick's interest in art was superficial, vanity playing a greater part than appreciation. This view is not supported, however, by his letters; for even during his absence at the Seven Years' War, he wrote to the Marquis d'Argens, his trusted adviser, friend and agent who lived in the palace of Sanssouci: "I demand as rental for the house that you write to me frequently on how you find the gallery and if the old garden and the Chinese garden have made any considerable progress during the four years in which I have not seen them."

The year of the foundation of the gallery, 1755, was also the year in which the merchant Gotzkowsky made eight important art purchases on behalf of the King. Gotzkowsky, who liked nothing better than to collect on a grand scale, amassed a huge quantity of pictures. The King bought a number of them until his collecting activities were interrupted by the war. Yet while he was at the front, beset by the innumerable responsibilities and dangers of his campaign, Frederick longed for the peaceful and cultured atmosphere of Sanssouci and could not help wishing that he might augment his collection by at least a few pictures. He wrote again to the Marquis d'Argens in March 1760:

I have, my dear Marquis, a small commission to give you. You know that Gotzkowsky still has some fine pictures which he has consigned to me. I pray you to inquire into the price and to find out whether he has the Correggio which he has promised me; it is a little curiosity which comes to me. I do not yet know what will become of me nor what will be the outcome of this campaign which seems to me most hazardous and, mad as I am, I am inquiring about pictures. But there, that is how men are made, they have their months of reason and their months of waywardness. You who are indulgence itself should sympathize with my weaknesses. What you will write will at least amuse me and fill my mind momentarily with Sanssouci and with my gallery. I assure you that deep in my heart these thoughts are more agreeable to me than those of carnage, murder and all the disasters against which one must guard and which would make Hercules himself tremble.

Although a bill exists to show that the King paid Gotzkowsky 115,520 reichstaler for a number of the pictures, he left the dealer with a considerable number on his hands. The latter as usual, though he claimed the action of the King had thrown him into bankruptcy, nevertheless, sold these pictures to Prince Dolgorouky for the account of the Empress of Russia. When Gotzkowsky a short time later offered him a Raphael for 30,000 ducats the King replied, "The King of Poland can afford to pay 30,000 ducats for a picture and to introduce a hundred thousand reichstaler headtax in Saxony; this, however, is not my way of doing things. I buy if the price is reasonable and I can pay it, leaving the things which are too expensive to the King of Poland, for I cannot manufacture money and I do not care for the imposing of taxes." Yet, Frederick the Great did not hesitate to pay 21,000 livres to Pasquier for Correggio's *Leda* which had been formerly in the collection of the French Regent, the Duc d'Orléans.*

* This was the picture which the Regent's son Louis ordered cut into quarters but the pieces were not burned as he directed them to be; they were saved by the director of the gallery, Coypel, who took possession of them and succeeded in putting them together again. At Coypel's death the picture was sold to Pasquier.

The closing decades of Frederick's life were years in which he reaped the harvest of his success. A treaty of alliance with Catherine the Great had been concluded and in 1770 he participated in the first partition of Poland. During these years he devoted himself to agriculture, industry and commerce. He was also greatly interested in the Academy of Sciences and in the problems of education. He gave a new judicial code to his people and encouraged many constitutional reforms, particularly in the field of religious tolerance, and he became a patron of literature and music.

Strange to say, throughout his life he never gave any support to the artists of his own country. He believed that the arts served only a decorative purpose and he spoke of artists as having "a mechanical skill." He was as ready to pay a high price for two crystal chandeliers as he was for a dozen pictures by Lancret and Pater put together. Towards the end of his life he lost his interest in art as easily as he lost his interest in French culture, and he was ready to pass on these interests to his brother Prince Heinrich and to his sisters. Prince Heinrich was a musician, an intimate friend of Madame Vigée Le Brun, an ardent collector himself who owned 150 pictures and one of the finest collections of Houdon's sculpture that was ever formed. With him and the death of Frederick the classic age of German collecting had, however, come to a close.

* * * * *

Collecting in the lesser eighteenth-century courts of Germany was even duller — if that is possible — than in Prussia and in Saxony. The same pattern, the same pretensions, were everywhere apparent. Nowhere does the general level of smug connoisseurship and carefully planned opulence seem to depart from the conventional imitation of Versailles. The courts were the little courts of little men who created a society that was more middle class than even the bourgeoisie. Each elector or grand duke aped his neighbor. A uniform lack of distinction prevailed not unlike that which we have known more recently on Fifth Avenue between the two World Wars. Germany was a paradise for the art dealers and the *amour propre* of each principality depended not only on the state theater, the opera and symphony which kept the burghers comfortable and happy, but on the picture gallery which so manifestly proclaimed the cultural pride of both the reigning prince and his loyal subjects.

Bavaria was the exception for she had started early in the game. Maximilian I, the great rival of the Emperor Rudolph II, had been a tireless collector of the works of Dürer. These, together with his Cranachs and Italian pictures, were housed in the Grüne Galerie. Maximilian II increased the collection to more than 1000 pictures. These he divided between the Residenz in Munich and the splendid Rococo palace at Schleissheim. Obviously this phlegmatic South German house had been contaminated by their Hapsburg neighbors whose blood coursed through their veins. Maximilian II bought *en prince*, never haggling over price; he bought pictures on one occasion at Antwerp to the tune of 200,000 florins in a single hour, and another time bought a hundred pictures on the spur of the moment from Gilbert von Ceulen. Among these were twelve of the famous Rubenses of the Munich Gallery – the *Helena Fourment*, various landscapes and portraits by Van Dyck. He rounded out the representation of the Netherlandish School and added to the Italian – Titian's *Charles V*, the allegory of *Vanity*, Veronese's *Jupiter and Antiope*, Correggio's *Satyr* – and some Spanish works. At Schleissheim alone there were to be seen 100 Flemish pictures, 65 Italian, 53 German, 18 French. The Austrian occupation of Munich in 1706 brought about the cessation of collecting which was not again resumed to any great degree until Napoleonic times.

The Munich Picture Gallery was greatly enriched in 1805 by the addition of the celebrated Düsseldorf Gallery, founded by the Electors Palatine. The collection was removed to Munich to save it from being carried off by the French; it testifies to the ability of this other branch of the Wittelsbachs as connoisseurs of art. The Elector Johann Wilhelm had brought back with him from Italy in 1691 a second wife, Anna Maria Louisa, daughter of the Grand Duke of Tuscany,* whose dowry included Raphael's *Madonna dei Canigiani*. He had

* We have already met with her in Florence as the widowed Grand Duchess, Anna Maria Ludovica, "the last of the Medici," who willed the Medici collections to Florence.

already established his reputation as a collector, having acquired Rubens's *Assumption of the Virgin* and other famous works. A special building was erected in his palace at Düsseldorf to house his pictures, which numbered, among many others, 40 by Rubens, 17 by Van Dyck and 7 Rembrandts. His wife was instrumental in obtaining Raphael's *Madonna dei Tempi* and paintings by Andrea del Sarto, Titian, Palma Vecchio and Tintoretto. There were also the masters of the Bolognese and Roman Schools, Domenichino, the Carracci and Reni. The minor Dutch and Flemish masters were fully represented. With his father-in-law, Cosimo III dei Medici, he exchanged several pictures by Rubens for an antique *Wrestler* and Giovanni Bologna's *Rape of the Sabine Women.* His younger brother, Karl Philip, sent him other pictures and he tried to procure through his sister, the wife of Charles II of Spain, a celebrated Veronese from Madrid. This great collection exercised an enormous influence over eighteenth-century Germany. Goethe visited it with Holderlin and Hemse wrote of it in 1776:

> We have a collection of paintings which is unequalled in the whole of Germany, even including Dresden, and if a city in Greece is famous for some one statue or picture by a celebrated master, what would not Düsseldorf be considered if art were still honored and treasured as it should be?

Meanwhile another branch had likewise been filling the palaces of Mannheim with masterpieces of painting and antique marbles. These were merged with the collections of Munich when the Elector Palatine assumed the rule of Bavaria in 1777. The latter prince appointed as the director of his galleries the Düsseldorf painter Lambert Krähe, who enlarged them, added to the collections and was responsible for having made the famous gallery of copies of the Old Masters – particularly those of Italy – that so excited the admiration of Goethe and Schiller. Karl Theodor was, in fact, the epitome of the German professor of a later age. No field of knowledge fell outside his monopolistic care. He founded the German National Theater, associated with the name of Schiller, and the Kurpfälzische Akademie which lent support to the medical and natural sciences and contained a library of 50,000 volumes. The Elector's *Antiquarium Kabinett* was filled with the debris of the Roman palaces – heads of emperors, lamps, Etruscan bronzes – the leavings which the more knowledgeable French and English connoisseurs had left behind. He was also an insatiable collector of prints, especially of maps, and he acquired some 400 drawings as well as prints and antiquities from the cabinet of Baron Stosch. Here he had better luck, for among the 9000 which were pasted into folders were found 373 etchings by Rembrandt. Most of these works of art ultimately found their way to Munich, where, during the reign of Ludwig I, they were blended with the treasures of the other branches of the Wittelsbachs.

The Brunswick collections were started about the same time (1691) as those of Düsseldorf. A century later they numbered 1200 pictures, including famous works by Giorgione, Tintoretto, Veronese and the leaders of the Netherlandish School – Rembrandt, Rubens and Van Dyck. The collections, too, were particularly rich in porcelains and glass – 1000 pieces of majolica have come down to us intact.

The Hesse-Cassel collection likewise rose to prominence in the eighteenth century. Started primarily as a cabinet of natural history by the Landgraf Karl, it was transformed into a splendid gallery of art by his successor, Friedrich II. The nucleus was the collection of Dutch masterpieces brought back to Germany by Wilhelm VIII, the Governor of Breda. It was this collection which Napoleon was later to allow Josephine to retain in lieu of alimony. A part of it was later purchased by the Czar.

It would be tedious and fruitless to enumerate the collections of the German principalities – they are all so very much alike. Here and there a happy acquisition of an Italian masterpiece; everywhere good pedestrian examples – and sometimes brilliant ones – of the Dutch School; invariably a Dürer, each one more tired than the last. The pattern of the millionaire's collection of the 1920's was finally a reality.*

* The splendid collections of Schwerin, Aschaffenburg, Darmstadt, Karlsruhe and Stuttgart bear eloquent testimony to the art activities of the German princes. Weimar and Cologne, whose Bishop-Elector was one of the most brilliant collectors of the eighteenth century, were among the most fortunate cities. Würzburg enjoyed world fame through its patronage of Tiepolo. The role of these artistic centers (alas almost totally destroyed in the recent war) for the Romantic movement of the nineteenth century will be discussed in a subsequent volume.

CHAPTER III

The Great Catherine

THE culmination of German taste was to be achieved not in Germany itself, however, but east of the Oder in Petersburg. The sudden awakening of Russia under Peter the Great had given her a new appetite for the products of European culture from which, for so many centuries, she had remained separated behind an "iron curtain" of Slavic self-sufficiency. She had been cut off from the normal evolution of Western taste and had been virtually untouched by the successive cycles of the Renaissance and the Baroque. Her interest in antiquity was primarily with the occasional treasures from the Hellenistic and Scythian graves discovered in her southern territories, particularly on the shores of the Black and Caspian Seas. What Russia had retained, however, from her common European past was an intense hieratic medievalism which was carried on with little or no deviation by the Byzantine Church for a thousand years after Justinian. The ikons of the time of Peter the Great were little different than those painted ten centuries before, except for the fact that the vitality of the earlier examples had dried out and withered from the limitations of an orthodoxy which was no longer a personal conviction but the carefully planned program of a state religion.

To be sure, both European and Asiatic influences had crept in, particularly in the popular art of the peasants in the more exposed borders of the empire. And whereas the schools of painting continued with extraordinary fidelity to the canons of the Church, it is in the accidental decorative elements of a dress or piece of furniture, or in the carving of the frame, that we see the introduction of foreign styles and motifs. Moreover, the reception given Byzantine humanists in the courts of Italy after the fall of Constantinople had established a point of contact between the scholars of both worlds. And the growing intercourse between the Russias and the cultures of Islam and western China provided constantly fresh elements to the decorative repertory of this isolated continent.

Prior to Peter the Great collecting as it was known in Europe had never existed; the court had seldom, if ever, ventured out of Russia and they knew nothing of the preoccupation of Western princes. The years of apprenticeship which Peter spent in Holland studying ship construction had opened his eyes to the prestige value of cultural collections in a nation's capital. Like so many "tycoons" of the present day he started in with Dutch pictures, particularly marine subjects, for he had the landlocked monarch's love for the sea. He purchased entire collections *en bloc* – the Bregue and Cottwold cabinets in Danzig, the Lieberkuen collection in Berlin, that of Lüders in Hamburg as well as several others. These formed the nucleus of his own art and curio cabinet to which he gave the German name of *Kunstkammer*. A new building was provided for it and a catalogue in German was issued. He spent much of his time there and, following the pattern of Saxony and Prussia, received ambassadors from foreign powers amidst his borrowed finery.

If the German courts were patterned after that of France, the eighteenth-century taste of Russia was essentially Teutonic. Following the example of Frederick the Great, who had given his favorite palace the French name of Sanssouci, Peter baptized his new Baltic capital Saint Petersburg and called his other palaces by the German names of Peterhof and Oranienbaum. A similar contrast may be seen in the fact that whereas the proceedings of the Prussian Academy in Berlin were conducted in the French tongue, his newly formed Academy in Petersburg spoke and wrote in German. French did not, in fact, become the court language until the accession of Catherine.

To Peter art was essentially an article of import, and although he did invite French and German artists to come to Russia, he totally ignored the little native talent that existed in his country. He tried in vain to establish a porcelain manufactory but was unable to obtain from foreign countries either the experts or their jealously guarded secrets of manufacture. He did, however, succeed in bringing an Englishman, William Elmzel, to Russia to found a native glass industry.

But to agents and art dealers from abroad he gave every opportunity for establishing themselves, urging the nobles to patronize them and to surround themselves with works of art suitable to their rank. Whenever he traveled in Europe he paid especial attention to the monuments, the churches and palaces along his journey. He took the time on his visit to London to sit for Kneller; and in Paris he tried, without success, to persuade Nattier to come to Russia as court painter. When he arrived late in the evening on his first visit to Dresden, he asked to be shown the art cabinet immediately and became so absorbed with the exhibits that he spent the entire night in studying them.

Peter's predilection for things German was carefully nurtured by Frederick the Great, who saw in it a way of weakening the power of Austria, by a strong alliance between Russia and Prussia. He managed to put a German princess, Catherine of Anhalt-Zerbst, on the throne of Russia despite the suspicions and misgivings of the reigning Empress. At the age of fifteen this Lutheran girl, for reasons of state, embraced the Greek Orthodox Church and embarked upon the unhappy marriage that was so soon to make her the most powerful woman of the world.

As a lover of art Catherine the Great was no less voracious than as a lover of men. She never posed as a connoisseur in either field and frankly exulted in satisfying her passions wherever she found them. In speaking of her collecting she said, "*Ce n'est pas l'amour de l'art; c'est la voracité. Je ne suis pas amatrice, je suis gloutonne.*" She slept with her several ministers in turn with the same abandon that she acquired her works of art, paying for them at the top of the market and discarding each one to satisfy some new refinement of body and soul; yet keeping in the aggregate a collection of objects and of people who were both stimulating to her imagination and useful to her lust for power. Her connoisseurship was as superficial as her philosophy, but both were indeed brilliant and characteristic of the age in which she lived. Durand, the French chargé d'affaires, gave the following account of her: "*La tragédie lui déplait, la comédie l'ennuie, elle n'aime pas la musique, sa table est sans la moindre recherche; le jeu n'est pour elle qu'une contenance; elle n'aime dans les jardins que les roses; elle n'a enfin du goût que pour bâtir et pour régenter sa cour, car celui qu'elle a pour régner, pour figurer dans l'univers, est passion.*" But above all it was her genius for personal rule and her ability for getting along with people that helped her through her most difficult situations. Princess Dashkov said of her, "Everyone, I believe, who has had the good fortune to approach her person must have more or less felt the influence of that irresistible eloquence and address to gain or to persuade which she had always at her command." "*Je plaisais: c'était mon fort,*" Catherine wrote freely about herself; she never misjudged either her strength or her popularity, and she could afford to relax the protocol and etiquette of court life to introduce instead into Russian society the informality of the Parisian salon.

Catherine despised her husband, Peter III, as cordially as he hated and feared her. "*Je vis clairement,*" she said, "*qu'il m'aurait quitté sans regret. Pour moi, vu ses dispositions, il m'était à peu près indifférent mais la couronne de la Russie ne me l'était pas.*" And it was the indescribable misery of her married life which led her to other men. At last her turn came with the bloodless revolution planned by her lover Gregor Orlov. One morning in 1762 she was awakened from her sleep to find Orlov standing at her bedside. "It is time for you to rise. Everything is ready to proclaim you," he said. Catherine dressed quickly, "*sans faire toilette.*" The guards marched to Peter's palace to take him prisoner, Catherine leading them on horseback wearing a Guard's uniform, and accompanied by a group of noblemen devoted to her. "Political action was indistinguishable from romantic masquerade." On this occasion Catherine displayed as usual her innate fitness to rule and her superior sense of the theater. Peter abdicated unconditionally. Catherine was inclined to send him in exile to Holstein, but Orlov and the nobles recognized that there would be no safety for any of them so long as Peter remained alive. Peter was put to death. In the words of Carraccioli, "*Le trône de la Russie n'est ni héréditaire, ni électif, il est occupatif.*"

Thus at thirty-three, Catherine, more beautiful and in better health than ever, became Empress, the sole Ruler of all the Russias. Immediately she set about the task of making her upstart regime the equal of the great courts of western Europe. Her original plan, which was never carried out, was to create an Académie du Nord with a huge art collection attached to it. Instead she added to the collections which Peter the Great had already started. Her predecessor, the Empress Elizabeth, had added nothing to them save a few mediocre objects in the Palace of Tzarskoje Selo. Her sole preoccupation had been her personal wardrobe which included some 15,000 gowns and 5000 pairs of shoes. The palace rooms formed a contrast of gilded finery, *à la Versailles*, and shabby neglect. Tapestries woven with gold thread rotted on damp walls. Clearly what was needed were comfortable apartments for living. She summoned the architects Trombara and Quaringhi from Rome. In 1765 she commissioned the Frenchman, de Lamot, to erect a pavilion connected with the Winter Palace to house her picture collections. It was to be a Hermitage after the manner of Jean–Jacques Rousseau's Hermitage on the estate of the Marquise d'Épinay. There, wrote Somov, "laying down the burdens of royalty, Catherine II became a woman of the world, charming her guests with '*les plus belles qualités de l'esprit et du coeur.*' "

Her first purchase in 1764 was the group of pictures which Gotzkowsky, the German merchant, had assembled for Frederick the Great, for which she paid 180,000 reichstalers. In this group were three Rembrandts, one of which, *Joseph and Potiphar's Wife*, is now in the Mellon collection in Washington. After this the collections followed furiously: 1768, the collection of Gaignat, the secretary of Louis XV; 1769, the collection of Count Brühl in Dresden for 148,000 florins *holl*. This purchase, one of the most brilliant, brought to the Hermitage many of its most treasured possessions: 2 Rembrandts, 4 van Mieris, 3 Ostades, 5 Ruisdaels, some Wouvermans, Terborchs, Rubenses, and a fine group of Italians. A group of pictures acquired by her agent in Amsterdam, Yver, from the Gerrit Braamcamp sale in 1771 was shipwrecked off the Finnish coast. Only a Mignard, which had been delayed in shipment, ever reached Russia. In the same year Catherine bought *en bloc* the famous collection of François Tronchin which his friends Voltaire, Diderot and Grimm had recommended to her. Grimm also acquired for her (in 1787) for 450,000 livres the incomparable collection of antique engraved gems of the Duc d'Orléans, for which Mariette had written the catalogue. The year 1772 saw the arrival at the Hermitage of some 400 pictures from the collections of the Crozat family which were purchased for 440,000 livres.* These included Titian's *Danaë*, and the *Portrait of Cardinal Pallavicini*, the beautiful Poussin now in Philadelphia, a number of canvases by Rembrandt, and above all the Raphael *Saint George*.

Other French collections of prime importance were acquired by Russia at this period of which the details may be found in Charles Blanc and Dumesnil. Prince Galitzin, the Vice-Chancellor, was sent to Paris expressly for the purpose of acquiring eleven pictures from the sale of de Choiseul d'Amboise, Comte de Stainville. Two of them were *The Fairs* by Teniers, which had belonged to the Comtesse de Verrue. Other celebrated cabinets to be drawn within the Russian orbit were those of Randon de Boisset and the Comte de Baudouin.

Catherine constantly complained of being "*pauvre comme un rat d'église*" and swore that she would stop buying. But always her agents turned up at the next great sale with the longest purse in Europe. As she had said herself, "*Je ne suis pas amatrice, je suis gloutonne.*"

The greatest coup of all, however, was the purchase in London in 1770 by the Russian ambassador, Moussin-Pushkin, for £40,000 of the great Walpole collection at Houghton Hall. This was sold to pay the debts of the second and third Earls of Orford, Horace Walpole reluctantly acquiescing. (The group of pictures sold comprised 198 pieces, including 79 Italians, 75 Flemish and Netherlandish, 7 Spanish, 22 French and 5 English.) England had lost its greatest ornament since the sale of the collection of Charles I.†

* Both collections of the brothers Crozat passed to Baron Thiers, Lieutenant General under Louis XV. These were again bequeathed to another nephew, who sold a portion of them at auction in 1757. The sale to the Hermitage was effected by Diderot. Cf. C. Blanc, *Le Trésor de la Curiosité*, and Dumesnil, *Histoire des plus célèbres amateurs français*. E. Dentu, 1856. Vol. II.

† The French Revolution was the signal for an activity which occurred not alone in Russia but in the capitals and cities of the Baltic and in Scandinavia. The nobility of Denmark and Sweden particularly were wedded to the fashions and intellectual pursuits of the French Court. But since their effects were not felt until long after the collapse of Napoleon, and contributed directly, as did the activity of King Ludwig II of Bavaria, to the Romantic Movement, they will not be discussed in the present volume. A full account of these eighteenth-century innovators will be given in the consideration of the collectors of the nineteenth century.

BOOK TEN

Collecting in the Napoleonic Age

CHAPTER I

The Growing Storm of Revolution

CATHERINE THE GREAT with her voracious appetite for other people's art was both a symbol and a cause. She represented the extremes of absolutism, the embodiment of personal power and self-interest; at the same time by her activity in art she offered a refuge for the capital which was in flight from the more uncertain countries of western Europe. This flight expressed itself not so much in the shipment of bullion – for there was precious little upon which the rank-and-file French aristocrat could lay his hands – as in the portable works of art which, easily removed from his château in the country or his apartment in town, could be converted into immediate cash in England or in the colonies. Already the rage for porcelain, touched off by Madame de Pompadour's extravagant support of the Manufacture Royale de Sèvres, had provided an excuse to the nobility to decorate their dining tables with the more fashionable and brittle ware, thus abandoning the family plate to the discretion of the smelter and the transfer of negotiable funds abroad. The process which had set in with the bursting of John Law's "Bubble" in 1720 continued slowly yet inexorably.

Only the few who blindly imitated the extravagances of the court itself failed to realize the disaster that impended not for the regime alone but for the whole European system. Democracy was perhaps the fashionable topic of the *salon* but beneath the powdered wigs of the *philosophes* and the billowing taffetas and coiffures of the blue-stockings, anxiety and reckless despair waged a constant and relentless warfare. The *style Louis Seize*, so sweet, so pure, so classically serene, was not the conscious proclamation of political or economic security; rather it was the declaration of principles of a new society to whose acceptance the *ancien régime* had arrived too late. If there were those who in the panic of the moment admitted the rights of man and the true justice of republicanism, more often than not it was a case of *sauve qui peut.*

The collections formed in the reigns of Louis XV and Louis XVI have one feature in common – each one was dispersed after the founder's death to foreign countries. Germany, Russia and Sweden were the principal buyers at the sales. The agents of Catherine pre-empted most of what was fine at the Gaignat sale in 1768 – Gaignat had been the secretary to Louis XV and had made a good thing out of it. Tronchin, the friend of the *Encyclopédistes*, sold his splendid pictures in 1771. The following year Catherine acquired at the sale of Crozat's nephew, Baron de Thiers, the *Saint George* by Raphael already mentioned, Titian's *Danaë* and several of the Rembrandts which have followed it to America from the Hermitage. In the same year Prince Galitzin paid over half a million livres for eleven pictures from the collection of Choiseul d'Amboise, Comte de Stainville. The collection of Randon de Boisset was sold piece by piece in 1777, Le Brun acting as agent for the Empress and buying most of it. And again in 1781 a celebrated sale took place disposing of the group of Rembrandts belonging to the Comte de Baudoin. During the same year the notable cabinets of Julienne and La Roque likewise went under the hammer.

There was at this time no national repository to which these collections might have been bequeathed had there been any disposition on the part of the owners to do so; for when Madame de Pompadour died her ambitious plans for the artistic development of the reign of Louis XV died with her. Marigny, her brother, continued for a while in office and Madame du Barry, to be sure, felt obliged to identify her passage with a gesture – *couleur de rose* – and a few trifling changes in the prevailing taste; but her art, though no less accomplished than that of her predecessor, was of another kind.

In 1750 an abortive effort had been made to open a museum for the public exhibition of the Royal Collection at the Luxembourg. One hundred and ten canvases were displayed adjacent to the galleries containing the series of the *Life of Marie de Medicis* which Rubens had painted for the Queen of France. The gallery was open, free, two days a week, but soon the court, anxious lest this concession on the part of the King to the radical demands of the day be misinterpreted as a sign of weakness, closed it except to a few artists who had the ear of the inner circle. The pictures lingered on there until 1785, when, the palace being turned over to the Comte de Provence, they were all shipped out to Versailles. Marigny in the meantime had obtained the permission of Louis XV to remove to the gardens of his private Château de Ménars the Greek and Roman sculptures which Colbert had so laboriously brought together for the crown. Another group of these marbles adorned the gardens of the Duc d'Antin.

* * * *

Louis XVI, it has been said, "*n'avait point de maîtresse; il faisait de la serrurerie.*" Historians are divided upon the question of his innocence and of his stupidity. To the historian of art neither quality is particularly important for he added little to the artistic thought of the French people and, save for a few excellent pictures, among which was Rembrandt's *Pilgrims at Emmaus,* virtually nothing to the national patrimony. In 1769 the Comte d'Angevillers, *Directeur des Bâtiments,* tried once more to enlarge the embryo museum at the Luxembourg by transferring all of the collections of the crown which had been neglected for half a century to the Louvre. Although the decree was signed by the King the plan was deferred until it was too late. The approaching Revolution drove d'Angevillers into exile as it had already done Monsieur de Calonne, Prime Minister of Louis XVI. The latter's collection, which he carried with him to England, "formed over a period of thirty-five years at an expense above 60,000 guineas," was to be a bright spot in London society until it was finally sold in 1794.

If Louis XVI does not loom large in the estimates of present-day historians, he nevertheless played a role in his own day as the symbol of the fury and terror of the Revolution whose victim he became. Horace Walpole, who had so admired Washington and Franklin and whose private sympathies had been always with the revolutionaries in America, recoiled in disgust and horror at those "tigers, hyenas, savages, Iroquois, that bloody and atrocious nation" of the French. In a letter to Lady Ossory he summed up the entire revulsion of his age:

Indeed, Madam, I write unwillingly, there is not a word left in my dictionary that can express what I feel. Savages, barbarians, etc. were terms for poor ignorant Indians and blacks and hyenas, or were some superlative epithets for Spaniards in Peru and Mexico, for Inquisitors or for enthusiasts of every breed in religious wars. It remained for the enlightened 18th century to baffle language and invent horrors that can be found in no vocabulary. What tongue could be prepared for a nation that should avow atheism, profess assassination and practise massacres on massacres for four years together: and who, as if they had destroyed God as well as their King, and established incredulity by law, giving no symptom of repentance! These monsters talk of settling a constitution – it may be a brief one and couched in one law, "Thou shalt reverse every precept of morality and justice and do all the wrong thou canst to all mankind."

Yes, Madam, yes, the 18th century could not close without carrying its improvements into execution and exhibiting the discoveries of philosophy. It had extracted an *encyclopédie* of all the guilt of former ages, and to avoid the charge of plagiarism had piqued themselves on refining on the cruelty of every crime, extracting the quintessence of all the tortures exercised on the early Christians. The most august senate of the world (as the French assemblies have called themselves), the Parisians for four years together have heaped every species of indignity, insult, terror, deliberate barbarity on five wretched persons, all the time in their power, and studiously augmented every dread of a father and mother for themselves and their two children, and gone on in that meditated inhumanity by retrenching every poor comfort, inflicting cold and want of necessaries, and every now and then enlivening their sufferings that might have grown torpid by use, by exhibiting to their eyes the bleeding head of their butchered friend, or assailing their sensibility by massacres of hecatomes of their innocent friends – no matter whether women or men! . . .

Religion, spotless virtue, good nature never impeached, abhorrence of spilling blood even to rescue himself and family, courage unshaken, dignity with not a shade of affectation, patience unexampled, and charity unwearied by indignities, and all this mass of virtues evidently both the emanations of his heart and the result of a propriety of good sense, for in all his trials did he either utter one silly sentence or not give the proper answers that truth and reason dictated? – Let the bloody peasants, his butchers, name the Roman or Greek, the Antonine or the Socrates, who lived as innocently or died so beautifully as Louis Seize.

It is ironical, perhaps, that it was one of the bloodiest of these hyenas who finally brought about the organization of the Louvre. On the twenty-ninth of May, 1791, Barère, *l'Anacréon de la Guillotine*, proposed to the Constituent Assembly of the Revolution the creation of a national museum. Two years later, on the 18th Brumaire, Year II (November 8, 1793), the Muséum Français finally opened its doors. The public was admitted free during the last three days of each *décade* or ten-day period, the artists on the first five days. David was made the chief of the committee directing the affairs of the institution. To bring about a public museum from the chaos of the Terror was no mean accomplishment, for the jealousies of the art world were easily translated into politics; denunciations and executions were frequent; pressure groups of artists were not unlike those which beset museum directors at the present time. Moreover, the dispossession and eviction of artists and their families who lived in small, jerry-built apartments subdividing the great galleries of the Louvre – many of whom had, indeed, lived there more than twenty years and had developed considerable prestige and power – made the work of the committee even more difficult. But what saved the latter was the urgent need for space to accommodate the thousands of works of art pouring in from the provinces – pictures and statues taken from the churches of France and Belgium by the victorious armies of the Revolution. The closing of the convents and monasteries, the sequestration of all ecclesiastical property and the appropriation of the private property of the *émigrés*, had put into the public domain the most extraordinary treasures, particularly of French art. While it was inevitable that chauvinism should be uppermost in the minds of the revolutionaries, the *Commission du Muséum* saw their responsibilities "with a largeness of spirit that did them honor." Since the collections of the crown had been richest in the masterpieces of the Italian Renaissance and in the Dutch and Flemish Schools, the Committee took a national pride in presenting the masterpieces of the French – Le Sueur, Poussin and Le Brun among many others – which "for their beauty contended successfully with the masterpieces of other countries."

As the Revolution gained momentum the demand for art became more and more a symbol of the new authority. The Jacobins were determined to show that culture, once reserved exclusively for the pleasure of the monarch and his favorites, was the natural right and endowment of the people. The Directoire pompously notified its young Corsican general that "the time has now arrived when the Muséum Français should encompass the most celebrated monuments; for the sovereignty of all the arts should pass to France in order to affirm and embellish the reign of liberty."

The French agreed that they were the people ordained by God to receive the spoils of antiquity; they were the inheritors of ancient Rome. Moving swiftly through Belgium they saw to it that the Flemish and Walloon churches shared the same fate as those of France. Her finest treasures – the Ghent altarpiece by the Van Eycks of the *Adoration of the Lamb* – were among the first to go, together with Rubens's *Descent from the Cross* from Antwerp Cathedral.* The usual excuses were made for further conquests of art – those of preserving and saving the most valuable treasures of history. From Belgium the Republican Army had moved on to Holland, where, since in this country of John Calvin there were no longer any monuments to seize on the grounds of superstition, they annexed the collections of the Stadhouder and the possessions of the Dutch burghers as objects of despotism and fanaticism. Always they acted in the name of humanity and for the good of mankind. By the time Napoleon was ready to cross the Alps a tradition had been firmly established.

There is a tradition in Amsterdam that when Napoleon and his looters came to take away Rembrandt's *Night Watch*, the picture had already been removed from the stretcher, laid flat and hidden beneath the floor of the gallery in which it was customarily exhibited.

* The Ghent altarpiece is one of the most widely traveled works of Flemish art. During World War II it was sent to France by the Belgian Government. The French then sent it to southern France, where in 1943 Abel Bonnard, Vichy Minister of Education, presented it to Hermann Goering for his birthday. It was subsequently recovered by the American army and returned to the Cathedral of Saint Bavon.

The Emperor demanded to know if there was not such a picture in the collection – while at the very moment he was standing upon it. The Dutch official replied, "Sire, the very fact that Your Majesty does not find the picture here must mean that it has already been taken down and at this minute may be on its way to Paris." The Emperor accepted the reply and no further search was made for it.

CHAPTER II

The Sack of Italy

I Francesi son tutti ladri
Non tutti, ma Buonaparte

People of Italy: The French Army is coming to break your chains. Meet it with faith. Your property, your religion, your customs shall not be touched. Everyone shall enjoy his property in security and, under the protections of virtue, exercise his rights. The people must remain quiet, we are the friends of all nations, especially of the descendants of Brutus, the Scipios, and of the great men whom we have chosen for our own model. To restore the Capitol and to erect there the statues of those heroes who have made it famous will awaken the Roman people who have been petrified through centuries of servitude. That shall be the fruit of our victories.

THUS, Napoleon, who knew the value of propaganda as well as art, proclaimed the entry of his armies into Rome. "*Je me plais,*" he wrote to Carnot, "*à voir Paris le rendez vous de toute l'Europe,*" and to fulfill this desire he left no stone unturned – particularly if it was a precious stone. If his proclamation to the Roman people gave voice to his concern for their welfare, his actions and his private utterances were lacking in such sentiments. "We will have everything that is beautiful in Italy," he said, "except a small number of objects at Turin and at Naples." Upon this basis he forced the Pope to sign the Treaty of Tolentino by which the Louvre (if only for a few short years) received a hundred of the greatest jewels of the Vatican. And it was the "violation" of this treaty by the Allies in 1815 which the French have ever since considered one of the blackest crimes of history. Was it not, they say, a diplomatic agreement contracted by two sovereign states? The case, moreover, had been fully stated by the painters Isabey and Gérard when they said, "*La République Française* *par sa force, la superiorité de ses lumières et de ses artistes est le seul pays au monde qui puisse donner un asile inviolable à ces chefs d'œuvre."* *

The greater part of the artists of France subscribed immediately to this point of view. "The more our climate seems unfavorable to the arts, the more do we require models here in order to overcome the obstacles to the progress thereof. . . . The Romans, once an uncultivated people, became civilized by transplanting to Rome the works of conquered Greece. . . . Thus the French people, naturally endowed with exquisite sensitivity, will, by seeing the models from antiquity, train its feelings and its critical sense. . . . All nations must come to borrow from our art, as they once imitated our frivolity."

Happily for the record this early doctrine of the *Herrenvolk* was questioned in responsible circles. Quatremère de Quincy, the perpetual secretary of the Académie des Beaux-Arts, in an open letter to General Miranda, protested against the grave prejudices to art and science which the removal of these objects from Italy might envisage. It is a noble and impassioned document which in the heat of present-day discussions regarding restitution of works of art and their possible use in payment of reparations gives pause to hasty actions and vindictiveness. He looks on Italy as the true homeland of the arts which must not be despoiled of her heritage, lest in their transplanting these very objects fail by some terrible disassociation to impart their fullest meaning:

Why does not France instead exploit the ruins of Provence? Why, after the discoveries made during the past century of so many statues among which was the beautiful *Venus* of the Gallery of Versailles, found at Arles, does she not investigate once more the knowledgeable and scholarly remains of Vienne, of Arles, of Orange, of Nîmes, of Autun, and many other places? Why does she not restore the beautiful amphitheatre of Nîmes, making it a depot for the wealth of antiquity in this Roman colony? Why does she not establish there a museum of antiquities corresponding to those of Italy? This, it would seem to me, more appropriate

* "The French Republic by its might, by the superiority of its enlightenment and of its artists, is the one country in the world which can give inviolable shelter to these masterpieces."

to accomplish before dismembering and despoiling the galleries of Rome and Italy.

Would it not be better, on the other hand, instead of removing from the great laboratory, which Rome is, her instruments of work and fragments for study, to reassemble there once more all those monuments which a misguided enthusiasm has from time to time removed from the city. . . . The most telling effect of these monuments upon those who study them is precisely this very impact of their accumulation . . . for we are incapable of judging them except by relation and comparison. The sense of beauty, the most independent and freest of all the senses, comes only from a comparative judgment that forms within our understanding. Knowledge of the beautiful, so necessary to all artists, is best achieved by climbing a scale or ladder in which the various classes of art are ranged according to an hierarchy of merit. . . . The number of masterpieces of all kinds which exist in the world is limited by the number of human geniuses. Each category increases in number in direct proportion to its decrease in merit; as the subaltern points of comparison become more numerous, the more the pre-eminence of the fewer is apparent and their beauty and instruction the more striking. Thus, the precious minority of antique statues owe their superiority directly to the infinite number of inferior ones against which they stand out and shine so brilliantly. . . . It will always be necessary that artists go to Italy to study, and particularly to Rome, for it is unlikely that the Pantheon, the Coliseum, or the columns of Trajan and Antoninus will be removed. . . . In vain may they take down paintings and remove frescoes but they will never take away the Sistine Chapel or the Farnesina or the beautiful galleries with their great pendentives, nor the cupolas and ceilings by Michelangelo, the Carracci, the Domenichini, the Guidi etc.

This protest of Quatremère de Quincy, to which was appended an artists' petition to the Directoire, was a gallant but none the less futile gesture. The French had tasted victory and were determined that they alone were entitled to its fruits. Napoleon, possibly in order to clarify his own equivocal position as a Corsican, wrote from Milan in 1796: "All men of genius, all those who have attained distinction in the republic of letters are French no matter in what country they may have been born." The terms of the Treaty of Tolentino were fully carried out. By its terms the Pope was required "to deliver to

THE GOTHIC GALLERY

THE RENAISSANCE GALLERY

LENOIR'S *MUSÉE DES MONUMENS FRANCAIS*

THE FRENCH ARTIST MOURNS THE FORTUNES OF WAR

the French Republic one hundred pictures, busts, vases or statues to be chosen by the Commissioners sent to Rome, among which would be notably the bronze bust of Junius Brutus and the marble bust of Marcus Brutus from the Capitol and five hundred manuscripts to be chosen by the said Commissioners."*

But the looting of Rome did not stop with the limits of the treaty. Private villas and palaces were ransacked, including the living apartments of the Vatican, fines and levies were imposed on the inhabitants. What the Commissioners did not acquire for their official purposes, they and the higher officers of the army took for their own use — Paul Louis Courrier wrote to a friend from Rome: "The monuments are scarcely better treated than the people. . . . Everything that was at the Certosa, at the Villa Albani, at the Farnese, the Onesti, in the Clementine Museum at the Capitol, has been pillaged, lost or stolen. . . . Soldiers who entered the Vatican Library have destroyed among other rarities the famous *Terrence* of Cardinal Bembo, one of the most precious manuscripts, which was stolen for the golden ornaments of its binding. The *Venus* of the Villa Borghese has been

* Translation of a Petition to the Directory supporting Quatremère de Quincy's pamphlet: "A love of the arts, a desire to conserve the masterpieces admired by all peoples, a common interest in this great family of artists spread out at all the various points of the globe, are the motives which prompt our addressing you. We fear that this enthusiasm which impassions us for the productions of genius might lead away their true interests even from their most ardent friends; and we come to you to beseech you to weigh with mature thought the important question of knowing whether it is useful to France, whether it is advantageous to the arts and to the artists in general, to remove from Rome the monuments of antiquity and the masterpieces of painting and sculpture which comprise the galleries and museums of that capital of the arts.

"We shall not allow ourselves to make any reflections on the subject in regard to any of the opinions heretofore publicly expressed in learned discussions; we shall limit ourselves to asking you, Citizen Directors, that before removing anything from Rome a commission be formed of a certain number of artists and men of letters to be named by the Institut Nationale, partly from its members and partly from without, for the purpose of making you a general report upon this entire question.

"Upon the basis of this report where all of the considerations will be discussed and weighed with the mass of reflections and indispensable illuminations for the development of so great a subject, and so worthy of yourselves, you will then pronounce the fate of the arts for future generations.

"Yes, you may rest assured, the decree which you will make will fix forever the destiny of these works; and it is thus in order to form the crowns destined for our triumphant legions that you will unite with the laurels of Apollo the palms of victory and the branches so deeply sought of the tree of peace."

Needless to say, no attention was ever given to this petition.

wounded by the hand of descendants of Diomedes and the *Hermaphrodite* (*Immane nefas!*) has a broken foot."

Throughout the peninsula the first Italian campaign of 1796–1797 had yielded untold treasures to the Gallic Caesar: Milan, Modena and Parma were plundered, Naples had been looted, and the troops helped themselves to the libraries of Pavia, Monza, Bologna and to the Brera and Ambrosian library at Milan. A clause in the Treaty of Tolentino had provided that in addition to the works surrendered from the Vatican and a levy of 300,000,000 scudi from the Papal States, the art treasures of Ravenna, Rimini, Pesaro, Ancona, Perugia and Loreto were to be given up. In April and May 1797 the French were in Venice where they removed the *Winged Lion of Saint Mark* and the famous bronze horses from the basilica. After the Peace of Campo Formio, Venice was assigned to the Austrian occupation troops, but not before a great part of the Titians and Tintorettos had already started on their journey to the French capital.

The Roman collections, packed and crated, were assembled at the port of Leghorn whence they went by sea to Marseilles. Here they were transferred to barges and floated up the Rhône, and then by numerous canals and inland waterways to the Seine. The first convoys arrived in Paris on the ninth Thermidor of the Year Six (July 27, 1798). One of the Commissioners, Thonin, indignant that these treasures were to be dumped on the Quai du Louvre "like so many cases of soap," suggested a pompous fete to celebrate their arrival in the city. A triumphal cortege left the neighborhood of the Jardin des Plantes where the barges had been moored and started its stately procession to the Champ de Mars escorted by troops, the members of the Institut marching in uniform and in a body and "a great multitude of distinguished personalities." Triumphal chariots, decorated with leaves and ribbons upon which were proclaimed the contents of the cases, and banners crying out "*La Grèce les céda; Rome les a perdus; leur sort changea deux fois, il ne changera plus*," carried the greatest objects: the bronze horses of Venice, the *Apollo Belvedere*, the *Laocoon*, the *Brutus* of the Capitol, Raphael's *Transfiguration*, Correggio's *Saint Jerome* and many others. Appropriate ceremonies took place before the Altar of the Revolution in the Champ de Mars, the Paris mob showing its appreciation of the culture of antiquity with the same enthusiasm that it received the wild animals destined for the Zoo and the miracle-working *Virgin of Loreto*, attributed by tradition to the hand of Saint Luke.*

The Louvre had already been closed for a year in order to make provision for the objects that were expected from Italy. The Muséum Français went out of existence and a new organization took its place, the Musée Central des Arts, which was presided over by a new commission. Obviously such a great enterprise was in need of a director but the Directoire was most penurious and the new museum had a struggle to get on its feet financially. Not until 1805 did the Palace of the Louvre come under the control of the Museum by order of the Emperor. In the meantime, Ennio Quirino Visconti, who had accompanied the sculptures from the Vatican, was charged with the problem of their exposition. He was the son of the earlier Visconti who, with Winckelmann, had created the Vatican Museum, and he quite naturally felt that, since he had become more Bonapartiste than the French themselves, he was the natural heir to the Museum of the Louvre.

It happened, however, that on a certain afternoon in 1797 a young man attended a reception given by the Marquis de Talleyrand, and fell into conversation over the punch bowl with General Bonaparte. The young man, who a few months later joined the General's staff for the Egyptian campaign, was none other than the Baron Vivant-Denon, the greatest impresario the art world has ever seen.

* Dorothy Mackay Quynn, "The Art Confiscations of the Napoleonic Wars," in the *American Historical Review*, April 1945. This article reviews and summarizes the researches of Saunier and Lanzac de Laborie from which much that follows has been taken.

CHAPTER III

Vivant-Denon and the Musée Napoléon

BARON VIVANT-DENON was one of those characters which only France and the eighteenth century together could produce. Having spent his early youth at Versailles under the protection of Madame de Pompadour, he forged a link between the *ancien régime*, the Revolution and the Empire. The bitterest years of his life were spent in that full cycle of the return of the Bourbons with Louis XVIII and Charles X. When he met Napoleon and went with him to Egypt, although he had the vigor and passion of youth he was already a man of fifty who had lived furiously and had known the widest variety of European society. At the age of seven a gypsy read his palm and said, "*Tu seras aimé des femmes, tu iras à la cour, une belle étoile luira sur toi.*" And the young Vivant-Denon never lost an opportunity to bring these prophecies to fulfillment. His earliest preferment was obtained when, scarcely more than a boy playing in the gardens of Versailles, he tossed a tennis ball in the pathway of the King. Louis XV took a fancy to him, enjoyed his scabrous wit, the indecent comedies and verses which he wrote so easily, and his accomplished flattery. Since he was a gentleman of the petty nobility of the provinces without fortune, Madame de Pompadour obtained for him a series of diplomatic posts, in Russia at the court of Catherine the Great – where undoubtedly he added to her repertoire on human relations – in Switzerland and at Naples, whose court was basking in the novel sunlight of the still fresh discoveries of Pompeii and Herculaneum. He was an excellent draftsman and engraver, enjoying a respectable professional standing with the artists, which, combined with a carefully cultivated intimacy with David, placed him on the side of the angels when the knife of Madame Guillotine began to fall.

When Vivant-Denon handed Bonaparte a glass of lemonade at the Marquis de Talleyrand's he was a person of stature and experience who could not be dismissed as either a sycophant or a soldier of fortune. If, indeed, he was a little bit of both it enabled him to play his larger role in a manner worthy of its dimensions. He is best known by his publications of the Egyptian campaign, the earliest monumental work on the ruins of the Nile Valley, and the records of his reckless exploits in the face of enemy fire prove the extent of his deep interest in archaeology. It is ironical perhaps that the great Egyptian wealth of the British Museum, the one institution which Vivant-Denon feared and detested, should be largely due to the good advice which he gave Napoleon. For the objects destined for the Louvre were taken by Nelson at Trafalgar and Paris never tasted the rich rewards of this campaign.

Upon Vivant-Denon's return from Egypt the works of art from Italy were already assembled at the Louvre under the care of Visconti. The First Consul visited the Museum for the first time in 1800 in the company of Le Brun, Josephine Bonaparte, Hortense Murat, the Councilor of State, Bënézech, who was acting Grand Chamberlain, Duroc, Eugène, the dealer Le Brun, and Vivant-Denon, who styled himself inoffensively "one of the scholars of the Egyptian Expedition." Napoleon at this time was beginning to show a taste for monarchy. Visconti had had no time to strike a medal for this inauguration and therefore contented himself with placing a bronze tablet on the base of the *Apollo Belvedere* containing this inscription:

*La statue d'Apollon qui se lève sur ce piédestal, trouvée à Antium sur la fin du quinzième siècle, placée au Vatican par Jules II au commencement du seizième, conquise l'an V de la Republique par l'armée d'Italie sous les ordres du Général Bonaparte, a été fixée ici le vingt Germinal, An VIII, première année de son consulat.**

The opening of the Museum was a great success, so much so that the members of the administrative council voted to perpetuate its

* "The statue of *Apollo* which stands on this pedestal was found at Antium at the end of the fifteenth century, placed in the Vatican by Julius II at the beginning of the sixteenth, conquered in the Year V of the Republic by the Army of Italy under the orders of General Bonaparte, has been placed here the twentieth Germinal, Year VIII, first year of his Consulate."

memory with an annual banquet. Newspapers celebrated the occasion, as did the theater; tourists argued as to whether the *Apollo Belvedere* was better seen at the Louvre than it had been at the Vatican. Miss Mary Berry, Horace Walpole's young friend, wept bitterly on its loss of dignity, and the German musician, Reichardt, congratulated the Louvre on having removed the dreadful fig leaves which ecclesiastical prudery had demanded at the Vatican.

The Museum, now very proud of its collection of sculptures, recalled to the Louvre the great collection of marbles which Marigny had taken from the Royal Collections and placed in the gardens of his Château de Ménars, with the consent of Louis XV. The French were not content to stop with the Treaty of Tolentino and they began to loot regularly and systematically the other public as well as private collections of Rome. Eleven objects, ceded by the Treaty of Tolentino, particularly the colossal groups representing the *Nile* and the *Tiber*, had been too heavy to be transported on the wagons to Leghorn and had remained in Rome in storage. After the retreat of the French army, the Neapolitans took them, together with a statue of *Pallas* recently unearthed at Velletri, and the antiques of the Villa Albani and of the Duc de Braschi, with the intention of transferring them to Naples. However, after a good many diplomatic maneuvers, they were finally sent to Paris in 1802. The ambassador of King Ferdinand of the Two Sicilies had said that Naples would never go to war for a statue.

A new system was devised for exhibiting the pictures as quickly as they arrived in Paris and could be put into condition to be shown. The most beautiful canvases, and the most famous ones, were provisionally shown in the Salon Carré, which was used as a hall of temporary exhibition. It was here that the public saw in succession Raphael's portrait of Leo X, the *Madonna della Sedia*, the great canvases of Veronese and Rubens, other Rubenses and Van Dycks that came from Genoa, and the Fra Bartolommeos; also the *Madonna* of Foligno and the *Death of Saint Peter Martyr* by Titian. An English traveler baptized the Salon Carré as the *bouquet de Bonaparte*. It was not, however, until long after the period of Napoleon that the idea prevailed of making the Salon Carré into the type of room that, since the time of the Medici, the *Tribuna* had been in the Uffizi in Florence.

The Louvre was regularly used as a reception hall for the great dignitaries that came to Paris at this time. On the occasion of the visit of the King of Etruria the Salon Carré was hung with the two great Veroneses, the *Marriage at Cana* and the *Feast at the House of Levi*, and the huge *Battle of Alexander* by Le Brun. The other Italian pictures had their definitive place in the waterside galleries of the Louvre, after which followed the French Schools, the German, the Dutch and the Flemish. The opening of the picture galleries created a furor; all of fashionable England poured over from across the Channel to see one of the Seven Wonders of the World.

The works of art had not withstood the journey too well. The Etruscan vases from the Vatican arrived in pieces and had to be put together by the painter and restorer Lagrenée, the decorator at the manufactory at Sèvres. The paintings had been rubbed, the varnish had been affected by the damps, and much had to be done to them before they were put up. Hacquin was in charge of the restoring of the paintings. It was indeed fortunate that the artists who comprised the council of the Louvre were men of such intelligence and taste, and so restrained in the question of retouching.

The cartoons of the *School of Athens* had been taken from Milan in several pieces. They were reassembled and exhibited in 1802 in the *Galerie d'Apollon*. The administration of the Louvre also tried to take possession of the famous Raphael tapestries of the Vatican. At the moment of the occupation of Rome by the Army of the Directoire in 1798, these tapestries had been put up for sale. There was a terrible protest and furor, the Commissioner Faipoult withdrawing them from sale and claiming them for France. They got as far as Genoa, where they were given up in consideration of some bonds underwritten by the Roman Republic. They nevertheless remained in the north of Italy until 1808 when they seem to have been picked up by a Jewish art dealer who sold them to Pius VII; they were finally brought back by the latter to their ancient places in the Vatican.

The history of the Louvre during this period followed inevitably the history of the nation. Having been organized at first as the Musée Central des Arts under the Directoire, it had become the Musée Napoléon under the Consulate and the Empire. These changes were accompanied by an administrative decree in November 1802.* The problem of who was to be the Director of the new Musée Napoléon was a burning issue in Paris in that winter. Visconti, the Roman archaeologist and classical scholar, was the favorite candidate and was convinced that he would receive the appointment. The Minister Chaptal had written the decree with his own handwriting, calling for a Director General at a salary of 12,000 francs. According to Lanzac de Laborie, he left a blank in which he intended to insert either the name of his own son or of Visconti. The Emperor returned the blank to him filling in with his own hand the name of Citizen Denon.

Six weeks after his appointment as the Director of the Musée Bonaparte, Vivant-Denon wrote to the First Consul, "*Je passe mes jours à mettre au fait de tout-ce que vous m'avez confié afin de me rendre maître et de justifier, peut-être, à l'avenir l'opinion que votre choix a donné de moi, et chaque fois que j'aperçois une amelioration à faire, je vous en fais l'hommage et vous addresse des remerciements de m'avoir élu pour l'opérer.*" † Accompanying Napoleon on all of his campaigns, directing the seizing of works of art and libraries throughout Europe, he stopped at nothing to create a flattering impression. At the time when Napoleon was planning the invasion of England, Denon conducted a frantic search for objects which in some way recalled the greatness of William the Conqueror; finding nothing, he took an old statue from the basement of the Musée des Monumens Français in the convent of the Petits Augustins, "*une statue anonyme, costume du onzième siècle, visage gras, les yeux à fleur de tête et l'air cholérique.*"

* "*Il y aura un directeur général du Musée Central des Arts. Il aura sous cette direction immédiate le Muséum du Louvre, le Musée des Monumens Français, le Musée Spéciale de l'École Française à Versailles, Les Galleries des Palais du Gouvernement, la Monnaie, les Medailles, les ateliers de Chalcographie, les gravures sur pierres fines et de mosaiques, enfin l'acquisition et le transport des objets d'art. Il sera assigné un logement au Directeur Général.*"

† "I pass my days familiarizing myself with all which you have confided to me in order to make myself master of it and to justify, perhaps, in the opinion of posterity your choice in me, and each time that I perceive some amelioration that might be made, I pay homage to you for it and address you my thanks for having elected me to execute it."

It was secretly packed up and carried out in a cart to a village on the banks of the Seine, then triumphantly brought back to Paris in a barge decorated for the occasion and proclaimed as a newly discovered statue of William the Conqueror found in Normandy. Notwithstanding, it is to the credit of this man, his courage, his willingness to fight, his importunities to get the proper moneys to pay the salaries of his employees, that we owe the present Museum of the Louvre. Vivant-Denon's financial battles were endless and he was in constant conflict with the ministers, particularly with the ministers of finance, who sought to put both him and his various functions into a strait jacket. This he would not tolerate. In a letter addressed to the Emperor in 1806, Denon points out to Napoleon that at the age of sixteen he had been a chamberlain to Louis XV and, later on, invested with diplomatic missions; he protested against a reform in the ministries which reduced him to the rank of a *chef de bureau.* "*Il est tout simple de n'avoir point d'emplois mais il faut que celui que l'on accepte convienne à l'état où l'on est né.*" *

At the end of March, 1803, the first convoy of antiquities ceded by the government of Naples arrived in Paris. "A lucky star," Denon declared at a public meeting of the Institut, "has guided the circumstances of these shipments." But despite this declaration, there were difficulties. The earlier things, the smaller pieces, came through at once but the very large pieces were held up by the drought, which had so lowered the water in the canals that it did not permit the barges to come through to Paris. The wild and exotic animals destined for the Jardin des Plantes suffered greatly and Denon was particularly concerned about a lion cub which had grown so much since the departure from Marseilles that it could no longer turn around in its cage. To these dilatory trophies of the Peace of Tolentino, which included the two colossal groups of the *Nile* and the *Tiber*, was added the *Medici Venus* from Florence.

The history of the Florentine collections which went to Paris is intimately interwoven with the Treaty of Madrid, by which, in 1801, the Grand Duke of Tuscany was replaced in Florence by the infant

* "It is all very well to have no employment but the employment which one accepts must conform to the position into which one is born."

Louis I (son of the Duke of Parma and of the daughter of Charles IV of Spain) who became the king of the short-lived Kingdom of Etruria. Already in 1797 at the approach of the French army, the Grand Duke of Tuscany, Ferdinand, had packed up 74 cases of objects of the Florentine collections and had shipped them to Leghorn. These cases, which included many of the finest things of the Florentine (and particularly the Medici) collections, were shipped from Leghorn in the autumn of 1800 to Palermo by the British navy, in order, so they said, to better guarantee the rights of their proprietor. The following year, the Republic of Tuscany, upon the initiative of the government of the First Consul Napoleon, was awarded to Louis de Bourbon Parma with the title of King of Etruria. The French envoy to Naples and the member of the revolutionary Convention, Alquier, were charged with the restitution to the Florentine court of the objects which had been taken away to Sicily. It was only natural that they should demand the *Medici Venus* on behalf of the Louvre as a commission for the French intervention. The "Venus of the Medici," wrote Foubert, "is one of the most famous and precious of antique statues, it will be glorious for France to make the acquisition of it," and he suggested an exchange of products of French manufactures in the value of 300,000 francs.

The puppet King of Etruria would have preferred, as he wrote to the First Consul, "an enlarging and a rounding out of the frontiers of my state," but Bonaparte was inflexible. His envy and cupidity had been aroused and he had the pretensions to place the *Venus dei Medici* beside the *Apollo Belvedere* in the Louvre. In 1802 the *Medici Venus* was shipped from Palermo to Marseilles. The Tuscans were inconsolable. The curator of the Uffizi, pointing his finger at the empty pedestal, had the temerity to observe to a French officer, "We have put nothing in its place because nothing can replace our Venus, it was the glory of Florence." In vain the Emperor sought to placate them by ordering later on a statue by Canova to occupy its place; the French director of police in Tuscany wrote, "The artists maintain that the *Venus of Napoleon* equals the *Venus of the Medici*," but the Florentine people were not to be satisfied again until its return after the battle of Waterloo.

The statue, although it had left Marseilles on the seventh of September, arrived at the Quai du Louvre only on the morning of the fourteenth of July, 1803, too late to be inaugurated in the celebrations of the day. This gave Denon adequate time to make preparations for its placing. He wrote to the First Consul, who was then in Belgium, "I will await your return to open the Museum of Statuary. It is you, General, who have brought it together, it is your prerogative to open it, since it is for all time the monument of monuments." This celebration took place on the fifteenth of August, Napoleon's birthday. Accompanied by Josephine, he spent the night at the Tuileries and after a solemn high Mass at six o'clock in the morning at Notre-Dame, he proceeded to the Louvre, accompanied by Denon, to open the doors of the Musée Napoléon. The ceremonies were brief and, because they were held so early in the morning, were free of formal addresses. But a few days later, Vivant-Denon, recently elected to the Institut, outdid himself in a pronouncement of rhetoric and criticism through which the chauvinistic genius of the French shone without mercy: "Today we may say assuredly to the arts that once more the *Venus* is under the safeguard of the most powerful of all nations and that the sanctuary in which it is deposited is for her the Temple of Janus against which the doors are forever closed." Finally he wound up with the inevitable parallel between the *Apollo Belvedere* and the *Medici Venus*. The *Apollo*, he declared, "would intimidate the boldest woman; the most timid young man would accompany with expression of sensibility the first words which he might address to the *Venus*."

Once Napoleon had proclaimed himself Emperor, Denon followed him in all of his campaigns and was constantly with him on terms of easy intimacy, never losing an opportunity to point out to the Emperor objects in the countries of his conquests which might add to the personal glory and ambitions of his name. When the *Pallas of Velletri*, discovered only six years earlier, was added to the gallery, he urged the Emperor to demand a further contribution of eight pieces of sculpture of the finest quality from Florence. These, he claimed, were not part of the Florentine patrimony, since they had come originally from Rome from the Medici Palace. The Emperor, however, was unwilling to make such demands upon Tuscany, but he did go along in the matter of the acquisition of the antiquities of the Villa Borghese, for in 1808 he forced his brother-in-law, Prince Camillo Borghese, husband of the lush Pauline Bonaparte, to sell to him what he wanted of the collection. These marbles were so large and so heavy that it required specially built carts drawn by as many as a dozen or fifteen oxen to move them. Upon another occasion, when Napoleon was lunching with Denon and Canova, the Director of the Museum expressed his intention of bringing the Farnese *Hercules* to France. But the sculptor, horrified, exclaimed, "May Your Majesty at least leave something in Italy. These ancient monuments form a chain which, with an infinity of other things, cannot ever be transported either from Rome or Naples." As a result the Emperor left the *Hercules* in Naples.

Napoleon's hero complex for ancient Rome expressed itself in many curious ways; he had set his heart upon the famous statue of Pompey in the collection of Prince Spada in Rome, at the feet of which Julius Caesar was said to have been assassinated. Spada asked 23,000 Roman ducats for it. The Emperor dispatched Denon to Rome to examine the statue, where, under the influence of the antiquary, Fea, who deliberately depreciated the object in order to keep it in Rome, he came to the conclusion, "*Ce n'était point Pompey qu'il répresentait mais un empereur mal determiné, et le travail artistique en était très mediocre.*" Denon was highly pleased. "It is my duty to warn Your Majesty," he wrote, "that the statue would add nothing to the collection of the museum and, if it were in Paris, it would be only with great difficulty that it could be placed. I would add that the head does not belong to the body. The statue seems to me to be one of those thousand and one rhapsodies which are daily made in Rome and to which great names are given in order to overwhelm the foreigners to whom they are sold at an exorbitant price." Visconti, possibly out of spite and in the hope of doing Denon one in the eye, hotly defended the statue. Napoleon, still spellbound by the classic legend of the Ides of March, none the less ordered the Director to conclude the negotiations. But for some reason or other the statue was never shipped from Rome and remains to this day in the Palazzo Spada.

A spectacular effort was made for the acquisition of the pediment sculptures from the temple at Aegina – the glory of the Munich Glyptothek. These seventeen statues, discovered by two English and two German archaeologists at Aegina, representing scenes from the Trojan Wars, were transported by the owner to Xanthis, where they were put up at auction. Upon the insistence of Visconti and to the annoyance of Denon, the French were the top bidder, 150,000 francs. But the year 1813 was a difficult one for Napoleon. The marbles were then transported from Xanthis to Malta, where, under the custody of the British, the sale was continued and the pieces knocked down, not to France but to Prince Ludwig of Bavaria, the future King Ludwig I. Napoleon, increasingly doubtful of his Bavarian alliance, wished to take no chance of offending the Germans on this point and grudgingly ceded them to the Munich gallery.

Towards the end of Napoleon's reign the number of antique statues exhibited at the Louvre, busts, bas-reliefs, exceeded four hundred. Napoleon had put the finger on practically everything that was worth while and available in Europe. He came perilously close to getting the Elgin marbles which went to the British Museum. Save for his misfortune at Trafalgar, the burden of explanation of how these sculptures were removed from Greece would now be on the shoulders of French archaeologists. He likewise lost out on the Aegina sculptures, and missed two more lots which went to the British Museum, the reliefs from Phigalia in Arcadia, the frieze attributed to Phidias, representing the *Battle of the Centaurs and Lapiths*, and the other, the *Combat of Theseus with the Amazons*, a frieze containing more than one hundred figures.

Denon and Visconti, who continued as curator of antiquities, naturally appropriated everything from the campaigns for the Louvre. One capital group of works they were, however, obliged to cede to the politicians and the soldiers; namely, the bronze horses from Saint Mark's in Venice. These were the original horses that were, according to tradition, made by Lysippus for Alexander the Great at Athens, given by Tiridates, King of Armenia, to Nero, who later placed them in the Hippodrome in Constantinople and were finally stolen by the Venetians from the Turks in the twelfth century. The horses were placed above the Arc de Triomphe of the Carrousel in the Garden of the Tuileries. There they were to commemorate Napoleon's military triumphs; he planned one more such monument, the Temple of Victory (which was never built), upon which were to be placed the *Quadriga* which in battered glory still adorn the Brandenburger Gate in Berlin. In order to make room for these steadily growing collections of the Museum, it was necessary to clear out from the Louvre organizations which had long been lodged there. In 1806 the Institut was moved out across the river to the palace which Mazarin had built for the Collège des Quatre Nations, the present seat of the Institut de France. The great Salle des Cariatides of the Louvre was readapted to contain the marbles of the Villa Borghese and the statues that were stolen from the Vatican.

* * * * *

The brilliance of the museum of antiquities cannot be overestimated, but Denon's principal preoccupation was in the organization of the picture collections of the Louvre where he pieced together the greatest picture gallery that the world had ever seen. Within a few months of his entering upon his duties as Director, he devoted a bay of the large gallery along the waterfront to the works of Raphael. Sixteen pictures by the master were grouped around the *Transfiguration* and it was possible to follow the entire evolution of his genius. "I will continue," he declared, "in the same spirit for all the schools and in a few months, in walking through the galleries, it will be possible to perceive the historic course of art and particularly of painting." Like all museum directors, he was dissatisfied with the lighting in his gallery and made all kinds of experiments to try to improve it. The architect Raymond, working with him, devised a moderately successful scheme for dividing the large galleries into bays and thus controlling the distribution of the light.

The alterations were finally terminated early in 1810 when the great picture gallery was designated to serve as the frame for one of the most memorable ceremonies of Napoleon's regime. Orders were given that the Grande Galerie of the Louvre was to be transformed into a chapel for the marriage of the Emperor with Marie Louise of

Austria. Only three weeks before the ceremony Denon received the following instructions from Daru:

> Sir, the religious marriage of His Majesty will be celebrated in Paris in the picture gallery which will be decorated as a chapel. There will be special places assigned for the Three Estates and everything will be so arranged that there will be no confusion. Along the entire length of the gallery of the museum will be two rows of benches on each side to seat three thousand persons, behind which there shall be two rows of gentlemen containing another three thousand persons, in all six thousand. Every possible precaution must be taken to avoid any accident occurring with so many persons in this gallery.

There were many difficulties in rearranging the gallery for this event, particularly as to the moving of very large canvases. Denon had had the temerity to point out that the *Marriage at Cana* by Veronese was too large to move. The Emperor replied, "Since it cannot be moved, then burn it," and Denon, against his will, was obliged to remove certain of the larger canvases from their stretchers, mounting them on rollers. Others he covered with damask and with silk and left them hanging on the wall. Denon wrote to the Intendant Général, Daru, "You may assure His Majesty that the public and the strangers will see, and his court will pass through, the most beautiful museum of the universe." An eyewitness of this ceremony, which took place on the second of April, 1810, has said, "As the Emperor advanced slowly through the bays of this gallery which, with his sword, he had hung with the masterpieces of the ages, and where, like trophies, the pictures recalled all of his greatest victories; the acclamation, at first discreet, increased, then spread and sustained and finally reinforced by the orchestras, filled the gallery with an astonishing tumult." The following day Napoleon and his bride paid the gallery a secret visit on which only Denon and his assistants were allowed to accompany the imperial couple.

* * * * *

The Louvre was now at its apogee; despite the wars which the Emperor was carrying on in every part of Europe, it was the acknowledged center of the world of art. Painters and sculptors flocked to

Paris to revel in the masterpieces from Italy and Flanders which filled its walls; it became the Mecca of the young French artists of the nineteenth century, who were never, indeed, to abandon the habits they had formed of coming to the Museum in these early years.

Still Denon was not satisfied with his incomparable collection. After the battle of Jena, when Napoleon was overrunning Germany, he urged the Emperor to demand as reparations from the King of Saxony certain of the most famous paintings of the gallery at Dresden, particularly the Correggios and the Holbeins. "The latter painter," he wrote, "is lacking in Your Majesty's collection. I should repeat again to Your Majesty that, in making the conquest of the rest of Europe, no opportunity will present itself of equal importance such as that of Saxony." Napoleon, however, would not concede this point, since he wished to make Frederick Augustus of Saxony an ally. Denon thereupon pounced upon Cassel, where he pre-empted 299 pictures, 153 objects of art, 367 pieces of lacquer, porcelain and pottery; he then proceeded to make heavy seizures in Brunswick, in Berlin and in Potsdam. Already fifty of the finest pictures of the Cassel gallery, particularly Rembrandt's *Descent from the Cross,* had been removed after the battle of Jena and were hidden by order of the Elector of Hesse in a game warden's house. General Lagrange seized them and sent them to Mayence, to the Empress Josephine, who had demanded them for herself, despite the protests of Denon, and placed them at Malmaison. These pictures, therefore, never entered the Louvre and were at a later date considered by the Emperor as part of his divorce settlement with Josephine. After her death in 1814 they were sold to the Czar Alexander I of Russia. Certain of them have remained at the Hermitage in Saint Petersburg, others are now in the Mellon collection in Washington.

The plunder of the German cities had been going on for years and exceeded, if that seems possible, what had already happened in Italy. Starting in 1794 the Revolutionaries had brought back from Aix-la-Chapelle the Hochminster marble columns, later incorporated in the galleries of the Louvre and the sarcophagus of Charlemagne, decorated with reliefs illustrating the rape of Proserpina. After the Peace of Lunéville the Commissioners, becoming more learned, and possibly more Germanic, took with them as *articles de voyage* carefully annotated copies of guidebooks such as *Le Voyage de Deux Bénédictins de Saint Maur* which conveniently inventoried the cloisters and abbeys they had visited. During the years 1806–1807 the collections and castles of the North German princes were systematically raided under the direction of Denon and two equally rapacious lieutenants, Daru and Henri Beyle (later to rise to fame under the pseudonym of Stendhal). The latter gave his personal attention to the property of the Duke of Brunswick – who was particularly hateful to the French and had a magnificent library at Wolfenbüttel containing 500 copies of manuscripts from the library of Cardinal Mazarin made for the Duke August the Younger. These were all shipped to Paris together with 78 paintings, many by Raphael, Titian, Rembrandt and Van Dyck. From Berlin and Potsdam a wide variety of objects were stolen, books, some annotated by Voltaire, paintings, a collection of medals worth 500,000 marks and a group of carved gems. By the end of the Napoleonic campaigns the shameless tally stood as follows:

> Berlin and Potsdam between them lost 60 paintings; Cassel, 299 after the first levy; Schwerin 209; Vienna lost 250 from the Belvedere alone and the galleries at Düsseldorf and Zweibrücken also suffered. In 1800 Munich and the magnificent collection of Schleissheim were raided and Nuremberg and Salzburg were robbed; in 1809 other objects were removed from Vienna. By 1814 they had taken about 4,000 books, an untold number of paintings and bric-a-brac, and all the valuable gems they could lay their hands on, including three Papal tiaras.*

The placing of Joseph Bonaparte upon the throne of Spain offered yet another opportunity for Denon's cupidity. He wrote to the Emperor, "Were any other prince than Your Majesty's brother occupying the throne of Spain, I should have demanded with Imperial orders the cession of 20 pictures of the Spanish School for the museum; it is entirely unrepresented in the collection and these would serve as perpetual trophies of this last campaign." After certain negotiations Joseph agreed in 1809 to place at the disposal of the French authorities important works of Velasquez, Ribera, Murillo, Ribalta and others, paintings which were to be seized from the convents and cloisters

* D. M. Quynn, *op. cit.*

in Spain. This was done, the King wrote, "in order that we may offer them to our august brother the Emperor of the French and thus manifest our desire to see them placed in one of the halls of the *Musée Napoléon.*" However, when these pictures arrived, they proved a great disappointment. Only six of them would Denon accept as being of sufficiently high quality for the Louvre. Later on Denon went to Madrid and chose a parcel of 250 pictures, which were demanded as indemnity for the campaign in Spain. Of the lot, only 150 were museum quality; the others were considered only suitable decorations for the imperial residences. But this was in 1813, when political affairs were going from bad to worse and the shipment was never made.

The reannexation of Tuscany to the Empire in 1812 was the signal for fresh demands by Denon. He wrote to the Emperor pointing out that the suppression of the monasteries and convents in Tuscany, the Duchy of Parma and the Papal States gave an opportunity for enriching the Museum with the works of masters who were not already well represented. "You may rest assured, Your Majesty," he stated, "upon my discretion I will ask only for pictures by those artists we do not have already in the Museum." And it is as a result of this political incident that, nearly half a century before the Pre-Raphaelite movement was to break out in England, the Louvre was enriched with its choicest Italian "primitives," ranging from Cimabue to Raphael. Fortunately, and to Denon's credit, the monstrous suggestion of two painters that they could take down the frescoes of the *Disputa* and the *School of Athens* in the Vatican was turned down with horror, although, on the other hand, he had the frescoes by Correggio removed from the refectory of the Benedictines at Parma, and had also authorized the removal from the church of the Trinità dei Monti in Rome of the famous fresco of *The Descent from the Cross* by Daniele da Volterra. On this same visit he stopped both in Milan, where he removed a certain number of the finest pictures of the Brera, and in Florence, where he also looted the Accademia. The pictures of the former museum he exchanged with Prince Eugene for some paintings by Van Dyck and Jordaens, and in Florence he wrangled with Cavaliere d'Alessandri, the director of the Accademia, over a painting by Fra Filippo Lippi which was to have been sent to him. His argument was that since the Louvre owned a fine example of the son, Filippino Lippi, the father should be at least equally well represented!

Shipments came frequently, although a final lot of primitives, due to depart in December 1813, never left Italy, again because of political conditions. In addition to the works of art which Denon acquired by conquest, in the early stages of the regime he was able to persuade the Emperor to make some distinguished acquisitions by purchase; but by the time that Napoleon's imperial ambitions had entered into their full scale, he refused to pay out money which might be spent on barques, cannon and frigates to take England for works of art which he felt he could acquire by military means instead. This was particularly true after his defeat at Trafalgar. He did, however, place at the disposal of Denon certain funds for the commissioning of works by contemporary artists and for the purchase of contemporary works.

* * * * *

In addition to the works of art received by military conquest, all of the works which had been stolen and seized from the Church by the Revolution were considered imperial property and were placed under the direction of Denon. After the Concordat of 1802, Napoleon wished particularly to pacify the Church. He obliged Denon to return to Notre-Dame many of the things which had been taken; further, he was required to give them in addition ten pictures of the Italian School. The Emperor also instituted a policy of returning, insofar as was practicable, the works of art that had been taken from ecclesiastical foundations that were still in existence. Naturally, there was a great residue left over of works of art that had been taken from churches, monasteries and convents which had been suppressed and destroyed. These pictures ran into the thousands; a large number had been disposed of during the Revolution in the auction room; others, again, were used for negotiations with ecclesiastical authorities. Denon, however, refused to return anything which he considered of prime artistic importance, stipulating that "the necessity of the Louvre was the necessity of the nation."

Not only was Denon bothered by the importunities of the Church, but the various government departments likewise made further demands upon the collections of the state for the furnishing of palaces and government offices. In this way many works of art found new homes in France. At Lunéville in Lorraine a palace was decorated for the signing of the treaty; later it was given to the museum at Nancy. The Empress Josephine, particularly during the days of the Consulate, was a perfect glutton for works of art (with a good eye for business, too) and demanded more and more; these she retained as her private property. Even Napoleon himself grew more and more demanding in the quality of the works of art which he requisitioned to decorate his private apartments; he issued a severe reprimand to Denon after his marriage to Marie Louise for having given him for the imperial apartments pictures which he considered "*des vieilles croûtes.*"

Most tiresome of the many annoyances to Denon was the pressure from provincial museums. It had been the policy of Napoleon from the days of the Consulate right on through the Empire to endow them with the surplus of the national collections. But it was against Denon's policy to starve the Louvre in order to feed the provinces. Notwithstanding, he was obliged to send certain very important canvases to the provincial museums, where they have remained ever since, partly because of the fact that when the pictures were returned abroad following the battle of Waterloo, those which remained in the local museums were not considered as part of the restitution.

* * * * *

CHAPTER IV

The Musée des Monumens Français

SIMULTANEOUSLY with the meteoric rise of the Musée Napoléon, Paris saw the emergence of another institution, the Musée des Monumens Français. Like Vivant-Denon's dream, it was also the intense, if short-lived, vision of another artist. Alexandre Lenoir, born in 1762, a painter of considerable energy and ability, seeing the hereditary collections of the French people which had been pillaged by the Revolution pouring into the capital, made a virtue of necessity and embarked upon a program that took from the cathedrals and parish churches, the convents and the abbeys, and from individual proprietors, anything and everything that was not either nailed down or incorporated as an integral structural part of a building. And whenever the opportunity offered to circumvent even so slight an obstacle as a sustaining wall or a supporting buttress, Lenoir gave scant consideration to the possible collapse of a historic monument provided he had first been able to remove the objects of his choice.

Lenoir's museum was, notwithstanding, the first real museum of medieval antiquities ever brought together, if we may except Westminster Abbey and the Royal Abbey of Saint Denis (of which it was to become the chief inheritor). It was the catalyst of the Romantic movement and the herald of the Gothic revival in France. It provided, moreover, an alibi for French chauvinism when the Napoleonic bubble burst and the art treasures of foreign countries were again restored to their proper owners. For the collections of the Musée des Monumens Français became the nucleus of the departments of French painting and sculpture of the present Louvre. As such the activities of Lenoir, however much they may have irritated Denon (who, though he did not have in actuality Colbert's title of *Surintendant des Bâtiments,* was none the less its tacit and effective inheritor), complemented the activities of the Musée Napoléon and gave ultimate form to the present governmental departments of Fine Arts.

From the earliest days of the Revolution the Constituent Assembly had decreed that all ecclesiastical property in France should be sold; all of the convents and parish churches should place their property at the disposition of the Assembly. And while much of the Church property was sold as real estate, nevertheless the Jacobins recognized the necessity of saving works of art – pictures, statues, books and manuscripts – and placing them in temporary deposits until the State should determine what would become of them. The principal depot for sequestrated property was, of course, in Paris. A commission of artists under the young Lenoir was put in charge of them. In 1790 he obtained the use of the convent of the Petits-Augustins on the corner of the Quai Malaquais and the rue des Petits-Augustins (today called the rue Bonaparte), the site of the existing École des Beaux-Arts. Here he brought together all of the principal monuments, first those in the Paris area and the monuments from Saint Denis, particularly the tombs of the Kings of France which had been despoiled and mutilated in the Terror. The graves had been opened, the royal bones dispersed and humiliated; it was Lenoir's idea to bring these remains together with the tombs of all the great men, the poets and philosophers of France, into the cloisters and gardens of the monastery. Among the famous tombs in his museum were those of Turenne, of Descartes, of Molière and La Fontaine. The tombs of Abélard and Héloïse were contained in a Gothic chapel, to which were added the remains of the Paraclete.

The preface to Lenoir's *Museum of French Monuments* is an eloquent justification of his purpose; it gives also a description of the monuments themselves. He first speaks of the decree of the National Assembly and their concern for "the Monuments of the Arts which the Country possessed":

> The Athenians were more favorably circumstanced, having effected the expulsion of their tyrants, they changed the form of their Government, and proclaimed a Democracy. From that instant the people took a

part in public affairs; the mind of every individual became more enlightened, and Athens raised itself superior to every other city in Greece. A correct taste being very generally established, and the opulent having obtained the admiration of their fellow-citizens, by the erection of public edifices, men endowed with talents of every kind immediately resorted to this magnificent city, where the arts and sciences fixed their residence; from thence, as from a common centre, they spread into foreign countries, and the progress of taste advanced in equal proportion with the prosperity of the state. Florence in more modern times has exemplified the truth of what we have advanced: no sooner had that city become opulent, than the clouds of ignorance were dispelled, and the arts and sciences were seen to flourish.

With this positive statement of his own belief in culture Lenoir proceeds to discuss the various types of monuments which he has assembled, paying tribute to those who aided him, and insisting that his fear lest the vandalism of the early revolutionary days might be repeated is his chief motive, he continues:

> I am enabled to exhibit to the public the saloons of four Centuries complete, and a Sepulchral Chamber, constructed expressly for the purpose of receiving the Tomb of Francis I which I have perfectly restored. . . . An Elysium appeared to me conformable to the nature of this establishment, and a garden adjoining to the house furnished me with ample means for the execution of my plan. In this undisturbed and peaceful retreat, more than forty statues are distributed; and upon a grass plot, tombs appear to elevate themselves with dignity, in the midst of silence and tranquility; pines, cypresses and poplars surround them. Effigies and urns, enclosing the "hallowed ashes of departed worth," placed upon the walls, concur to inspire this delightful spot with that tender melancholy, which appeals so forcibly to the feeling mind.*

In 1795 the Convention formally decreed the establishment of the Musée des Monumens Français; it continued as an independent unit until Napoleon as First Consul placed it under the jurisdiction of Denon and the Musée Napoléon. Here the difficulties began, for both

* *Museum of French Monuments*, tr. from the French of Alexandre Lenoir by J. Griffiths. Paris, 1803.

directors were ambitious and they were drunk with power and cupidity. Lenoir stopped at nothing within the territorial limits of France just as Denon considered all of Europe his exclusive and particular concern. But as the former filled his galleries with the loot from the churches, it was at last possible for the first time, indeed, anywhere in the world to see the evolution of the art of sculpture from antiquity to the eighteenth century. His difficulties, both financial and political, were endless. Efforts were made to liquidate the museum and transfer its contents either to Notre-Dame or to the Panthéon. But Lenoir held on, and as he gradually wore down the hostility of Denon, slowly gaining his confidence, the Musée des Monumens Français remained virtually intact throughout the Napoleonic era.

The duties of Vivant-Denon extended far beyond the Louvre into every aspect of the artistic life in France. It was he who gave the commissions for commemorative pictures and official portraits; the annual salons were likewise under his jurisdiction as well as the other collections and palaces at Versailles and Fontainebleau.* The Luxembourg, which still retained the splendid large canvases painted by Rubens for Marie de Medici, was turned into a public gallery in 1802 at the request of the Senate. Among the fine works exhibited there were Le Sueur's *Saint Bruno* from the cloister of the Carthusians in the rue de l'Empereur which had been purchased from them before the Revolution by Louis XVI; and the great series by Joseph Vernet, executed for Louis XV, illustrating the principal harbors and ports of France, and David's large canvases of *The Horatii* and of the *Sons of Brutus*. The Senate had also requested for the decoration of their building a work by Raphael; the large *Virgin and Saint Anne with Saint Catherine* from the Uffizi was placed there for exhibition.

There were also formed during this period some very important private collections; one in particular belonged to the connoisseur Séguin whose taste was renowned, and those of Cardinal Fesch,

* The exodus of the court from Versailles in October 1789 had left the palace and the town destitute. The townspeople vigorously opposed the removal of the art treasures and started a museum of their own. Denon, not wishing to offend the Emperor by bringing into the Louvre the portraits of the Bourbon kings, encouraged them in forming a museum of French art. By the time of the Consulate it contained 369 pictures.

Napoleon's uncle and ambassador to the Holy See, and Marshal Soult. One of the richest collections of all was that of Lucien Bonaparte. All of those were partially open to the public and contained many capital works.

Not the least of these was Vivant-Denon's personal collection, of which, as it must have appeared towards the end of the Director's life, Anatole France has given such a charming account in *La Vie Littéraire:*

In cabinets made by the cabinet-maker Boule for Louis XIV he had arranged the marbles, antique bronzes, painted vases, enamels, and medals collected during half a century of a wandering and interesting life; and he lived, smiling, in the midst of these riches. On the walls of his rooms there hung a few choice pictures, a fine landscape by Ruysdael, a portrait of Molière by Sébastian Bourdon, a Giotto, a Fra Bartolommeo, and some Guercinos, then highly thought of. The honest man who preserved them had a great deal of taste and few preferences. He knew how to enjoy all that gives pleasure. Side by side with his Greek vases and antique marbles he kept Chinese porcelain and Japanese bronzes. He did not even disdain the arts of barbarism. He would gladly show a bronze figure of Carolingian style, whose stone eyes and golden hands evoked screams from the ladies to whom Canova had taught all the suavities of the plastic art. Denon endeavored to class these monuments of art in a philosophical order, and he proposed to publish a description of them; for, wise to the end, he set age at defiance by forming new projects. He was too much a man of the eighteenth century to refuse sentiment a place in his rich collection. Being in possession of a beautiful reliquary of the fifteenth century, stolen doubtless during the Terror, he had enriched it with some new relics, not one of which had proceeded from the body of a saint. He was not in the least mystical, and never was there a man less fitted to understand Christian asceticism. The monks inspired him only with disgust. He was born too soon to taste, as a dilettante, like Chateaubriand, the masterpieces of penitence. His profane reliquary contained a little of the ashes of Héloïse, found in the tomb of the Paraclete; a small portion of the beautiful body of Inez de Castro, whom a royal lover had exhumed in order to adorn her with a diadem; a few hairs from the grey moustache of Henry IV; some of the bones of Molière and La Fontaine, one of Voltaire's teeth, a lock of the heroic Desaix' hair, and a drop of Napoleon's blood from Longwood.

Without cavilling as to the authenticity of these remains, it must be agreed that they were relics dear to a man who, in this world, had greatly loved the beauty of women, who sympathized with the troubles of the heart, had a delicate taste for poetry allied to good sense, esteemed courage, honoured philosophy, and respected power.*

* *On Life and Letters* by Anatole France, trans. by D. B. Stewart. John Lane Company, 1922.

CHAPTER V

Restitution and Reparation

THE artistic empire of Napoleon ended as abruptly and ingloriously as did his political ambitions. He abdicated at Fontainebleau on April 6, 1814, the plenipotentiaries signing a convention the following week for himself and his family. The new King, Louis XVIII, was in England, but his brother the Comte d'Artois had replaced him in the provisional government until the King's arrival in Paris in May. The armistice which d'Artois had signed with Austria, Great Britain, Russia, Switzerland and Portugal contained no provision for the return of works of art although he had separately agreed to return the archives of the Vatican and a number of articles used in papal ceremonies. Louis XVIII as a tactical gesture announced his willingness to return such works of art as had not already been hung or displayed in the Louvre or the Tuileries. Certain pictures had already gone back to the Low Countries and to Prussia, but the King, uncertain of his position, had carefully concealed this from his people. On the fourth of June, 1814, he declared: "The glory of the French armies has not been tarnished, the monuments to their bravery remain and the masterpieces of the arts belong to us from now on by stronger rights than victory." *

Feeling was running high throughout Europe and while the treasures in themselves were precious enough to the countries which Napoleon had conquered, they now became a symbol of liberation and revenge. The presence of the troops in Paris added a new note of futility and irony to the boasts of the new Bourbon King; these are summed up in an article from the *London Courier* for October 15, 1815:

* The basic data for this chapter are taken from D. M. Quynn, *op. cit.*, and from the various sources cited in the bibliography, particularly the works of Saunier and Lanzac de Laborie.

The disbanded officers of the army resort to Paris; and going about out of uniform influence the populace. As the foreign troops withdraw, the insolence of the Parisians increases. They clamor loudly against the removal of articles of art. And why? By what right? The right of conquest? Then have they not twice lost them? Do they persist in enforcing that right? Then why do not now the Allies plunder France of every article worth removing which she possessed before Bonaparte's time? They are entitled to do this by the example of Bonaparte's practice now so eagerly sanctioned by the Parisians.

Miss Quynn has shown that the restraint on the part of the Allies came from their realization that the King's popularity could not suffer too great a blow to the military pride of France. For the works of art, if they were a symbol to the countries of their origin, had during their sojourn at the Louvre become no less a symbol of French power and prestige. Prussia for this reason, while pressing heavy claims by virtue of the extent of the looting of Germany, and because of her interest in maintaining the Bourbon on the throne, "would not demand the immediate return of those of her paintings and statues then on display until they could be replaced in the Louvre by others, provided that they be returned in the course of the year and that all objects not on display be returned immediately."

After the return from Elba and the defeat at Waterloo the Allied position became much tougher. An effort of the French to insert a clause into the Convention of Paris (July 3, 1815) guaranteeing the "integrity of museums and libraries" was refused; Lord Liverpool taking the position that "It is most desirable to remove them (i.e. the trophies) if possible from France as whilst in that country they must necessarily have the effect of keeping up the remembrance of their former conquests and of cherishing the military spirit and vanity of the nation."

The role of the British and particularly of the Duke of Wellington is distinguished by its justice and intelligence. Those who look with jaundiced eyes today on the collections at Apsley House have chosen to forget that those pictures which he took from Spain were presented to him according to accepted and traditional conventions of war; and, too, they are ignorant of his splendid offer to return them to

King Ferdinand – a gesture which was as handsomely refused. The London *Courier* published another Paris letter in October:

> Things have suddenly taken a very different appearance here. To the great astonishment of everybody, and when there was least reason to expect it, the Duke of Wellington came to the diplomatic conferences with a note in his hand, by which he expressly required all works of art should be returned to their respective owners. This excited great attention, and the Belgians, who having immense claims to make, had been hitherto most obstinately refused, did not wait to be told that they might begin to take back their own. The brave people are already on their way to return with their Paters and their Rubens.

Not all of his countrymen believed in his magnanimity; the Prince Regent had instructed Lord Liverpool to try to get some masterpieces for the British Museum. But, according to Miss Quynn, both Wellington and Castlereagh refused. W. R. Hamilton, Lord Elgin's secretary, "that viper Hamilton" whom the French detested for his part in securing the Elgin marbles for England, and for having rowed out to a French ship in the harbor at Alexandria to take the Rosetta Stone away from France, wrote to the Earl of Bathhurst:

> We must necessarily give up the idea of procuring for ourselves any of the chefs-d'oeuvre from the Louvre. It would throw an odium upon our exertions to restore stolen goods and those French who are the most exasperated against the general measures of restitution already make use of this argument against our pretended disinterested exertions in the cause of justice. It will be very difficult and problematical to effect the restitution at all, and really for the former owners. If accompanied with any proposal to our own benefit, the whole will fall to the ground, and the French will remain undisturbed proprietors of what they are now afraid they are to lose; and they will have the additional gratification of owing it to our mismanagement.

But if the British were reticent and altruistic, their example was not followed by the smaller countries. During the entire autumn and early winter of 1815 Paris was day by day being depopulated of its art. How bitterly this was received by the Parisians, and how quickly the empire of Vivant-Denon had crumbled, may best be seen in the following series of letters written from Paris by a Scottish miniature painter who had gone there to see the great assemblage of the Musée Napoléon before it was too late. These letters, culled from his diary and written to his family at home, by Andrew Robertson A. M., "Miniature Painter to his late Royal Highness the Duke of Sussex," were never intended for publication. They are the observations of a competent artistic personality, the only disinterested eyewitness whose account has come down to us. The French comments on the activities of these three or four months are so filled with hate and rage that they are almost worthless. While the Congress of Vienna was in full and solemn session, the events in Paris were more practical but equally intense.

19th of September

Called on Dezier, he was not at home but saw his wife, and had an excellent sample of the feelings of the French – "Ah, when I came here four years ago I found my country the first in the world and now it is the last." Bonaparte had made France what it was – formerly all was filth, he made the streets to be kept clean and paved – then erected monuments, etc. – business was brisk – money and gold rolled in every direction – but now, ah Mon Dieu – last year this country was betrayed – sold – as to the King he is an unfeeling monster he came to Paris over the dead bodies of his people, his children as he calls them, he a father, what do the French know of him. – Twenty-five years ago the present race were all children, it is as if someone were to come and say, that is not your father, I am your father. I would say I do not believe it, I have known my father ever since I was a child and I will acknowledge no father but him – the King turned everyone away who had shed their blood for their country and took round him a parcel of nasty, beggarly emigrants; he cannot pass the Place de Louis XV because his brother was guillotined there but he can live in his palace and perhaps sleep in his bed – moreover he has called to be his advisor one of those who voted his death. France is ruined – it will never be what it was, if Bonaparte is to blame, he only loved France too much, that was his failing, he wished to make her too great! and the French love his very name – they will soon make another government and proclaim his son since they cannot have him – he landed with one thousand men and Louis could not get one man to fire a gun for him, how could he, there is that nasty Duc de Berri, when he was reviewing troops he would walk along the line and say to a soldier "What is that" – "It is the reward for courage in the service of my country for which I have often bled." "Take it away." The soldier was stripped of his honors, of his medals – was it not natural to join him who had given this reward – and they have taken away all the pictures and statues – there are the nasty Prussians too they have robbed the Invalides of those models of fortifications which had taken France 150 years to make – they were the property of France they have taken 24 out of 100. Now we are starving – nothing doing and heavy contributions to pay what will become of us God only knows.

September 20

Baron Gros is a fine figure of a man about 45 – full of animation and hate for the English – in other words he loves his country – and like myself has no objection to a dish of politics – he said the Romans conquered these works from the Greeks – the French were the Romans of the present day but now the English were – he expressed the utmost indignation that pictures and statues should be taken away to enrich England, a nation which did not know the value of art and gave no encouragement or something to this effect. I assured him that not one would go to England but that they were taken away by their respective proprietors. If the government were to bring one of these to England, people would be enraged, – with pleasure he added. I said England went to war for an object more noble and elevated, the peace and happiness of mankind – he shook his head – to restore the balance of power in Europe and to secure a lasting peace – in short that Great Britain was more the friend of France than the present generation would or could believe – he said Great Britain went to war on the same principle as Bonaparte to extend her Empire – look at our wars in India – this war in Ceylon. I replied that perhaps there was much of the conduct of Great Britain in India which was not to be defended but as to this war in Ceylon – the King of Candia had made incursions into our territories and cut off the ears of our people – would not France resent such an outrage and go to war – he was silent – He said we made war on France to secure all the commerce of the world to ourselves it was no difficult matter to upset this by proving how little if any the most commercial country can export. "It is the gold of England which has brought all this misery on France." I replied that England, to be sure, paid five millions to the Allies, five pounds per man, did that produce such an exertion – He continued he said there was England, Prussia, Germany, Spain, etc. all against France with its men. For seven or eight people to attack one man. I said Great Britain had the same as that for years and years. Ah but you were surrounded by the sea. So is Europe and look at the difference in the extent of the population. The sea was open to Europe united. What would have become of you but for the sea. It would have cost us more blood but Great Britain would still have been Great Britain. He smiled. I added that so patriotic, so firm and united was England that there was not a man who would not have died e'er it was conquered – fifteen millions of people united and determined can resist the power of the whole world – he spoke of the Battle of Waterloo, Mont Saint Jean they called it and acknowledged that the English fought better than all the troops they had met, yet I said they were the shabbiest the most ill-looking troops of all the allies. He paid a high tribute to the Scotch, he did not know I was Scotch, nor did I tell him. I said they were still worse looking troops. He said, however, that they were considered by far the best troops in the English army. I saw no portraits with Gros except a bad one of the King.

September 20th

Went to the Museum of French Monuments again. Spent the greater part of the day and was highly gratified, only was much interrupted meeting so many people whom I knew – the Louvre having been shut for three days was again open – it seems that the French would not agree to part with the pictures taken from Holland and Flanders – the Duke of Wellington at last said he must take them by force. Müffling, the Prussian Governor of Paris, yesterday was refused admittance – he flew into a rage – tore down the notice – sent for a Prussian guard and threatened to break down the doors which were immediately opened – and have continued so today – and a strange sight – English sentinels all along the gallery 71st Regiment Scotch – one division of the room almost entirely naked – the large works of Rubens being taken down made a dreadful blank in the wall. This gave the English artists an excellent opportunity to see them. I perceived some disputing and countermanding but I could not make it out. Mr. Salt told me that a few evenings ago at some great party not one of the Frenchmen would speak to Lord Wellington – at the door on the outside was a guard of one hundred men of the 71st. In the evening a little after seven when the passage through the Tuilleries is shut I happened to pass the Triumphal Arch where the gate is, two Prussian soldiers wished to pass through – the sentinels National Guard displayed the insolence of office and turned their back with considerable roughness. – The Prussians looked back – grumbled and threatened.

Thursday the 21st

Went to Monsieur Bon Maisons – saw a middling collection of pictures and two of Raphael brought from Spain by Joseph Bonaparte – the *Madonna de la Piché* and *Christ Bearing His Cross* – pictures of the highest class and his best time, particularly the latter – which although not half the size of *The Transfiguration* is almost equal to it – but alas they were in a terrible state – great pieces particularly of the former peeled off – it is said Joseph left them exposed to the weather – gauze was pasted over them to prevent them falling to pieces but the application of turpentine here and there showed their rich quality – and the general composition could be seen through it.

As I entered the Louvre a wagon was loading with pictures without packing cases chiefly of Rubens of immense size – many on panels – feeling tenderly for works of such excellence I was fearful that they might shake to pieces or at least be broken or injured – I spoke to the workmen – but what did they care – At last a gentleman who I found was from Antwerp and who superintended the removal came to the door and entreated the English officer who commanded the detachment not to take away the guard until five o'clock or as long as possible. He said there was to be a grand review tomorrow and the men must have time to prepare themselves – but consented to stop until then – the gentleman thanked him saying that they would work night as well as day but after the guard was gone they could not – this being settled I took the liberty to intrude – expressing my fears for the safety of works which every artist looked upon with tenderness as if they were his own children, adding that I was an English artist – he was delighted to find anyone take an interest in what was so arduous and painful to him. I had seen him yesterday engaged in altercations with the French. He told me that it was necessary to remove them without delay, the ministers had arranged that they must be taken away by force – they could only work under the protection of the guard but the French would not allow them to use even any hammer; that they were therefore obliged to remove them to a place of safety to pack them up properly at a distance of a mile and a half in the Rue Mont Blanc he questioned whether all had got there safe which had been removed – he thanked me most graciously for my attention and begged to know my name he gave me his address at Antwerp at some château – he told me also that the French wished to shut the Louvre and conceal all this but that the Allies wished the whole nation to know as the truth must be known at last it was better that it should be so at first. I found that the National Guard at the door had been removed – there were a few Prussians and a strong English guard – a Prussian sentinel at one side and a British at the other – the British guard were sitting near, their arms piled and not scattered over the place, looking at the show and listening to the people singing and playing. I found also sentinels at all the avenues leading to the place as if to prevent a surprise – terrible work this – upstairs I found the same scene of noise – hammering and confusion as before.

Among others I met [Sir Thomas] Lawrence who said that every artist must lament the breaking up of a collection in a place so centrical for Europe, for everything was laid open to the public with a degree of liberality unknown elsewhere – talking of the merits of the works he did not hesitate to give the preference beyond all comparison to the painter of the human soul and passion, Raphael, in his *Transfiguration* – he was delighted to find that all he had heard of its being injured and painted upon was false – it is in the most perfect state of preservation as the pictures in general were and if it was painted upon it was done with the utmost skill for he could not perceive it and whatever it was before it would not be so great a work were it otherwise than it is now – the next picture he thought was the *Peter Martyr* of Titian and after that a small Correggio. I said I was divided between that and the *Entombing of Christ* by Titian. He said we had given one Titian and that was enough – after him he gave the palm to Correggio. I pointed out *La Belle Jardinière* which he thought looked like a copy.

As I came out I surveyed the crowd of common people who were there all day long. There used to be nobody. I saw fury and despair in their looks like the brewing of an insurrection and the awful scenes of the revolution coupled with what I hear in the coffee houses – there is a volcano at hand and as soon as the Allies are gone from Paris it will burst forth and the whole will light on the poor King who, poor man, has resisted all this – they do not blame themselves but throw all upon him – they will throw off the Bourbons – and instead of a great victory they will gratify themselves with this – it will be all one to them – when they have not anything great to glorify over they will be at equal ecstasy with a trifle. In the absence of news they have all sorts of reports. Lord Castlereagh and Lord Wellington have quarrelled about this – it is all Lord W's doing the Emperor of Russia anything to encourage resistance and insurrection perhaps to the assassination of Lord W. Paris is in a ferment about these pictures and the review tomorrow of the whole army under Lord Wellington is a very prudent measure.

Andrew Robertson's letter of Friday, September 22, is devoted to a brilliant description of the review. Some 60,000 British and Scottish troops marched by the Tuileries and it must indeed have been a very brilliant sight.

Saturday, September 23rd.

The same scene of confusion at the Louvre – the guard in the room was doubled, about 50 – the 95th half on and half off – the gallery looks quite empty about two-thirds gone – little left but the French School and the Italian of which at least a part are gone.

Sunday, September 24th.

At the Louvre I found the Italian pictures going fast, the same scene of confusion, the guards trebled, there being also Prussian and Austrian guard – the French are in a fury and they are now admitted – it is open to all – the French ministers wish to conceal it – the fools – the King of Prussia walked through the room alone in uniform – a mob followed him – few of the Frenchmen took off their hats – some pretended not to see him, others stood in his way purposely and did so repeatedly to keep on their hats and look furious – soon after I met Gros. I have never seen a volcano – but after this interview I can conceive an eruption of Vesuvius – He would scarcely speak to me and when I introduced Mr. Salt he turned away – said a time of vengeance would come. France was the garden and cradle of the arts – the only place where these things ought to be – said nothing but what everyone acknowledges – but a Frenchman sees no further than his own interests – to consider how these things were brought together or the vengeance due on the part of the Allies towards France that they are content with having their own and leave all theirs while they would be justified in taking everything away – but to leave these works in the possession of France would only remind them what they have gained by war and encourage them to renew it – that it would be a precedent for armies to carry off works of art at every change of success which would end in their destruction – A Frenchman will not look thus far because he then would see the justice of restoring them to their original places, recognizing the principle that they are never to be removed for if they are left at Paris it would become a precedent for 50 removals by which they would be destroyed. It is true they were acknowledged to belong to France by treaties at the point of the bayonet – confirmed by their being left last year at Paris – justice requires their removal to their original place. "Justice equally required it last year," say they exultingly. True, but the Allies wished to induce France to conduct itself well, they therefore said nothing about the pictures and sketches. France has not behaved well. It therefore has no right to expect such a boon from this conduct – At all events they belong to the Allies by right of conquest – therefore for the future preservation of these works, in justice to the owners – in policy as regards France and by right of conquest they ought not to be again left at Paris.

Monday, September 25, 1815.

Not knowing what may happen in the present disturbed state of the public mind on account of the removal of the pictures and as in case of any commotion the bankers might refuse to pay, I went to Perrigeaux and drew what money I had remaining there, I then went to the Louvre which was shut against everyone, not excepting artists – and all my endeavors to gain admittance were unavailing. I therefore went and saw the Catacombs – The conductor of which walking through these depositories of the dead, described their beauties as if it were a flower garden, showing us here and there a beautiful specimen. In one cell was deposited a number of broken bones, at another was an inscription to say that it contained the ashes of those slain on one of the days of the revolution – at last we ascended the stair and blew out our tapers.

September 27th.

The Italian pictures going fast, went to Notre Dame, a fine structure but inferior to our Westminster Abbey.

September 29th.

Still the same crowds of people looking at the horses (these are the bronze horses of St. Mark's). One or two gendarmes riding about leisurely and whenever they saw a dozen or two people, walked through them to separate them. During the day half a dozen were so employed. The French are naturally bitter and satirical – even when they least wish it they are most so – the catalogues at the Louvre are bitter enough against themselves for as there has been no alteration they still contain their original bombast, this statue was conquered in Italy, that picture in Holland, etc. In the former catalogue they give a history of the *Venus de Medici*, her travels and the different nations which have possessed it – "but the victories of Napoleon the Great have forever fixed her destiny in France."

This would be the acme of everything that is ridiculous but for what at the Louvre I happened this day to observe. In the vestibule as you enter there is painted on the ceiling a figure holding a label "The Fruits of Victory" and anyone who reflects on what is now passing, the total breaking up of the collection when at last Europe has been roused to crush the serpent which has so long outraged every principle of justice and by a long series of crime he forgot that virtue, principle and justice ever existed – that mankind are endowed by nature with the same feelings as Frenchmen who corrupted by vice are so reconciled to sin and crime – so sunk in iniquity that they are blind to every moral principle – deaf to the voice of reason and truth – so inflated with self-love and pride that they would hardly believe that other men were of the same species with legs and arms until they now feel the force of the latter. To a reflecting mind this triumph of virtue cannot fail to point out the hand of providence which directed them twenty years ago perhaps to employ their own art in perpetuating their disgrace by writing on the entrance, "The Fruits of Victory" achieved by crime. For twenty-five years they have been the scourge, and now they are the laughing-stock, of mankind – Even England cried. But as if their disgrace were not complete their presumption was permitted to go so far as to place in the sacred assemblage of ancient art some of their own statues and (what could hardly be by chance) under the above ceiling they have placed as the first object that strikes the eye on entering (you can see no other indeed until you do enter) a colossal statue of Hercules killing the serpent and a frightful one it is, so much so that I can only compare it to the tigers and lions when I saw them fed the other day – or to themselves, being unable to conceive anything more ferocious or diabolical. The analogy held good even in the action and expression of Hercules whose gigantic power and benign expression afford a complete personification of Europe roused against France.

October 1, 1815.

The horses are gone – a number of people looking at the place which they occupied. I was anxious to hear what was saying but it rained and

I went into the Louvre to work – in the evening went to the Opéra Français – there were two pieces – the music chiefly compiled from Mozart – singing barely tolerable. After this came a ballet – the dancing is truly astonishing – there is always a ballet introduced in the operas, their knowledge of stage effect is very wonderful and the arrangement of color in the dresses admirable beyond conception – on the stage they display a spirit in taste and color which is seldom to be found in their pictures and the principle being distinctly shown I have learned much this evening – there can be no doubt that they try the effect repeatedly before the piece is represented – when they no doubt find that the figure in white must stand here, one in yellow there – another in pink next to it, one in light blue in another place varying all the colors as in a picture – becoming deeper as the figures are retired on the stage – hence a bit of red is wanted here – clap on a red body on a white dress – perhaps it requires an edging also – on a blue dress perhaps they want a bit of red – add a sash or a scarf – thus they give spirit and harmony to the whole by repeating the color of one dress – in another taking care not to break up the mass or predominant color of the dress, this principle is attended to in the retired figures – and were one to be out of its place, the harmony of color would be deranged – how different is this in our theaters where all is done by chance higgledy-piggledy – scarcely attending even to the harmony of one dress and totally neglecting the tout-ensemble – the ballet was political – expressing the enthousiasm of the people on the return of peace, thus were white flags, cockades, processions of national guards, etc. soldiers returning from the battles and joining the dance and embracing – a lady is in grief until she hears the fate of her lover – she is told he is killed – her agony was well expressed and would have its effect on the people but for the enraged and mortified state of their minds – at last she appears with an English Hussar officer who saved his life – the tune of Henry IV was repeatedly played to the dance, it was applauded but partially – all in one place – people were paid no doubt – these called for vociferously in the beginning of the evening before the curtain rose but they were not generally joined it was played however as casual and I could not help thinking how phlegmatic the French nation is compared with the English who without any convulsion show ten times as much gratification when God Save The King is played but the French nation we know only too well is not phlegmatic they are cold only to the Bourbons.

October 2.

The *Transfiguration* etc. gone – having been at the Luxembourg all day I just looked in at the Louvre – the whole gallery is now stripped except a picture here and there – they have now begun upon the pictures belonging to France it is said but not truly – *La Belle Jardinière* is gone but to be sent to Sèvres to be copied in porcelain etc. I believe the others are taken down by themselves. The *Madonna della Sedia* is gone and I understand all the rest will go in retaliation for Titian's Picture of *Christ Flagellated* which with some others disappeared a few days ago, nobody knows how – but must have been taken by authority some say that these were purchased, there is now no bounds to the rage of the French. I understand there were some high words in the gallery – when two or three soldiers were brought in and the picture in dispute carried off. I am surprised that no attempt has been made to rescue them as they pass along the street carried by unarmed soldiers with only a guard of five or six, sometimes only one, and often none – the Austrians have been at work until the last week – for the two or three days before, the guard were British while the Belgian pictures were taken away.

October 3.

I was not at the Louvre today but one man was heard to say that he had nothing to leave his son but, thank God for it, one thing and that was hatred of the English and thirst for revenge.

I understand that the name of Lord Wellington has been taken from a print of his portrait and the name Blücher has been put instead. Row in the Palais Royal this evening between some English and French officers in which it is said some people are wounded – for several nights there has been some disturbance it is said.

October 4.

I understand the French pictures belonging to France which have been taken down have not been taken by the Allies but by the French for the purpose of being hung in the department where the French School is – the first as you enter – so far good. Called on Prud'hon, his pictures are charming full of grace and elegance of feeling, good effect – fine color and free from much of the hardness of the modern French school – he does not have any edgy outline, all is blended – still preserving all the accuracy and undulation of form. Nothing can be more beautiful than his *Venus and Adonis* – the landscape beautiful and simple in composition, color and execution – he is called the Correggio of France and deservedly – portrait of a gentleman he was very sweetly painted but rather wanted vigor in the head, the background being bold, quite grand and forcible – in tone like a Titian or Gainsborough landscape, dark and the form simple.

October 5.

It is still insisted that the pictures are taken in retaliation for those seized by the French. I dare say that in their hurry the Allies have not inquired sufficiently respecting some said to have been presented to Bonaparte but they have taken all which ever belonged to certain powers and that the retaliation has begun with the French seizing the Titian *Christ Crowned.*

October 6.

Went to Mr. Samariva's, now in Italy, a great and rich amateur and patron of art – saw some beautiful pictures – a small Titian *Holy Family* equal to anything in the Louvre – a beautiful picture by Prud'hon – seems to be a Venus and Cupid in the clouds but I was so delighted with it but I thought only of the art – a charming picture by Guerin *Aurora Awaking Adonis in the Clouds,* her hands raised to remove the veil which had covered her, Cupid gently seizes his hand. Opposite was a large picture by Meynier – stiff and hard but well drawn. A beautiful little musical piece by Paul Vernay – but a still greater treat was offered by the two statues of Canova – his *Venus* very fine – but his *Magdalene* his chef-d'oeuvre is quite affecting and sublime – equal to the antique – grand in conception, beautiful in execution – such feeling I have not seen – the texture skin itself – particularly where the action of the foot bends the skin – it is a thing to be worshipped.

October 10th.

About one third of the statues now gone from the Louvre – the confusion is great and the appearance melancholy – to an artist it is affecting I said so to Gireaudel's assistant who was there – "it is to your government that we owe this." I said – "You pay too great a compliment to the power of England in conceiving that she should dictate to the whole world – and to her disinterestedness that she should do this as much to her own loss as that of France. Governments have their reasons but all artists must lament the event." With a shrug he made a certain motion with his hands as much as to say he admitted that it is a loss to the world—you admit everything—so far can a Frenchman see and no farther—they consider the arts the first step towards the happiness of the nation and of mankind—they neither know nor care what is most conducive to this latter object so as there is splendor, show, fêtes and fine pictures—among themselves they have no doubt that even English artists admit the loss to mankind, while it is only admitted to be a loss to the arts and this is sufficient proof to them of the atrocity of the act.

October 12.

The Louvre is truly doleful to look at now all the best statues have gone and half the rest, the place full of dust, ropes, triangles and pulleys with boards, rollers, etc. They have built up half way with stones and plaster those statues which are not solid below—in the picture galleries there are still many fine pictures the property of France. Entire autumn of 1815 was devoted to the problems relating to Napoleon's loot of art. The Congress of Vienna had reached politically a stalemate, this was the bone that was tossed to the politicians and to the populace.

Denon used every device known to man to stall, delay and to prevent the removal of the objects from the Museum. Finally he had to call in from the provinces many of the works of art which had been sent from the Louvre in order to fill the gaps of the objects which were taken away. A series of dispatches from Paris to the London *Courier* confirm the observations of the eyewitness Andrew Robertson:

October 2, 1815.

The public mind of Paris still continues in a state of extreme agitation; the people appear every day more and more exasperated against the allies. The stripping of the Louvre is the chief cause of public irritation at present; the long gallery of the museum presents the strongest possible image of desolation; here and there a few pictures giving greater effect to the disfigured nakedness of the wall. I have seen several French ladies in passing along the galleries suddenly break into ecstatical fits of rage and lamentation; they gather around the *Apollo* to take their last farewell, with the most romantic enthusiasm; there is so much passion in their looks their language, and their sighs, in the presence of this monument of human genius that a person unacquainted with their character or accustomed to study the character of the fair sex in England where feeling is controlled by perpetual discipline would be disposed to pronounce them literally mad – not the least of their griefs is the report that the *Apollo* goes to England, the *Venus Medici* was removed yesterday.

October 4, 1815.

Groups in public places have of late increased in numbers and boldness. The removal of the articles of art has afforded an occasion for bringing them together and an opportunity of venting their resentment against the allies. Upwards of 1800 pictures and other articles are said to have been removed from the Louvre. When the *Venus* was put in the cart on Monday, Sir T. Lawrence, Mr. Chantry and Canova burst into tears; but a German officer who stood by kissed her and laughed at them. When the last package was put into the cart the French mob collected around the door, hissed and goddamned the English troops who at the moment were on guard at the door just as if the pictures were going to be sent to England. The *Venus de Medici* is said to be dispatched to Florence. There is great talk of the *Apollo Belvedere* being destined for the Prince Regent, but we believe His Royal Highness's sentiments are far too dignified to accept a present which would but too generally be deemed as a bribe. The political conduct which he has pursued has been in entire coincidence with the manly and honorable feeling of the nation whose grand object was to re-establish the principles of justice. A thousand Apollos would be a poor compensation for the loss of that high character which Great Britain has maintained. The accident of employing British troops to seize the Flemish pictures in the Louvre has had injurious consequences in the state of the public mind towards England. The Duke of Wellington has explained that his sending a guard of the 53rd regiment to the Louvre on the requisition of General Müffling was an accident which he neither could nor sought to avoid. It happened to be the turn of the English to provide the guard for that day and the Duke had no discretion.

October 6, 1815. (Containing a statement from Canova.)

The cause of the fine arts is at length safe in port; and it is to the generous and unremitted exertions of the British Minister, Rome will be indebted for thus triumphing in the demands I came hither to make in her name. We are at last beginning to drag forth from this great cavern of stolen goods the precious objects of art taken from Rome. On the second instant amongst many fine paintings that were removed, we noticed that stupendous production *The Transfiguration*, the *Communion of St. Jerome*, the *Virgin* of Foligno; the next day several other exquisite pictures came away together with a group of *Cupid and Psyche*, the two *Brutuses*, the very ancient bust of *Ajax*, and other no less precious objects of sculpture. Yesterday *The Dying Gladiator* left his French abode and the *Torso*. We removed this day the two first statues of the world, the *Apollo* and the *Laocoon*.

The most valuable of them are to go by land and we will set off next week accompanied by the celebrated Venetian horses and all other precious articles belonging to Lombardy, Piedmont and Tuscany. The convoy will be escorted by strong detachments of Austrian troops. The remainder, which may belong to Rome, will be embarked and sent by sea to Italy.

Problems of restitution occupied all of the final months of the year 1815; first the Prussian pictures were taken away, then the Belgian, then the Italian and the Papal States and the works of art which had come from Austria. Canova was the representative of the Pope, coming from Rome with the special title of ambassador. When he was announced as *Monsieur l'Ambassadeur* at a reception of Talleyrand, the latter presented him to the company as "*M. l'Emballeur.*" Even so the activity, the persistent loss of memory of Denon, who could not remember where the objects had been placed, and the technical obstructions of Lavallée resulted in saving for France and for the Louvre a certain number of its very great Italian primitives, particularly those pictures which have occupied in our time the Galerie de Sept Mètres. The following list is given by Saunier of the pictures which were retained:

Albertinelli	*St. Jerome and St. Zenobias Adoring the Infant Jesus in the Arms of the Virgin*
Bronzino	*The Agony in the Garden*
Bartolo di Taddeo	*Virgin and Child with a Bird*
Botticelli	*The Child Jesus holding a Pomegranate*
Cimabue	*Virgin and Angels*
Empoli	*The Virgin*
Gentile da Fabriano	*Presentation in the Temple*

Taddeo Gaddi	*Altarpiece in several compartments*
Rafaellino del Garbo	*Coronation of the Virgin*
B. Ghirlandaio	*Christ Carrying the Cross*
D. Ghirlandaio	*Visitation*
R. Ghirlandaio	*The Coronation of the Virgin*
Giotto	*St. Francis*
Benozzo Gozzoli	*The Triumph of St. Thomas Aquinas*
Filippo Lippi	*Virgin and Child*
Macchiavelli	*Coronation*
Simone Memmi	*Christ with Angels and Virgin*
Orcagna	*Death of St. Bernard*
Pesellino	*St. Francis of Assisi with St. Comas and Damian*
Piero di Cosimo	*Virgin*
Pontormo	*Virgin*
Cosimo Roselli	*Virgin in Glory*
Vanni	*Virgin*
Vasari	*Annunciation*
Lorenzo di Credi	*Virgin and Child Adored by Sts. Julian and Nicholas*

These pictures were retained in Paris finally after negotiation conducted by Lavallée with the Tuscan government. Le Brun also was able to retain the Veronese *Marriage at Cana* because it was too large to be shipped, although the Austrian authorities had demanded its return to Venice. Stendhal observed, "The allies had taken 1150 pictures. I hope I may be permitted to observe we acquired them by a treaty, that of Tolentino. On the other hand the allies have taken our pictures without treaty." In addition to the restitution that was being made during the winter of 1816 in Paris there were a great many deals made on the side. The Czar acquired for 940,000 francs the pictures of the Empress Josephine at Malmaison. The collection of works of art taken under the Treaty of Tolentino from the Villa Albani in Rome were purchased in Paris by the Crown Prince of Bavaria for the Glyptothek in Munich. The following table is given by Saunier of the restitution made by the Louvre, showing the character and quantity of works of art returned to each state. It is interesting to note that in the case of Italy, where many of the owners were no longer living, there were created a series of municipal galleries and museums for the special purpose of receiving and exhibiting the restituted works of art.*

TABLE OF OBJECTS OFFICIALLY RETURNED TO THE ALLIES (signed by Lavallée, March 10, 1816)

Powers	*Pictures*	*Statues*	*Bas-reliefs and Busts*	*Bronzes*	*Etruscan Vases*	*Vases and Precious Objects*	*Ivory Vases*	*Wood Carvings*	*Cameos*	*Drawings*	*Enamels and Majolica*	*Diverse Objects*
Prussia	119	37	70	268		25	22	2	463		7	84
Cassel	421	11	6	5		1	19	10	4	2	9	28
Brunswick	230	1	6	3		1	54	25	1	243	1,154	55
Schwerin	190					18	10		3		29	15
Austria	323		16							2		
Bavaria	28											
Spain	284											108
Venice	15		2									
Milan	7									18		
Cremona	2											
Mantua			3	1						4		
Verona	6		2									
Modena	24		2	1						2		
Parma	30			7								
Tuscany	57	1				27 tables						
Sardinia	59	4	1									
Low Countries	210	1										
Papal States	60	44	14	4	16	1 chair 1 vase						
Albani		31	28			2 vases						4
	2,065	130	150	289	16	76	105	37	471	271	1,199	294

* Charles Saunier, *Les conquêtes artistiques de la Révolution et de l'Empire*, 1902. The list given above has been subjected to much research and revision. It will ultimately be published in detail by the École du Louvre.

Epilogue

THE NAPOLEONIC WARS brought to a close an era of art patronage and collecting which had continued almost unbroken for three thousand years. With the dawn of the nineteenth century there came a new philosophy and a new point of view. Democracy now claimed the picture and the statue for its own; generally speaking, the political concept of the royal collection – although its dying body was to twitch with the automatic reflexes of a Ludwig of Bavaria, a German consort to a British queen and an Opéra Comique hero – Napoleon III – was a thing of the past. Art had become emancipated from the audience chamber not so much by the Jacobins and by the Terror as by the Industrial Revolution and the growing cultural aspirations of the *bourgeoisie* and the workingman. No phase of our heritage of the past has undergone more radical changes in the past hundred years than have both the patronage of the contemporary artist and that accompanying sense of possession which from time immemorial has goaded the man of wealth into becoming a collector.

The purpose of collecting, however, changed even more than human nature. In the first third of the nineteenth century were established the great national picture galleries of Europe – the Prado and London heading the list. Archaeology achieved a new stimulus through the development of the eastern Mediterranean lands by English, Belgian and French capital. Napoleon's campaigns in Egypt had opened the gateway to the researches of Champollion and Mariette; Sir Henry Layard uncovered the romantic possibilities of the Holy Land and brought to England the incomparable series of Assyrian reliefs in the British Museum. The world of Islam was discovered and dutifully exploited. China, which had been known to the West only through the eyes of the Jesuits of the seventeenth century, poured its art into Europe with the establishment of the Treaty Ports. Japan was to be an American adventure following in the wake of Commodore Perry. The French devoted themselves to the philosophy of art and the recapturing of their long history – a task started by Lenoir in the Musée des Monumens Français and fully realized in the Cluny Museum in the 1840's and in the systematic care and preservation of the churches and abbeys, the palaces and castles of the country. Germany, lashed into intellectual fury by the mad King Ludwig, made the Glyptothek in Munich the shrine for a cult of classicism whose richest fruit was Schliemann, himself a commoner who provided through lowly manufactures the funds required to disclose the world of Homer to a fascinated public.

Across the seas a new spirit regarding art and culture was abroad. The democracy of Jefferson and the enlightened cynicism of Dr. Franklin created a new and precious pattern which during the later self-conscious years of lip service was all but lost to mid-Victorian snobbery. It was to be the pattern of the great democratic museums of the United States, filled with objects donated by private capitalists and supported by taxation and popular subscription.

The progress of patronage and art collecting in Europe following the Industrial Revolution and the rise of collecting in America must necessarily remain as the subject for another book – a book which can deal with the Romantic movement and the revolt against it which took place in modern art. The present volume has, we hope, prepared the ground which it must cover. In looking back over these pages certain conclusions and observations inevitably emerge.

It is axiomatic that the appreciation of art both for its intrinsic worth and for its value as an expression of the human spirit appears to be common to almost every age. The form which this expression takes varies as greatly as the climate, the language and the social usages of every people. But what so often escapes the visitor to a museum or the reader of the literature of the past is the homogeneity, the organic character of artistic tradition. The various chapters have sought to show much more than the relation of art to wealth; it is the relation of the precious object to the idea. And these works of art have been preserved and handed on from one generation to the next because the ideas that lie behind them are, and have always been, considered vital to the abundant life. They are the very things which distinguish the adolescence of one nation from the intellectual maturity of another.

The works of art here discussed are merely the timeless pieces of currency for which ideas, ideals and aspirations have been exchanged for thirty centuries. For this reason they have been treasured, often beyond price; they never have been static; like gold coins they have moved from one country to another as the economy or cultural stature of each people has required. It remains for our generation to decide whether we shall guarantee the ebb and flow of these spiritual values, or, whether we, the temporary custodians, shall bear the responsibility of debasing the one remaining currency of civilized man.

Appendices

APPENDIX A

On the Value of Money

No problem has presented greater difficulties to the historian and the economist than to translate the value of money into the value of commodities of daily life. A favorite – but totally unreliable – measuring stick has been the bushel of wheat. But here the prices vary according to the weather and the crops. Lean years are followed by years of plenty. Wars, the difficulties of transport, and acts of God have created unexpected famines. Even in the matter of livestock very little accuracy can be hoped for because animal husbandry has so improved. The following information is taken from Preserved Smith, *The Age of the Reformation*, Henry Holt and Company, 1920, pages 469–472:

> A fat ox now weighs two or three times what a good ox weighed four centuries ago. Horses are larger, stronger, and faster; hens lay many more eggs, cows give much more milk, than formerly. Shoes, clothes, lumber, candles are not in the same quality in different countries.

And, of course, there is an ever-increasing list of new articles upon which no comparison can be made.

Yet the supporting evidence is even clearer in regard to commodities and wages. While the bushel of wheat in Martin Luther's day is quoted by him in one of his letters at Wittenberg in 1527 at 80 cents a bushel – not too far from the prices of the twentieth century – wages were much lower. Wages followed the trend of prices.

> The remuneration of all kinds of labor remained nearly stationary while the cost of living was rising. Startling is the difference in the rewards of the various classes; that of the manual laborers being cruelly low, that of professional men somewhat less in proportion to the cost of living than it is today, and that of government officers being very high.

No one except court officials got a salary over $5,000 a year and some of them got much more. In 1553 a French Chamberlain was paid $51,000 per annum.

A French navvy received 8 cents a day in 1550, a carpenter as much as 26 cents, but a male domestic was given $7 to $12 a year in addition to his keep and a woman $5 to $6. As the number of working days in Catholic countries was only about 250 a year, workmen made from $65 to as low as $20. If anything, labor was worse paid in Germany than it was in France. Agriculture labor in England was paid on two scales, one for summer and one for winter, it varied from 3 to 7 cents a day, the smaller sum being paid only to men who were also boarded. In summer freemasons and master carpenters got from 8 to 11 cents a day for a terribly long day, in winter 6 to 9 cents for a shorter day, the following scale was fixed by law in England in 1563: a hired farmer was to have $10 a year and $2 for livery; a common farmhand was allowed $8.25 and $1.25 extra for livery; a manservant $6 and $1.25 respectively; a man child $4 and $1; the chief woman cook $5 and $1.60; a mean or simple woman $3 and $1; a woman child $2.50 and $1; all were, of course, boarded and lodged.

The pay of French soldiers under Francis I was, for a private $28 a year in time of war, this fell to $14 a year in time of peace; for captains $33 a month in time of peace and $66 in time of war. Captains in the English Navy received $36 a month, common seamen $1.25 a month for wages and the same allowance for food.

The Church fared little better than the Army. In Scotland, a poor country but one in which the clergy were respected, by the law of 1562, a parson if a single man was given $26 a year, if a married man a maximum of $78 a year; probably a parsonage was added. Doubtless many Protestant ministers eked out their subsistence by fees as the Catholic priests certainly did. Dürer gave 44 cents to a Friar to confess his wife, every baptism, marriage and burial was taxed by a certain amount. In France one could hire a priest to say a Mass at from 60 cents to $7 in 1500 and from 30 cents to 40 cents in 1600. At this price it has remained since, a striking example of religious conservatism, working to the detriment of the priest for the same money represents much less in real wages now than it did then.

Fees for physicians ranged from 33 to 44 cents a visit in Germany about 1520. Treatment and medicine were far higher. At Antwerp Dürer paid $2.20 for a small quantity of medicine for his wife. Fees were sometimes given for a whole course of attendance. In England we hear of such cures paid for at from $3.30 to $5. Very little, if any, advice was given free to the poor. The physician to the French King received a salary of £200 a year and other favors. William Butts, physician to Henry VIII had £500 per annum in addition to a knighthood and his salary was increased to over £600 for attending the Duke of Richmond.

Teachers in the lower schools were regarded as lackeys and paid accordingly. Nicholas Udall, Headmaster of Eton, received £50 per annum and various small allowances. University professors were treated more liberally. Luther and Melancthon at Wittenberg got a maximum of $224 per annum, which was about the stipend of leading professors in other German universities and at Oxford and at Cambridge. The teacher also got a small honorarium from each student. When Paul III restored the Sapienza at Rome, he paid a minimum of $17 to some friars who taught theology and were cared for by their Order but he gave high salaries to the professors of rhetoric and medicine. Ordinarily these received $476 a year but one professor of the classics reached the high water mark with nearly $800.

Rewards of literary men were more consistently small in the sixteenth century than they are now owing to the absence of effective copyright. An author usually received a small sum from the printer to whom he first offered his manuscript, but his subsequent royalties, if any, depended solely upon the goodwill of the publisher. A Wittenburg printer offered Luther $224 per annum for his manuscript but the reformer declined it, wishing to make his books as cheap as possible. In 1512 Erasmus got $8.40 from Badius, the Parisian printer, for a new edition of his *Adages*, in fact the rewards of letters, such as they were, were indirect in the form of pensions, gifts and benefices from the great. Erasmus got so many of these favors that he lived more than comfortably. Luther died almost a rich man, so many honoraria did he collect from noble admirers. Rabelais was given a benefice although he only lived two years afterwards to enjoy its fruits. Henry VIII gave $500 to Thomas Murner for writing against Luther but the lot of the average writer was hard. Fulsome flattery was the most lucrative production of the Muse.

Books were comparatively cheap. The Greek Testaments sold for 48 cents, a Latin Testament for half that amount. A Latin folio Bible was published in 1532 for $4, Luther's first New Testament for 84 cents. One might get a copy of the *Pandects* for $1.60, a *Vergil* for 10 cents, a Greek grammar for 8 cents, *Demosthenes* and *Aeschines* in one volume at 20 cents, one of Luther's more important tracts for 30 cents and the *Condemnation* of him by the Universities in a small pamphlet at 6 cents. One of the things that has gone down most in price since that day is postage. Dürer while in The Netherlands paid 17 cents to deliver a letter, or several letters, presumably to his home, from Nuremberg.

The most recently published table of the comparative values of European currencies for the year 1520 is compiled by Paul Wescher, *Grosskaufleute der Renaissance*, Basel, 1939, and is given here as a matter of interest. [The figures have not been verified, F. H. T.]

One Flemish pound or 1 Pound Groote = £1¼ = 4–4.5 Rhenish Gulden
= 5–6 Florentine Gulden or Florins
= 5 French Écus or Gold Crowns = 4.5 Spanish Ducats
= 3.25 Roman Ducats = 3 Hungarian Ducats = 3 Venetian Ducats
= 3 Portuguese Cruzadas

145 Rhenish Gulden approximate in value 100 Venetian, Hungarian and Roman ducats and about 115 Écus or Florins

The Mark Sterling (more generally known as silver Thaler) had 160 pence and was worth ⅔ of the £ sterling (or about 13 shillings). The value of the Écus amounted to 3–5 livres; a Spanish ducat was reckoned at 375–380 maravedis. According to modern estimates the gold value of a German gold gulden and the larger Florentine gulden was respectively 10 and 12 French gold francs but the purchasing power was from twice to three times that amount.

APPENDIX B

Notes on the Libraries and Collections of Ancient Egypt

THE sepulchre of Osymandias is described by Richard Pococke (1743) in his *Travels in Egypt*, which are included in John Pinkerton's *Voyages and Travels in All Parts of the World*, London, 1814, Vol. XV, pp. 253–256, as follows:

I viewed the remains of the large and magnificent temple there, which without doubt was a part of the ancient Thebes on the east side of the river. That grand building answers very well to the particular description Diodorus gives of the sepulchre of Osymanduas, which, he says, was a mile and a quarter in circumference.

First he says there was a gateway two hundred feet long, exactly answering to the measure of the pyramidal gate; it was sixty-two feet and a half high. From the upper part of two statues above this ground, without this gateway, it appears that the ground is very much risen; the gateway is now about fifty-four feet above the ground, and I should imagine that the gate was higher than Diodorus mentions, as the ground seems to have risen more than eight feet and a half; but these statues being thirteen feet and a half above ground, if we suppose they were sitting, they must be near twenty feet at least under ground, unless they were half statues, such as are mentioned in the temple of Carnack. They are of grey granite marble that has large spots of white in it; the shoulders are about three feet and a half above ground; the neck and head, to the cap, measure five feet, and the cap as much more. These are probably the statues mentioned by Diodorus, but he seems to speak of them as in another part of the temple, and describes them as twenty-seven cubits high, each of them made of one stone. The statue to the west differs little from the other, except that on the forehead there is an ornament of a serpent; the pilaster behind them, cut out of the same piece, in one is square like an obelisk, and comes half way up the cap behind; the pilaster of the other not being so thick; the ornament on the head seems to be the half of two dome leaves; the head itself may be supposed to have been designed to be as high as the part of the cap that sets out, being three feet deep, and the remainder of the cap three feet more, so that the head being near seven feet long, the whole statue, if standing, would be about fifty feet high, and sitting, about thirty-four feet high, computing seven heads to the whole body; so that if they were sitting, the ground must have risen above seventeen feet. To the north of these, are two obelisks, that probably are the finest in the world; they are now above the ground sixty feet high, and might be seventy or eighty according as the ground has risen. They are seven feet and a half square, and at bottom might be eight feet: the hieroglyphics are cut in with a flat bottom, an inch and a half deep; and the granite has perfectly retained its polish, which is the finest I ever saw. The hieroglyphics are in three columns down every side; at top, in each side, a person sits on a throne, and one offers something on his knees: These figures are likewise below. Lower are three hawks, then three bulls, and at about the distance of every four is an owl. I also observed among the hieroglyphics, serpents, insects, dogs, hares, monkies, birds, and heads of camels; they are exceedingly well preserved, except that about half of the pyramid of the western obelisk is broke off, and the south-west corner of the eastern one is a little battered for about six feet high.

In the front of the pyramidal gate there are windows over the false doors which are about ten feet from the top of the building; in the front of it, among other figures, is one represented sitting on a throne, holding out one hand, which has a staff or sceptre in it; the figures are in postures of adoration. On the other side, one who has on the same sort of cap as the other, is represented on a car as gallopping and shooting, with a bow, and many chariots after him. This may relate to the wars of this King against the Bactrians, which our author describes as cut on the walls in another part of the building; as the other may be the homage the captives paid to him, mentioned also as carved on the walls. Next he gives an account of a court four hundred feet square. This may be the colonnade, though the measures do not answer. Possibly it might have been near four hundred feet wide, extended a hundred feet further to the water, and as much on the other side. Instead of pillars, he says it was adorned with beasts cut out of one stone four and twenty feet high, executed after the ancient manner, and it was covered with stones twelve feet long, the ceiling being adorned with sculptures of stars, and painted with azure. In that manner a portico might be built on each side, with the colonnade as represented in the middle. This court is almost all inhabited, and filled up with little cottages, so that I could not go into it; but from the pillars I saw, I concluded the colonnade was continued as it is represented. I saw the top of the cap of a statue of red granite, just above the ground, which might be the remains of one of the smaller statues, and there seem to have been colossal statues at the pedestals. Beyond this colonnade he says there was another entrance and gateway much the same as the other, except that the sculpture was still finer. This seems to have been the pyramidal gate as I took it to be, which is much destroyed. At the entrance he mentions three statues, each of one stone, the work of Memnon Sicnites, who doubtless was a very famous sculptor; one of them was sitting, and the largest in Egypt, the foot of it being ten feet and a half long. He makes mention of many other particulars of the statues, and especially the very remarkable inscription that was on this vast colossus. "I am the King of Kings, Osymanduas: if any would know how great I am, and where I lie, let him exceed the works that I have done." This statue, without doubt, has been broken to pieces and carried away, as there are not the least signs of it. Beyond this gateway was another court much finer than the last, containing the history of the King, cut all round the walls, and there was a very large and beautiful altar in the middle of it, in the open air. This seems to comprehend the courts, unless the one might be looked on only as the entrance to the other, which is not improbable. The supposed gateway is only from conjecture, there being nothing but a rude heap of stones; and the area seems to be a very proper place for the magnificent altar that is described. And possibly those ruins I suppose in the plan to be remains of a pyramidal gateway, might be the buildings of this altar, which might be of such a design as that of the temple of Jerusalem, built of large stones. The pillars in this court are forty feet high. The work of the capitals is not in relief, but only cut out in lines. He next mentions a place like those rooms, that were built on purpose for music, which may be the apartment, though his measures do not agree. He after speaks of several apartments to walk in, and gives a particular account of the beautiful sculpture they were adorned with, which might be some porticos and rooms on each side, that are now destroyed.

He then gives an account of the sacred library, with that remarkable inscription on it: "The repository of the remedies for the soul." This might consist of the two rooms. In those rooms are several figures; one is a deity carried in a sort of boat by eighteen men, preceded and followed by a person with a particular ensign in his hand; the upper one has no person appearing on it, but a sort of cover in the middle of it, and is carried only by twelve men, there being no one before it. I observed one figure on the walls had a tortoise on the head for a cap, in another part a man leading four bulls with a string, which were cut as on four floors marked with a line one over another, and in several parts instruments of sacrifice. I remarked also in a compartment, a figure sitting, and one kneeling before it, on whose casque the sitting figure puts his left hand, having the cross, with a handle to it, in his right. Another with a hawk's head holds his left hand over the head of the person that kneels, having the same sort of cross in his right hand. Behind him is a short figure, which seemed to have wings on the side of his head. Below them are three persons kneeling, with hawk's heads. It is difficult to say whether or no this might be the King offering gold and silver to the deity, that he received yearly out of the mines of Egypt, which Diodorus says was cut on some part of the walls of the temple. I observed a door here with a strait top within; but without it was cut in an arch, something like the shell of a niche, which might first give the thought for the arch in Egypt. With the library he mentions about twenty apartments, in which were the representations of Jupiter, Juno, and the King, with several rooms about them, in which were cut in the most curious manner, all the sacred animals of Egypt. These seem to be those several apartments on each side, and many more that have been destroyed, which probably made the building all the way of the same breadth. At last he comes to the sepulchre itself. He speaks of ascending to it, and over the grand apartment there is another low room, where the body of Osymanduas might be deposited; in which, it seems, there was a plate of gold that probably often went round the room, so as to be three hundred sixty-five cubits in length and a cubit thick, or rather broad; on each of which cubits was cut the rising and setting of all the stars for every day in the year, and the effects the Egyptian astrologers attributed to them, according to their different dispositions. This great treasure they say Cambyses and the Persians carried away. The entablature round this room is very rich. Our author also observes that near the library were figures of all the gods of Egypt, with the King making a proper present to every one of them; and these I take to be the figures represented in the front of the building of the supposed sepulchre, where it is probable the middle figure sitting is Osiris, with five gods on each side. The stone below, which is represented with a dark shade, is a very particular red stone, which I saw went through to the upper room, and possibly on it might be cut a relief of the King offering his gifts to the several deities. This was certainly a very proper representation at the sepulchre of this great King, to set forth, as our author observes, to Osiris and the gods that were with him, that he had finished a life spent in acts of piety towards the gods, and of justice to mankind. Another thing is very remarkable in the front, that a building is marked out on it, that shews something of a very fine taste, and that the Egyptians had a notion of a beautiful disposition of lights, and of architecture in general, where it was proper to make use of such buildings, which we may suppose was not convenient for temples, that are generally built without windows, and with massive walls, that have no other variety in them, than that of hieroglyphics.

Pinkerton's *Voyages*, Vol. XV, page 808, gives two accounts of Alexandria; the first is by an Arabian physician of the thirteenth century, Abd Allatif – Abd Allatif's *Relation Respecting Egypt.* In this he refers to an earlier description of the fourth century A.D. by the Rhetor Apthonius.

ABD ALLATIF'S *RELATION*

I saw at Alexandria the column (of the pillars), called *Amood-alsawari.* It is of that red spotted granite which is so extremely hard. I can readily give credit to its being seventy cubits high. . . . Round the column of pillars I likewise saw some pretty considerable remains of these columns, part of them entire, and others broken; it was still evident, from these remains that the columns were once covered with a roof which they sustained. Above the column of pillars is a cupola which it supports. I conjecture this to have been the portico in which Aristotle gave his lessons, and after him his disciples; that this also was the academy erected by Alexander when he built the city, and in which he deposited the library consigned to the flames, with the permission of Omar, by Amron-ben-Alas.

Apthonius, after describing the site of what he denominates the *acropolis* of Alexandria, the elevation of the ground, the different roads leading thither, the hundred steps which were ascended in order to arrive there, and the propylaeum in which the entrance of it was decorated, thus continues:

On entering the citadel you find a site bounded by four equal sides; so that the shape of the building on it is of a brick mould. In the middle is a court surrounded by columns, and to this court porticoes succeed: the porticoes also are separated by columns of equal size. Each portico terminates at the angle of termination of another portico; being the last of the one and the first of another. Within the porticoes cabinets are constructed: some, which serve for containing books, are opened to those inclined to the study of philosophy, and present to all the city ready means of acquiring wisdom, others are consecrated to the worship of the ancient deities. These porticoes have a roof adorned with gildings, and the capitals of the columns are of copper gilt. The court is embellished with different ornaments, each part having its own: in one quarter are seen the combats of Perseus. In the middle of the Court rises a column of extraordinary dimensions, which serves as a point of direction to the building; for on arriving, you would not know whither you were going did not this column serve to direct you on the way. Round the capital of the column are placed all the elements of existence.

APPENDIX C

Extract from Venice, a Very Noble City Described by Mr. Francesco Sansovino, 1581 *

THERE is no city in Europe of greater size and with more palaces, both on & off the Grand Canal, than Venice – palaces which we call for modesty houses, giving the name of Palace only to that of the Doge. It is certain that if one were to stroll about the principal cities of Italy such as Rome, Naples, Milan, Genoa, Florence, Bologna, Padua, Verona & Pavia one would find that none have more than four or five buildings on any one street which deserve the title of palace. But here one encounters little less than a hundred, all of them the ancient as well as the modern, magnificent & grandiose in composition as well as in their arrangement & in their apartments; & it is true that one cannot see in any other place buildings more comfortable, intimate or better suited for the use of man than these.

Though the Venetians have been restricted in these islands, surrounded by the sea, they have extended as much as the site of the place permitted them, supplying the defection of nature with artifice & it is manifest that if all the palaces were to have *cortili* (which many have) & if the streets were wide & spacious as they are elsewhere, the city would be by far larger than any other in the world. On the edge of the quarter facing the mainland, the houses in their appearance (as built in the youth of Venice) demonstrate the parsimony of the early founders, where they are low with narrow windows & with few doorways, out of respect for the ill purged air of those times. But with

* *Venetia, citta nobilissima e singolare. Descritta in XIII libri da Mr. Francesco Sansovino.* Venice, 1581. (Book IX.) Translation by Giovanna Lawford.

the passing of time land was reclaimed & the air bettered through the concerted efforts of the people, by burning over, & through the continual rising & falling of the waters & they so built themselves palaces & dwellings of great size. German architecture was introduced; the Venetians doing as did the rest of Italy. The Goths for many years in Italy imposed everywhere their barbaric & corrupt customs, almost extinguishing the heritage of Rome. And, therefore, one sees that these churches & houses are composed in major part according to the manner of that nation. . . .

Nearly all of the palaces are on the best sites & with the best views of the city & placed for the most part on the water & nearly all of the dwellings of the inhabitants front on the water, this although useful as a means of servicing the family with all the necessary things the year round, cannot though so easily be explained. Apart from this every house has a terrace on its roof built of stone or of timber & which are called *Altane* & are used for hanging the laundry in the sun & from which can be seen a great tract of water & all the surrounding countryside. And all the roofs are of double curved tiles without any flat ones, so that the cost of building is greater here than on the mainland. Around the roof circle the eaves troughs of *pietra viva* through which the rain water runs by way of hidden drains into the wells where, cleansed of its rougher matter, it is turned to the benefit of the people, because there being no river, nor any bed of solid ground where one could find a vein of fresh water, one uses the cisterns, the waters of which are healthier & better to digest than the brackish underground waters. . . .

Now the foundations of these buildings are made of very strong poles of oak, which last eternally under water, out of respect for the slimy & not at all secure bottom of the marshland. These, driven by force into the ground & then secured with heavy beams & filled between with cement & broken rocks, make through their setting & coagulation, foundations so stable & solid they are able to sustain any heavy or high wall without giving a hair's breadth. The bricks or baked clay & the mortar come to us from the territories of Padua Treviso & Ferrara. . . . Sand comes from the Brenta or the Lido, but that of the fresh water is better. Timber is brought in great abundance by river, in the form of rafts, from the mountains of Cadore, Friuli & Trevisana. Iron comes from Brescia & various other places in Lombardy.

But the beautiful & wondrous material is the *pietre vive* brought in from Rovigno & from Brioni, villages on the coast of Dalmatia. It is white & similar to marble but so sound & hard that it lasts for ever under sun & ice. Even statues are made of it which when polished as one does with marble & then pomiced, resemble marble. With these so fashioned one incrusts entire façades of churches & palaces & fashions columns heavy & long as one would wish. . . . There are also façades incrusted with fine marbles, Greek, brought from the islands of the Archipelago & especially from Paros. However these are not as white as the usual marble & are quite different from the marble of Carrara in Tuscany. The stone also from Verona we hold in esteem because being red & with various markings it brings beauty to the buildings. . . .

The roofs of the buildings are generally pitched four ways so that aside from facilitating the draining of the water they add greater attractiveness to the buildings. The floor beams are closely spaced & alternating with slender voids they give to the eye a gratifying delight, aside from serving well for strength, & as so placed they are able to sustain great weight & the floors will not shake when walked upon. The dwellings are built ordinarily of three floors aside from the roof. All chambers have fireplaces, but not the other rooms, & this certainly with reason for when one gets up out of bed one's fire is near by which not only is good for drying the moisture one attracts to oneself during the night's sleep but also warms the room & purges the bad odors in the air & from wherever else they arise. The apartments were arranged by our ancestors in cruciform (that is to say T shaped) to the ill appearance of the building but this custom being done away with, they now run straight through the house from one façade to the other; the window openings correspond to each other as do the doors & as do the doors & windows of the chambers on the sides. Thus every window being amply proportioned the eye, apart from the beautiful view, can travel freely & the rooms are light & full of sun. Add to this that all windows are covered, not with waxed linen or paper screens but with thin pure white glass encased in frames of wood & secured with iron & with lead. Not only is this so in palaces & houses but in every other building, mean as it might be, to the surprise of strangers for in this alone there is infinite wealth, all of which pours out of the furnaces of Murano.

The façades of the buildings are plumb from the roof to the ground with no colonnades or projections or other impedimenta so that it comes to pass that in rainy weather man cannot shelter himself from the rain as in Padua or Bologna or anywhere else where there are colonnades. In the composition of the buildings the windows of the parlor are placed in the middle of the façade so that its location can be readily recognized, & at the windows are balconies projecting out with waist high columns all around – very useful in the Summer season for letting the fresh air by. Among the façades there are some with the *loggia* on the ground floor with columns, & with arches, but nevertheless all in line with the rest of the façade. This was done by our forefathers for, bringing home their provisions they used to unload them in the *loggia*, leading from which were the storerooms for putting them away. The doors are high & squared & every house on the water has two, the one serves the water & the other leads onto land. Every commodious dwelling has a *cortile*, with an uncovered well in the middle, as fresh water becomes purer in the open air than in the dark – note that the sun cleanses the water & exhales in this way all its impurities.

As for the ornamentation the furnishings & the incredible richness of the dwellings of the great, as well as of the common people & the humble, it is something impossible to imagine let alone to write of at length. And this is reasonable for 1159 years having now passed since she [Venice] was founded, without having been touched by predatory hands or enemies &, engaging all this time in commerce, through which she has continually brought home great wealth (as well as the relics of ancient cities maltreated & dispersed over many centuries by the barbarians), it naturally follows she has become opulent & rich. Moreover the noble houses for hundreds of years continued in flower through good government & through the commerce of the sea, & have continually increased their possessions to their greatest happiness; even those who in the past were given to parsimony bedecked their houses with great splendor. There are innumerable houses the ceilings of whose apartments are worked in gold & other colors & covered with paintings & excellent decoration. Nearly all of their interiors arc covered with the very best tapestries, coverings of silk, gilded leathers & other materials according to the different seasons. And the chambers are for the most part adorned with bedsteads & chests decorated in gold, & paintings with frames also covered with gold. The silver services & other wares of porcelain, pewter, & inlaid copper or bronze, are without end. In the halls of the great are arrayed the arms & the shields, & standards of their ancestors who had been with her sea & land forces. I have seen sold at auction the household goods of a nobleman (condemned for a sinister act) which would have been over much for any one of the Italian Grand Dukes. The same can be said for the common people & the humble ones in proportion, because there is no person so poor, and who has a home of his own, who has not chests & beds of walnut, green coverings, rugs, pewter ware, copper, gold chains, silver forks & rings — such is the state of well-being of this city. However with her extraordinary endeavor in all the arts & with the whole world contributing, her people, some more some less according to their position & intelligence, participated in this great wealth with such liveliness that they have become soft & licentious.

* * * * *

PALACES

Now choosing from among the many noble palaces & dwellings which we have mentioned above, we note the palace near the Church of Santo Antonio under the Procuratia de Supra, as being of extraordinary size. It contains about forty good & comfortable rooms, & was at various times a hostelry to different Princes, among the last of whom was Ferrante Sanseverino, Prince of Salerno, during his unhappy exile. It overlooks on the left almost all the lagoon and its several villages, & as far as Chioggia 25 miles away, & on the right as far as the Dogana di Mare. The garden is convenient to the body of the house as are the *Cortili* to the other parts, & it is kept at present by Marchió Michele Prior of Venice for the Order of San Lazero of the Duke of Savoy. Not far away it is accompanied by San Giovanni de Forlani, an ancient palace, but very comfortable, in which lived the Priors of those times. In the rear it has its ample gardens of great beauty. Not far from the Ponte della Madonna near the Pietà, one sees the palace of the Gritti family, painted on the outside by Battista Moro Veronese, & behind it the one of Procurator Alessandro Gritti, & near the Ponte della paglia a similar one, also of the Gritti. In the Rio di Palazzo is the palace formerly of the Trevisani & now of the Gran Duchessa of Tuscany, all incrusted with the finest of marbles, magnificent & very beautiful. On the Campo di Santa Maria there is another one, of marble, of the Malipieri family, & another across the way, la Ruggina, built a few years ago with a beautiful & richly adorned façade. Near the Malipieri is situated the famous palace of the Patriarch Grimani, built in the Roman style. It is divided into beautiful rooms & loggias on the ground floor, & adorned with antique figures & torsos & with inscriptions over all, in grand style. The stairway, adorned with paintings & stuccos, radiates the floors & landings. It is covered with beautiful soffits on which Francesco Salviati did a Psyche, & Camillo Mantovano worked the festoons, while beyond Giovanni da Udine did a whole room, all in stucco. Near by is found the palace of the Giorgia family, covered with white marbles, & near the bridge to the right is that of Francesco da Paoli Procurator of San Marco. Here are preserved illustrious paintings by Iacomo Palma Vecchio, who, being favored by this house, was not only supported by it but lived there for a long time & adorned it with very singular paintings. In the Rio of San Lorenzo is the palace of Luigi Giorgi, honest Senator; it is filled with many beautiful objects, portraits, & figures of marble & of stucco by Alessandro Vittoria. At the other end of the Rio loom the buildings of the Capelli, costly & magnificent. At San Benedetto one sees the palace of the Pesari, which covers a large plot of ground, worthy of its situation on the Grand Canal. The palace of the Loredani at San Stefano is equally illustrious, because aside from being built in the modern manner, it has several ornamentations of paintings & stuccos, & the façade was painted by Gioseppe Salviati. In the Calle of San Mauritio is situated the palace built by Nicolo' da Ponte for the present Prince of Venice, rich in various & beautiful paintings. On the Campo de Crocicchieri one sees the one of the Zeni, built after the model by Francesco Zeno, who was in his time a gentleman with knowledge of architecture. And a little farther on, this side of the bridge, one finds that of the Contarini, originally built by the Dolce family, & near by is that of the Giustiniani. In Canareio, across from San Job, is the very noble palace formerly of the Gonnella family & now of Monsignor Silvestro Valerio, whose salon is numbered among the best of the city. The one of the Grimani at San Boldo is equally noble. At San Paolo that of the Cornari built after the model by Michele da San Michele, is rich in varied ornament. And on the same Campo those of Bernardi & of the Soranzi are worth seeing. Gioseppe Salviati painted the façade of that of the Bernardi. At the Carmini the palace of Iacomo Foscarino Cavaliero & Procuratore of San Marco is to be noted, & it is furnished with many antiques. At San Pantaleone the Loredani built theirs, embellished by many ancient figures. At Santa Marina the buildings of the Emi, of the Mocenighi, of the Soranzi, & of the Bragadini are all to be remembered for their size, commodiousness, & for their rare & unusual ornamentation. At San Basilio one sees the very important edifice of the Molini. And near San Gervasio is the venerable habitation of the Barbarighi Doges, later rebuilt after the model by Sansovino, by the ever remembered Agostino Barbarigo. The Nani also have adorned their buildings, owned at present by Paolo Procurator of San Marco, with paintings & stuccos by the hand of Alessandro Vittoria. And in the quarter of San Luigi, are situated several palaces, of which that of the Michela family is very noble, & was occupied many years ago by Arnoldo Ferrerio, Ambassador of France. Then there is that of Doctor Negroni.

Also at the Misericordia is worth recording that of Luigi Thiepolo, Procurator of San Marco. Becoming undermined, its foundations were rebuilt with an artifice never before heard of, while people still lived above; they suffered no movement whatsoever to the great surprise of the city. By leaving a building standing & holding it up in the air, one can pour new foundations under it without discomfort to the inhabitants. This was discovered by Sansovino. With this invention he kept the Church of San Marco on its feet, for its middle dome was falling into ruins & threatening to pull the others with it. Finding nobody with enough courage to put their hands to it, Sansovino not only supported it but repaired it & rebuilt it. This was to his great honor & to the great delight of the Senate & the universe, for it had always been thought to be a hopeless task to preserve or restore it.

At San Ieronimo the house of the Mori, built to look almost like a large castle, was the work of Leonardo Moro. At Servi, the Grimani own beautiful & praiseworthy buildings, & not far away are the Vendramini whose palace, with a marble façade, was formerly the meeting place of the intellectuals of the city. Also when Gabriello, a great lover of painting, sculpture & architecture was alive, he had brought to it much ornamentation & many works by the most famous artists of his time. So that one sees here works by Giorgione da Castel Franco, by Gian Bellino, by Titiano, by Michel Agnolo, & others, preserved by his successors; & near by is the palace of the Dukes of Urbino, of good size, owned by them many years ago in accordance with the custom of other Princes who have or who have had places here for their amusement. At the Maddalena & at San Leonardo one sees the ancient buildings of the Donata family.

But without doubt the greatest number of palaces, of fine houses & of other notable edifices are seen on the Grand Canal which divides the city in half, & became the most important & desirable part of all. Our forefathers honored it with regal & splendid buildings. Beginning at the Dogana di Mare, & ending at Santa Lucia, they built it up solidly on one side as well as the other, with the richest of establishments which, such is their size & magnificence, one can with reasonableness call them palaces. But as it would be a tedious & over laborious matter to examine this quarter minutely, we shall take note of a few of the more obvious & largest palaces as we have already done for those previously mentioned which are situated inland, pointing out to the visitor a few of them, leaving the remainder to be explored by his own interest. Inasmuch as I hold firmly that man is not able (as I know by experience) to satiate his eyes with the variety of such beautiful buildings, the less can he do so adequately with writing.

It is enough to know that the most important of all the palaces on the Grand Canal are four in number (I speak of architecture, of the workmanship of the *pietre vive*, of their majesty, of their size & their cost, since these alone cost over 200,000 ducats). These are the Loredano at S. Marcuola, the Grimano at San Luca, the Delfino at San Salvadore, & the Cornaro at San Mauritio. These, generous in girth, in height, & in every other quality needed in a well conceived building, were built in our times & according to the doctrines of the ancient Vitruvius, from which it is wise for the best architects not to deviate.

The Loredano palace, of great body and of great height, & antedating the others & situated almost on an island, is a very noble one, because beside the abundance of its rooms, the façade is covered with Greek marbles & with large windows, all colonnaded in the Corinthian order. The Grimano, which exceeds it greatly in its regal halls & in every other thing, is very rich in work, so that the carving, scroll work, and other embellishment almost down to the foundations, are of excessive expense. There are also magnificent colonnades in the *cortile* & the façade abounds in the richness of its components & of its work by the hand of Michele di San Michele who was its architect. The Delfino, the first to be built in Venice after the Loredano, under architectural regulation is worthy of praise. It occupies a large plot of ground with a *cortile* in the middle surrounded by *loggie* in the Roman manner. The exterior façades are well conceived & inside it has large & commodious rooms done by order of Giovanni Delfino after the model by Sansovino.

The Cornaro, which ranks fourth for site, for magnificence, for size, for its wealth of stonework, and for its structure & symmetry, is among all the others memorable. Inside it has a large *cortile* embellished in the Roman manner & which can be opened or closed, & with other contrivances adapted to common use. It is ample enough on one side for the family of a Cardinal & on the other for all the men & women of his train. Because of its height it can be seen from every side & overlooks the lagoons. The façade with double tiers of columns, Ionic above, & with delicate rustication below with noble windows, appears full of majesty to the onlooker. In front, the *loggia*, with stairs rising from the water, gives nobility to this building. It was built by order of Giorgio Cornaro, son of the late Iacomo, Procurator of San Marco, after the model of Sansovino.

However, all of the four dwellings are surpassed in their sites, & in the greatness of their plants by the Foscaro palace, old & in the German style. As it is situated on the corner of the Rio di San Pantalone it overlooks, due to the bend in the Grand Canal, toward the left as far as the Rialto, & to the right as far as the Carità not far from San Marco. For this reason it is unusual and was chosen in the year 1574 as a worthy dwelling for the King of France. It is also as abounding as any other in the city in its apartments, & in its halls which were painted by Paris Bordone. This building belonged in other times to the Giustiniani family whose famous Bernardo sold it in 1428 to the Senate who presented it as a gift to the Marchese di Mantova but, being returned to the State & sold at auction, it was bought by Principe Foscari who transformed it so that it no longer is recognizable as the Casa Giustiniana. That same family owns also a very noble dwelling nearly as large as the other.

There are also on the Grand Canal the large & noteworthy palaces of the Duke of Ferrara at San Iacomo dell'Orio, venerable & built in the form of a castle in the German style; of the Duke of Milano at San Samuelo, which was begun in great style with columns & marbles & which afterward passed on to the Grimani family; of the Mocenighi, belonging to Giovanni brother of Principe Luigi; of the Cornari, built with blocks of rough stone, on the Corte dell'Albero; of the Cornari della Piscopia, which belonged at one time to the King of Cyprus & was given by him to the said Cornari, & which for a time received various foreign princes who came to this city; of the Gufoni at the Ponte da Noale, built after the model of Michele da San Michele, rich in its apartments & very well arranged; of the Troni at Santo Eustachio, in perfect symmetry & of dignified appearance; of the Contarini delle Torricelle; those of the Capelli on the Rio di San Polo, the one of Gian Battista painted by Paolo Veronese, the other of marble, formerly belonging to his brother Marino, of modern composition & with decorations by Maffeo Bernardo; of the Contarini at San Gervaso large in size & of well composed orderly form; of the Grimani at San Vito, in a rather beautiful & gracious manner; of the

Foscari at San Simeone, of beautiful appearance & with varied ornamentation for Pietro Foscari, spirited Senator delighting in the beauty of sculpture & painting as well as loving travel & the art of governing, not only decorated & restored this palace but also gave fame to his other palace situated in the Arena of Padua – the very worthy dwelling of the King of France; of the Pisani at Santa Maria Zebenigo, in the German manner but of solid & lasting form; of the Bonaldi at Santo Eustachio & that of the Coccina, so well planned inside & so graceful in appearance. On the outside it is not at all the inferior in structure or ornamentation of any other palace on the Grand Canal; & finally, that of the Giustiniani da San Moise & of others of many more families which at present I cannot remember.

There are also, praise the Lord, on the island of the Giudecca several buildings of importance of which two at the moment seem more important than the others. The one at the near point of the island is the palace of Andrea Dandolo, beautifully situated, copious in its apartments, *cortili*, *loggie* & gardens; & the other almost at the other end of the island, of the Vendramin family. These & many other buildings near by of more or less importance form a vast & great city which will appear to the subtle not as one but as many separate cities all joined together. If her situation is considered without the bridges, one will see that she is divided into many large towns & cities surrounded by their canals over which one passes from one to the other by way of bridges, which are generally built of stone but sometimes of wood, and which join her various parts together. The shops which are spread all over the city also make her appear many cities joined into one because every quarter has not only one but many churches, its own public square & wells, its bakeries, wineshops, its guild of tailors, greengrocers, pharmacists, school teachers, carpenters, shoemakers & finally in great abundance all else required for human needs, to the extent that leaving one quarter & entering another one would say without doubt one was leaving one city & entering another – to the great convenience & satisfaction of the inhabitants & to the great surprise of strangers.

* * * * *

Bibliography

THE works listed below are a selection from the vast fragmentary literature upon the collecting of works of art in ancient and modern times. No general work appears in English – the two most valuable sources have been the introductions to two works by German scholars, published respectively in 1854 and 1882 – namely, Waagen's *Treasures of Art in England*, and Michaelis's *Ancient Marbles in Great Britain.* Dumesnil's *Histoires des plus célèbres amateurs*, while covering much of Europe geographically, are primarily mid-Victorian excursions in biography and anecdote. The first really serious history of collecting – and that only in its bearing upon the collections of Vienna – is Julius von Schlosser's *Kunst- und Wunderkammern der Spät-Renaissance*, which, together with his *Die Kunstliteratur*, may be considered the point of departure for any investigator of the subject. To these and to certain other works this book owes its essential form and direction: Miss Miriam Beard's *A History of the Business Man* has been an endless source of inspiration, as have Bonnaffé's *Les collectionneurs de l'ancienne Rome* and Chambers's *History of Taste*. For the Italian Renaissance, in addition to the specific sources cited below, much profit has been derived from the great social historians of the nineteenth century, Burckhardt, John Addington Symonds, Ranke, Pastor, Gregorovius, Bishop Creighton, Lord Acton, Sir Richard Jebb, Michelet and Prescott. To Eugène Müntz, Francesco Pellati, Stark, and to Colonel Young is owed the pattern of the chapters on the Medici, and also to Müntz the basic data on collecting by the Papacy. These sources for the seventeenth century were supplemented by the data of Bertaux, Ranke and Michaelis. For France no study can be made without reference to Bonnaffé, Charles Blanc and Clément de Ris. The bibliography given by Miss Dorothy Quynn for the Napoleonic period underscores the debt of all students in this field to her and to Lanzac de Laborie and Saunier. The historian of collecting in Spain must always acknowledge obligation to Sir William Stirling-Maxwell and Miss Enriqueta Harris. Floerke's researches are basic for the study of collecting in the Low Countries. The sources for the Germanies and Austria were examined and synthesized by Dr. Clara Brahm, formerly of the Worcester Art Museum Library. They are listed below, many having been suggested by Dr. Hans Huth. Finally in England it would not be possible to overlook the great debt owed to Steegmann, Trevelyan, the publications of the Walpole Society and to many others. However it is to Horace Walpole himself, and to his commentators and biographers, that we must turn for an understanding of English taste. The generosity of Wilmarth S. Lewis, editor of the Yale University Edition of Walpole's *Letters*, has gone beyond the limits of ordinary friendship. Professor Dinsmoor and Ambrose Lansing have been more than helpful regarding the early chapters on Egypt and Greece. Professor C. R. Morey most generously took the time to read and criticize the proofs, as did Perry B. Cott. Charles Sterling of the Louvre and Jean Adhémar of the Bibliothèque Nationale opened avenues and vistas of French taste which otherwise would have remained unexplored. To Frits Lugt, however, the dean of all contemporary writers in this field, remains an immeasurable obligation for having studied and added to the proofs from the vast storehouse of his experience. Chapter II, Book V, has been entirely revised upon information and criticism supplied by him. To the latter, and to Edward Weeks, editor of the *Atlantic Monthly*, are given the most heartfelt thanks. But above all to my wife, my children, and to my associates both past and present at the Worcester Art Museum and at the Metropolitan, I wish to express my gratitude for their help and their forbearance.

F. H. T.

The Metropolitan Museum of Art
New York, 1948

Adam, Robert and James, *Works*. 1773–1778, 1779, and 1882.

Addison, Julia de W., *The Art of the Dresden Gallery*. Boston, 1911.

Alazard, Jean, *L'abbé Luigi Strozzi, correspondant artistique de Mazarin, de Colbert, de Louvois et de La Teulière*. Contribution à l'étude des relations artistique entre la France et l'Italie au XVIIe siècle. Paris, 1924.

Alison, Archibald, *Nature and Principles of Taste*. Edinburgh, 1790.

Allen, B. Sprague, *Tides in English Taste*. Cambridge, Mass., 1937. 2 vols.

Allen, George, *Occasional Thoughts on Genius*. London, 1749.

Ansell, Florence Jean, and Fraprie, Frank Roy, *The Art of the Munich Galleries*. London, 1911.

Antioch-on-the-Orontes, Publication of the Committee for the Excavation of Antioch and Its Vicinity. Princeton University Press, 1934. Vol. I and subsequent volumes.
Armstrong, Sir Walter, *Lawrence.* New York, 1913.
Avenel, Vicomte Georges d', *Découvertes d'histoire sociale.* Paris, 1907.
—— *Les Riches depuis sept cents ans.* Paris 1909.
—— *Histoire économique de la propriété, des salaires, des denrées, et de tous les prix en général depuis l'an 1200 jus qu'en l'an 1800.* Paris, 1894.

Bain, F. W., *Christina, Queen of Sweden.* London, 1890.
Barry, James, *The Works of James Barry, Esq.* London, 1809. 2 vols.
Bathoe, *A catalogue of the curious collection of pictures of George Villers, Duke of Buckingham, in which is included the valuable collection of Sir P. P. Rubens.* London, 1758.
Beard, Miriam, *A History of the Business Man.* New York, 1938.
Beardwood, Alice, *Alien Merchants in England 1350 to 1377, their legal and economic position.* Cambridge, Mass., 1931.
Beissel, Stephan, *Gefälschte Kunstwerke.* Freiburg, 1909.
Bell, H. I., Article on Alexandria, in *Journal of Egyptian Archaeology,* 1927.
Benesch, Otto, "Die Fürsterzbischöfliche Gemäldegalerie in Kremsier," in *Pantheon,* Vol. I (1928).
Berger, Adolf, "Inventar der Kunstsammlung des Erzherzogs Leopold Wilhelm von Oesterreich," in *Jahrbuch der kunsthistor. Sammlungen des allerh. Kaiserhauses,* Vol. I (1883).
Bertaux, Émile, *Rome: de l'avènement de Jules II à nos jours.* Paris, 1928.
Bertolotti, A., "Die Ausfuhr einiger Kunstgegenstände aus Rom nach Oesterreich, Deutschland, Polen und Russland vom 16. bis 19. Jahrhundert," in *Repertorium für Kunstwissenschaft,* Vol. V (1882).
Bildt, Charles de, *Christine de Suède et le Cardinal Azzolino. Lettres Inédites.* Paris, 1899.
—— *Les Médailles Romaines de Christine de Suède.* Rome, 1908.
—— "Queen Christina's Pictures," in *The Nineteenth Century and After,* December 1904.
Blanc, Charles, *L'Oeuvre complet de Rembrandt.*
—— *Le Tresor de la Curiosité.* Paris, 1857. 2 vols.
Blok, P. J., [Ed.] *Amsterdam in de Zeventiende Eeuw.* The Hague, 1897–1904.

Blomfield, Sir Reginald, *History of Renaissance Architecture in England*. London, 1897.
Bode, Wilhelm von, *Mein Leben*. Berlin, 1930. 2 vols.
Bolton, Arthur T., *The Architecture of Robert and James Adam*. New York, 1922.
Bonnaffé, Edmond, "Le Castiglione," in *Gazette des Beaux-Arts*, 1884.
—— *Causeries sur l'art et la curiosité*. Paris, 1878.
—— *Les collectionneurs de l'ancienne France*. Paris, 1869.
—— *Les collectionneurs de l'ancienne Rome*. Paris, 1867.
—— *Dictionnaire des amateurs français au XVIIe siècle*. Paris, 1884.
—— *Recherches sur les collections des Richelieu*. Paris, 1883.
Borenius, Tancred, *The Picture Gallery of Andrea Vendramin*. London, 1923.
Bouchier, E. S., *A Short History of Antioch*. Oxford, 1921.
Boulton, W. H., *Romance of the British Museum*. London, 1938.
Boyer, Ferdinand, "Les Antiques de Christine de Suède à Rome," in *Revue Archeologique*, Vol. 35 (1932).
Brandi, Karl, *The Emperor Charles V*, trans. from the German by C. W. Wedgwood. New York, 1939.
Breccia, Evaristo, *Alexandrea ad Aegyptum*. Bergamo, 1922.
Brewer, John S., *The Court of James I*. First published from an original manuscript in the Bodleian Library by Dr. Godfrey Goodman, Bishop of Gloucester. London, 1938.
Brice, Germain, *Nouvelle description de la ville de Paris*. Paris, 1725. 8th ed., 4 vols.
Brieger, Lothar, *Das Kunstsammeln*. Munich, 1918.
—— *Die Grossen Kunstsammler*. Berlin, 1931.
Brienne (Mazarin's Secretary), *Mémoires* of Louis Henri de Loménie, Comte de Brienne. Paris, 1828.
Briggs, Martin S., *Men of Taste*. London, 1947.
Browne, Edward, *Brief Account of Some Travels in Divers Parts of Europe*. London, 1685.
Buchanan, William, *Memoirs of Painting*. London, 1824. 2 vols.
Burckhardt, Jakob, *Beiträge zur Kunstgeschichte von Italien*. Berlin and Stuttgart. (Das Porträt, Das Altarbild, Die Sammler.) Basel, 1898.
—— *Die Kunstwerke der belgischen Städte*. Düsseldorf, 1842.
—— *The Civilization of the Renaissance in Italy* (translated by S. G. C. Middlemore from the 15th German edition containing the notes of Dr. Ludwig Geiger and Professor Walther Götz). New York, 1937.
—— *Kultur-Geschichte Vorträge*. (Collected Essays.) Leipzig, n.d.

Burgon, John William, *The Life and Times of Sir Thomas Gresham.* London, 1839.

Burke, Edmund, *A Philosophical Enquiry into the Origin of the Sublime and Beautiful.* London, 1761.

Càllari, Luigi, *I Palazzi di Roma.* Rome, 1944.

Cammell, Charles Richard, *The Great Duke of Buckingham.* London, 1939.

Campbell, Colin, *Vitruvius Brittannicus,* 1717–1770.

Campori, Marchese, *Raccolta dei cataloghi ed inventarii inediti dal secolo XV al secolo XIX.* Modena, 1870.

Cardinali, G., *Il regno di Pergamo.* Rome, 1906.

Cartellieri, Otto, *The Court of Burgundy.* New York, 1929.

Cartwright, Julia, *Isabella d'Este.* New York, 1903.

—— *The Perfect Courtier.* New York, 1927.

Cary, Max, *The Legacy of Alexander: A History of the Greek World from 323–146 B.C.* New York, 1932.

Casson, Stanley, "The Popularity of Greek Archaic Art," in *American Magazine of Art,* 1937. Vol. 30.

Castiglione, Count Baldassare, *The Book of the Courtier.* New York, 1901.

Caston, A., *Monographie du Palais Granvella.* Paris, 1867.

Catalogue of the Exhibition of the King's Pictures, Royal Academy. London, 1946–1947.

Cecil, Lord David, *The Young Melbourne.* New York, 1939.

Chambers, Frank P., *History of Taste.* New York, 1932.

Chambers, Sir William, *Designs of Chinese Buildings.* London, 1757.

—— *Dissertation on Oriental Gardening.* London, 1772.

—— *Treatise on the Decorative Part of Civil Architecture.* London, 1759.

Chancellor, E. Beresford, *Life in Regency and Early Victorian Times.* London, 1926.

—— *The Eighteenth Century in London.* London, 1920.

Chennevrières, Henry de, "Le Louvre en 1815," in *Revue Bleue,* XLIII (1889).

Clarendon, Edward Hyde, Earl of, *History of the Rebellion.* Oxford, 1717. 3 vols.

Clark, Sir Kenneth, *Gothic Revival.* London, 1929.

Clément, Pierre, *Jacques-Coeur et Charles VII.* Paris, 1866.

—— *Histoire de Colbert et de son administration.* Paris, 1874.

Cole, Charles Woolsey, *Colbert and a Century of French Mercantilism.* New York, 1939. 2 vols.

Collins-Baker, C. H., *Lely and Kneller.* London, 1922.

Constable, W. G., "The Foundation of the National Gallery," in *Burlington Magazine,* Vol. 44. 1914.

Conway, William M., *Literary remains of Albrecht Dürer.* Cambridge, 1889.

Cordier, Henri, *La Chine en France au XVIIIe siècle.* Paris, 1910.

Cosnac, Gabriel Jules de, *Les richesses du Palais Mazarin,* Paris, 1884.

—— *Recherches sur les collections de Richelieu.* Paris, 1883.

Courajod, Louis, *Alexandre Lenoir, son journal et le Musée des Monuments Français.* Paris, 1878–1887. 3 vols.

Cust, Lionel, *Notes on Pictures in the Royal Collections.* London, 1911.

Cust, Sir Lionel, and Colvin, Sidney, *History of the Society of Dilettanti.* London, 1914.

Daenell, Ernst Robert, *Die Blütezeit der deutschen Hanse.* Berlin, 1905.

Daressy, Georges, "Le Palais d'Amenophis III à Medinéb-Abou," in the *Annales du Service des Antiquités,* Vol. IV. 1903.

Dashkova, Ykaterina Romanovna (Princess), *Memoirs Written by Herself, Comprising Letters of the Empress, Catherine II.* (Ed. by Mrs. W. Bradford.) London, 1840. 2 vols.

Davidsohn, Robert, *Florentiner Welthandel des Mittelalters,* in *Weltwirtschaftliches Archiv.,* 1929

—— *Geschichte von Florenz.* Berlin, 1925.

Decamps, L., "Un collectionneur de l'an VI," in *Gazette des Beaux-Arts,* Vol. 7 (1873).

Defoe, Daniel, *The Anatomy of Exchange Alley.* London, 1719.

—— *The Complete English Tradesman.* London, 1738.

—— *A General History of Trade.* London, 1713.

—— *A Tour Thro' London about the Year 1725,* Being Letter V and Parts of Letter VI of *A Tour Thro' the Whole Island of Great Britain,* and containing a description of the City of London, as taking in the City of Westminster, Borough of Southwark and parts of Middlesex. Reprinted from the original edition, and ed. by Sir Mayson M. Beeton and E. Beresford Chancellor. London, 1927.

Degering, Hermann, "Französischer Kunstraub in Deutschland," in *Internationale Monatsschrift für Wissenschaft, Kunst und Technik,* XI (1916–1917).

Delen, A. J. J., *La maison de Rubens.* Brussels, 1939.
Delisle, Leopold, "Les archives du Vatican," in *Journal des Savants.* Paris, 1892.
Denis, Ferdinand, *Le Monde enchanté; Cosmographie et histoire naturelle et fantastique du moyen âge.* Paris, 1843.
Deschamps, Pierre, "Testament de Madame de Verrue," in *Gazette des Beaux-Arts,* Vol. 16 (1864).
Despois, Eugène A., *Le Vandalisme révolutionnaire.* Paris, 1868.
Deuvel, Thea, *Die Gütererwerbungen J. Fuggers des Reichen.* Munich, 1913.
Dibdin, E. R., "Liverpool Art and Artists in the XVIII Century," in *The Walpole Society,* Vol. 6. 1918.
Dobson, Austin, *Horace Walpole.* New York, 1890.
—— "The Bibliotheca Meadiana," in *Bibliographica,* 1895. Vol. 1.
Documenti inediti per servire alla Storia dei Musei d'Italia. Florence and Rome, 1878. 3 vols. (The most comprehensive body of source material for the Chigi, Pamphili, Odescalchi, Colonna, Barberini, Farnese, and the collections of the eighteenth century.)
Donath, Adolf, *Psychologie des Kunstsammelns.* Berlin, 1920.
Drioton, Abbé, *Annales du Service des Antiquités de l'Egypte.* 1936, 1937. (Cf. References to Egyptian libraries and colleges.)
Duchèsne, *aîné,* ed., *Musée français. Receuil des plus beaux tableaux, statues et bas reliefs qui existaient au Louvre avant 1815.* Paris, 1829. 4 vols.
—— *Voyage d'un Iconophile.* Paris, 1834.
Dumesnil, M. J., *Histoire des plus célèbres amateurs étrangers.* Paris, 1860.
—— *Histoire des plus célèbres amateurs Français.* Paris, 1856. 3 vols.
—— *Histoire des plus célèbres amateurs Italiens.* Paris, 1855.

Eastlake, Charles, *History of the Gothic Revival.* London, 1872.
Edwards, Edward, *Lives of the Founders of the British Museum.* London, 1870.
Ehrenberg, Richard, *Das Zeitalter der Fugger.* Jena, 1922. 2 vols.
—— *Hamburg und England im Zeitalter der Königin Elisabeth.* Jena, 1896.
Eigenberger, Robert, *Die Gemäldegalerie der Akademie.* Vienna, 1927.
Eisler, Max, *Alt-Delft.* Vienna, 1923.
Elton, Charles, "Christina of Sweden and Her Books," in *Bibliographica,* Vol. I (1895).

Encyclopedia Hispana Sud-Americana, España – Calpi – Barcelona.

Esdaile, Mrs. Katherine Ada, *English Monumental Sculpture Since the Renaissance*. London, 1928.

—— *The Life and Work of François Roubiliac*. London, 1928.

Fabricius, E., "Städtebau," in Pauly-Wissowa-Kroll, *Realencyclopaedie der klassischen Altertums-Wissenschaft*, III. A, 2.

Farington, Joseph, *The Farington Diary* (1747–1821). London, 1922–1928. 8 vols.

Finberg, Hilda F., "Canaletto in England," in *The Walpole Society*, Vol. IX, pp. 21–76.

—— "Canaletto in England. Additional Illustrations and Notes," in *The Walpole Society*, Vol. X, pp. 75–78.

Fisher, Irving, and Brown, H. G., *The Purchasing Power of Money*. New York, 1912.

Fizelière, A. de La, "Mme. de Pompadour," in *Gazette des Beaux-Arts*, 1859 (3), pp. 129, 210, 292.

Fleischer, Victor, *Fürst Karl Eusebius von Liechtenstein als Bauherr und Kunstsammler*. Vienna and Leipzig, 1910.

Fletcher, William Y., *English Book Collectors*. London, 1902.

Floerke, H., *Studien zur niederländischen Kunst- und Kulturgeschichte; die Formen des Kunsthandels, das Atelier und die Sammler in den Niederlanden vom 15.–18. Jahrhundert*. Munich, 1905.

Flower, Desmond, "Napoleon as a Bibliophile," in *Book Collector's Quarterly*. London, March 1932.

Forster, E. M., *Alexandria*. A History and a Guide. Alexandria, 1938.

Foville, Jean de, "Le Cabinet des Antiques," in *Les Arts*, Nr. 135, 1913.

Franckel, W., "Gemäldesammlungen und Gemäldeforschung in Pergamon," in *Jahrbuch des Kaiserl. deutschen archäolog. Instituts*. VI (1891), 49 ff.

Friedländer, W., "Die Entstehung des anti-klassichen Stils in der italienischen Malerei um 1520," in *Repertorium für Kunstwissenschaft*, Vol. 46. 1925.

Frimmel, Theodor von, "Ein altes Verzeichnis der Galerie Marino in Venedig," in *Beilage zu Blättern für Gemäldekunde*, October 1909.

—— "Gemäldesammlungen im Bilde," in *Beilage zur Allgem.* Zeitung, Nr. 140.

—— *Geschichte der Wiener Gemäldesammlungen*. Leipzig, 1898–1901. 3 vols.

—— "Materialien zu einer Geschichte der fürstlich Liechtensteinschen Galerie," in *Beilage zu Blättern für Gemäldekunde.* May 1907.

—— "Zur Geschichte der Galerie Borghese in Rom," in *Beilage zu Blättern für Gemäldekunde,* 1905.

Fugger News Letters, The, First and Second Series. Ed. Victor von Klarwill, trans. L. S. R. Byrne. London, 1924–1926.

Furtwängler, Adolf, "Über Kunstsammlungen in alter und neuer Zeit," in *Berl. Phil. W.,* May 13, 1899. (An address given at the 140th anniversary of the foundation of the Royal Bavarian Academy.)

Ganz, Paul, "Die Amerbach als Kunstsammler" in *Jahresbericht der Amerbach Gesellschaft.* 1920.

—— "Henry VIII and his Court Painter Hans Holbein," in *Burlington Magazine,* Vol. 63.

Gazette des Beaux-Arts. Cf. *Tables générales des cinquantes années de la Gazette des Beaux-Arts 1859–1908.* Vol. 5, Part 14, *Collectionneurs.* (Sales contained in Part 13.)

Gebhart, Emil, *Origines de la renaissance en Italie.* Paris, 1879.

Genard, Pierre, *Anvers à travers les âges.* Brussels, 1888–1892.

Georgian Art. New York, 1929. (Unsigned.)

German Museums. "Deutsche Kunststädte und Deutsche Kunstsammlungen um 1600," in *Museumskunde,* Vol. 13, July 1917. Pp. 43–52. (Unsigned.)

"Geschichte der Wiener Gemäldegalerie in den Jahren 1911 bis 1931," in *Jahrbuch der kunsthist. Sammlungen in Wien,* N.F., Bd. V. Vienna, 1931.

Gilpin, William, *Essay on Picturesque Beauty.* London, 1792.

—— *Observations on the Picturesque Beauty.* London, 1798.

Glück, Gustav, *The Picture Gallery of the Vienna Art Museum.* Vienna, 1925. (With 160 plates.)

Goethe, *Essays on Art.* Boston, 1845.

Goncourt, Edmond and Jules de, *Histoire de la société française pendant le Directoire.* Paris, 1864.

—— *La du Barry.* Paris, 1880.

—— (Edmond) *L'Art du XVIII Siècle.* Paris, 1906. 3 vols.

Granberg, Olaf, *La galerie de tableaux de la reine Christine de Suède.* Recherches historiques et critiques. Stockholm, 1897.

Graves, Algernon, *Art Sales.* From Early in the XVIII Century to Early in the XX Century. London, 1918–1921. 3 vols.

Green, Valentine, *Review of the Polite Arts in France compared with their Present State in England.* London, 1782.

Gribble, Francis, "Descartes and the Princesses," in the *Living Age*, 1913.

Gronovinus and Necorus, "De Museo Alexandrino," in Gronovii, *Thesaurum Graecorum Antiquitatem.* VII, 2741–2778.

Grot, Karlovich Yukov, *Lettres de Catherine II à Grimm (1774–1796).* Petersburg, 1878.

Groethuysen, Bernhard, *Origines de l'esprit bourgeois en France.* Paris, 1927.

Guerin, J., *La Chinoiserie en Europe au XVIII Siècle.* Paris, 1911.

Guiffrey, Jules, "L'Académie de France à Rome de 1793 à 1803," in *Journal des Savants*, 1908.

Gwynn, John, *Essay on Design.* London, 1749.

Haebler, Konrad, *Die Geschichte der Fugger'schen Handlung in Spanien.* Weimar, 1897.

Hamilton, Earl J., *American Treasure and the Price Revolution in Spain, 1501–1650.* Cambridge, Mass., 1934.

Hamilton, Sir William, *Collection of Engravings from Ancient Vases.* Naples, 1795.

Handler, Gerhard, *Fürstliche Mäzene und Sammler in Deutschland von 1500–1620.* (Doctoral dissertation at Friedrichs University at Halle-Wittenberg.) Strassburg, 1933.

Hansen, Esther V., *The Attalids of Pergamon.* Ithaca, 1947. Pp. 131, 289–290, 319–322, 332.

Hare, Augustus J. C., *Walks in Rome.* Philadelphia, n.d. 2 vols.

Hare, Christopher, *The Most Illustrious Ladies of the Italian Renaissance.* New York, 1911.

Harris, Enriqueta, *The Prado, Treasure House of the Spanish Royal Collections.* London, 1940.

Haskins, Charles Homer, *The Renaissance of the Twelfth Century.* Cambridge, Mass., 1927.

Hauser, Henri, *Les débuts du capitalisme.* Paris, 1927.

Haydon, Benjamin R., *Journal.* New York, 1853.

Hazlitt, W. Carew, *The Book-Collector.* London, 1904.

Heckscher, W. S., *Die Rom-Ruinen.* (Doctoral dissertation at University of Hamburg.) Würzburg, 1936. An English version of this has appeared under the title "Relics of Pagan Antiquity in Medieval Settings," in *Journal of the Warburg Institute*, I, 1938, pp. 204 ff.

Hervey, Mary F. S., *The Life, Correspondence and Collections of Thomas Howard, Earl of Arundel.* Cambridge, 1921.

Heyck, Eduard, *Florenz und die Medici.* Leipzig, 1927.

Heyd, Wilhelm von, *Geschichte des Levantehandels im Mittelalter.* Stuttgart, 1879.

Hind, Arthur M., *Giovanni Battista Piranesi.* New York, 1922.

Hoff, Ursula, *Charles I. Patron of Artists.* London, 1942.

Hofstede de Groot, C., *Die Urkunden über Rembrandt.* The Hague, 1906.

Hogarth, William, *Analysis of Beauty.* London, 1753.

Holmes, Sir Charles, and Collins-Baker, C. H., *The Making of the National Gallery.* London, 1924.

Holst, Niels von, "Frankfurter Kunst- und Wunderkammern des XVIII Jhs. ihre Eigenart und ihre Bestände," in *Repertorium für Kunstwissenschaft,* Vol. 52 (1931), pp. 34–58

Hope, W. H. St. John, *Windsor Castle; an Architectural History.* London, 1913. 2 vols.

Horsburgh, E. L. S., *Lorenzo the Magnificent.* New York, 1908.

Hübner, Paul Gustav, *Le statue di Roma.* Leipzig, 1912.

—— "Studien über die Benutzung der Antike in der Renaissance," in *Monatsschrift für Kunstwissenschaft,* II, 1909.

Huizinga, Johan, *The Waning of the Middle Ages.* London, 1927.

Humphreys, A. L., "Elias Ashmole," in *The Berks, Bucks and Oxon Archaeological Journal,* Spring 1924.

Hussey, Christopher, *The Picturesque.* New York, 1927.

Ilg, Albert, *Kunstgeschichtliche Charakterbilder aus Oesterreich – Ungarn Unter Mitwirkung von Hoernes, Schneider, Strzygowski u.a.* Vienna, 1893.

—— *Prinz Eugen von Savoyen als Kunstfreund.* Vienna, 1889.

Ilg, Albert, and Boeheim, Wendelin, *Das K. K. Schloss Ambras in Tirol.* Vienna, 1882.

Inventory of Philip II, published in *El Arte in España,* Vol. VII. Madrid, 1887.

Jacobs, Emil, "Das Museo Vendramin und die Sammlung Reynst," in *Repertorium für Kunstwissenschaft,* Vol. 46 (1925), pp. 15–38.

Jameson, Mrs., *Companion to the Most Celebrated Private Galleries of Art in London.* London, 1844.

Janzé, A. de, *Financiers d'autrefois.* Paris, 1886.

Justi, Karl, "Philipp von Stosch und seine Zeit," in *Zeitschrift für bildende Kunst*, Vol. 7 (1872), pp. 293–308, 333–346.

—— "Philip II als Kunstfreund," in *Zeitschrift für bildende Kunst*, 1881.

—— *Winckelmann und seine Zeitgenossen*. Leipzig, 1898. 3 vols.

Kent, William, and the Earl of Burlington, *Some Designs of Inigo Jones*. London, 1727.

Kerr, Albert Boardman, *Jacques Coeur, Merchant Prince of the Middle Ages*. New York, 1927.

Ketton-Cremer, R. W., *Horace Walpole*. New York, 1940.

Keynes, J. M., *A Treatise on Money*. New York, 1930. 2 vols.

Kleinschmidt, Arthur, *Augsburg, Nürnberg und ihre Handelsfürsten*. Cassel, 1881.

Klemm, Gustav, *Zur Geschichte der Sammlungen für Wissenschaft und Kunst in Deutschland*. Zerbst, 1838. 2 aufl.

Knight, Richard Payne, *Analytical Inquiry into the Principles of Taste*. London, 1808.

Knowles, John, *Life and Writings of Henry Fuseli*. London, 1831.

Kristeller, Paul, *Andrea Mantegna*. London, 1901.

Kyp, Johannes, and Knyfe, Leonard, *Britannia Illustrata, or Noblemen's Seats*. 1709.

Lafenestre, Georges, and Richtenberger, Eugène, *Rome*. Paris, 1905.

Lamb, W. R. M., *The Royal Academy*. London, 1935.

Lanciani, Rodolfo, *The Golden Days of the Renaissance in Rome*. Boston and New York, 1906.

Langley, Batty, *Treasury of Designs*. London, 1740.

Lansdowne, *Catalogue of the Sale of the Lansdowne Marbles*. London, Messrs. Christies, 1930.

Lanson, René, *Le gout du Moyen Âge en France au XVIIIe*. Paris, 1926.

Lanzac de Laborie, Léon de, *Paris sous Napoléon*, VIII. *Spectacles et Musées*. Paris, 1913.

Law, Ernest, *The Royal Gallery of Hampton Court*. London, 1898.

Lelièvre, Pierre, *Vivant-Denon*. Paris, 1942.

Lemoine, Robert J., *Les étrangers et la formation du capitalisme en Belgique*. Brussels, 1933.

Lenygon, Francis, "The Chinese Taste in English Decoration," in *Art Journal*. London, 1911.

Leslie, C. R., and Taylor, Tom, *Life and Times of Sir Joshua Reynolds*. London, 1865. 2 vols.

Lesueur, F., "Ménars, le château, les jardins et les collections de Mme. de Pompadour et du Marquis de Marigny," in *Société des Sciences et Lettres de Loir et Cher*, Vol. 21. Blois, 1912.

Le Suffleur, David, "Louis XIV Collectionneur," in *Revue de Paris*, March 1, 1927.

Levi, Cesare Augusto, *Le collezione Veneziane d'arte e antichità*. Venice, 1900. 2 vols.

Lill, Georg, *Hans Fugger und die Kunst*. Leipzig, 1908.

Louvre, *Commission du Muséum et la création du Musée du Louvre* (1792–1795). Paris, 1909.

Lugt, Frits, *Les Marques de Collections*. Amsterdam, 1921.

—— *Répertoire des catalogues de ventes*. The Hague, Vol. I. 1938.

—— "The History of Art," in *The Contribution of Holland to the Sciences*. A symposium edited by A. J. Barnouw and B. Landheer. New York, 1943.

—— *Wandelingen met Rembrandt in en om Amsterdam*. Amsterdam, 1915.

Luz, Pierre de, "Christine de Suède et Mazarin," in *Revue des Deux Mondes*. September–October, 1937.

Luzio, Alessandro, *La Galleria dei Gonzaga*. Milan, 1913.

Mackenzie, Faith Compton, *The Sibyl of the North*. Boston and New York, 1931.

Madrazo, D. Pedro de, *Viaje artístico de tres siglos por las Colleciones de cuadros de los Reyes de España, desde Isabel la Católica hasta la formación del R. Museo del Prado de Madrid*. Barcelona, 1884.

Manners, Lady Victoria, and Williamson, Dr. G. C., *John Zoffany, R.A.* London, 1920.

Manwaring, Elizabeth, *Italian Landscape in Eighteenth Century England*. New York, 1925.

Martin, Alfred von, *Soziologie der Renaissance*. Stuttgart, 1932.

Maspero, Sir Gaston, *Art in Egypt*. New York, 1912.

—— *Life in Ancient Egypt*, in *Manual of Egyptian Archæology*. London, 1914.

Mayer, Josephine, and Prideaux, Tom, *Never to Die – The Egyptians in Their Own Words*. New York, 1938.

Maze-Sencier, Alph., *Le Livre des Collectionneurs*. Paris, 1885.

Mead, Richard, *Authentic Memoirs of the Life of Richard Mead, M.D.* London, 1755.

Meltzing, Otto, *Das Bankhaus der Medici.* Jena, 1906.
Mely, Fernand de, and Bishop, Edmond, *Bibliographie générale des inventaires imprimés.* Paris, 1895. 2 vols.
Mercier, Louis Sébastien, *The Picture of Paris: Before and After the Revolution.* (Trans. and with introduction by Wilfrid and Emilie Jackson; includes extracts from *Picture of Paris.* 12 vols., published 1781–1788; *The New Paris,* published after the Revolution.) London, 1929.
Merriman, Roger Bigelow, *The Rise of the Spanish Empire.* New York, 1925. 4 vols.
Meteyard, Eliza, *Life of Josiah Wedgwood.* London, 1865. 2 vols.
Michaelis, Adolf, *Ancient Marbles in Great Britain.* Cambridge, 1882.
—— "Der Schöpfer der Attalischen Kampfgruppen," in *Jahrbuch des archaeolog. Instituts,* Vol. VIII (1893), pp. 119–134.
Molmenti, Pompeo, *La Storia di Venezia nella Vita Privata.* Origini alla caduta della republica. 7th ed. Bergamo, 1927. 3 vols.
Montaiglon, Anatole de, "Diane de Poitiers et son goût dans les arts," in *Gazette des Beaux-Arts.* Paris, April 1878.
Monum. Germ. Histor. Script, Vol. XX, p. 542. Henry of Blois—Bishop of Winchester A.D. 1150 in Rome, earliest English collector, brother of King Stephen. Cf. R. Pauly in *The Academy,* Nov. 6, 1880, p. 330.
Moryson, Fines, *Shakespeare's Europe.* London, 1903.
Mostra Medicea a Firenze, La. Florence, 1939.
Müntz, Eugène, *La Renaissance en Italie et en France.* Paris, 1885.
—— *Les arts à la cour des Papes.* Paris, 1878.
—— *Les collections des Medicis.* Paris et Londres, 1888.
—— *Mémoires de l'Academie des Inscriptions et Belles Lettres,* XXXV (1895), part II.
—— "Les annexations d'art et de bibliothèques et leur rôle dans les relations internationales," in *Revue d'histoire diplomatique,* IX (1896).
—— "Gem Collecting in the Middle Ages," in *Journal des Savants,* 1888.
—— "Les invasions de 1814–1815 et la spoliation de nos musées," in *Nouvelle Revue,* CV, 1897.
—— "Raphael Archéologue et historien d'art," in *Gazette des Beaux-Arts.* Paris, 1880.
Murray, David, *Museums, Their History and Their Use.* Glasgow, 1904. 3 vols.
Murris, Roelof, *La Hollande et les hollandais au XVIIe et XVIIIe siècles vues par les Français.* Paris, 1925.

Navenne, Ferdinand de, *Rome et le Palais Farnèse pendant les trois derniers siècles.* Paris, 1923. 2 vols.

Noack, Friedrich, "Kunstpflege und Kunstbesitz der Familie Borghese," in *Repertorium für Kunstwissenschaft*, Vol. 50 (1929), pp. 191–231.

Nolhac, Pierre de, "Les collections d'antiquités de Fulvio Orsini," in *Mélanges d'archéologie et d'histoire.* Paris, 1884.

Normand, Charles, *La bourgeoisie française au XVIIe siècle.* Paris, 1908.

North, Kennedy, "The Bridgewater Titians," in *Burlington Magazine*, Vol. 63. 1933.

Opitz, M., *Die Fugger und Welser.* Berlin, 1930.

Orbaan, J. A. F., *Deutsche Kunststädte u. deutsche Kunstsammlungen um 1600.*

Paine, James, *Plans and Elevations of Noblemen's Houses.* London, 1783.

Panofsky, Erwin, *Abbot Suger.* Princeton, New Jersey, 1946.

Parthy, Gustav, *Das Alexandrinische Museum.* Berlin, 1838.

Passerini, Luigi, *Gli Alberti di Firenze.* Florence, 1869.

Pater, Walter, *The Renaissance.* New York, 1919.

Pellati, Francesco, *I Musei e le Gallerie d'Italia.* Rome, 1922.

—— "Per la storia dei musei in Italia," in *Bolletino del R. Istituto d'archeologia e storia dell'arte*, 1922, Vol. I, pp. 4–6. A French translation has been given in *Museion* (VII year), Vols. 23–24, 1933, pp. 98 ff., under the title "Contribution à l'histoire des Musées d'Italie."

Pelli, *Saggio storico della R. Galleria di Firenze.* Florence, 1774.

Perrett, Antoinette, articles in *Country Life* (New York): "Amateur Architects of the Eighteenth Century" (April 1937); "Eighteenth Century Architecture: A Hobby for Gentlemen" (September 1937); "The Fashionable Connoisseurs" (November 1937).

Pevsner, Nikolaus, *Academies of Art Past and Present.* Cambridge, 1940.

Picot, E., *Les Italiens en France au XVIe siècle.* Bordeaux, 1901.

Pillement, Jean, *Livre de Chinois.* London, 1758.

Pirenne, Henri, *Le rôle économique et moral d'Anvers à l'époque de Plantin.* Brussels, 1930.

Plato, Dialogues of (Jowett trans., introd. by Raphael Demos), New York, 1937. (The index is particularly well arranged and useful regarding Plato's opinions on art.)

—— *The Republic*, Benjamin Jowett trans. Oxford, 1908.

—— *Socratic Discourses.* London, 1910.

The Elder Pliny's Chapters on Art, tr. by K. Jex-Blake with commentaries and historical introduction by E. Sellers. London, 1896.

Pollak, Oskar, *Die Kunsttätigkeit unter Urban VIII.* Vienna, 1928. 2 vols.

Posse, Hans, "Die Briefe des Grafen F. Algarotti an den sächsischen Hof und seine Bilderkäufe für die Dresdner Gemäldegalerie," in *Jahrbuch der Preussischen Kunstammlungen*, Vol. 52. Berlin, 1931.

Pye, John, *Patronage of British Art.* London, 1845.

Pyne, W. H., *History of the Royal Residences.* London, 1819. 3 vols.

Quynn, Dorothy Mackay, "The Art Confiscations of Napoleonic Wars," in *American Historical Review*, Vol. L, No. 3, April 1945.

Ranke, Leopold von, *The History of the Popes.* London, 1908. 3 vols.

Regalia, E., "Il museo dell'Imperatore Augusto," in *Archivio per l'antropologia e l'etnologia*, XIX, p. 449.

Reichl, Otto, "Zur Geschichte der ehemaligen Berliner Kunstkammer," in *Jahrbuch der Preussischen Kunstsammlungen*, Vol. 51 (1930), pp. 223–249. (A detailed description of the original art and curio cabinet at the royal palace in Berlin.)

Reinach, S., "Le Musée de l'Empereur Auguste," in *Revue d'anthropologie*, 1889.

Renard, Georges François, *Histoire du travail à Florence.* Paris, 1913. 2 vols.

Repton, Humphrey, *The Art of Landscape Gardening.* Boston, 1907.

Reumont, Alfred von, *Lorenzo dei Medici – "il Magnifico."* Leipzig, 1883. 2 vols.

Reynolds, Sir Joshua, *Discourses.* London, 1797.

—— *Letters*, ed. F. Wiley Hilles. London, 1929.

Rhodes, W. A., *The Italian Bankers in England and their Loans.* London, 1902.

Richards, G. R. B., *Florentine Merchants in the Age of the Medici.* Cambridge, Mass., 1932.

Richardson, A. E., *Georgian England.* London, 1931.

Richardson, Jonathan, *The Art of Criticism.* London, 1719.

—— *Science of a Connoisseur.* London, 1719.

—— *Theory of Painting.* London, 1715.

Riezler, Sigmund von, *Die Kunstpflege der Wittelsbacher*. Munich, 1911.

Rigby, Douglas and Elizabeth, *Lock, Stock and Barrel*. Philadelphia, 1944.

Ris, Louis Clément, Comte de, *Les amateurs d'autrefois*. Paris, 1877.

Robertson, William, and Prescott, William H., *History of the Reign of the Emperor Charles the Fifth*. Boston, 1857. 3 vols.

Robinson, A. Mary F., "Diane de Poictiers," in *Magazine of Art* (London), Vol. 9, 1886.

Rome in the Nineteenth Century, in a series of letters, 1817–1818. Edinburgh, 1860. 3 vols.

Rooses, Max, *Rubens*. London, 1904. 2 vols.

Rose, J. Holland, *Cambridge Modern History VIII, IX*. (Chapters on Napoleonic Period.)

Ross, Janet, *Lives of the Early Medici*. London, 1910.

Rouquet, André, *L'État des arts en Angleterre*. Paris, 1755.

Royal Academy, The (Ed. by Sir Ch. Holmes). New York, 1904.

Russell, William, *Letters from a young painter abroad to his friends in England*. London, 1750. 2 vols.

Russian Collections: *Les Anciennes Écoles de Peinture dans les Palais et Collections Privées Russes*. Brussels, 1910.

Sainsbury, W. Noel, *Original Unpublished Papers illustrative of the Life of Sir Peter Paul Rubens*. London, 1859.

Sansovino, Francesco, *Venezia Città Nobilissima e Singolare, Descritta, etc*. Venezia, 1581.

Saunier, Charles, *Les conquêtes artistiques de la Révolution et de l'Empire*. Paris, 1902.

Sayous, E., "La speculation dans les Pays-Bas," in *Journal des Économistes* (1901).

Scherer, Valentin, *Deutsche Museen*. Jena, 1913. A valuable manual on the history of German museums from the early beginnings up to the World War.

—— "Galerieeinrichtungen im XVIII. Jahrhundert," in *Museumskunde*, Vol. X, 1 (1914).

Schillman, Fritz, *Florenz und die Kultur Toskanas*. Leipzig, 1929.

Schlosser, Julius von, *Die Kunst- und Wunderkammern der Spät-Renaissance*. Leipzig, 1908.

—— *Die Kunstliteratur*. Vienna, 1924. (For those who are more familiar with Italian, the revised translation with appendix of this indispensable work is recommended: J. Schlosser – Magnino, *La letteratura artistica*, Florence, 1935; with appendix by Otto Kürz, 1937. An English edition is in preparation.)

Schulte, Aloys, *Geschichte des mittelalterlichen Handels und Verkehrs*. Leipzig, 1900. 2 vols.

—— *Die Fugger in Rom*. Leipzig, 1904.

Seidel, Paul, "Friedrich der Grosse als Sammler von Gemälden und Skulpturen," in *Jahrbuch der königl. preussischen Kunstsammlungen*, Vol. XIII (1892), pp. 183–213. Vol. XV (1894), pp. 81–94, contains highly important letters by Frederick II which reveal his attitude towards art and his ways of collecting.

—— "Die Kunstsammlungen des Prinzen Heinrich, Bruder Friedrich des Grossen," in *Jahrbuch der königlich preussischen Kunstsammlungen*, Vol. XII (1891), pp. 55–90.

Selfridge, H. Gordon, *The Romance of Commerce*. London, 1918.

Shaftesbury, Anthony Cooper, Third Earl of, *Letter Concerning Design*. 1713.

Shaw, W. A. ed., *Three Inventories of the years 1542, 1547 and 1549–50 of Pictures in the collections of Henry VIII – Edward VI*. Courtauld Institute, London, 1937.

Shelley, Henry C., *The British Museum, Its History and Treasures*. Boston, 1911.

Sismondi, Jean Charles Léonard Simon de, *History of the Italian Republics in the Middle Ages*. New York, 1906.

Sittl, Karl, *Archäologie der Kunst*. Munich, 1897.

Smith, A. H., "Lord Elgin and His Collection," in *Journal of Hellenic Studies*, Vol. 36, Part 2. London, 1916.

—— "The Sculptures in Lansdowne House," in *Burlington Magazine*, Vol. 6. 1905.

Smith, John Thomas, *Nollekens and His Times*. London, 1920. 2 vols.

Smith, Preserved, *The Age of the Reformation*. New York, 1920.

—— *A History of Modern Culture*. New York, 1930–1934. Vol. I, The Great Renewal (1543–1687); Vol. II, The Enlightenment (1687–1776).

Society of Artists of Great Britain, The Papers of, in *The Walpole Society*, Vol. VI, 1918, pp. 113–130.

Sombart, Werner, *Der Bourgeois*. Munich, 1913.

—— *Krieg und Kapitalismus*. Munich, 1913.

Sorel, Albert, *L'Europe et le Révolution française*, IV. Paris, 1903.

Stark, Carl Bernhard, *Systematik und Geschichte der Archäologie der Kunst.* Leipzig, 1880. (An indispensable guide to the antiquities of Rome and Greece and the formation of the early collections of Europe.)

Steegmann, John, *The Rule of Taste from George I to George IV.* London, 1936.

Steinmann, Ernst, "Die Plünderung Roms durch Bonaparte," in *Internationale Monatsschrift für Wissenschaft Kunst und Technik.* XI, 1916–1917.

Steneberg, K. E., "Portrait Collection of Queen Christina," in *Connoisseur,* Vol. 95. March 1935.

Stevenson, R. A. M., *Peter Paul Rubens.* London, 1939.

Stirling, William (Sir William Stirling-Maxwell), *Velasquez and His Works.* London, 1855.

Strabo, *Geographica.* (For description of Alexandria, XVII, I, 8.)

Strieder, Jacob, *Jacob Fugger the Rich.* New York, 1931.

Taine, H., *Philosophie de l'Art.* Paris, 1924. 2 vols.

Tardini, Giulio, *Basilica Vaticana e Borghi.* Rome, (1945?).

Taylor, Rachel Annand, *Invitation to Renaissance Italy.* New York, 1930.

Térey, Gabriel von, "Eine Kunstkammer des XVII. Jahrhunderts," in *Repertorium für Kunstwissenschaft,* Vol. XIX (1896).

Thirion, Henri, *La vie privée des financiers au XVIIIe siècle.* Paris, 1893.

Thompson, James Westfall, *The Medieval Library.* Chicago, 1939.

Toth, Karl, *Woman and Rococo in France.* Seen through the life and works of a contemporary, (Abbé) Charles-Pinot Duclos. Trans. by Roger Abingdon. Philadelphia, 1931.

Tourneux, Maurice, *Diderot et Catherine II.* Paris, 1899.

Tremayne, Eleanor E., *The First Governess of the Netherlands, Margaret of Austria.* London, 1908.

Trevelyan, G. M., *English Social History.* London, 1944.

Trofimoff, Andre de, *Du Musée Impérial au "Marché aux Puces."* Paris, 1938.

Turner, W. J. ed., *Panorama of Rural England.* New York, 1944. (Cf. V. Sackville-West, *English Country Houses.*)

Union Centrale des Arts Decoratifs (Paris) Ed. *Le Goût Chinois en Europe,* n.d.

Valentiner, W. R., "Rembrandt und seine Umgebung," in *Zur Kunstgeschichte des Auslandes*, Vol. XXIX. Strassburg, 1905.

Valle, Manuel R. Zarco del, "Unveröffentlichte Beiträge zur Geschichte der Kunstbestrebungen Karl V und Philipp II," in *Jahrbuch der kunsthistorischen Sammlungen des allerh. Kaiserhauses*. Vienna, 1888.

Vasari, Giorgio, *Lives of Seventy of the Most Eminent Painters, Sculptors, Architects*. New York, 1911.

Vaticano. Ed. by Fallani, Giorgio, and Escobar, Mario. Rome, 1946.

Venturi, Adolfo, *Il Museo e la Galleria Borghese*. Rome, 1893.

—— *La R. Galleria Estense in Modena*. Modena, 1882.

—— "Zur Geschichte der Kunstsammlungen Kaiser Rudolf II," in *Repertorium für Kunstwissenschaft*, Vol. VIII. 1885.

Venturi, Lionello, *History of Art Criticism*. New York, 1936.

Verne, Henri, *Le Palais du Louvre*. Paris, 1923. 2 vols.

—— *Le Palais du Louvre de Philippe-Auguste à Napoléon III*. Paris, 1924. 2 vols.

Vertue, George, *Catalogue of the Collections of Charles I, 1757, James II and Queen Caroline, 1758*. London, 3 vols. in 1.

—— *Notebooks*. The Walpole Society. Oxford, 1930–1938. 5 vols.

Villari, Pasquale, *The First Centuries of Florentine History*. London, n.d.

—— *The Life and Times of Girolamo Savonarola*. London and New York, 1889.

—— *The Life and Times of Niccolò Machiavelli*. London, 1879.

Vosmaer, Carel, *Rembrandt Harmens van Rijn, sa vie et ses oeuvres*. 2nd ed. The Hague, 1877.

Waagen, Gustav Friedrich, *Treasures of Art in Great Britain*. London, 1854. 3 vols. and supplement. Being an account of the chief collections of Paintings, Drawings, Sculptures, Illuminated Mss.

—— *Summary and Index to Waagen* (by Algernon Graves). London, 1912.

Wackernagel, Martin, *Der Lebensraum des Künstlers in der Florentinischen Renaissance*. Leipzig, 1938.

Waldmann, Emil, *Der Sammler*. Berlin, 1920.

Waliszewski, K., *Le Roman d'une Impératrice Catherine II de Russia*. Paris, 1894.

Walpole, Horace, *Aedes Walpolianae*. 1747.

—— *Anecdotes of Painting in England*. London (Henry G. Bohn), 1862. 3 vols. (With some account of the principal artists and incidental notes on other arts. Also a catalogue of engravers who have been born or resided in England, collected by George Vertue; digested and published from his original mss. by Horace Walpole with additions by the Rev. James Dallaway. New ed. revised with additional notes by Ralph N. Wornum.)

—— *Observations on Pleasure Grounds* (1774), *Treatise on Modern Gardening*, in *Collected Works*, 1798.

—— "Horace Walpole's Journals of Visits to Country Seats," etc. (edited by P. Toynbee), in *The Walpole Society*, Vol. 16, pp. 9–81.

Warburg, Aby, *Bildniskunst und florentinisches Bürgertum.* Leipzig, 1901.

—— *Flandrische Kunst und florentinische Frührenaissance.* Berlin, 1902.

Ware, Isaac, *A Complete Body of Architecture.* London, 1748–1760.

Waterhouse, Ellis K., *Baroque Painting in Rome.* London, 1937.

Waters, W. G., *Italian Sculptors.* London, 1911.

Watson, F. J. B., "On the Early History of Collecting in England," in *Burlington Magazine*, LXXXVI (1944), pp. 223–229. (Discusses here the copy of Richardson's *Account of the Statues, Bas-reliefs, Drawings and Pictures in England*, annotated by his son. This little known copy is preserved in the London Library and would appear to contain a wealth of gossip and detail.)

Weber, Max, *General Economic History.* New York, 1927.

—— *The Protestant Ethic and the Spirit of Capitalism.* London, 1930.

Wells, H. G., *Outline of History.* New York, 1922. 4 vols.

Welser, J. M., Freiherr von, *Die Welser.* Nüremberg, 1917.

Weniger, *Das alexandrinische Museum.* Berlin, 1875.

Wertheimer, Oskar von, *Christine von Schweden.* Vienna, 1936.

Wescher, Paul, *Grosskaufleute der Renaissance.* Basel, 1940.

Whitley, William T., *Art in England, 1800–1820.* Cambridge, 1928.

—— *Artists and their Friends in England, 1700–1799.* London, 1928. 2 vols.

—— *Gilbert Stuart.* Cambridge, Mass., 1932.

—— *Thomas Gainsborough.* London, 1915.

Wilde, Johannes, "Wiedergefundene Gemälde aus der Sammlung des Erzherzogs Leopold Wilhelm," in *Jahrbuch der kunsthistorischen Sammlungen in Wien*, N.F., IV, 1930.

Winckelmann, J. J., *The History of Ancient Art* (1764), trans. from the German by G. H. Lodge. Boston, 1873.

—— *Monumenti antichi inediti.* Rome, 1767. 2 vols.

Wyatt, Alphonse, "Le Cabinet de Christine de Suède," in *Gazette des Beaux Arts*, 1859.

Yriarte, Charles, "Isabella d'Este," in *Gazette des Beaux-Arts*, 1895.

—— "Les Relations d'Isabelle d'Este avec Léonard de Vinci," in *Gazette des Beaux-Arts*. Paris, 1888.

—— "Sabbioneta, la petite Athènes," in *Gazette des Beaux-Arts*, 1898.

N. B. Students wishing to pursue the bibliography of the history of collecting more in detail will find it helpful to consult the following:

Internationale Bibliographie der Kunstwissenschaft, 1903–1920. Cf. Sections under Kunstgeschichte, Austellungen, Museen, Sammlungen.

Repertorium für Kunstwissenschaft, 1876–1903. Cf. Bibliography at end of each volume. Sections 8, 9, and 10 deal with museums, exhibitions, collections, etc.

Répertoire d'art et d'archéologie, 1910–   . Cf. Index at end of each volume.

Gazette des Beaux-Arts. Cf. *Tables générales des cinquantes années de la Gazette des Beaux-Art*, 1859–1908. Vol. I, sections 13, 14.

If through inadvertence, or failure to trace present proprietors, the author has included any copyright material without acknowledgment or permission, he offers his apologies to all concerned.

Acknowledgments

The author wishes to make special acknowledgment to the following for permission to use material:

The Bobbs-Merrill Company for material from *The Young Melbourne* by Lord David Cecil, copyright 1939. Used by special permission of the Publishers, The Bobbs-Merrill Company.

Constable & Company, Ltd., for material from *The Young Melbourne* by David Cecil (British Empire rights only).

Crown Publishers for material from *The Works of (Pietro) Aretino* by Samuel Putnam. Copyright 1926 by Pascal Covici. Reprinted by permission of Crown Publishers.

Dodd, Mead & Company for material from *On Life and Letters* by Anatole France. Copyright 1922, reprinted by permission of Dodd, Mead & Company.

Faber and Faber, Ltd., for material from *Horace Walpole* by R. W. Ketton-Cremer (British Empire rights only).

William Heinemann, Ltd., for material from *The Century of the Renaissance* by Louis Batiffol (British Empire rights only).

Henry Holt & Company for material from *A History of Modern Culture* by Preserved Smith. Copyright 1930 by Henry Holt and Company, and for material from *The Age of the Reformation* by Preserved Smith, copyright 1920 by Henry Holt and Company.

Methuen and Co., Ltd., for material from *The First Governess of the Netherlands – Margaret of Austria* by Eleanor Tremayne (British Empire edition only).

John Murray for material from *Isabella d'Este* by Julia Cartwright (British Empire rights only).

Oxford University Press and the Phaidon Press for material from *Peter Paul Rubens* by R. A. M. Stevenson.

Routledge & Kegan Paul, Ltd., for material from *Roman Life and Manners* by Ludwig Friedländer (British Empire rights only).

Other acknowledgments are made in the footnotes.

Index